Education, Economy and Society

Series Editors: **Andy Green**, Institute of Education, University of London, UK; **Lorna Unwin**, Institute of Education, University of London, UK; **Karen Mundy**, Ontario Institute for Studies in Education, University of Toronto, Canada.

Titles include:

Andy Green
EDUCATION AND STATE FORMATION (2nd edition)
Europe, East Asia and the USA

Andy Green and Jan Germen Janmaat
REGIMES OF SOCIAL COHESION
Societies and the Crisis of Globalization

Maha Shuayb (*editor*)
RETHINKING EDUCATION FOR SOCIAL COHESION
International Case Studies

Emer Smyth, Maureen Lyons and Merike Darmody (*editors*)
RELIGIOUS EDUCATION IN A MULTICULTURAL EUROPE
Children, Parents and Schools

Education, Economy and Society
Series Standing Order ISBN 978–0–230–29007–9
Hardback ISBN 978–0–230–29008–2 Paperback
(*outside North America only*)

You can receive future titles in this series as they are published by placing a standing order. Please contact your bookseller or, in case of difficulty, write to us at the address below with your name and address, the title of the series and the ISBN quoted above.

Customer Services Department, Macmillan Distribution Ltd, Houndmills, Basingstoke, Hampshire RG21 6XS, England

---

Also by Andy Green

REGIMES OF SOCIAL COHESION: Societies and the Crisis of Globalisation (*with Germ Janmaat*)

EDUCATION AND DEVELOPMENT IN A GLOBAL ERA: Strategies for Successful Globalisation (*with others*)

EDUCATION, EQUALITY AND SOCIAL COHESION (*with John Preston and Germ Janmaat*)

HIGH SKILLS: Globalization, Competitiveness and Skills Formation (*with Phil Brown and Hugh Lauder*)

CONVERGENCE AND DIVERGENCE IN EUROPEAN EDUCATION AND TRAINING SYSTEMS (*with Alison Wolf and Tom Leney*)

WHERE ARE THE RESOURCES FOR LIFELONG LEARNING? (*with Ann Hodgson and Gareth Williams*)

FURTHER EDUCATION AND LIFELONG LEARNING: Realigning the Sector for the 21st Century (*with Norman Lucas*)

YOUTH EDUCATION AND WORK: World Yearbook on Education (*with Les Bash*)

EDUCATION LIMITED: Schooling and Training since 1979 (*with others*)

Education and State Formation

Europe, East Asia and the USA

2nd edition

Andy Green
Institute of Education, University of London, UK

palgrave
macmillan

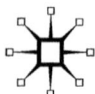

First published 2013 by
PALGRAVE MACMILLAN

Palgrave Macmillan in the UK is an imprint of Macmillan Publishers Limited, registered in England, company number 785998, of Houndmills, Basingstoke, Hampshire RG21 6XS.

Palgrave Macmillan in the US is a division of St Martin's Press LLC, 175 Fifth Avenue, New York, NY 10010.

Palgrave Macmillan is the global academic imprint of the above companies and has companies and representatives throughout the world.

Palgrave® and Macmillan® are registered trademarks in the United States, the United Kingdom, Europe and other countries.

ISBN 978–1–137–34173–0 hardback
ISBN 978–1–137–34174–7 paperback

This book is printed on paper suitable for recycling and made from fully managed and sustained forest sources. Logging, pulping and manufacturing processes are expected to conform to the environmental regulations of the country of origin.

A catalogue record for this book is available from the British Library.

A catalog record for this book is available from the Library of Congress.

Contents

Figures and Tables

Figures

Tables

Introduction

Education and State Formation was originally published in English in 1990, with subsequent translations into Chinese, Japanese and Greek.[1] This – somewhat belated – second edition provides a welcome opportunity to correct some errors in the original text and to add a substantial new section on East Asia.

The book originally grew out of my doctoral research, which began in 1985 as an investigation into the historical origins of certain 'peculiarities' in the English education system. In particular, I was interested in understanding why technical education was relatively underdeveloped in England by comparison with many continental European states, and why the impulse towards mass participation in post-compulsory education appeared to remain rather weak, even a century after the foundation of a national education system (NES). It soon became apparent that the comparatively unimpressive outcomes of mass education for many young people in England was the effect of a number of systemic characteristics which were quite exceptional by the standards of most Northern European countries and which had to do with the traditionally 'liberal' caste of the British state.

Consequently, and by degrees, the study became a broader comparative examination of the historical origins of national education systems in nineteenth-century England, France, Prussia and the United States of America (USA). Economic development was clearly part of the overall picture, but the focus became largely on the role of the state in educational change because that appeared to be the key factor which could explain the differential national patterns of educational development. The comparative theory propounded in the book sought to explain the formation of national education systems in the nineteenth century as part of the broader historical process of 'state formation'. The term equates to what historians used to refer to as 'nation-building' but is preferable in that it avoids the inherent ambiguity in the term 'nation', which can refer to 'the people' in general or the 'ethnic group', depending on the historical period or theoretical persuasion of the user.[2] The uneven development of national education, at least

1

in the countries studied, was seen as an expression of the different ways in which (nation) states were consolidated during the late eighteenth and early nineteenth centuries. More specifically, those states which underwent what I have called an 'intensive' process of state formation tended to form national education systems earlier than others which did not.

A number of valuable criticisms were made of the book when it first came out (which I have addressed at more length elsewhere).[3] Some commentators rightly pointed out that national-level studies such as this often pay inadequate attention to regional variation within states, and this is clearly an area where much work needs to be done, not least as globalization reconfigures the spacial dimensions of the world and requires new units of analysis in comparative work. There were also objections that state formation is a somewhat elusive 'portmanteau' concept, involving, on the one hand, both the economic and political development of states and, on the other, an ambiguity around state as political agent and state as 'nation state'. The first is, of course, true, although the primary emphasis in the term is on the construction of national identity and political statehood. Regarding the second, the ambiguity – or rather *double entendre* – is deliberate and necessary since, to paraphrase Edward Thompson on the formation of the English working class, states were present at their own making. However, it remains the case that 'nation state' is an inadequate concept, subject to the same ambiguities as the term 'nation-building'. Other useful points were made about the importance of patriarchy in explaining differential educational development.[4]

Overall, however, the argument about the role of education in the development of states seems to have been generally accepted and there are, of course, numerous historical studies of particular countries which similarly focus on the role of education and nation-building. I was fortunate enough to read Van Horn Melton's *Absolutism and the 18th-Century Origins of Compulsory Schooling in Prussia and Austria* before I finished revising my own original text, although not, unfortunately, Eugen Weber's great 1979 study of nation-building in France (*Peasants into Frenchmen: The Modernization of Rural France, 1870–1914*).[5] Few books have better captured what I would call the epic drama of national development. Since the publication of my book, other studies of education and state formation have appeared, including, amongst the major ones, Wong's *Hegemonies Compared: State Formation and Chinese School Politics in Postwar Singapore and Hong Kong*[6] and Chia's *The Loss of 'World Soul'? Education Culture and the Making of the Singapore Developmental State, 1995–2004*.[7]

In retrospect, two decades later, many of the concerns of the book still seem relevant. In England, debates around education still frequently focus on the perceived national deficits in outcomes by comparison with many European countries. Despite 'europeanizing' measures, such as the national curriculum and national testing, which appeared after 1988, there is still much that is 'peculiar' to the system in England. It has become more 'centralized', like many continental states, in terms of government control over curriculum and assessment, but is still unique in the degree of autonomy given to individual institutions. In fact, the latter singularity has been enhanced by the measures for local management of schools and colleges, school choice and diversity, and other quasi-market reforms introduced over the past 20 years, and also, more recently, by the proliferation of new school types, such as academies and free schools, which have been accorded even greater levels of autonomy. The debate around the roles of the state and the market in education still rages on. Several countries have followed the English lead in introducing more competitive 'quasi-market' relations into education, but England continues to be exceptional in its degree of adherence to this particular dogma.

'Exceptionalism' is not, of course, an English monopoly. All national education systems are peculiar in their own ways. Globalization may create certain trends towards policy convergence in education. Certainly, higher education is becoming increasingly internationalized, and there is a growing incidence of policy-borrowing between states, facilitated by the growing availability of international data and by the work of supra-national policy agencies. However, the evidence is that national systems, at least at the compulsory level, are not disappearing and not becoming much more like each other.[8] Governments may be increasingly losing control over their national economies but education is one area where they do still seek to pursue national policies.[9]

The policy issues discussed in this book thus do have modern resonances. Nevertheless, *Education and State Formation* is essentially an historical study, albeit brought closer to the present by the addition of post-war East Asian nation-building to the text. The theory applies to particular stages of national development and not to others. Developed democratic states increasingly emphasize the economic functions of education, rather than the ideological ones, at least in relatively 'normal' historical periods. Economic competitiveness has become the major rationale for improved education in all western states over the past 20 years. By comparison, the ideological role of schooling in reinforcing national identity and citizenship has been relatively underplayed in the older developed states.

In the older developed democracies, today, education still needs to address issues of cultural reproduction and identity formation. However, in pluralistic, multinational and multicultural states, this cannot be a question of forming a singular national culture and identity. It is still important for education to promote social cohesion and solidarity; never more so, in fact, than under the socially fragmenting effects of economic globalization. But education must embrace complex cultures and identities. State formation should be less about the reproduction of national identity and more about the formation of active and aware citizens in democratic society.

Education as a process of state formation appears to be primarily a function of early periods of nation-building, or of periods of political reconstruction after crises, such as in Japan after the Second World War. One would not expect the historical process described in *Education and State Formation* to apply in the same way in mature democracies today. However, it has been very evident in certain newly developed polities, such as South Korea, Taiwan and Singapore. Here, as in nineteenth-century France and Prussia, educational development since the 1960s has been closely associated with the consolidation of statehood and national identity, just as much as with economic growth. The rapid construction of national education systems has been precisely both a cause and an effect of the process of accelerated state formation (ASF).

The publication of a second edition of *Education and State Formation* at this time perhaps deserves some more explanation. The book is still quite widely read and cited, and this may provide some justification since the new version corrects some annoying mistakes in the original text and can be freshly presented to a new generation of readers. However, this could have been done some years ago. The reason for the delay is that I have been undertaking new research which is relevant to the themes of the original book and whose inclusion here I believe strengthens the original arguments as well as broadening their sphere of application. The new material, which all appears in the extended Postscript of this new edition, concerns theories of development and their relationship to state formation theory, and an application of both to understanding the role of education in the remarkable recent processes of economic development and state formation in East Asia.

The original arguments of the book were conceptualized entirely within the parameters of state formation theory. This seemed to be the appropriate theoretical framework for dealing with the role of national education systems in nation-building in the emerging capitalist countries in the West in the century after the French Revolution. The focus was largely on the social and political dimensions of that process, although, of course, economic development was also there in the background. However, the arguments did not engage substantively with the different theories of nationalism which are important in understanding different types of state formation in the 'Age of Empire' and after. And nor did they engage with a number of theories about 'late development' and 'developmental states' which were available at the time of my research but which have been increasingly refined over the past 20 years. These theories are primarily about economic development rather than the political and social dimensions of nation-building, but they are, in fact, highly germane to my argument. They are predicated on assumptions about the origins of particular kinds of economic development in certain forms of nationalism, and especially that which Chalmers Johnson termed 'situational nationalism'.[10] What I try to do here, which has not been done before, is to elaborate the two sets of theories in concert, since they reinforce each other. I do this through analysis of education and state formation in East Asia, since it is in this region where they have been most applicable in recent years.

The new section inevitably departs in some respects from the original text in terms of style, structure and emphasis. The point of departure for the original text was to understand the uneven development of national education systems in the West in the nineteenth century. This led to a consideration of how nation-building inspired educational development and, in turn, how educational development contributed to nation-building. The new section, on the other hand, reverses the order, starting from an analysis of state formation in post-war East Asia and then going on to look at the contribution of education to this. Furthermore, whilst the original study focused on the social and political aspects of state formation, the analysis of East Asia here is equally about the economic and socio-political aspects of development. This change of emphasis partly reflects the research I have been doing in the intervening period on skills formation and economic growth.[11] It is also partly influenced by the dominant theoretical paradigms used in the analysis which were developed for understanding more recent historical times. As technology has become more complex and advanced, and as globalization has made possible the acceleration of the development process, economics has come more to the fore in the frameworks that we use to understand the development process. This has probably now gone too far, as Amartya Sen has argued,[12] and I hope that the study here will contribute something to rebalancing the socio-political and economic dimensions in our approaches to development.

Methodologically, the original and the new texts are complementary but different. They both fall generally within the ambit of comparative historical sociology but the comparative logics applied in each case vary. Broadly speaking the original study exemplifies a comparative method which Skocpol and Somers have defined as 'macro-causal comparative analysis', whereas the East Asian study is more akin to 'parallel demonstration of theory'.[13]

My first efforts at devising a comparative approach to the analysis of the rise of national education systems in the West were largely intuitive and owed little to theories of comparative methods, of which I knew little when I started my PhD. It was only gradually that I groped my way to a more systematic approach to the analysis. I was clear from quite early on that the phenomenon that I was trying to explain comparatively was the uneven rise of national education systems. A number of countries which I had surveyed, such as Austria, France, Prussia and some other German states, were relatively precocious in developing national education systems. On the other hand, England and Italy had developed pubic systems relatively late, and the United States lagged behind also in the southern states. So there was a relatively well-defined outcome of interest or 'dependent variable', to use the statistical jargon. I was also clear from reviewing the literature that there were a number of possible causes of this uneven development, including levels of industrialization and urbanization, degrees of democratization, state centralization and religion. So these, in the statistical language, were the initial 'independent variables'.

However, it was quite evident that none of these factors alone could provide an explanation of uneven development. Some predominantly Protestant states (e.g. Prussia) were relatively advanced educationally, whilst others (England, the southern United States) were not. National education systems developed in most of my putative country cases (e.g. France, Prussia and Saxony) well before there had been substantial industrialization, urbanization or 'proletarianization' of the workforce, but in one case (the United States), national education systems developed in parallel with these phenomena (in the northern states), and in another (England) they lagged behind. Democratization coincided with educational development in the northern United States and, to a lesser extent, in England, but clearly post-dated the development of national education systems in most countries I was looking at (e.g. Austria, France, Prussia and Saxony). The most promising correlate of rapid educational development seemed to be state centralization since this was present in various 'positive' cases of educational development (e.g. France and Prussia) and absent in the negative cases (England and Italy). But the northern United States confounded this explanation since it was relatively decentralized but at the same time educationally advanced.

I chose to leave the United States in my initial sample of countries as a 'deviant' case and this proved to be a good decision. In trying to understand why the northern USA advanced so rapidly in education despite its being a decentralized state, I began to think in terms of accelerated state formation as a possible cause of rapid educational development. This explanation not only fitted some of the positive cases in continental Europe. It could also be seen to fit the United States since, though highly decentralized, the country post independence was most clearly an example of intensified state formation, albeit that much of the agency was at the level of individual states. On the other hand, the process of state formation was relatively muted in the laggard cases of educational development (England and Italy) during this period.

The theorist of comparative methodology, Todd Landman, cites the aphorism that 'to compare is to be human,'[14] and the logics of comparison described above could be put in this category of basic human thought processes. They were made a little more systematic by the use of primitive forms of what Charles Ragin[15] calls 'truth tables', although I had no knowledge of his important work on systematic logical forms of comparison at the time. A replica of the kind of truth tables I was drawing up then would look like

Table I.1 Truth table

	NES	Industrialized	Urbanized	Proletarianized	Protestant	Democratizing	ASF
Austria	yes	no	no	no	no	no	yes
England	no	yes	yes	yes	yes	yes	no
France	yes	no	no	no	no	yes	yes
Italy	no	no	no	no	no	no	no
Prussia	yes	no	no	no	yes	no	yes
N. USA	yes	no	no	no	yes	yes	yes

Table 1.1, where the only factor present in the positive cases and absent in the negative cases of national education system development – at, say, around 1830/1840 – was accelerated state formation. It should be noted that all of the categories used as column headings are a matter of degree.

The rough and ready procedure of tabulating the factors present and absent in each case was helpful but could not have been taken much further using Ragin's methods. As I later discovered, mathematical elaboration of these logical relations, as recommended by Ragin, requires 'discontinuous' (on/off) variables, whereas all of my variables were a matter of degree or of chronology, thus being 'continuous' rather than 'discontinuous'.

The ongoing analysis of 'positive' and 'negative' cases during the original research – tracing historical processes in each case and comparing these across cases – did finally lead to a more systematic mode of comparison and one that approximates to the macro-causal method described in the comparative methodology literature.

Ideally this method uses a logic which John Stuart Mill described as the 'Method of Difference'. This is essentially the method of the controlled experiment in natural science and is the most logically robust of the comparative methods. As he explained it in his classic account in *A System of Logic*,

> if an instance in which the phenomenon under investigation occurs, and an instance in which it does not occur, have every circumstance in common save one, that one only occurring in the former; the circumstance in which alone the two instances differ, is the effect, or the cause, or an indispensible part of the cause of the phenomenon.

The trouble is that in the social sciences, including historical sociology, it is never possible to find a set of cases with differing outcomes and where all the other circumstances are identical except the putative cause. Cross-national studies within regions are most likely to come closest to this since many of the basic geographical, geopolitical and cultural factors are likely to be similar, but generally comparative studies are not able to use the method rigorously. In practice, then, macro-causal analysis tends to use a comparative logic which approximates more to what Mill called the 'indirect' or 'joint' method.[16] This combines the Method of Difference with Mill's Method of Agreement (the latter being where all of the cases have the same outcome but where all other factors differ except for the putative cause). But it does not include the most exacting requirement of the Method of Difference, which is that the cases are identical except in cause and effect. In the joint method the investigator examines multiple instances where a particular phenomenon occurs, noting whatever conditions they have in common, and compares these with a range of instances where the phenomenon does not occur. If a certain condition (or conditions) is common to the first set and is absent in the second set, and especially if the cases are otherwise quite similar, you can assume that this condition represents the cause of the phenomenon in question in these cases.

The method is obviously not infallible. There may be causes which you have not observed, as can also occur in statistical comparisons. You cannot be entirely sure of the direction of causality, although this is less of a problem in historical analyses which are also tracing processes over time. Where there are several conditions which are all present in the positive cases and all absent in the negative cases, the logic will not tell you precisely which is the actual cause. There may also be several combined causes. But here it is the detailed historical examination of the cases, and of how the various factors inter-relate over time, which can provide an understanding of complex configurations of causality. This is a particular strength of the logical methods of comparative historical sociology, which involve a small number of cases, compared with 'large-N' statistical methods.[17]

The original research for *Education and State Formation* included initially a number of positive cases of national education system development (Austria, France, Prussia and the northern United States) and two negative cases (England and Italy). In the first set, early development of national education systems was accompanied by rapid state formation. In the second set, rapid state formation was absent during the period in question and national education system development did not occur until later. There were no other factors which were all common to the positive cases and absent in all of the negative cases. However, the other characteristics of the different states were not identical, although these were all broadly modernizing states. The Method of Difference could not be strictly applied in the comparative analysis for this reason, so I proceeded with a version of the Joint Method of Agreement and Difference. In the detailed historical accounts the case sample was reduced to three positive cases (France, Prussia and the United States) and one negative case (England).

The new section of East Asia uses different comparative logics. It might have been possible to do a larger study with many more cases which sought to apply the logic of Mill's Method of Difference. Many countries in East and

South Asia could have been included where some (Japan and the East Asian 'tiger' economies such as South Korea, Taiwan and Singapore, for instance) would have demonstrated a coincidence of accelerated state formation and the rapid development of education systems, whilst others (India, Sri Lanka and the Philippines perhaps) could have exemplified a weaker process of state formation and the slower development of national education systems (or at least of integrated national systems). Some other conditions would have been common to all countries (all being Asian) but perhaps only weakly so. Alternatively, the analysis could have been limited to the East Asian region, where there are more commonalities, but could have included a negative case (say the Philippines). Unfortunately, my expertise did not extend far enough to conduct comparative studies across all of these cases with any historical depth. So the approach adopted was to take a group of East Asian countries, including Japan, South Korea and Singapore, with Taiwan as an ancillary case, which all exhibited a process of accelerated state formation and rapid development of national education systems.

The 'parallel' method adopted here approximates to Mill's Method of Agreement inasmuch as the cases exhibit common causes and outcomes. As Mill, and later Skocpol and Somers, rightly observes, this comparative method is not as logically robust as the Method of Difference, and it is also prone to the danger of proof through biased case selection.[18] After all, there may be cases of rapid educational development in East Asia that were not accompanied by intensive state formation (as you might argue, for instance, for Hong Kong), although I cannot think of many. On the other hand, the comparative approach in this case is adopted as a sequel to a previous study which does include positive and negative cases, and so in principle, taken together, the studies can be seen as an extended use of the joint method. Furthermore, the parallel method has the advantage that it can be used to elaborate on an existing theory, using new cases to show how particular conditions create variants of the process described in the theory, thus forcing the theory to incorporate new complexities. This is what I have sought to do here, not least through the incorporation additional, but cognate, theories of late development and the 'developmental state'.

The structure of this study is as follows. Chapter 1 analyses the evidence for the uneven development of national education systems in the West by examining the opinions of contemporary educational 'experts' and comparative quantitative data on levels of enrolment, social access and literacy. This gives some provisional measure of comparative educational 'advance' in different countries, and this in turn is related to the chronologies for the development of 'state' forms of public education in different systems. The aim is to establish whether there were systematic differences in levels of educational development in different countries and whether this in turn related to the existence or absence of a public or state system.

Chapter 2 involves an examination and critique of different theories and interpretations that have been put forward to explain educational change in general and differential change in particular. These include traditional Whig or liberal perspectives; Durkheimian 'integration' theory and modern structural functionalism; theories relating to urbanization, proletarianization and the changing structures of family life; and Margaret Archer's Weberian systems theory.

Chapter 3 examines Marx and Gramsci's writings on the state and hegemony, and suggests that an analysis of the different modes of state formation in different countries offers a more coherent theoretical basis for understanding the origins of national education systems and their different national patterns of development.

The remaining substantive chapters in the original text use the theory of hegemony and state formation, as developed in Chapter 3, to develop an interpretation of the social origins of specific forms of educational development in the four countries. To do this I have focused on the *differentia specifica* of educational development in each country and the concomitant forms of state and hegemony by which this may be explained. The order of analysis in each chapter begins with a general theoretical discussion about the nature of the national state in question, and proceeds to analyse the development of education through broad periods, the boundaries of which are defined by major changes in state forms. This is followed by a conclusion which summarizes the argument about education and state formation in the western states.

The new extended Postscript in this edition is about education and state formation in East Asia. Part I starts with a theoretical discussion about theories of state formation and development, including a discussion of the points of intersection of state formation theory and contiguous theories of late development and developmental states. From here it moves to a comparative analysis of state formation and development in the East Asian states. Part II looks, comparatively, at the contribution of education to state formation and development in the case countries. In the first section it deals with the similarities across countries in the timing and forms of development of national education systems and how this was articulated with the broader state formation process. In the second section it looks at some of the differences across the cases, and how each country's education system was faring at the close of the twentieth century.

Andy Green
Nuffield, Oxfordshire
January 2013

1
The Uneven Development of National Education Systems in the West

The formation of national education systems in early nineteenth-century Europe marks the beginning of modern schooling in western capitalist societies. With the coming of the school system, education became a universal and national concern, embracing all individuals and having effects on all classes in society. Learning became irreversibly equated with formal, systematic schooling, and schooling itself became a fundamental feature of the state. The national education system thus represented a watershed in the development of learning. It signalled not only the advent of mass education and the spread of popular literacy but also the origins of 'state schooling' – the system which has come to predominate in the educational development of all modern societies in the twentieth century.

As an institutional form the national education system had a long period of historical gestation. Educational innovation had been a feature of all western societies since the Protestant Reformation. There were numerous seventeenth-century blueprints for national systems and in the eighteenth century the first inchoate attempts to realize these were pioneered by absolutist monarchs such as Frederick V in Denmark, Maria Theresa in Austria and Frederick the Great in Prussia. They lacked the resources to make their reforms effective but they certainly prefigured later developments with their provision of state funds for public elementary schools and with the enactment of legislation on compulsory attendance. However, it was during the French revolutionary era and the decades that followed that these embryonic national systems were first consolidated and given permanent institutional forms – initially in Prussia and France, and soon after in a host of smaller continental states, such as Switzerland and Holland. Thereafter, the broad parameters of reform in national education are clear: they involved the development of universal forms of provision, the rationalization of administration and institutional structure, and the development of forms of public finance and control.

11

National networks of elementary schools were consolidated with the help of the state, and gradually free tuition and compulsory attendance laws ensured universal childhood participation; secondary education expanded from its tiny elite base and progressively incorporated more modern curricula and pedagogy; technical and vocational schools proliferated, albeit unevenly, to meet new industrial demands. As educational provision expanded, so it also became more regulated and, by degrees, more systematic in organization. Diverse institutions were unified into a single structure, increasingly administered through an integrated educational bureaucracy and with teaching provided by trained staff. An age-graded, hierarchical system developed whose component parts were systematically linked and complementary, in time to become part of an 'educational ladder' whose different rungs were articulated through regulated curricula and entrance requirements. Lastly, educational control passed increasingly to the state. As public schools came to predominate over private and voluntary institutions, governments ineluctably increased their influence on education. Whether through central or local authorities, the state increasingly controlled education through the allocation of funds, the licensing and inspection of schools, the recruitment, training and certification of teachers and, in varying degrees, through the oversight of national certification and standard curricula.

These changes represented a decisive break with the voluntary and particularistic form of learning which had preceded them, where church, family and guild had provided for their own needs. As Michael Katz has suggested in his essay on the origins of public education in the United States, this change was radical and far-reaching:

> By the latter part of the nineteenth century, the organization, scope and role of schooling had been fundamentally transformed. In the place of a few schools dotted about town and country, there existed in most cities true educational systems: carefully articulated, hierarchically structured groupings of schools, primarily free and often compulsory, administered by full-time experts, and progressively taught by specially trained staff. No longer casual adjuncts to the home and the apprenticeship, such schools were highly formal institutions designed to play a critical role in the socialization of the young, the maintenance of social order, and in the promotion of development.[1]

The creation of a set of institutions solely devoted to education, and involving a putative monopoly of formal learning and training for diverse occupations, thus signalled a revolution in the concept and forms of education and a transformation in the relations between schooling, society and the state. Education not only became a mass phenomenon; it also became a central feature of social organization.

However, these developments, sketched here only in their broadest outline, occurred unevenly and in different forms from country to country. Although all western nations were eventually to adopt a system broadly in line with the model above, they did so at different times and with significant formal variations. The classic form of the public education system, with state-financed and regulated schools and an elaborate administrative bureaucracy, occurred first on the Continent, notably in the German states, France, Holland and Switzerland. All these countries had established the basic form of their public systems by the 1830s, although in France, universal attendance was not achieved until some 50 years later. The northern states of the United States followed, developing public education systems, according to their own more decentralized design, in the period between 1830 and the Civil War. Britain, the Southern European States and the American South lagged considerably behind, in England's case delaying the full establishment of an integrated public system until the following century. Although some countries were slow to recognize it, the achievement of high rates of attendance, competent teaching and widespread popular literacy were indisputably linked with the development of public systems because the old voluntary networks of schools were simply incapable of providing universal provision without state assistance. It followed that in countries such as Britain, or rather England and Wales (since Scotland and Ireland had distinctive educational arrangements) where public systems were slow to develop, educational levels were noticeably low. A brief sketch of the chronology of public educational development in the principal countries concerned in this study should illustrate the degree of national variation.

Prussia, 1780–1840

Prussia pioneered the development of national education in the eighteenth century, but it was in the years between the Prussian defeat by Napoleon at Jena in 1806 and the death of Altenstein, the Minister of Education, in 1840, that the national system was consolidated. Although free elementary tuition was not made law until 1868, a national public system was essentially in place by the end of Altenstein's ministry. Frederick II's compulsory attendance laws in 1763 marked the first important move in the direction of national education. The creation of a secondary-school board in 1787 was the first decisive shift towards state control. This was reinforced by the 1794 *Allgemeines Landrecht* law giving the state rights of supervision in all schools and requiring state regulation of all teachers.[2]

The organization of a state administrative structure, supervising a network of elementary schools, dates from 1808 when Humboldt became head of the Bureau of Ecclesiastical Affairs and Public Instruction, and created the celebrated *Volksschule* system. Each of the provinces were given a board for secondary schools and each district had a governmental board to oversee primary and junior secondary education.[3] A law of 1810 made education a secular activity and compulsory for three years.[4] Regulations of 1812 reformed the *Gymnasium*, making it a nine-year public secondary school able to confer the *Abitur* certificate, which controlled entry into higher education.[5] Further regulations in 1826 made schooling compulsory between the ages of 7 and 14, gave each parish an elementary school and prescribed training for all teachers. By 1837, detailed ministerial regulations for the *Gymnasien* covered the admission of pupils, the subjects taught, the length of terms, the distribution and working hours of teachers, and the nature of religious and physical education.

During Altenstein's ministry (1817–38), elementary education was extended and increasingly regulated, reaching its acme of illiberal, centralized efficiency and, at the same time, winning wide international acclaim.[6] By the 1830s there was thus a full national system of public elementary and secondary schools, which provided universal, compulsory schooling up to 14 years of age, and secondary education for the elite thereafter. Schools were public institutions, controlled by a complete state educational bureaucracy and financed largely through taxation. Public elementary schools already greatly outnumbered private schools and by 1861 they did so in the proportion of 34 to 1.[7] The state not only licensed and inspected schools, but also licensed and trained teachers, specified the curriculum and regulated national examinations. Elementary education was clearly quite distinct from secondary schooling but the rudiments of an articulated hierarchy of schools were developing, assisted by the creation, from the 1830s onwards, of various types of post-elementary and intermediate schools. Decades ahead of any other nation, Prussia had an integrated public school system which, not coincidentally, also exercised the most rigid control over what was taught.

France, 1806–1882

French educational development presents a more complex case where national education evolved in a less uniform manner over a longer period. The central administrative apparatus was created by Napoleon with the laws founding the *Université* in 1806 and 1808. The Napoleonic *lycée* was created in 1802, giving the state strategic control over secondary education. During the Bourbon Restoration the central administrative apparatus was maintained and the state consolidated its hold over education. An ordinance of 1816 required each commune to maintain a primary school for boys under the control of communal committees and the 1833 *Loi Guizot* extended state control over the licensing of teachers and inspection of schools, and extended primary schooling for boys and girls to each commune.[8]

By the time of the Second Empire one can already speak of a full juridical and administrative framework for national education. Public schools already dominated over private schools at primary level and state secondary schools were almost as numerous as private ones. In 1850 there were 43 843 public primary schools and 16 736 private institutions.[9] By 1865 the *lycée* and *collège* had virtually caught up with the private Catholic schools, accounting for 46 per cent of the country's 143 375 secondary-school pupils.[10] Of the 556 major secondary schools, the state controlled the majority, including 77 *lycées* and 251 municipal colleges.[11] Thus by the mid-century there was already a dominant public sector and an integrated educational bureaucracy at national and local levels which was responsible for licensing and inspecting schools, training and certificating teachers, organizing public finance and regulating national examinations. However, the spread of elementary education did not keep pace with the relative advance of secondary and vocational schooling, nor match the precocious bureaucracy of the administrative apparatus. It was not until 1882, with the Jules Ferry Laws, that elementary education became free and compulsory, and universal provision was not achieved before this time.

The United States, 1830–1865

The United States had no national education system as such since it had adopted a federal structure where each state had sovereign powers over its education. Each state had an individual system although certain federal regulations did require educational provisions as a condition of entry into the Union for the new territories. However, it would be broadly true to say that the southern states did not generally develop public education systems until after the Civil War, whilst most northern states did so during the Era of Reform between 1830 and 1860. It would be inappropriate here to attempt to summarize individual state legislation on schooling but, suffice to say, a number of general indices do demonstrate the existence of public systems in the northern states by the time of the Civil War.

During the reform era most northern states developed systems of public schools, financed from public sources and administered by the state and county education boards. Municipally owned and controlled, 'common schools' outflanked voluntary and charity schools during this period so that by 1850, 90 per cent of school and college enrolment was in institutions receiving public funds.[12] In New York City in 1850, public schools accounted for 82 per cent of the total; in Salem in 1846 they accounted for 76 per cent; and in Milwaukee in 1848 they accounted for 54 per cent. By 1865, 89 per cent of school children in Massachusetts were in public schools.[13]

Public high schools, financed out of taxation, developed in major towns from 1820 onwards, but these continued to be outnumbered by partially or totally independent academies. By 1860 many northern towns had so-called 'grade school systems' which reached up from the common school to the high school and provided an integrated, if rudimentary, educational ladder.

Public school systems in the northern states became increasingly regulated by the elected public education boards. These often appointed teachers, specified school books, regulated school terms and enacted compulsory regulation on attendance. By the 1860s, rate-bills (tuition fees) had been abolished in most states (Pennsylvania, 1834; Indiana, 1856; Ohio, 1853; Illinois, 1855; Vermont, 1864; New York, 1867; Connecticut, 1868; Rhode Island, 1868; Michigan, 1869; and New Jersey, 1871).[14] In 1850 public expenditure accounted for 47 per cent of all educational outlays, which otherwise included endowments, fees and other parental contributions. By 1870 two-thirds of educational spending had a public source.[15] Whilst less administratively centralized than education systems in Europe, the typical educational structure in the northern states had all the hallmarks of the public education system. They had achieved high levels of enrolment, a large measure of structural integration, complete predominance of public schooling, largely funded by the local state, and an incipient professionalization of teachers, at least in urban areas. Whilst there was considerably less teacher training than in Europe, high levels of literacy suggest that the reform movement did much to improve the efficiency of education.

England, 1839–1902

The development of a national public system of education in England and Wales lagged behind the continental states by a good half-century. Nothing like a full public system existed before 1870, compulsory attendance was not effected in most areas until the 1880s and elementary schools were not entirely free until 1891.[16] It was not until Balfour's Education Act of 1902 that state secondary schools were created and a fully integrated educational administration consolidated.

Throughout the nineteenth century the mainsprings of popular education were the voluntary societies. The majority of schools were owned and controlled by the National Society and the British and Foreign Schools Society, representing, respectively, the Anglican and non-conformist churches. It is true that from 1833 onwards governments did give some financial support to the societies but this remained a small fraction of their finance until 1870. By 1861 total government spending on education was only £250 000 compared with the £600 000 which was spent by the smaller Prussian state 30 years previously, and by 1869 still two-thirds of school expenditure came from voluntary sources.[17] Far from being undermined by Forster's Elementary School Act of 1870, the voluntary schools actually grew in strength within the quasi-public system which it created. By 1881 there were 14 370 voluntary schools to 3 692 public board schools, and attendance at voluntary schools was double that for the board schools. By 1902 the voluntary sector was still vastly dominant with 14 000 schools as compared with 6 000 board schools.[18] Secondary education, of course, remained exclusively private throughout the nineteenth century. There were no state secondary schools until the 1902 Act created the public grammar schools, exactly 100 years after Napoleon created the state *lycée*.

The lack of state involvement in schooling did not, of course, prevent the voluntary system from creating something approaching a national network of elementary schools, although there was a clear limit to their potential expansion. However, the weakness of the central administration in education had considerable consequence and it was in this that England was most exceptional. The Central Society for Education declared that 'the great deficit of English education [has been] the want of national education', adding that in this England represented the 'one great exception of the civilised world'.[19] It was most certainly correct. No national government apparatus for administering education existed at all until the creation of the Education Committee in 1839. This unusual body remained exceptionally weak, unpopular and ineffective, continually frustrated by its limited powers. By 1860 there were some 60 school inspectors, but many schools remained uninspected.[20] The function of the committee lay mainly in the allocation of government funds, and it can hardly be credited with supervising schools in the sense that applied in the northern US states or on the Continent. Government involvement in teacher training was also minimal and the creation of the 'pupil-teacher' system in 1846 was no substitute for a system of Normal schools (for teacher training). The supervision of curricula was slight before the instigation of 'payment by results' in the 1860s and this, in tying funds to educational results, had the largely negative effect of limiting education to the three Rs. There was no licensing of teachers, nor did any public authority coordinate public examinations. Most damaging was the absence of any integrated education administration. Elementary schools, technical schools and secondary schools remained supervised by separate authorities until the end of the century.

The 1870 Act, which created the local education boards, is usually credited with laying the foundations of a public system. However, it was never more than a compromise with the voluntary system. An integrated national education system was not properly consolidated until the 1902 Act, which created the local education authorities and brought all sectors of education under a unified administrative structure.

This distinctly uneven development of public or state forms in education, which, as the above summary comparative chronology suggests, particularly separated English from leading continental systems, inevitably had its effects on the quality of educational provision. Where school systems were systematically organized and well funded by public authorities, where teachers were trained and their work carefully monitored, and where education generally was considered a national priority, this inevitably led to higher 'standards' of education amongst the people who had access to it. This does not mean that what they were taught was necessarily desirable from all points of view, and, indeed, the kinds of knowledge and attitudes that were transmitted by the most efficient systems, notably in Prussia, often reflected most illiberal and doctrinaire purposes on the part of the state, and consequently engendered great suspicion amongst those with more democratic leanings. However, it did mean that whatever it was that was taught was taught effectively, leaving its mark on those who participated in the process.

This circumstance did not avoid the notice of contemporary observers. The relative merits and shortcomings of different national systems were a frequent subject of contemporary debate, informed by the first-hand observations of numerous well-travelled educationalists, and grist to the mill in many political campaigns over educational reform. Clearly then, as now, comparative judgements took account of what was taught in different school systems and therefore reflected political evaluations of what education was actually about, and how it was best organized. Thus those who praised the French and Prussian systems, such as many of the English middle-class Radicals, did so because they had notions that were relatively favourable to the idea of state intervention. Amongst these the more democratically minded, such as the English Radical MP Arthur Roebuck, remained suspicious of the authoritarianism of the Prussian system and advocated a type of schooling in England that combined Prussian efficiency with the democratic control of the US system. On the other hand, committed *laissez-faire* liberals, such as the educational polemicist Edward Baines, would have none of the Prussian system, not only because it was supposedly autocratic in its aims but also because it was étatist in its organization.[21]

However, despite the evident political dimensions to the debate, there was a level of consensus, within what might be called the international community of educators, about what constituted efficiency or effectiveness in education. This involved acknowledging the paradoxical fact that public education had advanced further in a number of continental states, including some which had barely thrown off the yoke of absolutist rule and had barely begun to industrialize, than in England, Europe's most industrial society. As the author of the preface to a popular book on US schools put it,

> It cannot be concealed, and ought not to be denied, that under one of the most arbitrary governments of Europe [Prussia], the children of all, even the meanest in the kingdom, are receiving, in their village and parish schools, more varied and solid, and in every sense valuable instruction, than in any of our schools, I had almost said academies, are accustomed or competent to furnish.[22]

Prussia was dubbed by Victor Cousin as the quintessential land of schools and barracks, and was universally admired, even by those most opposed to its political system, for the prolixity of its elementary schools and the vaunted efficiency of its teachers. Another well-known American educationalist, George Emerson, described with some envy the position of the Prussian teacher in the 1840s:

> The Prussian schoolmaster devotes himself to teaching for life, because he knows that, for life, it will yield him an adequate support. The government assigns him a post, and thus guarantees him, during good behaviour. It supplies him with a house and garden, and encourages him to collect round him all the comforts of life. It secures, also, that his salary shall be punctually paid; prescribes a course of study to which every child is obliged to conform, enforces a regular and universal attendance of all children of the proper age, and provides a system of rigid inspection and supervision. The school is so connected with the church and so honoured by the law as well as by usage, that the teacher is considered inferior only to the pastor.... finally, he has the cheering assurance that when, in the discharge of his high, but toilsome and anxious duties, he has worn out his best days, he will not at last be dismissed and forgotten, but will be held in honoured remembrance by those whom he has instructed, and will be permitted to retire on a pension from his government.[23]

Few other countries, outside the German states, could match the conditions afforded to the Prussian school teacher, but Prussia was not the only continental state whose education elicited the admiration of English and American educators. According to Alonzo Potter, Emerson's co-author,

> Provisions adequate to elementary instruction of all children in the land exist not only in Prussia, but also in Holland, in Saxony, Austria, and all other states of Germany; in France, Switzerland, Denmark, Sweden and Norway.[24]

We may question the validity of such sweeping endorsements of all these countries: France and Belgium, for instance, certainly did not have such evident superiority in all fields. However, many English observers, including those appointed to Royal Commissions, found much to applaud in the educational provision of numerous continental states. Matthew Arnold celebrated the academic excellence of the French *lycées*, which he attributed to the efficacy and acceptance there of state intervention; Huxley, the eminent scientist, praised Napoleon and, *inter alia*, the German states for declaring *la carrière ouverte aux talents*, and backing it with superior post-elementary education; Lyon Playfair, the scientist and tireless advocate of technical education, praised Prussia, Switzerland and France for the excellence of their higher technical schools.[25] Clearly, each nation had particular strengths and weaknesses, and the more prescient observers would make these distinctions, acknowledging, for instance, that if France had excellent *polytechniques*, it also had notable deficiencies in its elementary provision. However, the general distinction of Prussian education could not be gainsaid, just as the exceptional accumulation of English educational deficiencies could not be denied.

Contemporary testimony to English educational backwardness is ample. From the declaration of the Select Committee on the Education of the Lower Orders in 1818 'that England is the worst educated country in Europe', to Balfour's assertion in 1902 that 'England is behind all continental rivals in education', contemporary debates were littered with comparisons with European systems, almost invariably to England's detriment.[26] Numerous Victorian educationalists toured Europe and came home lamenting the state of English education. James Kay returned from Europe to remark that in England,

> where the aristocracy is richer and more powerful than that of any other country in the world, the poor are more depressed, more pauperised.... and very much worse educated than the poor of any other European country, solely excepting Russia, Turkey, South Italy, Portugal and Spain.[27]

In his parliamentary speech in defence of his 1837 education bill, the Whig politician, Henry Brougham, echoed the same theme: 'It cannot be doubted that some legislative effort must at length be made to remove from this country the opprobrium of having done less for the education of the people than any of the more civilised nations on earth.'[28]

Unfavourable comparisons were not only made with Europe. Benjamin Shaw, an English charity school advocate, wrote in 1817, after a tour of the United States: 'I am ashamed to reflect that in my native country, Great Britain, there are so many in opposition to the education of the poor, and to the system which is here an undisputed good.'[29] Nor were these solely domestic judgements or ones born of any national proclivity for self-deprecation. Whilst England had the dubious distinction of a temporary export of monitorial type schools, these were not long favoured outside the empire of their birth; few foreign experts commented favourably on English education, and foreign observers were conspicuous in their lack of interest in visiting or emulating English schools. De Tocqueville may have admired the British Constitution, but he did not have much to say about English elementary schools. The American, Alonzo Potter, wrote forthrightly that 'England has neglected the education of her labouring population, and the consequence is that the land swarms with paupers and vagabonds.'[30] His view seems to have been shared by many continental observers.

Recent historians have sometimes doubted the validity of contemporary 'expert' opinion on international comparisons, arguing that experts were often prone to exaggerate foreign superiority and domestic deficiency to enlist support for their reform proposals. The neo-liberal historian E. G. West has attempted to rehabilitate the reputation of English educational *laissez-faire*, arguing that reformers produced misleading enrolment statistics based on unrealistic age bases, and thus exaggerated English deficiencies.[31] However, comparative data, which West largely ignores, vindicates the deficiency verdict, at least in terms of the relative position of English education. Statistical indices of educational development, in the form of comparative data on enrolments, average length of schooling, literacy, public funding and teacher training, offer further comparative measures which make a reliance on the opinions of contemporary experts unnecessary, and they strikingly confirm the thesis of uneven educational development, not only in the English case but in general comparative terms.

Elementary enrolments

The first countries to establish near-universal enrolment at elementary schools were almost certainly Prussia and some of the other German states. Compulsory elementary education in Prussia was decreed by Frederick the Great and other absolutist monarchs before him, but the legislation of 1810, requiring three years of education at the *Volksschule*, was the first to be seriously enforced. Universal enrolment was largely achieved by the 1830s. Victor Cousin estimated in his report of 1831 that 42.4 per cent of all children were in attendance, whilst 42.8 per cent of Prussian children were of school age (7–14 years). Levasseur, in his classic comparative study of elementary schools, claimed that in 1861 Prussia had 2 875 836 students out of a total of 3 090 294 of school age. Saxony had even higher levels.[32]

Elementary education in the United States developed unevenly, with extreme ethnic and regional disparities. During the ante-bellum period, enrolments reached high levels in the northern states, particularly in the North East, whilst they remained low in all slave states, not only amongst blacks, where slaves were legally forbidden education, but also amongst whites. Albert Fishlow estimates that in 1840 the enrolment rate for white 5–19 year olds varied from 81.4 per cent in New England and 54.7 per cent in the Mid-Atlantic states to 16.2 per cent in South-Atlantic states and 13.4 per cent in southern central states. State-by-state enrolment figures illustrate this more exactly (see Table 1.1)[33].

The high rates of enrolment in the North East are corroborated by a number of local studies. Kaestle's research into 16 counties in New York State suggests levels of enrolment at 75 per cent of all 4–13 years olds even in 1800. Further data for eight towns in Massachusetts (1860), Michigan (1850) and Chicago (1860) showed 85–90 per cent of all 7–13 year olds in school.[34] Lawrence Cremin found that in Lowell, Massachusetts, an exceptionally education-conscious city, 80 per cent of all children between 4 and 16 were in daily attendance in 1856.[35]

Table 1.1   Percentage of white population
enrolled, 5–19 years, 1840

Maine	87.7
New Hampshire	85.6
New York	69.4
Massachusetts (1832)	68.9
Connecticut	65.3
Rhode Island	49.4
Pennsylvania	31.7
Kentucky	10.6
Virginia	9.8
South Carolina	8.1

Comparisons between elementary enrolment in Prussia and the United States are clearly made difficult by regional and ethnic variation. Whilst Prussia had standardized nationwide provision and legal requirements, US states had individual systems with their own state legislation. Even regional comparisons must remain tendentious since the attendance of those enrolled was not always regular in the United States and since estimates are, in any case, based on different age bases. However, it seems safe to say that overall, national enrolment was considerably lower in the United States than in Prussia until the latter half of the century. Cremin calculates a national figure for 1850 of 50.4 per cent of whites between 5 and 19 years and 42.1 per cent of all children of that age.[36] With the exception of the North East, no region had achieved universal provision before the Civil War. However, the New England states and rural areas in the North generally could claim near-universal attendance by this time.

French enrolments in primary school were considerably lower than in Prussia and the northern US states. According to Levasseur, there were 3 322 423 children in primary school in 1850 as against 2 875 836 in Prussia 10 years later. However, the population of France was some three times as great.[37] Although the number of elementary schools increased rapidly between 1810 and 1850, reaching a total in excess of 63 000 by 1847, there were still over 3 000 communes (out of 38 000) without schools by the mid-century. Near-universal enrolment was not achieved until the Third Republic.[38]

Enrolment in elementary schools in England and Wales, which as in France was not yet compulsory, was comparatively low by European standards, although possibly not lower than in France. According to Horace Mann's educational supplement to the 1851 census, the most reliable source we have, there were 2 144 378 day scholars in England and Wales. The total population aged 3–15 years was 4 908 696, which gives an enrolment rate of 43 per cent, assuming (generously) all day scholars to be under 15.[39] Given that the typical age base in US statistics was 14 years as against 12 years in England and Wales, this indicates that English enrolment was not only behind the 70–80 per cent rate for children in the north-eastern states but also behind the aggregate figure for the whole American population, including those in the southern slave states which banned the education of slaves. Comparisons with Prussia can only be approximate since statistics, again, are based on different age bases. Nevertheless, one may calculate, assuming that all 2 million or so scholars were below 14, and assuming an even age distribution of population, that 2 144 378 were in school out of 3 272 464 (4 908 696 × 8/12) children of 6–14 years – that is 65 per cent. The comparison with Prussia's near-universal enrolment for this age range is stark. In his detailed study of the 1851 census, D. I. Coleman found that in London only 56 per cent of 5–9 year olds and 46.3 per cent of 10–14 year olds were in school.[40] Enrolments in elementary schools in England and Wales did, of course, rise steadily throughout the century and particularly after 1870. However, according to Levasseur, the proportion of school-age children (7–14) enrolled in 1892 was still only 77 per cent a clear half-century after Prussia and other German states had near-universal enrolment.[41]

Another measure of enrolment rates is the proportion of the total population at school. Although this is a somewhat abstract statistic, and assumes equal national age distributions for comparative purposes, it was the favourite contemporary unit of comparison. Michael Mulhall, in his 1884 *Dictionary of Statistics*, gave the comparative estimates as set out in Table 1.2.[42]

There are certainly some eccentric figures in this series and they appear to underestimate enrolment in England and Wales. For instance, although Brougham's Select Committee report found 6.6 per cent enrolment in 1818, the Kerry Report found 9.1 per cent enrolled in 1833 (against Mulhall's 7 per cent for 1830) and some scholars have argued that the Kerry

Table 1.2 School children as percentage of total population

Country (by rank order, 1850)	1830	1850	1881
USA	15	17	18
Germany	16	16	17
Scandinavia	13	14	15
Switzerland	14	14	16
Belgium and Holland	15	17	18
Scotland	9	10	15
France	6	9	13
England	7	8	15
Austria	5	6	9

Table 1.3 Students as percentage of total
population, 1850

Maine	32
Denmark	21
USA (excluding slaves)	21
USA (including slaves)	20
Sweden	18
Saxony	18
Prussia	17
Norway	16
Britain	12
France	10

returns were underestimates.[43] The more reliable 1851 census report found 12 per cent of the population in school. England's relative position appears in these figures to have been higher than that of France, although not above those of Scotland and Holland, which are similarly underestimated.[44] However, recent research casts doubt on the accuracy of the comparison between England and France because the French population was aging in the second half of the century and the proportion of young people in the total population may well have been lower than in England[45] even at the mid-century. Cremin acknowledges that Mulhall's statistics can be out by as much as 20 per cent, but insists that they 'were essentially sound in the gross relative position they assigned to various nations'.[46] Whatever the judgement about its position relative to France, England, clearly, lagged behind not only the United States and the German states but also behind Scandinavia and Switzerland. This is confirmed by J. de Bow's statistical series for 1850, which uses the conventional English 12 per cent figure as the basis for enrolment in Britain (see Table 1.3)[47].

Thus, despite the attempts of E. G. West to undermine the experts' claims, it appears that by international comparisons, elementary education in England and Wales was considerably less widespread than in other major countries. In the middle of the nineteenth century the average Prussian child had 7 or 8 years of elementary education. Children in other German states, and in Scandinavia and Switzerland, had often had similar periods in school. Although attendance in the United States was less consistent, and although school terms were often shorter than in Prussia, it seems likely that 9 or 10 years of schooling between 4 or 5 and 14 in the rural North was quite typical. In England the average child had no more than 4 or 5 years of elementary schooling.[48]

Post-elementary enrolments

Nineteenth-century Europe and the United States experienced not only considerable growth in elementary education but also a proliferation of post-elementary and secondary schools. These can be divided into four main types. There were the traditional classical secondary schools, such as the French *lycée* and the German *Gymnasium*; the more modern secondary schools for the middle class, such as the French *écoles primaires supérieures* and the German *Realschulen*; the technical institutions, ranging from trade schools to the polytechnics; and, finally, various forms of university and higher-education institutions.

In France, after the creation of the *lycée* in 1802, there was a gradual increase in full secondary schools until the number of colleges finally reached and surpassed the pre-revolutionary levels. By 1865 there were 77 *lycées* and 251 *collèges*, and a similar number of private secondary schools. In all there were 143 574 students in secondary schools, 54.2 per cent of these in private institutions. In addition to these there were the advanced primary schools, known as the *écoles primaires supérieures*, of which there were 271 for girls and 436 for boys by 1850.[49] After 1839, a number of *enseignement professionnel* schools, providing a modern education for the lower middle and artisanal classes, were also developed. France was well provided with elementary trade schools, which numbered about 50 by the mid-century. It was also well known for its *polytechniques* and *grandes écoles*, the higher vocational schools whose standards greatly surpassed those of the English universities.

Prussia had a similar array of full secondary and intermediate schools. Legislation in 1812 defined the status of the *Gymnasium* as a nine-year secondary school able to confer the *Abitur* certificate, the prestigious passport into higher education. By 1860 there were 139 *Gymnasien* with 38 908 pupils. In the 1830s and 1840s, numerous other secondary schools emerged known as *Realgymnasien* and *Realschulen*, which offered a more modern curriculum for a predominantly bourgeois clientele. By 1860 there were 33 *Realgymnasien* with 11 416 pupils.[50] Later in the century these were joined by the *Mittelschule*, an intermediate secondary school. Prussia also had a number of basic trade schools, technical high schools and polytechnics which were highly regarded internationally.

The United States had a wide array of colleges and secondary institutions which tended to combine classical and vocational education. By far the most numerous of the secondary schools were the academies, some of which were private and others which were 'incorporated' and received public funds. By 1830, according to Hindsdale, there were 950 incorporated academies alone, and Inglis cites 6085 academies all told by 1850. By 1860 there were also 246 colleges, offering post-secondary education.[51] However, by far the most celebrated of secondary institutions was the high school, probably the first entirely free secondary school in the world and the jewel in the reformers' crown. The first of these, Boston's English high school, was inaugurated in 1821 and was followed by others conceived on similar lines. By 1850 Massachusetts had a high school in every other town and there were 102 in all by 1860.[52]

Secondary schools in England and Wales fell into three main categories, as the Taunton Commission found when it undertook its mammoth survey of schools in 1868. There were the 46 proprietary boarding schools which, along with the 9 famous public schools, gave classical education to the upper middle class and aristocracy; there were the 209 endowed grammar schools used mainly by the professional middle class; and finally there was the dense outgrowth of 'lesser' private schools, frequented by the children of independent artisans and the lower middle class. It is hard to know which of these to compare with the full European secondary schools. The Commissioners found most of the lesser private schools unspeakably bad so they can hardly qualify as full secondary schools. The endowed grammar schools were found to be generally 'very unsatisfactory' and in a 'chaotic' condition, but they often aspired towards full secondary schooling. However, as Bamford has shown, only around 70 of these ever sent children to university.[53] There were probably no more than 100 secondary schools in all that even aspired towards giving the kind of secondary education typically provided in the French *lycées* and *collèges* and the German *Gymnasien*; and one may doubt whether any of these matched the latter's academic standards. In any case, although exact numerical comparisons are not possible, it would seem that England had comparatively few adequate secondary schools, least of all to suit the middle class. The latter deficiency was exacerbated by the great scarcity of vocational higher education and the virtual absence of full-time trade schools until the end of the century.[54]

Comparative statistical analysis of enrolment rates in secondary education can only be very approximate given the nature of the data and the difficulty of comparing institutions which are not entirely cognate. However, if we limit the attempt to full secondary institutions which take children up to 17 or 18 and prepare them for university or higher vocational studies, we can make some proximate comparisons, using English public, proprietary and grammar schools, French *lycées* and *collèges*, German *Gymnasien* and *Realschulen*, and US high schools and academies.

Proportionate enrolment in these institutions was small in all countries, and largely male. In France in 1842, according to Villemain's official figures, only 1 in 493 of the population were in secondary schools, a rather lower proportion than before the Revolution. Fewer than 2.8 per cent of the age group were in attendance. However, enrolment grew steadily and by 1865 there were 143 574 recorded secondary students, roughly 1 in 260 of the population. Official estimates put this at 4 per cent of the age group, which may be generous, but certainly 5 per cent of male adolescents were attending.[55] There was no fully institutionalized system of secondary education for girls and consequently far fewer even attended post-elementary institutions. Paris alone was relatively well provided for in this respect. Whilst in the Department of Seine 19 317 boys were in secondary schools (1850), there were 17 000 girls (1842) who were in similar institutions.[56]

Prussian secondary education was no more widespread than in France. The proportion of the total population attending *Gymnasien* in 1830 was around 1 in 500.[57] However, modern secondary schools, including the *Realgymnasien* and the *Realschulen*, accounted for half as many again, bringing the Prussian rate for secondary education in line with the French level. In his important study of enrolment patterns in nineteenth-century secondary schools, Fritz Ringer shows that the mean secondary enrolments for the relevant age groups were 2.3 per cent in Germany (1870) and 2.5 per cent in France (1876). The lower figures are due to the numbers leaving before the end of the full secondary programme.[58]

Recruitment to US public high schools should by all rights have been more extensive given that, unlike their European counterparts, they were entirely free. Available data do not allow a conclusive answer to this. Orville Taylor estimated that 5 per cent received secondary education in 1835, which compares favourably with France and Germany. However, the figure may well have been higher. Figures for a somewhat later period suggest comparatively high levels of enrolment. There were 167 100 students in academies in 1880 and 202 926 students in public high schools in 1890, in all 370000-odd secondary students in a population of around 50 million. This would give a student/population ratio of roughly 1 in 135, about double the rate for France in 1865, and representing something like 10 per cent of the age group.[59] In some educationally advanced areas we know that high-school enrolment was relatively high before this. For instance, in a sample of 10 per cent of Massachusetts towns with high schools, Katz found that an average of 20 per cent of eligible children attended in 1860.[60] Relatively few of these would have ever completed high school. According to figures from the US Bureau of Census, it is estimated that in 1870 only about 16 600 students graduated from high schools – that is, 2 per cent of the population aged 17.[61] This may be compared with the 0.8 per cent of the age group who received the *Abitur* certificate in Germany (1870) and a similar proportion who were awarded the *baccalauréat* in France.[62] Whether the average high school or academy gave an equivalent education to that of the *lycée* or *Gymnasium* is hard to judge, but certainly it appears that secondary education of some sort was relatively more widespread in the United States than in other countries.

If this is so, the situation was quite the reverse in England and Wales. In their 1868 report the Taunton Commissioners carefully distinguished between endowed schools giving a full classical secondary education and those providing little more than an extended elementary schooling, and on the basis of these returns, and the figures for proprietary and public schools, Bamford estimates that some 25 000 boys were receiving a classical secondary education at this time.[63] Given the virtual absence of girls' secondary schools, it appears that scarcely more than 1 in 1000 of the population were in full secondary school at a time when 1 in 260 of the French population were in *lycées* or colleges.[64] Comparing the 25 000

English children with the 155 000 French children in secondary school, and allowing that perhaps only two-thirds of these latter were in classical forms, Lawrence Stone concludes that 'the French bourgeois elite was four times the size of the English, despite the fact...that the French population was only about two-thirds as large again as that of England'.[65] Any comparisons such as these are, of course, contentious and are as much about quality as quantity. If we ignore the level of education given and simply concentrate on bodies in schools, then the situation looks somewhat different. Retrospective figures in the Robbins Report suggested that 1 per cent of 17-year olds were in some kind of full-time attendance in 1870. Comparing this with the 0.8 per cent of German and French students who received the *Abitur* and *baccalauréat* awards at this time, Ringer comments that 'British secondary education around 1870 was practically as inclusive as its counterparts in France and Germany.'[66] However, descriptive evidence of the relative quality of endowed school education and continental secondary schooling does suggest that the gap in levels of secondary education was real. English contemporary opinion certainly confirms this judgement, most notably in Matthew Arnold's very unfavourable comparisons between English and French secondary education. 'Through the intervention of the state,' wrote Arnold, the middle class in France 'enjoys better schools for its children....than the same class enjoys in any country where the state has not interfered to found them.'[67]

Irrespective of the gross proportions in attendance, we do know that recruitment to English secondary schools was more socially exclusive than in other countries. The public schools were well known as the most aristocratic institutions of their kind in Europe. Bamford estimates that in the half-century before 1850, fewer than 10 per cent of students at Eton came from professional families: the vast majority were sons of gentry and landowners.[68] By comparison the French *lycées* were thoroughly bourgeois institutions. According to Duruy's comprehensive official survey of French secondary schools in 1864, only 17 per cent of students were children of landowners, whilst the majority were of bourgeois origin. Some 17 per cent came from leading business families, 18.65 per cent from professional families and 11.3 per cent were children of civil servants. Recruitment also included a substantial proportion of children from peasant and petit-bourgeois families (peasants, 12.3 per cent; white collar, 2.7 per cent; shopkeepers, 14.3 per cent; artisans, 5.1 per cent).[69]

By the mid-century the Prussian *Gymnasium* had become similarly bourgeois in character. Records for a somewhat later period, 1875–99, demonstrate how far this had gone. Whilst only 2 per cent of graduates were children of landowners, the majority, 71 per cent, were from bourgeois families, of which 21 per cent were from the learned professions, 25 per cent from lower professionals, and 25 per cent from industrialist and merchant families.[70] For the United States we have no such comprehensive statistics, but Michael Katz's research into high schools in Massachusetts suggests that they were similarly dominated by children from middle-class families. Out of a sample of 135 students who entered Summerville high school between 1856 and 1861, 44 had fathers who were business proprietors or merchants (32 per cent), 26 came from artisanal families (19 per cent), 11 were from professional or public service families (8.1 per cent), 10 had fathers who were employees in business (7 per cent) and 10 came from farming families (7 per cent). Only 1 had a father who was an operative or farm labourer.[71]

The primary social base of secondary education in continental Europe and the United States was the middle class, and this became increasingly the case as the century progressed. Secondary schools were dominated by children from the upper middle class, from professional, business and commercial backgrounds. However, they frequently included a substantial proportion from lower middle-class and artisanal families. English secondary schools were unique not only in the rather lower rates of enrolment in anything approximating to full secondary education but also in the extreme class differentiation of the institutions. There was no form of secondary education which brought together all these groups and could be considered normatively middle class. Public schools were dominated by gentry and aristocracy, and even when these were joined in the 1840s by the new proprietary boarding schools, these were overwhelmingly upper middle class in composition. Only the grammar schools recruited predominantly from professional families and these assiduously excluded children from the lower middle-class and artisanal families, who were mainly to be found in the lesser private schools.

Teachers

Comparative assessment of the quality of education in different countries is particularly difficult, especially for a period when there were no uniform assessment techniques. However, certain comparisons do stand out. One factor which clearly affected the quality of education was the competence of teachers. Contemporary expert opinion and general school folklore are hard to disentangle, and it is difficult to arrive at a coherent descriptive impression in this area, let alone concrete measures. However, it seems fair to say that whilst teaching in Prussia seems to have elicited rather widespread international acclaim, domestic judgements on English and American teacher competence were generally rather unfavourable.

In general the continental states had gone rather further in the licensing and training of teachers than was the case in England or the United States. Regulations regarding the licensing of teachers were common in continental Europe. In Prussia, from 1810 onwards, there were rigorous state examinations for secondary teachers and even elementary teachers had three years of training after leaving school at 14.[72] Elementary teachers in France, although not legally obliged to undergo training, could only practise after satisfying state licensing requirements. According to the 1833 *Loi Guizot*, which attempted to raise the status of teachers, new recruits had to show evidence of intellectual ability and receive a certificate of fitness from local councillors. Even after the 1850 *Loi Falloux*, which restored greater freedom for private teaching, there were tight regulations on those wanting to open private primary schools: the latter were required to have a *brevet*, *baccalauréat* or certificate of apprenticeship, unless they were ministers of religion.[73] In both countries, public schoolteachers were considered to be part of the civil service, which meant that they were carefully monitored, not only for their competence but also, at times, for their political loyalty. In France the humble *instituteur* and *institutrice*, the primary schoolteachers, though respected for their vocation, were poorly paid and probably worse off than the average labourer. In 1840 the minimum salary of a village teacher was 200 francs p.a. (and 23 900 communes paid exactly this amount), although this was marginally increased by parental contributions. Prussian teachers, as we have already seen, were comparatively secure and well paid even at the elementary level.[74] Even where the status and pay were modest, the teacher received training. Prussia had 45 Normal schools by 1837. At the same time, France had 75 *écoles normales*, and by 1863 there were an additional 11 for women.[75] Many of these institutions were rigid and narrow, scarcely different from the typical ecclesiastical seminary in their spartan regimes. Their academic standards were barely above elementary level but students were strictly drilled in their vocation. Much was expected of the French teachers, although they were hardly rewarded for it. 'I expect a lot of you,' wrote Guizot. 'There will be, so to speak, no private life for you: the state asks not only for the tribute of your intelligence and knowledge, but for the whole man.' But in return, teachers 'must expect neither fame nor fortune, and must be content with the austere pleasure of having served their fellow men, obtaining nothing beyond their obscure and laborious condition'.[76]

American teachers were no better off than their French counterparts. Their wages were low, their jobs were insecure and the short session required them to take additional jobs, often as farm labourers, tavern keepers, prospectors and craftsmen. Most of them did not stay very long. Whilst they shared their low status with teachers in France, they differed in that they lacked permanent employment and were normally untrained. The first Normal school was not established until 1839, and by 1860 there were only 12 state Normal schools and 6 private ones.[77] By the middle of the century no more than 1 in 4 of the higher-status urban schoolteachers had received a Normal school diploma.[78] In New York State in 1860 only 3 per cent of female teachers and 4 per cent of male teachers had attended Normal school.[79] Teaching in the United States did not begin to cast off its casual labour status until the mid-century. It was an occupation that anyone could enter without restriction and, according to Emerson, that a 'large proportion of common schoolteachers [were] not well qualified for their duties, is so generally admitted that proof would be superfluous'.[80] A mid-western school crusader claimed in 1842 that

> at least four-fifths of the teachers in the Common schools in Illinois would not pass an examination in the rudiments of our English education, and most of them have taken to teaching because they hadn't anything in particular to do.[81]

In England, the status of teachers was similar to that in the United States, and they came in for equal criticism. Dickens' famous description of Victorian teachers as a race of 'blockheads and impostors' may owe something to poetic licence, but there can be no doubt they were poorly qualified and mostly untrained. There were no legal requirements regulating entry into teaching in England, and many teachers drifted in and out of the business or supplemented it with other jobs as in the United States. The average pay was despicably low at around £85 p.a. for men and £60 p.a. for women in 1854, and this clearly did not act as a great inducement for those contemplating teaching as an occupation.[82] Teacher-training institutions were rare before the 1850s and the early efforts of the Education Department to set up more through government finance were fiercely resisted by the Church. It was not until after 1846, with the instigation of the pupil-teacher system, that the training of teachers became more widespread. However, even after this got under way, most of the teaching in schools was done by trainee pupils and untrained assistants. In 1860 there was fewer than one certificated teacher per school, and the number of pupil-teachers still outnumbered trained teachers by three to two in 1875.[83]

Not only were English teachers poorly trained but they were proportionally less numerous than in Europe. According to Mulhall's estimates of teachers, this was the case even in the 1880s after English enrolment levels had begun to catch up. Pupil/teacher ratios were evidently amongst the worst in Europe, and far behind those in the United States (see Table 1.4).[84]

A fuller comparative study of the quality of education in different countries, which cannot be attempted here, would need to consider the nature of the curriculum and the effectiveness of different pedagogic methods. Although this would be a difficult task there is some evidence that the English curriculum was notably narrow in relation to continental schools, particularly after the introduction of payment by results. Furthermore, in the opinion of many contemporary educationalists, it was the teaching method adopted in Prussian, Dutch and Swiss schools, derived from Pestalozzi, which was the most effective form of educational practice at that time, and

Table 1.4   Ratio of pupils to teachers

	Teachers (000s)	Pupils (000s)	Ratio
USA	273	9705	35.5
Switzerland	10	411	41.1
France	119	4950	41.5
Belgium	12	690	57.5
Scandinavia	18	1100	61.0
Holland	7	490	70.0
Austria	52	3690	70.9
Britain	57	5251	92.1

the 'simultaneous' method of the English monitorial school was, by comparison, a blunt instrument, more effective in stunning its pupils into sullen quiescence than in honing alert and intelligent minds. Whatever the truth of this, evidence of literacy rates, our only quantitative measure of educational results, does suggest that the quality of education varied and that England had little to be proud of.

Literacy

If elementary education in England was notable for its low enrolments and uneven quality, so levels of literacy were comparatively modest by the standard of the most literate European nations and the United States. Whilst in most European countries industrialization was associated with increasing general literacy, it is probable that in England rapid industrialization caused an initial decline in levels of literacy. This pattern was reversed in the course of the nineteenth century, as schooling began to keep pace with growing urban populations, but Britain did not regain its seventeenth-century reputation as Europe's most literate nation. Estimates for adult literacy levels are notoriously controversial, and variant definitions and unreliable data sources suggest considerable margins of error. However, Britain's relative position is confirmed by most estimates. On the basis of the Registrar-General's 1841 figures derived from marriage registers, adult male literacy was at around 67 per cent in Britain as a whole.[85] This would include many who were barely literate – that is, only able to write their own name. US literacy rates varied enormously by region and ethnic group. According to the 1870 census, illiteracy amongst those over nine years old was 21.9 per cent for females, 18.3 per cent for males and 81.4 per cent for blacks of both sexes. However, if we take Cremin's estimates for illiteracy amongst white adults from 1860 census data, a figure of 9 per cent emerges which compares very favourably with British levels.[86] Using Cipolla's comparative estimates for 1850 and including the US figure, various comparisons emerge

Table 1.5 Percentage of adult illiteracy, *c.*1850

USA (1860, white)	9
Sweden (1850)	10
Scotland (1851)	20
Prussia (1849)	20
England and Wales (1851)	30–33
France (1851)	40–45

Table 1.6 Percentage of adult illiteracy, 1878

USA	9
Germany	12
Scotland	15
England	23
France	30

(see Table 1.5).[87] Mulhall's figures suggest a similar rank ordering for 1878 (see Table 1.6).[88]

Lawrence Stone argues that by 1860 France had drawn level with England in levels of literacy.[89] Low literacy rates in England have an interesting correlate in the comparatively small number of libraries and books published in England compared with France and Germany. In 1848, England had 28 major libraries compared with 80 in Germany and 107 in France. During the preceding period the average number of new titles published was 1 000 as against 5 000 in France and 6 000 in Germany.[90]

The analysis presented here has concentrated only on the quantifiable measures of educational 'advance'. This inevitably has many limitations. However, it does seem to confirm the testimony of 'expert' contemporary opinion about the uneven nature of educational development in the nineteenth century. Furthermore, it also suggests that comparative educational development, as measured in data on enrolment, access and literacy levels, strikingly matches the chronologies of the development of national systems in different countries. Countries which developed state-funded systems of public education early, such as Prussia, Switzerland and Holland, did seem also to have achieved the higher levels of enrolment and literacy. This was also true of the northern US states, which developed public, though decentralized, education systems. It seems, therefore, that the organizational factor which was most clearly linked with educational development, as measured in levels of education received, was not necessarily the existence of centralized educational bureaucracy but rather the establishment of a public system funded and supervised by the state, whether at a central or a local level. Certainly, in countries such as England and Wales, which had no public system, either centrally or locally controlled, the results seem to have been largely negative for education. The following chapters will analyse the social causes of these differential national patterns of educational development.

2
The Social Origins of National Education Systems

The social origins of national education systems remain a relatively unexplored question in comparative sociology. Despite the extensive debates about the nature of schooling in the nineteenth century, none of the classical founders of social science provided a systematic analysis of the origins of mass schooling. Saint-Simon, Marx and Weber were all interested in the development of education and made more or less casual allusion to it, but nowhere produced a formal theory. Durkheim, alone of the 'founding fathers', devoted a study to it and gave regular lectures on the subject, but he never produced a comparative theory on the scale of his studies of suicide and religion. Modern sociology has only recently begun to fill this gap. However, theoretical studies of the functions of schooling, of which there have been many, have remained largely ahistorical and rarely include a full comparative dimension. Margaret Archer's two studies of the origins of education systems in France, England, Denmark and Russia represent a sole, courageous effort to explore the field in depth.[1] In the light of considerable advances made in recent years in comparative and historical sociology, this theoretical lacuna is somewhat surprising and leaves one of the most fascinating problems in historical development largely unexplored.

Whilst the problem of educational development has prompted little in the way of sociological theory, it has not lacked its historians. Within the now fulsome historiography of nineteenth-century education there is a veritable glut of single-nation studies which seek to offer historical explanations for the rise of mass schooling. A number of these offer a quite comprehensive set of factors which are said to have determined educational development. Michael Katz, for instance, in his 'Reassessment' of the origins of public education, has suggested that the four major factors affecting educational development were industrialization, urbanization, state intervention and changes in family structure.[2] Lawrence Stone, in an important essay on the development of literacy in England, has enumerated a rather longer list of causal factors, including social stratification, job opportunities, religion, theories of social control, demographic and family patterns, economic organization and resources, and political theory and institutions.[3] These and other historical studies have shown the pertinence of 'social factors' such as the ones enumerated here. However, the historians have often been highly eclectic and unsystematic in their theoretical treatment of this problem and many have not gone beyond mere itemization of historical factors. They have rarely examined their logical interconnections. Moreover, few of the histories to date have offered any comparative analysis of educational development and thus leave the problems of uneven educational development without due explanation. Nevertheless, their accounts deserve attention since they provide much of the raw material for a fuller theoretical analysis.

This chapter will seek to assess the validity of explanations of educational development by drawing on both modern sociological theory and historical accounts. Since sociological theories are often poorly grounded in historical analysis and since histories often lack an elaborated theoretical basis, this will necessarily involve a degree of theoretical reconstruction. Contemporary theory, where it has not been fully applied to the historical question, will be applied hypothetically. Historical accounts, which often contain an immanent or 'buried' theoretical problematic, will be reconstructed in the light of the theoretical paradigms on which they draw and assessed accordingly for their theoretical and historical adequacy.

Broadly speaking, there are four major theoretical paradigms for explaining the development of mass schooling. Positivist theory, from Durkheim to the American structural functionalists, has provided the traditional explanations of educational origins and functions, linking education with the rise of industrial society, the need for skilled labour and the general mechanisms of social integration. Marxist and Weberian theory has offered alternative explanations linking educational development with, amongst other things, the proletarianization of labour and the extension of bureaucracy. However, it is as well to start with liberal or 'Whig' explanations since, although they hardly constitute a developed theory, they have been very influential in early historical accounts.

Liberal theory

The classic Whig version of history is one which links gradual political democratization with liberal theories of freedom and is strongly Protestant in orientation.[4] It sees history as a gradual process of evolution, assumed to relate unproblematically to an idea of progress. The educational version of this, in simplified form, goes as follows. Mass education developed first and fastest in the Protestant countries of Northern Europe, and in the Puritan states of the north-eastern United States. The primary impetus for this development came from the early recognition of Protestants, from the Reformation onwards, of the powers of education as a vehicle of proselytization. The enormous educational advances of the nineteenth century were a product of this early impulse, coupled with the intellectual thrust of the Enlightenment, and of the gradual secular movement towards political democracy, under the banner of liberal capitalism. The advance of mass education was one of many institutional developments which exemplified the steady march of progress and civilization.

The role of religion in the early development of schools is beyond question and will be dealt with in detail at a later stage. Clearly, the churches were the major spur towards the development of schools from the sixteenth century through to the early nineteenth century throughout Europe. It is true that from the sixteenth century onwards one can find in the more populous urban areas, particularly those with burgeoning merchant and commercial classes, town and burger schools which were privately endowed. Grammar schools emerged in England, for instance, in the sixteenth and seventeenth centuries and contributed something towards the relatively high levels of literacy achieved at that time. Nevertheless, the vast majority of schools in Europe were organized by church and religious societies, and initially served largely ecclesiastical interests.

The first major acceleration in educational activity in modern times took place in the sixteenth century, stimulated by the spread of humanist ideas and the vernacular languages, particularly after the invention of the moveable type printing process. It is likely that education was also encouraged by the greater occupational value of literacy in crafts, business, navigation and war, which were added to law and the clergy as occupations requiring literacy. However, it was the onset of the Protestant Reformation that did most to galvanize education development. The sixteenth century witnessed the accelerated progress of literacy generally in England, but particularly so in the lands most influenced by the Reformation. The particular importance of education in Protestant communities lay in the nature of the religion and in the proselytizing spirit of the Reformation. Believing, as they did, that a 'right' understanding depended on a close study of the scriptures, the early Protestants were anxious to spread a knowledge of the Bible, and the importance of mass literacy to this was clearly appreciated. Furthermore, as Lawrence Stone has noted, it appears that Protestantism seized on the printing press with greater enthusiasm than Catholicism for this very reason. 'At a deepest psychological level ... [Catholicism] remained a culture of the image, of paintings, saints and sacred ornaments', whilst 'Protestantism was a culture of the book'.[5] The critical importance of Puritanism in the stimulation of education is well illustrated in New England and Calvinist Scotland. In Europe, the Lutheran areas of Germany and the Protestant cantons of Switzerland were important pioneers of mass education.

The trend towards Protestant ascendancy in education, according to Cipolla, remained a general one throughout the following centuries and contributed towards the steady advance of Northern Europe over the Mediterranean states in the nineteenth century. Rates of illiteracy around the turn of the seventeenth century are reckoned to have been at 55–65 per cent in Protestant Europe as a whole, and about 70–80 per cent in Catholic Europe.[6] However, the Protestant ascendancy in education was only temporary. After the initial Protestant thrust of the Reformation, Jesuit education made enormous advances, particularly in France, and literacy in the Catholic Rhineland and Tyrol regions was high. Catholic Austria under Maria Theresa witnessed the most startling of all eighteenth-century European efforts to create prototype national education systems. Equally, some Protestant areas, such as England and the southern United States, were not advanced in the later period. Other factors may well explain the retardation of educational development in Southern Europe. Italy, for instance, did not attain national unification until the 1870s and this, more than Catholicism, explains its late development of mass education which began at the time of unification.

Religions, and particularly Protestant religions, were clearly an essential element in the early development of schooling. However, as an explanation of the rise of national systems of education, religion will clearly not do. The fact is that national education systems were not simply elaborated networks of schools of the earlier type: they were qualitatively distinct. What characterized the national education system was its 'universality' and specific orientation towards the secular needs of the state and civil society. National education systems were, or became, institutions *sui generis*, and require explanations in kind. Whilst religion played a major part in the proliferation of early schools, it can hardly offer the primary explanation for the rise of new systems which were qualitatively different. In most countries the creation of public education systems involved, precisely, a break with the traditional clerical domination of schooling.

This is not to say that religion ceased to be an important influence. In all countries, church and sect made strenuous efforts to retain their influence, either through maintaining independent schools or by giving their services in public institutions. However, public institutions steadily over-reached the independent schools and became the dominant sector even, as in England, where this took a long time. Where the church or religious society continued to play a prominent part in public schools, as the Christian Brothers did in French elementary schools, it had to renounce sectarian interests and submit to state control.

The influence of enlightenment philosophy clearly offers a more likely candidate for the ideological basis of nineteenth-century mass education. Without the philosophical empiricism of Locke and the rationalist optimism of Voltaire, Rousseau and the French philosophers, it is hard to imagine what educational ideologies might have developed which could give coherence to the arguments of bourgeois educational reformers in the nineteenth century.

The baseline of all great educational theories, from Rousseau and Condorcet in France to James Mill in England, was that the environment formed the person. As James Mill wrote, 'All the difference which exists between classes and bodies of men is the effect of education.'[7] Whilst few denied some differences of birth, the informing spirit behind all bourgeois education theories was the predominance of nurture over nature and therefore the principle of universal educability. The philosophical basis of this, wholly revolutionary, idea clearly lay in Locke's famous description of the human consciousness as a *tabula rasa*, on which anything might be imprinted. The idea was developed in the materialist psychology of Hartley and Condillac, which asserted the optimistic belief that the human mind could be shaped by education, if only it proceeded methodically, recognizing the cardinal principle that the memory functions by association.[8] What transformed this psychological potential into a desirable human goal of general enlightenment through education was the long radical tradition which claimed that education was a human and political right. This clearly owed more to French revolutionary thought than to English empiricism, and finds only a weak echo in the utilitarianism of Mill and Bentham, but it was taken up powerfully in the radical writing of Tom Paine, William Godwin and William Lovett, who offered the clearest English articulation of the principle of education as a tool of human emancipation and a 'right of man'.

The cultural humus of the Enlightenment and revolutionary era certainly provided an essential condition for the development of emancipatory theories of education. However, one only has to look at the actual developments which occurred in education to see how far these often were from the ideas of the radical philosophers. The most popular educational treatise of the eighteenth century was Rousseau's *Emile*, which set out a programme of emancipatory and rational libertarian education for a middle-class child. But like Huckleberry Finn, after him, Rousseau clearly believed that the school was the antithesis of education, which was best gained from life, experience and the observation of nature. Although there were echoes of Rousseauesque ideas in Pestalozzian schools, the mainstream institutions of national education systems were, arguably, the antithesis of all that Rousseau believed in.

Empiricism, rationalism and emancipation were clearly fundamental touchstones in radical educational thought and gave coherence to many radical educational ideologies. They were not often, however, the dominant characteristics of school-reform programmes in the early years of the formation of national educational systems. This was true of most secondary education but the gulf between theory and practice was widest in elementary education where rote-learning, religious indoctrination and authoritarian routine were as likely to cramp the young mind as offer enlightenment and potential emancipation. Whilst radical reformers preached human freedom and intellectual development, dominant education ideologies, or at least those that informed the actual development of schools, were often more concerned with social control, moral conformity and political acquiescence than human emancipation.

This brings us to the third element in the triadic liberal mythology of education: democracy. This is certainly the most complicated of all of the aspects of the liberal interpretation and cannot be fully explored at this point. But certain preliminary points can be made. Whilst the advance of democratic forces have had an inestimable long-term effect on the shape of education, and whilst equality of opportunity has been the recurrent *leitmotif* in educational ideology in the era of the welfare state, it is by no means clear that it was a predominant factor in the rise of early national education systems, at least in Europe.

On a comparative plane, one is struck by the poor correlation in Europe between the spread of democratic ideas and institutions, and the geographical map of educational 'advance'. The most extensive systems of mass education were often found in those countries with the most enduring and authoritarian of absolutist monarchies. What is more, these systems were substantially constructed in the 'high' periods of the absolutist state – in Prussia under Frederick the Great and in Austria under Maria Theresa and Francis I. One of the great ironies of educational history is that the more 'democratic' nineteenth-century powers, such as France, England and the United States, which had all undergone political transformations, were forced to look to the autocratic German states for examples of educational reform to adopt at home. A. J. P. Taylor has written that the German education system was a 'gigantic engine of conquest' and that few of its Anglo-American admirers understood its real authoritarian purposes.[9] However, in due course, liberal and republican regimes were to show that they had their own uses for such an effective vehicle of social control.

The creation of national education systems in continental Europe was not for the most part the result of mass popular movements. The French Revolution certainly stimulated the development of radical educational ideas and the egalitarian educational plans of the Jacobins left an important long-term legacy. However, the construction of a French national system under Napoleon was not supported by popular agitation and bore few traces, at least at the level of popular schooling, of Jacobin ideas. In Prussia and Austria the early development of national education pre-dated the French Revolution and had no basis in popular movements. After the Revolution, the defeudalization of the German lands, brought about by the invading armies of Napoleon, was an important agent in educational change, both because it created a new social order and because it generated the nationalist reaction which more than anything propelled educational reform. However, it did not produce mass democratic movements. Such sporadic uprisings as there were had little connection for education, and even the upheaval of 1848, the great 'springtime of peoples', did little more in the educational field than politicize a group of university students and intensify the nationalism of sections of the middle class.[10] The educational ideologies that fired the reformers, such as Stern, Humboldt and Altenstein, were essentially nationalistic and paternalist and there was little in the elementary education system that could be attributed to democratic ideas.

If the formation of early national systems on the continent bore little connection with 'democratic movements', it certainly was connected with the emergence of the bourgeois state, as we shall see later. In as much as this was, as Marx recognized, a 'progressive' historical development, educational reform was, as Whig history would have it, a manifestation of social progress. However, change was generally neither particularly gradual and evolutionary, and nor was it necessarily most favoured by the ideas of middle-class liberalism. Many continental liberals, such as Turgot, Diderot and Voltaire, were hostile to popular education. Voltaire argued that the masses were destined to a laborious drudgery that only habit could make tolerable. 'To give the meanest of people an education', he wrote, 'beyond the station that providence has assigned them, is doing real injury.'[11] Prominent nineteenth-century liberals, such as Guizot, were equally afraid of over-educating the masses. The liberal was often no more friendly to mass education than the conservative paternalist.

The development of national education systems was not closely synchronized with the consolidation of liberal capitalist regimes in Europe. In fact it had a much longer arch of development originating in the mercantilist and étatist doctrines of the absolutist states, and developing in new ways during the revolutionary era, and in the constitutionalist and liberal regimes which followed. The functions of these early school systems had as much to do with social control and state formation as with the emancipatory doctrines and the growth of democratic forces.

The strongest case for linking the rise of national education systems with the advance of liberal and democratic ideas can be made with reference not to continental Europe but to the United States and Britain, where, of course, the idea is most current. In neither country was there an eighteenth-century absolutism which could sow the seeds of national systems, and, in both cases, the chronology of systematic educational development is clearly synchronous with the consolidation of liberal and republican regimes, punctuated as they were by the struggles of an emerging working class.

In England all major educational developments bore a close relation to shifts in political power. The early attacks on educational traditionalism in the first decades of the century were linked to the growing political challenge of the middle class in an, albeit uneasy, alliance with an emergent working-class radicalism. In its most radical philosophical guise of utilitarianism, the educational reform movement argued for changes in secondary education which would reflect middle-class scientific, rationalist and utilitarian beliefs, and for the extension of mass elementary education for moral enhancement, and political and social stability. Democratic arguments for the same were left largely to working-class advocates. The reforms in secondary and university education in the 1850s and 1860s followed on belatedly from the extension of middle-class political power with the Reform Act of 1832, and reflected, somewhat partially, the rise of bourgeois values. The Education Act of 1870, which established a quasi-national system, was a result, as much as anything, of the desire to control the political effects of the extension of the franchise in 1867 to the skilled working class. At each point, changes in educational provision reflected the shifts which occurred in the balance of political forces. Broadly, the gradual emergence of democratic political forms was reflected in the spread of mass education, and was connected with it.

However, the relations were more complex than they may appear and there can be no simple equation between the extension of national education and the rise of liberal, democratic forms. Firstly, it must be stressed that the dominant force in education right up until the 1860s was conservative, Anglican traditionalism. This was the case both in elementary education, dominated by the Anglican National Society, and in secondary schools and universities, where the ethos of the leading institutions was Anglican and traditionalist for many years and past the mid-century. Whilst some historians, such as Harold Perkins, have written of the triumph of bourgeois values, in the area of education this was by no means complete.[12] The educational debate may have been dominated by the growing voice of utilitarian experts, but their actual impact on the system was gradual indeed. Secondly, it was not clearly the case that the mainstream middle-class liberal ideology was particularly favourable to educational development. This point will be developed in Chapter 6 at length, but it is worth signalling here that the ascendant middle-class doctrines of pure *laissez-faire* were arguably a braking factor on educational development. The promotion of national education systems came entirely from, in different ways, working-class radicals and Chartists, and middle-class Utilitarians, whose state-enhancing liberalism was noticeably at odds with pure Political Economy and the *laissez-faire* of the dominant middle-class culture.[13]

The relation of liberal doctrines with the development of national education was thus complex and contradictory. Furthermore, the connection between educational expansion and the development of democratic forces was indirect. Whilst educational reform was ideologically influenced by democratic ideas and pushed from below by the demands of working-class organizations, the intentions of those who implemented it were largely to hold in check and control the results of democratic working-class advance. Educational reform was a reaction to political conflict, not an agent in transformation. Only in a very qualified sense can it be linked with democratic progress before, at any rate, the later part of the century.

In the United States the relation between education as a social force and the balance of political power was quite different. Education was clearly a key component of republican ideology and arguably a transformative force in the formation of an individualist, liberal capitalism. Certainly, it was so believed by its republican advocates who argued that the fragile forms of republican 'democracy' would not survive without it. However, even here, the claims of the educational progressives can easily be qualified.

The United States is the home of the most resoundingly 'triumphalist' tradition of education historiography whose primary exponents have developed an unalloyed progressive mythology, in a sense, more whiggish than Whig. Foremost amongst these was Ellwood Cubberley, formerly Inspector of Schools in San Francisco, and author of an influential history of US education, which tells of the triumph of public education as an expression of victorious democratic and humanitarian ideals.[14] Cubberley and his school have come under heavy attack from historians of the so-called 'revisionist' school, who have roundly condemned the pervasive historicism of Cubberley's 'heroic' history. 'Americans share a warm and comforting myth about the origins of popular education,' writes Michael Katz:

> For the most part, historians have helped to perpetuate this essentially noble story which portrays a rational, enlightened working class, led by idealistic and humanitarian intellectuals, triumphantly wresting free education from a selfish, wealthy elite and from bigoted proponents of orthodox religion.

Katz goes on, in a passage that could be accused of a reverse 'historicism': 'Popular education, according to the myth, started in a passionate blaze of humanitarian zeal; but most large urban school systems since the later nineteenth have been cold, rigid, and somewhat sterile bureaucracies.'[15]

Regardless of who is actually reading the past through the present, whether the Cubberleyan apologists of public schooling or Katzian critics, the specific charges against the Cubberley interpretation have a strong purchase. Katz effectively demonstrates that the high school, supposedly the democratic jewel in the reformer's crown, was largely a middle-class affair, despite its ostensibly egalitarian form. Katz's further argument, that elementary education for the working class was essentially a middle-class imposition, designed to control unruly urban populations, must be treated with greater caution. Although common schools in large towns had a decidedly paternalistic and moralizing attitude towards their predominantly working-class and often immigrant children, implying a model of imposition, this cannot be generalized for rural areas, which composed the majority of the population.

This case is considered in more detail in Chapter 5 but it is worth noting at this point two salient arguments about education and democracy in the United States. Firstly, it is clear that mass education did develop in tandem with 'democratic' republicanism in the United States and was an active agent in the process. Secondly, although it was underpinned by an exceptionally wide consensus of support from all classes, it was not conceived, nor did it act, simply as an emancipatory force, least of all for the working class.

In the same moment as republicans looked to education to secure the social and political basis of democratic, republican political forms, preventing any return to aristocratic reaction or authoritarian statism, European style, so they also looked to education to prevent anarchy, to uphold the values of competitive capitalism and to defuse the ideological attraction of militant working-class challenges wherever they occurred. Thus, even in the United States, where education was more closely entwined with democratic ideas than anywhere, it still had a contradictory function and wore a Janus face. On the one hand it was an ally of democratic forces, including working-class aspirations and, on the other, a powerful instrument of political conformity and an essential element in the construction of an individualist, capitalist hegemony.

Education and industrial revolution. Social integration and the provision of skills

Throughout much of the present century the dominant ideologies of education have been furnished by the theory developed within the American tradition of structural functionalism. The origins of this lay in the work of the French sociologist, Emile Durkheim, who wrote more on education than any other of the classical founders of social science. According to Durkheim, education had two major functions. One was to provide the skills needed for industrial economies. The other, which was more essential, was to act as a vehicle of social integration through the transmission of culture. Like the British political economists, Durkheim was concerned, above all, with the problem of social order, but he roundly rejected English individualism and the notion that social solidarity might inhere in the individual pursuit of self-interest in the free market. For Durkheim a social collectivity had to exist prior to, and beyond, the individual. The great problem for modern societies lay in the creation of a collective morality under new social conditions. With the historical dissolution of segmented, communal societies, where social solidarity had depended on the immediacy of community and in rigid subordination to tradition and collective consciousness, new forms of integration had to be located. For Durkheim the answer lay primarily in the nature of civil society. The inevitable and increasing division of labour had individualized populations and weakened the hold of collective beliefs, thus removing the former basis of mechanical solidarity. However, the division of labour also brought with it the potential for new forms of social cohesion which would ultimately be more binding. In societies based on specialization and individual contract, there was a mutual material dependence of each on everyone and this would provide the basis of a new 'organic solidarity'.[16] However, as Durkheim conceded, 'moral unity is not at all points what it should be', and therefore it was up to the state to enhance it. If it was not for the state to 'create the community of ideas and sentiments without which there is no society', the state must nevertheless 'consecrate it, maintain it [and] make individuals aware of it'.[17]

Education was one of the primary means for achieving this. Its main function was the development of social solidarity through the transmission of collective culture.

> Society can only exist if there exists among its members a sufficient degree of homogeneity. Education perpetuates and reinforces this homogeneity by fixing in the child, from the beginning, the essential similarities that collective life demands.[18]

Like the political economists before him, Durkheim accepted that the division of labour demanded that education should impart different skills depending on future occupation. However, whilst it developed these specialized functions it must also integrate children into collective ideas – a *culture générale*. Since education is a social function, and since the state is 'the very organ of social thought', the 'state cannot be indifferent to it'.[19] The state must educate.

The strength of Durkheim's educational thought lay in its deliberately anti-idealist and anti-individualist stress on the nature of education as a social process. Consciously avoiding educational utopias in the tradition of Rousseau and other 'romantics', Durkheim argued that the science of pedagogy should understand the historical role that education had performed in different societies and how it might reflect the social needs of the modern age. From his later historical vantage point he developed a theory of education, society and the state which expressed the singular novelty of the nineteenth-century education system. However, the weakness of his theory lay in its inability to theorize the contradictions in civil society, and thus to appreciate the class contradictions involved in the reproduction of a 'collective culture' through the state and its educational organs. Political Economy, particularly in the case of Ricardo, had discovered the economic basis of class contradictions and then proceeded to ignore them in its social thought, taking refuge in the philosophical individualism and abstractions of Bentham's 'felicific calculus' of the greatest happiness of the greatest number. Durkheim dealt with the subject of class antagonism but only to explain it away. Class conflicts were 'anomic' or pathological reactions to the new division of labour, temporary dislocations in the social order caused by rapid social change, the failure of morality to keep pace with technology, and the unwanted survival of feudal privilege in would-be meritocratic, bourgeois societies. The role of education in promoting particular cultures against others, in legitimating and consolidating a dominant culture, was thus ignored.[20]

Modern functionalism has lost much of what was useful in Durkheim's work without in any way mitigating its deficiencies. In particular it has forgotten the degree to which Durkheim developed his ideas against the grain of nineteenth-century individualism. Ironically, whilst French sociology of the Marxist *Annales* school has developed his ideas, in the English-speaking world he has been championed most vociferously in the United States, the archetypal home of individualism, where his ideas have become the textual reference for conservative educational theories. In so doing they have lost much of their historical dimension and relevance.

American functionalism, like much modern educational theory, has concentrated on the relationship between education and work. In the work of Talcott Parsons, education is seen as a 'focal socializing agency', responsible for preparing young people in future work skills and socializing them in the competitive and ostensibly 'meritocratic' principles of modern economic life. For Kingsley Davis and Wilbert Moore, school is the 'proving ground for ability and hence the selective agency for placing people in different statuses according to their capacities'.[21] Human Capital Theory, another variant of functionalism, is premised on the notion that technology is increasingly important to modern industrial economies, and that education has a major role to play in developing necessary technical skills. As Jean Floud and A. H. Halsey put it in their introduction to an influential volume of essays in 1961, advanced industrial society 'is dependent to an unparalleled extent on the results of scientific research, on the supply of skilled and responsible manpower, and consequently on the efficiency of the education system'.[22]

Functionalist theory has been decisively undermined in recent years from both Weberian and Marxist perspectives. The Weberian Randall Collins has argued that the content of most modern education is not very practical and that educational attainment correlates poorly with work performance, a conclusion verified in Ivan Berg's empirical studies. Most technical skills, argues Collins, are learnt on the job in any case. 'A close look at the evidence,' writes Collins,

> indicates that schooling does not supply specific technical skills, as functionalists contend... historical patterns of educational development have been caused by factors other than the increasing sophistication of industrial techniques.[23]

Marxist sociology has also argued a close connection between education and work but cogently refutes functionalist claims that education rests on a consensus of values, or that it operates in a meritocratic way. Nor does it serve primarily to reproduce necessary skills. By contrast, Marxist sociology has concentrated on the correspondences and homologies between educational structures and capitalist work relations, demonstrating how education reproduces and legitimates the power relations of the labour market through selection and differential socialization based on the class, ethnic and gender divisions of society at large.[24]

If functionalist theory offers a weak explanation of contemporary education it has even less purchase on the nineteenth century. Until the late nineteenth century, with the exception of specifically vocational schools, the degree to which schools actually prepared children for the skills of future work was relatively marginal. Equally, in societies where educational credentials were only necessary for a limited number of occupational positions, the selective functions of schooling had yet to become paramount. Certainly, schools were playing an increasingly important role in the formation of classes, particularly in countries such as France and Prussia, where secondary schooling was already an important vehicle for the consolidation of the bourgeoisie. This was especially true of those sections connected with public service, access to which depended on competitive examination. However, if the career open to talents was a slogan with some basis in post-revolutionary Europe, its meaning was less evident in England, which had no national examination system and whose civil service was yet to be put on a meritocratic footing. Even in the United States, where it also meant something, social mobility was not a primary function of the school and the road to social advancement often by-passed the school entirely. For the most part, the role of the school in the formation of social classes was more passive than active. It provided ideological legitimation for a process of class differentiation which occurred largely independently of it. Different types of school acclimatized each social class for which they were designed for their various social and economic roles where these were assumed in advance and were only partly dependent on any educational selection process. This was certainly changing, and faster in some countries than others, but in the early decades of the century, when national systems were first consolidated, most schools claimed to be meritocratic only in a very limited sense: they functioned more to sanction than to determine social stratification.

Despite the rather unpromising candidacy of functionalist theory as an explanation of nineteenth-century educational development, a large number of historical accounts are based on its theoretical premises. Many histories contain an implicit assumption that educational development was a product of industrial growth, arising out of the need for technical skills and contributing to economic development through the provision of these skills. H. G. Bantock, for instance, argues that mass education was a by-product of industrialization. 'Undoubtedly one of the basic factors', in the growth of education, he writes,

> was the coming of industrialization and the need to have workmen who could read and calculate if only to understand instructions relating to the machines they were called on to operate.[25]

E. G. West, in his book *Education and the Industrial Revolution*, endeavours to refute arguments that English education responded slowly to industrial needs. He concludes:

> Education expanded significantly during the period [of the Industrial Revolution] ... and ... significantly assisted economic growth throughout. There was an Education Revolution as well as an Industrial Revolution, and both were inter-related.[26]

Michael Sanderson has shown that this seemingly unremarkable assertion involves certain complications, not least in that literacy rates actually fell during the early industrial phase. However, he too concludes that English education promoted economic growth by encouraging an adequate provision to meet the rather limited literacy requirements of early industry, whilst avoiding levels of public expenditure that would have eroded profits.[27]

The evidence from economic historians does not support their view. New educational developments in England during the nineteenth century did not on the whole play a major role in economic development, nor is it clear that educational change was prompted in any direct way by the economic skill requirements thrown up by industrialization. Furthermore, whilst educational change corresponds with periods of industrial development in some countries, it does not do so in others. Strictly economic factors can hardly explain differential educational development.

Early industrial development required relatively few technical skills, and, by and large, these were acquired without much assistance from educational institutions. 'Fortunately,' writes Eric Hobsbawm,

> few intellectual requirements were necessary to make the industrial revolution. Its technical inventions were exceedingly modest, and in no way beyond the scope of intelligent artisans, experimenting in workshops, or of the constructive capacities of carpenters, millwrights, and blacksmiths. The flying shuttle, the spinning jenny, the mule, even its scientifically most sophisticated machine, James Watt's rotary steam-engine (1784), required no more physics than had been available for the best part of a century.

The technical requirements of the early Industrial Revolution could, in fact, be met by the pool of skills developed through traditional institutions. As Hobsbawm goes on to point out,

> The slow semi-industrialization of Britain centuries before 1789 had built up a rather large reservoir of suitable skills, both in textile technique and in the handling of metals.[28]

Carlo Cipolla has argued a similar case for Northern Europe in general. The Industrial Revolution was taken up first in countries that already had sufficient levels of literacy whose generation through education in previous centuries owed more to ethical than economic considerations. Literacy grew in European countries in advance of the industrial need for it. It was less an effect of industrialization than a prior facilitating agent.[29]

It was not until the second stage of the Industrial Revolution that education became more essential for the provision of new skills. By this time production techniques had advanced so far that, as Hobsbawm notes, 'the output of technological progress was a function of the input of scientifically qualified manpower, equipment and money into systematic research projects'.[30]

David Landes has isolated four types of knowledge required in production: the ability to write and calculate; the working skills of the craftsman and mechanic; the engineer's combination of scientific principle and applied training; and high levels of science, theoretical and applied.[31] During the early stages of industrial development, the need for the first two of these was fairly limited, and in any case sufficiently provided in the traditional forms of education, including the family and the apprenticeship. However, as industrialization developed, the requirements for scientific and technical skills increased, which put new demands on the education system. This related not only to secondary and higher education, which was under pressure to provide scientists and technicians for industry; it also affected elementary and working-class education generally. In mid-nineteenth-century England, there was not only an evident lack of scientifically trained managers and proprietors; there was also a virtual absence of suitably trained foremen and overseers. Since these were largely recruited from the ranks of ordinary labourers who generally made do with a short period of elementary education (four or five years), the onus was very much on the latter to ensure adequate training.

If the technical requirements of industry were rather limited in the early industrial phase, which was when national education systems were consolidated in most countries, it would seem unlikely that the latter could have been a direct response to economic needs. Even where needs did become more evident, education in England was generally slow to respond. Elementary schools were not greatly concerned with the provision of technical skills and barely gave a sufficient grounding in literacy and arithmetic, let alone elementary science, to facilitate later technical studies. A perennial complaint of those involved in the Mechanics Institutes and Department of Science and Art evening classes, later in the century, was that technical education amongst workmen was hampered by the paucity of their early education.[32]

If elementary education was slow to adapt, one might have expected the secondary schools to have done so more readily. For one thing, the main beneficiaries of economic advance were the middle class, its main consumers, and for another, one would expect that the skill requirements for middle-class occupations were rather more speedily affected by economic advance. The evidence here, at least for England, is that whatever economic pressures there may have been, with the exception of the dissenting academies, the response of the education system was almost non-existent, at least until the reforms of the Arnoldian era, and then it was only limited. It is certainly true that secondary education expanded considerably after 1840, and that had to do not only with the increased access facilitated by railways but also with increased affluence amongst the middle class. The extraordinary fact about English secondary education, however, is that whilst there was a clear quantitative response to middle-class demand, the form it took was almost entirely inappropriate to industrial needs. Secondary schools, whether 'public', proprietary or grammar, were notoriously detached from the needs of industry and wore their non-utilitarian classical ethos as a badge of status well into the second half of the century. The development of technical and vocational schools for working-class and middle-class students was notably slow in England and hardly compensated for the irrelevance of the secondary schools. As far as universities were concerned, the almost total absence of scientific and vocational education, at least until the mid-century, in Oxford and Cambridge, is well known. London University alone offered a more modern, professionally oriented education. One is tempted to conclude with Ashby that

> In the rise of British industry, universities played no part whatever... indeed formal education of any sort was a negligible factor in its success.[33]

Educational development in England does not appear to have been determined to any large degree by the need for technical skills. Even where the needs were apparent, schools were slow to respond; so inadequate was their provision that it seems likely, as both Hobsbawm and Landes have argued, that they contributed towards the failure of Britain to maintain its level of economic supremacy after 1860 and thus the beginning of the relative economic decline.

If we look at continental developments, the disjuncture between education and economic factors is even more evident, if for different reasons. The fact is that whilst in England the development of a national education system had to wait for near on a century after the onset of rapid industrial development, in continental Europe, education systems were developed largely before the rapid spread of industrialization began. By the 1830s, when Prussia, France and several other continental nations had substantially developed their education systems, industrial 'take-off' had not even begun. According to Rostow, this did not occur in France until 1840 and in Germany until between 1850 and 1875.[34] Austria was even later. Unlike the early Industrial Revolution in Britain, based on textiles, industrial take-off in France and Germany occurred first through the expansion of heavy industry – mainly via iron, steel, coal and construction industries stimulated by the railway boom of the 1840s. Swedish industrialization did not occur until the end of the century, and then mainly through timber production. During the first decades of the nineteenth century, France, Austria and the German states were still suffering from the ravages of the Napoleonic Wars, from complex political boundaries and restrictions on trade and commerce, and from a largely rural population too poor to create substantial home demand. Most industry, such as it was, existed to service the rich with luxury goods, or relied on state investment in construction and specialized industries. These latter, including the china and glass industries in Prussia and the tapestries, silks and fine goods from the Gobelins industrial centre in France, were highly labour-intensive and relied mainly on traditional craft skills. The development of mechanized production in large factories was only just beginning, and the French ironworks at Le Creuset, for example, were still something of a rarity.

The labour force in Prussia and France at this time consisted largely of rural and artisanal workers. Before the Revolution, 80 per cent of French workers were peasants, and agricultural labour continued to dominate in France and Prussia throughout the nineteenth century. By 1881, still 51 per cent of French workers and 43 per cent of German workers were in agriculture.[35] Those who did not work in agriculture were in proto-industrial activity in rural and urban areas. Most manufacturing was still based on small-scale household production and handicraft skills. Markovitz has estimated that by the mid-nineteenth century in France this sector still accounted for 59.9 per cent of production and employed 70–75 per cent of all workers engaged in industry. In Toulouse, for instance, France's sixth largest city, only 32.5 per cent of the workforce were employed in industry in 1851, and 74 per cent of these workers were handicraft artisans employed mainly in the production of food, clothing and housing, as bakers, tailors, masons and so on. The proto-industrial worker, labouring in workshops under a master artisan, continued to use traditional skills.[36]

Under these conditions it is hard to see how such limited demands for new skills as there may have been could account for the rapid developments that occurred in education, particularly in Prussia. Certainly there was not any general need to impose discipline in school as a preparation for the factory as may have been the case in England. As far as secondary and technical education was concerned, there was clearly an increasing demand for more scientists and trained engineers, not only to work in manufacturing but also to slake the growing thirst of the state for administrators and technically qualified personnel to work in the bureaucracy, the military and in public works. The major expansion in secondary education in France and Prussia in the eighteenth century was a response to these demands, mainly in the state; however, by the 1830s there is clear evidence of an over-supply of secondary graduates for professions and government service. The decline in enrolments in secondary education in Prussia after 1830 relates to this and to the growing attractiveness of careers in business which were not yet dependent on educational qualifications.[37]

Compared with England, Prussia and France had less strictly economic reasons for providing more education. The only greater area of demand that existed was in state service. Yet on the whole, whilst the response of educational institutions to economic needs was uneven, it was considerably more appropriate than in England. Not only did these countries develop national, rationalized systems earlier, but also they were more technically oriented than in England. French primary education, as in England, was not explicitly geared towards developing industrial skills, although it was admired by English royal commissions for their teaching of drawing. However, considerable advances had been made in the provision of working-class technical education, with the trade schools which abounded in pre-revolutionary France and Prussia and their post-revolutionary successors.[38] In secondary and higher education, considerable efforts were made to make institutions respond to economic needs; indeed, they were seen as pioneering economic development through technological expertise. In France the Jesuit colleges were renowned for their serious application to maths and physics, and the Napoleonic *lycées* and colleges, although predominantly classical, provided rigorous mathematical training. France also had a long tradition of advanced technical education from the Revolution's special schools down to the nineteenth-century *polytechniques* and *grandes écoles*. By the mid-nineteenth century, Prussia had a similar array of polytechnics and technical high schools. From the 1830s onwards we can see in both countries a growing state concern with the provision of scientific and technical education. Guizot created the practically oriented *écoles primaires supérieures*, and later, ministers, including Fortoul and Duruy, devised scientific courses for the colleges to divert students away from overcrowded learned professions and into industry. The same thing can be seen in Prussia with the creation of the *Realschule*, the *Realgymnasium* and other forms of more vocationally oriented middle-class education.

The relative advance of continental elementary and scientific education cannot be explained in purely economic terms. If technical requirements in the economy were the major factor in educational development, one would expect France and Prussia to have been behind England. But the fact is that they were not.[39]

Whilst the formation of national systems of education in Europe shows little correlation with the chronology of industrialization – occurring before industrial take-off in continental countries and after in England – the United States appears to offer an example of close synchronicity between the two phenomena. The crucial period for the consolidation of public education in the North was the age of educational reforms between 1830 and the Civil War. This was also the period of intensive economic development, as numerous commentators point out. During the period from 1830 to 1860, the United States as a whole, and the North East in particular, experienced considerable economic development. Intensive industrialization in the towns of the North East was accompanied by innovation and capitalization in western agriculture and, in the South, by the expansion of the plantation economy and the boom years of 'King Cotton'. In manufacture, the gradual shift from independent craft production to wage labour in factories and workshops was boosted by new technical advances: by the development of sewing machines, power looms, hot-air iron blasting, steam printing and the steam hammer for iron working, all of which increased production potential enormously. In agriculture the introduction of machines for threshing, reaping and harvesting had the same effect, and, together with a three-fold increase in farmed land between 1840 and 1880, made possible the enormous expansion in agricultural production that fed the growing urban population of the North East.[40] The period 1840–1860 was the era of railway boom, and as thousands of miles of new railway linked the eastern seaboard with the western frontier, markets for manufactures and agricultural produce swelled dramatically, triggering the economic take-off which Rostow attributes to this period (1843–1860).[41]

The fact that educational development in the North occurred most intensively during this period of industrialization and occurred fastest in those regions most affected (i.e. the North East) suggests certain correspondences between the two developments. Certainly there were contemporary reformers who believed in a strong economic motivation for educational development. Alonzo Potter, the author of popular school manuals, argued the value of education to productivity, claiming that it contributed

> most powerfully to render men more efficient both as producers and preservers of property . . . and affords the most certain and effectual means of developing the industrial resources of a country.

Quoting the case of a cotton mill owner, whose employment of well-educated operatives allegedly added 12 per cent to the speed of his machinery, Potter went on to state categorically that 'owners of manufacturing property had a deep pecuniary interest in the education and morals of their help'. Public education was the

> grand agent for the development or augmentation of national incomes . . . more powerful in the production and gainful employment of the total wealth of the country than all the other things mentioned in the books of the political economists.[42]

Such sanguine accounts of the economic benefits of education were also occasionally found in the writings of European educationalists, but it seems likely that American manufacturers were particularly receptive to this line of argument. Labour shortage was, after all, a major problem in US economic life and encouraged a sharp interest in the productivity of labour, manifest later in the early development of the scientific management of the labour process. Certainly US education was more modern and scientific in its approach than was the case across the Atlantic, the high school providing a prime example of vocationally oriented secondary education valued precisely for its potential economic benefits to the middle class.

However, it is easy to exaggerate any direct economic motives for education at this time, particularly as regards elementary schooling. As in continental Europe, by far the majority of productive activity was either agricultural or based on artisanal production. By the mid-century, still over 50 per cent of all employed people were independent farmers, and full-scale factory production, which did not really develop on any appreciable scale in northern towns until the 1860s, occupied only a small percentage of workers. It seems likely that the manual skills required in most areas of production, as in Europe, could have been adequately supplied through traditional forms of education, particularly in view of America's long-standing high literacy levels. The rise of mass elementary education can hardly have been an essential concomitant of early industrialization, at least as far as the provision of technical skills was concerned. The vast majority of common schools were educating children for agricultural work as they had done for generations. Even in towns where there was a growing requirement for factory operatives, the development of public schools seems to have owed little to any attempt to inculcate new skills. As Bowles and Gintis correctly point out, education had little relevance for the technical aspects of production. It is doubtful, they write,

> that any employer familiar with the daily working of their textile mills or other similar factories would seriously entertain the notion that the curriculum taught in the schools of the day had much connection with the production capacities of workers.[43]

It is undeniable that economic development, particular as manifested in the rising value of school land funds, was conducive to educational growth. However, it would seem that the motivation behind educational reform was not primarily economic. Major expansion of school enrolments occurred well before the period of industrialization in the North, and, equally, well before the later industrialization of the South. Furthermore, those who advocated educational expansion did so for a variety of reasons not necessarily economic. The primary concern of educational lobbyists and writers was, in fact, largely with political and social order, and the cultivation of republican ideals of virtue, morality and citizenship. It is hard to dissent from Kaestle's judgement that in relation to other arguments for education, economic benefits did not figure largely. Even in the treatises on political economy written by Americans in the 1820s and 1830s, education was a minor theme.[44]

We can summarize the relationship between educational development and the technical requirements of industrial growth as follows. Firstly, in no country does it appear that secular changes in educational provision were determined exclusively or even primarily by narrowly economic or technical factors. Secondly, even where economic change did call for educational response, schools did not, in general, respond either aptly or promptly. Thirdly, what educational responses there were varied considerably from nation to nation and bear no close correlation with the chronology of industrial advance. I would therefore concur with Lawrence Stone that 'before the middle of the nineteenth century, the role of purely economic factors... seems to have been a surprisingly limited on', and with Richard Johnson that attempts to 'link education and industrial revolution through some notion of "need" for labour skills (or literacy and technical know-how) have produced, so far, mainly negative results'.[45] Furthermore, it is clear that functionalist explanations of this sort can no more explain differential educational development than they can educational change per se.

Urbanization, proletarianization and the changing structures of family life

If the nature of labour skills provides a relatively weak explanation of the connection between industrialization and educational development, another approach has been to consider more broadly the connection between education and the wider social concomitants of industrialization. This approach is generally more in line with a Marxist analysis of the process of capitalist industrialization, which concentrates not only on changes in the forces (techniques) of production but also, more essentially, on the changing relations of production. The latter involves not simply changes in the relations between capital and labour, in the generalization of waged labour and the development of new forms of labour discipline, but also the social conditions necessary for the reproduction of capitalist relations. We are thus referring to new forms of labour socialization for work and new modes of class control in the community. It is this set of relations which has provided the point of purchase for a number of penetrating analyses of nineteenth-century education both from radical American sociologists, such as Michael Katz, Samuel Bowles and Herbert Gintis, and from English social historians, such as Richard Johnson.[46]

Growing urbanization and the proletarianization of labour can affect education in a number of ways. On the one hand, new forms of waged labour and subsequent changes in the dynamics of the family economy may affect the efficacy of traditional familial and community forms of education, disrupting and undercutting old forms and creating a hiatus in working-class education and child socialization. On the other hand, the spread of factory production and urban living may create new problems of labour control and social order, for which public education is seen as an important antidote. The spread of juvenile and female labour, outside the home, the proliferation of new forms of 'crime' and destitution under conditions of overcrowded urban living, and the multiple expressions of intensified class conflict were all aspects of the social problem most often quoted by educational advocates as pressing grounds for educational reform. This section will consider the ways in which these social factors related to educational development in different nations.

Whilst the consolidation of a national education system was delayed in England until the end of the century, the spread of mass elementary schooling through the voluntary monitorial schools was a developing reality from 1810 onwards. As such it can be closely related to the social changes that accompanied the early stages of industrialization. The period from 1780 to 1830 witnessed not only the rapid urbanization of the population, and the corresponding emergence of urban social problems, but also the transformation of the labouring population into a new proletarian class, living under new social conditions and acquiring an identity and consciousness of itself in relation to other classes. Education became an important element in the social management of this transition by the dominant class.

The century preceding 1850 was one of enormous demographic change. Between 1751 and 1851 the total population increased threefold and the majority of this additional population lived in towns. In 1801 only a third of the population lived in a town of any size, only one in six in towns of over 20 000 people, and most of these in London, the only city over 100 000. By 1851 half of the population lived in towns, over a third in towns of over 20 000 and more than a fifth in towns over 100 000. By 1861 London had 2 803 989 inhabitants; Manchester, Liverpool and Birmingham had over 250 000 and 25 other towns had over 50 000.[47]

The rapid growth of towns and the conditions of those who lived in them became an emblem of the dramatic changes wrought by industrialism: the town became the mirror of the new society, epitomizing both its achievements and its costs. It was at once the fount of wealth and industry and a place of unparalleled misery and human degradation. De Tocqueville visited Manchester in the 1830s and left a graphic account of what he saw:

From this foul drain, the greatest stream of human industry flows out to fertilize the world. From this filthy sewer pure gold flows. Here humanity attains its most complete development and its most brutish; here civilised man is turned back almost into a savage.[48]

For its working-class inhabitants the town meant overcrowding, unhealthy hovels and streets made foul by open drains and contaminated air. For the middle class it meant increased anxiety as they observed the conditions of the urban working class, their concentration and their potential for vice, immorality and sedition. The town embodied an unprecedented juxtaposition of extremes of wealth and poverty, and a graphic illustration of the growing division between classes. Above all, it conjured up in the middle-class imagination the fearful spectre of riot and rebellion. James Kay wrote after a visit to Manchester in the 1840s of 'the fearful strength of that multitude of the labouring population, which lies like a slumbering giant at their feet'.[49] Another traveller, William Coke Taylor, had similar apprehensions after touring the manufacturing districts of Lancashire:

> As a stranger passes through the masses of human beings which have been accumulated round the mills he cannot contemplate these crowded hives without feelings of anxiety and apprehension amounting almost to dismay. . . . [which] expresses something portentous and fearful.[50]

Equally traumatic and alarming, for the working and middle classes respectively, was the effect of new forms of labour on the working-class family. The transition from the proto-industrial, artisanal relations of production to those of the nineteenth-century factory was long and protracted but its social effects were felt particularly during this period. For the worker it meant a dislocating experience of transition from the relative independence of artisanal production or the slower and more 'natural' rhythms of rural labour, to wholesale subordination to the routine and discipline of the factory. For the working-class family as a whole, it involved the dissolution of old familial patterns and the strain of adapting to new ones, as labour became separated from the sphere of domestic life and children went out to work. This new division of public and private spheres, so important for the later construction of Victorian ideals of masculinity and femininity, was first experienced as dislocation. As David Levine writes,

> The ethic of equality and mutuality . . . disappeared from the marriage itself, replaced by a highly segmented form of nuptuality in which the worlds of husbands and wives barely overlapped.[51]

Contemporaries reacted to these changes with the greatest apprehension. Not only the anxious middle-class reformers but also working-class radicals and their revolutionary sympathizers considered the effects of industrialization on the working-class family as dangerous. To Frederick Engels it meant the dissolution of the family 'utterly and of necessity':

The children who grow up under such conditions are utterly ruined for later family life, can never feel at home in the family which they themselves found, because they have always been accustomed to isolation, and they contribute therefore to the already general undermining of the family of the working class.[52]

Educational reformers were concerned that with the partial breakdown of the traditional patriarchal control of the family, and the exposure of children to unwelcome and sometimes dangerous influences at work, the child would suffer from neglect and lack of discipline. The family was no longer equipped to educate and socialize children in the old ways and public education was seen as a way to mitigate the social consequences that might arise from this.

If urban conditions and disrupted family patterns gave middle-class reformers cause for concern, it was the rise in working-class political consciousness that did most to galvanize the middle class into educational reform. The period was, as E. P. Thompson has told it, the period of the making of the English working class, both sociologically and politically. In terms of political organization and thought, it represented a period of steadily growing class consciousness and activity, from the years of Tom Paine and the pro-Jacobin radicals, through to the era of the unstamped press and the Luddite uprisings after the war, and so to the high point of mass Chartist organization in the early 1840s. Within the Radical movement, working-class self-education, in societies, clubs, Owenite Halls of science and so on, amounted to a counter-educational movement of considerable potential and called forth a most resolute ideological counter-attack through middle-class educational reform.

These enormous social changes affected education in two, somewhat contradictory, ways, both undermining old forms and stimulating new developments, which were in turn held back by the very social conditions which they were designed to effect. On the negative side, the proletarianization of workers and the dislocation of traditional family structures led, as Richard Johnson and David Levine have argued, to a partial breakdown of old family-based educational practices. This traditional mode of education depended, as Johnson puts it, 'on a social basis of artisans and pre-proletarian workers'. It was gradually 'squeezed out by material changes, as capital secured a tighter control over the conditions of labour'.[53] Where father and mother were working away from home there was now little opportunity for this convivial, informal, family learning. Furthermore, as the family economy became increasingly dependent on the wages of the child, education became subordinated to material necessities. The child was likely not only to receive less home education but also to miss out on schooling, since work interfered with school attendance. Contemporary sources bear out Levine's conclusion that child labour was 'a major impediment to school attendance', and thus a constant frustration to the plans of educational reformers.[54] This was still the case in 1861, when the Newcastle Report gave its unsentimental opinion that work had to come before schooling and that compulsory education was thus impossible:

> Independence is of more importance than education, and the wages of the child's labour are necessary, either to keep the parents from the poor rates, or to relieve the pressure of poverty. It is far better that it should go to work at the earliest stage at which it can bear the physical exertion than that it should remain at school.[55]

If industrialization thus limited the extent to which working-class children could benefit from education, it provided a positive stimulus for educational reformers. The more traditional forms of education were undermined by social change, the more reformers felt justified in replacing them, particularly since industrial and urban development had provided urgent social reasons, as they saw it, for doing something about education. The least of these, but nonetheless important, was the factory itself. Whilst factory production required no new technical skills of its workers, it did require new habits of regularity, subordination to routine, and monotonous work and strict discipline, and these could only be achieved through systematic 're-education' of the workforce. Elementary schools clearly had a vital role to play in this, particularly in Britain, where the factory process was most advanced and the most rapid transformation was experienced. In this sense the early monitorial schools of Lancaster and Bell were ideally suited to economic needs. David Wardle gives a memorable description of the monitorial schools which bears out this point admirably:

> It was the factory put into the educational setting. Every characteristic was there, minute division of labour ... a complicated system of incentives to good work, an impressive system of inspection, and finally an attention to cost efficiency and the economic use of plant which was carried to far greater lengths than even the most modern advocates recommended.[56]

More important than the economic benefits were the social improvements which reformers believed could be achieved through education. Schooling would bring a sober morality to the destitute and 'godless' urban poor, and impose a social authority over the working-class child where the working-class family had failed. For Anglicans and Dissenters alike, the mission was very clearly one of controlling and 'moralizing' the urban poor, increasingly perceived as destitute, ignorant, irreligious, immoral and refractory. Vocal advocates of public education, such as Henry Brougham, Arthur Roebuck and James Kay, frequently referred to the proliferation of social unrest, vagrancy, crime and moral degeneration, and argued that education was a valuable means of countering such undesirable social trends. However, perhaps most important of all was their desire to counteract the spread of radical ideas through the education of working-class children and later adults in the benefits of middle-class morality and bourgeois political economy. The battle between working-class agitation and middle-class propaganda provided the underlying dynamic of educational change throughout the period. As Richard Johnson has written,

> One way of writing the educational history of this period ... is in terms of the shifting antagonism of 'provided education' and counter-cultural forms. Radicalism aimed to provide substitutes to sponsored forms. Philanthropic educators sought to regulate, destroy or replace the means of cultural reproduction that existed within the working class itself and which provided networks through which it could work.[57]

Urbanization, proletarianization and changes in the family thus formed an interrelated set of social factors which had contradictory effects on popular education. On the one hand they undermined traditional education and depressed school attendance, thus inhibiting the spread of mass schooling. On the other hand they encouraged reformers to redouble their efforts to implant the habit of school attendance in the working class and to provide the schools to cater for it. These contradictory effects go some way towards explaining the uneven way in which education developed during this period.

School attendance undoubtedly increased from the period of monitorial expansion in the first decades of the century. The Select Committee on the Education of the Lower Orders found that only 6.6 per cent of the population were in school in 1818, but in 1851 the census recorded 12 per cent in school. However, it developed with marked unevenness. The new schools made their most marked impact in the rural areas around London and in the counties where the National Society gained an early diocesan or district organization, such as Rutland, the North Riding, Northamptonshire and Suffolk. Within the best provided counties the new schools were especially numerous in market towns and the southern ports. Urban and industrial areas shared in the early growth, but by 1818 the industrial counties were still amongst the worst provided with new schools. Monitorial schools made little headway in the industrial areas of the North West, the East and West Midlands and in the rural counties of the East. Attendance varied enormously between counties. In 1818, Westmoreland and Rutland reported 1 in 14 and 1 in 20 at school, and Lancashire and Norfolk reported 1 in 46 and 1 in 47. The Kerry returns of 1833 suggest a consolidation of rural strengths and urban weaknesses during the 1820s. The biggest upsurge of educational activity was not until the 1830s and 1840s, and it was during this period that schools proliferated in manufacturing areas of the North, and began to rectify the uneven geographical spread of schools in the earlier period. Between 1833 and 1851, for instance, the ratio of school attenders to population in Lancashire and the West Riding increased from 1 in 36 and 1 in 42 to 1 in 17 and 1 in 16, respectively. However, by 1851 the best provided counties – Rutland, Berkshire, Hampshire, Northamptonshire, Sussex, Surrey, Oxford, Essex and Dorset – were generally not the major manufacturing regions, although some rural areas, such as Cornwall, lagged behind all others.[58]

An analysis of changing levels of adult literacy in England shows similar geographical unevenness and often a negative correlation with urban and industrial development. In his essay on literacy and education in England, Lawrence Stone argues that there was a rapid growth of literacy for 200 years after the development of the printing press in England. By 1675 the national average for men was not far off 40 per cent, although this varied from up to two-thirds in the cities to one-tenth in the remote rural backwaters of the highland zones in the North and West. During the century after 1675, literacy in the South and Midlands grew very slowly, only picking up again after 1780, when a rapid spurt drove the national average for adult male literacy up to two-thirds by 1840. However, between 1800 and 1840 'the big industrial cities were growing faster than their educational facilities, and urban literacy was most probably in decline'.[59]

Michael Sanderson extends this picture in his study of literacy rates in Lancashire during the period. After an initial rise in the early part of the eighteenth century, he finds clear evidence of decline in adult literacy rates after 1780 in industrial areas. Between 1750 and the 1820s, male and female literacy dropped in a number of typical industrial towns: Chorley (from 40 per cent to 23.9 per cent); Deane (from 31 per cent to 14 per cent); Eccleston (from 46 per cent to 34.6 per cent); Kirkham (from 53.1 per cent to 38.9 per cent); and Preston (56.1 per cent to 38 per cent). From the evidence of the parishes, Sanderson finds an even greater decrease in rural areas. This trend is not reversed, according to him, until the 1830s. He attributes this decline to the prevalence of juvenile labour, the migratory habits of families seeking work and the breakdown of familial controls:

> The fact that under the factory system, children and parents were working in different places removed the disciplines of parental control and led to the breaking of family ties. The result was a frequent desertion of the home by the children and a considerable juvenile vagrancy problem in the country. Needless to say, the last thing these juvenile vagrants considered was going to school to get an education.[60]

The immediate relationship between this set of social factors – urbanization, proletarianization and changing family forms – and educational change in England was thus complex and, in part, contradictory, but overall it is clear that they had an enormous impact in stimulating attempts at educational reform. However, the situation was quite different in continental Europe and such theories can only be applied with modification there. Large-scale urbanization came much later in Europe than in England and the transformation of labouring classes into proletarian workers was a more protracted process. Mass elementary education occurred quite early in a number of countries and was imposed on primarily rural, agrarian populations. There was thus little synchronicity between urban development, the emergence of specifically urban social problems and the elaboration of popular education. The latter was, as we know, relatively widespread by the third decade of the nineteenth century and owed much of its development to the previous century. However, Europe was still largely rural at this time. In fact, by 1855, when England had reached an urban majority, 72 per cent of the Prussian population was still rural, whilst in Saxony and Sweden the percentages of the rural population were 65 per cent and 90 per cent, respectively. France and Bavaria were not dissimilar, with less than 30 per cent living in towns (France, 1856, 27 per cent; Bavaria, 30 per cent). Of the continental states, only the Netherlands had undergone appreciable urbanization, with 36 per cent living in towns.[61] Whilst it is true that in several countries the population was rising steadily (27.7 million to 37.2 million in France, and 22.3 million to 36.4 million in Germany, between 1800 and 1860), the kind of urban problems experienced in England since the end of the eighteenth century were not a significant feature of European societies until 1840 onwards, by which time much of the early educational construction had already taken place.[62] Unlike in England, reformers rarely seem to have associated the need for educational reform with specifically urban problems.

Urbanization, however, is not synonymous with industrial development and the proletarianization of workers, and we should not assume that education was unaffected by changing family forms simply because there is no obvious correspondence with urbanization. The proletarianization of labouring populations was a protracted process that clearly pre-dated industrialization proper by several centuries. Like David Levine, Hans Medick and Alf Lüdtke associate this process with the growth of 'proto-industrial' forms which can be seen from the sixteenth century onwards. Proto-industrialization refers to the period of transition from agrarian to rural society, characterized by the emergence, expansion and final decline of rural industries. This occurred as the combined outcome of the 'destabilisation and decomposition of traditional European peasant societies', and the effects of the increasing penetration of merchant capital and an enforced orientation towards the market.[63]

During the seventeenth and eighteenth centuries there emerged in rural areas an increasingly under-employed population of small peasants and landless labourers, for whom the declining returns of small peasant and sub-peasant economies left only one alternative: 'the part-time or full-time transition from land-intensive agrarian production to labour-intensive craft production'.[64] In practice, this meant the emergence of household production based on a family economy and the capitalist organization of trade. Whether 'independent', or part of the 'putting-out' system, the home-industrial weaver, knitter or nailer was increasingly dependent on merchant capital and the logic of the market.

As David Levine has shown, the development of home production had considerable effects on the nature and structure of family life. Although the home producer was still partially independent, owning his own tools and organizing his own work and that of his family, the rhythm and meaning of work, and the social relationships which underpinned it, were changing. Pressure of survival in this market-oriented economy forced increased participation in production by all members of the family. Child labour amongst these 'cottage workers' extended far beyond that of ordinary peasants, and children were frequently hired out or left home early to work. Furthermore, the material conditions that governed customs of inheritance amongst peasant families did not apply to the cottage workers' families. This not only reduced the control of parents over the marital relations of the young but also loosened the structural connection of the generations, insofar as it had been guaranteed by property, inheritance and patriarchal domination. This often led to earlier marriage, and to greater individualization in the selection of partners, frequently interpreted by local contemporaries as a 'shameless' freedom typical of artisans. Within the family production unit the sexual division of labour became more blurred: hard economic exigencies could lead women to 'neglect' household 'duties' and the role-allocation process frequently became more flexible than in peasant families.[65]

In an impressive work on absolutism and the rise of compulsory schooling, James Van Horn Melton has shown how these and other changes in the relations of production in eighteenth-century Prussia underpinned the development of mass schooling.[66] The rapid advance in proto-industrial production, particularly in the Silesian linen and wool industry, created a labour shortage which encouraged the displacement of peasants from the land, increased the employment of child labour and required wholesale changes in working habits.[67] By the mid-century there was also a growing movement for agrarian reform and the commutation of labour services: measures designed to increase the incentives for efficient agricultural production.[68] These changes were closely related to a growing crisis of authority in rural and urban social relations. The decline of the guild system had led to the abrogation of the moral and educative duties of the master towards his apprentices and thus to the atrophy of an important form of social control; the declining importance of inheritance, due to the scarcity of land, weakened the patriarchal strength of the traditional peasant family; and the prevalence of noble absenteeism, with the spread of bourgeois leaseholding, and the growth of a class of landless rural poor, only loosely bound by seigneurial ties, all contributed towards the weakening of traditional forms of patriarchal authority.[69] Fears about the decline of traditional forms of social control in the countryside were heightened by frequent peasant uprisings.[70]

By the 1760s, cameralist state officials and agrarian reformers were campaigning vigorously for the extension of popular schooling as a way of compensating for the decline in traditional modes of social control and in an effort to instil an enhanced work ethic amongst the populace.[71] New forms of self-discipline and internal motivation had to be inculcated in the peasantry, in particular, if they were to work diligently as independent producers. As the Governor of Bohemia, Prince Carl Von Fürstenberg, remarked when contemplating similar problems in Habsburg Austria,

> The character of the peasant has been so neglected that the will and aptitude necessary for his self-improvement will require long and serious cultivation. In short, we must educate an entirely new generation.[72]

This, argues Melton, was in fact exactly what the absolutist rulers of eighteenth-century Prussia and Austria sought to do with their extensive educational reforms.

It is clear from Melton's detailed historical account of educational reform in the Habsburg and Hohenzollern territories that arguments about changing labour relations and family structures do have a part to play in explaining educational change in continental Europe, at least in these central regions. However, there are important shifts of emphasis. Whereas in England the argument revolves around proletarianization of labour in the strict sense of the term, that is the creation of a widespread industrial proletariat, here it concerns the gradual transition of a servile peasantry into new forms of independent agricultural and proto-industrial production. The dynamics of this are clearly different and pertain to another stage of capitalist development, if indeed changes in a semi-feudal economy can be characterized as such. In Prussia and Austria, major changes in education were occurring in a period prior to full-scale proletarianization and without significant impetus from urbanization. In England the period of proto-industry did not involve any such concerted efforts to reform education, and major changes in education did not occur until a much later stage in economic development. These discrepancies clearly need to be explained by other factors if there is to be a coherent comparative theory for the development of education systems.

North American society in the early nineteenth century was scarcely more urban or industrial than France or Prussia. Nevertheless, the United States has been the historical locus of the most ambitious theoretical attempts to relate educational development to these social changes. Most notable for their theoretical contributions are Michael Katz in his two historical works on nineteenth-century US education and the Marxist economists, Samuel Bowles and Herbert Gintis, in the historical sections of their celebrated volume, *Schooling in Capitalist America*. Taken together, their works demonstrate most clearly the strengths and weaknesses of this approach in its most theoretically elaborated form.

In both cases their analysis focuses on the consolidation of public education systems in the north-eastern states during the era of educational reforms from 1830 to the Civil War, and makes much of the degree to which this was synchronized with increasing industrial development, urbanization and the proletarianization of labour. Recognizing the relatively weak links between education and the provision of technical skills, they assess the function of education as a response to the broader parameters of social change, particularly as they affected urban communities where educational reform was most zealous. Broadly speaking, public education is seen as a response to, and way of controlling, new social problems thrown up by early industrial capitalism. For Michael Katz the period was one of cataclysmic social change:

> Within the lifetime of one man a new society was born, a society that smashed older expectations with the force of steam, that ripped apart and restricted the web of social relationships compressing the experience of men.[73]

Public education was essentially a response to the problems engendered in the transition to wage labour and in the trauma of urban life. Educational reform involved the 'imposition by social leaders of schooling upon a ... reluctant citizenry and most specifically on the new urban working class of whom it was a form of discipline and social control'.[74] In less dramatic language, Bowles and Gintis outline a similar argument, linking, somewhat more broadly, educational reform and expansion in the early nineteenth century with the 'growing ascendancy of the capitalist mode of production'. Particularly striking, they say,

> is the recurring pattern of capital accumulation in the dynamic educational sectors of the economy, the resulting integration of new workers into the wage-labour system, the expansion of the proletariat and the reserve army (of labour), social unrest and the emergence of political protest movements and the development of movements for educational expansion and reform.[75]

At the centre of the analysis, in both cases, is the movement from independent production to wage labour. Both authors accept that educational reform pre-dates the emergence of a large-scale factory proletariat, but argue that the gradual proletarianization of workers before this time was sufficiently traumatic to require social control through new systems of education. The task of public schooling was not so much to develop new skills for the industrial sector as to inculcate habits of conformity, discipline and morality, which would counter the widespread problems of social disorder and encourage acceptance of the values of competitive capitalism, both in the workplace and in the community at large. The argument, inasmuch as it relates to the more urbanized north-eastern areas, is powerful and one that has been partially anticipated, albeit unsystematically, in numerous earlier histories which have focused on problems of urbanization.

During the period from 1830 to 1860 the United States as a whole, and the North East in particular, experienced enormous demographic change. The total population in the United States grew at around 35 per cent per decade throughout the period.[76] In many areas, particularly in New England, this growth was exponential. In Massachusetts, for instance, which was already densely populated by American standards, each decade brought a higher rate of increase than the one preceding it. In 1820 the population was 8.7 per cent higher than a decade before, and by 1830, 15.2 per cent higher than this. During the following decade the rate of increase steadied, adding another 15.2 per cent to the population, but by 1850 population growth had leapt forward with an increase of 30.8 per cent.[77]

One of the major factors in population growth was immigration, which was also rising in a geometric curve: immigrants to the United States numbered over 143 000 in the 1820s, over 599 000 in the 1830s and over 1.7 million in the 1850s. By 1842 a third of the population of Boston were immigrants and children of immigrants, and three years later the same proportion of New York City were foreign born.[78]

Perhaps more significant even than the gross increase in population in this sparsely populated country was the change in its distribution. Urbanization, fuelled by immigration and employment-seeking internal migration, was of paramount social importance during this period, as increasing numbers of people adapted to life in middling and large cities. Between 1830 and 1860, the numbers living in towns of 2500 or more rose from 10 to 20 per cent: a rate of urbanization which peaked in the North East in the 1840s and in the Mid-Atlantic states in the 1850s.[79] In Massachusetts the population increased from 472 000 in 1810 to 1 231 000 in 1860, and in southern New England generally the proportion of people living in towns and cities of more than 10 000 inhabitants increased from 6.9 per cent in 1810 to 36.5 per cent in 1846.[80] Urbanization was considerably greater in the North than in the South, and particularly high and rising fastest in the North East, where educational change was most rapid.

Alongside this move towards the city was an equally important change in the nature of labour. The growth of manufacturing employment in relation to agricultural employment has already been mentioned. However, another kind of change was taking place, which affected all sectors, and this was the gradual shift away from independent employment to wage labour. In agriculture the traditional independent 'yeoman' farmer was slowly being replaced by wage labourers as the size and complexity of farm units increased. In the cities there was a rapid shift from independent craft production to waged labour in workshops and factories of increasing size. In New York City, for instance, between 1795 and 1855 there was a fourfold increase in the relative proportion of wage workers and a reduction of two-thirds in the relative numbers of independent merchants and proprietors.[81] In 1796 only 5.5 per cent of the population reported as labourers, whilst in 1855 27.4 per cent did so.[82] In Newark, New Jersey, one of the country's foremost industrial cities, 17.3 per cent of craftsmen who were heads of household were still self-employed in 1840. By 1860 a mere 8.7 per cent could have been classed as such.[83]

There can be little doubt that these changing contours of social and economic life had an impact on the development of mass education. Public education developed fastest and furthest in the northern states where the impact of urban and industrial development was greatest, and within these regions it was in the major cities where many of the innovations of the reform era were first promoted. As Carl Kaestle has said,

> The fact that state intervention in education succeeded in this period while earlier it had failed, and that it coincided with accelerating urbanization and immigration, suggests that there was a causal connection between education reform and social change in the years from 1830 to 1860.[84]

Educational historians have generally taken this period to be the critical moment in the formation of public education in the United States, and for those who have sought a functional relation between social forces and educational change, this has been the classic site for theoretical analysis. In their early seminal works, both Carlton and Cubberley saw the emerging industrial cities of the North East as the classic locus of educational reform, where social need and political will most favoured radical change. The rise of new cities, argued Cubberley, produced an entirely new set of educational problems to solve. In the older and more homogeneous village communities, church and charity education was adequate to social needs. However, as

> the cities now increased rapidly in size, became more city-like in character, drew to them diverse elements previously largely unknown, and were required by state laws to extend the right of education to all citizens, the need for a new type of organization began slowly but clearly to manifest itself to an increasing number of citizens.

Under such circumstances, argues Cubberley, the system of church, charity and private schools 'completely broke down under the strain', thus leaving the way clear for reformers to advocate an entirely new system.[85]

In Cubberley's classic account, the equation of public schooling and urbanization is made quite clear. What Marxist historians have added to this is an analysis of the class relations underlying the role of schooling, undermining Cubberley's 'heroic' vision and substituting a more insidious picture of social control through an education designed to combat the social tensions and unrest that went with proletarianization and urban development. Katz, in particular, underlines the way in which educational reformers attempted to address the problems of crime, vagrancy, immigration and social unrest, which were part and parcel of urbanization, and the institutional decline of the family and apprenticeship system that accompanied the proletarianization of labour. Of particular concern, of course, was the state of youth, which, according to Katz, had reached a point of 'crisis'.[86]

The fear of urban degeneration was, no doubt, a fundamental force behind educational reform. Underpinning almost all of the writing on educational reform in this period was a pervasive anxiety about order and morality in the cities, about the prevalence of crime, juvenile vice, prostitution, vagrancy and begging, and about the danger of crowds of idle and 'vicious' city workers roaming the streets. The extent of the problem was deemed to be growing alarmingly, following inescapably from the irreversible changes in the institutions that traditionally regulated social order. Proletarian family life was thought to have disintegrated. The apprenticeship system was corrupted and ceased to involve the traditional controls of youth by masters, and the decline of independent craft production loosened the ties which bound masters and journeymen. Above all, the very heterogeneity of urban life, mixing nationalities, creeds and diverse occupations, in a society no longer bound by the close web of community solidarity, seemed to challenge the very idea of social order. The single most important solution to these problems, it seemed, was education.

Public education, argues Katz, was essentially a form of state intervention in private lives, designed to maintain order. In their writings, many educational reformers do appear to have conceived of it in this way, notably Horace Mann, who had no hesitation in recommending public intervention where family life was failing:

> No one at all familiar with the deficient household arrangements and the deranged machinery of domestic life of the extreme poor, and ignorant, to say nothing of the intemperate – of the examples of rude manners, impure and profane language, and all the vicious habits of low-bred idleness which abound in certain sections of all populous districts – can doubt, that it is better for children to be removed as early and as long as possible.[87]

The urban school would be a protection for children against their parents and environment. No longer an extension of parental will, as in the ideal of the parentally controlled district and rural school, but now a bureaucratic apparatus that came between children and parents. School would succeed where the family had failed. The primary object, according to Mann, 'was not so much intellectual culture'

> as the regulation of the feelings and dispositions, the extirpation of vicious propensities, the preoccupation of the wilderness of the young heart with the seeds and germs of moral beauty, and the formation of a lovely and virtuous character by the habitual practice of cleanliness, delicacy, refinement, good temper, gentleness, kindness, justice and truth.[88]

The main concern of the reformers lay in the moral state of urban youth, and in particular with the morality of the children of the poor and the immigrant. The city itself was a temptation to vice. Barnas Seers, Mann's successor as Secretary of the Massachusetts Education Board, warned that the 'current of sensuality' is so strong 'that it often sweeps everything before it'.

> This life of congregated human beings, where money, leisure, shows and a succession of excitements are the objects of pursuit, is now, with inconceivable power, educating our children.[89]

The poor and the immigrant were deemed the most vulnerable to the corrupting influences of the city and for them especially the school was seen as a necessary salvation. In language which is strong but not unusual, the Boston School Committee described education as

> taking children at random from a great city, undisciplined, uninstructed, often with inveterate forwardness and obstinacy, and with the inherited stupidity of centuries of ignorant ancestors; forming them from animals into intellectual beings and from intellectual into spiritual beings.[90]

Public education offered a systematic remedy to urban social problems, or so the reformers believed. In addition to habits of order and routine, its curriculum represented a sustained inculcation of moral values designed at once to assimilate the immigrant into Protestant native culture, to acclimatize children into the virtues of hard work and clean living, and to produce future workers and citizens who would uphold the capitalist values of competition and property both at home and in the community. To Michael Katz this represented a sustained effort on the part of the middle class to control the unwanted social effects of a developing industrial capitalism. In the more Marxist language of Bowles and Gintis, schooling had begun to fulfil its primary purpose of reproducing the social conditions of capitalist labour.

This analysis has great force and provides what must be an essential element in any analysis of the social factors which promoted the development of public education systems in the urban North. Its power derives not least from its realistic assessment of the motives of leading reformers and of the class relations that underlay educational initiatives. It offers an important antidote to the rather naive humanist assumptions of the triumphalist interpretations of educational development. However, as a general theory of educational development in the United States as a whole, the argument has serious weaknesses.

The main difficulties with both of these accounts is that they rest on a manifest urban bias, that they involve seriously foreshortened periodization of educational change, and that their general analysis of class relations is skewed as a consequence. To take the urban question first, both interpretations give an unwarranted precedence to reform in urban areas and probably exaggerate the degree to which urban social problems actually underpinned educational change in general. Despite urban development, the United States was an overwhelmingly rural society throughout the entire period. It is worth repeating that even in 1860, 84 per cent of the population still lived in communities of less than 8 000 and the majority of these were independent farmers.[91] Yet educational development and the construction of public education systems was a nationwide phenomenon. It certainly was the case that innovations in public schooling developed first in the more urban north-eastern areas, and yet these also filtered out to the more rural areas of the Mid-West before the Civil War. It is often pointed out that school enrolment increased considerably during the period of intensive urbanization. In fact from 1840 to 1860 the proportion of white children (5–19) who were enrolled for school actually increased by 60 per cent.[92] However, less often mentioned is that this increase largely occurred in the more rural southern and mid-western states. The proportion of children enrolled in New England actually fell during the period. Albert Fishlow's analysis of regional enrolment rates neatly illustrates this (see Table 2.1)[93].

Clearly this does not obviate the fact that north-eastern towns, with their greater population increases, had to expand educational provision at a faster rate. However, it does show that educational expansion was not

Table 2.1   Regional enrolment rates

	1840	1850	1860
New England	81.4	76.1	73.8
Mid-Atlantic	54.7	61.9	61.3
South Atlantic	16.2	29.7	31.4
North Central	29.1	52.4	69.4
South Central	38.4	50.4	57.0

only, or even mainly, an urban phenomenon. Any general theory of the rapid development of public education in the North, or even of its slower emergence in the South, has to account for the fact that this involved the provision of schools in rural areas as well as towns, and that the rural areas often had higher levels of enrolment than neighbouring towns of the same state. Clearly an analysis which concentrates on the connections between urban problems and urban development does little to explain the origins of educational change in rural areas, especially given that the decentralized nature of American educational organization precluded the forced extension of educational innovation from urban to rural states. Certain effects can be attributed to ideological diffusion, but for the most part independent causes of educational change in rural areas must be sought.

Even regarding the urban areas themselves, where these theories have most pertinence, there may be some exaggeration of the degree to which educational change was an effect of urban problems. The social changes which accompanied proletarianization and urbanization were possibly neither so swift nor so traumatic as is sometimes implied. As Bailyn's account illustrates, the fragmentation of traditional family and community bonds had been occurring since settlement, and whilst this was no doubt intensi-fied during the period of rapid urbanization in the North East, it was not invariably as catastrophic as is sometimes suggested. Newark, New Jersey, for instance, was one of the nation's foremost industrial towns which between 1820 and 1860 experienced a steady change from being a community of tra-ditional craft production to one dominated by factories. Yet in her detailed study, Susan Hirsch found that workers did not experience industrialization as a cataclysmic event, and continued to aspire to traditional 'Victorian' family norms. 'The persistence of pre-industrial family values and concepts of male and female roles', she writes, 'limited the changes in family life that were caused by industrialization.'[94] Married women were only rarely employed in manufacture, 61 per cent of women workers in Newark being under 21. By 1860 only one in five Newark women over 14 were engaged in manufacture. Nor was child labour a widespread phenomenon, at least outside the textile towns.[95] Teenage labour did increase in the early years of industrialization but, as mechanization proceeded, semi- and unskilled adults, who were generally regarded as more reliable and skilful, replaced teenagers in jobs. Unlike in England, where the extent of juvenile labour was a major argument used by experts for educational reform, in the United States it was more likely to be the idleness of youth which preoccupied educational advocates.

Urbanization, immigration and the shift towards wage labour no doubt created considerable social problems in some cities, although the process was less traumatic than in England. However, it may be an exaggeration to see this as the primary social determinant of educational change; contemporary advocates painted lurid pictures of urban degeneration to advance their cause but, as Albert Fishlow points out, subsequent historians have possibly relied too heavily on their particular preoccupations. Their particular era, from 1830 onwards, was certainly greatly influenced by urban development, and was the seminal one for the consolidation of public education systems, but considerable educational development had occurred in the preceding decades when urbanization was not such a major preoccupation. Historians who have focused on the reform era have somewhat foreshortened the long span of educational development and paid too little attention to factors which were more evident in the earlier period. Figures for enrolment during the early republic are, unfortunately, considerably less complete than those for the reform period. However, from what evidence there is it seems that enrolment had been growing steadily from well before the beginning of the reform campaign and probably from the end of the previous century. On Fishlow's evidence, New York State had reached the level of enrolment attributed to 1830 by 1815, and that represented a substantial increase on 1798 levels. Fishlow concludes:

> The common school revival has served as a wrong focal point for the interpretation of that era. The movement for free schools was a fact, but that does not make it the transcendent feature of some six decades of educational experience. American efforts prior to the first such stirrings in the 1830's were exceptional by contemporary standards.[96]

Fishlow may underestimate the importance of qualitative changes during the reform era. However, he is correct to emphasize the importance of the earlier period, and the analyses of educational development that fail to explain the enormous educational activity of the revolutionary and early national periods in their singular emphasis on developments that paralleled urbanization, are surely missing an important dimension.

The relationship between educational change and the proletarianization of labour, which is most stressed in the work of Bowles and Gintis, is less liable to these criticisms since the process was not restricted to urban areas and had a much earlier history. The transition to waged labour occurred not only in the larger towns but also in the rural areas, both with rural industry and with the gradual transformation of agriculture. However, even here the emphasis is surely exaggerated, since independent producers remained in the majority for at least the first half of the century, when the most important changes occurred. Any account of the effects of changes in the structures of family life on education must also look more broadly at the way in which this affected the independent farmers and artisans.

The final problem which results from this unwarranted narrowing of focus is the way in which it skews the analysis of class relations. In the accounts of both Katz, and Bowles and Gintis, the typical target of reformers, the children of poor, probably immigrant, waged workers, holds centre stage.

Since the typical stance of reformers, and the education system as a whole, towards this group was one of authoritarian paternalism, a model of the outright imposition of education seems rather plausible. However, this generalization from one set of class relations cannot be sustained in a more general model. As Katz has more recently admitted, the situation was far more complex than this, and one of the most extraordinary features of the period was precisely the degree of consent amongst the population to public education. This does not mean that relations of class power were absent, or that education did not involve an attempt at social control with regard to certain groups. However, in the American case particularly, we must look for far more complex class relations than the concept of simple class imposition implies.

The arguments presented in this section are drawn from a diverse array of radical social historians who have sought to demonstrate the impact of social change on educational development in different countries. Although they have not generally been elaborated into formal theory, they do have considerable purchase on the problem of educational change, particularly in England and, to a lesser extent, in the United States. However, they do not, as yet, constitute a full comparative theory, and it is doubtful whether they could do so without considerable modification and the addition of new concepts. The major comparative problem remains the explanation of differential national development. Theories which concentrate exclusively on the effects of urbanization, proletarianization and changing family structures have yet to account for the rapid development of education in countries where these factors were least developed and the relatively delayed development of public education in England, where they were most developed.

Margaret Archer: A Weberian account

Another approach to the problem of differential national development in education is to curtail the search for underlying sociological determinants and to concentrate instead on explaining the actual mechanisms of educational reform in different countries. The chief exponent of this approach is the Weberian sociologist Margaret Archer, who has written a number of major comparative works on nineteenth-century education.[97]

Archer's starting point in her early work with Michelina Vaughan is a critique of existing theories of educational change which fail to explain differential development. Functionalist theory is dismissed because it posits a non-existent consensus of educational goals, fails to explain educational conflict and provides no explanation of differential educational development in countries where this cannot be explained by different economic relations. Marxist theory is said to have an initial advantage here because it incorporates the notion of class conflict. However, this superiority is only superficial, according to Archer, since Marxism also exhibits an unacceptable economic determinism, denying the efficacy of ideas in educational change and operating a crude bi-polar concept of class. Like functionalist theory, it cannot explain differential educational development. 'As a sociological theory,' writes Archer,

> Marxism does not satisfactorily explain the differences in educational development between [France and England]. In neither case does the economic infrastructure appear to have determined institutional change. The rapid rise of industrialization in England with the accompanying ascendancy of the middle class was not matched by a corresponding set of educational reforms which would have access, structure and content more consistent with the requirements of the class... [whilst] in France, rapid political change in the context of a stable mode of production led to the educational transformations culminating in the creation of the imperial university. This reform reflected the priority assigned to political rather than economic imperatives.[98]

Not content with a rejection of the major sociological theories, Archer goes on in a later article to dismiss the 'facile epiphenomenalism' of all theories which 'pinpoint some particular variable or process as universally responsible for expansion', and rejects, *tout court*, human capital theory, modernization theory, political integration theory, social control theory and ideological diffusion theory.[99]

In her own substantive analysis of educational change in Russia, Denmark, France and England in *The Social Origins of Educational Systems*, Archer adopts a form of Weberian macro-sociology which seeks to explain change in terms of group interaction. 'Education has the characteristics it does', she writes, 'because of the goals pursued by those who control it... Change occurs because new educational goals are pursued by those who have power to modify previous practices.'[100] However, groups are also constrained by structural factors and thus both human agency and structural conditioning are seen as equally important. Determinism is abandoned and replaced by a theory which posits the centrality of group interaction, where this is conditioned or influenced, but not determined, by prior structural or social factors.

Change in nineteenth-century education systems is brought about by the struggle between different educational interest groups. The dominant educational group are the churches, which have traditionally controlled education. Other 'adventitious beneficiaries' of the system are the legal profession, which benefits from traditional scholastic teaching, and the English ruling elite, whose objectives in political socialization and the reproduction of the class structure are well served by Anglican education. These are challenged by new 'assertive groups' drawn from those who are obstructed by existing education, either because they are denied access to it or because the content of existing education is irrelevant to their needs. The English dissenting entrepreneurs were obstructed in both of these ways and provided the core of the assertive group in England.[101]

The nature of educational challenge is conditioned by existing social forces. According to Archer, two main forms of challenge are possible. The assertive groups may engage in 'substitution', which involves creating rival institutions to ensure an educational provision compatible with their needs. Alternatively, they may adopt a strategy of 'restriction', which involves destroying the monopoly of the dominant group through legal constraints and subsequently replacing it through state provision. Which strategy is adopted depends on the nature of social forces in play, and, in particular, on the 'social distribution of resources'.[102] In order to employ restriction, the assertive group must have access to the national legislative machinery. Groups adopting substitutive strategies, on the other hand, must have sufficient wealth in order to finance substitute educational institutions. Thus the assertive group adopting substitution tends to be the economic elite, whilst the assertive group adopting restriction tends to be the political elite. Out of Archer's four national cases, two – France and Russia – exemplify the restrictive process and two – England and Denmark – the substitutive process. The French assertive group, for instance, is drawn largely from the professional and commercial bourgeoisie, which has insufficient wealth to compete with the Church in the educational market but does have sufficient political influence to initiate restrictions. The English assertive group, drawn largely from the industrial middle class, lacks political power for restriction but has sufficient wealth to adopt a policy of substitution. The future course of educational development in these countries follows from the structural implications of adopting the chosen strategy.

The following stage in Archer's analysis concerns the structural elaboration that ensues in different types of system, creating respectively the centralized and decentralized structures. In all systems, education becomes increasingly integrated with the state and with a plurality of other local institutions. Education ceases to be 'mono-integrated' and becomes 'multi-integrated', serving a number of social institutions and performing a number of different functions. However, this occurs in different ways. In systems with restrictive origins it occurs 'centrifugally', from the centre outwards. In systems with substitutive origins it occurs 'centripetally', from the outside inwards.

Thus in France, where old institutions have been abolished and replaced by new ones established by the state, education only becomes integrated with external institutions by central design. This happens of necessity because the assertive group needs to mobilize funds to finance the whole education system, which means that it must service many social groups to convince the public to devote their taxes to it. During the Empire the first priority was to devise an education system that would serve the bureaucracy and the military and would inculcate loyalty amongst the masses. Napoleon developed the *lycées*, the *polytechniques* and the *grandes écoles* to provide recruits for the state, whilst elementary schools remained concerned above all with inculcating morality rather than specific skills. However, by the 1830s, the demands of industry forced the state to develop more advanced education in the form of *écoles primaires supérieures*. This illustrates a form of integration of education with more extensive social institutions.

In England, multi-integration occurred directly and from the start. The aim of those employing substitutive strategies was 'to change the part of society which education serves, but to retain its mono-integrated status'.[103] This produced a 'primitive' form of multi-integration. Conflicting groups introduced education for their own purposes, and different parts of the social structure received the benefit. Thus there were three distinct systems in England, integrated with different parts of the social structure: the Anglican schools, which were dominated by the gentry and integrated with the conservative state apparatus; the middle-class schools, which were articulated with industry; and independent working-class schools, arising in tandem with working-class political organizations and institutions of self-help. However, as this pluralistic form of assertion became increasingly expensive, assertive groups began to look to the state to protect their institutions. In order to attract public funds they had to yield autonomy to accountability. They ended up with a state system that nobody intended and which, rather than constituting a whole, was merely the sum of its constituent parts. The diversity of national education in England thus stemmed 'from the incorporated networks retaining much of their early distinctiveness'.[104]

The distinction between centralized and decentralized systems is already apparent in the difference between those acquiring multi-integration centripetally and those acquiring it centrifugally. Archer elaborates this distinction with a further set of characteristics which describe the relations between education and the state, and education and society. Structural changes occurred in all systems and the most important of these are said to be 'unification', 'systematization', 'differentiation' and 'specialization'. The first couple arose from the relations between education and the state, and the second couple from relations between education and society.

Unification involves the 'incorporation or development of diverse establishments, activities and personnel under a central, national and specifically educational framework of administration'.[105] It involves various degrees of central control and standardization of procedures but is not invariably centralist. Systematization represents the transition from summativity to wholeness in the articulation of different elements in the system.

> Instead of national education being the sum of disparate and unrelated sets of establishments or independent networks, it now refers to a series of interconnected elements within a unified whole.[106]

Systemization is achieved through the articulation of different levels of education with one another through the manipulation of statutory entry and exit ages, the coordination or separation of curricula, and the use of national examinations and entry requirements to regulate access to different parts of the system.

Differentiation refers to the process by which education gains autonomy from different parts of society. A specialist educational collectivity emerges with a distinctive educational role structure and a definition of instruction which is not coterminous with the 'knowledge and beliefs of any single institution'.[107] In restrictive systems the state must serve various goals in order to maintain public support for state education, and thus cannot allow education to be too closely connected with any one institution. In systems with substitutive origins, groups have to concede some autonomy to education, accepting inspection and financial accountability, thus ensuring a degree of differentiation. Specialization refers to the ways in which educational institutions are developed to concentrate on specialized functions. In restrictive systems, again, the state must ensure some specialization to maintain the support of diverse groups that require education to service their particular needs. In substitutive systems, specialization is inherent from the beginning. 'Specialization is transmitted to the new system through the incorporation of independent networks.'[108]

Although, as Archer argues, all systems develop these four characteristics, they do so to different degrees. Those systems with restrictive origins tend to acquire strong unification and systemization, and weak differentiation and specialization. Conversely, the system with substitutive origins tends to develop with weak forms of unification and systematization, and strong forms of specialization and differentiation. 'In the case of systems with restrictive origins, unification is quicker and more dramatic, whilst it is slow and cumulative in substitutive systems.'[109]

Unification and systematization occur earlier in restrictive systems since, when replacement begins, it takes place within a unified administrative framework, created by the state after the abolition of the old system. From the start, all education provisions are initiated and coordinated by the central authority. It is not uncommon, writes Archer, 'for every decision concerning expenditure, appointments, examinations, curriculum and recruitment to be referred to a higher authority'.[110] Consequently the autonomy of educational personnel is not great, and it is common to find that teachers are civil servants and thus subject to more limiting legal statutes than other professions. Where the state cannot afford to get rid of all old, independent institutions, limited local autonomy may remain, but this is highly circumscribed by state regulations concerning authorization, licensing and certification of schools and teachers.

Strong systematization occurs in restrictive systems as a result of unified state control. Because the state has explicit objectives in education and a system of control which can realize these in practice, it ensures maximum effectiveness of the system by rigorously coordinating its parts. According to Archer, this does not necessarily entail positive articulation between different levels or the creation of an educational ladder. It merely means that overlap and disjuncture are avoided and the nature of links between levels is explicit.

In substitutive systems, unification and systematization are imposed on networks which are already specialized and differentiated. Independent networks fight to preserve their distinctive and specialized character, and resist standardization and central control. Depending on the degree to which the independent groups prevail on government to protect their interests after incorporation, administration unification and systematization is more or less inhibited. In England, unification remains weak even after 1870, and the level of systematization achieved even by 1902 is 'by far the lowest recorded in any of the four systems examined'.[111]

The brief summary of Archer's work presented here refers to the first half of *Social Origins*, which analyses the development of national education systems in the nineteenth century. Her declared intention was to provide a theory which can 'account for the characteristics and contours of national education systems and their processes of change'.[112] How far is this achieved for the early period? As a descriptive typology of different educational structures I would argue that Archer's account provides the most powerful comparative framework that has yet been produced. There are certainly some absences which are inevitable in a study of this magnitude and the selection of cases is open to some objections. Archer's typology is strong on organizational forms but has less to say on other interesting comparative issues, such as levels of enrolment and access, standards of literacy and so on. Also, by choosing two cases which exemplify the 'decentralized' system and two which exemplify the 'centralized' one, Archer produces a neatly symmetrical account but one which somewhat misrepresents the balance of types as they actually existed in nineteenth-century Europe. Most of these, including those in France, Holland, Switzerland and the German states, were on the 'state' model rather than the English 'voluntary' model. They were not all as centralized as the French system but they did provide 'public' forms of education. Archer's 'restrictive' pattern was really the typical form of development, and English 'substitution' the anomaly, and this is not fully brought out in her account. However, having said this, her anatomization of the different structural and organizational forms in nineteenth-century education systems, and her comparative assessments on the effects of these different patterns of development, are genuinely enlightening. Hers is certainly the first comparative account which gives due weight to the actual mechanisms of change in educational systems, and puts these at centre stage in her analysis.

However, as a theory of the social origins of education systems, the account is less than convincing. It has already been noted that Archer's focus on the institutional mechanisms of change supplies a level of analysis which has not always been sufficiently stressed hitherto. However, this in itself does not constitute the theory of social origins. The latter is contained in her analysis of structural conditioning and educational interaction, both of which are said to condition change.

In many respects Archer's analysis of interaction in terms of group conflict, the development of alliances and the elaboration of effective ideologies seems to go to the heart of the problem. It has much in common with interpretations which use Gramscian-type theories of hegemony, although it does not explicitly acknowledge these. Many of the differences between educational development in different countries can be read in this way, and Marxist historians, such as Brian Simon, on whom Archer draws heavily, have used a similar approach. For instance, the failure of English middle-class reformers to develop and sustain an effective alliance on educational reform with the working-class radicals was clearly a factor in the rather partial and slow attainment of their goals. So much is common ground. However, conflict theory without an analysis of the social and economic structures on which conflict develops is only half an explanation. Archer has delimited her study to exclude this level of analysis and is thus forced to rely on relatively unexamined concepts to explain the different forms that conflict takes. 'We do not try to explain the nature of the economy but treat it as given,' she writes.[113] Equally, there is no comparative theory of the state, which might support her analysis of why certain 'assertive' groups opt for a strategy of state 'restriction' and others for a policy of voluntary 'substitution'. This is the key moment in Archer's account and also the one where the theory is weakest.

According to Archer, the French assertive group chooses restriction because it lacks wealth for market competition, but has sufficient political influence to manipulate state policy. The English assertive group chooses substitution because it has little political power but adequate wealth. Unfortunately, this explanation of why each group adopts a different course is simply not credible. The French assertive group in the 1760s, when state education theory was first elaborated, had little political power in the state. It took a revolution to achieve that. It certainly had no more political power than the English middle class, say, in 1810, who were adopting the opposite strategy precisely because they lacked political clout, according to Archer. Furthermore, if her theory is correct in postulating that strategic choice is determined by the presence or absence of political power, why is it that after 1832, when the English middle class could win most of the political demands which it made on parliament, it was unable or unwilling to go wholeheartedly for a policy of restriction. Religious conflict, as Archer correctly says, is not an adequate explanation.

The answer surely lies not in the relative wealth or political power of the two bourgeois classes, although they did differ, but in their quite different orientations towards the state. The French bourgeoisie, parliamentarian, Jacobin, Republican alike, had thoroughly étatist conceptions of government, and consequently saw the road to educational change as leading through state legislation and state control. In the post-revolutionary period the state was seen by many republicans, including radicals, as a bulwark against aristocratic privilege and clerical tyranny. In England the bourgeoisie, on the contrary, saw the state as the source of all tyranny, whether in the form of oppressive legislation or extortionate taxation. English liberalism and *laissez-faire* were the crucial factors which gave the distinctive cast to English educational development. It was not so much that the middle class lacked the power to instigate reforms through the state, although in the early period they might have found it difficult; it was that they did not want to. The only group that was at all committed to creating a public education system through legislation was that of the Benthamite radicals, and their state-enhancing liberalism was decisively at odds with the philosophy of *laissez-faire* government, which prevailed amongst the majority of their class. For all the supposed flexibility and nuances of Weberian conflict theory, Archer barely distinguishes between the assertive group (the radicals) and the rest of the class. The failure of the middle class to adopt a united policy on education, no less than the failed alliance with the working class, sealed the fate of English education.

This *lacuna* in Archer's analysis would have been less significant were not the analysis of the conjuncture so important for her theory. However, as it is, it largely conditions what is to follow. There is a kind of systemic determinism in her theory whereby the choice of substitution or restriction at one point in time creates the structural/institutional limits which constrain all further development. The English assertive group thus advanced along the rails of the substitutive route, even after the conditions which determined the choice of this path no longer prevailed. Why, when substitution faltered after 1840, as Archer admits it did, did the assertive group not change trains? The answer must again lie in the nature of the liberal state and the *laissez-faire* ideologies which supported it, but this hardly features in Archer's account. The change of strategy did not come about until the 1860s because, according to her, substitution no longer seemed viable, involving, as it did, intolerable expenses for the middle class. What Archer again fails to stress is that a fundamental change in attitude towards the state was beginning to occur at this time, bringing with it the demise of pure *laissez-faire* and the voluntary principle in education.

For all its formal sophistication and comparative insight, Archer's study is missing a dimension which is crucial to explaining differential educational change during this period. This is the case not only for England and France but also for the countries which are not included in her study. In each case it was not only the nature of group conflict which determined educational change, but also the nature of the state and the relation of classes in civil society to the state. Chapter 3 will examine this issue.

3
Education and State Formation

We have seen in the preceding discussion the difficulties that arise from attempts to link the development of education directly with changes in the economic and social structure of society. The relationship between educational forms and changes at the level of productive technique and economic skill requirements is indirect and highly mediated by other factors. Equally, the connections between educational development and the changing social conditions of labour are complex and by no means constitute a relation of direct and immediate correspondence. Neither urbanization nor the proletarianization of labour are linked, in any simple or transparent way, with the development of new forms of schooling. The difficulties facing reductionist theories of this kind are fully apparent in the problem they face in explaining uneven educational development in different countries where this bears no clear relation with the levels of development of the forces and relations of production pertaining in them.

Such an evident disjuncture between social and educational forms has led Margaret Archer to abandon all notions of social determinacy and to develop a theory which relates the development of education to the interaction of different social groups and the internal logics of institutional development. She thus seeks the solution to the problem of the origins of educational change at the level of institutions and politics. As I have already noted, this represents, in some respects, an appreciable advance on earlier theorizations, not least in its greater purchase on the problems of comparative development. However, the overall coherence of the analysis is undermined by its own particular form of 'systemic' determinism and by the absence of a developed theory of the state. In her early work with Michelena Vaughan there were suggestive, if only provisional, considerations regarding the relations between educational development and the process of bureaucratization. However, there is no attempt to expand on these insights in the later work and, in fact, no serious attempt to theorize the general and specific forms of the capitalist state at all. What is needed, then, is a theory of the state which relates specific national differences in state forms to their economic and social conditions of existence. These specific state forms must in turn be related to the form of educational development which issues from them.

The analysis which follows is premised on the notion that the development of public education systems can only be understood in relation to the process of state formation, where this is understood in a non-reductive way which gives due weight to both political forms and their economic and social conditions of existence. State formation refers to the historical process by which the modern state has been constructed. This includes not only the construction of the political and administrative apparatus of government and all government-controlled agencies which constitute the 'public' realm, but also the formation of ideologies and collective beliefs which legitimate state power and underpin concepts of nationhood and national 'character'. This process occurred in all European nations in the eighteenth and nineteenth centuries, but it occurred in different ways and it is in the specific national forms of state formation, of which educational development is a part, that the key to the uneven and distinctive development of education systems lies. I will argue that these variant forms of state formation, and the corresponding systems of state education to which they give rise, can best be understood through the concepts elaborated within the Marxist tradition, and, in particular, with reference to Antonio Gramsci's theory of hegemony. The latter contains, at its core, a belief in the centrality of the 'educational' and moral role of the state, and, along with Gramsci's other suggestive writings on ideology and education, it provides the basis for an understanding of the historical genesis of state education.

To relate the development of the nineteenth-century education systems to the general development of the state would seem to be such an obvious analytical strategy that it is curious that it has not been systematically undertaken hitherto. After all, one would hardly attempt to analyse the construction of public health systems in the twentieth century without relating it to the evolution of the modern 'interventionist' or welfare state. Certainly, the relationship between the state and educational or other services was not as securely cemented in the earlier period as it was to become in the following century, but nevertheless the period was one where public education became, gradually but ineluctably, 'state' education, and state education was qualitatively distinct from anything that had gone before.

We must avoid retrospective foreshortening of historical events here. Clearly the rise of mass schooling, under state supervision, did not immediately displace earlier forms of education; nor can it be seen, without historical anachronism, as a ready-made version of public education as it exists in the era of the welfare state. Whilst education has become increasingly conflated with mass schooling, education and schooling were not yet synonymous; myriad forms of informal and community learning co-existed with the rise of formal schools, and indeed often conflicted with them.

Furthermore, the development of 'state' forms in these early national systems occurred at a time when few countries had anything approaching universal suffrage, even for males, and thus state regulation of schooling had no necessary relation with democratic control. With the partial exception of the United States, national education systems became state institutions before they became, in any real sense, democratic ones.

The point is well made by the American educational historians of the 'revisionist school'. In his powerful and path-breaking article entitled 'Education in the Forming of American Society', Bernard Bailyn criticized earlier generations of historians for a 'ubiquitous historicism' in their treatment of nineteenth-century education, which they depict as the education of the twentieth century writ small, merely as a primitive form of the present. In their 'heroic' vision, public education arose in a blaze of humanitarian and democratic idealism. 'Cubberley and others', writes Bailyn,

> told a dramatic story of how the delicate seeds of the idea and the institution of public education had lived precariously amidst the religious and other old-fashioned forms of education until the 19th century reformers, fighting bigotry and ignorance, cleared the way for their full flowering.[1]

Such an historical foreshortening, argues Bailyn, has led to a neglect of the earlier educational forms and the complex and varied contingencies which framed the rise of national education.

Bailyn has stressed the broad and diffuse nature of education's origins; his clear injunction is to see education as 'the entire process by which a culture transmits itself across generations', and not merely as the history of formal pedagogy.[2] The burden of his article is to trace the origins of public education in the decline of those variegated educational forms of the colonial period, as familial and community cohesiveness broke up under the strains of migration, dispersal, resettlement and the onset of industrialization under the already fragmentary conditions of frontier life.

Bailyn and others have rightly debunked the triumphalist mythology of the older historians and offered an important reminder of the essential variety of educational forms in this period. However, the old historiography did have a point. The public school system may not have been all they made it out to have been, but it certainly was a new and distinctive form of education and one that, in due course, was to increasingly colonize other modes of learning. Furthermore, as the older historiography was at pains to stress, the fact of formal education now being a public and state concern was of considerable importance. It signalled a decisive break with the voluntary and particularistic modes of medieval and early modern education, where learning was narrowly associated with specialized forms of clerical, craft and legal training, and existed merely as an extension of the corporate interests of the church, the town, the guild and the family. Public education embodied a new universalism which acknowledged that education was applicable to all groups in society and should serve a variety of social needs. The national systems were designed specifically to transcend the narrow particularism of earlier forms of learning. They were to serve the nation as a whole or, rather, the 'national interest' as conceived by the dominant classes in society. As such, education had to become a state concern and, ultimately, an institution of the state. It could no longer be left to the vagaries of individual or group action, nor could it be assumed that it would develop in the right ways or to the necessary extent through a process of spontaneous, molecular growth out of civil society. It had to be developed from the top downwards, with the deployment of the full bureaucratic machinery of the state. The fully fledged nineteenth-century education system thus became a species apart whose functions were relatively homogeneous and unique and which could hardly be equated, *tout court*, with those of earlier forms. It became an institution *sui generis*; an integral part of the state apparatus of the burgeoning nineteenth-century nation state and a vital pillar of the new social order.

We have already seen in broad outline how the national education system developed in parallel with the modern, capitalist state. The form of the national system was first prefigured in continental Europe during the absolutist monarchies of the eighteenth century. These not only developed many of the general features of the modern state – central bureaucracies, standing armies, national taxation – they also pioneered the first moves towards public education with the provision of state funds for schooling, the drafting of prescribed curricula and legislation on school attendance. Education was seen as an important means for furthering the mercantilist aims of the state. It was essential for providing the trained cadres for the government bureaucracy and the military, and had an important role to play in generating the skills needed for the fledgling state manufacturing projects. Not least, also, it was recognized as a powerful instrument for promoting political loyalty amongst the people and for creating a cohesive national culture after the image of the ruling class.

We have also seen that the decisive moment for the consolidation of national systems came during the aftermath of the French Revolution when the modern, capitalist state, in various guises, simultaneously took shape in regimes as diverse as those of the royal Junker state of Prussia, the Napoleonic Empire of France and the Early Republic of the United States of America. The importance of education grew with the increasing intensity of the process of state formation, and educational development was most dynamic and wide-ranging precisely in those periods and in those countries where state formation occurred in the most deliberate and compacted fashion. This was particularly the case where the reformed state emerged through profound social and political upheavals, as in France and the United States, and where it was directly involved in the process of forced industrialization 'from above', as in Prussia. However, even in England, where, for particular reasons, the reform of the state was notably gradual and protracted, one can see that the periods of most intensive educational development, as in the 1830s and after 1870, were also the periods when there was most activity in the reform of the state in general. That the chronology of educational reform and state formation should coincide so closely can hardly be surprising since education had become such an important and integral part of the whole project. Not only could it play an important role in furnishing industry and the state bureaucracy with personnel trained with the right skills and appropriate attitudes, but also it was of inestimable value for the dominant social classes in establishing their hegemony over the population at large.

The nineteenth-century education system came to assume a primary responsibility for the moral, cultural and political development of the nation. It became the secular church. It was variously called upon to assimilate immigrant cultures, to promote established religious doctrines, to spread the standard form of the appointed national language, to forge a national identity and a national culture, to generalize new habits of routine and rational calculation, to encourage patriotic values, to inculcate moral disciplines and, above all, to indoctrinate in the political and economic creeds of the dominant classes. It helped to construct the very subjectivities of citizenship, justifying the ways of the state to the people and the duties of the people to the state. It sought to create each person as a universal subject but it did so differentially according to class and gender. It formed the responsible citizen, the diligent worker, the willing tax-payer, the reliable juror, the conscientious parent, the dutiful wife, the patriotic soldier and the dependable or deferential voter. If, as Corrigan and Sayer maintain, 'state formation is ... cultural revolution', then education was clearly at the heart of this process.[3]

These are some of the more general relations between the construction of education systems and the process broadly referred to as state formation. But how can we theorize more precisely the relationship between education and the state during this period and what is the relationship between the state and the other levels of the social formation? Can education be seen unproblematically as part of the state apparatus and, if so, what is the relation between education and the social classes whose power is expressed in the state? A number of difficult problems arise here which have been partly anticipated in the earlier discussions. These concern generally the way in which different levels of the social formation are articulated one with another and what relations of determinacy can be said to operate between them. We have already seen the disjunctions that are apparent between the economic sphere and the forms in which education developed in different countries. Further, we have seen that the control of education does not correspond inevitably with those classes which are dominant in production at any given time. It would seem that the articulation of this particular part of the state with the economic and class relations which underpin the state are complex and specific to particular social formations. What then can the Marxist theory of the state add to our understanding of these complex relations?

Marx and Engels on the state

There is no one perspective that constitutes the Marxist theory of the state. In fact, it is debatable whether Marx actually left behind him a fully coherent theory of the state at all. The promised fourth volume of *Capital* on the state was never written and, although there are many passages in Marx and Engels' work where they discuss the nature of ideology, politics and the state, these do not constitute a theory of the social formation as a whole and the place of the state within it. There is nothing in Marx's writings on the state to compare with the power of his analysis of the capitalist mode of production in *Das Kapital*. His ideas on the state have to be culled from writings which vary considerably in tone and context. They include, *inter alia*, general but allusive theoretical statements in the classic passages which outline, often polemically, the general principles of historical materialism; extended historical analyses in a more empirical mode in writings on France and the historical sections of *Capital*; and scattered vignettes in occasional, journalistic writings and in sundry letters to friends and co-revolutionists.

Together these constitute a considerable corpus of writing but one which is uneven and often apparently contradictory in its conclusions. Nevertheless, it is possible to derive a general theory of the state and the social formation on the theoretical basis of historical materialism, and Marx and Engels' work has led subsequently to a vast body of theorization in this area. Perspectives on the state in the various traditions deriving from Marx and Engels obviously differ enormously and not all of them will be useful in a study of education and state formation. However, the debates that have been generated in this tradition are often highly germane to our purposes and one particular derivation of Marx's work on the state, which was epitomized in Gramsci's writings on the state and hegemony, is of particular value. Before considering this, however, it is important to go back, briefly, to the debate surrounding Marx's own writings on the question.

The starting point for Marx's analysis of the state lay in his early assertion that there could be no such thing as the 'neutral' or independent state. The idea that there exists an opposition or distinction between interests that are public and general, and those that are private and particular, was an illusion perpetrated by the modern state and had no foundation in reality. The state may appear to be independent, to stand above particular interests and treat all subjects as equal before the law, but in reality this neutrality only serves to mask the reproduction of substantive social inequalities which the state underwrites through its protection of private property. In his *Critique of Hegel's Philosophy of Law*, Marx refutes the idealism of Hegels' conception of the state, denying the hallowed notion of the separation of the state and civil society. He agrees with Hegel that there are two analytically distinct spheres in modern society: the sphere of the state and the sphere of civil society, which is the sphere of egoism or self-interest. But he denies that this separation was any more than a formal distinction and asserts that the capitalist state cannot transcend the 'war of each against all' or secure 'the common interest'. The universal state is an abstraction and 'the abstraction of the state as such belongs only to modern times, because the abstraction of private life belongs only to modern times'.[4]

In other works, Marx elaborates on the historical genesis of the idea of the universal state. In *On the Jewish Question* he acknowledges that the modern state has abolished some of the political significances of religion, birth, rank and occupation through the establishment of formal equality amongst its citizens. But it cannot abolish their continuing social significance in the reproduction of substantive social inequalities. The universal state thus in practice remains an illusion. Again, in *The German Ideology*, Marx and Engels pursue this theme:

> Out of this very contradiction between the interest of the individual and that of the community the latter takes on an independent form as the state, divorced from the real interests of individual and community, and at the same time as an illusory communal life...It follows from this that all the struggles within the state, the struggle between democracy, aristocracy, and monarchy, the struggle for the franchise etc.... are merely the illusory form in which the real struggles of the different classes are fought out among one another.[5]

The modern state arises with the increasing division of labour, the development of capitalist property relations and the division of the society into antagonistic social classes. Capitalist production requires the creation of 'free' wage labour, the extension of market relations and the assurance of private contract in law. Society is thus individualized, and formal legal equalities reflect the typical outward form of the bourgeois state. However, just as capitalism divides society into a collection of competing individual atoms, so it must create the universalizing state over and above them to ensure the conditions of continuing capitalist development. The 'anarchy' of competitive capitalism is predicated on regulation provided by the state. The state must be the guarantor of private property and legal contract. It must ensure the orderly conduct of the market and, above all, it must contain the increasing class antagonisms that the capitalist mode of production throws up. Thus,

Through the emancipation of private property from the community, the state has become a separate entity, besides and outside civil society; but it is nothing other than the form of organization which the bourgeois necessarily adopt both for internal and external purposes, for the mutual guarantee of their property and interests.[6]

The modern state is thus essentially the capitalist state.

In the materialist conception, then, the nature of the state is fundamentally shaped by civil society and the relation of production in any given period. As Marx expresses it in the celebrated 1859 Preface to *The Critique of Political Economy*, it is the relations of production, which correspond to a definite stage in the development of the material forces of production, which constitute the economic structure of society, 'the real foundation on which the legal and political superstructure arise and to which definite forms of social consciousness correspond'.[7]

It is not only that the state is historically determinate, that is specific in its general form to the mode of production which is dominant in any given period; its very function and nature is intimately connected with the operation of the economic structure at any given time. During the era of the capitalist mode of production it is precisely the mode of exploitation of labour by capital that contains the key to the nature of the state. This is firmly underlined in another well-known passage in *Capital*:

The specific form in which unpaid surplus labour is pumped out of the direct producers determines the relation of domination and servitude, as it emerges directly out of production itself and in turn reacts upon production. Upon this basis, however, is founded the entire structure of the economic community, which grows out of the condition of production itself, and consequently the specific political form. It is always the direct relations between the masters of the conditions of production and the direct producers that reveals the innermost secret, the hidden foundation of the entire social edifice, and therefore also of the political form of the relation of sovereignty and dependence, in short the particular form of the state.[8]

This is the so-called base–superstructure model of the social formation, which is generally taken to be the master concept defining the Marxist theory of the state. However, as many commentators have pointed out, it is riven with difficulties and in no sense constitutes a definitive conceptual schema for understanding the complexities of the social formation. The main problem is that if taken literally, this metaphor can lead to the crudest forms of economic reductionism. As Jessop has demonstrated, this has taken two main forms in the century after Marx's death.[9] It has led to the argument that the form of the state is determined purely at the economic level, thus effectively denying any independent efficacy to other levels of the social formation. It has also been used to justify a conception of the state as the pure instrument of rule by a single, unitary, dominant class. Both of these arguments involve a form of essentialism or historicism whereby the specific forms of the state are considered to be the direct expression of the economic relations and where the contradictions of the structure are automatically reproduced at the political and ideological levels. In this case the forms of politics and state can simply be read off from the contradictions appearing at the economic level.

There is certainly some textual support for this kind of reading in Marx and Engels' own writings. In the *Communist Manifesto* they refer to the state as a pure instrument of class rule: 'The executive of the modern state is but a committee for managing the common affairs of the whole bourgeoisie.'[10] Elsewhere in polemical passages this conception is reinforced. Furthermore, both Marx and Engels quite often refer to the state as none other than the collective will of capital, as if its express function is to act as the over-arching capitalist. Thus Engels writes in *Socialism: Utopian and Scientific*:

> The modern state, no matter what its form, is essentially a capitalist machine, the state of capital, the ideal personification of the total national capital.[11]

The problems with formulations like this are legion. They appear to ignore the considerable complexity of the relations between economy, class and political representation in modern social formations. Determinacy is seen to be exercised purely by the economic structure and other levels of the social formation are apparently denied any independent efficacy. The state is reduced to a mere epiphenomenon of the economic base. Clearly such a conception would make it difficult to comprehend a situation where the dominant political party does not reflect the economic interests of the dominant economic class and where the state is controlled by a class other than that which controls in the economic sphere. It would also seem to imply that classes are always unitary subjects, which embrace ideologies that directly reflect their class interests, rather than groups containing different fractions and often divergent ideologies. As far as the analysis of education is concerned, this reductionist conception of the state and of political representation would make it very difficult to explain how the British state, for instance, permitted the maintenance of an education system which failed to promote the best interests of the economically dominant manufacturing class.

The problems of economic reductionism are clearly a continuing part of Marx and Engels' theoretical legacy and will continue to occupy a controversial position in debates on the theory of the state. However, there is an alternative reading of their writings which, at least provisionally, suggests a way of avoiding these problems without abandoning entirely the limit premise of historical materialism, the determinacy of the economic in some form or 'in the last instance'. This reading has been suggested by Stuart Hall in an article re-examining the base–superstructure, metaphor and more recently by Jessop.[12] It derives to a large extent from a reading of Marx's more historical writings on France and England and leads directly into the type of analysis developed by Gramsci in *The Prison Notebooks*.

Both Marx and Engels were clearly aware of the problems inherent in their more general formulations on the state, and in their more conjunctural writings they showed a concern with the complexities of the social formation which belie any simplistic reading of the relations between the base and the superstructure. With the failure of the 1848 revolutions in Europe, they were forced to revise their formerly over-optimistic predictions about the imminence of the proletarian overthrow of capitalism. Clearly, the contradictions of capital would not simply unroll at the political level as a direct expression of the economic crisis. Marx's writings on England began to reflect the fact that the nature of politics and the form of the state did not unproblematically reflect the nature of economic relations. In an article on English politics, he was to write in 1855 that

> The British constitution is, in fact, only an antiquated and obsolete compromise made between the bourgeoisie, which rules in actual practice, although not officially, in the decisive spheres of bourgeois society, and the landed aristocracy, which forms the official government.[13]

Here and elsewhere, Marx explicitly recognizes the disjunctures between economic and political power which were particularly apparent within the British state. Rule by landowner Whig and Tory parties is time and time expressed as a form of compromise or as a 'masking' of real relations, whereby the economically dominant bourgeois class delegated political power to the landowner class so long as the latter ensured the maintenance of its essential interests. Arguably, Marx still underestimates the enduring real political and ideological sway of the capitalist landed class, but nevertheless it is clear from his shifting formulations in these articles on England that there is some conceptual unease with the over-compressed and elliptical way in which the relations between the base and the superstructure had been expressed in the earlier period. The exact relations between economic classes and their political representation is now put more into question. This continued to be the case in all of the historical writings of the subsequent period, both as they appear in *Capital* and in the political journalism. That Marx and Engels were now consciously wrestling with the problem and seeking to avoid the cruder forms of reductionism that could arise from an over-literal application of the materialist doctrine is made clear in subsequent correspondence.

In the historical sections of *Capital*, Marx is clearly working with the principle that the superstructure can exercise an independent effectivity on the economic base. In the passage from *Capital*, Volume 3, cited above, Marx refers to the way in which the political relations which emerge out of the form of exploitation in production 'in turn react upon production'. Elsewhere, in Volume 1, he describes how during the phase of primitive accumulation the power of the state is employed with the colonial system and national taxation 'to hasten, hot-house fashion, the process of trans-formation of the feudal mode of production into the capitalist-mode... to shorten its transition'.[14] Again in the famous passages in Volume 1, on the Factory Acts, Marx describes how state legislation, in the form of restrictions on the length of the working day, was instrumental in forcing the shift in the mode of exploitation from absolute to relative surplus value by encouraging greater productivity through the use of more capital intensive production techniques.

Although it does not always appear this way in the more compacted and elliptical formulations on the base–superstructure relation, it is clear that in practice Marx did allow that every level of the social formation could exer-cise its own determinacy on the social structure. After Marx's death, Engels was at pains to emphasize this and to rescue historical materialism from the economic reductionism apparent in the work of young followers. In a letter to Bloch written in 1890, he admits that he and Marx were respon-sible in part for the fact that the 'younger people' sometimes laid more stress on the economic side than was warranted. The need to emphasize the principle against adversaries and the pressures of time had forced them to pay less attention to the other aspects than was due to them. Accord-ing to the materialist conception of history, Engels insists, 'the determining element in history is the production and reproduction of real life'. But, he goes on:

> More than this neither Marx nor I have ever asserted. Hence, if somebody twists this into saying that the economic element is the only determining one, he transforms that proposition into a meaningless, abstract, senseless phrase.[15]

In a later passage, Engels struggles to reformulate the base–superstructure relation in a non-reductive way:

> History is made in such a way that the final result always arises from con-flicts between many individual wills, of which each in turn has been made what it is by a host of particular conditions of life. Thus there are innu-merable intersecting forces, an infinite series of parallelograms of forces which give rise to one resultant – the historical event.[16]

Such general formulations are admittedly not wholly satisfactory, but in their more detailed conjunctural analyses, Engels and, particularly, Marx were more successful in capturing the interdependent and reciprocal nature of determination.

An alternative reading of Marx and Engels' work on the state which avoids the reductionism common to the economistic and instrumentalist readings would seem to be possible and to have ample warrant both in *Capital* and in the historical writings. This reading, suggested by Hall and discussed by Jessop in his work, recognizes that the relationship between the state, the economy and the dominant classes is complex and often contradictory. Broadly speaking, the state is seen as a relatively autonomous force whose relations to particular classes and class fractions varies from one conjuncture to another. Its overall function remains determined by the economic base in that it seeks to secure the long-run survival of the mode of production on which it rests. It serves the dominant classes in their long-term interests but at any given moment may be dominated by this or that class fraction or, indeed, at certain exceptional moments, may appear to override all particular class interests.

Marx and Engels analyse a number of these moments in their historical writings. One was the era of the absolutist state. Engels remarks that

> Exceptional periods ... occur when the warring classes are so nearly equal in force that the state power, as apparent mediator, acquires for the moment a certain independence in relation to both. This applies to the absolute monarchy of the 11th and 18th centuries, which balanced the nobility and the bourgeoisie against each other, and to the Bonapartism of the first and particularly the second French Empire, which played off the proletariat against the bourgeoisie and the bourgeoisie against the proletariat.[17]

The most recent example of this, according to Engels, was the Bismarckian state where the capitalists and the workers were balanced against each other and both of them fleeced for the benefit of the 'decayed Prussian cabbage junkers'.

In Marx's analysis of France in the *Eighteenth Brumaire*, he employs a similar notion of class equilibrium or stalemate. Such is the balance of the different classes after 1848 that only the intervention of a force standing outside the immediate conflict can resolve the situation. Napoleon is the unlikely figure cast in this role. In a situation of stalemate between contending classes, where all classes are 'equally impotent and equally mute', they all 'fall on their knees before the rifle butt'.[18] However, the rifle butt in question is by no means a neutral weapon in the struggle. In fact, as Marx explains, what is actually happening is that, as a precondition of its continuing social power and economic domination, the bourgeoisie is induced to abandon its control over the state apparatus through parliament in favour of a strong executive under the personal sway of Louis Napoleon. Napoleon, in turn, consolidates his power on the back of the peasant class, who are incapable of enforcing their class interests in their own name, and who pliantly consent to representation by the master figure. Marx's account shows clearly how the executive power of the state can act momentarily as an autonomous force but only so long as it continues to represent the long-term interests of the dominant class. It also demonstrates a meticulous attention to the importance of different class fractions and the complex interplay of different political forces in the state, suggesting, unequivocally, that when it came to analysing concrete historical conjunctures, Marx acknowledged that a purely instrumentalist view of the state was untenable.

Another aspect of this reading of Marx's theory of the state, which has important ramifications for the concept of state formation, concerns the way in which the state represents the interests of the dominant class as the universal interest. This is a recurrent theme in all of Marx and Engels' political writings. The universality of the state is an illusion, but it is a necessary illusion for those classes seeking hegemony over subordinate classes. In fact, it seems a perennial rule of politics for the would-be dominant class to present itself as the class which represents the totality of interests of the dominated classes. As Marx and Engels put it in *The German Ideology*,

> Each new class which puts itself in place of the one before it, is compelled, merely in order to carry through its aim, to represent itself as the common interest of all the members of society, that is an ideal form: it has to give its ideas universality, and represent them as the only rational, universally valid ones.

Furthermore, with each new political revolution, the ascendant class has to achieve its hegemony 'on a broader basis than that of the class ruling previously'.[19] So it was with the radical bourgeoisie during the French Revolution, and so too it became during the Second Empire, when Louis Napoleon sought to claim the mantle of the universal interest, the French nation, through appearing as the saviour of all classes and, in particular, of the most numerous class, the peasantry.

In this specifically ideological role the state acts objectively as a force of social cohesion, seeking to mould all classes in the image of the dominant class. It is this dimension of Marx's writing on the state, undoubtedly underdeveloped but nonetheless significant in all of the historical writings, which is developed in later Marxist theories of hegemony where this specific work of political, moral and intellectual leadership is seen to be an essential function of the state.

The importance of public education in conducting this moral and intellectual work of the state should be readily apparent. Marx does not, in fact, make more than passing reference to education in his work, but what he does say confirms the idea that state education should be seen in this context. Criticizing the programme of the German Workers' Party on education in 1875, Marx raises sharp objections to the idea of 'elementary education by the state':

> Defining by general law the expenditures on elementary schools, the qualifications of the teaching staff, the branches of instruction etc., and, as is done in the United States, supervising the fulfillment of these legal specifications by state inspectors, is a very different thing from appointing the state as educator of the people.[20]

The Church and the government should never control what is actually taught in the school, says Marx. Better that the state should be educated by the people.

As a fervent believer in the educational potential of the working class, Marx clearly supported radical demands for a system of public education, funded directly by the state. The *Communist Manifesto* calls for 'free education for all in public schools'.[21] His remarks in *Capital* on the beneficial effects for children in factories of combining work with compulsory education, partially achieved by the factory legislation despite widespread employer evasion, suggest that Marx was also in favour of legislation on school attendance and supervision of schools by state inspectors.[22] However, like the English Chartists, he insisted that education should be under popular democratic control. Education must be wrested free from the tutelage of the ruling class. If this was not achieved then public education would merely be an indoctrination of the people in ruling class ideas. Marx's contempt for the 'servile belief in the state' and 'democratic miracles' evinced by the German Lassalleans with their 'education by the state' suggests that he was fully aware of the difficulty of achieving this. However, as we have seen, his view of the state is not monolithic, and the state does not invariably represent the undiluted class power of the dominant social group. The exact nature of state power will depend on the balance of class forces at any given time. Thus education, which has become part of the state apparatus, will also be the object of conflicting class demands. As it becomes a public and universal institution, so education becomes dragged into the general political arena. It becomes the site of continuing class struggles where antagonistic social forces seek to bring it into conformity with their own interests and particular needs.

Gramsci on state and hegemony

If the writings of Marx and Engels give us a provisional orientation to the problem of the relationship between education and the different levels of the social formation, it is in the work of the Italian Marxist Antonio Gramsci that this kind of analysis comes to fruition and takes on more concrete forms. Of all the major Marxist theorists of the twentieth century it is Gramsci who did most to illuminate the complexity of the superstructures in modern societies. Following in the tradition of Marx's historical writings, assessed above, Gramsci elaborated an analysis of the state, ideology and the political superstructures with an unparalleled sensitivity to the complex articulations of the different levels within the social formation, and an attention to the specificities of concrete historical conjunctures that has rarely been matched. Less concerned with defining the abstract laws of motion of capital, or the role of the state as an ideal collective capitalist, he concentrates on specifying the intricate relations amongst the plurality of social forces involved in the exercise of state power in a given social formation. This involves an exceptional grasp of the role of different class fractions and their competing ideologies in the maintenance of class domination, an attention to the broad 'educative' and moral role of the state in ensuring the hegemony of the dominant classes, and a sharp focus on the historical particularities of nation, region and cultural formation which provide the material context in which social leadership is won, consolidated and lost. It can be argued that Gramsci's writings are often fragmented and provisional, and that they do not constitute a fully elaborated general theory of the state as such.[23] However, it can scarcely be denied that they represent one of the most fruitful attempts to investigate the nature of class power in modern social formations.

Gramsci's writings on politics and the state, collected together in *The Prison Notebooks*, reflect the thinking of a social theorist and political activist who had lived through an exceptionally turbulent period of history. He saw the rise of Fascism in Italy and was ever conscious of the singular historical circumstances in his native land that had led to this. These latter factors, which will be considered later, were formative in directing his attention to the pertinence of concrete and nationally specific historical analysis, just as his upbringing in Sardinia was to make him acutely aware of the importance of regional differences. Furthermore, Gramsci's personal involvement in the Turin factory council movement, and development of the Italian Communist Party throughout the various twists and turns of political strategy during the 1920s, meant that his political thought was deeply marked by his reactions to the unfolding class struggles of the time, and his retrospective judgements on the role of strategies adopted. Thus Gramsci's analysis of the state and politics is not only an intellectual engagement with Marxist theory and the application of that to contemporary social structures. It is also an assessment and continual review of the utility of theory in the current struggle; an ongoing exploration in thought and practice of what he called the philosophy of praxis.

Gramsci rejects the economic determinism of much of the theory of the Second International (of the international socialist movement) because he has seen the sterile results of this in political practice. He holds neither with economism nor spontaneism, either in theory or practice, because he has witnessed their results in the failure of the German Communist Party's adventurist strategy in 1919 and in the disastrous later Comintern policy of no compromise with social democracy, the latter designated as 'social-fascism' during the Comintern's Third Period.[24] In the writings on politics and the state in *The Prison Notebooks*, where Gramsci is ever mindful of the lessons of the preceding decade, he categorically rejects simplistic notions of economic determinism and the idea of the purely instrumental class state. The nature of the state and the forms of political representation which are embodied within it cannot be simply read off from the economic relations and the class interests on which they are mounted. Rather, they are constituted through complex processes of mediation and alliance which are irreducible to particular economic contradictions. Likewise, ideologies and the conflict between ideologies must be understood in their full complexity and cannot be reduced to the expression of the economic interests of particular class subjects. As Gramsci points out, 'If for every ideological struggle one wanted to find an immediate primary explanation in the (economic) structure one would be caught napping.'[25] His theoretical perspective, developed out of his own political practice and from his readings of Marx's historical works, is clearly a development of that notion of 'relative autonomy' or complex articulation of levels that was outlined in the above reading of Marx's legacy. This is most forcefully underlined in his *Notes on the Philosophy of Praxis*, where he argues, echoing a phrase of Lenin's, that

> The claim, presented as an essential postulate of historical materialism, that every function of politics and ideology can be presented and expounded as an immediate expression of the structure, must be contested in theory as a primitive infantilism, and combatted in practice with the authentic testimony of Marx.[26]

If Gramsci's analysis of the superstructures is based on a deliberate refusal of theories which would reduce everything to the effects of economic and class determinism, his positive contribution rests on an analysis of the state as an active, organizing force in modern societies. The state is defined broadly as

> the entire complex of practical and theoretical activities with which the ruling class not only justifies and maintains its dominance, but manages to win the active consent of those over whom it rules.[27]

It includes, therefore, not only the central legislative and executive apparatus of government and the coercive machinery of the military and the police, but also those theoretical or moral organs, such as the courts, the schools, and the Church, where the intellectuals of the state are active in promoting certain views of the world and certain ideologies through which civil society is organized and brought into conformity with aspirations of the dominant class. State power is not only located in the central machinery itself; it is also rooted in civil society, in all those 'so-called private organizations' which it continually seeks to shape and influence. There is, as a number of commentators have pointed out, a recurrent ambiguity in Gramsci's work as to the exact boundaries of the state and what is called civil society.[28] At one point, he asserts that 'in reality civil society and the state are the same'. However, the point is that state power continually permeates those institutions beyond the boundaries of the state. The state works through civil society since one of its primary functions is to mould and educate society at all levels in conformity with its own historical goals.

Gramsci's intention is to understand the distinctive forms of class power and the role of the state in his own time, in a period when, despite the emergence of exceptional Fascist state forms, parliamentary democracy was the normal form of the bourgeois state. His analysis therefore starts from an appreciation of what is distinctive in the modern social formation. Comparing modern western states with pre-revolutionary Russia, where civil society was 'primordial and gelatinous' and where the state was everything, Gramsci finds that now civil society is infinitely stronger and better protected:

> In the case of the most advanced states, where civil society has become a very complex structure and one which is resistant to the catastrophic 'incursions' of the immediate economic element (crises, depressions etc.), the superstructures of civil society are like the trench systems of modern warfare.[29]

So much better developed is civil society in the West that the state is now only an outer ditch behind which lie the considerable 'fortresses' and 'earthworks' which are the main defence of the system. Such a system is no longer subject to any danger of 'frontal attack'. Revolutionary movements must now proceed through a 'war of position', likened to Lenin's theory of the united front, where the revolutionary party, described as the Modern Prince[30], must engage in a protracted effort to win for itself an alternative hegemony within civil society. 'A social group', says Gramsci, 'can, and indeed must, already exercise "leadership" before winning governmental power.'[31]

The modern state must be understood in relation to the ways in which power is exercised in complex social formations. The power of the dominant class, or the class alliance which forms the 'historic bloc', is now normally comprehensible only in terms of hegemony. This has a dual nature, which Gramsci likens to the double aspect of Machiavelli's centaur – half animal and half human. It involves both force and consent, violence and civilization, both the individual moment and the universal moment. Hegemony represents a form of class power that is maintained not only by coercive means but also by the winning of consent for it in civil society.

> The normal exercise of hegemony on the now classic terrain of a parliamentary regime is characterized by a combination of force and consent which form variable equilibria, without force ever prevailing too much over consent.[32]

If the distinctive, though not invariable, mode of class domination in the West is through the exercise of hegemony, this does not mean that the process of consent displaces or diminishes the power of coercion. Rather, the instruments of coercion are typically held in reserve, kept in the wings, until consent fails or the political authority of the dominant class is no longer secure.

It is through the concept of hegemony, to which he first gave currency, that Gramsci is able to think about the complex relations which constitute the superstructures of the social formation. It is a dynamic concept which attempts to capture the delicate balance that results from the interplay of multiple social forces. A hegemonic order represents a temporary settlement, the ideological balance of force in favour of the ruling class, not the homogeneous substance of an imposed class ideology. It is won through continual conflict which involves the creation of alliances, the attempted incorporation of subordinate groups and, even, the granting of concessions so long as these do not damage the vital interests of the dominant group. 'Undoubtedly,' writes Gramsci,

> the fact of hegemony presupposes that account be taken of the interests and the tendencies of the groups over which hegemony is to be exercised, and that a certain compromise equilibrium should be formed – in other words, that the leading group should make sacrifices of an economic-corporate kind.[33]

In winning hegemony the ruling class thus achieves a temporary mastery over the class struggle, but never its liquidation. A hegemonic order prescribes the limits within which ideas and conflicts move and are resolved, but these limits never attain permanence and within them antagonisms – political, cultural and ideological – are never fully eliminated since the contradictions at the level of the economic structure, effective through class, never cease to disrupt and disfigure the temporary unity of cultures and ideologies.

The state can thus only be understood with reference to this process of hegemony. It is partly through the state and through the influence of the state in civil society that hegemony is secured. Although acting in the overall interests of the dominant class or the dominant class alliance, the state presents itself, as Marx noted, as the universal interest. The following passage demonstrates Gramsci's indebtedness to Marx's *Eighteenth Brumaire* on this point.

> It is true that the state is seen as the organ of one particular class, destined to create favorable conditions for the latter's maximum expansion. But the development and expansion of the particular group are conceived of, and presented, as being the motor force of a universal expansion, of a development of all national energies. In other words, the dominant group is coordinated concretely with the general interests of the subordinate groups, and the life of the state is conceived of as a spontaneous process of formation and superseding of unstable equilibria ... between the interests of the fundamental group and those of the subordinate groups – equilibria in which the interests of the dominant group prevail, but only up to a certain point that is stopping short of the narrowly economic interest.[34]

If the political role of the state is to win the consent of the subordinate classes to the rule of the dominant bloc, it does this through a global reconstruction of all class interests and the reformulation of these in a new, more universal, language. This does not stop at the promulgation of particular class slogans or the mere representation of the individual class interest as the general interest. At certain historic moments it involves the reconstitution of society as a whole on new terms. This involves both moral re-education and the transformation of the economic structures themselves:

> In reality, the state must be considered as an 'educator', in as much as it tends precisely to create a new type or level of civilization. Because one is acting essentially on economic forces, reorganising and developing the apparatus of economic production, creating a new structure, the conclusion must not be drawn that superstructural factors should be left to develop spontaneously, to a haphazard and sporadic germination. The state, in this field too, is an instrument of 'rationalization', of acceleration and of Taylorisation. It operates according to a plan, urges, incites, solicits, and 'punishes'.[35]

In this passage, Gramsci clearly indicates the very close relation between state and all aspects of society. The state is an educator in the ideological realm but it is also an organizer and initiator in production. The relationship between the two is one of reciprocal determination.

Clearly education is central to the whole concept of hegemony in Gramsci's work. The process of winning consent and transforming the consciousness of the people to conform to modern conditions of production is precisely a process of education, and the schools are therefore a crucial instrument in the process of state formation. If one of the most important functions of the state is to raise the great mass of the population to a 'particular cultural and moral level', writes Gramsci, the two most important institutions are the courts and the school, 'the school as a positive educational function, and the courts as a repressive and negative educative function'.[36] The exact location of the school in the social formation is somewhat ambiguous in Gramsci's writings. At some points it is referred to as part of the state and at others it is in civil society, one of those 'so-called private organizations, like the church, trade unions, schools and so on'.[37] However, it is clear that the school is a site where the state intervenes and through which it attempts to accomplish its objectives.

The role of the school in Italy is to create 'citizens' in conformity with a universalizing dominant culture; that is, to detach them from the localized and traditional habits of 'magical' or 'folkloric' culture, and remake them anew after the image of the dominant culture. The function of the 'old primary school', that is as it existed before the Gentile reforms of 1923, is described as a dual formation of children:

> Scientific ideas were intended to insert the child into the *societas rerum*, the world of things, while lessons in rights and duties were intended to insert him into the state and civil society.[38]

The school is always at odds with the culture of the children, notes Gramsci. It continually has to confront the 'the tendencies toward individual and localistic barbarism' in its attempt to mould the youth of the new generation in the 'universal' ideas of the dominant culture. The successful teacher is the one who understands these folkloric or common sense notions in the culture of the children but who also knows how to transform them.

Gramsci's writings on education, which constitute a considerable part of *The Prison Notebooks*, are always suggestive and deeply considered. They have to be taken seriously since they were undoubtedly an essential part of his thought. Gramsci himself was a tireless popular educator both in his work in the Turin factory movement and in his agitational journalism. He clearly considered popular education as an essential part of his political work, and even during his period of incarceration his thoughts continually returned to the question. However, his educational writings are not always easy to interpret. They are often somewhat cryptic and even more than usually subject to misinterpretation if read out of context.

One difficulty that is immediately apparent is that Gramsci often slides from the descriptive to the prescriptive without any clear signals as to what he is doing. When he is writing about the importance of combating popular folklore in education or of the importance of rigour and structure in pedagogic method, his comments can at different times appear to apply both to what is and to what should be. The reason for this is that he concentrates in his general passages on the process of education rather than on the content. The importance of education in the construction of hegemony is such that these comments apply equally to the work of the school in promoting the ends of the state and to the form of schooling which is necessary for the revolutionary movement to prepare the working class for power. Whilst the content would clearly be different, in both the actual and putative cases, the same processes must be adopted in transforming popular common sense. In each case the teacher must start from the common sense perceptions of the students but proceed to transform these in a process that involves effort and discipline. Learning 'is a process of adaptation, a habit acquired with effort, tedium and even suffering'.[39] Certain elements of the curriculum are necessary in establishing counter-hegemony as in the maintenance of the status quo. Thus Gramsci is insistent on the importance of scientific knowledge and a broad general education. He makes no concession to dialect in the school and insists that all children need to master the standard forms of the national language. His own transition from the underdeveloped and traditionalistic culture of his Sardinian origins have clearly left their mark in his strong belief in the importance of a broad general education for the advance of the working class. He thus appears broadly sympathetic with the universalizing principles of a schooling designed to transform popular culture through an uncompromising struggle against folklore. Education must adopt rigorous methods to take 'the healthy nucleus which exists in "common sense"' and to transform it into something more 'unitary and coherent'.[40]

The apparent conservatism of Gramsci's educational ideas has to be seen in the context of his reaction against the developments occurring in Italian education at the time. He was strongly opposed to what he saw as the romanticism underlying the educational reforms put forward by the philosopher Giovanni Gentile when he was education minister in Mussolini's first cabinet. He saw the demotion of factual learning as a regressive step and strongly opposed the early specialization that resulted from the development of vocational schools which determined in advance the future destiny and occupation of working-class students. The new type of schooling appeared to be more democratic but in reality it would not only perpetuate social differences but 'crystalize them in Chinese complexities'.[41] Gramsci is clearly opposed to the instrumentalism of the new educational philosophy. Elsewhere he writes that technical schools should not be allowed to become 'incubators of little monsters aridly trained for a job, with no general ideas, no general culture, no intellectual stimulation, but only an infallible eye and a firm hand'.[42] Although a 'conservative' in his insistence on discipline and rigour in education and the importance of acquiring what he calls factual baggage, in other respects Gramsci is true to time-honoured socialist educational principles. He advocates a broad general education to high standards for everyone. Obdurately opposed to the private school which reproduces 'class and caste' divisions, Gramsci advocates a common schooling in public schools funded by the state.

Despite their fragmentary and often unfinished appearance, Gramsci's writings on education, like all of his work, embody a peculiar profundity and deep sense of reality. There is a sense of the multifaceted nature of social forms and the contradictory quality of experience that is often absent in the more formally perfected productions of social theory. The complex and sometimes allusive nature of his intellectual explorations reflect, in their very unevenness, the tensions and contradictions of his dual role as a social critic and a political activist. His ideas about schooling exemplify, in a particularly acute form, a recognition of the dualistic nature of education, a process which can be at once an instrument of social control and a force for liberation. As a political activist Gramsci is an educational optimist. He sees possibilities in popular education and believes, above all, in the importance of education in transforming popular consciousness and developing that level of popular culture which is an essential prerequisite for achieving an alternative hegemony. At the same time, Gramsci, the unsentimental analyst of class society, must be a realist and a pessimist. He recognizes the uses to which the school can be put by the state in the interests of the ruling classes: the school as an organ of state power. In a sense, his work is a sustained meditation on a single, but double-sided, theme: the way in which the dominant and the subordinate classes seek to educate society into their own conceptions of the world.

The underlying reality of the whole process is, of course, the struggle between classes and, in particular, the struggle in the realm of ideas. It is no accident that Gramsci is so fond of quoting those lines of Marx about the 'ideological forms in which men become conscious of this conflict and fight it out'. To Gramsci, ideas are a material force; 'they "organise" human masses, and create the terrain on which men move, acquire consciousness of their position, struggle, etc.'[43] The school is thus a strategic battleground, a uniquely important site of struggle. It is because he is so aware of this continual conflict within education that his presentation of the subject is never static. Whilst clearly locating the school as part of the process of class reproduction, he never forgets its contradictory nature or its Janus face. Unlike some more recent Marxist educational theorists, who have erred too far into a functionalist and static view of the educational process, where schools unproblematically reproduce the necessary conditions of capital without contradiction or struggle, Gramsci holds together both ends of the chain, forgetting neither the coercive force nor the emancipatory potential of the school. Education is a weapon in the struggle for hegemony, the school a vital agency in the process of state formation. But the process is ever contested and the results of the struggle are never decided in advance.

State formation and uneven educational development

To see the origins of public education in terms of the historical process of state formation, and the shifting modes of hegemony which characterized it, is to locate the problem, so to speak, in the correct conceptual field. However, this does not, in itself, constitute a theory of educational change capable of explaining uneven national development. This would require a theory of state formation which not only outlines the general conditions for the development of the capitalist state but also specifies the conditions for specific national and regional variations. Such a theory does not exist at this level. Indeed, it is doubtful whether such a thing is possible. In the *Critique of the Gotha Programme*, Marx argues that whilst one can generalize about 'present society' across national boundaries, it is impossible to do so about the 'present state'.[44] Thus, whereas capitalism can be found in all civilized countries and varies only in its degree of development, the form of the state varies with each country's border, differing markedly, for instance, between the Prusso-German Empire and Switzerland, and between England and the United States. Whether Marx's distinction between the mode of production, which can be considered in the general or abstract, and the social formation, which can only be apprehended in its concrete specificity, as the product of many determinations is sustainable, it remains the case that neither Marx nor Engels attempted a general theory of the state which would provide the conditions determining national variations. In fact there is relatively little attempt in their work to describe particular national paths of development at all, and neither were as curious as subsequent historians have been about the peculiarities of individual national formations. The most striking aspect of the time was the secular advance of the capitalist mode of production in all western societies, and this served, in a sense, to eclipse the importance of the question of national differences.

Given this relative absence of a full comparative dimension in Marx's analysis of the state, our exploration of variant national paths in the development of the state and of state education will necessarily draw most heavily on the more recent debates in which this topic has been more thoroughly examined. However, it is worth indicating, briefly, how Marx's historical writings have provided some preliminary pointers for the analysis of comparative development.

Although Marx's main preoccupation lay in unravelling the general conditions of development for the capitalist state in the West, he did draw a number of comparative distinctions between forms of development typical in different countries. It appears that in general terms he considered England to be the classic or typical case of economic development. It provided the very laboratory of capital and the primary subject for the immense labour of research that culminated in his major work.[45] However, English political development was more of a mystery to him and appeared at times somewhat anomalous. Likewise to Engels who, despite his early and considerable research into English social conditions, found the logical incongruities of British society a 'sore trial to the reasoning mind'.[46] Both Marx and Engels seemed to regard French political development as somehow more typical, providing the classic example of the bourgeois revolution.

Whilst Marx devoted most of his research on the development of the capitalist mode of production to the British case, his most detailed historical work on the development of state forms related to the period of French revolutionary history. *The Eighteenth Brumaire*, for instance, contains Marx's most detailed analysis of political development for any country. However, there are numerous references in his journalistic writings to British institutions and politics, and it is clear that Marx saw a number of significant distinctions between political structures in Britain and in France. The singularity of the British case lay not only in the fact that it exemplified the most complete development of capitalist relations in the economic sphere but also in that its state forms were unique. Britain not only had the most polarized class structure; it also had a set of political institutions that had no immediate parallel anywhere else. These were the historical product of a long-standing alliance between the bourgeoisie and the capitalist landowners dating back to 1688. This had resulted, amongst other things, in those 'aristocratic' trappings to the state which often seemed so incongruous in the world's most capitalist country. Furthermore, as Marx repeatedly noted, the state machine itself was in many ways a minimal apparatus, and, as such, in sharp contrast with the growing bureaucracies of France and Germany. Even in 1872, Marx was still remarking that Britain lacked a 'military-bureaucratic machine' of the kind typical of continental countries.[47] Marx was, of course, by no means alone in making this observation. De Tocqueville frequently remarked on this feature of English society and Weber later maintained that Britain was the last of all western countries to bureaucratize.

By comparison the French state had a sprawling bureaucratic machine, not only larger in absolute terms and more pervasive, but in certain respects more rationalized. The French state had at its disposal an army of more than half a million officials by the middle of the nineteenth century. In Marx's vivid description in the *Eighteenth Brumaire*, this state

> enmeshes, controls, regulates, supervises and regiments civil society from the most all-embracing expressions of life down to the most insignificant motion, from its most general modes of existence down to the private life of individuals. This parasitic body acquires, through the most extraordinary centralization, an omnipresence, an omniscience an elasticity and an accelerated rapidity of movement which find their only appropriate complement in the real social body's helpless irresolution and its lack of consistent social formation.[48]

Marx's formulations in this passage are most precise and contain a number of contrasts which are particularly revealing. This vastly inflated state machine is parasitic but also dynamic. It is capable of a rapidity of development which contrasts ironically with the relative immobilism of civil society. As Marx goes on to show, the étatist and centralized nature of the French state was historically the legacy of the absolutist monarchy but it had been appropriated by the revolutionary movement and subsequently became an indispensible tool of the bourgeoisie, not only for the maintenance of its political hegemony but also for forcing the development of civil society. Through its concentrated and directed power it could compensate for the relative stagnation and underdevelopment of the economic forces. Thus the Revolution first appropriated the centralized state of the absolutist monarchy to break down the localist, feudal barriers of the *Ancien Régime* and to create the civil unity of the nation. Napoleon perfected the state machine which he inherited. By means of the state he consolidated the gains of the Revolution, and with the bureaucracy he prepared for the 'class rule of the bourgeoisie'.[49] The vast and centralized French state, on which large sections of the bourgeoisie were utterly dependent, was thus both a parasitic and a strangulating force, and an essential and, at times, dynamic agency for developing capitalist relations in civil society.

In the writings on France and elsewhere, Marx recognizes that the state plays a critical role in the development of bourgeois society. This is true not only for France but also in Germany, where the autocratic Junker state of the post-Napoleonic period, and the later Bismarckian state, are crucially important in the forcing, hot-house fashion, of the process of capitalist industrialization. This relation of state and civil society, where the state has a pivotal role in bourgeois rationalization, was arguably typical of continental modernization. In their single-minded focus on the supposedly classic form of British economic development, Marx and Engels sometimes appear to overlook the fact that precisely because of its temporal priority English industrialization, in which the state played little part, could not be typical. All other countries had to follow in the wake of the first country to industrialize and consequently had to do it differently. In most cases this involved using the state as a directive force to prime the pump of industrial development in a concerted attempt to catch up with the leading industrial nation (see Postscript). However, if their economic analysis appears to overlook the singularity of the British case, Marx and Engels' assumptions in the political realm about the typicality of the French route appear to endorse the view that in most continental countries bureaucratization was inevitable and necessary for the development of capitalist society, and that therefore the relative lack of this in Britain was significant.

Marx's writings on Britain demonstrate the singularity of the British state in relation both to its conservative forms and to its relatively limited apparatus. According to Marx the conservative state was not, as Guizot argued, the result of a moderate and essentially religious seventeenth-century revolution which avoided the destructive excesses of the French one. It should be explained rather by the early capitalist nature of the landowning class which meant that the English Revolution, which was a genuine revolutionary transformation, could be followed by an alliance between the landed and bourgeois classes which shared the same essential interests:

> The great puzzle of the conservative character of the English revolution ... is in fact explained by the lasting alliance of the bourgeoisie with the great landowners, an alliance which fundamentally distinguished the English from the French revolution ... [50]

The lasting political dominance of the landed class, which could be maintained only because that class was essentially capitalist, in no way blocked the development of economic supremacy for the new industrial bourgeoisie.

> A new bourgeoisie of colossal proportions arose; while the old bourgeoisie struggled with the French Revolution, the new one conquered the world market. It became so omnipotent that, even before it gained direct political power as a result of the Reform Bill, it forced its opponents to legislate in its interests and in accordance with its requirements.[51]

From this point on, Marx's analysis of political power in Britain is typically characterized in terms of that 'delegation' and 'masking' which was noted earlier. Landed dominance of the political machine is seen as a facade which conceals the true nature of bourgeoisie power. The aristocracy may occupy the leading positions in the state but they rule only on behalf of the bourgeoisie, whose essential interests they share.

However, Marx does tacitly acknowledge that this bifurcation of power does represent a genuine singularity in British political structures and has significant effects. It is not merely an illusion but a real national peculiarity which derives from that historic alliance which is stressed at the outset. After the victories of 1832 and 1846 the bourgeoisie 'neglected to draw the necessary political and economic conclusions' and allowed the party of the landed class to retain the reigns of political power. The latter's influence thus remained considerable:

> The whole business of government in all its details – including even the executive branch of the legislature, ... remained the guaranteed domain of the landed aristocracy ... the aristocracy ... enjoys exclusive power in the

cabinet, in parliament in the army and the navy, and which is one half, and comparatively the most important one, of the British nation ... [52]

Marx did not believe that this power of the landowners could last. In the same passage he goes on to talk of how they would be forced to sign their own death warrant. In this he was clearly over-optimistic and it is arguable that Marx did generally underestimate the long-term efficacy of landowner influence. Nevertheless, it is evident that he did recognize the peculiarly conservative caste of the British state and attributed this to the survival of landed influence. Whether this constituted, for Marx, a serious long-term limitation on the extent of bourgeois hegemony, as some have argued, is debatable but certainly some of its effects were already apparent.

The other peculiarity of the British state which Marx repeatedly mentions is the extent to which the *laissez-faire* doctrine had been taken. These ideas are associated primarily with the Manchester free-trade school, the representatives of capital, par excellence. Their last word, says Marx, is the bourgeois republic,

> in which free competition rules supreme in all spheres of life; in which there remains altogether that minimum only of government which is indispensible for the administration, internally and externally, of the common class interest and business of the bourgeoisie, and where this minimum of government is as soberly, as economically organised as possible. [53]

The kind of state that was created in Britain by the mid-century, and which continued throughout the heyday of *laissez-faire*, certainly did reflect in large measure the aspirations of the pure free-traders. The British state comprised the smallest central bureaucracy of any major western power. It had no continental equivalents either in the austerity of its means or in the conscious limitation of its domain. It was expressly forged to ensure the effective regulation of the market and the maintenance of social order with least cost and the minimum of interference in commercial and social affairs. That Marx and Engels took this peculiarity seriously is demonstrated by the fact that Engels found it necessary to remind English socialists in 1886 of Marx's comments on the absence of a military-bureaucratic machine in England. He deduced from this that of all countries in Europe, 'England is the only country where the inevitable social revolution might be effected entirely by peaceful and legal means.'[54] Whatever the political prescience of this remark, it does betray a conviction that the exceptional nature of the British state was critical.

These suggestive but summary distinctions certainly do not exhaust the supply of comparative reference in Marx's work. Both he and Engels were, after all, cosmopolitan Europeans in their culture and internationalists in their politics, and had numerous pertinent comparative observations to make about the state of political forces in different nations. However, it is true to say that the specification of national differences in the development of the state was not amongst their foremost concerns. However, for very good reasons, this was not the case with Gramsci. As someone who had made the personal transition from the Sardinian periphery to the metropolitan heartland of Turin, in a country where the difference between developed and underdeveloped regions was of extreme importance, Gramsci was especially sensitive to the question of regional variation. What is more, he lived through the rise of Mussolini and was inevitably curious about what it was in Italian history that made the advent of Fascism possible. Why should Fascism occur there and not, for instance, in France or England. It is just such questions, about why particular countries adopted exceptional regimes during that period and, incidentally, about why some national economies fared better than others in the post-war period, that have prompted the recrudescence of comparative studies in more recent times. Gramsci's work, then, is of considerable interest when it comes to analysing specific and uneven forms of state development in western countries.

Like Marx, Gramsci was particularly concerned with the different nature of the ruling class alliances that characterized the emergence of the modern state in different regions. His comparisons between the nature of development in France, England, Germany and Italy largely hinge on the different forms of hegemony or class domination that obtained at crucial periods in each country, and how these were reflected in the roles of intellectuals and of parties. French development is again taken to be archetypal in the sense that Gramsci continually uses the example of the Jacobins as a yardstick for comparison.

The Jacobins, says Gramsci, 'created the bourgeois state, made the bourgeoisie into the leading, hegemonic class of the nation, ... gave the new state a permanent basis and created the compact French nation'.[55] The example of the Jacobins was important because it was they who first demonstrated how, through effective leadership, a revolution could develop where the aspirations of one class, the bourgeoisie, could be stretched beyond their natural limits and become a focus for the people as a whole. Helped by the intransigence of the nobility and the international situation, successful in harnessing the peasantry through their agrarian policy, and thus forming a bond between town and country, the Jacobins were able to become, for a while, a truly hegemonic force. They represented the 'revolutionary movement as a whole, as an integral historical development. For they represented the future needs.... not only the needs of those particular physical individuals, but also the needs of the national groups which had to be assimilated to the existing fundamental groups.'[56]

With the 1791 *Loi Le Chapelier* and the Law of the Maximum, which refused rights of combination and put a ceiling on prices and wages, the

Jacobins showed that the limits of the Revolution had been reached, and Thermidor[57] gained the upper hand. However, the Jacobins had, for a period at least, acted as the 'national-popular' force and had in a sense accomplished their historical mission.

Italy presents a quite different case of state development which Gramsci continually contrasts with that of France. In his pencil sketches of the course of Italian history since the Renaissance he shows how a number of national circumstances inhibited the process of state formation, leading, finally, to the extreme 'solution' of Fascism. Unlike the Jacobins, the Italian bourgeoisie failed to develop an effective hegemony. 'The Italian bourgeoisie was incapable of uniting the people around itself, and this was the cause of its defeats and the interruptions in its development.' [58] Since the time of Machiavelli, Italy had been handicapped by regional division and national disunity. The Renaissance had seen the development of a cosmopolitan humanist culture that severed the intellectuals from the people. The strife between municipalities, and the nature of the papacy, international in orientation rather than a force for internal cohesion, had resulted in an 'economic-corporate' form of society, the most stagnant of all forms of feudal society. The *Risorgimento* finally united Italy but it was a revolution without a revolution, a 'passive revolution' which failed to mobilize the people. Politically, the national bourgeoisie had never established that form of hegemony which the Jacobins had successfully achieved in France. Intellectually they had failed to create a national-popular culture rooted in local traditions but bent on social transformation such as would have welded together the bourgeoisie and the popular forces in a revolutionary alliance:

> An effective Jacobin force was always missing, and could not be constituted; and it was precisely such a Jacobin force which in other nations awakened and organized the national-popular collective will, and founded the modern states.[59]

Gramsci's writings on England are not extensive but such fragments as exist do suggest that he considered the English case also as significantly different from the French case. Following Marx, he sees the revolutions of the seventeenth century as bourgeois revolutions, where these were succeeded by a 'fusion' between the old and new classes which left the old aristocracy as the governing stratum acting as the 'intellectuals' of the bourgeoisie. The bourgeoisie did not face a major antagonist in the landed classes, and allowed the latter, who were better organized politically, to act as their representatives. As in Italy, the bourgeoisie failed to become the hegemonic class; they were never 'conceived of as an integral part of the people, but always as an entity separate from the latter'.[60] Initially it had been the nobility which had formed the national-popular bloc against the Crown, creating the basis for the later popular Toryism. During the nineteenth century it increasingly acquired the character of a 'bourgeois aristocracy' and after 1832 brought the state into conformity with needs of the middle class. Thus, like Marx, Gramsci portrays aristocratic rule as a surrogate form of bourgeois power which calmly represents the interests of capital, but nevertheless puts its own stamp on the state, upholding tradition and preserving a particular 'mentality' which protects the state from sudden upheavals. If this represents, as in Italy, an incomplete bourgeois hegemony, it does not, however, have the same serious consequences. State formation occurs under the assured leadership of an old class which creates a popular basis.

Laissez-faire policy, which Gramsci also sees as a distinguishing English feature, is not so much an abdication of state formation by the dominant class as a particular form of it adapted to English conditions. The argument of Political Economy, which presents the state as separate from the economy and civil society, is illusory. In fact, *laissez-faire* is just another form of state regulation 'introduced and maintained by legislative and coercive means'.[61] However, it does involve particular social relations which are specific to England. Elsewhere, Gramsci writes an interesting note about the specific conditions which made the decentralized state, or what he calls 'self-government', possible only in England. It was the existence of a landowning class, deeply implanted within the localities, with long experience of public affairs, a certain prestige which was never fully undermined by a 'savage confrontation with the people', and the abundant leisure which accrued from its living off rents, which made possible the typical forms of decentralized gentry rule which were unique to England.[62] Liberal politics in the nineteenth century were thus an adaptation of earlier state forms to meet the new conditions of bourgeois society, but they never effected a major structural reform of the state. They did not involve 'the foundation or organization of a new political society, and even less of a new type of civil society'.[63]

Like Marx, then, Gramsci is arguing that a specific process of state formation occurred in Britain in the nineteenth century as a result of its earlier history. This produced a state apparatus that was adequate for the needs of capitalist society, but the process of reform was peculiarly gradual and conservative in its outlook. It represented a secure form of capitalist rule but never a complete form of bourgeois hegemony.

It is in these different national forms of hegemony, which are provisionally outlined in Marx and Gramsci's work, that we can find the key to the uneven and nationally differentiated ways in which education developed in the nineteenth century. The detailed explication of these different educational histories and the way in which they relate to different modes of state formation can wait until the following chapters, but a number of provisional conclusions can be drawn here.

The first conclusion is that the general theory of the state derived from Marx is not an impediment to understanding national difference. If we adopt a theory of the complex articulation of different levels within the social formation, some of the problems that arose earlier concerning the disjunctures between economic development and rates of educational change become more easily explicable. The fact is that whilst economic relations do exercise a influence on educational forms, precisely how they do this is determined by the nature of the state, because it is always at the political level that competing demands on education are resolved. Education is part of the superstructure of the social formation, in a broad sense already part of the state itself. How it will respond to particular economic needs, arising for instance out of the development of new techniques of production, or new forms of capital–labour relations, will depend on how these different needs are represented through the state by different social classes who have an interest in them, and therefore on the balance of social forces as they are embodied and organized within the state. Typically, then, it was not necessarily the countries with the most developed economic relations which exhibited the most far-reaching adaptive responses within education. It was where, for particular reasons, the state was conceived as an important instrument of economic development or where the balance of class power condensed within the state was favourable to the state intervening in this way through education that corresponding changes in education did occur. This was most obviously the case in countries such as France and Germany, where economic advance was particularly dependent on state direction and where the social and political composition of the state was such that such strategies could be effective.

The second point is that many of the ways in which Marx and Gramsci have signalled the singularity of different national forms of state formation do in fact substantially prepare the ground for an analysis of differential educational development. Education works primarily through ideas and therefore corresponds most closely to that aspect of state formation which concerns ideology. It is essentially part of that process of state formation which Corrigan refers to as cultural revolution. It should not be surprising then that educational development through the state was most dynamic in those countries and during those periods when the state was most intensely involved in this kind of cultural transformation. We can see from Marx and Gramsci's work how this occurred differently in different countries.

In a number of nineteenth-century states, most notably France and Germany, the state was a particularly active force in the development of the economy. However, it could also play an important role in the consolidation of the political and ideological hegemony of the ruling classes. Where this occurred through an acute social and ideological polarization, as in France, or through a very deliberate effort of national reconstruction from above, as in Prussia, the state often became an enormously important instrument of cultural transformation. It engaged in a wholesale and calculated process of social transformation, and schools were necessarily an important part of this process. The latter's development was thus seen as peculiarly important and great efforts were made to stimulate it. Where, on the other hand, state formation was relatively delayed or feeble, reflecting a partial or unconsolidated bourgeois hegemony, as in Italy, or where it was unusually gradual and conservative, on account of the nature of the ruling alliance, as in England, cultural transformation through public schooling had less sense of urgency. State involvement in education was less deliberate and less far reaching. Left more to its own devices, schooling developed with less dynamism and less coordinated effort. Where, as in England, political traditions strongly opposed the development of a more expansionist and interventionist state, the counter-pressure against the promotion of education through the state was particularly strong, making it more unlikely that state forms of public education would develop.

Another factor which distinguishes state formation in certain countries and which had important repercussions for education was nationalism. In those countries where the attainment of national unity, both cultural and territorial, was particularly delayed and protracted, or characterized by long periods of military conflict, nationalism became an important factor in state formation. In many states, in fact, the creation of the modern bourgeois state and the rise of nationalist movements were inseparable. Prussia is a good case in point. In these cases, education thus became inextricably tied up with nationalist sentiments. As Eric Hobsbawm has remarked, schooling was the 'most powerful weapon for the forming of nations'.[64] Not only did it provide a means for training efficient and patriotic soldiers; it also became a conduit for channelling nationalist aspirations where these involved the desire to forge a new national identity or a distinctive national culture. The school was uniquely well placed to promote the use of a particular national language, and to popularize those aspects of national culture and those images of national identity which most appealed to the ruling or ascendant group. This function of the school appealed not only to Napoleon, who made ruthless use of it, but also to the nationalist pioneers of the reformed Prussian state after their national humiliation at the hands of Napoleon. Similarly, although in different ways, the leaders of the Early Republic in the United States consciously used education as a means of fostering a new national identity and securing the ideological basis of the new polity.

If education thus received a strong shot in the arm from nationalist sentiments, and often developed with particular rapidity in those countries where nationalist reconstruction was paramount, it was often correspondingly neglected in those countries where these forces were not operative. England is the obvious case in point. Of all the nations in this study, England was the first to attain national unification and was consequently least bothered by the issue in succeeding periods. Nationalism was a uniquely muted and conservative force in eighteenth- and nineteenth-century Britain. The sense of national identity was complacently secure and national superiority more often assumed than stridently asserted. Moreover, national identity was typically and potently represented in the ancient institutions of the ruling class, and the latter felt little need to develop a popular nationalism which would be hegemonic in Gramsci's sense of the 'national-popular' or in any sense transformative. National identity was essentially the past. It did not need to envision the future. Thus educational development in England was deprived of one of its historically most potent rationales. Tradition could accomplish what, in other nations, required education.

In this section I have tried to provide a broad theoretical framework which locates the development of public education within that general process which I have called state formation. The particular forms which this took in different nations is said to provide the key to understanding differential educational development and some of the critical areas of difference have been outlined. In the case studies which follow I will endeavour to trace these interrelated historical processes with greater historical specificity, focusing on those critical historical conjunctures where particular configurations of class forces decisively conditioned major turning points in educational development.

4
Education and Statism in Continental Europe

The origins of formal schooling in continental Europe lay with the churches and religious societies. They were the instruments of early educational expansion and the first authors of systematic forms of teaching. However, the transformation of religious education into formal systems of schooling, designed to serve secular and national ends, was the work of the state, in a protracted process which went back in many cases to the sixteenth century. It was the Reformation which first thrust education into the political arena and prompted extensive royal interventions in schooling. Later the absolutist state also 'acted on' religious education, always dependent on it, but consciously bending it to its particular requirements. Most notably it was during the eighteenth century, the high period of absolutism and the era of 'enlightened despotism', that the machinery of national education was first decisively prefigured in legislation on compulsory attendance, state funding and inspection for schools. The infant education systems which these two forces spawned were consolidated in the early nineteenth century either by absolutist states in their final, sometimes 'liberal', hour, as in Prussia and Austria, or by post-revolutionary bourgeois regimes, as in France, Switzerland and Holland.

The historical span across which these developments occurred was thus characterized by momentous social and political change. National systems were born in a period of declining feudalism, the progeny of transitional absolutist states which developed many of the 'rationalized' features of modern government whilst still committed to the maintenance of aristocratic rule. Yet they came to maturity in societies that were essentially capitalist, reflecting the nationalism of the emergent nation states, the hegemonic aspirations of the rising bourgeois class and being generally key institutions of the emergent modern capitalist state. The national education system in continental Europe was thus the product of state formation in a transitional period. Its typical forms and objectives were first delineated according to the priorities of the absolutism but were subsequently decisively transformed through bourgeois revolution. It is to the early period that we must first turn.

The Reformation marked the first major advance in education in the early modern period and demonstrated the effectiveness of a combined initiative by church and state. The initial impulse behind the expansion of schooling was religious. Lutheran doctrine stressed the importance of education for religious enlightenment: if the clergy were to preach effectively they had to be both knowledgeable and trained in the techniques of oratory; if the people were to understand they had to be literate. However, as Luther was quick to realize, education was also a political issue. To train youth right, he argued, was essential not only for their own spiritual sakes 'but also for the welfare and stability of all our institutions, temporal and spiritual alike'.[1] The peasant wars in Germany convinced Luther of the urgent need for a widespread system of education which would act as a mechanism of social control, and he argued that this should be financed and administered by the secular power. His proposals were readily taken up by German princes, who welcomed the attacks on the papacy as a means of bolstering their own independence and fully appreciated the value of education in establishing secure and socially cohesive Protestant states. The full Lutheran education programme, first set out in 1528 in Melancthon's *Articles of Visitation*, was soon adopted by the Elector, John of Saxony, and many other territories, including Hesse (1526), Pomerania (1535), Braunschweig (1543) and Brandenburg (1573), adopted new school regulations. Altogether more than 100 such school ordinances were adopted in Protestant states during the sixteenth century.[2]

The educational ferment in Europe generated by the Reformation was echoed, though not quite matched, by the considerable efforts of the Counter-Reformation, and the ensuing religious competition over educational control continued to be a major feature of educational development for several centuries, until supplanted by the conflict between church and state in the nineteenth century. The major instrument of Catholic educational advance was the Society of Jesus, officially recognized in 1540 and specifically designed as a teaching order. The Jesuits quickly achieved ascendancy in education in Portugal, Spain and Italy, and were destined to become the major force in French secondary education. They developed a rigorous educational method, codified in the *Ratio Studorum*, which was, arguably, more advanced pedagogically than anything else in Europe at the time, stressing uniformity and high standards.[3] They also developed a stress on discipline and central administration, the influence of which was still felt in the Napoleonic *lycées* of the early nineteenth century. Although their work extended throughout Europe, it was in France that they had the greatest impact on secondary education, creating 126 colleges prior to their disbandment in 1762.[4]

As in Protestant states, education in Catholic countries also attracted royal sponsorship, well illustrated in the French case by Louis XIV's support for the Jesuits and suppression of Huguenot education after the revocation of the Edict of Nantes.

The second major wave of educational reform in Europe occurred in the late seventeenth century when, after a period of relative stagnation, educational development was revived in both Protestant and Catholic states through the impact of German Pietism, an austere religious movement which sought through education to restore the unfulfilled spiritual promise of the Reformation. However, here again it was the secular state which typically took up the educational ideas promoted by the religious groups and used them for its own purposes, most notably in the absolutist Habsburg and Hohenzollern territories. The growing importance of education for the state during the period can be understood by analysing the typical structures and functions of absolutism in the European social formations.

The absolutist state had arisen as a result of the prolonged crisis of feudal society and represented, as Perry Anderson has described it, 'a redeployed and recharged apparatus of feudal domination... the new political carapace of the threatened nobility'.[5] Feudalism as a mode of production was originally characterized by the organic unity of economy and polity, wherein the institution of serfdom fused economic exploitation and political-legal coercion at the molecular level of the village. With the abolition of serfdom in Western Europe and the commutation of dues into money rents, this cellular unity of the political and economic repression of the peasantry was weakened, thereby jeopardizing the power of the feudal lords. The centralized monarchies of the sixteenth century which decisively broke with the 'pyramidal, parcellized sovereignty of the medieval social formations' were one response to this crisis.[6] The absolutist state took this one stage further, displacing 'politico-legal coercion upwards towards a centralized, militarized summit'.[7]

The absolutist states were, as Anderson puts it, 'machines built overwhelmingly for the battlefield'.[8] The typical medium of inter-feudal rivalry was military, and the primary vocation of the noble class was warfare. In societies based economically on land, which unlike capital is not infinitely extendable, the categorical imperative of noble rule was the acquisition of territory through military conquest. The absolutist state was therefore characterized by almost permanent international warfare. During the entire sixteenth century, there were only 25 years without large-scale military operations in Europe, and in the whole of the seventeenth century, only seven years passed without major wars between states. On the eve of the French Revolution, according to Necker, two-thirds of French state expenditures were military.[9]

Whilst presiding over essentially feudal societies, the absolutist states also pioneered many of the institutions of the modern state apparatus. They introduced standing armies, permanent bureaucracies, legal codes and national taxation, all of which suggested a transition to Weber's rationalized legal administration in contrast to the jungle of particularistic dependencies which characterized earlier periods. They also hosted the development of early capitalist relations in the towns, witnessing the beginnings of unified commercial markets and early pre-industrial manufactures. Concerned as they were with war, the absolutist states also promoted manufactures and trade, regulated the guilds, encouraged exports and protected their economies against the import of foreign goods.[10] According to the French mercantilist and German cameralist doctrines, it was the role of the state to intervene in civil society both to develop social institutions and to augment the economic power of the state through acquiring a greater fraction of world trade than their foreign rivals.[11]

The promotion of education clearly fitted in with the objectives of the absolutist state, particularly in its later years when the importance of expert administration and technical knowledge in the arts of war and industry became more important. Secondary schooling was increasingly important to provide the bureaucracy with trained and efficient staff, whilst technical and vocational schools could supply the military with capable recruits, and the state manufactures and public works departments with expert engineers. Elementary schooling was likewise increasingly necessary to provide disciplined and loyal military and naval cadets, and to promote patriotic beliefs amongst the people.[12] The attempt to create universal, state-controlled and bureaucratically administered national education systems can thus be seen as a typical product of state formation in the period of absolutism.

If the general connections between the forms of the absolutist state and the early development of forms of national education are apparent, it is important to specify somewhat more precisely national differences in this respect. This can be approached by considering some of the significant differences between the absolutisms of Eastern and Western Europe. As Anderson has observed, whilst exhibiting everywhere the same essential characteristics, the absolutist state took distinctly different forms in the East and the West. This was epitomized in the much greater repressive powers of eastern absolutisms and in their tendency towards extreme militarization. The explanation for this lay in the different economic basis of eastern aristocratic power and in the different relations pertaining between the nobility, the peasantry and the urban bourgeoisie.

> The Absolutist state of the West was the deployed political apparatus of a feudal class which had accepted the commutation of dues. It was a compensation for the disappearance of serfdom, in the context of an increasingly urban economy which it did not completely control and to which it had to adapt. The Absolutist state in the East, by contrast, was the repressive machine of a feudal class that had just erased the traditional communal freedoms of the poor. It was a device for the consolidation

of serfdom, in a landscape scoured of autonomous urban life or resistance. The manorial reaction in the East meant that a new world had to be implanted from above, by main force. The dose of violence pumped into the social relations was correspondingly far greater.[13]

The pressures which resulted in the centralized, militaristic states of the Habsburg and Hohenzollern dynasties came from without and within. It was the international pressure of western absolutism, the political apparatus of a more powerful feudal aristocracy, ruling more advanced societies, which obliged the eastern nobility to adopt an equivalently centralized state machine to survive. The construction of Prussian absolutism by the Great Elector from the 1650s onwards, for instance, was in large measure a response to the continuing military threat of Sweden, whose armies had only recently occupied Brandenburg. Equally, it was the frontier character of the eastern social formations with their scattered populations which made it difficult for rulers to enforce liege obedience on their subjects and corresponded with a much less cohesive network of intra-feudal relations than in the West. 'One consequence of this', writes Anderson,

> was to concentrate seigneurial power over the peasantry to a degree unknown in the West... territorial, personal and economic Lordship was generally fused in a single manorial authority, which exercised cumulative rights over its subject serfs.[14]

Whilst in the West, overlapping and plural jurisdictions over villeins were objectively propitious to peasant resistance, in the East the position of the serf was one of abject dependence.

These objective differences in the nature of absolutist regimes go some way towards explaining the differences between the nature of state intervention in education in different regions. The typical policy of the absolutist state in France was to encourage the development of technical and vocational schools, seen as important for promoting the military and mercantilist policies of the state. However, for all the might of French absolutism, the state never seriously tried to impose compulsory education on the peasantry, as did Frederick II in Prussia and Theresa and Joseph in Austria. It is certainly of note that all of the most sustained attempts to create state control over schools and to enforce compulsory attendance in this period occurred in the eastern states. It may well be that only certain distinctive characteristics of eastern absolutisms were favourable to this outcome. Eastern absolutisms developed later than their western counterparts and in addition to their relative late-comer status had numerous handicaps to overcome. They were territorially vulnerable, linguistically diverse and demographically dispersed. Without that dense network of intra-feudal relations that characterized western feudalisms, they were in particular need of surrogate mechanisms of vertical solidarity and social control. Education was an obvious candidate. Furthermore, the dependent and geographically shackled condition of the peasantry, combined with the concentrated local power of the noble class, may have made the imposition of compulsory education more feasible than in France, where the peasantry were less hamstrung and where there was in any case perhaps less urgent reason for using education as a means of social integration.

Another important distinguishing characteristic of eastern absolutisms was that they lasted considerably longer than in the West. This was inevitably to have considerable importance for education since in numerous countries, in particular Prussia and Austria, education systems were to be finally consolidated under absolutist or only partially reformed royal states. A brief consideration of educational development and state formation in Prussia should show the comparative significance of this fact.

Education and absolutism in Prussia

The consolidation of a full national education system in Prussia dates, as we have seen, from the first three decades of the nineteenth century. It occurred during the 'era of reforms' which followed the occupation of Prussia by Napoleon and represented just one aspect of that process by which the Prussian state was regenerated in the wake of military defeat and national humiliation. The immediate causes of those subsequent educational developments, which were to so impress western observers, must therefore be sought in that specific conjuncture, in that historical moment of state formation when the Prussian Junker class, buoyed up by a fierce nationalistic reaction to French occupation, managed to re-establish the foundations of its power after the abolition of serfdom through a reformed state apparatus and the imposition of new social relations amongst its subjects. However, the origins of state education in Prussia actually lay further back in the work of the eighteenth-century absolutists.

Prussian absolutism developed in the century-and-a-half after 1648 in a period of intensive state-building and military activity which created the European power that was to lead German unification in the following century. The Elector, Frederick William I, laid the foundations of Prussian absolutism after the Thirty Years War, building up the military, centralizing the bureaucracy and increasing state revenues. His successors, King Frederick and Frederick William I, further strengthened the military, creating a new secret police and promoting manufactures and agriculture through drainage, dikes and settlement projects in the country. Frederick II finally consolidated Prussian power, creating a disciplined and efficient bureaucracy and a formidable 150 000-strong army, which contributed towards the notable successes in the Austrian War and the Seven Years War, and the consequent acquisition of Silesia.[15]

The bold educational reforms undertaken by the state in this period were clearly not unconnected with this general fortification of Prussian state power. An effective system of secondary schooling was important for providing able administrators in the bureaucracy and technical expertise for state manufacturing projects. Elementary schools could also help to instill discipline and patriotism in future military recruits. However, there were further reasons for developing education which have been well analysed in James Melton's recent work.

During the late seventeenth and early eighteenth centuries, changes in Prussian social and economic structures created what Melton calls a crisis of legitimation. In the towns the decline of the apprentice system was undermining the traditional patriarchal controls over youth, whilst in the countryside the growth of the landless poor, the absenteeism of noble landlords and the rise of proto-industry were all undercutting the traditional structures of authority in the family and the feudal structures of the estates. The state saw an urgent need for new forms of labour discipline to make peasants and industrial workers more productive and for new forms of social control to compensate for the decline in traditional forms of authority. It sought answers in education and, particularly, in the new reforms advocated by the Pietist movement.

German Pietism had arisen in the late seventeenth century as a movement which sought to rekindle the neglected spiritual values of the Reformation after the ravages of the Thirty Years War. Spiritual leaders such as Philip Spener believed the Lutheran faith to be in a state of crisis, its leaders absorbed in abstruse theological debates and its followers practising the externals of the faith alone. Spener's followers, who were strongly influenced by Calvin, eschewed scholastic argument and the sensual display of the Church, advocating in its place a new spiritual purification and inner renewal. The Pietist celebration of 'inwardness' also led to a renewed concern with the role of education in shaping personality. Stressing the importance of bible reading, Pietism promoted popular literacy on an unprecedented scale.

The educational policies of the Pietists found ready support from the absolutist rulers. The Hohenzollerns were a Calvinist dynasty ruling a predominantly Lutheran population, and the Elector, Frederick I, saw it as being to his advantage to promote a movement which put faith above theological controversy and which might provide a counterweight to the Lutheran nobility. Pietist pedagogy was also particularly attractive to the Elector and his successors because it stressed austerity and the work ethic, upheld the social hierarchy, and believed in authority in the classroom. With its stress on universality and social obligation, Pietist schooling was a useful instrument for regenerating social authority. It was also uniquely adapted, so the mid-century cameralists were to argue, for creating the kind of voluntary submission and self-discipline which was needed for the new industrial workers and the peasantry when they were granted more independence. The appeal of Pietist pedagogy, according to Melton, lay in 'its simultaneous promotion of submission and autonomy'.

> Pietism provided a pedagogy that encouraged both activity and passivity, entrepreneurial enterprise and an acceptance of existing social and political structures. It represented, in short, a pedagogical compromise between the demands of state-building and a hierarchical social and political order.[16]

The general revival of German education at the end of the seventeenth century thus began with the Pietist movement and was developed through the efforts of the absolutist monarchs. The first and most illustrious of the Pietist reformers was August Francke, Spener's successor as the leader of north German Pietism, and it was he who pioneered the new pedagogy which was to act as a model for widespread reform in the Hohenzollern and Habsburg territories. Francke's educational work began after his appointment to a post at the University of Halle. Convinced that only education could raise the morals of the poor, he set up his first school in Halle in 1695. This was originally intended for beggars but it gained such a reputation for piety and orderliness that middle-class children started enrolling as well. Soon a Latin school was added and later his educational complex was crowned by the creation of the Padagogium, an elite boarding school preparing the children of the nobility and prosperous merchants for university and the bureaucracy. In 1696 he also created a new *Seminarium* which served as a model for teacher training during the next century.

Francke's successor in Pietist educational reform was Johann Hecker, himself a graduate of Francke's *Seminarium*. Like his mentor, Hecker developed a network of pauper schools and a pedagogical institute for methodical teacher training. However, his most notable achievement was the creation in Berlin of the first *Realschule* (1747), a vocationally oriented establishment designed for the children of middle-class parents who were dissatisfied with the classical diet of the *Gymnasium*.

Francke and Heckler were responsible for a host of pedagogical innovations which were widely copied throughout the rest of Europe. They pioneered the simultaneous method of classroom teaching, which was greatly more efficient than the prevailing system of individual teaching in class, which reputedly led to poor order and gave children only a few minutes of instruction per day. They were also responsible for the practices of student hand-raising and the roll-call, the introduction of the hour-glass into classrooms and the concept of 'free-time' in school, all of which illustrated their attention to method and the cultivation of self-disciplined work. Most importantly, they developed the system of methodical teacher training which was arguably more rigorous than anything else of the time. The

Pietists established the German reputation for the use of the most advanced pedagogic techniques, which was to continue in the next century when German schools were ahead of all others in the application of the new Pestalozzian methods.[17]

The other legacy of the period was the development of forms of state control in education, and this was the contribution which the absolutist rulers grafted onto the reforms pioneered by Pietism. It was the decrees of Frederick William I and Frederick II on schooling which really signalled the first steps towards education by the state and represented the decisive imprint which the late absolute monarchs left on Prussian education. In 1715, legislation instituted state inspection of schools, albeit still at this stage conducted by the clergy. Two years later a compulsory attendance law made parents responsible for ensuring the education of their children from 5 to 12 years up to prescribed levels. The *Principia Regulativa* of 1736 gave the state and local public authorities responsibility for building schools, and in 1763 the celebrated *General-Landschul-Reglement* consolidated these earlier laws in one piece of legislation. According to this latest law, children between 5 and 13 were required to attend school daily between 8 and 11 a.m. and 1 and 4 p.m., except on Saturday afternoon and Sunday, until they reached certain prescribed standards in religion, reading, writing and elementary arithmetic. Although there was widespread evasion of the 16 groschen fine for non-attendance, the legislation set an important precedent which would habituate the Prussian population to compulsory schooling. Some 50 years later, when such regulations were fully enforceable, they would rarely need to be applied. The legislation also fixed teacher-training requirements, specified textbooks and provided state funds to supplement tuition fees as sources of funding for schools, thus anticipating many future characteristics of the national education system.[18] From here it was no great step to the establishment of full state control over education.

The construction of national education in Prussia

The Prussian state education system was finally consolidated by successive reforming ministers from Humboldt to Altenstein during the three decades after the French occupation. It represented, for its time, a unique achievement, and whilst the political concerns which motivated its development were highly questionable, its extensiveness and forms of organization elicited widespread admiration from western educational reformers. Its distinguishing features, as we have seen, included the very broad base of its elementary schooling, which achieved universal enrolment years ahead of other European nations; the efficiency of its teacher-training and systematic pedagogical methods, which produced high general levels of literacy and academic excellence amongst its secondary classical scholars; and the general advance of its technical and vocational training, at both intermediate and advanced levels. The political corollary of this educational 'efficiency' was its authoritarian ethos. Prussian education developed under rigid central control, with a disciplined and hierarchical organizational structure and a level of political policing over the curriculum which was scarcely matched in any other country. Such an admixture of qualities led to both admiration and consternation amongst contemporaries. Subsequent historians have reacted with equal bewilderment. To A. J. P. Taylor, Prussian education was the 'wonder of 19th century Europe', but it was also a characteristic product of Prussian militarism, 'a gigantic engine of conquest, the more effective in that it was conducted by volunteers'.[19]

The characteristic forms of Prussian education were clearly rooted in its historical origins in the absolutism of the eighteenth century. The prerogative of the state to impose compulsory schooling on the masses, and the patriotic duty of the latter to conform to this, had been well established in the earlier period and required no major cultural revolution to be made effective in the following century. The stress on military power and bureaucratic efficiency which had prompted educational development earlier was still an active force and continued to provide the shaping spirit behind educational innovation. What was added in the subsequent period was a virulent nationalistic impulse and a desire to use education to promote the reform of the Prussian state and later to galvanize industrial development through technical expertise. Educational development was to become one of the most active ingredients in a process of compacted and forced state formation that transformed a society based on serfdom and royal absolutism to the reformed Junker state that was capable of dragging Germany into the capitalist world.

The social and political nature of the conjuncture which saw the rise of Prussian national education has already been indicated. With the crushing Napoleonic victory at Jena in 1806 and the tough terms of the subsequent Treaty of Tilsit, Prussia lost much of its territory to the newly created Grand Duchy of Warsaw and was required to accept a French army of occupation as well as paying a crushing financial indemnity. The Prussian population was reduced to 5 million and the army was stripped to 42 000. However, it was the very scale of defeat and the sharpness of national humiliation which propelled the intense programme of national reconstruction that followed, and through which the ruling Junker class managed to restore its power in the post-feudal conditions that Napoleon had imposed.

The first series of reforms were the work of Stein, a francophobe Rhinelander whose objective was to stir peasant and middle-class nationalism through agrarian and state reforms and thus to repel the French and promote a unified German nationalism.[20] In his brief period of office, Stein introduced plans for civic equality, agrarian reform, local self-government and nationalist mobilization against Napoleon. Serfdom was abolished in the countryside, which benefitted the richer peasants but left the remainder marooned in rural areas with small scraps of land and little chance of urban migration. Enhanced centralization of the state was only nominally offset by the limited autonomy granted to the towns.[21] Stein had achieved limited reforms but in the process had antagonized the Junkers, providing them with a pretext to reassert their power.

Under Stein's successor, Hardenberg, the governmental apparatus was subject to further reform and its administrative machinery strengthened, but nothing was attempted which would undermine Junker power. A policy of agrarian clearance known as *Bauernlegen* (literally, laying the peasants flat) swept away communal lands, creating enlarged manorial estates, and a growing mass of landless agricultural labourers. These were disciplined by a feudal *Gesindeordnung*, which imposed a ruthless manorial discipline over them with imprisonment for striking and strict limits on mobility. Military expansion was restricted by Napoleon, but this did not prevent a strong army from being built up by the rapid training of reserves. Schnarnhorst and Gneisenau, the Prussian military organizers, developed a system of universal military service – putting 'the people in arms', as its radical rhetoric proclaimed, but in reality just a further example of popular subservience. The net effect of the reform era, according to Anderson, was thus 'to strengthen rather than moderate the royal state in Prussia'.[22]

It was in this context that Humboldt, Head of the Bureau of Ecclesiastical Affairs and Public Instruction, set about creating the machinery of a national education system, instituting the *Volksschule*, establishing provincial and district school boards, and decreeing, in 1810, that education was a secular activity and compulsory for three years. The philosophy behind this determined effort of educational construction was pre-eminently one of furthering the national strength and efficiency of the Prussian state.

Johann Gottlieb Fichte, the intellectual doyen of German nationalism, had argued the importance of education to Prussian reconstruction since Tilsit. In his celebrated *Addresses to the German Nation* he had called for a total effort from the Prussian people to build a new corporate state. This was to be based on 'a new moral order' to whose 'sublime will' each individual should be subordinate. Fichte argued that each child must be made to realize that

he is not merely a member of human society here on earth for the short span of life which is permitted to him. He is also, and is undoubtedly recognized to be, a link in the chain of spiritual life in a higher social order.

Education would be the expression of this corporate spiritual identity and the means for national regeneration. 'By means of education we want to mould Germany into a corporate body, which will be stimulated and animated in all individual members by the same interest.'[23] The means to this end would be the construction of a popular national education system operated according to the pedagogic principles developed by the educationalist Pestalozzi at his successful school at Yverdon in Switzerland. Fichte credited Pestalozzi with making an educational discovery that would revolutionize the world:

> By the force of his genius and his love, he has created a true national education that is capable of rescuing the nations and humanity…from the deplorable conditions into which they have now fallen.[24]

Such a noble aspiration, argued Fichte, should impel national regeneration through education in Prussia.

With somewhat less of Fichte's ecumenical idealism, Prussian political leaders argued the same case, reflecting always on the importance of national revival through education and on the characteristically Germanic ideal of individual subordination through education to a collective corporate spirit. 'In order to transform the people,' wrote Stein,

> to inspire them with confidence and to make them endure any sacrifice for independence and national honour, we must educate the youth of the country. All the forces of the spirit must be developed and no ability on which the dignity of man rests must be neglected. We shall see a generation growing up which is physically and morally of such vigour that a better future will open before us.[25]

Such was the ideological motivation behind Humboldt and future Prussian educational reformers. It not only inspired the zealous and highly paternalistic programmes of reform in elementary education but also furnished, in different ways, the informing spirit behind secondary and higher education. This could be seen particularly in the development of the *Gymnasium* and the universities. Legislation in 1812 reconstituted the *Gymnasium* as a state institution providing nine years of classical education for the elite and authorized to issue the *Abitur* certificate, which gave access to higher education. The classical secondary school became the main mechanism for preparing young people for bureaucratic careers and, with recruitment now based on a meritocratic footing, competition amongst aristocratic and, increasingly, middle-class youth for state office became intense.[26] The universities, likewise, played an important role in supplying the state with its top functionaries. Their revival was also initiated by Humboldt, who founded the University of Berlin in 1810, which established the characteristic ambience which was to infuse all Prussian higher education. German universities generally became renowned for the excellence of their research and the enormous breadth of learning which they cultivated in their students. But even this was conceived as a way of rendering service to the state, and higher education became permeated with that Hegelian idealization of the state and the bureaucracy that Marx was to find so objectionable. The whole classical idea of *Wissenschaft* – the cultivation of high levels of general education through detached scholarship – could hardly be separated from the further glory of the state. Ostensible freedom for academic research did not prevent swift retribution for those who flouted this sacred concept. When student dissent did emerge in the universities after 1815 it was quickly put down by King Frederick II through the instrument of the notorious Karlsbad decrees.

If furnishing the state with efficient bureaucrats and loyal subjects was the primary motivation behind the educational developments of the reform era, in the following period it was the needs of industrialization that were to become paramount. Forms of capitalist development had become increasingly visible since the Napoleonic occupation. With the abolition of serfdom, Junker farming was successfully converted to capitalist methods. The Junker estates were transformed into larger and more efficient *latifundia*, relying entirely on waged labour but still benefitting from semi-feudal controls which were exercised over labour. Meanwhile, agrarian reform encouraged increasing bourgeois investment in land.[27] By the 1830s this capitalist development had shifted markedly into industrial growth, notably with the acquisition of the industrially advanced Rhine-Westphalia regions after the conclusion of the wars with France and with the proliferation of railway construction. In the absence of a vigorous and independent bourgeois class, this industrial development took necessarily distinctive forms. It had to be forced from the top down. This 'revolution from above', as Barrington Moore describes it, was led by an essentially agrarian Junker aristocracy and vigorously promoted by the state and bureaucracy.[28] The Prussian bureaucracy was instrumental in the provision of technical and financial aids to nascent industrial enterprises and in the establishment of the *Zollverein*, a united German trading zone. Above all, the state was to cultivate that abundance of scientific and technical expertise which was so important for continental states which industrialized after England and had, perforce, to make concerted efforts to catch up. It did this through the education system.

The period of the 1830s and after thus saw further vigorous doses of educational reform, this time under the ministerial tutelage of Prussia's most celebrated educational reformer, Altenstein. It was during his ministerial tenure that Prussian elementary schooling, already legally compulsory for seven years since 1817, became effectively universal. Not only did the average Prussian child now receive an extensive period of schooling but this was conducted with rigorous discipline and efficiency. Teacher training had already been developed on an extensive scale, so that by 1837 there were already 50 Normal schools and even elementary teachers had training that lasted several years. They carried their dutifully acquired pedagogic methods with them into the classroom, which was consequently organized along the most methodical lines and often according to the most progressive Pestalozzian principles of graded learning. The curriculum was broad, at least by English standards of the time, but its contents were carefully monitored by the state. It thus represented a most exemplary mode of educational practice but one subordinated in the most illiberal manner to the instrumental aims of the state. As Schnabel has described it, the state school

> became merely an instructional institution, the task of which was to transmit a definite volume of knowledge for the future battle of existence and for the purposes of economic life and the life of the state, and for the rest to inculcate obedience and subordination to adults and superiors.[29]

Secondary education continued to be dominated by the needs of the bureaucracy but here also there were increasing signs of this desire to put education at the service of industrial development. The *Gymnasium* remained mainly classical in its curriculum but less rigidly so than the English public school since it appeared able to reconcile a serious approach to science with the classical ethos which the latter could not. According to the 1837 regulations, Greek and Latin occupied 46 per cent of the curriculum, physics and natural history 32 per cent, maths 17 per cent and French 4 per cent.[30] This at a time when still around 80 per cent of the English public school curriculum was based on classics. In addition to these schools, a number of new institutions were also developed which were specifically designed to offer a more modern education to the middle class. After 1832 the *Realschulen* were entitled to confer their own certificates. These new schools multiplied, and in the following decades other modern institutions were added to them, such as the *Realgymnasien*, which combined classical and scientific education. At the same time, new trade schools were being developed. The intermediate trade schools known as the *Gewerbeschulen* proliferated after 1817, and by 1827 a new advanced trade school called the *Gewerbeinstitut* had emerged, later to be transformed into the highly regarded polytechnic and *Technical Institut*.[31]

Prussian post-elementary education for the middle class thus considerably outstripped its English counterpart, adapting more readily to the needs of both the bureaucracy and the industrial sector, much as French education was to do. It catered only for a small elite – according to Ringer, no more than 2.4 per cent of the age group were enrolled at any one time by the 1870s, but it was increasingly oriented towards the growing middle class, whose social status depended in part on its acquisition of educational credentials.[32]

At the beginning of the century the *Gymnasium* already had a high representation of students from non-commercial middle-class families. A representative sample of *Gymnasium* students for the period 1784–1808 shows that 40 per cent came from families with fathers who belonged to the service and professional class (officers, officials and members of learned professions) whilst 33 per cent had fathers who were clergymen or secondary teachers. By comparison only 2 per cent were children of landowners. Children of peasants and day-labourers represented around 5 per cent and the remainder, some 14 per cent, came from lower middle-class and artisanal backgrounds.[33] During the course of the century the service and professional class retained its predominance in elite secondary education, particularly in the *Gymnasium*, but there was a marked increase in participation by children from the commercial and industrial middle class and the technical professions, often in the new modern secondary schools. Ringer comments that by the late nineteenth-century, German secondary education was 'really rather progressive for its time', by no means dominated at its summit by aristocratic and landed classes, as in England, and including a considerable proportion from the lower middle classes.[34]

A comparative analysis of the social origins of German and French secondary students during the second half of the century helps to illustrate the nature of German secondary education as it evolved through the century. Table 4.1 draws on Ringer's analysis of the official data on the social origins of students gaining the *Abitur* between 1875 and 1899, and on Harrigan's analysis of the data in Duruy's survey of French secondary schools between 1864 and 1868.[35]

The data has to be interpreted with some caution since the occupational categories are not entirely congruent in the two sets of figures. Harrigan's French categories, for instance, separate commercial leaders from *petit-commerçants*, whilst Ringer combines merchants, innkeepers and commerce in one category, making it difficult to distinguish the big and the small fish. Secondly, the strikingly low figure for German landowners may

Table 4.1 Social origins of secondary students in Germany and France (in percentages)

Father's occupation	German secondary			French secondary	
	Gymnasium	Realgymnasium	Oberrealschule	Lycée	Collège
Top professional and official	21	7	5	21.9	13.1
Landowner	c.6	c.6	c.6	18.9	15.5
Industrialist	5	9	13	3.8	3.1
Merchant and *petit-commerçant*	20	26	27	25.4	21.9
Lower professional and administrative	23	26	24	14.3	14.4
Peasants/farmers	11	8	4	8	16.2
Artisans	7	13	17	3.1	9.1

be suspect and one wonders, given the typically active role of the Junker on his estate, whether some of these may have reported as farmers. The strikingly low proportion of landowners in the German figures must therefore be noted with some qualification. However, some other differences are relatively clear. Considerably more children in the German secondary schools were from industrial backgrounds, either industrialist or artisanal, and there is a markedly greater representation of lower professional and administrative workers. The latter certainly accords with what we know of the close connection between education and bureaucracy during the history of German education, and the former is probably partly explained by the later date of the German survey, coming at a time of enormous industrial expansion in the country.

These differences are interesting but overall the comparison shows a remarkable similarity in the social class distributions. Children of professionals and senior officials dominate in both secondary systems, whilst the industrial and commercial middle class provide the second largest single group of students. Ringer has argued that the *Gymnasium* was more 'progressive' in social intake than the *lycée*. Comparing data for three *lycées* with the figures for the *Gymnasien* above, he claims that the *lycée* was dominated to a greater extent by the upper middle class than was the case with the *Gymnasium*, having a higher proportion of *rentiers* and proprietors and rather fewer from the lower middle class. This may well have been true of the *grands lycées*, such as the ones in Ringer's sample, since, as Harrigan has also shown, these were often frequented by the wealthy urban bourgeoisie. However, as indicated above, it was certainly not true of the *lycées* in general.

What seems to distinguish the German and French patterns most is the rather different set of internal relations between the various component parts of their systems. Whilst the difference in social composition between the French *lycée* and college is relatively small, the same cannot be said for the three types of German school. The *Gymnasium* is quite clearly an institution dominated by children from professional and bureaucratic families with a relatively modest industrial representation. The *Oberrealschule*, on the other hand, has the majority from commercial and industrial families and a rather smaller number of children from professional and civil service families come from its lower ranks.

French secondary education formed a relatively unitary system. There were, of course, status differences between the different types of school. The *grands lycées* were certainly the elite schools and the *lycées* in general were more dominated by the landed, professional and service upper middle class than the communal colleges. However, the differences were never sharp and the type of school probably divided social groups less than the type of course followed. The classical programmes continued to attract the majority of children from professional and bureaucratic families, whereas children of peasant and *petit-bourgeois* families, and those wishing to follow business careers, often opted for the new vocationally oriented courses set up by Victor Duruy in 1862. However, the co-existence of different programmes within the same schools, the wide overlap in the curriculum and the lack of clear class differentiation between schools were all testimony to the essentially homogeneous nature of French secondary education.

German secondary education by contrast represented a clear social hierarchy. Each type of school had a distinctive social clientele, a different curriculum and different rights with regard to the conferring of certificates. The *Gymnasium*, which was the pre-eminent secondary institution, was still dominated by the landed and service class. By the 1875–1899 period over 50 per cent of *Gymnasium* students had fathers in the professions, the civil service or farming. Three-quarters of graduates anticipated employment in public service or in the liberal professions. The curriculum was still predominantly classical and was seen as the route into university and professional training. The *Gymnasium* had a near monopoly of access to the universities for its graduates throughout the century. It was not until 1900 that the other secondary schools were given ostensibly equal access to higher education and this did not really become a reality until the Weimar period. The other secondary institutions were much less prestigious and attracted more of the industrial and commercial middle strata. Whereas only 25 per cent of *Gymnasium* pupils came from industrial or commercial families, these represented the largest single group in the less prestigious *Realgymnasien* and *Oberrealschulen*: 35 per cent and 40 per cent, respectively. Equally, the artisanal contingent in the *Oberrealschulen* was more than double the proportion for the *Gymnasien*. German secondary education was thus highly segmented and hierarchical. As Ringer notes, it represented a status ladder where the apex was dominated by the traditional service class comprising the old professions and the top civil servants. The newer, rising middle-class groups tended to be segregated in discrete institutions and thus there was little of the social integration that characterized the French secondary system. The French system was certainly more uniformly 'bourgeois' but the German system was not so much more 'progressive', as Ringer contends, but rather more traditional.[36]

The reasons for these differences lay in the historical interrelations between education and the formation of the class structure in the two countries. French secondary education, as we shall see, emerged through the post-revolutionary period as an important bastion of bourgeois power. It represented one of those gains of the Revolution which the bourgeoisie was determined to retain since its relatively meritocratic structure was one of the means by which the bourgeois could maintain social ascendance in the face of threats from above and below. One consequence of this was that the *lycée* and *collège* became normatively middle-class institutions, welding together socially disparate middle strata in a common bourgeois culture. Prussian post-elementary education by contrast exhibited less of this incipient democratization. It was not so much the creation of an ascendant bourgeois culture but the child of a landowner state which by necessity had to make room for a growing but subordinate bourgeoisie. The structure of Prussian post-elementary education was consequently more hierarchical and more socially segmented.

Both in its ideological ambience and in its structure, Prussian education thus represented the hegemony of a dominant Junker class but one that was determined to modernize even if this meant giving greater power to the bourgeoisie. Unlike the English landed classes, who could remain aloof from the industrial process in the safe knowledge that the class 'below them' would take care of it, the Prussian Junkers had to pioneer it themselves. Consequently there arose the strange spectacle of an education system solidly dominated by the traditional class but embodying many of the needs of the new industrial order which it was assiduously trying to promote. A more autocratic regime by far than in England produced, paradoxically, as David Landes has noted, a 'more open' and modernized structure through its education, whereas the latter allowed education to remain stagnant and closed in the very moment of its political democratization.[37]

The character of the Junker hegemony which thus imprinted its forms on Prussian education is well illustrated by a passage in Gramsci's work, where he describes the relative class locations of the intellectuals in different societies. Industrial development in Prussia, he writes,

> took place within a feudal integument that persisted up to November 1918, and the Junkers preserved a politico-intellectual supremacy considerably greater even than that of the corresponding group in England. They were the traditional intellectuals of the German industrialists, but retained special privileges and a strong consciousness of being an independent social group, based on the fact that they held considerable economic power over the land, which was more 'productive' than in England. The Prussian Junkers resemble a priestly-military caste, with a virtual monopoly of directive-organizational functions in political society... Furthermore, unlike the English landowning aristocracy, the Junkers constituted the officer class of a large standing army, which gave them the solid organizational cadres favoring the preservation of an esprit de corps and of their political monopoly.[38]

We can see from this passage how the military and bureaucratic origins of state formation in Prussia continued to characterize the forms of Junker hegemony in the nineteenth century and how this was reflected in the education system. Conceived as a tool of bureaucratic and military advance in the eighteenth century, state education in Prussia was finally consolidated in the following century during the course of, and as part of, that 'revolution from above' by which the Junker state propelled a scarcely 'defeudalized' social formation into capitalist industrialization. The distinctive features of Prussian schooling – its dynamic, state-impelled development, its bureaucratic efficiency, its hierarchy and segmentation, its technological advance and, above all, its authoritarian ethos – thus emanated from the specific historical forms of state formation in that country and exemplified the precise forms of class domination as they evolved throughout the period in question.

Education and absolutism in France

A national education system in France was first conceived by the *philosophes* of the eighteenth-century Enlightenment and later created by Napoleon during the Empire. In contrast with Prussia and Austria, it was thus essentially the creation of a post-revolutionary period of capitalist state formation. However, as de Tocqueville observed, many of the institutions of the nineteenth-century French state owed their character to the legacy of the centralized royal bureaucracies which preceded them, and education was no exception. Although the elementary and secondary education of the *Ancien Régime* was entirely dominated by the Church and religious orders, and was yet to be subject to any effective state control, the state had already demonstrated its interest in education through constant interventions in technical and vocational training. What is more, detailed plans for a national education system had already been drawn up by several leading French philosophers and it was these to which Napoleon referred when he did finally lay the basis of such a system. Thus, whilst French absolutism cannot be credited with laying the foundations of national education, as in Prussia, it certainly did establish certain principles which re-emerged in a transmuted form to influence later developments. The most important of these, of course, was the principle of administrative centralization, of which the Napoleonic education system was to be a pre-eminent example.

The development of a centralized state apparatus in France occurred in the seventeenth century, notably through the efforts of Sully, Richelieu and Colbert, its great administrative architects, and under the royal aegis of Louis XIV, the most powerful of absolutist monarchs. Richelieu, the effective ruler of France for many years, first created a rationalized central state apparatus capable of sustaining direct royal control throughout France. The main instruments of central authority in the localities became the *intendants*, a corps of non-hereditary officers who were to become progressively more powerful and authoritarian in their practices. These were the object of widespread popular revolt during the crises of the *Fronde*, but this was successfully stamped out by Richelieu's successor, Mazarin, in 1653, and the state emerged strengthened to usher in the period of fully consolidated absolutism under the new king. Louis XIV presided personally over a highly centralized state apparatus, directed from the *Conseil d' en Haut*, the supreme executive body of the state, and the *Conseil des Dépêches*, which dealt with provincial and domestic affairs. France was now divided into 32 *généralités* controlled by the tentacular network of *intendants*, which covered the entire realm. The army increased from 30 000 to 300 000 by the end of the reign and a permanent police force was created in Paris, which was later extended throughout France.[39] Meanwhile the aristocracy were encouraged to remove themselves from their provincial estates and to reside at court in Versailles. They thus demonstrated their loyalty to the Crown and effectively denuded themselves of any important role in the structure of administration and control in the localities, whereby they so clearly distinguished themselves from the English gentry.

This was the state which was to survive without major modifications until the Revolution. It represented an extreme form of administrative centralization without countervailing local powers, such as the English gentry maintained in the county shires. Its anatomy has been vividly portrayed in *The Ancien Régime and the French Revolution*, where de Tocqueville sought to show how the forms of the nineteenth-century French state were derived from the institutions of the old order. These latter were subject to such extreme centralization that even the most trivial of local decisions depended on central authority. Such was the control of the state over even the most minute of local details that, according to de Tocqueville, it could take over a year to get permission to repair a church steeple or the priest's house. Summarizing the nature of the old regime he wrote:

> We find a single central power located at the heart of the kingdom and controlling public administration throughout the country; a single minister of state in charge of almost all internal affairs of the country; in each province a single representative of government supervising every detail of the administration; no secondary administrative bodies authorised to take action on their own initiative; and, finally, 'exceptional courts' for the trial of cases involving the administration or any of its officers.[40]

The significance of this pre-revolutionary administrative centralization for the future development of education was immense, and some of its effects were already being felt. As in Prussia and Austria, the French state was well placed to intervene in education and, inasmuch as this would promote its policies, it frequently did. However, as we have already noted, the nature of state intervention in French education during the seventeenth and eighteenth centuries varied somewhat from the typical pattern of eastern absolutisms, such as Prussia and Austria. Like them the absolutist state in France frequently intervened in education through patronage and decree, and occasionally through creating its own institutions, and its efforts were inspired by similar military and mercantilist goals. However, there were significant differences also. Firstly, it is reasonably clear that in France the primary locus of state interest in post-elementary education was with the technical and vocational schools rather than with the colleges themselves. Richelieu and Colbert were well known for their opposition to the expansion of the Jesuit colleges, which they believed diverted energies away from the important economic and military affairs of the nation, and produced a surplus of non-productive classical scholars.[41] What concerned the leading ministers of the seventeenth century more was the development of adequate technical and military training which would support the efforts of the state in the development of commerce and manufactures, in the development of public works and in the pursuit of military conquests. Secondly, whereas in Prussia and Austria there were considerable royal efforts to improve popular education in elementary schools, in France, apart from a totally nominal school attendance decree in 1698, there appears to have been little intervention in this area by the state prior to the Revolution.

Part of the explanation for these differences lay, as has been suggested, in the different structures of the respective absolutisms. France was relatively early to form itself into a unified nation. The movement towards the national unification had been initiated by the Capetian monarchs of the fourteenth century. Although the Hundred Years War, the persistence of regional particularisms and the dynastic rivalries that followed the religious wars were to delay the consolidation of the centralized royal state until the seventeenth century, by 1500, according to Seton-Watson, 'the essential steps had been taken towards the creation of the French state and the French nation'. In 1539, Francis I had made French the sole official language, symbolizing the relative homogeneity of the French nation. The French were thus, in Seton-Watson's words, 'the first European people to be formed into a nation and French governments were the pioneers of the European form of the centralized administration and uniform national culture'.[42] Although it would be hard to offer conclusive proof of the point, it may well have been that this relative national homogeneity, as compared, for instance, with the great territorial and ethnic instability of German dynastic realms, may have reduced the absolute importance of national integration through popular education which so preoccupied Prussian and Austrian monarchs. Furthermore, the social structure of the absolutist state as it emerged in the seventeenth century was significantly different from that of eastern absolutisms. Despite the intensity of noble exploitation of the French peasantry, the latter gained a relative independence quite early. Serfdom had long been abolished, and in the absence of widespread enclosure and with the frequent splitting-up of noble estates, there was a large class of peasant cultivators both large and small. These still suffered under crippling tax burdens and forced military service, and, despite the near extinction of the *corvée*, still had to perform compulsory labours for the state, as in the construction and maintenance of roads. However, they had a relative degree of personal freedom compared with other European peasantries and their situation bore no comparison with the abject subservience of the Prussian serf. Peasant uprisings were a frequent occurrence in the seventeenth and eighteenth centuries.[43] Under such conditions a Frederickan style imposition of education on the peasantry was probably not only less of a priority than in Prussia; it would no doubt also have proved very difficult to sustain. When the drive towards mass education was undertaken during the July Monarchy, there was, even then, considerable peasant opposition to it and this did not abate until the peasantry slowly began to recognize the benefits of education in enhanced social mobility.[44]

The other distinctive characteristic of French education in the period of absolutism was the marked development of technical and vocational provision compared with the relative stagnation in the colleges and universities. This can also be related to the distinctive structures of the French state and, in particular, to the nature of the bureaucracy which, by the seventeenth century, had already reached an advanced state of sclerosis.[45] This was due largely to the royal practice of selling offices, institutionalized by the *Paulette* of 1604, which rendered such offices inheritable subject to annual payments. Colbert and several ministers after him later tried to abandon the practice, but without success, since royal revenues were highly dependent on this source of income. The sale of offices had become the price of royal independence from the aristocracy and of any effective control by a parliament.[46] However, the price was considerable. As a result, writes de Toqueville, the bureaucracy had become

> so intricate and so inefficient that it had to be left running idle, so to speak, while alongside it was set up another instrument of government, at once simpler and easier to manipulate, which in practice carried out the functions only nominally performed by the hoards of office holders who had bought their way into the bureaucracy.[47]

Unlike the highly efficient Prussian bureaucracy, the French one thus stagnated and was subject to no similar pressure towards efficiency. It was not until the Revolution swept away the old feudal privileges that the bureaucracy was reformed and set on a more meritocratic basis. This had important consequences for secondary education. Whereas in Prussia this had become an important avenue for the recruitment of efficient young bureaucrats, thus stimulating secondary reforms, in France, where offices were sold, no such close equation existed and the state consequently had less interest in it. It was not until after the Revolution when the civil service began to recruit on a competitive basis that Napoleon was prompted to set up the *lycées* to act as an efficient incubator for young officials.

The advancement of military and economic efficiency, on the other hand, was close to the hearts of ministers, and the development of effective vocational training was recognized to be crucial to these ends. French agriculture and industry had not developed on any scale parallel to that in England, due partly to the frequent neglect of their estates by the nobility and partly to the preference of the bourgeoisie for earning safe incomes from official sinecures rather than from enterprise. Ministers such as Richelieu and Colbert were determined to set this right, which they attempted to do through constant state interventions. The general principles of mercantilism have already been discussed inasmuch, at least, as they related to the promotion of national strength through state intervention in industry and trade. What should be noted in addition is that successive ministers directly sponsored industry and coupled this with the promotion of training. During the seventeenth century, several state industries were set up. Others received state patronage, were granted privileges and subsidies, and received protection from the competition of the guilds. A prime example of this was the great industrial centre, the Gobelins, which Colbert reorganized under state control as an exemplary centre for the production of furniture, tapestries, silks and fabrics.

These ventures inevitably stimulated the development of technical skills and, according to Frederick Artz, historian of French technical education, they prompted a 'great technical revival' in France.[48] They were also accompanied by the creation of a number of state training establishments. Richelieu founded a trade school for war orphans at Langres, which provided instruction in maths, construction theory and practical training in cloth- and shoe-making. In 1657 another trade school was started at Saint-Germain-des-Prés. The Government also established academies for the teaching of art and design and architecture, such as the Académie Royale de Peinture (1648), the École de Rome (1665) and the Académie Royale d'Architecture (1671). In 1688 another art school was established at Bordeaux, as a result of Colbert's efforts, and this was copied by many municipal authorities in the next century.[49]

The period also saw the inauguration of a number of military academies sponsored again by the state. Richelieu had been a great advocate of military and trade schools. 'Letters and arms', he wrote, 'are both equally required for the establishment and maintenance of great empires, the former regulating and civilizing within the state, the latter extending and protecting it.'[50] It was he who set up the first military academy in France and by 1684 there were 4275 *cadets-gentilhommes*. In 1682 a state school for navigation was set up, which was useful for both peaceful and wartime maritime needs. These early ventures in vocational training were all a reflection of the priorities of the seventeenth-century state. Artz rightly emphasizes this point in his summary of developments during this period:

> Throughout the seventeenth century the efforts to initiate and reform technical education were based on the theories of mercantilism. To make the state strong in a military and naval way, to improve the quality and output of manufactures so that they would command both domestic and

foreign markets were the steady aims of statesmen. Unless this is grasped, the efforts to improve technical education cannot be understood.[51]

The following century saw a growth of economic activity. Textile, iron, steel and coal production made considerable advances, trade quadrupled between 1720 and 1780, and total output increased by about 60 per cent.[52] At the same time, military commitments continued so that by the end of the *Ancien Régime* over half of the state finances were devoted to them. Official state policies continued to favour the sponsorship of military and vocational training.

The century saw the rise of the higher elementary schools designed to meet the need for engineers in the army and navy, and in the state construction projects. In 1716 the Government of the Duc d'Orléans initiated the Corps des Ponts et Chaussées to supervise state construction schemes. The École des Ponts et Chaussées derived from this, providing an education in architecture, maths, physics and chemistry. An early example of the close relation between technical education and government service, and probably the finest civil engineering school in Europe, this school became, during the Revolution, one of the more advanced technical schools (*écoles d' application*) to which students went after completing the course at the École Polytechnique.[53] In 1749 the famous École du Corps Royal du Génie was established at Mézièrs, providing two-year courses in civil engineering and also establishing an international reputation.[54] Shortly before the Revolution the Government also authorized a school of mining, later to become the École des Mines, which offered scholarships for three-year courses in chemistry, mineralogy, metals, physics, hydraulics and mine ventilation.[55] The century also saw an increasing development of the trades schools first established by Richelieu and Colbert. Schools of drawing were set up by the municipalities in Nancy (1702), Toulouse (1726), Bordeaux (1744), Marseilles (1753), Lille (1755), Lyon (1756) and Rheims (1757).[56] In 1767 the École Royale Gratuite de Dessin was established by the Government in Paris, and in 1781 a school of commerce was opened at Mulhouse. Probably the most famous of the trade schools was the one established privately by the Duc de la Rochefoucauld-Liancourt in 1780 for orphans of former soldiers, which later became the celebrated École des Arts et Métiers.[57]

The other main focus of state activity in education was on the provision of military and naval training. France had long maintained a highly developed interest in military science, and improvements made during the century were an important factor in the military successes of the revolutionary and imperial armies. In 1751, Louis XV, who was keen to strengthen the army after its defeats at the hands of the British and the Austrians, issued an edict ordering the foundation of the École Royale Militaire, which was duly opened at Chateau de Vincennes in 1753 and ready to cater for 500 students aged 8–13. Efficient artillery schools existed already at Metz, Strasbourg,

Perpignon and Grenoble, and in 1764 new cavalry schools started in Metz, Dovai, Angers and Besançon.[58] A number of initiatives were also made in naval training during this period. The École de Marine opened at Le Havre in 1773, offering a four-year course to 50 paying students. Naval colleges were also created at Vannes and Alais, offering more elementary courses. These lasted for six years, four of which were spent on board ships. Teachers were appointed by the state, and courses included maths, geometry, mechanics, physics, hydrography and navigation. This was the best system of naval education that the *Ancien Régime* devised but it did not survive the Revolution.[59]

These initiatives in technical and vocational training, sponsored by the absolutist state throughout the seventeenth and eighteenth centuries and designed to further the military and mercantilist objectives of the state, represented the most significant developments of the period in terms of the anticipation of later forms of state education. They also put France ahead of any other nation in this field at the time. According to Artz,

> schools like the Écoles des Ponts et Chaussées and the École du Genie stood first in Europe. In the higher technical school of the eighteenth century is prefigured most of the accomplishments of the nineteenth and twentieth centuries in advanced technical education.[60]

Blueprints for national education

Thus far the contribution of the absolutist state towards the development of education in France consisted only of strategic interventions in specific areas, where these were seen to be of particular national significance. There was as yet no conception of a full national education system under state control. However, during the pre-revolutionary period this was to change. With the rapid ferment of Enlightenment thought, the increasing strength of the bourgeoisie, and the conversion of the latter and sections of the nobility to novel and radical ideas, a new political climate was emerging which was favourable to educational innovation. This period was to produce, within a short space of time, an extraordinary renaissance of educational thought in France, and in the process the conceptual basis for national education was first elaborated.

Rousseau's *Emile* was published in 1762 and became probably the most popular education treatise of all time. It described in idealized terms the rational education of a young gentleman learning from life under the wise protection of his mentor and guide. Romantically counterposing a 'natural' intellectual development to institutionalized learning, Rousseau's novel articulated popular antipathy to the arid scholastic teaching of the Jesuit school. In the same year the Jesuits were expelled from teaching by the increasingly anti-clerical *parlements*, and replaced by the more gallican

Oratorian schools with their new emphasis on science and the vernacular literature. The *parlements* were active in proposing new schemes for secular education. La Chalotais' famous 'Essay on National Education' came out the following year and this, coupled with the detailed blueprints for reform devised by luminaries such as Rolland and Diderot, laid out the basic principles of a state education on which Napoleon was to draw when he set up the *Université* after the Revolution.

The educational plans of La Chalotais and Diderot can be seen both as a culmination of the movement towards state centralization, which we have already discussed, and as an embodiment of new revolutionary principles. In a sense they represent the crossover of two historical times where the statism of the absolutist period is redeployed to serve the ends of the future bourgeois revolution. La Chalotais' prescriptions are unashamedly étatist in conception. 'I claim for the nation', he writes,

> an education which depends upon nothing but the state, because it belongs to it in essence; because the nation has an inalienable and imprescriptible right to educate its members; because in the end the children of the state must be brought up by members of the state.[61]

Rolland's proposals embodied the same principles. In his 1768 report on national education, which he drafted as president of the *Parlement* of Paris, he recommended a scheme for a national hierarchy of schools from a central university down to local primary schools. He sought 'to turn Paris into the centre and fountainhead of public education' and in this well expressed the dominance that Paris had attained in French national life through centuries of absolutist centralization of power.[62]

The plans of the *philosophes* also represented a radical break with the past and the centralized state was to be the instrument whereby education could shake off its feudal garments. They were born out of the growing anti-clerical movement which had infected the bourgeoisie and sections of the nobility alike, and their most immediate purpose was to challenge and replace the Church's domination of schooling. By giving control of education to the state, narrow clerical restraints could be removed and education could begin to serve the general interests of the nation. Education would become secular, rationalist and designed on a meritocratic basis so that it could most effectively supply the nation with the skills that it required. The purpose of schooling, said Rolland, was to 'successfully fill the different occupations of the state'.[63] With the growing ambitions of the bourgeoisie, education would increasingly become the competitive proving ground of ability and the mediator of occupational selection. The competitive examination was to symbolize this, and for Diderot 'all posts in an empire, including the most important, [should] be filled by competitive examination'.[64]

This secular meritocracy was, of course, for the middle class only. The parliamentarians maintained a rigid and elitist dualism whereby the middle class would be enlightened through rational education to give leadership to the masses, whereas the latter would continue to receive a religious instruction which should not seek to raise them above their station. 'The goal of society'. wrote La Chalotais, 'requires that the knowledge of the people should not go beyond their occupations. Any man who looks beyond his dismal trade will never practice it with courage and patience.'[65] Other 'enlightened' *philosophes* agreed. Rousseau, for all his republican leanings, was no supporter of egalitarian education. 'The poor have no need of education,' he wrote in *Emile*, 'it is shaped by their situation. They can have no other.' Voltaire, who was a great admirer of Frederick the Great's educational reforms, was of the same mind. Commenting on the exclusion of the common people from the college, he wrote to La Chalotais: 'I thank you for proscribing studies for the peasantry.'[66] Napoleon was to return to this same notion of limited meritocracy and selective secularism 40 years later.

The educational blueprints of the eighteenth-century philosophers thus represent both the high water mark of educational thought in the period of absolutism and the prefigurement of republican education as it was to become. The étatist and centralizing conceptions of the *philosophes* were in a sense quite compatible with the structures of the absolutist state and, as we have seen in the case of Prussia, the absolutist state was quite capable of conceiving a form of national education. France had already gone some way towards this, although not as far as Prussia or Austria. The expulsion of the Jesuits had been a clear indication that the state was quite prepared to take over educational control from the Church, and indeed the state had already intervened considerably in the development of technical and vocational schools. Furthermore, as Bourdieu and Passeron have pointed out, two of the more 'meritocratic' features of the Napoleonic *Université*, the competitive state examination for secondary teachers known as the *aggrégation* and the prize competition between Parisian *lycées*, the *Concours Général*, both originated during the *Ancien Régime* (1766 and 1747, respectively).[67] As de Tocqueville remarked, 'there had existed under the old regime a host of institutions which had quite a "modern" air', and this was true of education as much as other areas.[68]

However, the national education system was in practice not constructed during this period and whilst its future forms were already taking shape in the minds of progressive men and women, it took the Revolution to provide the material conditions for their implementation. National education, in France at least, can hardly be conceded to the absolutist state. The modern ideas of the *philosophes*, with their secular rationalism, their concern for liberty, their defence of an elitist meritocracy and their erastian conception of the state, were essentially the voice of the vanguard of a rising and increasingly anti-clerical bourgeoisie; a class which was soon to overthrow the *Ancien Régime* if not quite all of its works.

Education and the French Revolution

The outbreak of revolution in France marked a new era of state formation in Europe and the development of education was inevitably closely interwoven with this process. Its most immediate achievement was the destruction of the feudal basis of the *Ancien Régime* and this, in paving the way for the development of those bourgeois relations that were emerging in the earlier period, permitted the realization of the educational plans of the enlightenment philosophers. It culminated in the centralized and elitist bourgeois state of the Napoleonic Empire and it was in this context that the apparatus of national education could first emerge with the creation of the Napoleonic *Université*. However, it is important to consider the Revolution not merely as a bridge which created the material conditions for the fulfilment of the educational plans of the earlier period but also as a revolutionary process which, in its most radical phases, strayed far beyond the bounds intended by its leading bourgeois class. During these periods, new educational ideas were adopted which were way in advance of the blueprints of the eighteenth-century *philosophes* and, although few of these were to survive the *Consulate*, they left an important legacy which would influence education in later periods. We must consider, therefore, not only the Revolution's immediate outcome and the educational arrangements it ushered in under Napoleon, but also the revolutionary process itself and what the various revolutionary assemblies hoped, but ultimately failed, to accomplish.

The Revolution began with an offensive by sections of the nobility, following a summer of peasant uprisings. It became progressively more radical at each successive stage, reflecting the changing balance of forces between bourgeois and popular elements, until with Robespierre, who carried it far beyond its bourgeois limits, it finally succumbed to its own class contradictions. Each new assembly thus owed its power to new class alignments and expressed a conception of the world in accordance with these. Education could hardly be a major priority during these turbulent periods but nevertheless numerous educational plans were put forward and these reflected the political conceptions of each successive assembly to which they were submitted. Education thus became an important site of ideological struggle. Intense debates over alternative proposals, as with a barium meal, revealed the course of the Revolution itself.

The early years of the Revolution were important more for the dismantling of the existing educational structure than for the development of alternative forms. The main concern of the Constituent Assembly (1789–91) was the abolition of the powers and privileges held by the Church and nobility during the *Ancien Régime*, and so in sweeping away the old feudal structures it also undercut the material basis of the old education system. The elimination of tithes and the *octrois* (1789), which was the principal source of finance for community and church schools, and the nationalization of church properties destroyed many existing schools. The civil constitution of the clergy in 1790 reduced the number of clergymen available to teach and dealt a further blow to church schooling. This process of abolition culminated in the disestablishment of all religious corporations and schools, and the suppression of the universities during the following three years.[69]

Despite the largely destructive work of the early assemblies, a number of educational plans were also produced. The Constituent Assembly acknowledged the importance of public education. It placed amongst the fundamental provisions guaranteed by the constitution 'public education for all citizens, which should be free in respect of that teaching which is indispensible for all'.[70] However, their commitment to these things remained somewhat notional. The political outlook of the Constituent Assembly reflected the ideals of the property-owning liberal bourgeoisie. In their eyes the Revolution was for legal equality and political rights, but should extend neither to the abolition of private property nor to the creation of social equality. Thus the early educational plans of Mirabeau and Talleyrand, submitted to but never debated by the Assembly, embodied the abstract principle of universal rights to education but not the desire to see everyone educated equally. The reports called for universal and free state education but only along the elitist lines already marked out by the parliamentarians. For the popular masses it would mean only a limited elementary instruction. For girls it would be no more than a preparation for domestic roles. Nothing in fact came of the plans and the Assembly did little more for education than delay the abolition of the colleges by delaying the sale of their lands and granting them state subsidies.

The Legislative Assembly (1791–2) seemed concerned to produce something more concrete and set up a Committee of Public Instruction. This produced the plan on the 'General Organization of Public Instruction', which was read to the Assembly by the Girondin, Condorcet, on 21 April 1792. This proposal expressed the great optimism of the Revolution in its belief in the power of education to reshape society and popular consciousness, and represented the first major break with pre-revolutionary educational ideologies. Unlike the parliamentarians, Condorcet considered education to be a right and a legitimate source of popular enlightenment and freedom. Strongly condemning its use by the state as a tool of social control, he advocated a fully secular system of education under popular democratic control, with elected teachers and the state acting as paymaster alone. Education should embody the greatest possible freedom of individual thought, and therefore its role in furthering republican ideas should be balanced by a commitment to individual development. The ideal of education was

> to afford to all members of the human race the means of providing for their needs, of serving their welfare, of recognising and exercising their rights, of understanding and fulfilling their duties.

Education, Condorcet proclaimed, should

> assure for everyone the opportunity of perfecting their skills and rendering themselves capable of the social duties to which they had a right to be called; to develop to the utmost the talents with which nature has endowed them, and in so doing to establish among all citizens a true equality and thus to make political equality realised by the law.[71]

This envisioned equilibrium between the rights of the state and individual freedoms reflected the liberal and decentralizing spirit of the Assembly, and was a far cry from the authoritarian statism of the parliamentarians and the early educational plans of La Chalotais and Diderot. So too was the emphasis on education as a vehicle for social equality. For Condorcet the commitment to egalitarian principles was axiomatic and intimately linked with the quest for freedom. 'Inequality of instruction', he wrote, 'is one of the main sources of tyranny', and the purpose of education is to 'bring [classes] closer together by instruction.'[72] Nevertheless, Condorcet's plans inevitably stopped short of a fully egalitarian system. Primary education was to be universal and free, and run according to egalitarian principles; but secondary education was to remain highly selective, offering only a limited meritocracy. Secondary schools, offering a general and technical education, would be largely for the middle class, whilst the *lycées*, with a broad modern humanities curriculum, would be reserved for a tiny elite.

With the fall of the Legislative Assembly and the advent of the period of revolutionary government, the importance of education to the revolutionary process became more clearly articulated. The years of the Montagnard Convention (1793) and the subsequent Jacobin dictatorship (1793–4) represented the furthest point of the Revolution, where the aims of the liberal bourgeoisie were increasingly stretched by the egalitarian demands of the popular forces. For the Jacobins the Revolution was not only for political equality and civil rights but also for social equality and the elimination of differences in wealth. Political and social equality were indivisible. Unable to jettison entirely the defence of property, the Jacobins were forced at least to heed the demands of the popular masses for 'an equality of consumption' and, with the Law of the Maximum, the state took over central control of the economy. Seeking to hold together the alliance between the middling bourgeoisie, the artisanal Parisian *Sans Culottes* and the peasant masses, the

Jacobins espoused an egalitarian democracy based on universal suffrage and the multiplication of small independent producers. Their policies on education reflected this desire to achieve not only civil liberties but also a measure of social equality, and with the establishment of a more directive central apparatus they showed their willingness to achieve this by more deliberate and prescriptive means. They sought in education a universal system that would maximize social levelling and promote to the fullest republican ideals.

The Montagnard Convention placed education unequivocally amongst the rights of man. 'Education is the requirement of us all', maintained article 22 of the Declaration of Rights: 'Society must favour with all its might the progress of public reason, and must place instruction within the grasp of all citizens.'[73] This was more than a declaration of principle. The Convention and the people were looking for positive measures. Condorcet's plans came under increasing attack. According to Sieyès, a member of the Committee for Public Instruction, Condorcet's aristocratic origins had led him to take a 'universalist and olympian' view, mistaking his war against prejudice for the struggle of the popular classes.[74] What was now required was a more deliberate and radical attempt to encourage social equality through education. The most thoroughgoing expression of this was probably Lepelletier's plan, read to the Convention by Robespierre in July 1793. This called for gratuitous and obligatory elementary education in common state boarding schools to be known as *Maisons d'Egalités*. In support of his plan Lepelletier said:

> I ask you to decree that between the ages of 5 and 12 for boys and until 11 for girls, all children without distinction be brought up in common at the expense of the state and that all, in the sacred name of equality, will receive the same uniform, food, instruction and care.[75]

The schools would teach the three Rs, practical skills and republican principles, thus combining a notion of practical service to the Revolution with Robespierre's idea of creating a 'new type' of republican man. The proposal was accepted, although it was not until December that a decree on primary schools sanctioned a system of free, compulsory instruction under state supervision. This was to be decentralized in accordance with popular demands.[76] However, due to the pressures of the war and to the great disappointment of the Sans-Culottes, it was never fully implemented.

Lepelletier's plan represented the educational ideals of the Revolution at its furthest stretch, shortly before the over-reaching Robespierre finally fell. With the ensuing Thermidorean reaction, the accent in educational planning began to shift back to the priorities of the bourgeoisie. Gradually the principles of free and compulsory schooling were abandoned. The decree of November 1794 called for the institution of primary schools at the rate of one school per 1 000 inhabitants. Teachers were to be appointed by a committee of the district administration and paid for by the state. However, education was not put on a compulsory and gratuitous basis and this signalled a retreat from the earlier principles. The primary concern of the Thermidorean bourgeoisie lay in secondary and higher education, and with the training of the cadres of the new society and the new state.

On Lakanal's instigation the new *écoles centrales* were set up in each department to represent a model of a modern secondary education. Pupils between 12 and 14 were to be taught modern languages, natural history and design; pupils aged 14–16 would learn maths, physics and chemistry; and 16–18 year olds, grammar, belle-lettres, history and legislation. The lack of free provision reflected the conservative reaction, but the syllabus and methods were fully in keeping with the ideological movement of the Enlightenment and the provision of 25 per cent scholarship places suggested that the meritocratic idea was not wholly dead.[77]

The Thermidoreans also put their minds to developing new institutions of higher education, designed to supply the state with its top functionaries. In September 1794 the Convention set up the Central School for Public Works, later to become the École Polytechnique. Medical schools were also set up in Paris, Montpellier and Strasbourg. However, their crowning achievement was the 1795 *Loi Daunou*, which consolidated these new developments in what was the major piece of educational legislation during the revolutionary period. This maintained the commitment to secular state control and a curriculum based on a broad scientific humanism, which were to be the hallmarks of republican education thereafter, but it abandoned the notion of free or compulsory education. The law included the intention to create primary schools in each canton and a central school for every 300 000 citizens. Although it was not fully implemented, 87 Central schools were created and these had a lasting influence on secondary education. Whilst hastily abolished by Napoleon in 1802, they left an important precedent for a modern scientific schooling. As Frederick Artz has said,

> In spite of their disappearance, the *écoles centrales* represent the most interesting experiment in secondary education in France between the foundation of the Jesuit schools in the seventeenth century and the opening of the modern *lycées* in the second half of the nineteenth century. The modern *lycée*, moreover, derived many of its methods from those of the *écoles centrales*.[78]

With the Directory (1795–9) came the restoration of the liberal, bourgeois state. Economic freedoms were re-established, a property franchise excluded the masses from political power and the central powers of the state continued to be augmented despite the maintenance of limited municipal administrative autonomy. The drift away from revolutionary egalitarian principles in education continued. Whilst elite education was conscientiously promoted, primary education was neglected and, in the absence of state funds for the payment of teachers and the establishment of new primary schools, religiously oriented teaching sprang up, though it was subject to municipal supervision.[79] The major achievement of the Directory lay in the development of special schools which were designed to produce trained recruits for manufacturing and for the service of the state. Numerous special schools were established between 1793 and 1803 catering for such diverse occupations as soldiers, sailors, midwives, pharmacists, veterinarians, teachers, musicians, miners, agriculturalists and craftsmen. The most famous of these was the École Polytechnique opened at Palais Bourbon in 1795. The school took 360 students of 16–20 years, selected by competitive examination in 22 cities. It provided a rigorous three-year course in a wide curriculum of applied science and engineering. With such intellectual eminences as Laplace, Monge, Hatchette, Bertholet and Chaptal on its staff, it formed probably the most distinguished scientific faculty in the world, and provides a clear example of the Revolution's contribution to the development of science. Standards were fiercely competitive and graduates had a virtual monopoly on future state employment. By 1806, 1 664 students had been admitted and about 1 000 of these held state positions, including 194 in military engineering, 29 in the department of mines, 194 in the servicing of bridges and roads, 14 in civil administration and 312 in the artillery. A considerable number also entered commerce and manufactures. The Revolution also founded a number of specialized *écoles d' application*, such as the École des Mines (1783) and the École de Mars (1794).[80] Together they represented a fine example of the way in which education could be put into the service of the state and how subsequently it came to mediate the relations between substantial sections of the middle class and their future class positions. They also left a significant legacy which would be invaluable to Napoleon's Empire. There were nowhere in the world, according to Artz, 'even in the disastrous years of 1814 and 1815, better schools offering training for industry, for the army and navy, and for the designing and constructing of public works, than those in France'.[81]

The Revolution clearly never achieved all of its objectives in education. However, its importance can be in no doubt. During a period in which successive regimes attempted and substantially achieved a comprehensive restructuring of the entire French state and the social relations on which it was based, the importance of mass education had been unequivocally established. Education was now acknowledged to be an indispensible instrument for forging national unity, for supplying the state with its trained cadres and for raising popular consciousness in line with ideologies of the new classes. The Jacobins, unique in their passion for recasting social institutions according to the pure logic of their democratic and republican ideals, and masters of the art of universalizing their beliefs to inspire revolutionary alliances between disparate classes, recognized mass education for what it was: the

means *par excellence* for winning popular hegemony. The concrete achievement of the Revolution in the field of education thus lay in four areas.
It consolidated the principle of secular, state-controlled education whose
object was the service of the state and the fostering of a national and republican ideology; it continued and reinforced the tradition of technical and
vocational training through state institutions; it developed a model, in the
Central schools, of a modern meritocratic secondary school; and, finally, it
established an ideology, during the life of the Convention, of education as a
right and education as a vehicle of social equalization. Not all of this was to
survive the *Consulate*, but its ideological legacy was to continue to influence
education throughout the nineteenth century.

Napoleon and national education

If the idea of national education was thus first conceived in France by the
enlightened *philosophes* of the *Ancien Régime* and subsequently developed in
new ways by the Revolution, it was not until the period of the Consulate
and the Empire (1799–1814) that the basis of a national education system
was really established. It was Napoleon who first laid down a lasting legal and
administrative framework for national education with the foundation of the
Université and the legal powers that went with it. In order to understand the
distinctive form and purpose of Napoleon's creation, we must first examine
the nature of the bourgeois state that the Revolution had brought into being.

Despite the unrealized aspirations of the Jacobins, the Revolution had
made a decisive historical contribution towards the creation of a unified
bourgeois state in France and thus the transition to capitalist social relations.
The early years of the Revolution had swept away the entire structure of the
Ancien Régime, removing the legal foundations of aristocratic power and with
them all the autonomies, local privileges and provincial particularisms that
characterized the old order. The suppression of feudal rights, the elimination of tithes and the sale of national (ecclesiastical) lands had stripped the
aristocracy and the Church of much of their privilege and power. The abolition of the Three Estates and the elimination of primogeniture, hereditary
nobility and venal offices meant that the clergy and the nobility had disappeared as orders. The Declaration of Rights in 1789 made all eligible to civil
posts and guaranteed the protection of natural rights for all. By the end of
the Constituent Assembly, civil, if not social, equality had been proclaimed.

The Revolution thus permanently transformed the relationships between
social classes in France. The suppression of seigneurial powers and the confis-
cation of émigre lands permanently weakened the aristocracy and, although
many were to re-emerge chastened but still powerful under Napoleon, this
could only be on the basis of new forms of wealth. The peasantry were also
permanently transformed. The abolition of the tithe and feudal rights over
property and the introduction of fiscal equality had mainly benefited the

landowning peasants, enlarging their share of national land and allowing the future development of many into capitalist farmers and *petit-bourgeois* office holders. The smaller peasants had benefited from the disappearance of feudal rights over persons but not to any great extent from the splitting-up of émigre estates and church lands, and many were to be gradually proletarianized in the coming years. The old bourgeoisie – that is, those who had been integrated into the privileged structures of the old regime – shared the fate of the aristocracy and many, particularly the old office-holders, were ruined. However, a new bourgeoisie was emerging which was more vigorous than before. In the following years, speculation, the sale of national lands, equipping and provisioning armies, and exploiting conquered territories all gave businessmen fresh opportunities for acquiring wealth and greatly concentrated bourgeois fortunes. The development of capitalism was still, of course, slow. Commercial capital still predominated and only a few large manufacturing concerns existed, mainly in textiles. However, commercial and financial capital was expanding fast, continually swelled by lucrative state contracts, and it was the buoyancy of these financial family fortunes which would provide the impetus for the industrial enterprises of the capitalists of the next generation.[82]

In terms of the state apparatus itself, the Revolution had both completed and transformed the work of the absolute monarchies, creating a unified and centralized bureaucratic machine, exercising its powers over the whole nation, and committed now to furthering the essential interests of the bourgeoisie. The first years of the Revolution had destroyed the absolutist state and in its stead it brought in a liberal and secular state based on principles of national sovereignty and civic equality. The monarchy was abolished, the executive was subordinated to the legislature, venal offices were eliminated and universal male suffrage was proclaimed. Without abandoning altogether strong central powers, a degree of administrative decentralization was effected in accordance with liberal principals. The years of revolutionary government saw a massive recentralization of power as the Jacobins responded to crisis by taking control of the economy and announcing the 'despotism of liberty'. After Thermidor, the Directory briefly restored a liberal economy but continued to augment central power, subordinating the municipalities to departmental administrations, expanding the police and excluding the masses from political life through the property franchise. With the Brumaire *coup d'état* and the beginning of Napoleon's consular rule, the liberal state was finally abandoned in favour of military dictatorship, thus signalling the definitive end to the revolutionary process.

The state which emerged during the Consulate and Empire was the product of bourgeois revolution, but it was an exceptional form of bourgeois rule. It represented essentially a restoration of order through the concentration of power in a single office combining executive and legislative powers. After a decade of class antagonisms, Napoleon sought a new stability. He endeavoured to achieve this through re-integrating sympathetic sections of the aristocracy with bourgeois property-owners and ruling personally in their joint interests by means of massively increased personal and central state power. Napoleon's achievement was essentially to complete and perfect the centralized state machine that had been pioneered by the absolutist monarchs and to turn this to the development of bourgeois social relations in France. The watchwords of government were now authority, order, bureaucratic efficiency and, of course, military strength. With legislation in 1800, Napoleon suppressed elections and instituted a cadre of public officials directly appointed by himself. All administrative authority in the departments was placed in the hands of the prefects, appointed from Paris and with sub-prefects under them, and these proceeded effectively to rationalize administration in the provinces. Besides creating a unified administrative machinery, Napoleon laid down the legislative basis on which it was to operate. The Civil Code, drawn up by a committee of lawyers and amended in the Council of State, was finally accepted in 1804.[83] Finally, with the Concordat of 1802, Catholicism was acknowledged as the religion of the majority of the French people, and its public practice permitted but only under strict state control. Napoleon recognized that religion could be used as an effective instrument of government and thus placed the bishops under the close control of the prefects.[84]

The Bonapartist state represented an exceptional form of class rule characterized by Gramsci as a form of 'Caesarism'. At certain historical conjunctures, according to Gramsci, a situation arises in which 'the forces in conflict balance each other in a catastrophic manner; that is to say, they balance each other in such a way that a continuation of the conflict can only terminate in their reciprocal destruction'.[85] At such a time, when there is a 'crisis of authority' within the state, the way is open for the 'man of destiny', the charismatic leader who 'alone is capable of solving an overriding problem . . . and fending off mortal danger' to the state.[86] To Gramsci, Napoleon Bonaparte represented a classic instance of the process where both personal power and bureaucratic control are augmented to effect a new class alignment capable of resolving the crisis in state authority.

Despite its authoritarian means and its renunciation of the Jacobin principles of democracy and equality, the Bonapartist state represented, to both Gramsci and Marx, a progressive force. Within France, wrote Marx, Napoleon

> created the conditions which first made possible the development of free competition, the exploitation of the land by small peasant property, and the application of the unleashed productive power of the nation's industries. Beyond the borders of France he swept away feudal institutions so far as this was necessary for the provision on the European continent of an appropriate modern environment for the bourgeois society in France.[87]

Whilst abandoning the Jacobin ideals, Napoleon stood by the principles of the bourgeois revolution of 1789, preventing the reassertion of aristocratic and church privilege, and using the state to defend and extend the gains of the bourgeoisie. Most notably this manifested itself through the opening up of state offices to competitive recruitment and thus declaring the career open to talent.

The educational innovations of the Empire reflected the aims and structures of the Napoleonic state. The development of centralized educational bureaucracy and the subordination of education to state control was an extension of the étatist policies already described and demonstrate Napoleon's desire to use the state in education to promote the interests of the bourgeoisie and the collective goals of the nation state. The development of the public *lycée* embodied the secular rationalist philosophy of the revolutionary period and offered a limited form of meritocratic promotion for the middle orders. The continuation and development of the vocational and special schools reflected the desire for efficient and well-trained recruits for the military and public authorities, providing a technical education that complemented the broad humanist curriculum of the *lycée*. Finally, the readmission of the Church into primary education illustrated the limitations of bourgeois meritocracy and clearly proclaimed Bonaparte's aim to ensure that education for the masses offered not a ladder of social advance but more an instrument of social control and political loyalty. Throughout, the accent was on the use of education to promote a unified and cohesive national culture which would celebrate the glory of France and underwrite the hegemony of the Bonapartist state. 'To instruct is secondary', said Napoleon, 'the main thing is to train and to do so according to the pattern which suits the state.'[88]

The centrepiece of educational legislation and the main embodiment of educational centralization during the Empire were the two decrees of 1806 and 1808 which created the *Université*. This unique institution represented a giant secular teaching corporation whose cardinal principles were supreme central control and state monopoly over instruction. The rigid hierarchical structure of administration which it embodied reflected these principles. At the apex was the *Grand-Maître* appointed by and directly responsible to the head of state. Below him were the regional academies, which had little effective autonomy, and below them the local organization of the individual communes. The *Université* was designed to supervise the entire system. Although legislation did not make every school government property, it placed them all under official control, ensuring both geographical uniformity and ideological orthodoxy. National curricula were standardized and a national system of examinations, including the *baccalauréat*, the *licence* and the *doctorat*, regulated entry into different levels of state service or into institutions of higher education. Teachers became part of the state bureaucracy, swearing an oath of allegiance to the *Grand-Maître*, and encouraged by 'professional' status and career ladders to form a disciplined and loyal corps which would take official policies into their individual institutions. With the creation of the École Normale in 1808 there was in addition a centre of official pedagogical orthodoxy which would provide a pipeline for the transmission of approved educational policies and methods.[89]

R. D. Anderson has warned against 'exaggerat[ing] the centralization of French education', pointing out the relative autonomy of the *Université* before the Second Empire and the absence of state control over the primary schools. 'In centralist France,' he writes, 'the state did not itself run a single primary school in 1848; even teacher training colleges were run by the departments.'[90] The reminder is a salutary one and it is certainly important to avoid an empty fetishization of the concept of centralization which already looms large in the mythology of French education. However, even in this period, when the state had indeed not taken all schools into public ownership and control, the degree of state influence was nevertheless remarkable. Even where it was the local authorities that supervised education, as with the primary schools, these were subject to strong central control. As Zeldin reminds us, the local state was in effect merely an 'outpost of central administration' during most of this period.[91]

During the Empire it was only with the *lycées* and the communal colleges where one can talk of full public ownership and control of educational institutions. Primary schools were still largely run on a day-to-day basis by the religious organizations, and private secondary schools still outnumbered public ones. According to Aulard, church schools accounted for about 50 per cent of institutions in 1811.[92] However, these were all subject to increasing state controls. The decree of 1808 had tried to give the state a monopoly over education, and further legislation in 1811 had enhanced state supervision over private schools. All schools had to be authorized by the state before opening and were subordinated to *Université* regulations. Schools could not offer their own diplomas. Private schools were weakened financially by being obliged to pay a per capita contribution to the *Université*, and all private pupils had to submit a certificate attesting to two years of study in a public *lycée* before entering the *baccalauréat*. Catholic secondary schools were limited to one per department and were prohibited in towns where a *lycée* already existed. Religious orders continued to run elementary schools but they had to register with, and swear allegiance to, the *Université*, follow a prescribed syllabus and submit to supervision by local state officials.[93]

In secondary education, Napoleon's aim was to create a system of schools under state control and to uniform standards which would ensure the development of a loyal, nationally minded and competent educational elite to supply the state with its technical and administrative experts. To this end he closed the Revolution's central schools, which he considered too liberal in curriculum and regime, and replaced them with the new state *lycées* and the communal *écoles secondaires*, which were to be run with military-style discipline and efficiency. According to the decree of 1802 the *lycées* were to receive 20 per cent of their funds from the state and the rest from fees; staff were to be appointed by the *Université* and all schools would follow the same curriculum in preparation for uniform national examinations. The schools would provide a mixed classical and scientific course of studies and follow a highly disciplined daily routine. The *écoles secondaires* were conceived of as preparatory schools to the *lycée* or as a preparation in their own right for the lower rungs of the bureaucracy. They were also put under state control and, in the case of those run by the municipalities, were to become known as collèges. By 1808 there were 37 state *lycées* and 300 state *écoles secondaires*.[94] Although this represented considerably fewer state secondary schools than private ones, they were well on the way to becoming the prestige institutions, thus giving the state the leading edge in secondary education.

Only a very small minority at this time ever received secondary education; according to official figures, fewer than 1.8 in 1 000 were enrolled in 1809, and these schools were certainly not designed to be anything other than elite institutions.[95] Entrance to the *lycée* could only be attempted after five years of elementary schooling, and the level of fees meant that this transition was exceedingly rare. The Napoleonic system clearly did not have anything resembling an educational ladder. However, Napoleonic regulations were designed to incorporate an element of meritocratic competition and did offer a window of opportunity for social advancement for the few through education. The decree of 1802 had provided for selection by merit for the *lycées* and some 6 000 national *bourses* were available to cover the cost of fees, although a third of these were reserved for the sons of officials and officers.[96] The overall effect of Napoleon's promotion of competitive secondary education, and the linking of state appointments to academic credentials, was not so much a wide increase in social mobility but rather a means of consolidating the gains made by the bourgeoisie during the Revolution. The career open to talents was essentially the career open to the middling ranks of society, although this group was somewhat more broadly defined than before.

Technical education saw no major innovations during this period but rather a continuation of the developments of the revolutionary era. The trade school founded at Liancourt in 1786 was moved to Chalons-sur-Marne and renamed the École des Arts et Métiers. Teaching was to a high standard and students followed courses in theoretical and applied sciences for periods of 3–10 years. According to Artz, it provided the best elementary trade school training in Europe.[97] After 1800, schools of design were founded all over northern and eastern France, some supported by the state and some by the municipal authorities. New special schools were founded by Napoleon for military and cavalry training, most notably with the École Militaire Spéciale.[98] Together with the institutions created during the previous period, these probably set France in the vanguard of technical education in Europe.

However one assesses the record of the Empire in secondary and technical education – and in comparison with the dismal state of the latter in England, for instance, it looks quite impressive – the developments in elementary education were comparatively slight. Napoleon's attitude towards education for the masses represented a complete abandonment of the revolutionary principles of education as a right and as a vehicle for social equality. Rather, it represented a return to the elitist notions of the *philosophes*. Secular, rational education was alright for the middle class but for the masses, education should be little more than a training in morality and political loyalty, and, as Napoleon was quick to realize, religion was an eminently useful vehicle for this so long as the Church could be kept under tight state control. 'God and the Emperor', said Fontanes, 'are the two names that one must engrave in the hearts of children. It is to this double thought that all the system of national education must address itself.'[99] These were Napoleon's sentiments entirely and inasmuch as Napoleon attended to elementary education at all, it was with these aims in view. According to the imperial catechism, 'to serve our Emperor is to honour and serve God himself', and this was precisely what primary education was to teach the children of the people to do. Napoleon's re-admission of the teaching orders into primary education was thus not so much in contradiction of his policy of controlling education through the state but rather another means to achieve the same end. In case there could be any doubt about the subordination of the primary schools to the state, Napoleon appointed state inspectors to supervise schools run by the religious orders.

Education and state after the Bourbon Restoration

By the end of the Napoleonic Empire the basic framework of national education in France was thus securely in place. It was by no means yet a complete or universal system but the administrative and legal framework was there, distinctive institutional models had been developed, if not yet generalized, and the typical characteristics of French education were already clearly discernable. During the Revolution and the subsequent consolidation of the bourgeois state under Napoleon, a distinctive form of national education had emerged, which, as we have seen, reflected in its unique character the specific forms and objectives of the French state. Centralized in administration, standardized and uniform in its procedures, state-defined in its objectives, French education well expressed the nature of the French bureaucracy and the priorities of the ruling class. It had been vigorously promoted by successive regimes and had developed as far as it had because it was rightly seen as a means to promote the hegemony of the French state and the classes that it represented. It could provide the state with its technical experts, it played an important part in fostering that uniform and patriotic national culture which was seen as an essential precondition of national unity and strength, and it consolidated the social position of the bourgeoisie. By establishing a credential link between education and state office, it safeguarded the bourgeois from the reassertion of aristocratic privilege from above and, by excluding the popular masses from this limited educational meritocracy, it saved them from pressure from below. The latter would be reconciled to their subordinate social position through a limited and traditional education whose main objective was to inculcate political loyalty and civic morality. It remains to be seen how this emergent education system was consolidated in the succeeding period and how new regimes and state forms shaped its development.

Despite the restoration of monarchy which followed the downfall of Napoleon, and the increasing prominence of the financial and industrial interests during the Restoration, the basic forms of the centralized Napoleonic state did not change. To the ruling class it was the consummate mechanism of their power. It appeared to the bourgeoisie and also to the peasantry, at least in de Tocqueville's opinion, to guarantee against any restoration of the old order or the revival of aristocratic privilege. Even some radical republicans, such as the theorist Dupont White, defended centralization as an instrument of popular liberation, arguing that it was necessary to destroy privileges and prevent against the evils of localism and *laissez-faire*.[100] To all political parties the central state represented in the last analysis the guarantor of order and national unity.

Marx, as a revolutionary, clearly saw little merit in the French state but he did recognize the important service that it performed for the bourgeoisie. In the *Eighteenth Brumaire*, in a passage as remarkable for its historical sweep as for its rhetorical power, he traces the evolution of the central state in France, indicating clearly its importance as a universalizing force and one that contributed greatly to the hegemonic power of the bourgeoisie.

The first French revolution, with its task of breaking all separate local, territorial, urban and provincial powers in order to create the civil unity of the nation, was bound to develop what the absolute monarchy had begun: centralization, but at the same time the extent, the attributes and the agents of governmental power. Napoleon perfected this state machinery. The Legitimist and the July monarchy added nothing but a greater division of labour, growing in the same measure as the division of labour within bourgeois society created new groups of interests, and, therefore, new material for state administration. Every common interest was straightway severed from society, counterposed to it a higher, general interest, snatched from the activity of society's members themselves and made an object of governmental activity, from a bridge, a schoolhouse and the communal property of a village community to the railways, the national wealth and the national university of France. Finally, in the struggle against the revolution, the parliamentary republic found itself compelled to strengthen, along with the repressive measures, the resources and centralization of governmental power. All revolutions perfected this machine instead of smashing it. The parties that contended in turn for domination regarded the possession of this huge state edifice as the principal spoils of the victor.

Under Napoleon this central state was, according to Marx, 'the only means of preparing for the class rule of the bourgeoisie'. During the Restoration it became the instrument of the ruling class, of the large landowners who predominated under Legitimist Bourbon rule, and then of the financial aristocracy, the bankers, stock-market and railway barons, who predominated during the July Monarchy of Louis Philippe.[101]

The education system which developed during the Restoration continued to reflect the basic parameters of the French centralized state. With the reassertion of clerical influence and the more liberal policies of the July Monarchy, there was to be a certain movement towards greater 'freedom of education', restoring somewhat the influence of the Church; and with the advances of industry during the 1830s, there was also a renewed emphasis on vocational teaching. But these changes aside, education continued to develop along the lines mapped out by Napoleon. The state maintained its overall control, despite pressure from the Church, and the relative proportion of state to private schools increased.

The most important educational achievement of the period was probably the extension of primary schooling, which, by the end of the July Monarchy, had developed into something approaching a national network of schools. This network was still some way from delivering the universal education that had been achieved in Prussia but it was a considerable improvement compared with the neglected state of primary education under Napoleon. The first step towards improving elementary education came with the law of February 1816, which made schooling compulsory and free to the poor, and instructed each commune to set up a primary school under the supervision of a communal committee. This latter included members appointed by the Rector of the Academy, who ensured continuing state control but was presided over by the local *curé*. At the same time a national budget was inaugurated for primary schooling. The net effect of these provisions was to increase somewhat the total number of schools but at the same time to increase the influence of the Church. Local committees frequently allowed the religious congregations to provide the schools so that the Christian Brothers, for instance, could acquire a total of 320 schools by 1830. Furthermore, during the 1820s, Catholic opposition to state schooling became intense and a strong lobby emerged for greater freedom of teaching. The Church gained considerable influence on local school committees and in 1821 bishops were given the right to supervise all religious matters in secondary schools. With the appointment of Abbé Dennis Frayssinous to the ministry of education, Jesuit influence in education reached a new high until the final years of the Bourbon monarchy finally reversed the trend, removing the bishops from control over the local school committees.[102]

The July Monarchy saw a continuation of the conflict between the Church and state in education, and this led to greater freedom for religious schools but not to any serious reversal of the principle of state control. The Charter of 1830 increased the freedom to open schools and represented a victory for the cause of *liberté d' enseignement*, whilst the 1833 *Loi Guizot* conceded more to clerical influence by putting moral and religious instruction at the head of all subjects in the primary school.[103] However, the state maintained its right to inspect all schools and the *Université* consolidated its position at the head of education, aided by the support of Louis Philippe who, significantly, sent his own sons to the state *lycée*. Whilst the Ultramontanes wanted a completely Catholic education system, most Catholics were in fact content to see church schools co-exist with state schools and did not envisage a rival system. State monopoly had been somewhat loosened, but the state was still the leading force in education and would remain so even during the Second Empire, when clericist reaction invaded education.

The major piece of educational legislation during the period was the *Loi Guizot*, which attempted to improve and extend education in all areas and particularly in primary education. A major report by Victor Cousin had exposed great apathy amongst parents and local notables towards education, and Guizot himself deplored the state of education. The law adopted a number of measures to rectify this situation. It reasserted that every commune should have a school, instructed communes to provide a schoolhouse and pay the teacher, and provided a state subsidy for poorer areas. All communes of over 6 000 were to have a public secondary school (Collège Royale) and an *école primaire supérieure*. Normal schools for teacher training were to be set up in the departments. The state was to provide a third of the initial expenses of school building in each commune but otherwise finance would come from fees and municipal funds. The minister was to appoint inspectors for each department.[104]

Guizot's legislation was a response to two pressures: one pushing for the extension and improvement of primary education and the other for more opportunities to be made available to the middle class. Both of these reflected the economic development of the period and thus the increasing need for skilled labour. The effects on primary education were not dramatic but they did encourage the trend towards the establishment of a national network of schools. According to Guizot's report, there had been 28 000 primary schools in 1821, about half of which were run by the state. These had risen to 30 000 in 1829 and 42 092 in 1832. By the end of the July Monarchy there were 63 000 primary schools, and only around 3 000 communes out of 38 600 were without a school.[105] The quality of education had no doubt also improved as much greater attention was paid to the training of teachers and the inspection of schools. By 1843 there were 87 state inspectors for schools who had between them 114 assistants, and the number of Normal schools had increased to about 76 by the mid-century.[106] This was altogether a rather better record than across the channel. Attendance, however, was still by no means universal and children had on average around six years of schooling, barely more than in England and considerably less than in the German states.

Developments in bourgeois education reflected widespread pressure, notably from liberals and technologically minded republicans, such as Saint-Simon, for a greater emphasis on the teaching of science and modern subjects. One response to this was the creation of the *école primaire supérieure*, a new type of scientifically oriented post-elementary school for the lower middle class. In his 1831 report, Victor Cousin clearly expressed the purpose of the schools:

> This education, while remaining inferior to that of the royal and communal colleges, will bear precisely on useful knowledge which is indispensible to that numerous class of the population that will not enter the learned professions but needs a broader and more varied culture than the lower class properly so-called, the peasants and workers . . . At present primary education in France is very superficial; and there is nothing between it and our colleges.

Like many of his contemporaries, Cousin was most concerned about the excessive production of classically trained young lower middle-class men which society could not absorb into the liberal professions or other commensurate positions. These *déclassés* had a dangerous propensity for radicalism and Cousin wished to see them directed into other useful pursuits.

> These young men acquire connections and tastes which make it difficult or impossible for them to enter into the humbler career of their fathers; whence comes a race of disturbed men, disconnected with their own and their father's position, enemies of social order, ready to hurl themselves, their knowledge, their more or less real talent, and their vaunting ambition into the paths of servility and revolt . . . Certainly our colleges must remain open to any who can pay the fee, but it is not necessary to admit indiscreetly the lower classes; hence we must have intermediate establishments between primary schools and our colleges.[107]

The purpose of these new schools was clear, but it was not so easily effected in practice. Although by 1841 there were some 161 of these schools run by the state and another 191 in private control, they were not considered a great success and were later converted into trade schools.[108] They never acquired the prestige within the middle class of the colleges and many people were reluctant to abandon a classical training for their children.

The same problem emerged in attempts to modernize the college curriculum. Salvandy and successive education ministers attempted to instigate new scientific streams within the colleges to attract the middle class away from the over-crowded liberal professions and into business and technical careers. They had some success, particularly with the industrial class, and during the Second Empire were to run the classical streams a close second in their ability to attract students. However, they continually ran up against the conservative classicism of the *Université* and the *lycée* professors, and the popular prestige attached to classical education denied the scientific streams parity of status.

Since the creation of the Napoleonic *lycée*, French secondary education had acquired the appearance of a distinctively modern system. France was the first country to develop a national system of secondary schools run by the state, and the secular, rationalist ethos which informed it had, as Robert Anderson puts it, 'a remarkably modern air'.[109] Its regular administrative pattern, its uniform curriculum, its serious application to science, its meritocratic principles and, above all, its competitive and rigorously intellectualist spirit did indeed mark it out from secondary schooling elsewhere, not least as it existed in contemporary England. Victor Cousin once quipped that in France even babies would compete over who could dribble best, and the remark clearly points towards something distinctive in the cultural ambience of nineteenth-century France. However, this appearance of modernity was in some ways deceptive.

The dominant ethos in French secondary schools remained classical throughout the period even if this classicism was adapted to a rationalist world view. The principle subjects in the *lycée* and college continued to be grammar, rhetoric and belles-lettres. This remained the case even after the introduction of bifurcation into classical and modern streams. By the mid-century the study of letters still dominated in the *lycées*, in both the classical and the modern streams (see Table 4.2)[110]. Science was certainly taken seriously and occupied a much greater part of the curriculum than

Table 4.2 Percentage of time spent on each subject during seven-year *lycée* course in 1852

	Classical	Modern
Philosophy	2	2
Letters	67	47
Modern languages	5	5
History and geography	13	13
Science	13	32

in the English public school. However, it was the philosophy and letters classes in the final years of the *lycée* which continued to attract the most prestige and which gave the distinctive style to French secondary education. As Zeldin remarks,

> French schools distinguished themselves from those of most of Europe by the teaching of philosophy to children.... To finish off their education, the elite of the nation were neither given responsibility as prefects, nor encouraged in athletic distractions, as were British children, but instead were offered a very peculiar intellectual training.[111]

It was this concentration on rhetoric and philosophical abstraction, sometimes to the point of excessive formalism, which developed the distinctive style of the *lycéens*. At its best, it engendered a fluent eloquence and a remarkable agility in argument which impressed itself on French cultural life. At its worst, it led to intellectual pomposity and empty verbalism as young students grappled with a subject quite beyond them and, unable to master the content of their studies, merely acquired the formal veneer which would see them through their examinations. In either event it was this literary style and refinement, more than any scientific knowledge, that constituted the *culture générale* which the aspiring bourgeois so wished to cultivate to mark their social status. The 'modernity' of the secondary school thus lay primarily in its bureaucratic forms of organization and its limited meritocratic principles. What it actually taught had the appearance of modernity in its pursuance of that secular rationalism which was characteristic of the French Enlightenment. But it was not the modernity of the scientific, industrial world.

By the end of the July Monarchy, secondary education was still very much a minority affair. The number of secondary schools had barely surpassed its pre-revolutionary levels and no more than 5 per cent of French boys received a full secondary education. According to Ringer, 'the total output of educated men per population in France in 1842 was no greater, and was perhaps a little smaller, than it had been around 1700, in the 1780s and about 1809'.[112] Provision for girls was, of course, considerably lower. The extent of secondary schooling was nevertheless considerable by English standards and probably somewhat higher than in Germany. Most importantly, secondary schooling had come to be thoroughly dominated by the middle class and, even if it sometimes failed to address the concerns of industry, it was a powerful instrument of bourgeois cultural hegemony.

Education and bourgeois hegemony

We have traced the development of a national education system in France as it emerged during and after the Revolution, and seen how it related to the formation of the bourgeois state in different periods. More specifically, we have seen how the impetus for its development emerged from the military, bureaucratic and ideological requirements of the state and how the typical forms of French education reflected the character and priorities of this state apparatus. State control, bureaucratic uniformity and systematic organiza-tion were indeed, as Archer has maintained, the distinctive characteristics of French education. The legend of the French education minister who listened to the chiming of the clock and observed with satisfaction that he knew what each and every child in France would be studying at that moment, down to the precise chapter of Virgil, is not entirely without foundation, although its significance is not always fully understood. The significance of centralization in French education was not so much that it exemplified some national fetish for uniformity but rather, historically, that it provided such a potent vehicle of bourgeois hegemony in France. Both Marx and Gramsci frequently observed the ability of the bourgeois vanguard in France, from the Jacobins down to Bonaparte, to project bourgeois culture as the uni-versal norm, and indeed it was the abstract and sweeping universalism of revolutionary ideology that made the French Revolution unique amongst bourgeois revolutions. Education in nineteenth-century France was above all a manifestation of this ideological dominance, often less than impres-sive in its practical accomplishments, particularly with its relatively low enrolments in primary education, but enormously potent as an ideologi-cal force. It played a major role in the securing of bourgeois hegemony in France, both in the way in which it constructed classes occupationally and in the mentality which it nurtured in each.

The single most important contribution of French education to bour-geois society was probably its role in fostering the idea of national unity through its assiduous cultivation of patriotic values and of a particular conception of French nationhood. As Zeldin has remarked, its stress on cul-tural uniformity and standardization represented an 'organized onslaught on regional and local eccentricity'.[113] Whereas the centralized state had only managed to impose an administrative unity on the nation, it was mass edu-cation which first made possible the spread of a uniform national culture. It was this potential which allowed education to become such a national obsession in France during the nineteenth century, invested at different times with almost magical properties; capable, so it was often thought, of curing almost every social evil. The desire to impose a 'national' cul-ture was most clearly expressed in the prominence given to civic education and, particularly, in the efforts made to promote the national language and literature.

The political importance of encouraging the spread of the standard French language and combatting local patois had already been a preoccupation of the Jacobins. In the second year of the Revolution, Saint-Just had made a famous attack on the 'old idioms', the symbols of reaction and localism:

Federalism and superstition speak in bas-breton; the emigres and hatred of the republic speak in German . . . The monarchy has its own reasons for resembling the Tower of babel; in a democracy, however, to allow citizens to remain ignorant of the national language, and incapable thereby of supervising the exercise of power, is to betray France. The French language, which has had the honour of being utilized for the Declaration of the Rights of Man, must become the language of all Frenchmen. It is our duty to provide citizens with the instrument of public thinking, the most certain agent of revolution, that is, a common language.[114]

The nineteenth-century French state had less interest in linguistic standardization as a means of social levelling, but it was equally concerned to promote national unity and loyalty to the state through a nationalistic celebration of the language, and this became one of the great obsessions of schools. It was not simply a matter of spreading a standard tongue but equally a celebration of the allegedly unique properties of the national language, the precision and clarity which many liked to believe was its quintessential characteristic. As Zeldin says, 'nowhere was language so highly esteemed as embodying the national genius'.[115]

The importance of education in nurturing common ideas of national identity can hardly be in doubt, and, as Gramsci has insisted, the achievement of ideological hegemony frequently works through such 'national-popular' conceptions. Nowhere was this more true than in France. However, education did not, of course, except in the vaguest sense, create a common culture. It was too clearly structured along class lines for that to be the case. What it did instead was to construct a system whereby different classes were schooled in different ways so that each was part of a so-called common culture but inserted differently within it. In 1810, Destutt de Tracy observed that to 'sensible men' it was obvious that 'in every civilised society, there are necessarily two classes of men', and that consequently there must be 'two systems of education' having nothing in common with each other.[116] Throughout this period the French bourgeoisie adhered to this apparently self-evident principle, taking care to provide the middle class with one education and the worker with another, where these were appropriate to their different stations in society. Whilst promoting an ostensibly indivisible national culture, in practice they apportioned different bits of it to each social class.

French primary education was thus designed to impart a limited version of the national culture that would encourage political loyalty and civic obedience amongst the working class, and impart a modicum of useful and appropriate skills without encouraging excessive ambition or the desire for social advancement. Whether they were church schools or municipal schools seems not to have made much difference. Both were concerned with what was essentially moral education. Catholic schools placed great stress on teaching the catechism and preparing children for their first communion. They sought to inculcate a pious and receptive attitude and to instill the Christian virtues, but avoided exciting any worldly ambitions:

> Traditional Catholic teaching was designed not to awaken the child but to teach him that desire could never be satisfied, except in the next world. It sought to fill him with humility, to warn him of God's severity as well as of his justice and mercy.[117]

The purpose of the state in primary education was similar. Guizot told his prefects in 1833, in words that Durkheim would echo 60 years later, that 'we have tried to create in every commune a *moral force* that the government can use at need'.[118] The government sought civil obedience and popular acquiescence in that hegemonic concept of nationhood which it promoted and on which its power rested, but its language in education differed little from that of the Church. 'Faith in providence, the sacredness of duty, and the respect due to law, to the ruler and the rights of all, such are the sentiments which [the teacher] will endeavour to impart', read Guizot's ministerial instructions to teachers.[119]

Guizot was a liberal and did as much as any education minister to improve working-class education, but any idea of promoting social equality through education was far from his thoughts. He wrote in his memoirs:

> The tendency to widen ... universal primary instruction does not deserve legal encouragement; the purpose of laws is to provide for what is necessary, not to go ahead of what may become possible, and its mission is to regulate social forces, not to excite them indiscriminately.... Far from education being a means of social change, it should accept to be limited by the divisions in society.[120]

At primary level, education was thus essentially an instrument of social conformity. Its effect on the class structure was regulatory and consolidative, specifically designed to foil excessive ambition and to limit social mobility. *Déclassement* was in essence a negative term and education was designed to limit not promote it.

Secondary education, however, was a different matter and stood in a different relation to the process of class formation. The difference lay chiefly in that secondary education was, in a sense, a vehicle of social transformation. It was one of the means by which the bourgeoisie was formed as a class. It symbolized the career open to talent and the means by which the middle class could ensure its continued social ascendancy. It had to proclaim itself meritocratic because only through this could it remain a bulwark against aristocratic privilege. In this sense it continued to represent the 'principles of 1789'.

It was in defending the status of the middle class that the *lycée* and the state college excelled. They had to remain more efficient than the private Catholic schools, frequented by the aristocracy, and usually did, precisely because their *raison d'être* was to win the credential race for the middle class and thus secure the positions for them that would guarantee their status. Whilst the Catholic schools remained popular, particularly with the aristocracy, because they developed character and moral values, and were thought to provide better pastoral care and a more sympathetic boarding atmosphere, the state schools were always more effective in training for examinations and thus maintained the loyalty of the majority of the bourgeoisie.

Secondary schools had to protect the bourgeoisie not only from above but also from encroachments from below, from the masses who were pressing at their heels. It was this desire to keep ahead that gave the classical programme its phenomenal appeal amongst sons of the industrial, professional and petit-bourgeois strata alike. Far from being associated exclusively with the aristocracy, as in England, classicism was the insurance policy of the bourgeoisie, an exclusive badge of status, a medium of social advance, and the sign of its social distinction from the lower orders. So close was this association between middle-class ambition and classical education that liberal propagandists such as Bastiat were able to argue that the classical curriculum was the nursery of radicalism and the yeast of those popular ambitions that led to social dislocation.

Duruy later candidly expressed the importance of education for the middle class. The sons of the Bourgeois, he said, must receive

the widest and richest intellectual culture, in order to strengthen the aristocracy of intelligence amid a people that wants all sorts of aristocracy, and to provide a legitimate counter-weight to this democracy which is rising in full-flood … the people are rising; the bourgeoisie must not stand still, for to stand still would be to fall behind.[121]

Education had become increasingly important in the process of occupational selection and thus in the forming of classes. Although advancement in business careers still depended largely on influence, patronage and demonstrated ability, entrance into professional careers and into state service now required educational credentials. The *baccalauréat* was the new symbol of a meritocratic middle-class elite. This was strikingly borne out by Jean-Baptiste Dumas in a passage which anticipates the notion of cultural capital favoured by modern Marxist sociologists of education:

Alongside the wealth represented by landed property and transferable stocks a new form of wealth has been established and developed: that whose capital consists in a solid and practical education, whose symbols and the title deeds are the degrees and diplomas which are the sanction and reward... Knowledge becomes at all levels... a form of wealth and property of fixed value.[122]

Dumas was perhaps too optimistic about the fixity of credential value but in other respects his description admirably sums up the importance of education to the French middle class.

There were contradictions in the bourgeois philosophy, however, despite its apparent coherence. Meritocracy was alright so long as it could be restricted to the middle class, but in practice this was never entirely possible. It was not only sons of the industrialists, bureaucrats and professionals who gained from the secondary schools but also on occasion the children of *petit-bourgeois* and peasant families. This had little to do with the scholarships since these had declined markedly since the Empire, but rather resulted from the fact that schools selected on merit from amongst those who could pay, and the fees were not always beyond the reach of artisanal and peasant families. Zeldin calculates that by the mid-century about half of the population were in a position to afford secondary schooling if they so wished.

For the 1860s, valuable data on secondary enrolments exists in the records of the survey carried out by Duruy in 1864. The American sociologist Patrick Harrigan has done detailed statistical analyses on this and has found a surprisingly wide degree of class access. Out of recorded college enrolment returns for 1860–6, he finds that nearly 50 per cent of graduates from provincial *lycées* and colleges were sons of peasants, shopkeepers, white-collar employees, workers and enlisted servicemen. A more detailed summary of the data for enrolments in *lycées* and colleges, respectively, shows the class backgrounds of students (Table 4.3)[123].

The data clearly only shows us the proportions of students in secondary schools from each social class and not the proportion of each social class that attended secondary schools. The fact that the numbers of students in colleges from peasant and *petit-bourgeois* backgrounds exceeded those from landed and professional backgrounds should not be allowed to obscure the fact that, since students from the former were recruited from a considerably larger group, their proportional representation was relatively considerably lower. Only a tiny fraction of peasant or lower middle-class children ever went to secondary schools. Furthermore, students from upper middle-class backgrounds clearly dominated secondary schools, particularly the *lycées*, but also the colleges. The children of top professionals and officials, landowners and business leaders accounted for over 55 per cent of the students in the *lycées* and over 40 per cent of the students in the colleges. Nevertheless, the figures do show a significant degree of social mixing, and this was one of the significant characteristics of French secondary schools.

Status distinctions clearly did exist between the different types of secondary school. The lower middle class had little access to the *grands lycées*,

Table 4.3 Social origins of students in *lycées* and *collèges* between 1864 and 1868 (in percentages)

Father's occupation	Lycée	Collège
Professional	21.7	15.9
law	8.0	4.8
high	10.0	7.1
low	3.7	4.0
Landowner	18.9	15.5
Business leader	16.0	9.8
commercial	12.2	6.7
industrial/managerial	3.8	3.1
Civil service	12.3	10.3
high	3.9	3.2
middle/low	8.4	7.1
Peasant	8.0	16.2
Petit-bourgeoisie	18.5	27.8
white collar	2.2	3.3
shopkeeper	13.2	15.2
artisan	3.1	9.1
Workers	1.4	1.2

the most prestigious secondary schools often preferred by the wealthy bourgeoisie and landowners, and the *lycées* in general tended to attract the greater share of children from top professional and bureaucratic families. However, the distinctions were never sharply defined in class terms. In fact the most important division was probably not between schools but rather between the classical and modern streams, especially during the 1860s when Duruy's Special Programmes, oriented towards more vocational learning, gained popularity. These tended to attract more children from industrial, commercial and farming families, whilst the classical streams continued to be favoured by professionals, civil servants and even workers. However, despite these distinctions, there was considerable class overlap in all types of school and between the different courses which shared a common curricula core in any case. Unlike the sharp divisions of rank which existed in English secondary education, with its public, proprietary, grammar and lesser private schools, all carefully distinguished in their social clientele, the French secondary sector formed a relatively unitary system bound together by a common set of bourgeois values.

One should not exaggerate the degree of social mobility afforded by the secondary education since it was never more than a tiny fraction of any class that actually benefited from it. Of those who did, most did not derive social mobility from it. In Harrigan's sample of graduates, 48 per cent maintained familial status, 32 per cent were upwardly mobile and 20 per cent suffered loss of status.[124] However, their expectations were high and when these failed to be realized it could have important social consequences. Harrigan shows that 50 per cent of his sample, including children from all social classes, expected to go to professional schools, whilst only 20 per cent anticipated becoming agriculturalists or *petit-commerçants*, and only 10 per cent expected to be employed at lower levels in industry, the military or in clerical work.[125] Inevitably, large numbers of secondary graduates did not fulfill their occupational ambitions and had to take work that was not commensurate with their qualifications. The bureaucracy and the professions could not provide enough openings for the growing class of educated people, and the fiercely competitive system of recruitment, vitiated by nepotism and political bias, made frustrated ambition a common fate. Balzac was to predict that 'youth will explode like the boiler of a steam engine', and indeed many déclassés did turn to political radicalism.[126] *La Jeunesse Républicaine* played a significant part in the Revolution of 1830, for instance. Thus whilst secondary education produced relatively little real social mobility, it fostered unrealizable ambitions amongst many, which contributed significantly to the radical political ferment.

Secondary education was thus essentially a middle-class meritocracy, although this class was sometimes quite broadly defined. The general tendency over the previous century had been to enhance greatly the hold that the middle class had over the upper reaches of the education system. It seems that just as education was becoming increasingly important to occupational and social status, so the middle class managed to deepen its investment in it. Comparison between records for this period and for the mid-eighteenth century suggests that the bourgeoisie had considerably increased their representation in secondary schools at the expense of both the aristocracy and the lower social groups. An analysis by Frijhoff and Julia into records for colleges at Auch, Avalon and Gisors during the *Ancien Régime* shows that class intake at that time was relatively broad. The proportion of students from bourgeois backgrounds (professionals, senior officials, merchants and industrial bourgeoisie) was at around 42 per cent in Auch (*c*.1600); 55 per cent in Avalon (*c*.1745); and 13 per cent in Gisors (*c*.1770). Children from small farming and artisanal backgrounds were almost as numerous, although not, of course, in proportion to their relative numbers in the population, with up to 30 per cent of college students coming from these groups.[127] If we compare these with Harrigan's figures on the 229 secondary schools during the Second Empire, we can see that the proportion of students from peasant and artisanal families had decreased considerably, whilst children from bourgeois families were considerably better represented. Over 56 per cent of college students now came from bourgeois families (top professionals, business leaders, industrial managers, top officials), whereas only 18 per cent came from artisanal or peasant families. Analysing these and similar comparative statistics, Ringer concludes that secondary schools had actually narrowed their class intake since the beginning of the eighteenth century. It would seem safer to say that what had actually happened was that the bourgeoisie had extended its representation in secondary schools and that artisanal and peasant representation had declined in proportion to the decline of these groups in the population as a whole. The group that had made the most obvious advance in this respect was the lower middle-class, which now represented over a third of all secondary students.

As well as consolidating the occupational status of the middle class, the French secondary schools played an important role in cementing a common culture within the middle class. Unlike the English secondary educational system which favoured gentry values and maintained a rigid hierarchy of rank, separating the landed classes from the manufacturing class, and both from the lower middle class, which had little provision at all, French secondary education was distinctive in that it was dominated by a pervasive bourgeois culture and united the various ranks of the middle class within it. It is quite true that the classical emphasis of the French secondary school still tended to reproduce the divide between the industrial and professional sectors, although arguably less so than in England. But where it certainly differed was in its ability to cement a cohesive cultural bond between a broad range of professional, bureaucratic and technical groups which were the backbone of the French state. In England the ruling class was not only fractured along the lines which divided the gentry from the 'productive' bourgeoisie but it was also subject to secondary social fissures between the manufacturing class and the aristocratically inclined old liberal professions, and also between the latter and the growing technical and engineering strata which were hardly recognized as professions at all. The comparative breadth and cultural homogeneity of the French professional and official class was indicated by the relative ease with which the engineer was assimilated into it. The technocrat and the liberal professional were subsequently to find more in common than their counterparts in England. Saint-Simonians in France had already abolished the distinction, whereas, in England, C. P. Snow was still lamenting the division between the 'two cultures', the liberal and the scientific, a century later.

Despite its continuing detachment from the values of the industrial world, the common culture promoted by the secondary schools was pre-eminently bourgeois. It applauded ambition and defended meritocracy; it encouraged dedicated commitment to study and painstaking application; above all, with its secular, rationalist principles, it promoted the belief in expertise which was to prove so important for the development of the French state. Whilst vehemently elitist, its genuine commitment to rewarding merit could not but give access to powerful positions to an increasing numbers of those with talents from whatever class they came. As R. D. Anderson concludes in an important essay on French secondary schools, there was a kind of openness about these schools which was highly significant and which set them apart from their English counterparts:

It was the result of the institutional evolution in the revolutionary and Napoleonic period, and reflected the general approval which individual ambition, intellectual merit and the power of money found in the ethos of bourgeois society. It was a reminder that the 'principles of 1789' really did make France a more democratic society in certain ways. The country was ruled by an elite, but the elite remained open, and education could not be used to consolidate intellectual and social influence in the hands of a self-perpetuating clique ... the system did in fact favour déclassement, enabling the lower middle-class to push their sons a rung or two up the social ladder and the newly rich to push their sons into the liberal professions, but at the same time it contributed social stability and continuity by linking the process with the absorbtion of traditional values.[128]

This relative openness of French state secondary schools, and the culture of ambition and expertise which it fostered, was indeed the singular achievement of French education in this period and set it apart from many other nations. It was essentially the product of the state and of a particular kind of relationship between the state and civil society. In Gramscian terms it was that universalizing, hegemonic drive of the Jacobin tradition, later re-articulated by Napoleon to serve the interests of the emerging bourgeoisie, which had pioneered this development. In the useful terminology of David Marquand's recent book, it was the product of the 'developmental state', the state which actively intervenes to force the development of civil society in line with modern conditions.[129] Whatever the terms of analysis, it is clear that such developments did not occur spontaneously from the social relations of society – they were actively organized from above. Their historical importance can be gauged from the reciprocal contribution they made to the future development of economic and state structures in France.

5
The US Experience: Education, Nationhood and the Decentralized State

> There emerged during the first century of national life an authentic
> vernacular in education that stands in retrospect...among the two
> or three most significant contributions the United States has made
> to the advancement of world civilization. Lawrence Cremin[1]

The consolidation of public education systems in the United States began in
the North East in the 1830s, during the early phase of industrialization, and
extended to all northern states during the ante-bellum period. The process
was more protracted in the southern states, which had only made tentative
steps in this direction before the Civil War, and it was not until the Reconstruction period that equivalent systems developed there. Whilst uneven in
its regional and ethnic penetration, the spread of mass public education in
the United States was a remarkable process, rivalling in its extent that of
most European nations and, arguably, more democratic in form than any.

The origins of American public education lay further back, in the colonial
and revolutionary periods, and were closely connected with the formation of
the American nation. As in Europe, where education had proved to be 'the
most powerful weapon for forming nations', in the United States, public
schooling proved to be a formidable tool for shaping national consciousness and it was largely in the pursuit of this that the initial impetus for
public education lay.[2] From the period of the Revolution onwards, education was held to be uniquely important for the cultivation of a national
identity, for the maintenance of social cohesion and for the promotion
of republican values, especially so in a country of dispersed and heterogeneous communities and in the early years of a new and fragile republic.
As in Europe, the development of public education was a crucial aspect of
nation-building, and in its early phase performed a cultural and ideological
role which was paramount over any other function. However, the process
of its development was quite distinct from European models and contains
a number of paradoxes. Not only were the ethnic and class relations which

underpinned the emergence of public education in the United States quite distinctive, contributing their own effects on the unique forms of American education, but also the whole nature of state and civil society was different. Whereas education systems in Northern Europe arose, for the most part, in extremely centralized states and owed much to the étatism and constant interventions of monarchs and governments alike, in the United States, public education arose in a decentralized system, and one, at least according to the official version, that owed more to spontaneous forces in civil society than to any central state direction. Ironically, the country which developed the quintessentially 'public' form of schooling was also that which had the least visible state machine. To understand this it is necessary to examine the nature of the American state.

The classic conception of the American state is one of relative statelessness. As Stephen Showronek has pointed out, 'The exceptional character of the early American state is neatly summarized in the paradox that it failed to evoke any sense of the state.'[3] This was also the initial impression of de Tocqueville, who first observed the United States in the 1830s and whose analysis of the country in *Democracy in America* has been immensely influential. To de Tocqueville, nothing was more striking in the United States 'than the absence of what we term the government or the administration'.[4] Indeed, the country appeared to be governed by an 'invisible machine', so unobtrusive was central government and administration. De Tocqueville, and many subsequent writers, equated this apparent lack of a central state with the pervasive spread of democratic ideas, the fortunate legacy of a country without a feudal past, and blessed with boundless land and opportunity.[5] In the United States, he said,

> Society governs itself for itself ... The nation participates in the making of its laws by the choice of its legislation, and in the execution of them by the choice agents of the governments; it may be almost said to govern itself, so feeble and restricted is the share left to the administration, so little do the authorities forget their popular origins and the power from which they emanate.[6]

One happy result of this relative lack of central control was, according to de Tocqueville, the degree to which it liberated individual initiative: 'The action of individuals, joined to that of the public authority, frequently accomplishes what the most energetic administration would be unable to do.'[7]

De Tocqueville's view of the United States was undoubtedly an idealized picture, even for the populist Jacksonian period of government. It is true that underlying his laudatory account is an uneasy awareness of contrary realities. Despite the advanced democratic spirit which he finds, he can think of 'no country in which there is so little independence of mind and real freedom of discussion as in America', and at one point asserts that 'far from the American government being not sufficiently centralized, I shall prove hereafter that they are too much so'.[8] However, despite these acute observations, the overriding impression of *Democracy in America* is one of admiration for democratic institutions and culture. The weakness of the account, for all its perspicuity about manners and ideas, is the superficiality of its understanding of the material basis of civil society. De Tocqueville's overwhelming emphasis is on institutions and ideology; the real class and ethnic divisions in the distribution of power and wealth in civil society are simply absent.

Marx and Engels, needless to say, took a different view. They recognized the exceptional character of the decentralized American state but also stressed that it performed the same function in relation to capital there as it did in Europe. Engels acknowledged that in certain frontier regions of America , where class antagonisms were still 'undeveloped', the central state might be 'very insignificant, almost infinitesimal', yet this did not mean that the United States was a capitalist society without a state.[9] In fact, the United States was the 'most perfect example of a modern state', in that, above all, it protected the rights of private property and most effectively ensured the development of capitalist society.[10] The dichotomy can best be understood by referring back to the Marxist argument analysed in Chapter 3. For Marx and Engels, and later also for Gramsci, the state could not be considered separately from civil society. Its nature and functions were formed by the social relations on which it rested. If American society was distinguished by the prevalence of small capitalist farming and the relatively wide basis of the white suffrage, this would give particular forms to the state, and, along with other historical reasons, would go some way towards explaining its decentralized forms. However, this in no way altered the fact that a state apparatus existed, at both federal and state levels, and that this machine was successful in its primary functions of defending property, social order and the conditions for capital accumulation in general.

The central state apparatus in the United States was nevertheless clearly small by European standards. The nation had inherited no hereditary monarchy and no national church, and it had neither an insulated bureaucratic class nor great national corporations and formal estates.[11] The constitution framed during the revolutionary period was, moreover, explicitly designed to avoid the concentration of central state powers which was considered to be the hallmark of the old European systems from which America was breaking loose. The primacy of the legislature in the original constitution, the inbuilding of numerous checks and balances to central power, and the adoption of a federal system were all aspects of a deliberate political aversion to overweening central control. Constitutional federalism inhibited the penetration of central power throughout the nation by ensuring the integrity of these states, each with its own institutional organization, legal code and law-enforcement apparatus. After the Revolution, no standing

army remained and the establishment of state religions was formally pro-
scribed. As Showronek has pointed out, it was this 'broad-based diffusion
of power among the localities [that] was the organizational feature of early
American government most clearly responsible for the distinctive sense of
statelessness in American political culture'.[12]

The real decentralization of power, and the illusion of statelessness
that issued from it, were clearly important features of American political
individuality. Not least for our concerns here, the notion of the minimal
state was important in that it weakened the typical Anglo-Saxon popular
fear of the state which might otherwise have been, as in England, a powerful impediment to the development of state forms in public education.
However, it should in no way be confused with the absence of state power,
in the broad sense of the term. Capitalism in the United States, as elsewhere,
relied on the apparatus of law which sustained the interests of private property and profit, and required for its development an environment of social
order and regulation which local government, churches, courts and schools
sought to maintain. Above all, American capitalism benefited from the ideology of competitive individualism which the agencies of the state, as well as
civil society itself, were successful in promoting. As the nineteenth century
wore on, aspects of central state control became more evident, the federal executive gained more powers, parties developed which, through the
'spoils system', created the central and local bureaucracies, and the legal
system grew to become a major pillar of state power. At the end of the
century a revolution in government was occurring which created a more
European-style central state apparatus.

The decentralized and diffuse nature of the American state clearly
had important repercussions for the nature of the education systems
which developed there. The involvement of the central state in the early
development of public education was correspondingly less than in Europe,
and, to a remarkable extent, the early schools were the product of private
initiatives in civil society, from both corporate bodies and individuals acting
collectively in the community. The experience of self-determining communities on the frontier in creating local schools was important not only for the
mythology it created but also in actuality. There was undoubtedly a kernel of
truth in Cubberley's assertion that 'everywhere development has been from
the community outward and upwards, and not from the state downward'.[13]
However, this deeply embedded ideology of American localism, whilst pointing to certain important realities, has also served to mask the degree to which
the state, both central and local, was actually involved in the development
of education. As David Tyack has pointed out recently, 'Much of the recent
historiography has been apolitical, almost stateless.'[14]

The importance of education for the forming of the American nation has
been generally accepted. In a land settled by immigrants with different cultures and speaking different languages, and where there were no ancient

national institutions to build on, education was uniquely important for the construction of nationhood. However, the degree to which this was the result of concerted political effort on the part of generations of political and community leaders has been somewhat obscured by the strong emphasis on local self-activity. Education in the United States, as elsewhere, was an important factor in the construction of a hegemonic ideology and a social order which was not, in fact, a classless Americanism as in republican myth, but involved relations of power and domination between different ethnic and class groups. As such it was clearly not merely the result of spontaneous action amongst equal individuals in the community. Demands and activity clearly issued from 'below' but they were inevitably organized from above, even where not specifically by the federal state itself.

Education did not come into prominence as a national issue and one that fundamentally concerned the state until the revolutionary era and, of course, could not have done so whilst the country was still a collection of colonies. However, there was an important shift towards a conception of public education in the colonial period and one that did at times involve the local colonial administrations. The change was essentially one involving a movement from community and church-based education to the institution of formal schooling.

Education in the colonial period

The education of the first generation of settlers was essentially a family and community affair, and the forms it took were a direct inheritance from the medieval past. 'Serving the needs of a homogeneous, slowly changing rural society,' writes Bailyn,

> they were largely instinctive and traditional, little articulated and little formalized. The most important agency of transfer of culture was not formal institutions of instruction or public instruments of communication, but the family.... What the family left undone by way of informal education the local community most often completed. It did so in entirely natural ways, for so elaborate was the architecture of family organization and so deeply founded was it in the soil of stable, slowly changing village and town communities in which intermarriage among the same groups had taken place generation after generation, that it was at times difficult for the child to know where the family left off and the greater society began ... the youth moved naturally and gradually across the borderline that separates the personal from the impersonal world of authority.[15]

Alongside the family and the community generally, the Church was the centripetal force in integrating society and a major force in education. For the older children the apprenticeship formed the last stage in the process of childhood education.

These traditional forms, however, could not be sustained under the material conditions of colonial settlement, and a number of factors served to undermine this organic and informal provision of education. Plentiful land and opportunity made it easy to set up a household, and families soon dispersed into smaller, geographically separated units, as resettlement continually disrupted stable communities. A new family form emerged, typically the isolated conjugal unit with dispersed lines of descent and partible inheritance. At the same time the spread of wage labour undermined the traditional paternalism of certain forms of labour. Bonded servitude declined in the seventeenth century as the scarcity of labour and the demand for servants gave bondsmen the power to reduce their obligations. Voluntary indenture, the system by which impoverished immigrants repaid the cost of their transportation, also declined, whereas the apprenticeship, which still involved paternal obligations on the part of the apprentice master, became increasingly perfunctory as masters sacrificed their obligations for greater profits.[16] In sum, there was a general loosening of community ties and mutual obligations on which the traditional form of education depended.

As traditional educational forms were undermined, so education was increasingly transferred to external agencies. Initially, it was the towns and neighbourhoods which decided to set up schools. Sometimes families formed groups to organize subscription schools and sometimes they sent their children to private-venture schools or small dame schools.[17] Churches also played an increasing role in providing schooling. As religious sects became more prolific and as their competition for membership from dispersed populations became more intense, evangelicalism increasingly turned to schools as a vehicle for spreading the word. Quakers, Presbyterians, Baptists, Mennonites, Lutherans and Moravians set up schools in abundance, and it was not until the mid-eighteenth century that this educational sectarianism began to break down due to a lack of financial resources and schooling gradually became more secular.[18]

Whilst the church and township was the most dynamic force in the spread of schools during the colonial period, colonial governments were far from disinterested in the question. A number of New England colonies enacted laws concerning education. In Massachusetts, legislation in 1642 and 1647 introduced property taxes for schools, required towns of 50 householders to appoint and pay teachers, and towns of 100 householders to provide a grammar school.[19] Officers of the town were required to ensure that families were fulfilling their educational obligations, a measure which reflected the concern expressed in the preface to the 1642 Statute regarding 'the neglect of many parents and masters in training up their children in learning and labour'.[20] Similar laws were enacted in Connecticut in 1665, Plymouth

County in 1658 and New Hampshire in 1680.[21] Not all of these laws were enforceable and certainly the broad stream of enforcing legislation dwindled during the eighteenth century, as rural communities failed to keep up. However, as an early demonstration of the state's interest in education, they were clearly important.

Overall, schools multiplied during the colonial period well in excess of the increase in population, and although the majority still did not go to school, there was clearly a shift in educational provision away from the family and community, and towards the public and formal.[22] Whilst obviously not yet concerned with any clear sense of nationhood, schools were already seen as a means of maintaining social control where family and community restraints and control were lacking.

Education and the American Revolution

It was during the revolutionary era that education in the United States first became a national issue and one that was seen to be a central concern of the state, even if the role of the state remained largely exhortatory. The struggle for independence from Britain, whilst falling far short of a domestic revolution in social relations, was the moment in which the American nation, as a political entity, was constituted, and in the extraordinary intellectual ferment of those years, every aspect of the nation's character and destiny was probed, contested and constantly reformulated. The importance of education for the nation as a whole became abundantly clear. A newly formed nation, especially one composed of disparate national groups without a common heritage or ancient national institutions to draw on, required a national identity and a national culture. Republicanism as a political system was thought to be uniquely dependent on the virtue and character of its people for survival; the more so if the United States was to realize its destiny as a land of unparalleled opportunity and liberty. In all of these respects, education was held to be a crucial factor – in the words of Andrew Lunt some years later, the 'very bulwark of the republic' and the 'pillars' on which American democracy was supported.[23]

To many of its early founders, the American Republic was distinctly fragile. They believed, as David Tyack has put it, that 'republics were as evanescent as fire-flies on a summer evening', that Europe was conspiring to wreck the nation and that internal disorders and factions were threatening to shatter the republican community.[24] Some, such as Thomas Jefferson, feared a new absolutism. 'Experience hath shewn', he wrote, 'that even under the best forms [of government], those entrusted with power have, in time, and by slow operations, perverted it into tyranny'.[25] Others, such as the more conservative Federalist, Noah Webster, worried that republican government might prove anarchical. 'The United States', he wrote, are in no danger of monarchy or the aristocracy of hereditary estates and offices. But these states will always be exposed to anarchy and faction, because these evils approach under the delusive but specious guise of patriotism.[26]

Whatever their fears they believed that only intelligence, wisdom and virtue amongst the people would protect them from future catastrophe. Independence from Britain had been won, and a new constitution had been written, but only an ongoing revolution would achieve the lofty ideals which, they believed, destiny had entrusted to them. According to Benjamin Rush, a Republican and signatory to the Declaration of Independence, they had only finished the first act of the great drama: 'We have changed our forms of government, but it remains yet to effect a revolution in our principles, opinions and manners so as to accommodate them to the forms of government we have adopted.'[27]

This revolution was to be accomplished, above all, through education, and to men such as Webster, Jefferson and Rush, there could be no doubt that education was a political process, designed to promote certain values and beliefs. To Benjamin Rush, it was both possible and desirable that education should nurture certain political ideas; indeed, it should endeavour to 'convert men into republican machines'.[28] The converts would then follow, as if automatically, the duties and principles connected with the republican ideal. 'While we inculcate these republican duties upon our pupil,' he wrote,

we must not neglect at the same time to inspire him with republican principles. He must be taught that there can be no durable liberty but in a republic and that government, like all other sciences, is of a progressive nature. The chains that have bound this science in Europe are happily unloosed in America. Here it is open to investigation and improvement.[29]

The connection between education and liberty was one that was fundamental to enlightenment philosophy. Freedom could only be vouchsafed by the vigilance and educated judgement of the people; democracy could only work if those who elected representatives to govern made enlightened choices. 'Enlighten the people generally,' wrote Jefferson, 'and tyranny and oppression of body and mind will vanish like evil spirits at the dawn of day ... the diffusion of knowledge among the people is to be the instrument of vast progress.'[30]

The preservation of liberties and the republican form of government involved the development of new citizens both devoted to national ideals and able to conduct their civic duties. In his preamble to the 1779 Bill for Free Schools in Virginia, Jefferson called on schools to develop in pupils the skills and qualities necessary for citizenship in a republic. The republic needed able leaders chosen on merit, virtuous lawmakers and citizens who could choose them wisely. Women, according to Rush, should also be instructed in the 'virtues of liberty, government and patriotism'. However, this was not so much for performing their own role as citizens as for 'instructing their sons in the principles of liberty and government'.[31] For the most part their education was to be preparation for 'the discharge of [their] most important duty [as] mothers'.[32] The education of girls was also concerned with citizenship, but their role was clearly defined in terms of what they provided for others. To Noah Webster, 'a good education is that which renders the ladies correct in their manners, respectable in their families, and agreeable in society'. Their education should 'enable them to implant in the tender mind [of their children] such sentiments of virtue, propriety and dignity as are suited to the freedom of our governments'.[33]

In promoting the values of republican government, political leaders were also trying to form a distinctive American national culture and character. The manner in which the American Republic was created, through a decisive rupture with Europe, made the stress on American values all the more important. To justify the break from Britain, the principles for which the United States was to stand had continually to be cast in distinction to the corruption and servitude to the state, which was believed to be characteristic of the Old World. Again, education was important because it was through a vernacular US education that an American character could be formed, and the independence of American from European culture sealed. According to Webster, 'our national character is not yet formed'. As he exhorted his compatriots:

> You have been children long enough, subject to the control and subservient to the interest of a haughty parent. You have now an interest of your own to augment and defend: you have an empire to raise and support by your exertions and a national character to establish and extend by your wisdom and virtues. To effect these great objects it is necessary to frame a liberal plan of policy and build it on a broad system of education.[34]

This involved not only the inculcation of republican values but also the development of a specifically American cultural tradition. Webster, himself, played an important role in this enterprise as the author of numerous readers and spelling books which attempted to homogenize the American language, instruct in patriotic principles and hasten the development of an American literature, through judicious selections of speeches from representative leaders.

The harnessing of education to the project of US national development clearly had enormous repercussions for the education system as a whole. Not only had the state and political leadership come to feel a definite interest in its development; from now on it would be subject to continuous pressure from above to develop in particular ways and perform particular functions. American leaders were highly prescriptive about the forms that education should now assume. Numerous plans were drawn up for public education systems and the ideas which education should convey were explicitly stated. Men such as Jefferson and Rush wanted students to think critically but they also wanted political and cultural uniformity. In his bill for education in Virginia, Jefferson wrote that every teacher should 'give assurance of fidelity to the Commonwealth', and in granting a charter to the University of Virginia he insisted that the 'Board of Visitors' should prescribe textbooks that would avoid pernicious federalist materials.[35]

From the moment that education became thus yoked to national ambitions and, in effect, became a political issue, it was clear that it would no longer be left to the spontaneous initiatives of ordinary Americans in their towns and neighbourhood communities. Despite the libertarian rhetoric of political leaders and educationalists, in which education was the guarantor of freedom and individual rights, a new function was emerging which had more to do with control and cultural conditioning, and this was clearly not to be left to chance and local caprice. Public education has everywhere been Janus-faced, at once the very fount of enlightenment and liberty, and a vehicle for control and political socialization. During the American revolutionary period, both of these aspects were equally evident. Ideologically, it was essential that education in the United States should be seen to embody the ideas of liberty and opportunity. At the same time, politically, it was necessary that education should serve the libertarian capitalist state by ensuring the order and stability which it required. The American ruling classes were concerned equally about order as about liberty. In fact, the republicanism of the revolutionary era was essentially a very conservative revolutionary force. There were as many who feared anarchy as those who feared the return of aristocratic tyranny. The political constitution that was adopted was certainly democratic by the standards of France, Germany and England at the beginning of the nineteenth century. However, it was far from being a full democracy. The limitations on the franchise and the constitution of an upper house in Congress were specifically designed to put a brake on popular sovereignty. Education was caught between the twin poles of liberty and control. Its function, in a sense, was precisely to reconcile freedom and order, to make sure that the liberties of a democratic state did not conflict with the basic structure of the capitalist system. Nor were the principles of many who wrote about education exactly egalitarian. Jefferson, for instance, believed that people could be divided into two classes. For the labouring class, three years of education in the three Rs and republican values were adequate, whilst for the 'learned', who would provide the elite of leaders in society and form an aristocracy of talent, the highest levels of education were necessary. The political ideals of the early republican leaders were closer to those of the eighteenth-century enlightenment thinkers, the *philosophes*, than to the Jacobins of the French Revolution. This preoccupation with reconciling liberty and order through education was not, in this sense, so far away from that held by educationalists in Restoration France. Where they differed was primarily in their conception of the state.

Education in the early republic

Despite the intense interest of federal politicians in the issue, education in the United States after the Revolution and during the early national period remained a decentralized affair. The Constitution itself made no mention of it, and in the Tenth Amendment it was reserved as a function of the individual states. The development of schools, whilst encouraged by an ideological climate established by political leaders, continued for some time to rest primarily on the efforts of private groups. In the rural areas the local community remained the mainspring of development, whilst in the towns and major cities it was increasingly the charitable organizations that made the running.

During the early Republic the typical school in the rural North East and the new Mid-West was the district school, organized and controlled by a small locality and funded through taxes on property, fuel contributions, tuition fees and, latterly, through state aid.[36] The district system had been adopted from the late eighteenth century onwards as populations dispersing from towns into outlying areas sought control over their own schools. Maine, Vermont, New Hampshire, Rhode Island and Connecticut had adopted this system early; other states did so later: New York in 1812; Ohio in 1821; and Illinois in 1825.[37] District school committees controlled these schools, selecting teachers, deciding what subjects should be taught and determining the length of the school term.[38] Rural schools were anything but uniform, reflecting in religion and language the communities they served, but within each area they tended towards commonality. Small, dispersed communities could not afford to keep more than one school. During the reform period the district system was increasingly attacked as inefficient and corrupt, and, under the centralizing and standardizing pressures of the time, districts were slowly consolidated into larger areas and schools became more dependent on state funds.

In contrast with the community schooling of rural areas, urban schooling tended to be more specialized and class-divided.[39] During the early decades of the century, numerous types of school co-existed in the growing urban areas. Those whose parents could pay, perhaps four-fifths of the population, tended to go to independent pay schools and academies.[40] The wealthy hired private tutors or patronized select boarding schools, whilst the middle classes used private-venture day schools whose fees were often not beyond the reach of clerks and skilled labourers.[41] Complementing these numerous independent pay schools were the dame schools, operated by women in their homes for small children, providing custodial care and rudimentary training at low fees.[42] For those children whose parents could afford neither of these, such education as they received was largely through apprenticeships and church or charity schools.

Charity schools became the forerunners of the mid-century common schools, but they did not start out that way. The expansion of charity schooling through church and philanthropic organizations began in the first decade of the century as a response to fears about the growth of the urban poor. Their aim was essentially to bring morality and discipline to a growing army of churchless poor and, unlike the rural district schools, they were less an extension of parental values than an attempt to substitute for a culture which parents were deemed to lack. Schools for blacks and whites were generally separate, but in both cases free philanthropic education was an attempt to condition the poor in the values of the Protestant middle class.

The urban common schools of the mid-century were largely the result of the consolidation and transformation of these early charity schools into a public education system. Charity schooling was the innovative sector. As Kaestle points out, 'Here began the pedagogical, organizational and financial reforms that extended public schooling, and with it Anglo-American protestant culture, to growing numbers of poor people.' As charity schooling expanded, independent schooling was on the wane. In many cases 'the charity schools literally became the public schools'.[43] This process of osmosis began with the agglomeration of various charity schools under the aegis of leading philanthropic organizations, which subsequently began to commandeer public funds and broaden their clientele, thus aspiring towards 'public' schools. The New York Free School Society was a case in point. Initially incorporated in 1805 to serve children of churchless, indigent parents, it changed its character in 1808 to include the churchgoing poor. Thereafter it gradually consolidated other charity schools under its control and began to command a greater proportion of public money. Finally, changing its name to the Public School Society, it opened its doors to all children, charging fees to those whose parents could afford it. In 1832, instruction became free to all students and by 1835 the society had become by far the largest school organization in New York City.[44] This process of systemization involved more than just consolidation. 'The trustees of the public school society attempted to standardize procedures and content, introduced supervision, carried on teacher training, and articulated more clearly the different levels of the system.'[45] In this drive towards rational organization and standardization they prefigured the work of the reformers of the following decades.

Schooling in the southern slave states developed more slowly than in the North and conformed to neither the rural nor the city patterns of the North East and Mid-West. The greater level of class and racial division in the South pre-empted the possibility of adopting the common district school, whilst aristocratic ideologies of philanthropy were less conducive to the systematic development of city schools for broad sections of the population than was the more democratic, public spirited philanthropy of northern puritan culture. Colonial education in southern areas, such as Virginia, had consisted of private tutors and private schools for the rich, with charity schools for pauper families, but there was little state interest in the problem of education except to see that orphans and children of the indigent poor were properly apprenticed and trained in some useful trade.[46] During the early Republic, schools continued to develop along highly stratified lines with the proliferation of private, church and pauper schools. Any notion of 'public' schooling was strictly limited and in many states there was great resistance to state intervention other than for pauper children. School attendance was generally lower than in the North, not only for the children of slaves who were largely debarred from formal education, particularly after 1830, but also for white children, many of whom made do with *ad hoc* private schools established by itinerant school masters.

Enrolment rates increased overall during this period but exhibited very uneven regional patterns. The greatest increases appear to have occurred in the small towns and rural areas of the North, where an increasing acceptance of the district system, plus a greatly enhanced interest in education for girls, created a greater demand which increased, if limited, state funds helped to satisfy. According to Kaestle, in New York State in 1800, approximately 37 per cent of all children under 20 went to school, whereas by 1825 this had increased to 60 per cent.[47] Enrolment rates in cities, however, appear to have remained fairly constant, probably due to the difficulty of meeting sharply rising demands due to increased population size. Between 1790 and 1850 there was a fairly constant rate of enrolment for under 20s in New York City of 26 per cent. The South remained considerably behind in this. Albert Fishlow estimates that between 1800 and 1839 the average enrolment rate may have been as low as 16 per cent.[48]

Education in the early Republic thus developed in a variety of ways according to the cultural traditions of the region and the political complexion of the state. Puritan morality and democratic republican traditions stimulated education in northern states, whilst slavery and aristocratic ideologies retarded it in southern states. In northern rural areas, dispersed populations and as yet unformed class relations allowed the growth of more common schools under substantial local control, whereas in the cities a social structure of already sharp class distinctions underlay a more hierarchical provision of schooling which owed less to local democratic initiative and control, and exhibited more clearly the relations of power and class inequality that would characterize school provision of the later period. As Kaestle shows, the charity school was clearly 'antagonistic to the child's family and peer influences', whereas the district school tended to reflect an extension of parental control. With such a variety of forms, clearly there can be no single model of educational development for the United States during this period. However, certain qualifications need to be made to the orthodox account of schooling by spontaneous local and democratic initiative.

Educational development in the United States was certainly distinct from any European patterns. The social conditions of the early Republic, in particular the dispersal of populations and relative fluidity of the class structure in the North, allowed the early development of forms of common school, particularly in rural areas, which were apparently more 'democratic' in structure than schools in Europe. Furthermore, the spread of republican values, with their stress on individual opportunity and initiative, combined with the relatively weak presence of the federal state apparatus, encouraged an ideology of localism that attempted to maximize community control over schools. However, these differences, whilst being the source of a potent educational mythology, were only relative and applied only in certain regions. The hierarchical school provision of the southern states and the charity schooling of northern cities already exhibited keen class distinctions and had departed considerably from the model of local democratic control. The classic view of American educational development as proceeding from the bottom up in a process of spontaneous local self-activity is hardly tenable as a general explanation.

The degree to which educational development was promoted by an ideological climate established by republican leaders during the revolutionary era has already been suggested. However, the contribution of the state could also be more direct than this and has often been underplayed. Certainly, the role of the federal and local state apparatus was limited in the early period by certain factors. As Tyack says,

> The influence of the federal or state governments on public education was diffuse... public hostility to centralization of power, weak federal and state bureaucracies, executive vetoes, splintered administrations, and court review of legislation – to say nothing of legislatures themselves – all combined to attenuate the influence of federal and state governments on the county and local governments.[49]

However, both the federal government and the state legislatures had a significant impact in the sense that they could exhort, persuade and enable through legislation local authorities to adopt specific educational policies.

The federal government exercised its influence through land grants and conditions attached to new territories entering the Union. By the 1785 Ordinance, one lot in each new township, where these comprised 365 lots or square miles, should be laid aside for educational purposes. Between 1803 and 1896, federal government gave more than 77 million acres to western and southern states to support common school funds. These lots increased considerably in value over time and by the later decades of the nineteenth century, most states west of the Mississippi gained 10 per cent of school revenues from school funds based on land. In 1833 President Jackson withdrew $10 million from federal reserves for distribution to state banks for educational use. Congress also required territories to devise state constitutions, and thereby induced leaders in new states to think systematically about how to provide education as one amongst an array of institutions designed to build a republican form of government.[50]

State constitutions did frequently include educational provisions. Of the 45 state constitutions written between 1792 and 1912, 29 included provision for state superintendents, 15 for state boards, 10 for county supervisors, 35 for land grants, 36 for school funds, 19 for state taxes and 18 for nonsectarian education.[51] Individual states also passed numerous laws both empowering and prescribing local areas to provide schools and raise taxes for their financing, and creating state inspectors and boards of education. Not least, also, was the influence of politicians and state superintendents in arguing for public education. Whilst in most areas of social provision the American state was slow to become involved, public education was one major exception.

Although it was some time before the argument in favour of state control of education was won, and public education systems were created, it is clear that the origins of public education systems lay in the political impulses that were generated by the Revolution and the ascendance of American nationalism in the early years of the Republic. This close connection between the development of public education and nation-building in the United States goes some way to explaining how a county opposed to central state control and deeply attached to localism and voluntary initiative in education could produce a public education system years in advance of a country such as England, which held an equal aversion to state controls in education. The exceptional character of education development in the United States lay in the fact that a potentially disabling liberal philosophy of *laissez-faire* educational development was counterbalanced by forces particularly favourable to the development of public education. On the one hand, the impetus towards nation-building through education was particularly powerful in a country with diverse populations, unformed political and civil institutions, and lacking other obvious instruments of social control and ideological hegemony. On the other hand, the development of democratic political forms and ideologies was sufficiently advanced to encourage a belief in widely diffused education and to neutralize those more reactionary 'aristocratic' ideologies which, for instance, in England proved to be a powerful barrier to education development. In a country whose ruling classes had relatively little to fear from educating politically unorganized popular classes, and whose people believed that they were largely free from any danger of European-style state tyranny, the arguments against allowing the development of state-supervised public education were relatively weak, in all quarters. In the absence of such impediments, and with the powerful motivation of forming an enlightened and ordered nation, it was possible and desirable to make an exception of education and to allow it to grow as a public, state-organized institution where in other areas of social provision the attitude was strictly of 'state – hands off'.

The reform era

By 1830 the United States had numerous schools of various kinds but no school systems as such. It was during the next 30 years, the period of the so-called 'era of reforms', that systems of public education were first consolidated in the northern states, initially in the Puritan strongholds of the North East, and spreading out from there into the states of the Mid-West and Mid-Atlantic region. The main directions of reform were remarkably consistent in all of these areas, although the composition and depth of opposing forces might vary, and in the course of three decades the basic framework of public education systems had been settled in all northern states.

The process involved consolidation, standardization and increased public control. The district system of locally controlled schools gradually, and not without fierce local resistance, gave way to more centralized systems of town schools; private schooling steadily waned and lost ground to public schools, as public funding increased and tax support replaced the rate bill (or tuition fee) as the primary source of funding. Schooling became more standardized and its organization more professional; teacher training was encouraged and teachers were increasingly engaged in the reading of professional journals and attendance at educational seminars. Supervision by the state, through the offices of school superintendents, limited the autonomy of local school committees, and, through the unremitting efforts of reformers and officers, new policies and practices were disseminated throughout the different schools to unify the curriculum and standardize teaching procedures. By slow degrees, attendance became more regularized and included a growing proportion of children. Enrolment increased most slowly in the large cities, but in the rural areas of the North it had become more or less universal by the mid-century. Whilst elementary education was thus extended and systematized, public secondary education, in the shape of new high schools, was extended, creating in urban areas systems of grade schools which provided a rudimentary educational ladder, at least for white children, although, of course, the majority still made no use of the high school itself.

Why efforts to create these public school systems should have prevailed in the North during this period, when previously they had failed, has been the subject of much speculation. Because their development coincided with accelerating industrialization in the North East, increasing immigration and growing urban populations throughout the North, and the emergence of more defined ethnic and class antagonisms, particularly in urban areas,

many writers have concluded that these were the social forces which underlay reform. The strengths and limitations of these arguments have already
been considered in some detail. It seems that although all of these factors were relevant in part, they cannot fully account for the ubiquitous
spread of reform in the North, which was still dominated by communities of
small, independent farmers living in small towns in essentially agricultural,
rural areas. This was still a period of transition from an agrarian small producer economy and, although there were early features of the new industrial
order, they had scarcely remade American consciousness or transformed the
ideology of 'free soil', small-farmer republicanism.

For all of the growing signs of social change, it would be a mistake to see
this period as if it were quite singular and distinct from the early national
period. In social and economic terms it witnessed considerable changes, but
little that was not an extension of trends already in operation before; in
education it was certainly an era of qualitatively distinct development but
in a sense this too was a continuation of the earlier movement towards
universal and systematic elementary education, only shifted, as it were,
into a higher gear. The ideology which would support the idea of public
education was established before, and it was the mechanism which was now
developed, albeit with a renewed sense of urgency prompted by burgeoning
social problems.

Essentially, this period represents a consolidation and culmination and,
although the reforms met with considerable resistance, which created an
aura of crusading zeal amongst proponents, this was not an educational
revolution and 1830 represented no revolutionary rupture. The reforms are
probably best understood as the product of that same movement towards
nation-building which was their basis in the revolutionary era – but in a new
context and subject to changing forces. Where before education had been
promoted as an essential vehicle for creating a new national identity and
character, and as the main ideological bulwark of republicanism in its fragile post-revolutionary incarnation, now it was required to perform a similar
integrating function, but in a context where the forces of social fragmentation were more varied and deep-seated. In addition to the potential sources
of disorder and anarchy which politicians had believed characteristic of the
new nation, new and potentially disruptive contradictions were emerging,
not least in the concentration of new waves of immigrants in large cities,
in intensified cultural and ethnic divisions, and in emergent class contradictions. Added to this were further threats to the nation and the Union,
both from abroad and at home, which revivified the fervent nationalism
and republican unionism of the dominant culture. The War of 1812 had
stoked up the nationalist feelings of a generation, whilst the ever-present
threat to the integrity of the Union from the seemingly 'irrepressible conflict'
between southern slave power and northern republicanism provided continuous stimulus for fervent celebration of the values of the American Union

and of cohesive nationhood. Now, as before, education was invoked to promote republican values and to integrate disparate social forces. However, to do this it had to confront problems that were greater than hitherto: there were more diverse and antagonistic groups to be assimilated, incipient class divisions to be managed, social problems to be controlled and, above all, widening political and ideological wounds to be sutured. Of course, no system could be adequate to these problems, but American faith in the power of education was, as ever, boundless.

The immediate causes of the reforms in education lay in the successful campaigns of the reforming lobby. These involved advocates both in and out of political office, and their allies in the press and amongst the public at large. The reform movement of 1830–60 has been repeatedly described as a victorious moral crusade by sympathetic historians. Whether or not one sympathizes with its aims, this characterization captures a certain truth: the movement constituted, above all, an ideological battle which was won more through persuasion and dexterous political manoeuvring than through coercion. The battleground was the individual state, and whilst the objective involved greater centralization and 'state' control of education, the means adopted were essentially consistent with the decentralized and localist traditions of American democracy, such as it was. The process of reform thus had little in common with developments in Europe or in England. Unlike the educational reforms in Prussia and France, which were disseminated from the centre outward, and largely by decree, reforms in the American North owed relatively little to central federal initiative, and where they rested on public authority proceeded usually by legislation that was enabling rather than prescriptive. The main locus of public intervention remained at the level of the individual state's legislatures and county authorities, and the degree to which these were reflective of popular opinion can be gauged from the continuous vacillations, reversals and re-enactments which characterize the educational legislation of this period. In its continued opposition to 'Prussianizing' central control, this process reflected the Anglo-Saxon roots of its pioneers; however, in other respects it had little in common with the process of educational reform in England. Where educational reform in England was politically stalemated by contending political factions, in the United States it enjoyed a wide basis of support, despite fierce localized opposition; whereas in England educational reformers were obliged to operate a covert policy of administrative incrementalism that by-passed political factions, in America the process of reform was always overtly political and had a high public profile. Fortunately for American reformers, they could rely, at the end of the day, on cementing a political alliance in favour of reforms that could overwhelm most of the pockets where opposition was most entrenched.

The leading reformers themselves, men such as Horace Mann, John Pierce and Henry Barnard, were largely from Puritan middle-class families of

Anglo-Saxon descent. Their values were those of the dominant Protestant republican culture of the North and their aims clearly involved the imposition of these on other disparate communities, which inevitably resisted this cultural domination. However, despite their sectional roots, their reform platform was articulated in broad democratic terms and enjoyed wide support. At the basis of the movement for education reform was a wide bedrock of support for education improvement generally. Aside from southern opposition to the education of slaves, which was adamantine, there was no significant constituency which opposed the development of education *per se.* The whole ideology of American republicanism rested so firmly on a belief in freedom, opportunity and moral virtue that opposition to mass education would have been unthinkably un-American for most northerners. In the more aristocratic culture of the southern slave states, many slave-holders opposed reform in public education but there were few in the North who would stand out against the rights of individual citizens, at least whites, to improve themselves through education, as for many years Tory Anglicans did in England. The only serious argument concerned what form educational development should take.

There were basically two camps in the struggle over educational reform: those who supported the creation of a more uniform public school system, and those who opposed greater centralization and favoured the retention of the district system. Those who opposed what they termed 'Prussian influence', which meant public common schools, state supervision and tax support, formed an extremely heterogeneous alliance and one that was never capable of mustering a sustained and coherent opposition. They included German Lutherans and Mennonites who wished to maintain their cultural identity and favoured separate schooling in their native language; Catholics who objected to Protestant hegemony and anti-Irish prejudice in public schools; and some free blacks who argued that separate schooling was preferable to racism and low teacher expectations of black pupils in public schools. To these were joined some special interest groups, such as private school proprietors, who naturally opposed measures which limited their influence.[52] In addition to these were those of all social groups who were suspicious of reforms that would increase taxation and reduce local control. The last group consisted to a large extent of democrats loyal to the Jeffersonian tradition of state minimalism and who opposed centralizing measures.

In aggregate, although rarely together, these groups managed to stall reform in some areas for a number of years. Opposition to the abolition of the district system was particularly fierce. In Massachusetts, for instance, there was legislation in 1853 which encouraged the voluntary abolition of districts, and again in 1859 which required it. Within a year, opposition had forced the repeal of this legislation and it was not until 1869 that abolition was again required through legislation, only to be repealed the following year in an act which allowed the re-establishment of districts. They were not finally abolished until 1883.[53]

There was similar opposition in many areas to the creation of free schooling. In Kenusha, Wisconsin, the electorate voted for a free school system, then abolished it, and finally recreated it in the 1840s.[54] The most successful resistance to school reform came from Catholic communities which, although unable to prevent reforms in the public school system, successfully fought to maintain a network of independent Catholic schools. The legacy of opposition to reform survived in these and other independent schools, and in the degree both to which local influence was retained despite increasing central control, and in the way in which cultural pluralism persisted in common schools despite the overweening Protestant assimilationist aims of the reformers. However, opponents of reform could not permanently block the movement towards common public education in the long term, not only because they themselves were a fragmented opposition but also because of the breadth of support on the other side.

The ideological bloc in favour of school reform was altogether more widespread in its constituency and more coherent in its aims. It included Whigs and Democrats, and supporters from all social classes. Although the reformers' characteristic stress on central supervision, uniformity, state intervention and cultural assimilation was more characteristically Whig than Democrat, the reformers counted amongst their supporters many Democrats who favoured public education as a force for greater social equality. When the Ohio legislature established a state superintendency of public schooling in 1837, the measures were passed by a majority of the House of Representatives with 19 Whigs and 16 Democrats voting for, and 15 Whigs and 19 Democrats voting against. Such were the overlapping boundaries of party support on educational issues.[55]

That education reform enjoyed a considerable base of support from different social classes has been generally agreed by educational historians of this period.[56] Although we know relatively little about the views of unskilled workers and agricultural labourers, there is considerable evidence that the working men's organizations of the 1830s gave their support to extended public education.[57] These organizations flourished particularly between 1828 and 1834 during which time they effectively publicized their demands for tax-supported common schools. Working men in New Castle, Delaware, for instance, pledged in the preamble to their 1830 constitution to 'unite at the polls and give our votes to no candidate who is not pledged to support a rational system of education to be paid for out of public funds'.[58] A meeting of 'Working men, mechanics and others friendly to their interests' in Boston on 17 August 1830 resolved 'that the establishment of a liberal system of education, attainable by all, should be among the first efforts of every law giver who desires the continuance of our national independence'. In 1836 the General Trades Union of Cincinnati, Ohio, issued an 'Appeal to working men of the West' in which it pledged to fight for a 'national system of education'.[59]

It may be objected that these organizations had an extremely broad class membership and could hardly be taken as representative of working-class opinion. Certainly they contained not only mechanics but also small employers, and excluded few from their definition of working men except where they were considered not to belong to the producing class. Andrew Jackson had defined 'the producing classes' as all those whose work directly involved the production of goods, including farmers, labourers, mechanics and small businessmen. Only those who profited from the work of others, such as speculators, bankers and lawyers, were excluded. Such a catholic definition of 'working men' was common in the North, and where organizations represented this broad constituency it is difficult to be precise about the class basis of their support for education.[60] However, there is little evidence of any concerted opposition to public education reform from the wage-labouring population where this was based on class issues rather than ethnic or religious loyalties. Even where these did exist they were often attributable to local circumstances rather than being indicative of general ideological opposition. Michael Katz, for instance, has argued that the vote to abolish Beverly High School in 1861 was due to working-class dissent, but recent research by Maris Vinovskis has shown that whilst the negative vote correlates with occupational wealth and status, a closer correlation existed with neighbourhood resistance, suggesting that the issues concerned geographical access and localism, not the existence of a high school as such.[61]

The key to the relatively rapid development of public education in the northern states during this period undoubtedly lies in the breadth of support which it could command. Well orchestrated by politically astute reformers, the reform programme could appeal to both collective and individual interests of large sections of the population. As Carl Kaestle summarizes it,

> The reforms prevailed because they served the predominate ideology, and because a majority of the people in the North appear to have been convinced that a cosmopolitan school system would serve not only the collective goals of republicanism, Protestantism and capitalism, but individual goals of enlightenment, morality and personal advancement as well.[62]

That this should have been so clear has to do with the way in which educational policies and values articulated with the fundamental values of North American society; most importantly, in the concepts of class and nation on which republican ideology rested.

One reason for the popularity of educational reforms lay in the way in which they appealed to notions of personal freedom, opportunity and social mobility. The common stance of educational reformers on these issues was broadly progressive in the Jacksonian and ante-bellum periods, and amounted to a diffuse but consistent egalitarianism. Public schools were preferred to private institutions not only because they were held to be more efficient but also because they were considered to be more democratic.

Private schooling was rejected by many advocates, such as Henry Barnard, because they believed that they classified society at the root 'by assorting children according to wealth, education, or outward circumstances of their parents, into different schools' and so educated 'children of the same neighbourhood differently and unequally'.[63] The idea of social mobility through education was certainly stronger amongst Democrats and in the proclamations of the working men's groups than amongst the prominent educational reformers and the Whig theorists whom they relied upon. However, if reform advocates put relatively little emphasis on social mobility in their writings, often assuming that children would continue for the most part in the social 'station' of their parents, they did claim to believe in opportunity and advancement by merit where deserved. As John Pierce, the Superintendent of Michigan Schools, wrote in his report of 1837 (Common School Report),

By means of the public schools the poor boy of today, without the protection of father or mother, may be the man of learning and influence tomorrow, and he may accumulate and die the possessor of tens of thousands, he may even reach the highest station in the Republic.[64]

The common school was proclaimed as the most democratic institution which could offer opportunities for all. As the popular educational author Alonzo Potter put it, 'If the school is an essential agent of civilization, it is the common school that forms the appropriate agent of modern and democratic civilization – if that civilization is one which aims at the greatest good for the greatest number.'[65] In their stress on hard work, advancement by merit and the availability of opportunity for all, the educational reformers reflected the dominant themes of republican doctrine which were shared by broad sections of the American population. If these themes had a cross-class appeal, it was because the values of populist US capitalism also had a relatively broad class appeal. From the inauguration of Andrew Jackson's presidency in 1828 through to the formation of the Republican Party in the early 1850s, the essential values of small-producer capitalism – the belief in free soil, free labour and the validity of productive entrepreneurial capitalism – formed the basis of an ideological hegemony which persisted despite the emergence of nascent class ideologies.

This unique ascendancy of popular capitalist ideology, and the relative failure of class-based political organizations in the United States during this period, has rightly preoccupied many analysts of American society. For despite de Tocqueville's assertions about the pervasive 'equality of condition' that characterized the United States, this was clearly already a class society and was becoming more so. As Edward Pesan's research has shown, the wealthiest American families had already amassed fortunes equal to those in European class societies. In this, the 'era of the common man', there was already a vast inequality of condition, particularly in the major cities, and the gaps between the richest and the poorest were widening. In Boston on the eve of the Revolution, the richest 10 per cent had owned over 50 per cent of all wealth. By 1833, the richest 14 per cent owned 86 per cent of wealth, and by 1848 this had increased to 96 per cent. In New York City, by 1828 the richest 4 per cent owned almost half of all wealth.[66]

Not only were there vast inequalities of condition, but wealth was far from being the impermanent, fluid commodity that de Tocqueville described. To a large extent, wealth and status were inherited as in Europe. According to Pesan's research, 95 per cent of New York City's wealthiest members were born into high status and wealthy families. Only 20 per cent of Boston's 100 wealthiest citizens had been poor. 'The pursuit of wealth in Jacksonian America was marked not by fluidity,' remarks Pesan, 'but by stability and rigidity.'[67] In fact, social mobility in general was probably not as great as has often been suggested and certainly in the major cities of the mid-century it involved relatively few people. In his research into Boston residents in the nineteenth century, Stephen Thernstrom found little occupational career mobility. Only about 10 per cent of the city's manual labourers moved into middle-class occupations in the 1830s and 1840s. Studies of other cities have produced similar results.[68] Dawley found that about 10 per cent of shoemakers in Lynn were occupationally mobile in their lifetime and, in her study of Newark craftsmen, Susan Hirsch found that 97.7 per cent retained their status during 1836 and 1840, and 98.5 per cent between 1856 and 1860.[69] The popular notion that the skilled labourer would, by hard work, and, in time, become an employer is not borne out by these studies. The republican belief that all workers could become capitalists, best represented in the Horatio Alger novels about rags to riches success, was, to a large extent, myth.

If the material realities of the ante-bellum North offer no immediate explanation for popular acquiesence in the mythology of egalitarian capitalism, how then is it to be explained? Numerous theories have been proffered to explain the relative absence of class consciousness in nineteenth-century America. De Tocqueville stressed the absence of feudal history and the prevalence of democratic structures in Jacksonian America. Frederick Turner, in his famous thesis, argued that the western frontier provided an essential safety-valve for those whose lack of opportunities in the East might otherwise have turned to oppositional ideologies. The German sociologist Werner Sombart argued that there was no socialism in the United States because various special circumstances gave the promise of success to many of the oppressed, and gave credibility to the universal promise of capitalism: 'One tolerates any oppressive situation more easily if one lives under the illusion of being able to withdraw from it if forced to', and many believed they could.[70] Boundless resources, cheap land and a relative labour shortage offered the chance of mobility, or at least the belief in that chance, to rather more people than in Europe. The absence of pre-capitalist social relations and the relatively democratic caste of culture and political system made the distance between social groups appear less than in reality it was. Those who had not yet prospered from the system believed that the chance was available to them.

More recent research has inevitably qualified many of these notions. Even after the 1863 Homestead Act, relatively few of the poorer eastern families benefited from migration to the West, which was mainly a movement of middle-class farmers.[71] Social mobility may have been somewhat greater than in Europe, and class lines were more blurred in frontier areas, but the rigidity of the class system in the cities remained and hardly warranted the illusion of a society so dynamic and fluctuating in its social boundaries as to be virtually classless. It is probably misleading, in any case, to search for permanent sociological features to explain US exceptionalism, and certainly no single explanation will do.

The relative absence of class organization during this period has its basis, no doubt, in a number of specific material conditions, of which some were durable and some transient. However, it was the interaction with these of particular cultural and political formations that produced the hegemony of the republican capitalist ideology and the relative subordination of alternative ideologies. Abundant land and natural resources, where these had not been subject to prior appropriation by a feudal class, did give rise to a unique social formation in which small capitalist farmers were numerically dominant. This provided social anchorage for an explicitly *petit-bourgeois* politics celebrating the sanctity of private property and the virtues of capital accumulation. Where a traditional factory proletariat did emerge it often lacked the class organization of its continental equivalents. The 'boom town' nature of industrial development in the West created an industrial class without prior organizational traditions. The factory made the town, rather than the town preceding the factory, which meant that the labour movement in the United States, with the partial exception of the New England valleys and the older eastern seaports, arose without those deep roots in artisanal resistance to industrialism which were a determining factor in the emergence of militant unionism and working-class organization in Europe.[72] This, coupled with rather high rates of geographical mobility, inevitably reduced the potential for collective action.

Where organizations did emerge, as with the working men's parties by which Marx set great store, and with the heroic struggles of the New England shoemakers, they could generate militant consciousness, but they failed in the long term to create sustainable socialist organizations. Amongst other reasons this owed much to the disorganizing effects of ethnic and cultural division within the working class. When poor German and Irish immigrants arrived in their millions after the 1840 crop failures to work on the railroads, in the factories and in the Pennsylvania coal fields, native workers rioted against them, refused them admission to trade unions and tried to exclude them from the franchise. Protestant nativism was always a significant element of popular republicanism and it bore down hard on the Irish Catholics in particular. At the very moment when Catholic immigrants began to flood the eastern labour markets, Protestant evangelism was, as Mike Davis puts it, 'stoking the pietism of the Yankee working class to a white heat'.[73] From the late 1840s onwards a clear cultural and political divide separated the Catholic immigrant from the native Protestant. This was sealed in the formation of the virulently anti-immigrant Know-Nothing Party, one of the most successful third-party movements in American history, which later joined with free-soilers and sections of Whigs to form the Republican Party. The latter became the main political organization of Protestant America, whilst immigrant communities aligned with the Democrats, thus producing a primary political division owing more to ethnicity than class consciousness.

Lastly, and by no means least, even in the age of ascendant anti-slavery politics in the North, white workers, both native and immigrant, failed to unite with black, freed men. Black communities were attacked, abolitionists were hounded and colour bars were imposed on crafts. Despite notable exceptions to nativist and racist sentiments, any cohesive movement towards collective working-class politics was decisively undercut by these ethnic divisions.

A social formation dominated by a class of small farmers and with a new industrial working class which had emerged with scant class traditions and rebarbative ethnic divisions was unlikely to have developed pervasive anti-capitalist ideologies, let alone organizations. What made this more unlikely, and made the positive attraction of popular capitalist ideas more plausible, was the nature of the American political system. Unlike the major proletariats of the Old World, the American working class was created after the attainment of substantial levels of political democracy. In 1750, well over 50 per cent of the white male population in the North East already exercised a local franchise. By the time of Jackson's second election victory in 1832, property qualifications on the male franchise had been abolished in all but four states and whilst only five states, all in New England, allowed even a restrictive franchise to blacks, this represented a more broadly based suffrage than in any other county at the time.[74] The importance of this relative extension of democratic rights on the formation of American political ideology can hardly be exaggerated. The American bourgeoisie had gained power not through any revolution against an indigenous feudal class but by winning independence from a colonial power. Whereas European proletariats organized and struggled for political rights, the white American working class emerged when popular sovereignty was already established. These factors go far in accounting for the relatively conservative and self-celebratory caste of US democratic ideologies which more frequently looked backward to rights already won and enshrined in the Constitution than forward to future struggles and victories.

It was on the basis of these social and political conditions that a hegemonic republican ideology of popular democratic capitalism was possible. Elaborated in different ways by radical democrats, free-soilers and later Republicans, certain elements of a shared ideology were recurrent. The United States was a free and democratic nation with a 'manifest destiny' to lead the way for other nations. Effective democracy rested not only on the maintenance of social order but also on the active participation of citizens, whose intelligence and virtue were the bedrock of the republican order. Small-scale, producer capitalism was an ideal which offered opportunities to all, and those who failed to benefit from it did so only through their lack of application, or, to the more generous, through unavoidable ill fortune. Only the capitalism of the speculators, the banks and the large corporate interests was reprehensible and in the rest of the economy employers and workers should be united by common interests in the system. During the periods of depression and increasingly in the years before the Civil War, voices were heard which proclaimed the inevitability of conflict between classes, but at no point was the dominant ideology of the majority Protestant population seriously undermined.

Public education was both the result and an important vehicle of this republican hegemony. The consensus behind democratic republican ideas was a major factor in the rapid advance of public education systems in a country where *laissez-faire* culture might otherwise have proved to be a major obstacle to state involvement in educational provision. Not only was there a relative absence of those reactionary 'aristocratic' ideologies which in other places blocked educational improvements which might have put the popular classes 'above themselves', but also the working class was not such a political threat as to alarm those who might have feared their better education. The working class itself, and particularly the native Protestant working class, did not necessarily see the state as an instrument of oppression and state schooling as an imposition of alien powers. Rather, the American workers tended to cling to the notion of an ameliorative popular sovereignty which, so long as it controlled the state, could bring benefits through state welfare measures. Public education could offer opportunities for workers, and, if schools heavy handedly preached Protestant pieties and republican ideals, then native workers, at least, could acquiesce in this.

As in Europe, education in the United States had a significant role in relation to the formation of classes. However, its importance at this time lay more in the legitimation of that populist capitalist ideology that sanctioned the relations between classes as they already existed, rather than in any more active process of class reproduction. The relatively democratic forms taken by public education – the common school, the grade school system and the free high school – reflected the democratic slant of republican capitalism. Whilst the experience of schooling was clearly not equal at this time for different social classes, neither was it deliberately constructed to maintain class divisions quite as it was in Europe. Class reproduction in the United States depended rather less than in Europe on the process of educational selection. The United States was far less of a credentialist society than was France under the July Monarchy or Prussia during the 1830s and 1840s. The United States had no system of national qualifications and of close links between secondary schooling and the state bureaucracy as in Europe. Professions were slow to instigate standardized national entry requirements. Nor did the selective 'cultural capital' imparted by schools play such an important role in determining future occupational roles in a society where money counted more than style or manners. It seems likely that besides other avenues to wealth and power, education was relatively insignificant and that routes to social mobility frequently by-passed the school system. At this time, although not in our own, class reproduction was relatively independent of schooling for most social groups in the United States, and in this American schooling differed considerably from that in Europe, where class formation through educational selection was already becoming a major function of the school system. Education in the United States functioned not so much to create classes as to legitimate their existence. As Stephen Thernstrom has put it,

> In Europe, education has helped to make social differences seem more profound and indelible. In America ... the education system has had no such effect. If anything, it has fostered the notion that social stratification is 'merely' a matter of money, of good luck in the market.[75]

However, if schooling in America adopted a rather permissive role in relation to the formation of classes, being more of a sanction than an instrument of class formation, in relation to nationalities and cultural differences it was highly prescriptive. Whilst the common school system might appear agnostic in relation to class, where class manifested itself as race or national difference, it was highly selective in structure and discriminating in purpose. Most obviously it discriminated against blacks and American Indians, and there was no common schooling for them. For the 4 million slaves who constituted roughly half of the population of the slave states in 1860, education was simply outlawed.[76] Slave states passed laws prohibiting the teaching of slaves to read: Louisiana in 1830; Georgia and Virginia in 1831; Alabama in 1832; South Carolina in 1834; and North Carolina in 1835.[77] Some slave states prohibited the teaching of free blacks as well. Maryland and Kentucky were alone in having neither prohibition.[78] This did not mean that slaves were totally uneducated: there is plenty of evidence of slave literacy in surviving diaries and memoirs, and in contemporary advertisements for literate runaways.[79] In Du Bois' estimation, some 5 per cent of slaves were fully literate in 1860.[80] Slaves formed clandestine schools in plantations and slave masters generally allowed some 'oral' education of slaves; some even ignored state laws and allowed slaves to learn to read and write. However, slaves were, at least after 1830, totally excluded from educational institutions and from any concept of 'common education'.

The situation of free blacks, of whom there were 488 000 in 1860, mostly living in towns of the upper South and the North, was better, but only relatively so.[81] Although they were not legally debarred from public education in the northern states, they generally experienced *de facto* exclusion or segregation. Most black children who received schooling attended either independent black charity schools or segregated schools. This remained the case despite the absorption of black charity schools into public education in some states, and even after the enactment of mandatory integration laws in Massachusetts, where whites managed to reorganize segregation on a residential basis. Clearly blacks were not excluded from the concerns of educationalists during this period, as they were in the South, but nor were they an equal element in the reformer's concept of the nation's youth.[82] Racial stereotypes abounded. Boston Primary School Committee, for instance, stated its reasons for rejecting integration in 1841 in these terms: the 'peculiar physical, mental and moral structures (of black children) require an educational treatment different' from whites. Black children, they continued, could memorize and imitate, but 'when progress comes to depend chiefly on the faculties of invention, comparison and reasoning, they quickly fall behind'.[83] Free blacks in the North were educated but rarely in common with whites and never on an equal basis. Apart from the Indians, whom American society was more intent on liquidating than educating, no other minority ethnic groups suffered similar levels of discrimination, or were excluded from common schools by design. However, Irish Catholics and immigrants from continental Europe all faced prejudice in common schools and justifiably felt excluded by the overbearing Protestant culture purveyed through the school system. It was the immigrant poor whom the urban reformers most wished to control and 'civilize' through education, and to the extent that they did this through the imposition of an alien culture on a group which formed a substantial proportion of the new industrial working class, the schools could certainly be accused of an oppressive form of class domination. Michael Katz's comment that 'educational reform and innovation represented the imposition by social leaders of schooling upon a reluctant, uncomprehending, skeptical and sometimes . . . hostile citizenry' is somewhat wide of the mark as a description of the relation between schooling and American workers in general, but in the case of the immigrant poor it would seem fully justified.[84]

As in Europe, education in the United States played an important part in the formation of nationhood and state. Whilst less directly involved than in France or Prussia in the training of state personnel for the military, bureaucracy and public works, it was equally significant in the development of national consciousness and in reproducing the hegemony of those dominant republican ideologies on which the state rested. Schools functioned above all to legitimate the values of popular capitalism, to assimilate minorities into the ascendant Protestant culture, and to instruct men and women in their differentiated roles as citizens. Whilst in Europe class remained the fundamental unit of social organization, in the United States class divisions were overlaid with strong ethnic and cultural divisions. The nature of schooling in the two continents reflected this different balance of social contradictions. Whilst in Europe schooling was most coercive in relation to class formation, in the United States it showed its most authoritarian face in relation to the subordination of ethnic minorities, in the marginalization and segregation of blacks and in the coercive assimilation of immigrant cultures. In the construction of different gender roles for men and women, schooling also played an important part, no less in the United States than in Europe.

The intense drive towards assimilating minority cultures stands out as one of the most singular features of American education, and was one of the most powerful motivations behind the reformers' campaign for common, that is common Protestant, schooling. As Michael Katz writes in his 'Reassessment' of the origins of public education,

> This massive task of assimilation required weakening the connection between the immigrant child and the family, which in turn required the capture of the child by an outpost of native culture. In short, the anxiety about cultural heterogeneity propelled the establishment of systems of public education; from the very beginning public schools became agents of cultural standardization.[85]

The task was joined most fervently in the major cities where immigrant children were most numerous, in towns such as New York where foreign-born residents made up over 50 per cent of the population by the mid-century.[86] Assimilation involved the promotion of linguistic and cultural uniformity, the inculcation of the American political creed and a general submersion in the values of Protestant morality. In a country dominated by religious sects, the latter, to be effective, had to be broad and non-denominational. Most Protestants finally accepted the idea that religion in schools should be limited to bible reading and prayers common to most Protestants, whilst cautioning against the discussion of any controversial doctrines, such as those of the Trinity and transubstantiation. For the most part it was an education not in doctrine but in individual morality. As the educationalist Orville Taylor wrote, 'It is our duty to make men moral.'[87]

Making a child moral involved instilling respect for private property, obedience to authority and law, and acceptance of the social system. It involved
the cultivation of habits of self-discipline, orderliness and industry. Alonzo
Potter urged teachers to 'inspire the young with deep reverence for parents
and for old age', and Charles Northend in *The Teacher and the Parent* advocated a 'spirit of obedience and subordination', which he believed would
prepare children 'for higher spheres of usefulness and happiness'.[88] Next
to moral virtue and self-discipline, most valued was the spirit of industry.
Grammar books frequently included a wealth of aphorisms on the virtues of
hard work and the dangers inherent in idleness and sloth. Joseph Burleigh's
The Thinker, a Moral Reader included terse injunctions, such as: 'Remember
that all the ignorance, degradation and misery of the world, is the result of
indolence and vice.'[89]

Even the teaching of language was seen as a moral exercise. In writing his popular textbooks, Noah Webster had made it plain that he saw
them as a vehicle for the standardization not only of language but also
of morals and principles. These books were still in use in 1855 when
Illinois' superintendent of schools recommended *Webster's Dictionary* with
the words:

> Great care should be taken to eradicate provincialism and to procure that
> purity and uniformity of language so much to be desired. It will operate
> as a kind of national brotherhood.[90]

The assimilation of immigrant children into American culture, which
was a primary function of urban schools, meant not only sharing a
common language but also accepting the dominant Puritan morality of
the day.

Schools not only sought to prepare children, native and immigrant alike,
to be virtuous and morally upright adults in the Puritan mould, they also
sought to train them to be active and intelligent citizens, involved in the
democratic process. In his book *The District School*, first published in 1835,
J. Orville Taylor based his defence of public schooling almost exclusively on
the argument that good education was an essential pillar of a democratic
republic. 'A free government', he wrote,

> demands virtue and intelligence: it cannot prosper, it cannot exist, with-
> out them. Then, if you desire the perpetuity of your liberties, the equal
> rights and privileges of your liberties, and the honour and glory of your
> happy country, educate your children.[91]

Knowledge is necessary, he argued, to see the nature and necessity of civil
government. The half-educated will not know when their government is
well administered, and not knowing the value of the privileges they enjoy

will be too ready to seek a change in their rulers. Education is important so that people may choose their legislators well. 'In a government where the people not only make the laws, but select those who are to administer them, there is an imperious necessity', he wrote, 'for high intelligence and moral worth in every individual.'[92] Knowledge is necessary for seeing the necessity of obeying just laws as it is for selecting those who make them, and it is important for performing the lesser duties of citizenship, such as serving on juries. An educated public is necessary, according to Taylor, not only to encourage men to perform their patriotic duties but to ensure that they defend their democratic rights and use these wisely. 'Obedience to the constitution and laws of the United States is. . . . a patriotic and moral duty', but citizens have another duty which is constantly to seek to improve the system.[93]

Education in citizenship was also thought to be important for girls. However, since the role of women in ante-bellum America was defined quite differently from that of men, their education was to have different objectives. Women were not thought to have an active or participating role in the democratic process; their function was to bring up their male children to be active citizens and their education should be limited to this purpose. In his *Thoughts upon Female Education*, Benjamin Rush typically defined the role of women in terms of their duties as mothers: 'Our ladies should be qualified to a certain degree, by a peculiar and subtle education, to concur in instructing their sons in the principles of liberty and government.'[94] The generations that followed had not altered this precept but merely re-emphasized the importance of the domestic sphere.

The 1840s had seen something of a crusade about the nature of the woman's role. This both celebrated the importance of the home and the woman's pre-eminent place within it, and sharpened the divide between the public sphere of men and the private realm of women. Women had three main roles in the home: to create a sanctuary from the busy, corrupt, daytime world which their husbands inhabited; to manage a frugal household and assist their men as guardians and stewards of their property; and to nurture and instruct their children to make a virtuous new generation in a perilous society. As the public world of men increasingly drew apart from the home, male school advocates argued that girls received too much academic education. Arguing for the adoption of sewing classes, the Salem School Committee reported in 1840:

> It is a matter of complaint in our city, and seemingly just, that girls have too much intellectual and too little home education . . . Boys need, strictly speaking, a more intellectual education than girls, since the latter are destined to the duties of the home, while the main province of the former, as men, is ever abroad, in the complications of business, requiring the rigid analysis and calculation happily spared to the wife and mother.[95]

Such criticism of academic learning for girls in no way implied that female education was unimportant. On the contrary, levels of schooling for girls had increased notably during the century, and the 1840s witnessed a renewed emphasis on the importance of a specific form of female education. A new interest in methods of child-rearing and domestic science were characteristic of this period. In her *Treatise on Domestic Economy* in 1841, Catharine Beecher argued the necessity of the subordination of women, the separation of male and female roles, and the importance of more domestic education for girls: 'A little girl may begin, at five or six ... to assist her mother and if properly trained can render essential aid.' From 10 to 15 years, 'though some attention ought to be paid to intellectual culture, it ought to be made altogether secondary in importance'.[96] Beecher then went on to provide details on anatomy, diet, exercise, manners, household budgets, child-rearing, leisure, house construction, cleaning, washing, sewing, gardening and other areas of female interest. This and other works on domestic economy tried to promote the dignity, complexity and importance of housework, whilst they disseminated practical suggestions on household management, health and other matters important in the woman's sphere.[97]

As interest in the domestic sciences increased, so concern with the best forms of child-care also preoccupied social commentators. This is most obvious in the literature on childhood development, which expressed a new view of the importance of a gentle, protective and appropriate environment for the nurturing of children. In the course of a century there had been a decisive shift from the harsh Calvinist view that children inherited the original sin of Adam, to the more romantic view of the educator Pestalozzi, influenced by Rousseau, that children were not only innocent but naturally good, and that educational methods should shield them from a corrupt world and encourage the natural development of their characters. This shift towards a softer, more child-centred pedagogy was accompanied by an increasing employment of female teachers during the reform era. They were believed to be generally more capable of providing a more sympathetic environment for younger children in particular, and their wages were considerably lower.

This widening division of male and female roles, and the increasing 'scientific' interest in feminine occupations, was accompanied by renewed reverence for 'femininity'. Whilst the rigours of frontier life and the relative absence of domestic servants in the American North had traditionally encouraged more emphasis on the practical virtues of womanhood than was common amongst the more pampered European middle class, American ideology was not immune to the cult of graceful femininity. Like other educational authors, Alonzo Potter believed that a specific education was needed to cultivate feminine virtues:

> One cannot look at the female – with less muscular vigour and more sensibility than the other sex, with more timidity and gentleness, with

deeper affection and more acute sensitiveness – without perceiving that she has been appointed to a sphere very different from that of man.[98]

Her mission was to bring a humanizing influence on the world and education should support her in this purpose:

> To fit her for such a noble ministry, she needs a training quite different from that given to the other sex. Her delicacy and purity must remain untarnished. Her diffidence and even bashfulness, at once a grace and a protection, should be cherished as a peculiar treasure.... The strifes and tumults of the senate-house and the platform are too rude even for her eyes to rest upon, much more for her voice to mingle in...

To prepare for her womanly role, she needs both intellectual and domestic skills, writes Potter:

> Instead of reading, as seems to have been the opinion of Locke and Fénelon, but little intellectual culture, she should have a mind well disciplined and stored with knowledge. She ought also to be thoroughly versed in whatever belongs to domestic life and occupation. She should have, on the one hand, such a taste for books and study, that she will never willingly remit the work of self-culture, and, on the other hand, she should be so imbued with a sense of dignity and responsibility of woman's mission in life, and so instructed in its duties, that she will always be ready for the humblest and most arduous of its claims. And above all things, that feminine grace, which results from the possession of delicate feelings and gentle thoughts and manners, should be preserved, and she should be taught to shrink from noise and notoriety.[99]

If American girls were to be educated as the future guardians of male fortunes, then boys were to be schooled to vouchsafe the very destiny of the United States and the 'free world'. The idea of education for nationhood took its most lofty forms when politicians self-consciously examined the nature of America's historical destiny. The founding fathers, somewhat nervously, considered the fate of the American Revolution and called for the education of virtuous citizens to ensure the success of an historical experiment, and thus to justify the high hopes that had been placed on it. As Thomas Jefferson had proclaimed sombrely,

> The eyes of the virtuous all over the world are turned with anxiety on us, as the only depositories of the sacred fire of liberty ... our falling into anarchy would decide forever the destinies of mankind and seal the political heresy that man is incapable of self-government.[100]

Americans of the mid-nineteenth century were altogether more confident, proclaiming ever more inflated ambitions for the role of the American nation in world affairs. To Jesse Olney, author of *A History of the United States*, Americans were 'to work out, not alone our destiny, but that of the whole world.... The inferior races shall be educated and made fellow labourers in the great work of human progress.'[101] In pursuit of this, some said manifest, destiny, education as nation-building aspired to its apotheosis. In his popular apologia for republican education, J. Orville Taylor ends with the characteristically rhetorical injunction:

> He who wishes his country to take a high standing among the nations of the earth; he who wishes for the growing improvement and prosperity of his countrymen and who wishes the perpetuity of this glorious example of liberty and self-government, will desire to do all in his power to educate the people.[102]

Behind the pious ideals of this most nationalistic of educational philosophies we can find a deep irony. The very impulse which created one of the world's most advanced public education systems was also that which did most to deny it credibility as a truly national system. So much the product of an ascendant Protestant majority and its crusading moralities, American public education remained regionally uneven and ethnically divided. No country has claimed so much for national education and nowhere has the reality fallen so short of its aims.

6
English Education and the Liberal State

The development of public education in England contrasts sharply with both the European and the US examples in this study. For the greater part of the nineteenth century, governments consistently rejected the continental solution of educational development through the state. The dominant tradition in education remained instead the voluntary system, a form of school organization based on private initiative and independent control. This rejection of centralized state control resembled aspects of education in the northern United States, but it failed to match the vigour and dynamism of the latter's educational development through concerted local initiative. At no point did educational reform achieve the kind of broad consensus over objectives and means which characterized the American experience. Consequently, England remained almost deadlocked over education for many years, postponing major changes long after their importance had been recognized by many of those most closely involved in schooling.

England was the last of the major nineteenth-century powers to create a national system of education and the most reluctant to put it under public control. The slow and partial development of state forms in education was manifest in a number of related areas, as Chapter 1 sought to show: a statutory framework governing attendance and the licensing of schools and teachers was late to develop, as were teacher training and national examinations; the level of public finance and control remained low throughout the period, leading to weak forms of inspection and curriculum control; and, finally, the development of a unified central authority for education was an exceptionally fraught and protracted business.

The consequences of this lack of central direction and support could be seen in terms of the low enrolments and uneven standards in elementary education, the retarded growth of technical schooling and the very slow pace of change in secondary education. Overall, the education system was characterized by a singular diversity of institutions and a chronic lack of integration between the various parts. This pervasive state of comparative educational underdevelopment, apparently recognized by most contemporaries with any

knowledge of developments in other countries, was the legacy of a voluntary system which had been maintained long after the point where it had
any chance of delivering an adequate national provision. The foundations
of a national system were not laid until 1870, and even then this remained a
compromise with past voluntary traditions. It was only in 1899 that a single
authority was created to oversee education. State secondary schools were not
created until 1902: a century after their inauguration in France and Prussia.

The most interesting question about the development of national
education in England is thus not so much why it occurred but why it
occurred so late and in the peculiar manner in which it did. Why did the
country which had been the most literate in Reformation Europe emerge
during the Victorian era as one of the most illiterate and under-educated
in all of Western Europe? And how could this occur in a nation which had
been amongst the most open and liberal of all states during the eighteenth
century, which pioneered the Industrial Revolution and which, by 1860, at
the high point of Victorian capitalism, enjoyed yet unchallenged economic
supremacy, producing half of the world's manufactures and a third of its
cottons, iron and coal? Such a limited educational provision in a society
which took pride in its industry and liberal values appeared contradictory.
As David Landes has noted, comparison of the educational structures of
nineteenth-century England and Germany presents

> One of the strangest paradoxes of modern history: on the one hand, a
> liberal society [England] standing out from others in the 18th century
> for equality and mobility of status, should have lost something of these
> during the very period of its progressive political democratization, while
> on the other, a far more authoritarian society [Germany], characterized in
> the pre-industrial period by a clearly defined, fairly rigid hierarchy of rank,
> should have developed a more open structure without corresponding
> political change.[1]

The problem is the more paradoxical because there were in England many
of the social preconditions most likely to stimulate educational reform.
Demographic change occurred early in Britain, with the population reaching
an urban majority by 1850, half a century ahead of any other nation. This
brought with it all of those social problems which were foremost amongst
the arguments of educational reformers in other countries. The proletarianization of the English labouring class had been more complete and certainly
more traumatic than in other countries which had maintained sizeable peasant populations throughout the early industrial phase. It led to the creation
of the world's first, largest and most class-conscious proletariat and a level
of open class conflict well above that which had prompted educational
remedies in other countries. Above all, there was a rising bourgeois class
which was fully aware of its historical importance and which recognized the

value of education in its battle for ideological hegemony over other groups. Certainly, education did develop in response to these factors, and in many ways England offers the most explicit example of the use of schooling by a dominant class as a means of winning hegemony over subordinate groups. However, of all of the countries in this study, England was the least successful in developing educational institutions which could achieve these goals, and thus provides the biggest challenge for explanation.

These educational peculiarities clearly have complex causes, yet few accounts have adequately explored them and none in their full comparative context. The classic explanation for the slow development of a public educational apparatus rests on the so-called religious difficulty. Anglicans were reluctant to cede control over education, which they considered the hereditary and natural prerogative of the Established Church. They feared that state control would lead to secularism or increased influence for Dissent. The High Church was more hostile to state intervention than other sections of the Anglican establishment, but none could entertain the idea with much enthusiasm, except perhaps for the small clique of administrative experts amongst them. Dissent by and large accepted the idea of non-denominational schooling and this suggested a rational alternative to a fully secular education, which few except the Benthamites could abide. However, for the most part they were equally suspicious of state intervention because they recognized the dominance of the Anglicans within the establishment and believed that this would lead to unequal state support for Anglican education. The situation appeared intractable. As G. M. Young put it, 'Dissent could not abide the parson in the classroom and the church would have no-one else.'[2]

The confessional division was certainly a real problem and countless bills for enhanced state intervention fell because their proponents failed to navigate between the Scylla of non-conformist suspicion and the Charibdis of Anglican intransigence. In Lord Ashley's words, after the defeat in the Commons in 1843 of Graham's Factory Education bill,

> The Dissenters and the church have each laid down their limits beyond which they will not pass, and there is no power which can either force, persuade or delude them.[3]

History was to prove him wrong, but it remained the case that many contemporaries believed that the religious divide in education was insurmountable. Historians have generally agreed. As Derek Fraser, the historian of the British welfare state, has summarized it, 'The rivalry between Church and Dissent precluded the growth of a state system.'[4]

The conclusion appears more or less definitive and is generally taken to encapsulate the quintessence of the peculiar English problem. However, there are a number of reasons why the issue should not simply be left there. Whatever the salience of the religious difficulty, and clearly it had considerable importance, it cannot provide comparative explanation for the uniquely underdeveloped state of English education. There are a numbers of reasons for asserting this point. Firstly, in no other country had religious schism prevented the growth of national education or delayed it for so long, not even in the United States, the archetypal land of religious sects, nor in other countries with an established church. The typical solution to the problem, which, after all, arose in most countries, was either to declare education a secular matter or to allow church involvement in schools on a non-denominational basis and under state supervision. These options were theoretically also available in England but they were not taken up. The second point is that when the climate of opinion did finally change in favour of greater state intervention in education during the late 1860s, this had little to do with changing religious attitudes or any waning of the antagonism between Church and Dissent. Rather, it had to do with changing attitudes towards the state and the belated realization that the voluntarist ideal was an impossible one. Lastly, and most importantly, the religious difficulty, which was more or less surmounted by the compromise of the 1870 Act, cannot explain the persisting backwardness of English education throughout the twentieth century. The problem clearly goes deeper than the religious schism and has had a much more sustained historical influence.

Another approach to the problem has been to look at the class relations pertaining during this period and to ask how these have affected educational development. In a sense this leads on from the earlier problem since religious division was in large measure a refraction of antagonistic class relations. Anglicanism was by and large the religion of the establishment. It was espoused by the landowning class, who were dominant in parliament during the first half of the century and who continued to dominate the cabinet until the end of it. It was also the religion of important sectors of state personnel and of the structures of rural local power. Dissent, by comparison, was largely urban, embracing large sections of the manufacturing middle class and also of the 'respectable' working class. The clash of churches was thus also a clash of class and cultural politics. Another way to explain the *impasse* in educational development is thus to focus on the irreconcilable nature of bourgeois and gentry/establishment cultures and educational objectives. Historians, such as Carl Kaestle in the United States and Harold Silver in England, have thus rightly stressed the stultifying effect of landowner opposition to educational improvement in the early decades of the century, emphasizing aristocratic prejudices against educating people 'above their station'. Margaret Archer, as we saw earlier, also grounds her argument on the effects of nineteenth-century class relations. In her view it was the political subordinacy of the middle class, and its lack of control over the state apparatus, which determined its choice to transform education through 'substitution' rather than state action.

There is no denying the salience of Britain's particular class relations in this period, but there are two overriding problems with this type of explanation. Firstly, countries with an equally prominent landowner class – such as Prussia – did not experience the same obstacles to educational development. One would therefore need to explain why a landed class in one country should come to provide a block on educational reform whilst the same group in another should not. The second problem is that landowner intransigence cannot explain the situation during the second half of the century. If 'aristocratic' dominance was a major retarding factor in the early part of the century, it remains to be explained why radical bourgeois advocates of educational reform were so unsuccessful in the post-reform era, when in other respects this was pre-eminently a period a bourgeois ascendance. Even if one rejects Harold Perkins' classic account of the triumph of entrepreneurial values in mid-Victorian Britain and argues, for instance, with Perry Anderson that the age was still one of landowner hegemony, explanations of educational underdevelopment still face critical difficulties. One must explain not only why educational reform failed, whereas in other crucial areas reforms were achieved which reflected the priorities of the middle class, but also why large sections of the bourgeoisie failed even to strenuously advocate them. Concerned as the middle class was with education, it did not generally advocate those types of reform which had proved successful in other countries. With the exception of a small group of Benthamite experts and their radical Whig allies, the middle class as a whole was either lukewarm or intransigently opposed to state control of education, not only because it feared Anglican influence but also because it disagreed with it in principle. Even had the middle class achieved undisputed hegemony over the political and state apparatus during this period, it would almost certainly not have developed a state education system for the simple reason that most of them did not want it. The peculiarities of English education clearly owe as much to the political profile of the middle class as to the gentry and establishment.

The peculiarities of the English

The main contention of this book has been that the development of education can only be understood as part of the wider process of state formation that led to the emergence of the modern capitalist state. Following from this, it has been argued that it was the specific national characteristics of this process in different states which explains the individual and distinctive nature of different education systems. The fortunes of education in England relate no less to this process of state formation, even if the state appears to have played a less directive or leading role. The key to understanding the particular characteristics of English educational development must also be sought, therefore, in the nature of the British state as it emerged from the settlement of 1688 and in the relations of class power on which it rested.

The singular characteristics of the modern British state and social formation have been a favourite theme of historians for over a century. De Tocqueville first wrote of the 'peculiarities of the English' in the 1830s, and nineteenth-century Whig historians, like their peers in other countries, frequently wrote of what they liked to term the 'national genius'. However, more recent explorations of English peculiarities have tended less towards celebration and more towards lament.

The underlying concern of modern historians has been with the relative decline of Britain as a world economic and political power. This is generally reckoned to have begun in the 1870s, when Britain's hitherto undisputed economic ascendancy was first challenged by Germany and the United States, and, as most historians and economists agree, has continued ever since. The main problem has been seen as a failure of modernization and adaptation which dates back to the mid-Victorian period. After a supremely successful first Industrial Revolution, Britain failed to adapt to the new realities of capitalism during the so-called second stage of the Industrial Revolution. In particular, it failed to adopt new technologies and thus increasingly fell behind its more dynamic competitors.

A number of social factors have been associated with this blocked development. The long nineteenth-century political ascendancy of the landowner class has been related to the allegedly 'amateur' and conservative caste of the establishment and state elites. The landowners promoted an 'anti-industrial' and 'anti-urban' culture which is said to have caused the gradual atrophy of those entrepreneurial values which fuelled the first Industrial Revolution, and to have prevented vigorous development in the later period. Alternatively, the allegiance of the political and industrial elites to ideas that were formed and seemed appropriate to the early industrial phase is said to have hindered development in the later phase when they were no longer relevant. These include the empirical, rule-of-thumb methods of the industrialist, the dominance of finance over manufacture and its typical 'colonial' orientation towards overseas investment, and, finally, the adherence of the ruling class to free trade which well suited the first and dominant industrial power but which was less appropriate in the later period of intense national economic rivalry. Overarching all of these problems in civil society was the failure to create what has been called the 'developmental state'. Britain was the first country to industrialize and, unlike the continental states which did so later, this occurred organically, from the bottom up, and involved minimal state intervention. However, whilst the economy could prosper in the early nineteenth century with a minimal, non-interventionist state, in the period of high technology and international monopoly capital, such a liberal regime was inimicable to coordinated industrial development.

The issues involved here may seem remote from the apparently circum-scribed and more local issues involved in the history of nineteenth-century education. However, as I hope to show, this is not the case. In many ways the problems of educational development in the early nineteenth century actually anticipated later problems in the development of the state gen-erally. The underdevelopment of education was one of the causes of the onset of relative economic decline, closely tied up as that was with the slow adaptation of Britain to the use of modern technology in the later stages of industrial development. There has continued to be a connection between educational 'backwardness' in relation to science and technology and slow industrial innovation throughout the twentieth century. Fur-thermore, the forces which retarded educational development in the early nineteenth century were arguably the same forces which re-emerged in the later period as developmental hindrances. Education thus in some ways presents a microcosm of the whole problem.

It is clearly not difficult to draw connections between these national characteristics and the problems of nineteenth-century educational devel-opment. Landowner power and culture, particularly in its anti-scientific and elitist manifestations, certainly goes some way towards explaining the nature of secondary education in the nineteenth century. The success of early indus-trialization, which had little need of extensive formal education or highly scientific technology, suggests one reason for the enormous complacency of the Victorian elite towards scientific and technical education. Liberalism and the doctrine of the minimal state was clearly a crucial factor behind the reluctance to put education under state control, or to use the state as the leading instrument of educational advance. However, if these gen-eral connections suggest appropriate avenues of investigation, their relative obviousness also belies the considerable complexity of the debate surround-ing the question of the peculiarities of the British state. In the following I shall try to locate the problem of educational underdevelopment within the parameters of this more general debate and suggest how a reading of the peculiarities of the English debate can also provide the basis for an understanding of the peculiarities of English education.

The historical controversy over the origins of the modern British state began in 1964 with Perry Anderson's polemical article in *New Left Review*, entitled, 'Origins of the Present Crisis'. The debate which ensued included E. P. Thompson's celebrated rejoinder, 'The Peculiarities of the English', fur-ther elaboration of the *New Left Review* theses from Anderson and Tom Nairn, and a number of other critiques of their position. Simultaneously, Eric Hobsbawm was developing his own historical explanations of the origins of Britain's economic decline in *Industry and Empire*. These seminal analyses were followed by further contributions to the debate, notably from Andrew Gamble and Martin Wiener, and later in another Anderson article and in a somewhat different analysis from David Marquand.[5]

Broadly speaking these works all seek to provide historical explanations for what are taken to be the key problems of modern British development: relative economic decline and the apparent failure of governments to achieve modernization through the state, as has occurred most successfully in countries such as France, Sweden and Japan. The historical arguments are complex and detailed, and each of the contributors have drawn on a number of the themes which were suggested above. However, it is possible to distinguish between three primary forms of explanation. The first, which is developed most consistently in the works of Anderson, Nairn and, more recently, Wiener, relates to the so-called failure of bourgeois revolution and the political and cultural ascendancy of the landed class during the nineteenth century. The second thesis, developed most consistently in Hobsbawm's work, concentrates on the logical results of Britain's 'developmental priority' – that is, its singular position as the first industrialized nation. The third form of explanation, which is most evident in the work of Gamble and Marquand, is an extension of the 'priority' thesis but stresses more strongly the pervasive social and political effects of liberalism. The latter involves a complex of singular English attitudes concerning the state, 'freedom' and individualism, which have prevented the creation of an effectively interventionist state such as might have given a positive lead to the process of modernization. None of these theses is necessarily irreconcilable. In fact, versions of these arguments exist in all of the major accounts in stronger or weaker forms. However, there are a number of important disagreements on particular issues. In what follows I assess these differences and suggest how such theories can add to the understanding of English educational development.

Anderson and Nairn and the failed bourgeois revolution

Of all of the analysts of the British social formation in the nineteenth century it is Anderson who has most consistently stressed the relative power and influence of the landed class. Indeed, in a series of arguments sustained over 20 years, he has never deviated from the proposition that it was the landowners who constituted the true regnant class throughout the century and whose political power and ideological influence constituted the real hegemonic force. By comparison the history of the industrial bourgeoisie was characterized by a series of failures and compromises, and it was this very self-limiting and subordinate role played by the would-be revolutionary class which constituted the primary English peculiarity and explains many of the problems faced by British capitalism in subsequent periods.

In his early polemical essay, Anderson delineated the broad contours of the development of the state and class structure from 1688 to the present day, concentrating on those factors which he claimed marked out British development from the more 'classical' paths followed by continental states and, in particular, by France. England, he claimed, had 'the first, most mediated and least pure bourgeois revolution of any major European country'.[6] The seventeenth-century revolutions had transformed the structure of English society, paving the way for the development of capitalist agriculture and commerce, but they had failed to transform the superstructure. The heirs of the revolution were not the bourgeoisie but the landed, albeit capitalist, gentry class, and subordinate to them the merchant capitalists. The revolution failed to displace the aristocracy from political power and left almost no revolutionary ideology. After 1688 there followed

> a permanent partial interpenetration of the 'moneyed' and landed interests, which simultaneously maintained the political and social subordination of merchant capital, and gave the city the aristocratic colouration it has to this day.[7]

In the centuries that followed there was to be no fundamental antagonism between the old aristocracy and the new industrial bourgeoisie. By the end of the eighteenth century, when the bourgeoisie were poised to challenge the power of the landowner state, the French Revolution catapulted them back into an alliance with the old regime for fear of the more dangerous class rising below them. With the Reform Act of 1832 they were content to acquire only partial political representation and thereafter their revolutionary impulse waned. Throughout the mid-Victorian period the bourgeoisie continued to aspire towards the style and status of landed classes rather than develop a universal or hegemonic philosophy of their own. With the increasing interpenetration of agrarian, mercantile and financial wealth, a process of osmosis occurred between the upper bourgeoisie and the aristocracy which consolidated the typical ruling elite of the period. 'In the supremely capitalist society of Victorian England,' writes Anderson, 'the aristocracy became and remained the vanguard of the bourgeoisie.'[8]

What distinguished the English from the more revolutionary French 'route' was thus the lack of any genuine revolutionary polarization between classes. Without such an historical confrontation there was no cause for the English bourgeoisie to fundamentally question the old order, or to systematically replace traditional ideas with a new vision of the world. The British intellectual class never broke its umbilical connection with the conservative establishment; it never made the radical break with tradition, such as the *déclassé* continental intelligentsia, and thus never elaborated a more typical bourgeois ideology to challenge the dominance of the rural and conservative gentry culture. The result was the 'suffocating traditionalism of English life' and the 'aristocratic, amateur and normatively agrarian' model of political leadership.

In a series of parallel essays, later collected in a volume entitled *The Break-Up of Britain*, Tom Nairn elaborated a similar thesis.[9] Claiming that Marxist history was bound to investigate 'the developmental uniqueness of states

as well as their uniformities', he went on to anatomize the singular characteristics of English development using the familiar formula of the failed
bourgeois revolution.[10] The modern British state was the creation not of the
bourgeoisie, as in the more classical continental pattern, but rather of a capitalist but 'patrician' landlord elite. From its origins in the Whig regimes of
the eighteenth century it was marked by its unusual subordination to civil
society and by the dominance of the landed class within it. Early industrialization within the context of this liberal heritage served only to reinforce
those distinctively conservative and colonial traits. Thus the 'pioneer liberal-
constitutional state never itself became modern: it retained the archaic
stamp of its priority'.[11] The first industrial country thus failed to generate
that revolution within the state which alone could have achieved the kind
of concerted modernization which later capitalist development required.

Thus far Nairn's account diverged little from Anderson's original thesis,
except perhaps in his somewhat greater stress on the effects of developmental priority. However, in his most original contribution to the debate,
Nairn further argued that Britain had failed to develop that kind of popular nationalism which often constituted the core of those universalizing
bourgeois ideologies which in continental states had played such an important role in winning consent for policies for national development. The
latter, argued Nairn, typically arose from the need to defend against external
military threats, or else from the desire to reverse a history of economic
backwardness. Britain had neither stimulus and so developed no radical mythology of popular nationalism. Its nationalism was rather that of
the 'great power' variety: celebratory, complacent and essentially conservative. In the epoch of British imperialism, this self-regarding and stultifying
patriotism came to characterize the inertia of a backward-looking state.

Nairn and Anderson's polemics against the conservatism of English historical development called for treatment in kind. E. P. Thompson's furious
philippic in *The Peculiarities of the English* gave just that, whilst a number of
more measured critiques from Richard Johnson, Nicos Poulantzas and others
echoed many of Thompson's themes. Nairn and Anderson were accused of
self-indulgent anglophobia and of perpetuating a false mythology of contrasts between English and continental development. Their treatment of
class was 'static' and 'idealist', and they had misused Gramsci's concept of
hegemony. Most seriously, they had failed to appreciate the essentially capitalist nature of the English gentry and had thus fallen into the classic liberal
trap of mistaking the class enemy. As Thompson put it, they were continually hunting an 'aristocratic snark'. By concentrating on the form and style of
'aristocratic' rule, Nairn and Anderson had neglected its underlying capitalist
content.

A number of Thompson's criticisms were admittedly no more than debating points. Anderson had, for instance, repeatedly asserted the capitalist
nature of the landed class since the Civil War and, despite his polemical

use of the term, was clearly not arguing that nineteenth-century Britain was a feudal society. However, Thompson's main objection was a powerful one: Anderson had repeatedly and critically over-stressed the nature of landed hegemony during the nineteenth century. There were two aspects to this.

According to Thompson, Anderson had greatly exaggerated the importance of intellectuals and generalized ideologies in the maintenance of hegemony. Certainly, in France there had been a more total confrontation between the old and the new classes, and this had prompted the elaboration of 'totalizing' bourgeois ideologies. Catholicism also played a part in this. As Thompson put it,

> The intelligentsia of other countries have been more fortunate. They have been able to fight their battles with more panache and more appeals to universals because they have managed to preserve Holy Church as their foil to this day.[12]

Certainly, also, the English bourgeoisie had been more pragmatic in their politics, and their ideology had been more diffuse and less systematized. Nevertheless, argued Thompson, if they did not put their whole society in question it was not because they were weak but rather because they did not need to – they largely controlled it. The problem here, as Johnson later summarized, was the persistent tilt towards idealism in Anderson's work. By unduly stressing the political and ideological moment, he had ended up writing a kind of 'totalizing history...of an idealist kind, a history of the superstructures in the manner of Lukács'.[13]

Thompson's other main line of argument was that not only did Anderson overrate the general importance of intellectuals and systematic ideologies but he also failed to appreciate the strength and pervasive nature of bourgeois culture as it existed. Anderson had never 'imagined the great arch of bourgeois culture', which stretched from Bacon and Protestantism down to Adam Smith and Charles Darwin, who formed the two great landmarks in bourgeois thought. Whilst the conservative cultural traits of the landed class continued to be influential in the Anglican Church, in the army and navy, in the Lords and education and the legal profession, the ideals of the bourgeoisie were dominant in manufacture and commerce, in Dissent, in urban local government, in the police force and in sections of the bureaucracy. Above all, it was the pervasive middle-class culture of the Protestant churches and of liberal political economy which formed the solid core of what was an indisputably bourgeois hegemony in Victorian England.

Neither Thompson nor Johnson could find any warrant for Anderson's notion of landowner hegemony. Despite the 'aristocratic' trappings of the state, the bourgeoisie were the dominant class both economically and ideologically. If their world view was unsystematic and empiricist, it was no less pervasive for that. The 'absent centre' of bourgeoisie culture, for which Anderson had searched in vain, was so obvious that he had missed it. It was liberalism and bourgeoisie religion, and these two components, later transmuted into social reform and Fabian movements, had more claim to constitute the characteristic content of English ideology, wrote Johnson, than any kind of 'pseudo-feudalism'.[14] Furthermore, at the political level, the major objectives of the bourgeoisie were also achieved. If the gentry maintained hold of the levers of political power, this did not diminish bourgeois hegemony since both classes had essentially the same interests. The aristocratic mask of political power was useful to the middle class since it provided stability, as in Bagehot's 'dignified parts' of the constitution, and also since it diverted the wrath of radicals away from the critical centres of capitalist power and on to its relatively dispensable parts. Marx's classic account of the British state as a mask or camouflage disguising true bourgeois power thus remained the most convincing description of hegemony in mid-Victorian Britain. The landed class ruled but only as delegates of the bourgeois interest.

In a later contribution to the debate, Anderson went some way towards meeting the charges that were made against his earlier work and produced what must be the most sophisticated version of the landowner hegemony thesis to date. The polemical and highly metaphorical undertow of the earlier article, which had engendered some of the more spurious polemical obfuscation of the debate with Thompson, went and a number of significant revisions were made. The comparative argument was made more sophisticated by locating English peculiarities in greater specificity. The demonstration of landowner dominance now rested less on an analysis of culture and more on an assessment of the comparative economic strength of the different classes. And finally, liberalism re-emerged as a determinant and defining characteristic of the mid-Victorian hegemony. However, Anderson still defended his original thesis. The industrialists, he wrote, 'remained junior partners in the natural order of things, without compelling economic motives or collective social resources to transform it'.[15]

The starting point in Anderson's later article, 'The Figures of Descent', was a recognition of the continuance of landowner power in all post-revolutionary continental regimes down through the nineteenth century. This appears to undercut the argument about the peculiarities of the social formation in Britain and therefore its role as an explanation of Britain's subsequent relative decline. Anderson acknowledged this but went on to show that there were, nevertheless, decisive distinguishing factors about the landowner class in Britain that marked it out from its continental counterparts. English landowners had a longer history as a capitalist class than any comparable group; their interests ranged more widely than any other, from commercial agriculture to finance and urban development; their experience as a stable ruling elite was unrivalled, and they were also the wealthiest. In the 1870s, no less than 80 per cent of private real estate in

Britain was controlled by 7 000 persons, with some 360 magnates owning estates upwards of 10 000 acres, representing a quarter of all land in
England. In continental states, where the major landowners had to co-exist
with considerable peasant classes, there was no equivalent of this enormous
concentration of landed wealth. Whilst in England an agrarian elite, defined
by estates of over 1 000 acres, accounted for some 55 per cent of English
soil, French landowners with only 300 or more acres accounted for only
20 per cent of French land in the early nineteenth century. In Prussia, where
large estates were said to start at 375 acres, their owners controlled no more
than 40 per cent of land at the mid-century. This concentration of land, combined with the higher productivity of English agriculture and their extensive
interests in urban land speculation, coal, canals and railways, made the
English landowners the most economically powerful class of their kind in
Europe.[16]

In comparison with the industrial bourgeoisie, the landowners remained,
according to Anderson, the wealthier class and their political power was thus
based on solid material foundations. The fortunes of the greatest aristocrats
towered over those of the most successful industrialists and there were many
more of them. Drawing on W. D. Rubenstein's detailed work on probate
records, Anderson argued that during the first half of the nineteenth century,
virtually all of those with property proved at over £500 000 were landowners
and until about 1880 these still comprised over half of the very wealthy in
Britain.[17]

Alongside the landed class was the City financial sector, by the nineteenth century the centre of world financial transactions. Although it was
the dominance of the British manufactures in world trade that secured the
hegemony of the City, London's commercial and financial transactions grew
at a faster rate than the export of manufactures during the middle half
of the century. City profits were 30 per cent of the total value of exports
in 1820 and 50 per cent by 1880. Outside land, the financial sector created the majority of the largest fortunes, with families such as the Loders,
the Morrisons and the Rothchilds coming high on the list. Thus, whilst in
late nineteenth-century Germany and America the summits of capital were
uncompromisingly industrial, in Britain, land and finance still commanded
the leading place in the hierarchy of capital.

The nature of the Victorian ruling elite thus reflected the material basis of
class power. Its leading personnel continued to be supplied by the landed
and financial factions. Finance capital had always been sharply distinguished from manufacture in Britain, playing no major part in supplying the
investment for the expansion of early manufacturing enterprises, and it continued throughout the century to be oriented economically towards overseas
investment rather than domestic industry. Culturally it was Anglican and
conservative in outlook, like the majority of the landed class to which it was
closely allied. It was thus a Tory regime, representing the interests of these

groups, which presided over the early stages of industrialization and rallied the forces of order against an insurgent working class in the early decades of the century.

After years of agitation the industrial bourgeoisie did finally assure its entry into the political system in 1832. However, although the Whigs extended the franchise by some 300 000 to include middle-class house-holders, they carefully skewed representation towards small borough seats. This contained urban representation below the threshold where it could sustain an autonomous bourgeois party. Despite the resistance of some bourgeois radicals, the middle class was thus absorbed into the existing system and its reforming zeal was consequently blunted before the point where it might have created its own political party. The consequence, according to Anderson, was 'a fundamentally unaltered aristocratic ascendancy in English politics'.[18] Between 1818 and 1900 there was no increase in the number of commoners in the British cabinet. Between 1868 and 1886, 28 cabinet ministers were aristocrats and only 22 were from the middle class. If the British parliament was, as Engels once remarked, 'the most fashionable debating club in Europe', the central core of government was even more exclusive. The gentry also continued to dominate in the Commons. By contrast, in mid-century Prussia the *Landtag* was dominated by civil servants. In the French Chamber of Deputies and in the US Congress it was the lawyers who predominated.

Clearly, as Anderson acknowledges, the entry of the middle class into the political system had considerable effects on the policies of governments. The party which could command the support of the growing industrial and commercial class was likely to gain power and it was this which ensured the Whigs their long period of ascendancy during the mid-Victorian period. Peel's repeal of the Corn Laws, which split the Tory party, heralded the conversion of large sections of the ruling class to free-trade liberalism, and guaranteed Liberal ascendancy during the golden years of Victorian capitalism. However, within 30 years the political alignments were to shift again. A growing plutocracy of landed magnates, financiers and brewers was joined from below by sections of the bourgeoisie and the professions who were increasingly drawn to the status and values of the ruling elite. Together they cemented a new conservative ruling bloc. The crisis of liberalism and home rule in the 1880s encouraged increasing sections of the middle class to shift to the Conservatives and led to the Unionist ascendancy of Salisbury and Balfour that consummated the century. With the decline of mid-century liberalism, Anderson was thus again on surer ground and returned to his theme of conservative cultural hegemony. 'What was new in the late 19th century', he wrote

was the secretion of a deeply conformist and conservative cult of countryside and club, tradition and constitution, as the predominant outlook among the intelligentsia, repudiating bourgeois origins and miming seigneurial postures in a synthetic gentility and ruralism extending far into the 20th century.[19]

Anderson's analysis of the political and cultural dominance of the landed elite was thus not substantially modified. What was new, however, was his analysis of the state in Victorian England. One of the most trenchant criticisms of his earlier accounts had been the degree to which they underplayed liberalism as the truly hegemonic ideology of the age. In his later treatment of the state, however, Anderson was bound to concede that one of the most singular aspects of the British social formation in the nineteenth century was the relatively minimal nature of the state bureaucracy and this, of course, owed precisely to the power of liberal orthodoxy. The Victorian state was indeed, as Anderson maintained, exceptional in both the austerity of its means and the simplicity of its functions. In absolute figures, overall public expenditure registered nil growth between 1830 and 1850, actually falling in per capita terms. Thereafter it rose by a mere 20 per cent per capita over the next 40 years, during a period when public spending more than doubled in France, and trebled in the United States and Germany. At the middle of the century, the Victorian Civil Service numbered just under 40 000 and by 1861 it had fallen to 31 000. If local government is included, English officialdom numbered no more than 60 000 when Palmerston died. The French bureaucracy at the time numbered 450 000. By 1881 the British Civil Service, both central and local, had risen to 80 000, by which time its German equivalent numbered 450 000.

The British state apparatus was not only uniquely lean and compacted compared with the sprawling continental bureaucracies, but its functions were also significantly less wide ranging. Industrialization had occurred from the bottom up, as an organic or molecular process which required little direction from the state. Furthermore, as Anderson noted, it played almost no part in developing the infrastructure of transport in contrast with continental states and deferred creating public education long after universal elementary schooling had become established elsewhere.[20]

It is hardly possible here to do justice to the complexity of Anderson's argument in this later version of his thesis, but it should be clear that it was substantially adjusted to take account of the earlier criticisms. It would be difficult, for instance, to dismiss his arguments about landowner dominance on the grounds that his reading of history was culturalist or idealist, as his former critics were wont to do. The case for the economic dominance of the landed and financial sectors of capital may still be open to debate, but Anderson certainly put a challenging defence and one which successfully shifted the locus of his argument from the realms of ideology to the material basis of class power. However, there will still be many historians, Marxist and otherwise, who will continue to assert the orthodox interpretation of Victorian Britain as the bourgeois society *par excellence*, and from this perspective there can be little room for Anderson's distinctive argument about landowner hegemony. Eric Hobsbawm, for instance, has recently dismissed the whole idea of a failed bourgeois revolution – which, as he rightly notes, has right-wing versions as well – as simply 'mistaken'.[21] There can be no attempt to resolve this debate here but a number of points should be made which have particular bearing on the question of education.

Anderson undoubtedly strengthened the argument about the singularity of landowner power in Britain, both as it relates to the comparative position of equivalent classes in Europe, and in relation to the other tiers of the indigenous class structure. The problem is that he only achieved this by placing increasing emphasis on those aspects of the landed class that were most 'capitalist' and most 'urban'. Consequently, it amounted to proving that the landowners were dominant by showing just how bourgeois they were. What distinguished the English landed class from their continental counterparts was that they had been capitalists for longer, that they had maintained closer connections with urban life through their financial involvement in urban development and their social connections with the London 'season', and that politically they had learnt to adapt to the realities of bourgeois liberal politics at a time when aristocratic intransigence in France was leading to revolution and partial extinction. In terms of their relation to the industrial class at home, they had so far adapted to the *laissez-faire* spirit of capitalism from the Napoleonic Wars onwards that there remained, according to Anderson, no real antagonism between them and the bourgeoisie proper at all. If this was the case, where does it leave the thesis of the dominance of a peculiarly conservative 'aristocratic' culture? If the landowners retained power essentially on the terms of the bourgeoisie, equally committed, as Anderson claims, to liberal political economy, then surely we are back to the classic Marxist conception of a delegation of bourgeois power through a landed governing class? If so then there can be no warrant for talking about landed hegemony.

The question really boils down to the theoretical issue of how one defines hegemony. If the hegemonic ideology is that which is most typical of the class which furnishes the governing stratum then there might be a case for arguing landowner hegemony during the Victorian era. However, as Nicos Poulantzas pointed out in his early rejoinder to Anderson's arguments in the 1960s, this cannot be the correct way to define hegemony and it was certainly not Gramsci's. Hegemony resides in the nature of the power *relations* and the ideologies that legitimate them which objectively represent the dominant interests in those relations of power. It is not the property of any one class and least of all can it be equated with the traditional ideology of the class which happens to provide the political leadership:

If in general, the politically dominant ideology in a formation is that of the politically dominant class, this is not because it can be identified with some political will of the class subject as if ideologies were 'political' number-plates social classes wore on their backs; it is because the dominance of this ideology is related to the set of objective co-ordinates which result in a given political domination, a given class-state and a given dominant ideology.[22]

The dominant ideology will comprise various elements, not all of which arise out of the class consciousness of the dominant political class but which will serve to keep that class in power. Only in the latter sense can it be termed 'their' ideology. In other words, one cannot deduce from the typical ideology of the class that supplies the governing elite the content of the dominant or hegemonic ideology, any more than one can deduce from the relative paucity of political representation of another class the notion that their ideology is not represented in the dominant ideology. In terms of Victorian Britain, then, it was the nature of the dominant ideology and the objective relations of class power that it legitimated that constituted 'hegemony', and not the typical ideology of the landed class which provided the political leadership.

The problem with Anderson's account of hegemony was that it concentrated too much on the traditional ideology of the landed class, which provided the majority of the political leaders, and too little on the actual nature of the politics and ideas which were dominant. Two, somewhat contradictory, patterns of argument emerged. Firstly, Anderson conceded the dominance of liberal political economy within the state apparatus since this was evidently the case, but far from conceding this as a quintessentially bourgeois philosophy, he traced its antecedents in the liberalism of 'laissez-faire landlords' in the eighteenth century. The Whig liberalism of the eighteenth century was easily transformed into the political economy of the nineteenth century:

> The basic design transmitted by laissez-faire landlords proved eminently adaptable and suitable to the needs of the first industrial revolution. The tensions between aristocratic and bourgeois politics within the post-reform framework did not coincide with any conflict over the role of the state in a common capitalist economy.[23]

Whilst it may be true that bourgeois political economy had its origins in eighteenth-century liberalism, the idea that by the next century there was minimal antagonism between the radical bourgeois philosophy of Ricardo and the traditional philosophies of sections of the landed class is quite untenable. It was certainly the case that the majority of landlords finally succumbed to the principal tenets of political economy. As Thompson pointed out, large sections of them finally even supported Peel in the repeal of the Corn Laws. However, this only illustrates the degree to which the ideas of the bourgeois economists had become accepted. It can hardly be used to support the notion of landowner hegemony.

In other respects, elements of what may be termed the traditional landed culture survived in opposition to political economy. Tory paternalism was not extinguished and remained at odds with the harsher aspects of market liberalism. The 'romantic' or 'organic' conservative tradition of Carlyle and Ruskin totally rejected the 'dismal science' of political economy and the bourgeois cash-nexus, and the culture of Anglicanism and Tory tradition-alism was often considerably discordant with the Benthamite culture of secular expertise. In other words, precisely those conservative aspects of rural landowner culture which Anderson most wished to stress were frequently in opposition to the spirit of Manchester liberalism which epitomized bour-geois aspirations in the mid-century. Why else would Richard Cobden, the scion of the industrial middle class, maintain that 'the spirit of feudalism was rife and rampant in...the age of Watt, Arkright and Stephenson'.[24] To minimize these conflicts as a way of establishing the concordance of liberal political economy and landlord ideology contradicts Anderson's case in respect of the conservative cultural hegemony.

Anderson's attempt to annex liberalism to the idea of landlord hegemony thus leads to the major problem with his account. Throughout his writings he has consistently emphasized those aspects of the hegemonic ideology which can be equated with conservative landed culture and equally consis-tently underplayed those elements which were distinctively bourgeois. Thus the importance of Benthamism and Dissent in the overall cultural config-uration of the period are consistently neglected. There can be little doubt, for instance, that by the mid-century large sections of the landed class, and indeed the labour aristocracy, had been substantially won over to the principal moral themes propagated most vociferously by middle-class non-conformism and the evangelical movement. One does not have to go as far as Harold Perkin and Trygve Tholfsen have done in claiming an unal-loyed triumph of bourgeois morality to appreciate the deep implantation of middle-class ideas of propriety, hard graft, self-reliance, enterprise and indi-vidualism within the dominant culture. Samuel Smiles' *Self Help*, one of the most widely read books of the period, epitomized this well. For all of its shrill moralism it was a deeply populist text and its strident individualism provided the core motif of the dominant ideology of the period.

Benthamism certainly had fewer claims to represent the hegemonic ideology. Despite the adherence of its main proponents to the key notions of political economy, its tendency to promote even limited state enhancement and its secular rationalism were unpalatable to many sections of the mid-dle class. Nevertheless, its influence within the state apparatus in the period until 1840 was considerable and it receives scant attention in Anderson's account. The state apparatus is a crucial site for the propagation of dominant ideologies, as Gramsci stressed, and the cultural milieu of its leading functionaries is clearly an important issue here. Anderson's account was again somewhat lopsided here. Recognizing that the state apparatus was at least partially reformed during the era of the Napoleonic Wars, Anderson depicted this as the 'rationalization of the aristocratic state at its own behest'.[25] This involved departmental reorganization along more rational lines and the reduction of patronage in government office. However, this did not represent, in Anderson's view, its transformation into a bourgeois apparatus. Even the Northcote–Trevelyan reforms of the 1850s did little to democratize the civil service. Rather than displace the upper-class hold on state office, they merely entrenched it by ensuring that the gentlemen personnel were better trained. The picture of an amateur and traditionalist state intellectual caste is thus hardly redrawn.

The reality was actually somewhat more complicated than this. Some of the older branches of the state were indeed classic repositories of aristocratic styles and values, most notably the army, the foreign office and the home office. But, as Robbie Gray has pointed out, we have to set against this those branches of the state, such as the Board of Trade, the Local Government Board, and the Education Department, which were often heavily influenced by Benthamite expertise and conformed much more closely to utilitarian models of a public bureaucracy. Equally, if local administration in rural areas was controlled by gentry sitting on the magistrates bench, urban local government was increasingly the province of shopkeepers and tradesmen.[26] Any characterization of the state apparatus as uniformly amateur and traditional in style is clearly only half of the story.

If we abandon the idea, as we should, that the nature of hegemony is constituted solely by the culture and interests of the dominant political class, and see it rather as a relation established between classes, under conditions of unequal power, then it is hard to dissent from the traditional belief that the nature of that hegemony constructed during the Victorian period owed less to landed culture than to ideologies and aspirations that were objectively bourgeois. Certainly there were aspects of the traditional landed ideology that remained distinctly influential in some areas, particularly in the Anglican Church, in the rural areas and in certain branches of the state. There was also a powerful current of thought amongst sections of the intelligentsia which was overtly antagonistic to the dominant bourgeois ethos of the time. The romantic conservative tradition, which extended down from Coleridge to Carlyle, Ruskin and even Dickens in his later years, was deeply opposed to the narrow materialism and harsh self-interest of the liberal creed, and at times appeared both unsympathetic to the urban world and hostile to industrialism itself. As both Wiener and Anderson rightly insist, these influences, combined with the lure of the gentlemanly, pastoral lifestyle, proved uniquely attractive to sections of the bourgeoisie and the old professional class. However, the wide resonance and compelling attraction of this view of the world owed precisely to the very dominance of liberal and materialist values in this the most urbanized and industrial country in the world. It was an inevitable reaction and had important consequences, particularly in the later period, but it hardly dislodged the mainstream bourgeois values from their hegemonic position. The overwhelmingly dominant values of the Victorian era were those of individualism, enterprise and *laissez-faire* liberalism, at once both tempered and sharpened by religion. Whatever their antecedents, these were nothing now if not the values of a confident and predominantly bourgeois capitalism.

The arguments put forward by Anderson, Wiener and others have an important part to play in explaining some aspects of the peculiarities of English education even if they cannot provide the entire explanation. Clearly the conservative, traditionalist cultural milieu which they depict was one of the main factors behind that most peculiar of national institutions: the English public school. Since the Anglican Church and gentry also controlled most of the other major secondary schools, it would be no exaggeration to say that Anderson's conservative landowner hegemony was the operant force here. As middle-class radicals repeatedly complained at the time, there really was no secondary education on a national scale for the middle class.

Other connections are readily apparent. The long-lasting absence of any adequate technical training and the relative inattention of schools to science and vocationally useful subjects was at least partly a product of the pervasive influence of those conservative and anti-utilitarian values which we have discussed. If the Anglican Church controlled the major part of education, from elementary schools up to the universities, this was hardly surprising, particularly since the only countervailing force, parliament, could rarely muster a majority against the Church. When it did urge the Church to reform its educational institutions it had to move with the greatest of caution. The influence of the landed class within the state apparatus, and the persistence of elements of old-style patronage there, must have also been one of the factors which blocked the development of the kind of meritocratic linkage between secondary education and state service which existed in European countries, notably in France and Germany. If gentlemanly status was a sufficient criterion for government office, who needed a system of credentials? In fact, British civil servants were not without expertise or higher levels of education but the ethos of competitive entry and credential qualification for it was not as prominent as on the Continent and this deprived the secondary schools of one motivation for putting themselves on a more meritocratic footing. In the absence of a credential culture there was less pressing reason for ensuring high academic standards or for measuring these scrupulously with examinations. When the Northcote–Trevelyan reforms threatened to make civil service entry more competitive, this was one of the reasons for the reforms of the secondary schools which occurred belatedly in the 1860s.

Traditionalist cultural values also had significant effects on elementary education. The Tory/Anglican establishment was very late to recognize the value of working-class education and it was not until the Lancasterian schools of the rival churches began to move in on popular education that the Anglicans were persuaded that they had better take the issue more seriously. When they did meet the non-conformist challenge with their own National Society schools, the educational ideology that they espoused was distinctively patrician and paternalistic. Whilst the British and Foreign Schools Society (BFSS) schools preached humility, discipline, obedience and respect, they also encouraged self-improvement, which could not be logically entirely separated from ideas of social advancement. National Society schools, on the other hand, stressed the importance of social hierarchy, the need for deference and the virtue of being satisfied with one's allotted station in life. The distinction was perhaps slender and working-class leaders were as ready to condemn the paternalism and indoctrination in either type of school, but there was something in the improvement ethic of the dissenting schools that was in the long run more acceptable. The stultifying condescension of the Anglican schools, deriving from the ritual conservative belief in rank and status, no doubt did much to alienate the working class from education.

So much can the thesis of the 'conservative culture' explain. However, beyond this it leaves many questions unanswered. To explain the existence of the uniquely traditionalist public school by reference to landowner power is one thing. To say why the middle class did not fare better in achieving alternative types of school is another. 'Aristocratic' schools existed in many European countries. France, for instance, still had many Catholic secondary schools, which, like the public schools, were popular amongst the old elites, putting a similar emphasis on morality, manners and character training, and being rather less concerned with academic standards than the public *lycées*. However, France also had the state secondary schools, which provided a national apparatus for middle-class education, and this had no equivalent in England. Landowner power may thus explain the nature of the public school but it does not explain why a middle class, which could obtain most of its central demands through parliament, did not attempt to win a system of middle-class schools as in France. Similarly, the prevalence of landed influence in the state may go some way towards accounting for the absence of that credentialist or 'meritocratic' ethos that so affected continental education, but it is not entirely convincing as an explanation. The Prussian bureaucracy, for instance, had a similar preponderance of officials from aristocratic or landed backgrounds and yet it had many of the French features of a modern, rationalized and credentialist public administration. Secondary education was articulated with it by a system of national examinations, just as in France.

The failure of scientific and technical education in England is also only partially explained by the conservative culture thesis. Whilst the Anglican/Tory establishment must carry some of the blame, it was by no means only they who failed to see the importance of scientific and technical education. Many industrialists were also totally oblivious to it. In some cases this could be explained by the fact that they themselves had gone to a secondary school that failed to take it seriously, but this was not always the case since many of them had left school at 14 anyway. In any case, to suggest that the influence of schooling could override the lessons of years spent in industry is somewhat implausible. The fact is that the majority of industrialists were not really much influenced by this conservative culture but nor did their own middle-class culture or their experience in the world of industry apparently convince them of what was self-evident to continental industrialists: the fact that education was essential for economic advance. The explanation of this must lie elsewhere.

The last and most perplexing problem remains the absence of a continental-style system of national elementary education. Here the argument about conservative hegemony is of little help. If Anglican and Tory fear of extended working-class education was a factor in obstructing advance in the early decades of the century, it certainly cannot be held principally responsible thereafter. By the 1820s, all parties were committed in principle to improving popular education and the churches and middle-class philanthropy proved it by their considerable charitable investments in it. The major barrier to development was, as we have argued, the resistance to state intervention. This was not an exclusively Anglican or Tory problem. Benthamites and administrative experts aside, the majority of middle-class opinion was, as amongst the gentry, vehemently opposed to state education. The argument that state-led development in education was prevented because of the lack of middle-class political muscle or because of inadequate implantation in the state machine, as Archer claims, is quite untenable. It did not happen because virtually no large constituency wanted it to happen.

Hobsbawm and the early start

To return again to the debate around the nineteenth-century state, it should by now be apparent that the chief theoretical difficulty is to give due weight to the unusual preponderance of landowner influence within the state, which did indeed constitute one of the English peculiarities, without slipping into the untenable thesis of landowner hegemony. In many respects, Eric Hobsbawm's classic account of British development in *Industry and Empire* and later in *The Age of Capital* does achieve this. His distinctive trait as a historian has always been his extraordinary ability to capture the whole panorama of social change across different continents. Like Marx, he has been principally concerned with the broad currents of economic and social change which have accompanied the spread of capitalism throughout the world. However, as a comparativist he retains a sharp eye for national variation, and it is these dual qualifications which give his account of the nineteenth-century debate particular authority.

In the course of his analysis of the nineteenth century, Hobsbawm notes many of those characteristics which for Anderson have constituted the core of the argument about the conservative culture. The British aristocracy and gentry were little affected by industrialization except for the better. They remained a formidable economic force. Equally prosperous were the 'numerous parasites of aristocratic society', the rural, small-town functionaries and professionals who became 'increasingly reactionary' as the century wore on. The universities, the lawyers and 'what passed for a civil service' were 'unreformed and unregenerate'.[27] Moreover, there was an upper stratum of the bourgeoisie, including the merchants and financiers, and increasingly top industrialists, who were often inclined to assimilation into the world of landed society. For the industrialist, 'success brought no uncertainty so long as it was enough to lift a man into the ranks of the upper class'. He would become a gentleman, doubtless with a country house, perhaps eventually a knighthood and a peerage. There would be a seat in the house for him or his Oxbridge-educated son. His wife would become a 'Lady', instructed in her duties by a multitude of handbooks in etiquette. This group, typically represented by the Peelites in parliament, were essentially assimilated into a landed oligarchy though at odds with it, says Hobsbawm, when the economic interests of land and business clashed.[28] But for the last crucial qualification this evocative account could have come straight out of Anderson.

Nevertheless, Hobsbawm stops some way short of the idea of landowner hegemony, and refers to the 'Wiener thesis' as 'quite unconvincing'. The argument is straightforward. Although, as Hobsbawm agrees, there is 'some truth in the theory that aristocratic, amateur values were dominant', and although it was certainly the case that trade was stigmatized, the value of these observations is limited because 'many British businessmen did not conform to them' and because the majority of the middle class were not assimilated.[29] The reasons for the persistent failures of modernization in the period after 1860 must be sought, therefore, not so much in these cultural forces but rather in more directly economic factors where possible.[30]

The main purpose of *Industry and Empire* is thus to explain, in terms that would satisfy social and economic historians, the factors that underlay Britain's early industrial success and its later decline. It is the second part that most concerns us here since it was arguably the same inhibiting factors which retarded educational development. Hobsbawm's characteristic answer to this problem has been to show how many of the social conditions that favoured early industrialization were the same factors which would inhibit its later development. In other words, the answer to the question of English exceptionalism lies in what Nairn called the 'logic of priority'. Only one nation could be the first industrialized country and in being so it was necessarily exceptional.

In Hobsbawm's account, three characteristics distinguished the first industrialized country from all those that followed it. Firstly, the wealth that made possible the early economic take-off in Britain was largely derived from colonial trade and investment. This gave the merchant and financial sectors of capital unprecedented predominance in the English social formation and the economy generally. Their historical priority created an exceptional division between finance and later manufacturing capital, and ensured their continuing overseas or 'colonial' orientation. Secondly, the first-comer nation could industrialize with relatively little technology or formal training. That was because the first Industrial Revolution 'required little scientific knowledge or technical skill beyond the scope of a practical mechanic of the early 18th century'. Thirdly, the first Industrial Revolution could occur within a liberal regime precisely because it came first and had no real competitors. This meant not only free trade and minimal government but also a whole attitude of mind which was empirical and individualistic. 'Only so lucky an industrial power', writes Hobsbawm, 'could have afforded that distrust of logic and planning...that faith in the capacity to muddle through, which became so characteristic of Britain in the nineteenth century.'[31]

Clearly none of these characteristics would be appropriate to countries industrializing later. Germany and France had no equivalent build-up of pre-industrial wealth in the spoils of colonial trade. Their manufacturing and finance capital would have to advance hand in hand since both were equally interdependent. By the time Germany and France entered into full-scale industrialization, state-of-the-art technology had advanced to the point where formal training in applied science could not be avoided. Nor could latecomers afford Britain's liberal regime. Free trade did not favour them equally and catching up economically could only be achieved through concerted, state-supported development. In the case of Germany and France, previous historical development had in any case developed an apparatus and a philosophy of the state which was more amenable to its later use as a leading-edge instrument.

After its successful early start, British economic advance continued unabated through the mid-century 'golden years' of Victorian capitalism. Those institutional features that were entrenched during the early years were substantially unchanged but as yet they provided no apparent impediment to short-term capitalist development. 'By the middle of the nineteenth century,' writes Hobsbawm, 'government policy in Britain came as near *laissez-faire* as has ever been practicable in a modern state.'[32] Few countries had ever been dominated by an *a priori* doctrine to the extent that Britain was by *laissez-faire*. Government was small and comparatively cheap, and as time went on it became cheaper by comparison with other states.[33] Alone amongst industrial powers, the British state performed no major role in infrastructural development. But this scarcely seemed to affect economic progress. Railways, for instance, were effectively financed from the surplus of private capital and, although they did not always develop according to a rational plan, they did develop. The state was not completely reconstructed and still bore the traces of the old regime, but the industrialists feared revolution too much to risk direct challenge to the established order. In any case the cost of institutional inefficiency was 'never more than petty cash to the most advanced industrial economy in the world'.[34]

So matters stood in 1860 when Britain was at the peak of its economic ascendancy. However, within 20 years, the inexorable process of relative decline was clearly apparent. The reason, according to Hobsbawm, was that the chickens finally came home to roost. Those institutional peculiarities, which had been associated with Britain's early economic achievements, now appeared as so many fetters on economic development. Lack of scientific and technical training deprived industrial managers, scientists and foremen of the very skills that were so essential in the second stage of industrial development. Heavy investment in old industrial plant and once successful techniques discouraged industrial innovation. Lack of coordination between finance and manufacturing capital caused shortages of domestic investment and prevented the development of systematic economic concentration – the formation of trusts, cartels and syndicates which were so characteristic of Germany and the United States in the 1880s. The state remained at least partly committed to the old principles of liberalism and was poorly equipped to lead the way in modernization. In short, Britain was too committed to the old ways, which had once been so successful, to adapt vigorously to the new. It left one way out. By relying on the strength of its overseas Empire and the profits of trade and investment there, it could maintain economic strength without the pains of modernization. Imperialism thus allowed Edwardian capitalism to survive into the new world without ever quite abandoning the old.

Gamble and Marquand on liberalism

Our third paradigm explanation of the 'British route' is more of an extension of the above account than an alternative, and as such can be dealt with rather more briefly. Andrew Gamble in *Britain in Decline* and, subsequently, David Marquand in *The Unprincipled Society* both wrote excellent long-range accounts of British development which seek to explain the failure of modernization in modern Britain. The accounts, at least for the nineteenth century, are similar, and Marquand acknowledges his debt to Gamble if not to other precursors. The underlying theme in both books is taken from Hobsbawm's widely acclaimed thesis about the transformation of early strengths into later weaknesses. Hobsbawm has subsequently indicated his agreement with 'some parts' of Marquand's thesis and the explanation for the failure of economic modernization is essentially the same in all three accounts. What Gamble and Marquand have added is a more wide-ranging analysis of the political and social structures of the nineteenth century which extends the argument about economic developmental blockages into a specific critique of social and political structures.

Like Hobsbawm, both Gamble and Marquand see Britain's relative economic decline after 1870 as a failure to adapt after the first Industrial Revolution. Marquand's eloquent introduction summarizes the general argument well:

> In at least three related aspects, twentieth century Britain has been a prisoner of her nineteenth century past. She was the first industrial society in history, the pathfinder of the modern world. The values and assumptions of her elites, the doctrines disseminated in her universities and newspapers, the attitudes and patterns of behaviour of her entrepreneurs and workers were stamped indelibly by this experience. But because she was the pathfinder – because she made the passage to industrialization early, at a time when technology was still primitive, when the skills required were still rudimentary and when it could be managed efficiently by the small scale, fragmented structures of liberal capitalism – the experience taught the wrong lesson.[35]

It was the early Industrial Revolution, successfully accomplished under a liberal regime, which entrenched the damaging notion that liberal doctrines would be applicable for all time and under all circumstances. The Industrial Revolution provided the aspic which would preserve the ideas of Adam Smith in a kind of deadly suspended animation to the present day. However, as both authors stress, the origins of British liberalism lay further back in yet earlier and more precocious British achievements. Thus to Gamble it was not so much Britain's early start that was the cause of the failure to keep up with later competition but 'the very social relations that made the early start possible, and which remained intact and strengthened by that start'.[36]

Gamble's account of British development starts with the early achievement of territorial integrity and the nation state. It was the successful early consolidation of the strong state under the Tudors, combined with the strategic advantages of island insularity (and so naval power) and successful commercial agriculture, which allowed royal absolutism in England to be cut short in the seventeenth century. The heirs of 1688 were the Whig gentry and it was they who laid the foundations of centuries of liberal capitalism. The settlement created a state where individual liberties were highly regarded and where suspicion of central state power was widespread.

England in the eighteenth century, writes Gamble, became the acknowledged land of liberty, and the freedoms and relative social mobility that this engendered were in no small part responsible for the early Industrial Revolution. However, by the late nineteenth century it was this very liberal order that became the major impediment to the creation of the kind of dynamic state without which modernization could not occur. It was the 'permissive orientation of the state to the market order [and] the tradition of suspicion towards the government and its initiatives [that] have constantly hampered the development of an interventionist state in the last hundred years'.[37] It was not so much that these attitudes prevented such a state from arising but rather that they prevented it from being as successful as its advocates had hoped or as other more intrinsically corporatist states had been.

Marquand likewise traces the origins back to 1688, from which point, he says, Britain followed an aberrant path. The Stuarts failed to sustain an absolute, patrimonial monarchy, strong enough to impose its will on the gentry. Cromwell failed to create the alternative republican form of the strong state and thus never 'trenched the freedom of the landed class to do what it wished with its own'. The result was the familiar pattern of fragmented and decentralized liberal rule:

> The medieval particularism of the past blended with the 'possessive individualism of emergent capitalism'. The old corporations, the old precedent-bound common law, the old houses of parliament all survived; and they, not the will of a reforming monarch, became the conduit of modernity. The end product was a political culture suffused with the values and assumptions of Whiggery, above all with the central Lockean assumption that individual property rights are antecedent to society. In such a culture, the whole notion of a public power, standing apart from private interests, was bound to be alien.[38]

For both Gamble and Marquand the overriding and determinate British singularity has been the longevity and pervasiveness of a uniquely doctrinal commitment to the principles of nineteenth-century liberalism. Like Anderson they trace the origins of this back to the role of the eighteenth-century gentry but unlike him they are far from arguing that this was the basis of a landowner hegemony in the next century. Their point is rather that such was the heritage of the past and its influence on all classes that liberal individualism became the dominant mode of a specifically bourgeois hegemony. Even the Benthamites, the nearest equivalents to continental bourgeois ideologists and the group least suspicious of the state, were at heart liberal individualists. The community to Bentham was a 'fictitious body', just as for modern neo-liberal Thatcherites 'society does not exist'. Then as in the 1980s, political economy recognized only the individual. The public good was no more than the happiness of the greatest number of individuals, and this could only be achieved through the individual pursuit of enlightened self-interest. What singled out Britain from the continental republics and monarchies alike was thus not so much the predominance of landed culture as the deep infusion of liberal individualism in all sections of the ruling class and, in different ways, in the working class as well. Because of the power of the individualist creed, because of the decentralized nature of government and the relative absence of the cohesive or, as Marx would say, universalizing public power, because of the fissiparous nature of civil society, British society was unique. It had adopted a form of bourgeois social organization that marked it out from all other leading continental states during the nineteenth century.

For Marquand, in particular, this has been more than a political philosophy: individualism and hostility to the state have constituted almost a whole way of life. The ethos of early nineteenth-century market liberalism was 'more deeply embedded in her culture than in other European culture'. More completely than elsewhere, Britain's culture was 'permeated with the individualism which its intellectuals codified and justified'.[39] The result has been a singular inability to create the kind of 'developmental' or 'entrepreneurial' state which could provide a positive interventionist force capable of directing modernization within civil society. With a social fabric deeply divided by 'non-encompassing' interest groups and lacking an effective set of corporate structures linking government, banking, industry and unions, Britain has been unable to develop a long-term and coordinated approach to economic development. Exceptionally amongst leading Western European nations, it has been unable to create the structures which constitute what the French call the *Economie Concerté*, which has been so critical in successful modernization in countries such as France, Sweden, Austria and Japan.

The analyses suggested by Hobsbawm, Gamble and, to an extent, Marquand seem to me to provide a uniquely powerful way of assessing the specific form of the British State in the nineteenth century. They have generally incorporated the most useful features of Anderson's original polemical thesis whilst abandoning those arguments about landed hegemony which seem untenable in the light of recent work on the theory of hegemony. They have addressed themselves, as Thompson never did, to the central issue in Anderson's argument – the question of modernization and relative decline – without falling into Anderson's somewhat overdrawn notion of centuries of national 'failure'. It is an argument about early strengths and later weaknesses rather than a global picture of failed bourgeois revolution. The analysis also seems to provide the most satisfactory theoretical basis for understanding the nature of education in nineteenth-century England.

The concept of the early start is clearly central to understanding the way in which education developed in the first half of the century. The fact that industrialization occurred first in England meant that there was never an equivalent of that intensely nationalistic and concerted drive towards development through the state that existed in continental nations. England did not need to use education in such a deliberate way to pursue national development because it had occurred anyway without any great assistance from education. The fact that industrialization occurred at a time when science and technology were relatively unimportant for its success explains why it was so long before it became apparent to most people that education and training were essential for economic development.

There were, of course, other pressing reasons for developing education which were well recognized, but there was an overriding factor which inhibited such efforts, and that was the nature of the state and public attitudes towards the state. The development of public education in Europe had been an expression of that intense belief in the importance of the public realm and the leading role of the state in national development. This was true in different ways in both republics and monarchies. The revolutionary state, with the universalizing ideologies of its bourgeois cadres in the Jacobin tradition, was one, more democratic, version of this. The authoritarian bureaucratic state of the Prussian tradition was another. Even in the United States which, like Britain, held fast to liberal notions of the state, there was a strong nationalistic drive towards development and at the local level a vigorous, democratic concept of the public domain which supported educational reform. Only in Britain was individualism and hostility to the state so entrenched that support for public education through the state could not be won.

Education and liberalism, 1780–1839

Pre-industrial origins

If the most striking distinction between English and continental education in the nineteenth century was the relative reluctance of the British state to play a fully interventionist role, the pattern had not always been thus. During the first efflorescence of educational reform in the modern period, at the time of the Reformation, the English monarchy played an active role in promoting changes in education just as, for instance, the Lutheran princes did in German states. The Reformation had made education a directly political concern and how to use it to secure certain political and religious objectives became a vital question of statecraft.

The sixteenth century saw major developments in English education. The influence of renaissance humanism broke the hold of medieval scholasticism on educated thought and brought learning more in touch with the temporal world; the spread of the vernacular, facilitated by advances in printing, provided stimulus for a literate public; and the development of navigation, commerce and crafts encouraged a new demand for literacy and learning. If the humanists had challenged the Church's monopoly on education and encouraged the foundation of new reformed institutions, the Reformation carried on where Erasmus and Vives had left off. The spread of Lutheran ideas encouraged the promotion of popular literacy as an aid to religious understanding and as a means for political stability, and in making education a concern of the state it further eroded the traditional ecclesiastical domination of schooling.

The Tudor state was never far removed from developments in education, as Joan Simon has demonstrated in *Education and Society in Tudor England*.[40] Cardinal Wolsey had sought to reform education under the aegis of the Church, prescribing school and university studies to stem the spread of Lutheran heresy. After the break with Rome, the Church became subject to the Crown, and the reform of universities and schools henceforth occurred under the aegis of the state. Cromwell demanded university allegiance to the King, set about purging scholastic teaching and issued injunctions to parents to educate their children. Education became intimately connected with the state-building policies of the Tudor monarchy as the revolution in government put a new premium on the presence of educated men at court. 'By the close of Henry's reign', writes Simon, 'there had been a wholesale transference of rights over schools to the crown, bringing to a climax the long process of lay encroachment on ecclesiastical powers over education.'[41]

The Tudor state performed an important role in education, not so much in founding new institutions – many of the new grammar schools created during the sixteenth century were lay foundations, mostly by wealthy London and provincial merchants – but in reorganizing and adapting existing schools, in supervising the local schools under lay governing bodies and in generally encouraging the idea that schooling was important. During the seventeenth century there was also significant state involvement in education, particularly during the period of the Commonwealth. Grammar schools already pertained to something like a national network and leading educational writers were beginning to draw up blueprints for reform, inspired by the Baconian revival of scientific learning. Notable amongst these was a plan for a national system of common and mechanical schools, submitted to the Committee for the Advancement of Learning in 1653 by Samuel Hartlib and John Dury, two writers influenced by Comenius. Nothing came of this but during the revolutionary era parliament also directed educational development to some extent, diverting money from confiscated church lands to increase the incomes of school masters and the smaller colleges of Oxford and Cambridge, and to found the new university at Durham.[42]

Although the English state in the sixteenth and seventeenth centuries achieved no sweeping measures to compare with the legislation which prefigured national education in Prussia and Austria in the following century, its role was not markedly different from that in sixteenth-century continental Europe. Certainly England had the reputation at the time for being amongst the most literate of nations.[43] Furthermore, some parallels can be drawn between the motivations of the continental absolutists and the state-building and nationalistic preoccupations of the Tudor monarchies. To be sure, the overt issue was usually religion, but as Namier once remarked, religion was a sixteenth-century word for nationalism.

However, after 1660 the divergence between English educational development and that on the Continent became more apparent. The educational movement of the revolutionary era was eclipsed by the restoration of King, court and the Established Church and the resumption of church control over education. The reforms of the earlier period were too closely associated with Puritan and republican policies to survive. The eighteenth century represented a period of marked decline for the older educational institutions and witnessed no positive state interest in education to parallel the work of the absolutist states in continental Europe. School endowments lost much of their value and, as enrolments at the grammar schools and at Oxford and Cambridge went into sharp decline, traditional education became increasingly stagnant and corrupted. The aristocracy and gentry withdrew their children from all but the most exclusive schools so that they might be educated at home, free from the contamination of children of lesser rank. Plebian children were squeezed out from the grammar schools as scholarships were appropriated by clergy and gentry. Meanwhile, the middle class were increasingly alienated from traditional institutions by the barriers erected to Dissent, by the cost of university education and by the limitations of classical learning. With the Test Act of 1673, Dissenters were debarred from graduation at the ancient universities and these became exclusively Anglican institutions, with scant claims for either scholarship or teaching. So began a period of catastrophic decline in Anglican secondary education which was to last into the 1830s.

Initiatives in educational reform thus passed to the dissenting academies which represented by far the most dynamic area of educational development in the eighteenth century. First established by ejected clergy for the sons of non-conformists, these offered classical, modern and vocational subjects up to university level and became the main vehicle for a utilitarian middle-class education. The academies were often transient and little is known about their numbers during this period, but they clearly played an important role in providing vocational training for the middle class analogous to that offered by the continental academies and technical schools.

Before the spread of Sunday Schools at the end of the eighteenth century there was relatively little education made available to the poor, most of whom acquired their education through the family or the apprentice-ship. The Restoration was generally unfavourable to popular education, which was often seen as a dangerous stimulant to sedition and unrest, and what independent elementary schools there were went into decline in the latter part of the seventeenth century. Soame Jenyns probably expressed the general view of the propertied classes when he wrote in 1757 that ignorance 'is necessary to all born to poverty and the drudgeries of life... [since it is] the only opiate capable of... [enabling] them to endure the miseries of the one and the fatigues of the other'.[44]

What most distinguishes English educational development in this period is the almost total absence of those state initiatives which were so significant in continental development. The central state intervened in education only to shore up the privileges of the Anglican Church and beyond this played no positive role at all. To some extent this may be explained by the relative absence of those causes which prompted continental states to intervene in education.

Britain was exceptional in its early achievement of territorial and cultural unification as a nation. It was initially favoured by its insular geography and ability to avoid foreign invasion. The Tudor monarchs hammered it into a national mould with the suppression of baronial and Church independence, the successful early centralization of state power and the establishment of English as the sole official language. As Seton-Watson writes in his classic text on nationalism and nation-building, 'By the end of Elizabeth's reign the process of formation of English national consciousness had been virtually completed.'[45] The British state was, of course, still not an established entity. England had been unified with Wales in 1536 but the union with Scotland was not consolidated until 1707, whilst Ireland was to undergo a long and bitter process of colonization. National and ethnic divisions thus remained but there was nothing of the order of those protracted national conflicts which, in continental Europe, propelled absolutist monarchs into those deliberate efforts of nation-building in which education had played such an important part.

Nationalism and educational development in England did, arguably, fuse briefly during the Reformation, but thereafter there was no basis for a fervent indigenous nationalism and no impulse from the central state to link nationalist aspirations with educational development. In his comparative thesis on *Nationalism and Education*, Edward Reisner has argued that in this and later periods, 'England seems to have used schools hardly at all as a means of nationalistic propaganda'.[46] The truth was probably more, as Nairn has argued, that the nationalism was rather of the complacent 'great power' variety, reflecting in education a taken-for-granted national superiority rather than stridently asserting national identity as in the Prussian school. However, the point remains that the need to forge national unity and consciousness through education was not a major factor in England, and thus one of the factors that did most to detonate educational development in continental Europe was simply absent.

Another factor that had prompted state intervention in continental education was the need to furnish the state apparatus with trained personnel. Such concerns do not appear to have weighed heavily with English

236 Education and State Formation

rulers during this period and the reasons for this are not difficult to divine. The personnel requirements of the state during this period were exceedingly modest. Protected by its surrounding seas and politically committed to the avoidance of foreign military entanglements, the eighteenth-century state had no need of large armies and therefore little need to school officers and soldiers. Furthermore, a state which taxed its subjects rather lightly by comparison with its continental neighbours needed no large army of tax-collectors. In fact, officials of all kinds were rather small in number. The state apparatus which was left after the revolutions of the seventeenth century was exceedingly streamlined and its administrative class not so large that it required any great educational innovations to furnish. Thus one of the major reasons for the lack of any strong central drive in education was simply the early termination of absolutism in England and thus the absence of those swollen bureaucratic and military machines the staffing of which on the Continent required considerable educational innovation.

To put the case more positively, however, it was not only the absence of motives which pre-empted any major state involvement in education but also a deliberate political antipathy to enhancing the central powers. The liberal state was predicated on the notion that the government should intervene in the affairs of civil society as little as was compatible with the maintenance of civil order, the protection of property and the defence of the realm. As Gamble has argued, what was exceptional about the eighteenth-century state was the very subordination of the state to civil society. The liberal state which emerged after the seventeenth-century revolutions was essentially the creation of a capitalist gentry class, jealous of its freedoms and determined to retain as much power independent of the state as was possible. The typically decentralized nature of administration, with relatively limited central apparatus and resting in the shires on the unpaid justices of the peace, was an ideal form of government for a commercialized gentry class with strong implantation in the structures of local power.

The notion of the liberal state was not only the self-serving philosophy of the gentry class; it also had wide popular reverberations. As Gamble says,

> It mean[t] widespread suspicion of government power and constant pressures to limit it. The English claimed the right to revolt against tyranny, the right to freedom from arbitrary arrest and search, the principle of equality before the law and the right to trial by jury. When these were added to a degree of freedom of publication, speech and conscience, and a much wider freedom to travel and trade, there was a body of rights which, although often infringed and abused, provided a distinct sphere of legal equality, the basis of the bourgeois order.[47]

The popular concept of freedom was not so much democratic as anti-absolutist. But in an age of European absolutism, the strength of the liberal creed as a manifesto of individual rights and freedoms was evident. Less evident, at least until later, was that individualism and the hands-off attitude towards the state could become a positive impediment to the creation of national institutions which capitalist civil society would not of itself generate. Education systems, which were a remarkable product of reforming continental states, would not arise spontaneously in a liberal capitalist order.

The middle-class challenge

The period from 1760 to 1840 was the classic period for the formation of education systems in continental Europe, and a similar time span frames the first stage of major educational innovation and expansion in England. Beginning in the 1780s, the first important upsurge in popular education was the Sunday School movement. This was followed in the first decades of the next century with the spread of the monitorial schools and thus the beginnings of a network of voluntary elementary education. The period also saw the development of the mechanics institutes for the education of working-class adults and the first efforts to reform secondary and higher education in conformity with the needs of the middle class. The period may for convenience be held to end in 1839 with the creation of the Education Committee. This represented a new form of government intervention in education and thus the beginning of a new phase of educational development.

This simultaneous process of reform across Europe, on both sides of the channel, no doubt owed something to similar objective determinants. In each case its most idealistic proponents took their intellectual inspiration from the optimistic rationalism of enlightenment thought; education responded, albeit slowly and unevenly, to new economic demands; and in all countries, educational reform represented a significant aspect of the development of the bourgeois state, most notably as a means of perpetrating the ideological hegemony of the rising class. However, the nature of educational change in England differed markedly in form from that which occurred in most continental states. Whilst on the continent, educational reform meant the creation of national systems through state intervention, in England it meant educational expansion without system. The underlying principle was not state direction but rather voluntaryism.

The first pioneers of middle-class reform in England, and those perhaps closest in orientation to the continental reformers, were the Radicals of the revolutionary era. These were the small coteries of radical industrialists, scientists and rationalist non-conformists who congregated around the Lunar Society and other literary and philosophical societies which sprang up during the 1780s. They included luminaries such as the engineer James Watt, the pottery manufacturer Josiah Wedgwood and the scientist Joseph Priestley. Close to them and most important as a writer on education was the philosopher of human perfectibility William Godwin. In the main they were supporters of the French Revolution and of American Independence.

At home they were prominent in campaigns opposing slavery and the Test Acts, and they championed the cause of parliamentary reform.

Their educational thought was profoundly influenced by Rousseau and the *philosophes*, and exuded that rationalist optimism and faith in the powers of education which was the hallmark of all Enlightenment writings on education. The purpose of education was to develop rational thought, to open the mind to all areas of human knowledge, and thus to create enlightened and useful citizens to participate in the challenges of the new world. Existing institutions, needless to say, they considered to be hopelessly archaic and quite inadequate for these purposes. Only the dissenting academies, where many had received their own education, were considered appropriate to middle-class needs. Their ideas clearly echoed many of the broadly humanist themes of their contemporary French revolutionary educationalists, particularly those of Girondins, such as Condorcet.

However, in two respects they were quite distinct. In the first place the main preoccupation of men such as Priestley was clearly not with popular education but with the education of their own and other middle-class children. He addressed himself not 'to low mechanics, who have not the time to attend to speculations of this nature, and who had, perhaps, better remain ignorant of them'.[48] Their pedagogy, like Rousseau's, spoke of the education of the privileged child and in this they had more in common with the thought of his era than with that of the Revolution. The second notable difference lay in their respective attitudes towards the role of the state in education. The French educationalists were designing plans for national systems of education to be controlled by the state. The English educationalists were not talking of national systems at all and were certainly not friendly to the idea of state involvement in education. Priestley and Godwin both declared themselves to be against education becoming a function of the state, which they believed would lead towards the imposition of uniform beliefs.[49] Even Tom Paine, who was closer to the Jacobins than any of the others, was opposed to the notion of state control of education, suggesting rather that taxes should be reduced so that those who could not currently afford to pay for education could in future do so.

Despite their revolutionary sympathies the middle-class Radicals thus remained true to their liberal heritage, rejecting the Jacobin means of universal change through the command state. Nevertheless, they represented a uniquely radical moment of educational thought. After them, few middle-class educationalists would offer such a generous and rounded vision of human enlightenment without, at the same time, pushing their own brand of class dogma. The next generation of middle-class radicals emerged, as Brian Simon points out,

> as a class whose characteristics had changed, whose purposes were narrower, and who were engaged on two main fronts – against the landed

aristocracy on the one hand, and against the emerging proletariat on the other. In these conditions the educational tradition of the 18th century took on a new form, tending towards a narrower utilitarianism and having, to some extent, an abstract, doctrinaire quality ... [50]

The period of reaction that followed the French Revolution saw the wholesale repression of the Radicals, marked by the treason trials, the suspension of *habeas corpus* and the persecution of the radical press. Many dissenting academies closed and Priestley fled to America. However, in the subsequent period the new classes re-emerged with a greater consciousness of themselves and of their historical roles. The French Revolution had strengthened the position of the English manufactures and after the wars the growing divisions between industrial and landlord interests were increasingly evident, cogently expressed in the writings of the economist David Ricardo. The middle class now increasingly saw itself as the rising hegemonic class, the bearer of a new set of universal values. By 1826 *The Westminster Review* was writing of it in euphoric terms:

> Of the political and moral importance of this class there can be but one opinion. It is the strength of the community. It contains beyond all comparison, the greatest portion of intelligence, industry and wealth in the state. In it are the heads that invent, and the hands that execute; the enterprise that projects and the capital by which these projects are carried into operation ... The people of the class below are the instruments with which they work; and those of the class above, though they may be called their governors, and may really sometimes seem to rule them, are much more often, more truly, and more completely under their control. In this country at least, it is this class which gives the nation its character.[51]

The middle class sought not only to reform the political and economic structure in line with its own beliefs but also to transform education into an instrument of its own purposes. At the same time, radical activity within the working class was developing and represented a mounting challenge not only to the conservative establishment but also potentially to the middle class, which now aspired towards political leadership. With this sharpening class antagonism, educational ideologies became increasingly polarized.

Middle-class ideologies

The aims of the middle class in the education of their own children were determined by their own distinctive economic needs and by their particular ideological perspectives on the world. The economic position of the class demanded an education for their children which would impart the relevant knowledge and useful skills such as would serve them in their future productive occupations. Their values were conditioned by the doctrines of non-conformist religion and evangelical Anglicanism; by the economic individualism and political liberalism of political economy; and increasingly by the utilitarian social philosophy which Jeremy Bentham and his followers had derived from these. These values suggested a distinctive form of middle-class education: one which would reflect in its content the notions of piety, respectability, hard graft and utility, and in its forms the desirability of independent control, methodical instruction and reward for achievement.

The traditional institutions of secondary and higher education offered little that was compatible with these ideals. Schools and universities were seen as corrupt and indolent, their instruction poor and for the most part irrelevant. They were controlled by a conservative alliance of the gentry and the Anglican Church, which showed little desire for change. James Mill attacked the universities for their medievalism and preoccupation with religious indoctrination.[52] Their religious obscurantism and general laxity had led to the virtual abdication of teaching and thus to a staggering ignorance amongst their undergraduates. Baden Powell claimed that not more than two or three Oxford degree candidates out of ten could add vulgar fractions, tell the cause of night and day, or explain the principal of the pump.[53] Public schools were similarly attacked as useless, old-fashioned and corrupt. Radicals were quick to expose the prevalence of sexual immorality, fagging, student riots and other manifestations of moral barbarism. Aside from the remaining dissenting academies, there was thus little education available to suit the middle class. As Radical MP Thomas Wyse was to put it in 1837,

> The middle class, in all its sections, except the mere learned professions, finds no instruction which can suit their special middle class wants. They are fed with the dry husks of ancient learning, when they should be taking sound and substantial food from the great treasury of modern discovery.[54]

Middle-class Radicals not only campaigned against existing institutions. They also tried to develop their own theory for an alternative system of education. An influential example of this was Bentham's plan for a school for his friends' children which was published in 1816 under the title of *Chrestomathia*. The scheme was designed according to the principles of utilitarianism, emphasizing useful knowledge, methodical learning and individual competition. All knowledge, according to Bentham, must serve a social function; it must prepare children for their future occupations and have relevance in everyday life. In place of classical learning he put science and technology at the head of subjects and all other subjects had to be justified by their vocational utility. The teaching method was derived from Hartley's materialist psychology. This taught that the mind functioned by associations and thus education had to be systematic and proceed according to a rational plan. Bentham thus outlined a graded curriculum which laid subjects out in an order of 'facility', proceeding from the simple to the complex and from the particular to the general. Pedagogic principles were derived from the utilitarian principles of pleasure and pain, and involved the use of frequent rewards as well as punishments. Stimulus would be provided by encouraging competition through frequent testing and the use of a graded 'setting' system.[55]

Bentham's school never materialized, mainly because of his insistence on the exclusion of religion from it. However, one can get an idea of the utilitarian scheme of education in practice from examining Hazelwood School, set up in Birmingham by a friend of Priestley, Thomas Wright Hill. At Hazelwood, every moment of the school day was organized. The bell would be rung some 250 times each week, each time signalling a precise activity. Marks were awarded for good work or behaviour, and these could be used to pay off fines awarded for bad behaviour. Behaviour was thus moderated by a system of positive and negative stimulations connected with an elaborate banking system. This was organized with proper account-ing techniques by an appointed student treasurer. The whole reflected the psychological principles of utilitarianism and the spirit of entrepreneurial capitalism, and was quite clearly the antithesis of what went on in the traditional grammar school.[56]

Middle-class plans for popular education, needless to say, embodied rather different objectives. Unlike the Anglican gentry establishment, which had traditionally doubted the political wisdom of educating the lower classes at all, the middle class had generally come to support improvements in popular schooling. Adam Smith and Thomas Malthus had both been early supporters of charity schooling, and by the early nineteenth century the middle class, and particularly Dissent, had accepted their arguments and were giving their philanthropic support to the new monitorial schools. However, their ratio-nale for this new commitment to working-class education was different in every conceivable way from their ideals in middle-class education. Far from intending popular education as a way of bringing universal enlightenment to the working class, or seeing it as a means for their social advancement, either individually or collectively, it was rather a way of ensuring that the subordinate class would acquiesce in their own class aspirations. Popular education would inculcate the ideas of political economy and Christian morality; it would encourage social conformity and loyalty to middle-class political ideals and it would produce a more productive and willing class of workers in their mills, factories and foundries.

The classic middle-class defence of popular education was clearly outlined in *The Wealth of Nations*, where Smith argued that the very nature of modern industry made education a necessity for the working class:

The man whose life is spent in performing a few simple operations . . . has no occasion to exert his understanding, or to exercise his invention in finding out expedients for removing difficulties which never occur.

He naturally loses, therefore, the habit of such exertion, and generally becomes as stupid and ignorant as it is possible for a human creature to become. The torpor of his mind renders him, not only incapable of relishing or bearing a part of any rational conversation, but of conceiving any generous, noble, or tender sentiment, and consequently of forming any just judgement concerning many even of the ordinary duties of life. Of the great and extensive interests of his country, he is altogether incapable of judging; and unless very particular pains have been taken to render him otherwise, he is equally incapable of defending his country in war.[57]

Popular education, argued Smith, had two great merits. It could make the craft worker more productive and would be beneficial to the morals and behaviour of all workers:

The more they are instructed, the less liable they are to the delusions of enthusiasm and superstition ... An instructed and intelligent people besides are always more decent and orderly than an ignorant one ... they are more disposed to examine, and more capable of seeing through the interested complaints of faction and sedition, and they are ... less apt to be misled into any wanton or unnecessary opposition to the measures of the government.[58]

Thomas Malthus was another early champion of popular education. Whilst generally opposed to charity, which he saw as an incitement to overpopulation and working-class dependence, he made an exception in education by supporting the charity schools. His arguments, like Smith's, stressed the importance of inculcating the right ideas in the working class:

If ... a few of the simplest principals of political economy were also taught, the benefit to society would be almost incalculable ... A knowledge of these truths so obviously tends to promote peace and quietness, to weaken the effect of inflammatory writings and to prevent all unreasonable and ill-directed opposition to constituted authorities.[59]

The immediate intellectual heirs to Smith and Malthus, and the leading middle-class ideologues of popular education during the first three decades of the nineteenth century, were the so-called Philosophical Radicals and, in particular, the circle of utilitarian thinkers around Jeremy Bentham. These were amongst the leading supporters of the early Lancasterian schools and in theory stood for a radical notion of a universal, rational, secular and scientific education for all. The egalitarian and democratic rhetoric of their writings, however, scarcely masked their affinity with the rather limited and class-based conceptions of Smith and Malthus. Whilst seeking the support of the working class for their own bid for parliamentary reform, they never really conceived of the enfranchisement of the workers. Bentham himself was a very late and half-hearted convert to democratic ideas and dismissed the notion of natural human rights as a 'mere figment'. Their defence of popular education thus had little connection with the revolutionary tradition of Condorcet in France or Tom Paine in England. Rather, it derived essentially from their desire to convince the working class that their interests lay in supporting the goals of the middle class. The universal enlightenment which they claimed to seek in education was in fact only the perpetration of their own ideas of political economy: a means for winning hegemony over the working class.

The contradiction between universal ideals and class interests in popular education were perhaps most evident in the writings of James Mill, who was a pupil of Bentham and one of the leading middle-class writers on education of his time. In his famous article on education written in 1818 for the *Encyclopaedia Britannica*, Mill developed an argument for universal education from the materialist premises of Hartleyan psychology and the utilitarian arguments of Bentham. The aim of education was to bring happiness to the greatest number: 'to render the individual, as much as possible, as an instrument of happiness, first to himself, and next to other beings'. The guarantor of its efficacy was the belief that the mind was shaped by the environment and methodical training. Thus whilst natural differences in ability could not be denied, it was not these that created most divisions amongst men but rather differences in education. 'All the difference which exist between classes or bodies of men ... is the effect of education.'[60]

If education was capable of moulding all minds, and if the object was to bring the greatest happiness to all, then it should seek to impart those characteristics, such as intelligence, temperance, justice and generosity, which were most conducive to happiness. These, argued Mill, should be the universal objects of all education. However, according to him there was a preventing cause making it impossible that the working class should acquire the intelligence of their superiors. Since 'a large portion of mankind is required for this labour', and since the cultivation of intelligence requires leisure, 'there are degrees ... of intelligence which must be reserved for those that are not required to labour'.[61] Without exploring the contradictions of his argument, or questioning the justice of the economic system which denied the majority the leisure to learn, Mill thus simply accepted that education for the working class must be of the most limited kind.

During the 1920s and 1930s, with the rising tempo of class struggle and increasing signs of urban social unrest, the middle class increasingly looked to education as a means of social pacification and amelioration. To its most optimistic advocates, education was a cure for all social evils, from crime, immorality and ungodliness, to sedition and revolutionary sympathies.

To Leonard Horner, an early factory inspector, education was a necessity if for no other reason than policing the poor:

> To put the necessity of properly educating the children of the working classes on its lowest footing, it is loudly called for as a matter of police, to prevent a multitude of immoral and vicious beings, the offspring of ignorance, from growing up around us, to be a pest and a nuisance to society; it is necessary in order to render the great body of the working class governable by reason.[62]

Some of the more democratically minded reformers, such as Radical MP Arthur Roebuck, would argue the case for popular education in less adversarial and contemptuous terms. Popular education was about making England safe for democracy. The working class, he argued in defence of his 1833 bill for National Education in the Commons, was a growing political force:

> Anyone who will look before him must see the growing political importance of the mass of the population. They will have power. In a very short time they will be paramount. I wish them to be enlightened, in order that they may use that power which they will inevitably obtain.[63]

Roebuck's tone was more conciliatory, and indeed his bill was one of the most radical to come from middle-class reformers; yet the political objective was fundamentally the same. He wanted everyone to 'receive a good political education', to 'understand their social condition' right, so that there would be no more discontents, no more rick-burning, no more combinations and 'futile schemes of reform'. In essence, this meant teaching the working class middle-class political economy, and in this Roebuck well represented the primary political goal of his class in espousing the cause of popular education.

If middle-class ideologists were clear about their aims in education, they were less certain about the means. Existing institutions were clearly inadequate and were badly in need of reform. However, the educational establishment had long been dominated by the Anglican Church and the gentry, and these showed little inclination towards change. Radicals repeatedly campaigned for reform to existing institutions but their efforts were of little avail. The remaining options were to create alternative middle-class institutions through private efforts, or to use the state as an instrument of reform. The first course was expensive and fraught with many practical obstacles. The second raised the whole problem of the legitimate role of the state in such matters and was a critical area of controversy in middle-class thought throughout the period.

The conception of the state which dominated middle-class thought by the 1830s was derived from the classical tenets of political economy.

Adam Smith had given one of most definitive statements of this in his *Wealth of Nations*, where he categorically rejected the mercantilist notions of state intervention in the economy and proclaimed instead the fundamental beneficence of a 'natural' market order. According to the theory of the 'free market', it was the pursuit of individual self-interest, unfettered by government restrictions, which would lead to the mutual benefit of all and the maximum public good. The market order had multiple advantages. It allowed the greatest degree of individual liberty; it provided incentive to enterprise, a competitive spur to efficiency and guaranteed success to the most meretricious; and by encouraging the pursuit of individual self-interest it inadvertently promoted the good of the whole community. By pursuing his self-interest, wrote Smith, a man is 'led by an invisible hand to promote an end which was no part of his intention' – the common weal. The necessary corollary of the free market was the limitation of government power. There was, according to Smith, 'a strong presumption against government activity beyond the fundamental duties of protection against foreign foes and the maintenance of justice'.[64]

The political economy of Adam Smith remained the baseline of middle-class thought in the first decades of the century. His economic ideas were developed by Ricardo, McCulloch and others, whilst Bentham and his school extended his principles of economic individualism into the realms of political and social thought. Although he made more exceptions to it in practice than some political economists, Bentham was ideologically committed to the limitation of government:

Nothing ought to be done or attempted by government for the purpose of causing an augmentation in the national mass of wealth ... without some special reason. Be quiet ought on those occasions to be the motto, or watchword of government.[65]

Even John Stuart Mill, who by the mid-century had increasing reservations about pure *laissez-faire*, was still publicly opposed to any but the most cautious state intervention and only where there were exceptional reasons. In 1848 he still thought 'letting alone ... should be the general practice'.[66]

Laissez-faire did not mean weak government. As Polanyi has argued, the achievement of liberal market order where it most mattered, in trade, land and employment relations, required strong state action of a negative kind, both to pass the initial legislation and to enforce and regulate it thereafter.[67] Nor did *laissez-faire* invariably prohibit positive state intervention. There were some areas of public concern where it was acknowledged that only state action would suffice. In addition to its cardinal role in national defence and maintaining order, the commonwealth had a duty, wrote Smith, in erecting and maintaining those public institutions and those public works, which though they may be in the highest degree advantageous to a great society are, however, of such a nature, that the profit could never repay the expense to any individual or small number of individuals, and which therefore cannot be expected that any individual or small number of individuals should erect or maintain.[68]

However, precisely which public concerns could justify breaking the general rule of non-intervention was the subject of continual debate.

The political economists of the nineteenth-century, such as Smith, found various matters of public concern that might warrant government intervention. Nassaur Senior, for instance, though against government limitation of the working day, supported action on urban sanitation and the economic affairs of Ireland. McCulloch, although a doctrinaire individualist in most ways, supported state intervention in transport and public health. Bentham and his followers found many causes for government intervention, including the poor law reform, public health and education. However, their attitudes in all cases remained equivocal. In principle they believed, as J. S. Mill later put it, that 'every departure from the laissez-faire principle, unless required by some great good, is a certain evil'. And yet there were numerous great goods that came to their attention and many social problems that could not be avoided.[69]

The debate over education, and the role of the state in it, reflected these ambivalences. Adam Smith provided an early minimalist rationale for state interference in education. For the reasons already discussed he considered education of particular public importance and thought it should be encouraged by government. However, he was against the government setting up schools. Free tuition, he said, would deprive teachers, parents and children of incentive, whereas an educational market would provide competition amongst suppliers of education and reduce corruption in schools. Arguing that all children should be able to read, write and account before they went to work, he recommended a legal requirement to pass certain exams before setting up in a trade, and probationary training before admittance into the professions and public office.[70]

The Philosophical Radicals of the nineteenth century, whilst generally in favour of state support for education, were similarly equivocal on the exact role that the state should play. McCulloch was in favour of state schools and said that government 'interference would be in the highest degree beneficial'. However, Ricardo was opposed to this. He wrote to Brougham concerning the latter's plans for infant schools in London, that if it involved the state taking responsibility for the education of the poor 'I should be exceedingly inconsistent if I gave my countenance to it.'[71] James Mill was in favour of limited government intervention in education but retained considerable scruples about its effects. 'When the government undertakes to do for any man,' he wrote,

> what every man has abundant motives to do for himself, and better means than the legislature, the legislature takes a very unnecessary, commonly a not very innocent trouble.[72]

His son, John Stuart Mill, was more positive about the role of the state. 'Education', he wrote, 'is one of those things which it is admissible that the government should provide for the people.' It could be exempted from the rule of non-interference 'because the case is not one in which the interest and judgement of the consumer are a sufficient security...the uncultured cannot be competent judges of cultivation'.[73] However, even Mill was wary of state control over education. He wrote in *On Liberty*:

> A general state education is a mere contrivance for moulding people to be exactly like one another...in proportion as it is efficient and successful, it establishes a despotism of the mind, leading to a natural tendency to one over the body.[74]

His solution was to avoid a state monopoly of schooling through a combination of public and private schools. But the emphasis was clearly on the latter. The state would regulate the system through control over compulsory public examinations.

The ambiguity in the Radicals' approach to state intervention stemmed, as Halévy has pointed out, from an underlying contradiction in their philosophy.[75] On the one hand, they argued with Adam Smith that there was a natural harmony in the market order such that individual interests would ultimately coincide with the common good. On the other hand, they recognized that this did not always occur spontaneously and that social conflicts could thus arise. The problem, as they saw it, was that the pursuit of individual interests could only further the common good where individuals recognized their best interests, and this did not always occur. The role of education was thus to help individuals to understand what was in their best interests. However, this, it seemed, could only be achieved through state intervention since private individuals had insufficient motive to promote an adequate general education, and this recourse to the state was in contradiction of their general conviction in state non-interference. The problem was logically insoluble. Thus the solutions that were adopted had to be justified despite philosophical convictions on pragmatic grounds alone.

The result in education, as in other areas of social policy, was compromise and not a little muddle. The Radicals concurred with general middle-class sympathies in supporting the development of voluntary education, and in middle-class schooling they made no attempt to go beyond this. However, as far as popular schooling was concerned, they had to concede that voluntary provision was inadequate to meet their goals and so sought further state remedies. The Benthamites thus became leading supporters of bills put forward by men such as Brougham and Roebuck for a system of national schools supported by the state. However, they failed to create the effective political alliances which were necessary to bring these to fruition. Liberal middle-class opinion was not generally favourable to state intervention and the Radicals were arguably not the most effective of advocates for it. They were themselves too ambivalent and sceptical about the whole project to make a convincing case. State intervention was invariably justified in negative, almost prophylactic, terms; it was an expedient or a measure of last resort that was offered almost apologetically. A. J. Taylor has written of nineteenth-century social reform in general that, although parliament legislated widely, and although administrators often laboured heroically within limits set by government, 'Victorian social policy was basically negative and unconstructive.'[76] This verdict must apply particularly in education. The middle-class Radicals signally failed to provide a positive and compelling rationale for a leading state role in education.

Working-class ideologies

Working-class educational traditions which developed during this period had an altogether different history – one which was rooted in the material realities of working-class life and which grew alongside the struggle for emancipation. Whilst sharing in, and perhaps over-reaching, middle-class optimism and faith in the powers of education, which both drew from enlightenment traditions, the working class set itself different goals in education and harnessed the powers of reason to its own class objectives. Drawing strength from Paine's phenomenally popular volumes, *The Age of Reason* and *The Rights of Man*, the working-class movement looked upon education as a 'natural right' and celebrated the power of rational thought to advance its secular and egalitarian aims. Central to this project was the importance of the collective pursuit of knowledge, both for individual self-realization and fulfilment, and for that understanding of the condition of the class which was an essential precondition for collective political advance.

Whilst notions of rights and emancipation were common themes throughout working-class writings, it is important to recognize that working-class culture in this its period of formation was necessarily heterogeneous and attitudes towards education no doubt varied considerably. Whilst the often positive response of working-class parents to Sunday Schools, and indeed the many institutions of self-education which the class evolved, suggest a positive evaluation of the importance of learning, this could take many different forms, both formal and informal, and material realities were such that in practice children often had to forego their education early for work. Our impressions of working-class attitudes towards education, drawn from the writings of their most literate representatives, suggest at least two somewhat different perspectives. On the one hand, there is the perspective of the 'practical man' wanting as much useful education as could help 'him' in his daily life; on the other, there is the rather more ambitious perspective, typical of the mostly artisanal leaders of the class, who desired a broader understanding of the world through learning and books, and for whom there was no limit to the range of knowledge which they might wish to acquire.

For many ordinary labourers one might surmise that a practical education was their main objective. William Cobbett was not of this class himself, but in his populist journalism he cultivated a persona which claimed to represent the ordinary man. His principle in education was the cultivation of useful knowledge. He stressed the value of education in 'rearing-up' children with useful skills which would benefit them in their daily lives. The rural child should learn about the skills required for gardening, rearing animals, making bread and butter, ploughing and hunting. But when it came to formal education, or 'Heddekashun' as he parodied it, he was generally hostile. This was partly because he objected to the instrumental aims of the 'education-mongering' middle-class reformers, but it was also because he did not set such store by knowledge derived from books, or at least did not think it was important for ordinary workers. 'Book learning is by no means to be despised,' he wrote, 'but nor was a man to be called ignorant merely because... [he] cannot make upon paper certain marks with a pen... [it] is a wrong use of words to call a man ignorant, who well understands the business he has to carry on.'[77] Such was Cobbett's antipathy to 'provided' education that in his later life he actually opposed measures to grant state aid for the building of new schools. When in 1833 parliament first made such treasury grants available, Cobbett objected, saying it would raise taxes unnecessarily and probably only encourage idleness and vice to boot.

Cobbett undoubtedly represented one element of popular opinion on education. His was the traditionalist and somewhat sentimental view of the 'practical man', full of the dignity of labour but rather suspicious of things of the intellect. In his paternalistic and rather conservative way he celebrated certain anti-intellectual values in popular consciousness which in the socialist tradition were rather to be deprecated as signs of deference and cultural defensiveness. Engels once commented sardonically on the type of English worker whose ' "practical" narrow-mindedness.... can really drive one to despair', and Cobbett's hostility to schooling was no doubt a representation of the kind of inward-looking parochialism that Engels and others found inimical to socialism.[78]

However, there was another side to the story, which Engels, incidentally, was just as quick to note, and that was the extraordinary thirst for knowledge which was typical of many of the Chartists and others in the vanguard of the working class. Engels declared that he had 'often heard working men, whose fustian jackets scarcely held together, speak upon geological, astronomical and other subjects, with more knowledge than the most "cultivated" bourgeois in Germany possess'.[79] This other, perhaps more usually, skilled working-class tradition, which prized learning with an almost abstract passion, and sought the most encyclopaedic knowledge through voracious habits of personal study, was clearly distinct from the rather self-limiting concept of learning embodied in Cobbett's 'practical' man. Indeed, in the years of Chartism, working-class leaders were to become increasingly contemptuous of the parochial attitudes expressed by the ex-Tory convert to popular causes, William Cobbett. Bronterre O'Brien, for instance, found himself on opposing sides to Cobbett over the issue of the 1833 grants to schools, and wrote a series of articles in the *Poor Man's Guardian* claiming that Cobbett did not care if workers were educated or not provided that they could plough and make hurdles and had plenty of home-brewed ale and bacon. Contrary to Cobbett, he believed that workers should avail themselves of every opportunity for intellectual improvement.[80]

The alternative tradition of the working-class autodidact cum political radical is epitomized in the career of William Lovett, the foremost Chartist champion of educational causes. A former apprentice cabinet-maker, Lovett came to London in 1823 and was introduced to a small literary association composed of working men, known as The Liberals, which met regularly in Gerard Street. It was in their company that he first started out on his intellectual odyssey. In his autobiography he recalls his first intellectual awakening:

> I now became seized with an enthusiastic desire to read and treasure up all I could meet with on the subject of Christianity, and in a short time was induced to join my voice to that of others in its defence whenever the question became the subject of debate; and often I have sat up till morning dawned reading and preparing myself with arguments in support of its principles. Political questions being also often discussed in our association, caused me to turn my attention to political works, and eventually to take a great interest in parliamentary debates and questions of the day. In short my mind seemed to be awakened to a new mental existence; new feelings, hopes, and aspirations sprang up within me, and every spare moment was devoted to the acquisition of some kind of useful knowledge.[81]

Lovett's lifelong and disciplined habit of self-education was not untypical of working-class activists, as the considerable number of surviving autobiographies show, and it provides a clear demonstration of the high value which was placed on the acquisition of the widest possible intellectual culture.

If Lovett himself provides a model of a certain type of attitude towards education, his own writings on education were amongst the finest of his generation, showing a generosity of spirit and a profound commitment to human emancipation that was rarely matched by his middle-class contemporaries. In his *Address on Education by the Working Men's Association* (1837) he proclaimed a broad, humanist approach to education as a 'universal instrument for advancing the dignity of man and gladdening his existence'.[82] Like Godwin and the eighteenth-century materialists, Lovett celebrated the potential for development in all people and recognized the positive power of education to achieve this. 'All men are not gifted with great strength of body or powers of intellect,' he later wrote, 'but they are all so wisely and wonderfully endowed, that all have the capacities for becoming intelligent, moral and happy members of society.' Education was a force for awakening sensibility and expanding mental and political horizons: 'Give to a man knowledge and you give him the light to perceive and enjoy beauty, variety, surpassing ingenuity, and majestic grandeur, which his mental darkness previously concealed from him.'[83] Lovett was a utopian but not a dreamer. He recognized that ultimately human happiness would depend on the achievement of political and social justice but education would be a powerful weapon in securing this.

In his writing on educational method, Lovett championed ideas of creative learning that were to become current a century later. He sharply criticized the passive and mechanical methods of learning which prevailed in schools at the time:

> This word-teaching, rote-learning, memory loading system is still dignified by the name of education; and those who are stored with the greatest lumber are esteemed its greatest 'scholars'. Seeing this, need we wonder that scholars have so little practical or useful knowledge – are superficial in reasoning... [84]

In its place, Lovett argued for a pedagogy of self-activity, personal discovery and creative understanding. Teaching should be based on observation and step-by-step development of the child's understanding, and writing should be related to experience. Science, on which he placed great stress, should be taught using models, observation and experiment. Competition and corporal punishment should not be encouraged and the classroom should be a place of 'lively and interesting enjoyments'.

Working-class leaders showed no want of desire and imagination in their visions of an education fit for an emancipated class. However, they were less sanguine about the means of achieving it, and their scepticism owed to their understandable suspicions of the motives of the middle-class reformers who were their only potential allies for progress. Cobbett had described the latter in the most unflattering terms, arguing that the likes of Henry Brougham, the Whig educational reformer, were mere 'shoy-hoys', scarecrows set up to divert the workers from their true interests.[85] Many were suspicious about the monitorial schools which were frequently seen to be imposing education in a purely instrumental way to shore up middle-class interests. Radical economist William Thompson wrote that many reformers were

> viciously determined to make use of the new instrument to diffuse, without enquiry, their particular views on moral subjects...the object of which was not to give the people knowledge for their own sakes, but to swell the numbers of the future partisans of some unimportant dogma.[86]

If the voluntary system won less than whole-hearted support from working-class leaders, and indeed from ordinary parents, by no means all of whom ensured the attendance of their children, plans to create a national system under state control also met with a sceptical response. Although the working class was hardly converted to the ideas of bourgeois political economy during this period, its traditions had been greatly influenced in different ways by the liberal traditions of the last century and there remained a quite marked residual hostility to the powers of the state. Unlike in France, there was no successful model here of Jacobin-style social reform through the state to look to. Such a strategy would, in any case, have required united action with a middle class genuinely committed to democracy and popular emancipation, and there was little evidence that this existed. Plans for state education appeared to be just another means whereby the ruling class could force its ideas on the workers. Cobbett thus remained an opponent of national education until his death in 1835, and most Chartist leaders remained ambivalent about state involvement until such a time as the state came under democratic control. William Lovett wrote from his captivity in Warwick Gaol in 1840:

> While we are anxious to see a general system of education adopted, we have no doubt of the impropriety of yielding such an important duty as the education of our children to any government, and the strongest abhorrence of giving any such power to an irresponsible one...If ever knavery and hypocrisy succeed in establishing the centralizing, state moulding and knowledge forcing scheme in England, so assuredly will the people degenerate into passive submission to injustice, and the spirit sink into the pestilential calm of despotism.[87]

These were strong words and ones frequently repeated by other working-class leaders. However, opinion on this was not as united as it may appear. A distinction has to be made between proposals for an education system under the control of the central state, as for instance in Prussia, and other schemes for a national system of education financed from public sources but under democratic control. The former was universally reviled as a species state tyranny, whereas by the 1840s the latter had some supporters, not least amongst whom were Lovett and Marx himself. Lovett's own demand, anticipating Marx's in *The Communist Manifesto,* was for a national system of non-sectarian schools, financed by the state, but under the control of local committees, elected by universal suffrage.

The lines of debate within the working-class movement were thus between those, such as Lovett, who believed that it was right to campaign for such a system even before the attainment of democracy, and others, such as George Harney, who believed that this was a utopian diversion from the real political struggle, and that under prevailing conditions it was best that the working class should pursue its own independent means of education without reference to the state. During the embattled years when Chartist agitation was at its height, this debate became increasingly bitter. Lovett's approach, dubbed by Fergus O'Connor as 'Knowledge Chartism', came under increasing attack and he finally dropped out of the mainstream of the Chartist movement. Meanwhile the bulk of the movement continued to view plans for national education with suspicion, and rather than give their support to them concentrated instead on the struggle for the franchise and the six points of the Charter. Working-class self-education continued to develop independently from the efforts of middle-class reform.

Given the quite intransigent response of the middle class to Chartist demands, it is quite understandable that the likes of Harney should have concluded that 'any system that meets with the acquiescence of our foes will have as its object the perpetuation of the people's slavery'.[88] However, it is also possible to see Lovett as one whose powerful utopian imagination put him before his time, but whose ideas were of seminal importance for the development of working-class thought on education. It was to his demands that the labour movement later returned in the 1870s when circumstances were more propitious for genuine advance towards democratic control of education.

The failure of a campaign for national education

Reforms in education during the first four decades of the nineteenth century reflected both the strengths and the limitations of the political ideologies which motivated them. On the one hand, there was an increasing consensus over the importance of schooling and a growing consensus within each class about the objectives which they sought to pursue through it. On the other, there was a continuing ambivalence as to the means which might be employed to bring this about. The result was a period of frenetic activity on a number of different fronts which had all the sound and fury of a minor educational revolution but signified sadly little in terms of systematic development. The two forms of educational initiative which must be distinguished reflected the basic dualism embedded in the ideologies of the reformers. Firstly, there were the attempts by different social groups to develop systems of voluntary education independent of the state. This initially took the form of attempts to reform existing educational institutions and, as this failed, led to the creation of substitute forms more appropriate to the needs of the different classes. Secondly, there was the ongoing campaign to create some kind of national education system through legislation and state support.

The campaign for national education was spearheaded by the radical wing of the middle class. Its primary ideologists were, as we have seen, the bourgeois intellectuals of the Bentham circle and later the educational administrators in and around the Education Committee. Its parliamentary agitators were radical MPs such as Arthur Roebuck, Thomas Wyse and George Grote, and their occasional Whig allies, such as Henry Brougham. Between them they produced a number of parliamentary bills for national education, most notably those of Brougham in 1820 and Roebuck in 1833. However, these all failed to get parliamentary consent, giving rise to parliament's reputation as a 'cemetery for the interment of defunct education bills'.[89] By the end of this period there was still no legislation pertaining to national education, excepting parliament's 1833 approval for some rather small sums to be made available annually from the treasury for school development by the voluntary societies.

The reasons for these repeated failures can be gleaned partially from the parliamentary debates which attended the proposal of the various bills. Samuel Whitbread's Parochial Schools bill of 1807 was defeated by aristocratic opposition and finally fell in the Lords. The Chancellor had objected to the damage it might do to voluntary schools, but the underlying tenor of the opposition can be gauged from Davies Giddy's famous speech against the bill as rendered in Cobbet's parliamentary papers:

> However specious in theory the project might be, of giving education to the labouring classes of the poor, it would, in effect, be found prejudicial to their morals and happiness, it would teach them to despise their lot in life, instead of making them good servants in agriculture, and other laborious employments to which their rank in society had destined them; instead of teaching them subordination, it would render them factious and refractory, as was evident in the manufacturing counties; it would enable them to read seditious pamphlets, vicious books, and publications against Christianity; it would render them insolent to their superiors; and in a few years, the result would be, that the legislators would find it necessary to direct the strong arm of power against them, and to furnish the executive magistrates with more vigorous powers than were now in force. Besides, if the bill were to pass into law, it would go to burthen the country with a most enormous and incalculable expense, and to load the industrious orders with still heavier imposts.[90]

The opposition to Whitbread's bill reflects the extreme paranoia of the ruling class during the period of the French Wars. By the 1820s the case for popular education had generally been won, even if members of the aristocracy were still lukewarm about the idea. However, Brougham's 1820 bill, the first to propose universal, compulsory, state-funded education, met with the same fate. Although it gave considerable powers to the Church in education, it was clearly inspired by Benthamite thinking, and provoked organized Anglican opposition from those who feared that state provision meant secular control. At the same time it was opposed by Catholics and Dissenters, who resented the powers it gave to the Church, and by industrial representatives who feared the loss of child labour.[91]

Roebuck's bill of 1833 was the most thoroughgoing of all plans for national education. He recommended a universal and compulsory system of elementary schools financed by the state, and controlled by elected district committees. This would be supported by schools for infants, industrial schools and teacher-training schools, the whole to be overseen by a minister of state. The bill was opposed by Lord Althorpe, who feared prejudicial effects on the voluntary schools and wished to see popular education without 'interference from the government', and by O'Connell, who argued that 'nothing could be more destructive than to imitate the example of France in respect to her system of national education'. Peel finally killed the bill with liberal sentiment, arguing that in a country such as England, which was proud of its freedom, education ought to be left free from state control.[92]

The failure of plans for national education thus had amongst its most immediate causes both aristocratic conservatism and religious divisions. However, underlying all of these was the traditional liberal hostility towards the state. The general social and economic basis of this peculiarly English ideological configuration has already been mapped out. Its origins lay in the nature of gentry capitalism and its corresponding state forms as they emerged after 1688, and its persistence into the nineteenth century owed much to particular factors associated with English developmental priority. We have seen how in England the specific forms of educational development were constrained by the liberal character of the state and by the absence of those forces which engendered nationalist and étatist solutions to problems of development in continental Europe. Chiefly amongst these it was the advantage of an early and 'spontaneous' Industrial Revolution that removed the need for concerted state action in economic development and associated educational initiatives. Where reasons for educational development were acknowledged to exist, as clearly by now they were, solutions were constrained by this otherwise entrenched ideology. It remains to add, concluding the argument of the preceding pages, that there were also more immediate reasons why those who did seek to create state solutions to the problems of education were so unsuccessful.

Against a climate of liberal hostility to state initiatives, it may seem that advocates of national education had little chance of success. However, it must also be acknowledged that they were not the best advocates of their cause. Middle-class Radicals were themselves extremely ambivalent about state involvement in education. They failed to offer a positive or coherent rationale for public education and never managed to evolve a strategy or programme that might have provided the basis of a popular alliance on the issue. The utilitarian educational philosophy was an abstract, doctrinaire and uncompelling creed. Lacking the egalitarian and democratic aspiration of the French Jacobin educational tradition, it offered an education to the working class that appealed neither to the language of democratic rights nor to aspirations for collective economic advance. Denuded of the popular rhetoric of American capitalism, it held out no promise of individual mobility through education and expressed no concept of active citizenship for the working class. It was an impoverished and limiting pedagogy; quite uncompelling when it affirmed some abstract good, such as happiness or moral virtue, most eloquent in negation when it argued the powers of education to prevent crime and disaffection. It offered the working class not a liberating force but a restraining, paternal hand. Not a vision to command universal assent, it failed to sustain even the most temporary of popular political alliances and thus had no chance of shifting the dead weight of aristocratic complacency and middle-class prejudice and self-interest.

The voluntary system

If 'national education' never quite took root on English soil during this period, there was an alternative policy that was more adaptable to the domestic political climate, and that was 'voluntaryism'. The term was often used by contemporaries and roughly described a mode of educational development free of state control which relied on the independent initiative and financial resources of private individuals and organizations and on the uncompelled attendance of children. For the working class it meant a whole nexus of educational activities and institutions which developed in close concert with political organizations. It ranged from informal workplace discussions and reading groups to the Corresponding Societies and secular Sunday Schools of the 1790s, and through to the Chartist Halls and Owenite Halls of Science of the later period. Its activities included adults and children and these were hardly separable from the overtly political activities of the radical unstamped press. Middle-class philanthropic education for the working class can be seen as a response to this: an attempt to counter the radicalism of working-class self-education with an alternative system of school indoctrination.

The development of mass elementary education thus occurred through a series of rival philanthropic initiatives from the 1780s onwards whose competing efforts reflect the ideological struggle for hegemony over the working-class mind. The first and most explosive burst of philanthropic enthusiasm for schooling occurred with the Sunday School movement, which began in the 1780s triggered, as Richard Johnson puts it, by a 'moral panic' over the dangers of the juvenile crowd. Robert Raikes' system was first publicized in his *Gloucester Journal* in November 1783 and was taken up widely in the provincial press. Backed by a heterogeneous mixture of justices, bishops, scientifically minded Unitarians and some landowners and manufacturers, it first developed local organizations in Leeds, Manchester, Derby and Liverpool and remained consistently strong in industrial areas. Crude and brief as a form of working-class schooling, it had the merit of being free and sufficiently flexible to be adaptable to working-class conditions. The schools were sometimes 'appropriated' by working-class groups who also set up their own secular Sunday Schools.[93]

After 1790 a period of educational reaction set in. Sunday Schools were considered potential vehicles for the spreading of radical ideas and Pitt even considered closing them down. The movement soon fragmented and, although it had a vigorous afterlife in certain areas, it was soon overtaken by a new initiative. The monitorial school, developed after 1803, was the first form of mass schooling in England and provided the central unit of 'provided' education for the next 30 years. The concept of the school, first elaborated by non-conformist Joseph Lancaster and Anglican Andrew Bell, was uniquely suited to English conditions. Based on the use of pupil teachers or 'monitors', the system provided a cheap, mechanical and narrow form of mass schooling which was easily reproducible through local philanthropic initiative in loose aggregation under central societies.

The first of these, inaugurated in 1808, was the Royal Lancasterian Society which later became the British and Foreign Schools Society. Initially backed by an influential group of educational sponsors, including Whitbread and Brougham, it drew support from Baptists, Quakers, Evangelical Anglicans, leading Whig aristocrats, Utilitarians and independent liberal politicians. From the outset it was committed to interdenominational education. In 1811 the Anglican Church matched the Dissenters' initiative with its own National Society, dominated by bishops, and thus clearly declared its intention to maintain the Church's traditional dominance in the field of popular education. With the formation of these two societies began the pattern of religious rivalry in the provision of schools which initially stimulated growth and later helped to block the emergence of any more rational provision until 1870. By the 1830s there was already a considerable network of these schools up and down the country and, if they were far from achieving an even geographical coverage or any consistency of standards, they had established themselves as the pre-eminent providers of elementary education such that, when parliament agreed to give public grants to schools, it was through these societies that it channelled them.

The education provided by these schools was narrow and regimented in the extreme. The Spicer Street Lancasterian school, for instance, the first of its kind in Spitalfields, was conducted in a room measuring 106 feet by 39, which could accommodate 660 children in 33 rows of desks each designed for 20 boys. In this educational battery farm, one teacher, relying on the services of his monitors, could teach these 600 or so children for a cost of five shillings per annum per child. Needless to say, in schools of this type there was much regimentation and drilling, and what little learning was acquired depended largely on passive memorization.[94]

The curriculum in both the National Society and BFSS schools was narrow, aiming to do little more than inculcate the three Rs and Christian morality. The main textbook was the Bible, sometimes supplemented by religious tracts and improving publications from the Society for the Promotion of Christian Knowledge, or written by Evangelicals such as Hannah More. After 1830 the religious societies began to employ inspectors in their schools and the curriculum began to expand to include more secular education, but this was mainly to teach 'correct' moral and political thinking. An 1840 BFSS reading series, for instance, included a special section on political economy, warning about the dangers of challenging the economic order. In their *Daily Lesson Book 111* of the same period, authors Dunn and Crossley included homilies 'on the folly of thinking it unjust that one man should receive more than another for his labour', and 'on the impossibility of regulating wages by law'.[95]

The voluntary system also included the secondary schools, and here the principle of independence was followed even more rigorously. Despite the domination of this sector by the Anglican Church and the rural gentry, and the complete unsuitability of the schools in it for the middle class, there were no middle-class campaigns for a system of state secondary schools such as existed in France, Germany or the United States. The strategy, rather, was to reform the existing grammar schools through a campaign which involved vociferous public lobbying and the relentless public exposure of school corruption and inefficiency. Middle-class reformers also attempted to infiltrate the governing bodies of some schools and by this means achieved some measure of reform in a few schools, such as Macclesfield Grammar School, where modern subjects were introduced into the curriculum. However, they frequently ran up against the argument that ancient statutes would not allow school reform or the abandonment of the classical curriculum. In some cases the issue went to court, as in the case of Leeds Grammar School, but they were not successful here either. In 1805 the Lord Chancellor, Eldon, decided against the petitioners on the grounds that their scheme for modernizing the curriculum was no more than an attempt 'to promote the merchants of Leeds' at the expense of poor classical scholars.[96] The case provides a good local illustration of the more general reasons for the overall failure of the middle-class reform campaign in this period. Their approach appeared to be merely a plea for special interests; they failed to universalize their objectives beyond their own class and thus created no hegemonic movement for secondary school reform. With the failure of the grammar school reform movement, the middle class increasingly turned towards a strategy of substitution; they created their own independent private schools and 'proprietary' secondary schools, run as joint stock companies, and anticipated later university reform with the inauguration of the modern University College of London (1828), based on models developed in Edinburgh and Berlin.

By the end of this period, voluntary initiatives had developed a network of schools, both elementary and secondary, which some would claim provided an alternative model to the national state system. Schools were spread unevenly and their standards were variable, but they were expanding fast, particularly so after government grants became available in 1833, and their advocates could claim that they were on the road to creating a national network. Although the schools were not public institutions in the continental or American sense of the term, the national societies certainly believed they had claims to represent the 'public interest'. They were an example of that peculiar form of decentralized 'self-government' which Gramsci saw as a particularly English phenomenon.[97] The monitorial and grammar schools were 'independent' but they were not profit-making. Whilst not controlled by elected authorities, they sought their warrant in English tradition and custom. The Established Church was the guardian of public morals and felt it needed no further mandate to provide the public's education. Schools were run by local organizations which, whilst not elected, claimed the traditional authority which the squirearchy and magistracy had assumed in rural social organization: they were composed of local notables and subscribers acting in 'the best interests of the community at large'.

However, whatever the achievements and legitimacy of the voluntary system, all was not well. English education was still perceived to be trailing far behind US and continental rivals. Enrolments in elementary schools, which, as we have seen, scarcely topped 50 per cent of the school-age population, were well behind those abroad, particularly in Germany and Holland, which had almost universal attendance. Post-elementary education was still greatly inadequate, particularly in its lack of modern and vocational schools for the middle class and trade schools for the working class. Middle-class Radicals would continue to point to grave deficiencies. Arthur Roebuck lamented in 1833 that education in England had been 'so long, so steadily and so perniciously neglected', whereas 'in America, the magnificent provision for this same object surpasses all that the world has seen before'. In 1843 Joseph Hume could still maintain that 'England stood at the bottom of the scale of the civilized world' in educating its people. Only Portugal had a worse record.[98]

The most obvious underlying deficiency, of course, was the lack of any national apparatus. England, alone of major states, still had no central government authority for education. Public finance was minimal, there was no national examination system, little in the way of legal regulation or positive state inspection of schools, and practically no teacher training.

As most of those involved in the administration of education were to become increasingly aware, such deficits were a distinct hindrance to improvement. Whatever the political merits of a voluntary system, it was not one that could deliver the best in the way of education either for the middle class or for the workers. As Thomas Wyse, the Radical 'Member for Education', put it in 1837,

> The voluntary system of public instruction, with no central power to guide, aid or control it, has not only not worked well, but worked nearly as ill an any system well could.[99]

Bureaucracy by stealth, 1839–69

The mid-century state

The fortunes of educational reform during the years of the mid-century reflect the ambivalences and contradictions of state and society during the high period of Victorian capitalism. The period from 1840 to 1870 was, as argued earlier, an era of confident and secure capitalist hegemony. Bourgeois policy and ideology were in the ascendant, both in the organs of state and in civil society. With the widened franchise of 1832, the repeal of the Corn Laws, church rates and knowledge taxes, and reforms to local and central government, the policies of the middle class were increasingly winning ground. The ruling class had conceded a portion of political power in the interests of capital and property, which they shared alike with the manufacturing class, and if the landowners continued to dominate the political machine, they would now do so in the interests of the bourgeoisie, at least where these counted most. However, if we see the period as one of bourgeois hegemony, where in Marx's classic formulation, bourgeois power was delegated through 'aristocratic' rule, the ideological sway of the middle class was nevertheless qualified in crucial ways. If the period marked the final conversion of the ruling class to political economy, decisively represented in the liberalism of Peel and Gladstone, it also saw the waning of a more thoroughgoing middle-class radicalism and the accommodation of the bourgeois politics within the Liberal Party. The final moment for a radical middle-class politics had passed by. Joseph Sturge's Complete Suffrage Movement, which sought to ally working-class radicalism under the wing of a radical middle class, had foundered, and with its final parliamentary victory the Anti-Corn-Law League had no more reason for existence. Liberal politicians had conceded enough to middle-class radicalism to draw its fire whilst successfully pre-empting the formation of a middle-class political party. Whilst 150 Radical MPs had been elected to the reformed parliament of 1837, by 1841 this group had dwindled to 50 Radicals and 100 Liberals.[100] Content with its partial political successes and assured free reign for its economic interests, the middle class lost much of its antagonism to a landed class, now more close to it, and saw instead its main opponent in a still refractory proletarian mass below it. The effort to isolate and finally repress the Chartist movement only drew the two wings of capital closer together politically, just as the coming decades were to witness an increasing social interpenetration of leading segments of the two social groups, forming the unified Victorian elite of the upper middle class.

The ambivalences of class power in mid-Victorian England were matched by contradictions at the level of the state. If liberal individualism and political economy were the dominant dogmas of the time, both deeply implanted within the mass of the middle class, and publicly espoused by the majority of politicians and ideologues, this was also a period of significant administrative reform, much of which pushed well beyond the limits of what was allowable within the doctrine of pure *laissez-faire*. Whilst these changes fell somewhere short of the 'revolution in government' proclaimed by historians of administration, and whilst they hardly yet constituted the triumph of collectivism as feared by the most ardent individualists, they were certainly evidence of incipient counter-movement occurring, as it were, despite and behind the back of the dominant *laissez-faire* culture. Inasmuch as this reform occurred through the gradual efforts of administrators and civil servants, sometimes without clear parliamentary sanction, and often against the grain of the dominant culture, it represents a kind bureaucracy by stealth and this nowhere more than in the field of education.

The pattern of educational development during this period reflected these dominant forces and their ancillary contradictions. The trajectory of change, however gradually it occurred, was definitely in the direction of those goals sought by the middle class. Reforms in elementary education continued to aspire to an effective and efficient mass provision which would educate the working class in the beliefs of their social superiors. With the inevitable prospects of further extensions of the franchise, the importance of making the country 'safe for democracy' was increasingly pressing. Reforms in secondary education, whilst gradual indeed, generally reflected the middle-class desire for a more relevant curriculum, a more purposeful ethos and a system of examinations which would embody the spirit of competition and rewards for merit. However, the very slow and faltering progress made in these directions also reflected the deep entrenchment of conservative and landed interests, particularly in the universities and grammar schools.

Regarding the means to these ends, and the conceptions of the state which would determine them, the dominant tradition remained that of educational voluntaryism and this was in accordance with the liberalism of the age. The earlier campaigns of the Radicals for a national system went into temporary abeyance after the failure in 1843 of Joseph Hume's bill and the controversy over the educational clauses of Graham's Factory Act. Reformers such as Kay-Shuttleworth were resigned to the impossibility of major legislation and seemed to settle for a more protracted battle from within the administration, accepting for the moment the invincibility of the voluntarist lobby. Up until 1870, elementary schooling was thus still entirely dominated by the religious societies, and not a single school was actually owned or controlled by the state. Secondary schooling remained even more fiercely independent and managed to resist even state inspection, although it did have to submit to the scrutiny of several government commissions of enquiry. However, behind the scenes an educational bureaucracy was developing which was part of the more general movement of administrative reform, and it was from this redoubt of 'Benthamite' expertise that the impetus for state reform would later occur, when objective circumstances were more propitious for interventionist solutions.

The underlying causes of England's unique response to the problems of national education remained in this period much as they had been before. Underpinning all other arguments for independence in education was the dominance of a certain set of values pertaining to the proper relations between the individual and the state. Middle-class sentiment valued cheap and efficient government and low taxation, resisted state interference except where it was absolutely unavoidable, and generally believed individualism to be better than collectivism in all things. Whatever might be the necessary exceptions to these principles, they remained the ultimate yardstick. In comparison with forms of government that came before and after, and placed aside the practices of other European states, England came, as A. J. Taylor has put it, 'closer to experiencing an age of *laissez-faire* than any other society in the last five hundred years of world history'.[101] As we have already seen, this meant maintaining a state apparatus and levels of public spending incomparably lower than in all major European states.

The mid-Victorian period cannot be credited with having added much in a theoretical sense to the doctrines of political economy considered before. But what it did contribute to liberal ideology, and this was no less important, was a popularization of the earlier doctrines through the work of Herbert Spencer and Samuel Smiles. Spencer transposed Darwin's ideas from the realms of natural evolution to social organization, thus spurning a 'social Darwinism' which neatly sanctioned capitalist self-interest with the natural law of the survival of the fittest. Smiles, on the other hand, deepened popular attachment to individualist values by constructing a moral framework which stressed the dignity of working-class independence and individual aspiration.

The popularity of Smiles' thought was illustrated by the enormous success of his book, *Self-Help*, which sold 55 000 copies in the first four years and went into countless later editions.[102] To Smiles, self-help was not the paternalistic philosophy of philanthropy but rather what Richard Cobden once called the 'masculine species of charity'; it not only encouraged people to 'help themselves', as all good Victorians thought proper, but also sought to convince them that all had the resources to do this, and therein lay the reasons for its great popularity. To Smiles, charity and help 'from without' were disabling and demeaning.[103] Rather than be enfeebled by middle-class charity, the working class must help itself, which was after all just what, if in a different sense, the working-class movement had always known. The philosophy appealed not to deference but to aspiration:

> The healthy spirit of self-help created amongst working people would more than any other measure serve to raise them as a class, and this, not by any pulling down of others, but by levelling them up to a higher level and still advancing the standards of religion, intelligence and virtue.[104]

Smiles helped to purvey the belief that entrepreneurial capitalism offered to the industrious full opportunities for success. Little did it matter that the idea of the self-made man was a myth, perhaps the most successful one that any class has fostered to serve its own interests. It was effective because it appealed to that deep-seated strain of individualism which would give credence to all manner of hopes and illusions.

Smilesian individualism, the Spencerian struggle for existence, the traditional liberal hostility towards the state – all of these constituted part of an interwoven cultural fabric which provided the backcloth to all thinking on education in this period. There were, of course, alternative traditions to draw on but the point here is that individualist notions were so pervasive that no arguments could ignore them. Small wonder then that voluntaryism remained the favoured philosophy in education.

There were other frequently repeated reasons for avoiding state involvement in education and there are other ways of analysing their root causes. Many claimed that state involvement in education would lead to secular schooling and based their opposition on this premise. Anglicans still feared loss of control and non-conformists still doubted that the state would deal even handedly as between Church and Dissent. Aside from the religious argument there was the fear that a state educational bureaucracy would merely be a fetter on voluntary effort. According to Mill,

> The mischief begins when, instead of calling forth the activity and power of individuals and bodies, it substitutes its own activity for theirs; when, instead of informing, advising, and upon occasion denouncing, it makes them work in fetters, or bids them stand aside and does their work instead of them.[105]

Some would support state involvement in elementary schooling but oppose it in middle-class schools on the grounds that the middle class could look after themselves. One such was school inspector J. P. Norris, who wrote that 'the more civilized the homes the less need the government interfere with the education of the children'.[106] However, what most probably underlay this argument, as John Roach has pointed out, was the middle-class belief that state education would endanger their social position, denying them the social privacy of their own schools and forcing their children to mix with those from lower social classes.[107]

Some social critics also believed the middle class to be too narrow in their interests and culture to bother much about education, and that this was why they would not have the state spend their taxes on it. Engels once wrote that

> So short-sighted, so stupidly narrow-minded is the English bourgeoisie in its egotism that it does not even take the trouble to impress upon the workers the morality of the day, which the bourgeoisie has patched together in its own interests.[108]

John Stuart Mill felt a similar contempt when confronted with the 'petty preoccupations' of English 'society' and 'the absence of high feeling which manifests itself by smearing deprecations of all of them'.[109] Matthew Arnold, the high-minded scourge of middle-class philistines, was perhaps most prone of all critics to find in the middle class a narrow materialism and perverse resistance to the cultivation of 'sweetness and light' which was the essence of education.[110]

There was no doubt a limited truth in these observations. The manufacturing class was certainly very busy in the making of money and sometimes appeared to have little time for the affairs of state or even of culture. Charles Knight found this when he toured the industrial North in 1828 to drum up support for educational projects:

> It was not always easy to interest the busy mill-owners in the objects for which I came amongst them. Some were too absorbed in their ledgers to hear long explanations; others were wholly indifferent to matters which had no relation to the business of their lives.[111]

However, this picture of pervasive philistinism and obdurate narrow-mindedness was only half the truth. It ignores the enormous sentimental and financial investments that were made in education and other charitable causes, and misses the rich variety of middle-class culture that existed, albeit sometimes within rather limited social and moral horizons. Kay-Shuttleworth, who knew Manchester somewhat better than Knight, remarked in 1847 that 'on Sunday many thousands of the middle class devote three hours of their rest from the business of life to the pious office of instructing the children of the poor', and the very existence of a voluntary tradition was surely proof of this point.[112] The middle class in England no doubt often had less education than their continental counterparts, and émigres such as Marx and Engels were inevitably prone to notice the difference, but to cite their cultural philistinism as a reason for the backwardness of English education was really to confuse cause and effect. The middle class on the whole well appreciated the value of education even if some of them knew little of it. That they would not promote it through the state was due less to disinterest in education as such than to their great dislike of state intervention.

Mill and Arnold, elsewhere in their work, well recognized this to be the underlying cause. Although he saw good cause for not allowing the state a monopoly of education, Mill recognized in his later years that total hostility to state intervention could be a mere prejudice and was one to which the English middle class were particularly prone. In his autobiography he professed that, in England,

> Centralization was, and is, the subject not only of rational disapprobation, but of unreasoning prejudice; where jealousy of government interference was a blind feeling preventing or resisting even the most beneficial exertion of legislative authority to correct the abuse of what pretends to be local self-government, but is, too often, selfish mismanagement of local interests, by a jobbing ... local oligarchy.[113]

The argument that centralization could be justified democratically as a bulwark against entrenched local power groups was reminiscent of the French Republican argument and showed how far Mill had travelled from pure political economy. Matthew Arnold was, like his father, a long-time advocate of state intervention, and roundly condemned the English middle class for their opposition to state secondary education, which he believed to be the only way to achieve schools for the middle class comparable in excellence to the *lycées* of France. The great impediment to this he believed was English individualism:

> Our prevalent notion is ... that it is a most happy and important thing for a man to be able to do as he likes. On what he is to do with his freedom, we do not lay too much stress ... We have no notion, so familiar on the continent and to antiquity, of the State – the nation in its collective and corporate character, entrusted with stringent powers for the general advantage in the name of an interest wider than that of individuals.[114]

That it was the dominant *laissez-faire* ideology and the liberal conception of the state, rather than the religious controversies through which they were refracted, that underlay middle-class opposition to state schooling and therefore the failure of many proposed reforms can be well illustrated with the case of educational polemicist Edward Baines Junior. He was a Dissenter by birth, an author of a history of cotton manufactures and the editor of the *Leeds Mercury*, a leading organ of manufacturing interests and liberal opinion. He was also an educational advocate who had been active in the promotion of the BFSS and a strong and vociferous opponent of state education. In a series of ten open letters in 1846 to Lord John Russell, whom he takes to be a supporter of state education, Baines outlines the case against state involvement. It is an outstanding polemic and must stand as a *locus classicus* of the voluntarist case. Denying purely religious motivation, he claims to speak for English traditions and asserts that not only Dissenters but also the Church and Catholics share his opposition to state education.

The basis of Baines' arguments rests on his exposition of the liberal creed which is the English heritage: 'I stand', he wrote,

> for the English, the free, the voluntary method, which I hold accordant with the national character, favourable to civil and religious liberty, and productive of the highest moral benefits to the community.[115]

The duty of government is to protect property and personal safety, to maintain peace and social order, and to defend the realm.

> It is not...the duty of government to interfere with the free action of the subject beyond what is necessary for these protective and defensive objects. It is not the duty of the government to feed the people, to clothe them, to superintend their families, to cultivate their minds, to shape their opinions, or to supply them with religious teachers, physicians, schoolmasters, books or newspapers.[116]

Where governments ignore these principles they only 'undertake to do for the people what they are better able to do themselves'. State education is thus 'in total opposition to the liberty and mental independence of the British people'.[117]

Baines' argument, clearly established from the outset, rests on classic liberal principles. He underlines the point by turning his polemic to the continental systems of state education, under whose spell, he claims, have come 'our philosophical radicals'. Admitting that their educational standards are superior, he attributes this to better teaching based on the advanced ideas of Pestalozzi. As for the system in which it occurs, it is inherently despotic:

> A system of state education is a vast intellectual police, set to watch over their young at the most critical period of their existence, to prevent the intrusion of dangerous thoughts, and turn their minds into safe channels.[118]

What is more, its educational advantage may only be temporary. 'The tendency of the system is to stagnation, a perfunctory discharge of routine, and a positive resistance to improvement.'

In a further letter, Baines considers state education in the United States. This, he admits, is 'consistent with liberty', but only under those special conditions which prevail in America, with its 'universal' [sic] suffrage and absence of any established Church.[119] Such a system could not be transferred to England, with its Established Church and still preserve liberties. The common schools in the United States he recognizes as 'highly beneficial' but, just as in Europe, state education is unfavourable to liberty, so here it is detrimental to religion.

Baines' primary argument is that liberty and state education are irreconcilable. However, returning the debate to England, he also argues for the positive educational advantages of the voluntary system. The present state of schools may be defective, but its defects can be remedied by the existing institutions. State involvement would not improve them as fast as they can improve themselves. The effect of government intervention would be to undermine the vigour of voluntary effort, remove the stimulus of competition and deprive parents of responsibilities. Government interference 'relieves men of their duties, and ... robs them of their virtues'. Having made his case, Baines ends, in a vein more prophetic than he probably realized:

> It is my confident belief that any measure of state education, unless designedly made so slow and imperceptible in its advances as to elude popular opinion, would be resolutely opposed by a majority of the Church, a great majority of Dissenters (including Wesleyans), the Scotch and the Welsh.[120]

The Bainesian defence of the voluntary method was an incarnation of *laissez-faire* in the educational field, and as this was the age of *laissez-faire* in government and economics, so it was, in the main, in education. However, this was not without contradiction and, as often happens, history was advancing by the contrary side. Whilst political economy dominated the age, and the middle class in particular, it had its equivocal, not to say contradictory, side, and this was represented in the growing fault line between its pure *laissez-faire* and Benthamite wings. Doctrinally the distinction was not always easy to make, but it involved significant political differences and was based, in part at least, on the distinctive experiences of different fractions of the middle class. Whilst pure *laissez-faire* was more congenial to the manufacturing bourgeoisie and capitalist gentry, Benthamism, or more accurately the growing culture of professional expertise and bureaucratic efficiency, reflected the rise of a partially distinctive class fraction of professionals, civil servants and experts of various kinds. Whilst for the most part *petit-bourgeois* in their economic relations and, at base, intellectual defenders of the bourgeois order, the professional stratum had a distinctive insertion into the social order, neither 'producers' nor yet quite 'parasites', and thus often had a different perception of social realities. Some, such as J. S. Mill, well understood the incipient contradictions of the *laissez-faire* capitalist system and could see the necessity of future changes. Others were simply more in touch with the social problems of the day and knew better than industrialists what pragmatic government interventions would be necessary to deal with them. All of them were distinguished by their own occupations which in their nature encouraged the belief in merit, expertise and efficiency in government bureaucracy. Hardly transcending class relations in the romantic mythology of Shelley's 'acknowledged legislators' or Arnold's class 'remnants', they were yet partially displaced from mainstream class relations and whilst most became in a sense the 'intellectual' representatives of their class, others, as Marx remarked, could easily break away, such as Robert Owen and William Thompson, and become the intellectuals of another class.

This social grouping was thus, politically, inherently unstable and therefore best placed to crystallize the contradictions of the dominant ideology of the day. The main contradiction was that whilst maximum economic advantage was to be gained through limitation in the cost and scope of government, the longer-term interests of capital would require such reforms in administration and social policy as to make government expansion necessary. Government concessions to the working class could be forestalled temporarily, to economic advantage, but in the longer term the working class could only be successfully incorporated into the existing order by some amelioration of their condition. The ideologists of the professional class most clearly expressed these contradictions. Bentham, for instance, despite keeping faith with the principles of political economy, became in his chosen field of government, as Perkin puts it, 'the apotheosis of the professional ideal'.[121] He stood for expert, efficient administration, cautious reform and the principle of meritocratic selection, and those who pursued the reforms he supported inevitably breached the *laissez-faire* principles of minimal government. As the century wore on, such contradictions became more plain. J. S. Mill, perhaps the supreme ideologist of his class, met with similar contradictions. Still holding to the principle of *laissez-faire* in theory, he found more and more reason to depart from them in practice. He wrote in *The Principles of Political Economy*:

> In the particular circumstances of a given age or nation, there is scarcely anything, really important to the general interest, which it may not be desirable, or even necessary, that government should take it upon itself, not because private individuals cannot effectively perform it, but because they will not.[122]

In fact, Mill's views had so far evolved under the influence of his wife, Harriet Taylor, that he considered himself a socialist. In his autobiography he wrote: 'Our ideal of ultimate government went far beyond democracy, and would class us decidedly under the general designation of socialist.'[123] It is a sure mark of the continued hold of political economy that Mill could have thus described himself, yet there was a shift in his thinking, and as such he represents the deepening fissure in middle-class ideology that was to split the Liberals in the coming period.

It was within this widening ideological gap that the professional experts of the mid-century operated. Men such as Chadwick, Horner, Trevelyan and Kay-Shuttleworth were not so much bearers of a new 'collectivism', as Brebner and others have argued; their conceptions were too equivocal for that and many of them indeed, such as Chadwick, still professed adherence to classical political economy. They acted rather, as Polanyi has argued, out of a spirit of pragmatism, seeking practical solutions to intolerable social facts.[124] The social reforms which they pioneered, in public health, in factory inspection and in the civil service, hardly represented a wholesale shift towards state collectivism but rather a series of compromises designed to alleviate social conditions within the limits of prevailing liberal opinion. Where they appeared to advance too far, their initiatives were quickly checked. Trevelyan's proposals for civil service reform were partially enacted with the opening up of the Indian civil service to competitive entry in 1853, but such was conservative opposition that it was 20 years before the same principles would be applied to the home services. When Chadwick's implementation of the Public Health Act of 1848 threatened to go too far in the direction of centralization, his efforts were quickly thwarted. Marx referred to liberal legislation as 'homeopathical doses of reform', implying that with small measures they only hoped to forestall larger ones, and there was no doubt truth in this, and yet the movement was significant and did decisively anticipate the new conception of the state which would emerge in the 1870s. The educational reforms of the mid-century period were a part of this more general movement, reflecting both its promise and its limitations.

The voluntary system and administrative reform

With the failure of legislation for national education, elementary schooling remained, throughout this period, on an essentially voluntary basis. However, a central administrative authority was, by slow stages, developing which reflected the desire of that growing body of experts for greater coordination and central control, and this increasingly prodded, exhorted and, occasionally, compelled the voluntary system to adopt new measures.

The first government financial support for elementary schools came with the 1833 grant which allocated £30 000 to schools, most of which was channelled through the two societies. The sum was derisory, barely topping the allocation to West Indian planters in compensation for the emancipation of their slaves, but it nevertheless set the precedent for public funding.

This increased gradually during the period, so that by 1861 total public expenditure reached £250 000. The extra funds clearly stimulated the spread of voluntary schools. The 1820s had seen a dip in the upward curve of new school buildings with only 1 265 new foundations. Between 1831 and 1841, this rose to 3 035 and the next decade saw 5 454 new schools inaugurated.[125] Government aid reinforced voluntary schooling, thus giving the lie to the voluntaryist argument that government intervention would undermine voluntary initiative. However, it did not, and was never intended to create a public, tax-supported school system. Central government spending remained at below half of the Prussian level, and by 1869 still two-thirds of school expenditure came from voluntary sources. Not a single elementary school was owned or directly controlled by elected public authorities.[126]

Government grant aid did bring with it other changes, nevertheless. If the state was to provide money for education then it must monitor how this money was spent. This was the original brief of the Education Committee, first proposed in 1838 by Lord John Russell, and adopted in 1839 by an Order in Council. The manner of its formation was indicative of the political limits of educational reform during the period. It was instigated without full parliamentary sanction and developed by administrative sleight-of-hand, thus by-passing the parliamentary deadlock over educational reform in the only way possible. Thus 'one of the weirdest pieces of government machinery England has ever known was about to begin its sixty years of eccentric and improbable existence'.[127]

This surrogate central educational authority became a significant force in the debates of the following period, not least in its assiduous compilation of facts and statistics subsequently used by parliamentary advocates. However, it had little effective power and its efforts at educational reform were frequently thwarted by parliamentary opposition. Its early initiative to establish non-denominational Normal schools for the training of teachers was opposed by the Church and failed to pass through the House. A subsequent motion to rescind the Orders in Council which had created the Committee failed by a mere five votes. In 1844 the Committee in Council issued its notorious minutes regarding school supervision. State inspection of schools had been minimally instigated through the Factory Act of 1833 and the New Poor Law of 1834. The Committee now wished to extend this system under its own aegis. The minutes stated that

> The right of inspection will be required by the Committee in all cases; Inspectors, authorized by H.M. in Council, will be appointed from time to time to visit schools to be henceforth aided by public money; the Inspectors will not interfere with religious instruction, or discipline, or management of the school, it being the object to collect facts and information and to report the results of the inspections to the Committee in Council.[128]

The Committee asked for powers of inspection that were hardly extensive by continental or American standards. However, they were too much for the Anglican Church, which strongly objected to this proposal. The 'Concordat' which was finally reached made major concessions to the Church, giving bishops a veto over the appointment of inspectors for Anglican schools.

Denied effective powers, understaffed and functioning without agreed principles of action or settled rules of procedure, the Committee was a poor substitute for the central educational authority for which reformers canvassed. In the course of time, according to one of its historians, A. S. Bishop, 'the Committee of Council became first an irrelevance, then an anachronism and finally a laughing stock'.[129] In 1849 its first secretary, James Kay-Shuttleworth, resigned from overwork and nervous exhaustion. He was replaced by Ralph Lingen, who presided over the Education Department for the next two decades until the creation of a new system under Forster's 1870 Act. The Lingen era was characterized by a gradual increase in the department's power although not by any increase in its popularity. Parliament strongly objected to the lack of accountability of the department to itself, and teachers and inspectors were alienated by its work. Bishop writes:

> The administration...was conducted by officials who, by all accounts, knew little and cared less about the education of the poorer classes and who, on the admission of one of their number, treated elementary schools with contempt.[130]

The main changes over which it presided included the increase in public funding, the extension of the Inspectorate, the development of the pupil-teacher system and the implementation of the 1862 Revised Code. None of these measures can be said to have fundamentally reformed the voluntary system. The Inspectorate were hard-working and often zealous about improving teaching in schools but they were unequal to their task. By 1860 there were 60 inspectors, but these between them had to visit 10 403 schools. Often they visited three each day and still the majority of schools remained uninspected. If they had little time they had less authority. As their most celebrated member, Matthew Arnold, complained, they could do little more than report, and schools often took little notice of them. The English squire, he said, liked to have an inspector down from London occasionally, as he might call in a landscape gardener or an architect, to talk to him about his school, to hear his advice and be free to dismiss him as soon as his advice became unpalatable. They had little influence on policy-making and were hardly consulted over the formulation of the Revised Code.[131]

The development of the pupil-teacher system (1846), another singular English educational institution, represented the first serious attempt to train teachers, and characteristically assumed the form of an apprenticeship. Pupil teachers were rigorously selected, chosen as much for their morality and obedient attitudes as for any other attributes. Female apprentices, who by 1860 outnumbered males, had to come from decent and respectable homes, preferably not from those large families which were thought to breed coarse and indelicate habits.[132] Their training was accordingly humble, much time being taken up in religious instruction and moral preparation. As one college principal reported,

> The object being to produce schoolmasters for the poor the endeavour must be, on the one hand to raise students morally and intellectually to a certain standard while, on the other, we train them in lowly service, not merely to teach them hardihood and inure them to the duties of a humble and laborious office, but to make them practically acquainted with the conditions of the community among whom they will have to labour.[133]

The standards required for the teacher's certificate were not high. According to the Newcastle Report, pupil teachers were expected to read with 'proper articulation and expression', to be acquainted with English grammar, to be prepared to compose an essay on a subject connected with teaching, and to be able to do sums and algebra up to simple equations.

Not only did the system provide little beyond the most rudimentary of skills, but it did little to enhance the status of teachers. By 1850 there were only 1 173 certified teachers in England and Wales, which was less than one for each school. Pupil teachers outnumbered their qualified colleagues by two to one. The average teacher's salary remained low, no more in 1854 than £85 per annum. A school mistress earned about two-thirds of her male colleague's wage. The status of teachers was still relatively menial: it was not a job for a 'young man of an adventurous, stirring or ambitious character', warned the Newcastle Report. In fact, it was an occupation frequently ridiculed and abused, not merely in fiction but publicly by people in high office. Lord Macaulay described school masters as 'the refuse of all other callings...to whom no gentleman would entrust the key of his cellar'.[134] It was not until 1870, with the formation of the National Union of Elementary Teachers, that the fortunes of teachers began their slow and precarious ascent.

The major legislation on elementary education during the period was the 1862 Revised Code, unpromisingly introduced to the House by Robert Lowe as guaranteeing neither efficiency nor cheapness, but assuredly one or the other. The Code, best known for its introduction of a teacher piece-work system known as 'payment by results', had been the main recommendation of the 1861 Newcastle Commission, which, on the basis of some highly dubious statistics had found nothing much wrong with the voluntary system. In the event the new Code offered cheapness more than efficiency, and certainly not quality, drawing from Matthew Arnold the complaint that it reduced education to a more mechanical process. 'In a country', he wrote,

> where everyone is prone to rely too much on mechanical process and too little on intelligence, a change in the Education Department's regulations... inevitably gives a mechanical turn to school teaching, a mechanical turn to inspection, and must be most trying to the intellectual life of a school.[135]

By tying two-thirds of government aid to tested results in a limited range of subjects, it made learning more rigidified and narrow, if that were possible, reduced teachers to ciphers and turned educational administration into a vast exercise in accountancy.

By the mid-1860s, elementary education was thus still an exceptionally narrow and limited affair. At its maximal point of development the voluntary system, pepped up by doses of the bureaucratic tonic, was still unequal to its task. Its unique forms and singular failures were highlighted by international comparison. The voluntary system was built on independent institutions. It received less public funding than in any comparable country, raising the bulk of its finance from fees and subscriptions. Public supervision of schools was still slight by European standards. Where state intervention had increased central control, as through 'payment by results', it was less to promote good practice as was the endeavour of the American superintendents, but to codify and cramp teaching in the interests of cost efficiency. Teacher-pupil ratios were amongst the worst in Europe and teacher training minimal by German standards. Enrolments were lower than in almost all comparable states. Not surprisingly, the product reflected the process. Aside from France, England was Europe's most illiterate major power.

Secondary schools

Secondary schooling in mid-Victorian Britain was notable for its elitism, its resistance to modern curricula and its segmented and hierarchical structure. We saw in Chapter 1 that English secondary enrolments were probably low in comparison with other countries, at least in anything approximating to full secondary education. But most distinctive was the level of differentiation between different types of school. Contrary to the continental and US pattern, all English secondary schools had remained financially independent of the state and within this independent system manifold distinctions of rank and prestige had developed, reflecting the byzantine social divisions in the middle and upper rungs of the English class structure. However, despite these social divisions, which were characteristic also of the German secondary schools, there was little corresponding differentiation of curricula, such as might have given an education designed for the needs of different classes. The major secondary schools, including the public, grammar and proprietary schools, remained predominantly classical in orientation and even the lesser schools remained under the influence of an ethos developed by the traditional gentry institutions. The most significant result of these factors was the absence of any normatively middle-class secondary education to compare with the French *lycée*, the German *Realschule* or the US high school.

Secondary schools were divided into three distinct tiers corresponding to the different class strata which formed their respective clienteles. The aristocracy, the gentry and some of the wealthy industrialists generally sent their sons to the nine famous public schools. Pre-eminent amongst these were Eton, favoured by Anglicans and Tories, and Harrow, favoured by the Whig aristocracy. For the middling rich, including the poorer gentry, those from the older professions and the majority of substantial manufacturers, secondary schooling was obtained from the better endowed grammar schools and the new proprietary schools. The lower ranks of the middle class, including the smaller tradesmen and farmers, if they could afford secondary education for their children at all, were likely to make do with the lesser grammar schools and the private schools, amongst which the latter were quite numerous and often very poor. At no level was an education provided for the mainstream of the middle class, which reflected its interests, excepting in those exceptional private schools which continued the traditions of the dissenting academies.

Of all schools, the public school was the most alien to the middle-class mentality. 'During the early industrial phase,' writes Ringer, 'the public schools were notoriously the most aristocratic institutions of secondary education to be found in Europe and probably in the world.'[136] During the half-century up until 1850 the gentry and aristocracy accounted for over half of the enrolments in major public schools. Sons of clergy and officers accounted for a further 16 per cent, whilst only 1 in 20 pupils came from professional families. In contrast, by the 1860s, 65 per cent of students in French *lycées* came from business, professional or civil service backgrounds and over 69 per cent of those in German *Gymnasien* were from similar class backgrounds. Clearly the difference in period explains some of the difference: the public schools had widened their class intake somewhat by the later period. However, the discrepancies were no doubt still considerable.

Largely patronized by the landed and clerical groups down to the mid-century, the ethos of the public schools had reflected the culture of the rural upper class; they had little interest in the promotion of 'useful knowledge' and regarded their very distance from worldly affairs and industrious pursuits as a mark of social status and honour. Most valued as a preparation for a life of genteel leisure, where they did aspire to public service, it was within an ethos which exalted careers coloured by ideals of honour and public leadership – in the military, in politics and colonial administration, and latterly in the professions and the civil service. Within this frame the pursuit of intellectual excellence and particularly scientific knowledge had been regarded with some contempt, either as unworthy or positively dangerous, whilst classical learning was celebrated as a badge of status and a mechanism of social exclusion.

Throughout the mid-nineteenth century the dominance of classical culture in the English public school was almost total. In practice, little more than the rote learning of Latin and Greek, classics continued to occupy four-fifths of the timetable even in 1870, and this despite the fact that, as the Clarendon Commission reported, it was often extremely poorly taught. It was stoutly defended by headmasters as the pre-eminent mental discipline and the classical class was extolled as the crucible of civilized culture.

What the public school had, traditionally, most prided itself upon was the development of character. In his first address at Rugby in 1827, Thomas Arnold himself laid down a credo to which many defenders of classical education would have subscribed. 'What we must look for here is first,' he said, 'religious and moral principles, second gentlemanly conduct, [and] thirdly intellectual ability.'[137] The order of priority was symptomatic of the precedence of character over learning, which was the hallmark of the classical public school. Indeed, even the Clarendon Commissioners, who found many faults in public school education, could not resist ending their report with a statement on the gentlemanly virtues of these, the 'chief nurseries of our statesmen', which was nothing short of a paean of praise:

> It is not easy to estimate the degree in which the English people are indebted to these schools for the qualities on which they pique themselves most – for their capacity to govern others and control themselves, their aptitude for combining freedom with order, their public spirit, their vigour and manliness of character, their strong but not slavish respect for public opinion, their love of healthy sport and exercise...they have had perhaps the largest share in moulding the character of the English gentleman.[138]

The advance of science and vocational studies into this classical shrine was fiercely resisted. Science was tarred by association with industry and base utility. Even general vocational subjects were infected with the stain of social inferiority. Thring, the successful headmaster of Uppingham, had found it

> absolutely impossible to direct the studies of a great school to this end [professional education] beyond a certain degree, without destroying the object of a great school, which is mental and bodily training in the best way, apart from immediate gain.[139]

Dean Farrar, a rather exceptional clerical advocate of useful education, wrote about reactions within the public school establishment to his ideas:

And no sooner have I uttered the word 'useful' than I imagine the hideous noise which will environ me, and amid the hubble I faintly distinguish the words vulgar, utilitarian, mechanical.[140]

Even after 1840, when public schools began to attract more children from the industrial and professional strata, the disdain for scientific and applied knowledge persisted. Less of an impediment for the professional group, whose professional ideal could be domesticated to one of gentlemanly service, more 'amateur' than expert, for the industrialist's son the public school meant a process of cultural denial and relearning. They were tolerated, eventually, so long as they became 'gentlemen'. The schools continued for the most part to ignore science and modern education, stressing the values of an ancient and conservative rural culture, sympathetically framed in the grandiose and pastoral setting of the school environment.

The survival of the public school in this entrepreneurial age seemed to many contemporaries, and to subsequent historians, as something of an anachronism. However, its persistence had little to do with any cultural lag and was no local institutional aberration. It reflected a central feature of the Victorian class structure, resting on the solid material basis of continuing landowner power and cultural prestige. The public school survived because the landed class retained sufficient influence to guarantee its survival. Its ambiguous relation to the entrepreneurial values of the day reflected contradictions within the dominant culture itself.

Secondary schooling both reflected and retrenched these social and cultural divisions within the dominant classes. The public school provided the social nexus for this fusion of class cultures that created the ruling elite in Victorian England. Drawing the majority of its students from the landed class, it increasingly absorbed those from the upper layers of the industrial and professional classes and provided their inter-socialization with the aristocracy. It trained them neither for industry, trade nor commerce, but primarily for rule, in politics, in the military and in administration. At Rugby, the favourite destination for pupils before 1840 had been the Church, but subsequently it became the army and then law. The favourite destinations of Harrovians between 1830 and 1850 were the army, politics and administration, with law and the Church running second. In 1830 almost half of all MPs came from public schools. Public schools produced few scientists of note and it was not until the 1870s that any significant number of its graduates went into business.[141]

The remaining secondary schools, the endowed grammar schools and the new proprietary schools catered for the broad mass of the middle class but hardly on their own terms. The grammar school continued to be controlled in the main by the gentry and the Anglican Church, providing a largely classical education which sedulously aped the public schools. In this they reflected the continuing sway of the landed class both politically and culturally. It was only in some of the newer public schools such as Wellington, Rossall and Marlborough, and in private schools controlled by the nonconformist churches, such as the Presbyterian Mill Hill School, that a more modern form of education flourished. But for the majority of the middle class there were no schools that catered for their particular needs.

The reforms of the mid-century modified the content of secondary education but not its structure. Mostly it was a case of *plus ça change, plus c'est la même chose*. The reform effort began in the 1840s, after the public schools had gone through a period of decline and disrepute and as they became in greater demand with access facilitated by the new railways. The revival, which was most associated with the regimes of Thomas Arnold at Rugby and Samuel Butler at Shrewsbury, was more in morality than education and aimed to salvage the diminished reputation of public schools. Arnold was notable chiefly for his high moral standing and espousal of muscular Christian virtues, which raised the moral tone of schools if not their scholarship. He was a man of broad faith rather than dogmatic religion, but his liberalization of the teaching curriculum was probably less significant than his encouragement of athleticism and gentlemanly conduct. Butler is remembered for his attempts to encourage a greater competitive spirit at Shrewsbury and thus to improve standards, and certainly that was the drift of the following decades.

However, the classical curriculum retained its sovereign status, and the position of science was not improved. Thomas Arnold actually stopped the teaching of science at Rugby under the traditional pretext:

Physical science alone can never make a man educated; even the formal sciences [grammar, arithmetic, logic, geometry], valuable as they are with respect to the discipline of reasoning power, cannot instruct judgement; it is only moral and religious knowledge which can accomplish this.

It was the old shibboleth of the gentleman all-rounder: 'The purpose and ideal of education was the good, open and full life coupled with the manly spirit.'[142] Little had changed at Shrewsbury even by the 1870s, of which period ex-pupil and later Fabian Graham Wallas recalled: 'We had no laboratory of any kind, and I never heard in my time of any boy receiving a science lesson.'[143]

The main reforms in secondary education came in the 1860s, forced to a large extent by the movement towards a greater emphasis on competition and merit in government service and on qualifications in the professions. The India Act of 1853 had opened appointments to the Indian Civil Service to competitive examination and the Northcote–Trevelyan Report of the same year recommended the adoption of the same procedure in the Home Service. Meanwhile the professions were becoming more conscious of the need to safeguard standards of practice. Professional associations had been formed for civil engineers in 1818, lawyers in 1825, architects in 1837 and mechanical engineers in 1847. With the Medical Registration Act of 1858 it was clear that the future for the professions would increasingly involve compulsory registration by qualifying examinations.[144] The importance of good secondary education for middle-class children was thus becoming increasingly obvious. Efforts to reform secondary education in line with these new realities can be seen both in the independent efforts of schools and universities to improve themselves and in the initiatives of government. The most obvious expression of the new climate within the schools lay in the movement towards examinations. The formation of the College of Preceptors in 1850 as an independent examining body for secondary schools was followed in 1857 and 1858 by the introduction of local examinations by Oxford and Cambridge universities, which finally led to the Oxford and Cambridge Joint Examination Board in 1873. These various bodies conducted examinations in numerous subjects from different centres around the country and certainly had an appreciable effect on raising standards in secondary education. However, the system ran up against innumerable problems which limited its effectiveness, and its goals were arguably some way from the meritocratic concept so dear to the Benthamite tradition.

The practical problems stemmed from the uncoordinated nature of the projects. Different independent bodies were conducting examinations according to different criteria in a host of different subjects. Furthermore, the examining bodies were not in close touch with the teaching in secondary schools and consequently exams often assessed things which students had never learnt at school or could only get from private crammers, and developments in assessment were not closely linked with reform in the school curriculum. Since the exams were not designed to assess schools but only individuals who put themselves forward, they only had an effect on a limited number of pupils and encouraged schools to concentrate on cramming their best scholars rather than to improve their general standards. These problems somewhat undermined the credibility of the exams and, given also that there were still rather few occupations that required formal qualifications or which selected on a competitive basis, it was not surprising that the exams continued for a long time to lack prestige and gain acceptance as a national institution for assessing merit and selecting for occupations.

It is also probable that many of the advocates of the new exams did not see them as a means to any full-blown meritocratic system. In the main they favoured only the very few who had the means to buy the best education, and of this advocates of competition were well aware. Gladstone had been very clear that in supporting open competition for posts in the Civil Service he would not be damaging the position of the ruling class. His letter on the subject to Lord John Russell in 1854 makes this abundantly clear:

I do not hesitate to say that one of the great recommendations of the change [to competitive recruitment] in my eyes would be that it would be its tendency to strengthen and multiply the ties between the higher classes and the administrative power...I have a strong impression that the aristocracy of this country are even superior in natural gifts, on the average, to the mass; but it is plain that with their acquired advantages, their insensible education, irrespective of book-learning, they have an immense superiority.[145]

Without any extensive system of scholarships to good secondary schools, and there was none, it is clear that the introduction of examinations in secondary education would only favour those who were already favoured. The underlying motive of advocates of secondary examinations was often, in any case, not so much to create a middle-class meritocracy in secondary education but rather to make a pre-emptive strike against state inspection and control of schools. So long as reformers in independent schools could show that they were making efforts through examinations to improve standards, it was possible to argue against advocates of state intervention that they were capable of putting their own house in order.

Independent action did not, however, completely forestall government concern, and the 1860s witnessed increasing government intervention in secondary education, not least with the major inquiries which the government instigated. The first of the commissions was set up in 1861 under the chairmanship of the Earl of Clarendon and was briefed to investigate the public schools. Its main concern was the inefficiency of these schools which, in Clarendon's words, placed the 'upper classes in a state of inferiority to the middle and lower'. The report, which was duly submitted in 1864, found much value in the character training provided by the public schools but reported low standards in the teaching of classics and still lower achievements in maths and English. Their recommendations included the improvement of standards in these areas and the inclusion of science and modern language teaching, but most significant was their insistence on the maintenance of classics as the central core of the curriculum. In so doing they helped to improve the efficiency of the public school in grooming the upper class for its leadership roles in a more competitive society. However, they also sealed its isolation from other secondary institutions and from the mainstream of the middle class. Classicism continued to operate as a mechanism of social exclusion and this, coupled with the removal of many scholarships, limited still further their accessibility. As Brian Simon has summarized it, the Clarendon Commission 'created an efficient and entirely segregated system of education for the governing class – one that had no parallels in any other country'.[146]

The remaining secondary schools were investigated by the Schools Inquiry Commission set up in 1868 under Lord Taunton. This, the most far-reaching inquiry ever undertaken, which ran to 20 volumes in its final report, was quite unceremonious in the presentation of its findings. With the exception of the proprietary schools, whose standards were acknowledged to be good, the majority of grammar and private schools were found to be very unsatisfactory, employing untrained teachers whose methods were poor. The middle class wanted a more modern curriculum which was not provided in these schools. The Committee's solutions were twofold. Firstly, they recognized the need for greater central supervision of secondary schools, and recommended that the state be given control over secondary school inspection and examinations and that a national registry of teachers be set up. Secondly, they proposed a three-tiered structure for these schools which would reflect the divisions of rank within the middle class and provide at each level an efficient education geared towards the specific needs of its consumers. The first grade would cater for those with inherited wealth, the top professionals and the poorer gentry, who wished to retain a cheaper form of classical education up until the age of 19. The second would provide a more modern and vocational education, retaining some Latin, up to 16 years, and would cater for children of engineers and those in the lower branches of the medical and legal professions. The third grade would offer a basic education in reading, writing and arithmetic up to 14 years for the sons of smaller farmers and tradesmen, and superior artisans. This intricate system of social differentiation was to be achieved through market manipulation, by adjusting scholarships, fees, curricula and statutory leaving ages to produce a *de facto* limitation on entry to different types of school to different social groups.[147]

These proposals were only partially incorporated into the Endowed Schools Act of 1869. The government balked at any centralization in secondary education and ignored the recommendations on state inspection, whilst supporting various measures to encourage the creation of three tiers of schools along the lines suggested by the enquiry. Overall, the measures did help to increase the efficiency of middle-class education and did something to modernize the curriculum, although unevenly. At the same time they seriously reduced working-class access to secondary education which had already been extremely limited, but was available through free places in some grammar schools. Most remarkable about the reforms was the deliberate way in which they perpetuated and in fact intensified these multiple class differentiations. Far from creating a normative form of middle-class education based on uniform principles of utility, merit and relevance, as the French *lycée* and US high school had at least partially done, they institutionalized the social and cultural fragmentation of the middle class and circumscribed the meritocratic principle to exclude the majority of the population.

Secondary schooling for girls was still extremely limited during this period, and when it could be found it was more concerned with the cultivation of genteel manners than with education as such. Upper middle-class families often did not send their daughters to school at all, preferring education in the protected environment of the home. When a school education was sought it was hard to find. This was still before the period of the creation of girls' public schools, and most endowed grammar schools excluded girls.[148] Some early prototypes of the girls' secondary school had emerged, such as Cheltenham Ladies' College (1854) and the early girls' high school, North London Collegiate (1850), but as the Taunton Commission reported, these were few and far between. Where prosperous middle-class families did choose to send their daughters to school, it was normally for about three years at a local school, or occasionally at a select boarding school.

Where it existed, the education of girls in secondary schools was clearly far removed from the experience of boys. Its main objective was to cultivate domestic skills, graceful accomplishments and an ethos of service, in line with the Victorian middle-class notions of femininity. If it aspired towards academic objectives at all, it was to make girls sufficiently knowledgeable to be interesting companions and useful help-mates for their husbands. As the headmistress of one girls' high school reported in her school magazine, the 'note' of the school should be a 'delicate, womanly refinement, a high-toned courtesy, a gentle manner (and) a dignified bearing', adding that this was far removed from the 'loud, romping vulgarity of the Hoyden, called "the girl of the period" '.[149] What the girls' school did share with its male counterpart was a super-sensitivity towards class distinction. Girls were discouraged from mixing with anyone below their social rank, and girls' schools assiduously strove to maintain their social exclusivity. Social snobbery formed part of the hidden curriculum of the school and, as the Bryce Commission later found (1895), this was the main object of most girls' schools. In her evidence to the Commission, Mrs Armitage, who visited about 70 schools in Devon, found that almost half were indifferent or worthless. The majority of private girls' schools were distinguished only by their 'unblushing assertion of caste exclusiveness'.

> The dominant idea about girls' education is that it should be as far as possible cloistral, that girls should be kept from any contamination with people who drop their H's or earn their salt.[150]

Technical and scientific education

One of the principal casualties of the tradition of *laissez-faire* in education was scientific and technical instruction. With the exception of pure science which developed largely independently of formal educational institutions, England was, by the mid-century, incomparably backward in most areas of scientific and technical education. For the working class, elementary education was too sparse and narrow to provide a proper foundation for technical and scientific study, and facilities for full-time post-elementary education were largely absent. State-organized trade schools for artisans and engineers, which were common in continental Europe, had not developed in England, where received opinion regarded the workshop as the only fit place for learning a trade.

Provision for the middle class was, as we have seen, equally deficient in this area. Public and grammar schools remained frozen in the classical mould, and, until the last quarter of the century, universities contributed virtually nothing towards scientific and technical needs. This again was in striking contrast to major continental states where not only was secondary and university education more scientific, but where also a layer of technological institutions had emerged in the form of the *Polytechnique*, the French *grande école* and the German *Technische Hochschule* (technical high school). Equivalent polytechnics and civic universities did not begin to emerge in England until the 1870s and 1880s.

English skills training was based on the apprenticeship, and this remained the paradigmatic form of all future technical education. Privately organized by employers and independent craftsmen, the apprenticeship system received no public funds and embodied a characteristically practical approach based upon on-the-job experience rather than theoretical study. The same principle was adopted in training for professional engineering. Whilst vocational education for doctors and lawyers was widespread, particularly with the numerous medical schools, a scientific and technical education for engineers and manufacturers was hard to find, reflecting the bias against science and the new professions in much middle-class education. As a contemporary report on civil engineering put it, 'Every candidate for the profession must get his technical, like his general, education, as best he can; and this necessity has led to conditions of education peculiarly and essentially practical.' Whilst the French engineer emerged after three or four years in the *école* with a high level of theoretical training, the English engineer had 'a simple course of apprenticeship'.[151]

Where government intervention later supplemented this system it was in an ancillary role that left its fundamental features intact. State-assisted technical education was predominantly part time, practically oriented and in administration largely marginalized from mainstream educational provision. When anxieties about the superiority of French design in silk manufactures prompted the government to create a school of design and later to fund other such schools in industrial areas (of which there were 17 by 1852), the council which administered them was characteristically located within the Board of Trade, insulated from contact with educational administration.[152] The schools were bedeviled by bureaucratic and factional conflicts and represented a very inauspicious beginning for state intervention in technical education. They were intended as a stimulus to technical education but never as an alternative form to the apprenticeship. The system had its own particular merits but the cultivation of expertise in applied science and technology was not one of them. Matthew Arnold's later judgement on this seems incontrovertible:

> In nothing do England and the Continent at the present moment more strikingly differ than in the prominence which is given to the idea of science there, and the neglect in which the idea still lies here.[153]

The reasons for this startling absence in Europe's most industrialized nation have already been suggested. In part it resulted from the deep penetration within traditional education institutions of those conservative and 'anti-industrial' values of the ruling elite. But it was not just an infirmity of older institutions or of the 'old' classes. It was also a failure of the new, and one that centrally concerned middle-class values. Its major cause lay in the particular forms of British industrialization and the liberal state which presided over it.

In continental Europe, industrialization occurred under the tutelage of the state and began its accelerated development later when techniques were already becoming more scientific; technical and scientific education had been vigorously promoted from the centre as an essential adjunct of economic growth and one that was recognized to be indispensable for countries which wished to close on Britain's industrial lead. By contrast, Britain's early industrialization had occurred without direct state intervention and developed successfully, at least in its early stages, within a *laissez-faire* framework. This meretricious industrial start had two consequences for technical education. Firstly, state intervention was thought to be unnecessary for developing technical skills, where the initial requirements were slight and adequately met by traditional means. The customary empirical approach of the apprenticeship seemed adequate and eminently practical. In fact, political economy suggested that state intervention might be positively injurious. Not only would it offend against liberal principles and create an unwanted additional tax burden, but it would interfere in the market, undermine the manufacturer's own training provision and endanger trade secrets. Secondly, the very success of Britain's early industrial expansion encouraged a complacency about the importance of scientific skills and theoretical knowledge which became a liability in a later period when empirical knowledge, inventiveness and rule-of-thumb methods were no longer adequate.

By the 1850s the limitations of this approach were becoming increasingly evident. Industrial development was entering a new phase which made different demands on education. As Eric Hobsbawm has written,

> The major technical advances of the second half of the 19th century were essentially scientific, that is to say they required at the very least some knowledge of recent development in pure science for original invention, a far more consistent process of scientific experiment and testing for their development and an increasingly close and continuous link between industrialists, technologists, professional scientists and scientific institutions.[154]

What was absent in England was precisely this link between pure science and its application. In short, technical education. This became increasingly obvious with the development of new technologies – the electric telegraph, the synthesis of aniline dyes, artificial fertilizers, and so on – which were highly dependent on scientific knowledge, particularly on chemistry, and in which Britain was at some disadvantage.

The pragmatic approach of on-the-job training appeared to be inadequate, and a more rigorous and systematic form of training was required. However, private and voluntary initiatives were not responding sufficiently. This was not surprising, since there was an inherent limitation in the *laissez-faire* approach to training which lay in the very nature of the market itself. Capitalist enterprise was, by definition, competitive and individualistic, and recourse to any collective strategies to improve technical skills – for instance, setting up technical schools – went against the grain of entrepreneurial values. As James Kitson, a Leeds ironmaster and advocate of technical education, later explained in evidence to the Select Committee on Scientific Instruction (1867–8), the problem was not confronted 'because the question is so extensive that individual manufacturers are not able to grapple with it, and if they went to immense trouble to establish schools they would be doing it in order that others might reap the benefit'. He added, 'We do not do that in Yorkshire'; but he might well have said, 'it is not done by sensible capitalists', at least not without encouragement from the state.[155] Competitive entrepreneurs would not sponsor schools for technical training because they feared for their trade secrets, suspected that others would poach their trainees, and reckoned that the investment was not warranted by its potential return in immediate profit. Their judgement was not untypical of their class. In no country did individual capitalist enterprise produce a collective strategy for training without state intervention. In this, the area of education with most economic importance, the market principles of political economy were found wanting.

Thus by the mid-century there was increasing anxiety about the state of technical education. The Great Exhibition of 1851 had alerted more far-sighted observers to the potential industrial challenge from the Continent. Lyon Playfair, a leading chemist and champion of scientific education, returned from a tour of the Continent to warn of the superiority of its technical schools. In a much publicized lecture entitled 'Industrial Instruction on the Continent', he argued that science and technical skills were becoming increasingly important in modern industry and that England was failing to respond. The attitude towards technology was marked by a failure to relate theory and practice:

> We see many producers in our own country practicing their arts by the aid of empirical experience only, little guided by scientific laws. Hence also has arisen an overweening respect for practice and a contempt for science.[156]

This dichotomy was reflected in social divisions:

> We have eminent 'practical men' and eminent 'scientific men', but they are not united, and generally walk in paths wholly distinct. From this absence of connection there is often a want of mutual esteem, and a misapprehension of their relative importance to each other.

Changing economic circumstances and the agitation of men such as Playfair and Henry Cole, the recently appointed Secretary of the School of Design, prompted government intervention, and in 1853 the Department of Science and Art was created under the Board of Trade. The aim was to create a more effective central body to stimulate and coordinate efforts in technical education, including existing schools and sundry public institutions, such as the Government School of Mines and the Division of Practical Geology. However, the system it supported would remain 'local and voluntary...(and) in the main self-supporting'.[157] The department had mixed fortunes. Under Cole's energetic supervision the existing design schools were revived, and by 1858 there were 56 flourishing schools of art with 35 000 students.[158] The science division was less successful, initially; most of the new science schools failed and by 1859 only 450 students attended courses. Aid to science classes from the department between 1853 and 1859 amounted to a mere £898. However, in the following decade, with Henry Cole as sole secretary of the department and Captain Donelly as Inspector of Science, a more energetic regime evolved and pupils in science schools and evening classes increased to 10 230.[159] Payment by results was instituted throughout the schools and classes receiving funds, and outside examiners were brought in to assess the school results.

However, this limited government action still left scientific and technical education in an inadequate state. Criticism of existing provision continued and intensified, as burgeoning economic realities kept this issue alive in public debate. The Paris Exhibition of 1867 had a chastening effect since the failings of Britain's industrial performance were now evident. In all of the ninety classes of manufacturers, Britain was pre-eminent in only ten.[160] Lyon Playfair, who was one of the jurors, reported back on the exhibition with some foreboding. In an open letter to Lord Taunton he claimed that with few exceptions, 'a singular accordance of opinion prevailed that our country has shown little inventiveness and made little progress in the peaceful arts of industry since 1862'. The one cause of this 'upon which there was most unanimity of conviction is that France, Prussia, Austria, Belgium and Switzerland possess good systems of industrial education and that England possesses none'.[161]

By 1870 Playfair was arguing that 'the industrial supremacy of England is endangered for the lack of knowledge, in spite of the practical aptitudes of her people'. England was the only state in Europe that was 'neglecting the higher education of the working classes, and of those men who superintend their labour'.[162] However, it was not only the working class whose education was deficient and detrimental to industry. Managers and proprietors were increasingly criticized by contemporaries for neglecting research, failing to adopt new techniques and losing markets through poor salesmanship. And this was frequently attributed to their inadequate education. Engels commented sardonically that the middle class were as a rule 'quite uneducated upstarts' qualified only by 'insular conceit, seasoned by business sharpness'.[163] The judgement was harsh but not entirely unjustified by comparison with their continental counterparts. Many had left school at 14, and those who went to secondary school learnt little about science or business there. Huxley, the eminent scientist, complained to one audience that if you went to a public school

> You shall learn not one single thing of all those you will want to know directly you leave school and enter business life... you may become a manufacturer, but you shall not be provided with the means of understanding the workings of one of your steam engines, or the nature of the raw products you employ.[164]

Growing anxiety about the scientific ignorance of foremen, industrial managers and proprietors, and the deleterious effects of this on the economy, prompted a series of public enquiries into the state of technical education. In the year following the Exhibition, the Select Committee on Scientific Instruction reported. This was followed by eight reports from the Devonshire Royal Commission on Scientific Instruction and the Advancement of Science (1872–5) and then in 1884 with reports from the Samuelson Royal Commission on Technical Instruction. Each report praised the achievement of continental education and noted the industrial advances that could not have occurred but for 'the system of high technical instruction in their schools, for the facilities for carrying on scientific investigation, and for the general appreciation of the value of that instruction and of original research'.[165] Whilst all reports defended the notion of workshop training, they each found many defects in English provision. The 1868 report concluded that 'the facilities for acquiring a knowledge of theoretical and applied science are incomparably greater on the Continent than in this country'.[166]

The primary concerns of the reports lay in the results of inadequate training for supervisors, managers and proprietors. Most managers and 'capitalists of the great industrial enterprises' were only educated up to higher elementary level, although in 'rare' cases they followed courses at institutions such as the Royal College of Mines or Owen's College, Manchester. There was a great insufficiency of modern grammar schools. In public and endowed grammar schools, 'science is as yet very far from receiving the attention to which it is entitled'.[167] Although some improvements had been made since the Clarendon Committee reported, still only 18 out of 128 schools investigated had more than four hours of science teaching. Various witnesses noted the effects of this inadequate scientific background in managers and proprietors: many of them did not understand the manufacturing process and thus failed to promote efficiency, avoid waste and instigate innovative techniques. Furthermore, having little interest in science themselves, they did not value it in their workmen.

The second area of deficiency lay in the ignorance of foremen and supervisors. Ordinary workmen were not thought to require much scientific education but since the foremen and sometimes the managers also were drawn from this class, it was desirable that there should be a pool of expertise there. The absence of this was put down to a number of causes. The Revised Code had narrowed the focus of elementary schools to such an extent that they imparted little scientific or technical knowledge. Their standards were inadequate as a foundation for further study. Continuation schools and evening classes were 'unsystematic' and 'desultory' in their provision, and they were hampered by the lack of preparation and fatigue of their students, whose efforts to acquire further education after work were not recognized by employers. Furthermore, there was a shortage of qualified science teachers, and the administrative separation of Department of Science and Art classes and the remainder of elementary and secondary education was a handicap. Professor Huxley, in evidence to the Newcastle Commission, berated the split between the Department of Science and Art and the Education Department, which was like 'cutting education in half'.[168]

As to the apprenticeship system, opinions expressed in the reports varied. The Samuelson Report acknowledged the benefits of continental trade schools, concluding that 'secondary instruction of a superior kind is placed within the reach of children of parents of limited means to an extent (of) which we have no conception in this country'.[169] However, a number of witnesses criticized the overly theoretical nature of these schools and maintained the superiority of the workshop as a means of imparting practical skills. Some of the most perceptive comments were offered in evidence given by Flemming Jenkins, a professor of civil engineering at University College

London. Explaining that in his experience apprentice supervision was often very lax, he maintained that whilst the best apprentices learnt a good deal, the idle ones learnt nothing at all. Comparing the apprenticeship system with the continental trade schools, he argued that in terms of practical ability and common sense, the English apprentice was a match for anyone, and even for the products of the polytechnic. However, he continued,

> When in after life, the two men came to fill the higher stations, the English engineer would begin to feel the want of elementary training very severely, and he is at a disadvantage compared with the man abroad, in the judging of new problems which come under his eye.[170]

The reports made various recommendations for the improvement of science teaching in elementary and secondary schools and the better training of science teachers. Most significant was probably the recommendation of both the Devonshire and Samuelson commissions that means should be found to integrate the work of the Department of Science and Art and the Education Department. Samuelson found much to criticize in the confusion and overlapping between the two departments and suggested that scientific and technical education was best advanced in the context of a broad and integrated secondary provision. Unable to go beyond the technical brief, the report recommended the creation of a central authority for all matters relating to scientific and technical education.

Despite widespread acceptance of the findings of the commissions, their more wide-ranging proposals were not immediately adopted. During the next ten years, technical education expanded within its existing structures. The Department of Science and Art, which had become linked to the Education Department in 1856 but still remained essentially separate, expanded its support and supervision of science and art schools and classes. However, these remained unintegrated with elementary and secondary education, and the dual administration of these sectors became increasingly fractious, wasteful and inefficient. With the instigation in 1880 of the independent City and Guilds London Institute for the Advancement of Technical Education and with the creation of the new polytechnics in the 1880s, this *ad hoc* proliferation of technical provision was becoming increasingly muddled and chaotic.

The last decade of the century did finally bring some important advances in technical education. The Technical Instruction Act of 1889 allowed the new local councils to set up technical instruction committees which could be financed by a one penny rate and the Local Taxation (Whiskey Money) Act of 1990 provided public funds which could be spent on technical education. Together the measures contributed to considerable growth in technical education and encouraged many towns to build their first technical colleges.

This was the golden age of the technical education movement. However, despite this late outbreak of good sense, the long record of neglect left an enduring legacy. Technical education had been cast in a mould that subsequent legislation would find hard to break. Growing up as an extension of the apprenticeship system and reliant on employer initiatives, it developed in a fragmented and improvised manner; initially of low status, conservatively rooted in workshop practice, and hostile to theoretical knowledge, publicly funded technical education became normatively part time and institutionally marooned between the workplace and mainstream education. A century later it would still be seen as the Cinderella of the educational system.

The compromise system, 1870–1902

The 1860s marked a decisive period of transition in English education. The modest reforms in secondary and technical schooling discussed above were only part of a broader shift in educational thinking which was finally to reorganize elementary education and to institute, for the first time, a national system of education in England. The question was no longer about piecemeal state intervention but rather concerned giving the state overall responsibility for provision, and the form that this would take.

The decade after 1860 represented, in effect, the day of reckoning for the voluntary tradition. Its energies and potential had been largely exhausted and even its most ardent advocates, such as Edward Baines, had now abandoned the cause. The question now was how to replace it. This transition and the options open were well summarized in Horace Mann's retrospective survey in a speech delivered in 1869:

> There was much to be said in the years gone by, for the theory of individual action, and a dream, in which some of us indulged, of a state in which every parent should be paying, fully and directly and consciously, for his children's education, presented as a fair and lofty ideal, as a rival theory can boast. But the dream had vanished; even the arch prophets of the faith have now abandoned the shrine; and the only question is what faith to substitute, whether to adopt a policy of 'thorough' or a policy of compromise: to focus on the theory of co-operation, a perfect system, covering the whole community and consistent with the self respect of all, or to try to satisfie ourselves with half a system, touching only a portion of the people, and touching them with the long, numbing hand of charity.... if we cannot now hope to do it by another – if not by separate then by combined exertion.[171]

The reckoning had perhaps been inevitable for some years, as it became apparent that the voluntary system could not deliver adequate provision.

But it was the political and economic changes of the 1860s that made change seem both necessary and possible. The challenge of continental industry had made the importance of sound education fully apparent for the first time. As manufacturers grappled with modern scientific techniques, the danger of neglecting education was now readily apparent. At the same time, the greater mechanization of domestic industry reduced the need for child labour, thereby removing a major obstacle, at least in the minds of industrialists, to the acceptance of an extended education.

On the political front, new alignments were emerging which were favourable to educational reform. With the extension of the franchise in 1867, middle-class liberal opinion became increasingly favourable to educational reform. Men such as Bright, Mundella and Forster were optimistic that the newly enfranchised working-class householders could be persuaded to vote for industrialists and education could play an important role in this. As Robert Lowe put it, it was necessary to 'compel our future masters to learn their letters'.[172] Meanwhile, the growth of reformist trade union politics amongst skilled workmen and the so-called labour aristocracy portended a limited *rapprochement* between the organized working class seeking the right to vote and liberal manufacturers seeking access to power. The stage was set for the emergence of the classic mid-Victorian liberal alliance of the radical middle class, Dissent and the skilled working class.

Political re-alignment coincided with the modification of traditional attitudes towards the state. The breach between political economy and the culture of Benthamite experts, evident since the 1830s, had now widened to the point where 'letting alone' and social reform could no longer be reconciled and the era of pure *laissez-faire* was waning. The shift in perspective was perhaps more pragmatic than anything else. It was not so much, as Dicey maintained, that the liberal middle class was suddenly overwhelmed by a socialist conspiracy of collectivism, but rather that irresistible practical arguments had forced a recognition of the necessity of a more positive role for the state. The Victorian middle class had gradually become more aware of the extent of poverty and deprivation, and found their consciences stirred. At the same moment as they were realizing the extent of the social contradictions in capitalism at home, they also began to recognize its vulnerability to foreign competition. Both factors argued for a more positive role for the state.

In the decades after 1870, new ideologies, of course, were to emerge which would embody different conceptions of the state. Chamberlain's radical liberal followers were to break with orthodox liberalism and develop a new ideology of 'social imperialism'. This would yoke together ideas of imperial strength abroad and social efficiency at home in a new reactionary collectivism under the sign of the strong state. Fabianism would emerge to combine the traditions of Benthamite expert administration with reformist socialist demands and so create a distinctive 'top-down' concept of reform through the state. And finally, the working-class movement was to develop in new directions; a resurgence of Marxist thought would lead to the emergence of distinctive indigenous brands of revolutionary socialism, embodied in the work of William Morris and the Social Democratic Federation, and the new mass trade unionism of the 1880s and 1890s would embody the reformist aspirations of the mainstream of the labour movement. These developments are clearly beyond the scope of the present work but it is important to signal that the changing conceptions of the state which were already evident by 1870 and which lay behind the new developments in education were also the beginning of larger movement which would herald the birth of the welfare state and a century of further reform in education. L. T. Hobhouse later well captured the shift from the 'old' to the 'new' liberalism in his remark that 'There are other enemies of liberty than the state and it is in fact by the state that we have fought them.'[173]

Attitudes towards state education changed accordingly. Amongst the middle class, with the softening of non-conformist hostility towards state education, and the realization of the political and economic benefits of extended elementary education, there was a growing consensus on the virtues of reform. The trade union movement was increasingly calling for a national system of non-sectarian education. The product of these converging forces was a new educational alliance, the National Education League, founded in 1869 by radical Liberals and Dissenters and led by Joseph Chamberlain. Their demand was for a free, compulsory, non-sectarian and rate-aided national system of education. Campaigning against them for the claims of the Anglican Church was the rival National Education Union.[174]

The Education Act of 1870 was the result of these new forces and represented a crucial turning point in educational legislation. It did, as is frequently claimed, lay the foundations of a national system of education. For the first time, government was accepting responsibility for ensuring that universal elementary provision existed. The most important feature of the act was thus the provision for locally elected school boards, empowered to levy a rate for the provision of elementary schools. The country was divided into school districts corresponding to boroughs and parishes. Where a district was judged to have insufficient provision it would be allowed six months to rectify the position through voluntary effort, and failing this a school board would be set up, consisting of members elected by rate-payers. This board would be required to provide new schools where these were needed, and if it failed in this the Department of Education could set up a new board. The act was designed to 'fill the gaps' in voluntary provision and to create a national system worthy of the name. Systematic it may not have been, but it did in time create a national provision, thus fulfilling W. E. Forster's ambition of bringing 'elementary education within the reach of every English home for the first time'.[175]

The act fell far short of the demands of the Education League, however. It provided neither free nor compulsory education at elementary level, nor did it attempt to create an integrated and unified system. It was essentially a compromise with the voluntary system or, in Horace Mann's less kindly description, 'a composite contrivance'.[176] Forster himself had never intended to dismantle the voluntary system nor abandon completely the principles it stood for. His speech in defence of the bill in the House made this quite clear and, in fact, few pieces of major new legislation can have proposed with such reluctance to abandon past traditions.

> We must take care not to destroy in building up – not to destroy the existing system in introducing a new one ... our object is to complete the voluntary system, to fill up the gaps, procuring as much as we rightly can the co-operation and aid of those benevolent men who desire to assist their neighbours.[177]

Nor would such an attempt have found sufficient parliamentary support. Many Liberals, such as Gladstone himself, were only half-hearted converts to state education and were reluctant, as he put it, to 'undergo the risk of extinguishing that vast amount of voluntary effort which now exists throughout the country'.[178]

Voluntary principles were thus maintained in certain areas. Legal compulsion was not introduced and it was left to the boards, if they so wished, to enact by-laws requiring education between 5 and 13 years. Fees were also maintained, since Forster was opposed to relieving parents of this responsibility. However, school boards were permitted, with government approval, to set up free schools under special circumstances. On the question of religious instruction, some restrictions were imposed since grant-aided schools were obliged to exempt children who so wished from religious observances and lessons on a particular dogma, and denominational schools were unable to claim grants for religious instruction.

In the aftermath of the act it became clear that the creation of elected school boards opened a significant breach through which the working class could struggle for control over education, and for many the board schools came to be seen as the beginning of an education system that could provide genuine opportunities for working-class children, particularly so when radical boards created the post-elementary higher-grade schools. However, it should be stressed that there was nothing particularly egalitarian about Forster's Act. It said nothing about secondary education and the lack of access to it for the working class, and completely failed to address the question of potential inequalities where the voluntary sector remained largely autonomous. The voluntary sector was actually strengthened by the act and remained the leading sector for many years after. In 1882, double the number of children attended voluntary schools as board schools and by 1902 there were still twice as many voluntary as state schools.[179] John Bright well summed up the bill in an address in 1870. 'The fault of the bill', he said,

> is that it extended and confirmed the system which it ought...to have superceded...it was a bill to encourage denominational education, and where that was impossible, to establish board schools. It ought...to have been a bill to establish board schools.[180]

Forster's Act thus created a national provision without an integrated system. Horace Mann's earlier question of whether to adopt a 'policy of thorough' or a 'policy of compromise' had been resolved in the latter direction. What now existed was a 'dual system' where the voluntary principle had been transformed but not replaced. If the state was now the guardian and guarantor of a national provision, the guiding principle for that provision was still the maintenance of maximum independence and 'freedom' within a publicly accountable system. One result of this was the failure to address those educational divisions which contributed the most enduring characteristic of English education – its extreme segmentation along class lines.

After 1870, education remained multiply fragmented, in terms of both administration and provision. Elementary education was sharply demarcated from secondary education, and technical schooling remained adrift from both. In their administration, technical schools continued to be separated from other sectors, remaining under the control of the Department of Science and Art, which was almost permanently estranged from the Education Department. Secondary schools also remained largely independent in organization. The Taunton Report had described a system in which

> innumerable bodies of trustees continued in perpetuity, whose schools were submitted to no public test, least of all of an official kind, whose actions were virtually uncontrolled save by the terms of statutes.[181]

The Endowed Schools Act of 1869 had appointed three commissioners to review secondary schools and empowered them to insist on the adoption of new methods where these did not reform themselves. This they did too effectively for the liking of the schools' patrons, and in 1874 the Disraeli government effectively reduced government control by transferring the Commissioners' powers to the Charity Commission. The major public schools had always resisted state interference and their organization, the Headmasters' Conference, which was founded in 1869 to ensure that public schools 'should be free from any form of guidance or control', had widespread support within the Anglican and Tory establishment. Tory governments, from Salisbury to Balfour, consistently tried to limit the power of the Charity Commission and maintain the independence of the voluntary sector.

By the mid-1890s, educational administration was characterized, according to Archer, by a 'chaotic array of bodies...which represented a low degree of administrative unification'.[182] The Liberal Bryce Commission, which reported in 1895, urged greater unification. Surveying the development of English education it found that 'growth has not been either continuous or coherent, that is it does not represent a series of logical or even connected sequences'.[183] It found administration in a poor state and recognized the need for a system which would be a 'coherence, an organic relation between different authorities and different kinds of schools'. However, it was caught within a dilemma. It wanted secondary schools to retain their autonomy and balked at the idea of centralization and uniformity. On the other hand, it wanted greater coherence and administrative efficiency. In the end it came down on the side of a single unified education department, controlling primary, secondary and technical education. Many of the Commission's proposals were too much for the Salisbury government, and the 1899 Act ignored most of its recommendations. It did institute a consolidated Board of Education, incorporating the Charity Commission, but ensured separate status and autonomy for secondary schools.

The corollary of a weakly unified administrative structure was a system of schools which lacked any systematic linkage between its various parts. In her study of the origins of education systems, Archer has shown how systems which develop through 'substitution' inevitably lack systematization since they represent not a planned structure but rather an agglomeration of independent institutions. The likely effects of this are described as follows:

> Instead of a teaching profession, recruited and trained in a uniform fashion (according to level and discipline) and subject to stringent legal statutes, it is more likely that there will be diverse bodies, differentially recruited and responsible to different authorities. Instead of uniform methods, curricula and examinations, these may vary from area to area, and from one type of school to another. Instead of an integrated policy of pupil intake for the whole system, there may be divergent sets of practices.[184]

This well describes the state of English education at the end of the century. There were no uniform regulations governing the training and certification of teachers in different sectors, and many teachers were still untrained. The curriculum was only weakly regulated and not in such a way as to promote compatibility between the different sectors. There was still no national system of examinations. The linkages between different sectors were constructed according to what Archer calls the 'negative hierarchy principle' – that is, allowing minimal promotion through the different parts. All in all it reflected a principle of maximum class differentiation.

Balfour's Act of 1902 hardly changed this. It was pushed through by a Conservative government, despite widespread popular opposition. It replaced the school boards by the new local education authorities, thus undercutting the movement towards popular control that had occurred under the school boards. It strengthened the hand of the voluntary lobby by providing rate aid for church schools so long as these accepted local authority representation on their boards. Finally, it created the first state secondary schools, but did so in a way that deliberately pre-empted the objectives of the working class in secondary education. The autonomy and elite nature of independent secondary schools was preserved, whilst the new state grammar schools were kept deliberately separate from elementary schooling to discourage any notion that the majority of children could transfer into secondary education. The act also introduced a legal ceiling of 15 years for elementary schools and effectively killed off the higher-grade schools which had come, under the old school boards, to offer a surrogate form of secondary education for working-class pupils. Robert Morant was later to reinforce the separation of elementary and secondary education by having the grammar schools adopt an 'academic' curriculum, on the public school model. Effectively, two education systems had now been created where the majority of working-class children would leave at 13 or 14 whilst the middle class monopolized secondary education.

With the passing of the Act of 1902 a national education system had finally been consolidated, bringing England and Wales into line at last with the rest of Europe. However, it had been done in such a way as to perpetuate many of the singular and most undesirable historical characteristics of English education. Administrative unification of the education system had been partially achieved without there being any serious attempt to integrate its parts in an educational sense. The limited number of scholarships provided for secondary schools meant that the exclusion of the working class from secondary education was still almost total. The average child still left school at 13 with roughly the same years of schooling as the Prussian or North American child of the mid-nineteenth century. The independent secondary schools remained more elitist than any of their overseas counterparts, reflecting an obsession with caste exclusiveness. Lastly, technical education remained underdeveloped and marginalized from mainstream education.

The liberal tradition in education would leave a mixed legacy. Whilst its many apologists would continue to celebrate the virtues of vigorous independent forces in education, the very strength of the voluntary interests would continue to undermine the coherence and credibility of public education. The Bryce Commission had celebrated the English educational tradition for its 'freedom, variety and elasticity', and indeed this has been its credo ever since.[185] However, there were other constructions that could be put on this. Frequently in practice, elasticity had meant *ad hoc* and unplanned development; variety had meant class differentiation and freedom meant the unchecked authority of the powerful to provide education solely in their own interests. A more accurate characterization of the English educational tradition was later made by Tawney: 'The hereditary curse of English education', he wrote, 'is its organization along lines of social class.'[186]

Conclusion: Education and State Formation in the West

The aim of the first part of this book has been to analyse the social origins of certain historically specific forms of education known as national education systems. These were defined as systems of formal schooling at least partly funded and supervised by the state which provided universal education for all children of school age in a given nation. A set of educational institutions constituted a national system when it supplied the majority of the nation's needs in formal education and did so through an integrated and coordinated network of institutions. For the most part such systems were consolidated in the West in the nineteenth century and they represented the precursors of modern state schooling.

As the empirical analysis in Chapter 1 demonstrated, such systems arose unevenly in the major nations of Europe and North America. Countries developed their school systems at different times and according to different organizational models. Some of these differences are historically quite significant. A gap of nearly a century, for instance, separated the formation of an integrated administrative apparatus of state schooling in France and Prussia from England. Similarly, almost a century separated the creation of state secondary schools in France and Prussia from those in England. Whilst Prussia legislated for compulsory attendance at school until 14 years in 1826, similar provisions were not applied in England until 1921.

The speed with which countries adopted education systems also appears to correlate with the extent of their education provisions as measured in enrolment, access and literacy rates. This would seem to be hardly surprising since the extent of popular participation in schooling depended to a large degree on the availability of finance for schools and the determination or otherwise of governments and dominant social groups to encourage attendance. Mass schooling did not arise spontaneously from popular demand or from the action of market forces alone. It was to a large degree organized from above by the state. This conclusion clearly contradicts the neo-liberal argument that education developed in response to the market and that in a liberal England the market provided quite adequate schooling through voluntary initiatives. In comparison with other states, English education was most inadequate and this appears to be related to the slow development of state intervention in education.

Chapter 2 examined existing theories of educational change. It was found that none of these can adequately explain the social origins of national education systems nor their different chronologies of development. Traditional Whig explanations have stressed the role of Enlightenment philosophy, Protestant religion and institutional democratization. However, this perspective cannot explain why education should have developed fast in an undemocratic state, such as Prussia, and relatively slowly in a supposedly more 'democratic' state, such as England. Nor can Protestantism offer an adequate explanation of differential educational advance since some Catholic countries, such as Austria, were pioneers in national education and since several Protestant areas, such as England and the southern US states, do not fit the pattern of Protestant educational ascendancy. Functionalist theories which have linked education with economic skill requirements fare no better as general theories since the international pattern of educational development bears no close correlation with the process of industrialization at all. The first industrial country, England, was not the pioneer in educational change, whereas many of the less industrialized nations in Europe reacted much more speedily to bring education in line with the needs of developing economies. Lastly, theories which have attempted to link educational change with urbanization, proletarianization and the changing structures of family life, whilst suggesting many significant connections between the development of schooling and these social variables, are unable to explain significant degrees of educational development in regions which were predominantly rural and pre-proletarian.

The key social factor in explaining the timing and form of the development of education systems is rather, as I argued in Chapter 3, the nature of the state and the process of state formation. The major impetus for the creation of national education systems lay in the need to provide the state with trained administrators, engineers and military personnel; to spread dominant national cultures and inculcate popular ideologies of nationhood; and so to forge the political and cultural unity of burgeoning nation states and cement the ideological hegemony of their dominant classes. This inevitably entailed at different times using education to perform some of the functions suggested by existing theories. In societies undergoing the proletarianization of labour, education could be a useful tool in acclimating workers to waged employment whether in workshops, factories or on the land. Equally, in regions undergoing rapid urbanization, numerous social conflicts were thrown up which it fell to schools to attempt to control and ameliorate. The break-up of traditional pre-proletarian family forms caused particular problems for youth socialization in the context of antagonistic class societies, and education was frequently seen as a substitute mechanism to achieve this in ways which were acceptable to the dominant classes. However, it was specifically the intervention of the state which affected the formation of national education systems, and it is therefore the nature of the state in different countries which must carry the largest burden of explanation for the particular national forms and periodizations of the development of school systems.

The formation of national systems occurred first and fastest in countries where the process of state formation was most intensive. Three historical factors have been particularly associated with this accelerated and compacted process of state formation or nation-building. One has been the existence of external military threats, or territorial conflicts, which have often propelled the victim nations into vehemently nationalistic responses and deliberate actions to strengthen their state machines. Another has been the occurrence of major internal transformations resulting either from revolution, as in France, or from a successful struggle for national independence, as in the United States. In each case the country concerned has emerged from major conflagrations with an urgent task of national reconstruction, not only to repair the ruins of war but also to establish a new social order which will reflect the principles for which the struggle was originally undertaken. Lastly, there have been the situations where nations have been prompted into state-led programmes of reform to escape from relative economic underdevelopment. Where one country is significantly behind other competitor countries economically it has generally not been possible to catch up simply through the spontaneous initiatives of individual entrepreneurs. Liberal politics have not been of much use to underdeveloped countries, since they favour the already powerful, and nations which have successfully reversed histories of underdevelopment have generally done so either under the wing of other more powerful states or through concerted, centrally directed programmes of reform.

The development of national education systems has been historically closely connected with these phenomena, not only during our period here but also in the modern day, where education has been a major priority of countries undergoing national reconstruction after war or successful struggles for independence. In the eighteenth and nineteenth centuries it was those nations which underwent this kind of state formation which were most prone to developing national education, and generally they did this at the precise time when the process was at its highest pitch. Militaristic state-building first propelled the eighteenth-century Prussian state into educational development, and the pressures of economic advance kept the process on the boil in the next century, as absolutism gave way to constitutional bourgeois rule. Absolutism played a similar if lesser role in France. But here it was principally revolution and bourgeois social and economic reconstruction under Napoleon and after that fuelled a similar educational drive. In the United States, another leading country for educational reform, it was the need to consolidate a new US state after the break with Britain that did most to galvanize educational reform. Unlike in continental countries, this was achieved less through the work of the central state and more through the initiative of individual reformers and the local state and county administrations with which they were closely allied. If the process here appears to have been based on broader democratic foundations and owed less to the étatist spirit that characterized continental development, it was still clearly understood as a means of developing the national culture and securing the political system and was no less a process of organized state formation.

Not only the timing but also the forms of national systems reflected the nature of the state which created them. Most obviously, centralized states created centralized educational bureaucracies whilst more liberal states, such as the United States, created more decentralized systems. This had effects on the nature of the schooling provided, as Archer has shown. A centralized bureaucracy was better placed to engineer education systems where the various parts were more systematically linked with the whole. This tended to promote national systems of examinations, organized teacher training and policies on the curriculum that dovetailed between the various parts. Decentralized public systems, on the other hand, typically involved less draconian controls over the practice of education, making it more difficult for the state to use schooling as a means of securing uniform ideological beliefs. The voluntary system, as in England, was neither genuinely public nor really a system, and had less coordination or integration than any other arrangement.

However, it was not only the degree of central control which affected the forms and content of education. Schooling was a product not only of the state but also of civil society, and it was the nature of class relations there which finally determined the purposes of schooling. It was the different forms of hegemony operating between the dominant and subordinate classes which was ultimately responsible for what schools did, for who they allowed to go to what type of school and for what they taught them when they were there. The modernizing but still hierarchical and militaristic Junker state of Prussia produced an education system that was universal but authoritarian and multiply segmented. The working class received what was for the time an ample and ruthlessly efficient education in the public *Volksschule* system, but its objective was most clearly not only to train them to be skilled and productive workers but also to be loyal servants of the state. For the middle and upper classes, secondary education was as extensive as anywhere in Europe at the time, but it was clearly divided between the traditional classical education received by the upper strata in the *Gymnasien* and the more utilitarian education received by the mainly middle-class clientele in the *Realschulen*. The more thoroughly bourgeois state of Napoleonic and Restoration France achieved a less comprehensive and efficient elementary school system but its secondary education was arguably more modern than any, imbued with a circumscribed but potent meritocratic ideology and reflecting a notably cohesive and unified bourgeois culture. US education, as befitted a state which had gone furthest down the road of political democracy, had a less authoritarian system of education and one that undoubtedly offered more in the way of egalitarian access to post-elementary education than any other nation. However, for all the populist rhetoric of America's 'democratic' capitalism, this was still severely circumscribed along class and ethnic lines; if what the schools taught was not so tightly controlled by the central state and owed something to an exceptionally broad social consensus, it still reflected in the main the ideology and political purposes of the dominant, white, Anglo-Saxon middle class.

England represents the most exceptional case of educational development. Of all the countries considered here it had the greatest accumulation of unsolved educational problems and was probably further behind in reform than any area except the southern US states. Although religious divisions and the continuing sway of a conservative gentry culture played some part in this, it was the nature of the state which was most responsible. During this period, Britain never experienced the kind of deliberate and concerted process of state formation that occurred in the other countries and which was the driving force behind their educational reforms. Absolutism was cut short by early seventeenth-century revolution, and in the eighteenth and nineteenth centuries there were no major external military threats, social revolutions or problems of economic backwardness of the sort to engender intensive programmes of nation-building. National identity, strong institutions and a relatively stable ruling-class hegemony had already been established by earlier revolutions. Economic ascendancy was achieved on the back of this without concerted state direction. Instead it was the liberal market order and the doctrine of the minimal government which shaped the relations between society and state. Such an order served the capitalist economy well, at least for the first half of the nineteenth century, but it was inimical to systematic educational development. The result was the distinctive Victorian voluntary system of schooling which dominated education throughout the century and has left a strong imprint ever since.

The decisive feature of English education was the relative weakness of state or public forms. This not only limited the overall extent of educational provision, since there were clear limits to what voluntary initiative could achieve, but also gave distinctive forms to the system as a whole. Lacking whole-hearted state encouragement and with no effective central authority to coordinate it, education developed in an unsystematic and almost haphazard fashion. Teacher training and inspection were weak, curriculum and examination reform was exceptionally slow and guided by no comprehensive or rational plan, and the various parts of the system were not methodically articulated one with another. Overall the system reflected the contradictory nature of mid-Victorian bourgeois hegemony. Its main purpose in popular schooling was to promote acquiescence in middle-class morality and the nostrums of liberal political economy, and it did this in a typically partisan and doctrinaire fashion. However, the system also reflected the individualist and fissiparous character of the liberal order. Different parts of the school system were dominated by powerful interest groups which maintained exceptional levels of autonomy.

The result in secondary education was the survival of an antiquated system of gentry education in the public schools and the absence of any normatively middle-class schooling such as had been achieved with the continental *lycée* and *Realschule*, and the US high school. The result in working-class education was faction and conflict, and thus the long delay in reforms which were necessary to improve the system. These factors alone well justified England's poor reputation in education. When to these problems were added the very partial development of technical and scientific education and the rather limited extent of higher education generally, an overall picture emerged of pervasive neglect of an essential national and public resource. Such was the record of nineteenth-century liberalism in education.

The legacy of Victorian policies on education had a profound influence on the development of education in the twentieth century. Many of the typical features established then continued to characterize English education even during the era of the interventionist welfare state, and in many respects the system still suffers from the pattern of relative underdevelopment first inscribed in those years. Technical education has remained rooted in the apprentice model of practical, on-the-job training, marginalized from mainstream education, anti-theoretical and low in status. Attitudes towards mass education have been marked by that Victorian blend of ruling-class paternalism and working-class deference and defensiveness which have contributed much towards the alienation felt by students and parents to state schools and the widespread preference for early school leaving which only began to be rectified at the end of the twentieth century. Our public schools continue to represent a uniquely independent, influential and elitist private sector which has no real foreign equivalents and which contributes to our well-deserved reputation for class division in education. They have done much to undermine the public sector, syphoning off a certain amount of talent from state schools and ensuring that many of those in power who control the state system have no direct personal interest in it. The corollary of this entrenchment of private interests has been a relatively weak commitment to collective or public provision, the legacy of a stubbornly individualist culture.

English education has continued to pride itself on its 'freedom', diversity and independence. 'Among the splendours of the English system', Shirley Williams once remarked, 'are its flexibility, its imagination, and the freedom of the teacher in the classroom.'[1] Whatever the merits of this independence at the local level – and it has led to much creative curriculum development –

it has also come at some cost. The system as a whole has remained multiply fragmented and unsystematic. For a long time it stubbornly resisted modernization and measures to increase standardization and rationality, which on the Continent had long been considered essential for the promotion of equality. The result has been the structural incongruities of the system which are manifest at every level. The survival of voluntary schools, which make up some 30 per cent of all state schools, led to numerous different types of establishment with varying degrees of public accountability. Permissive legislation on comprehensive reform in the 1960s allowed the development of many different models of secondary schooling, encouraging considerable regional disparities. Failure to plan post-16 provision created an uncontrolled institutional diversity which is both wasteful and incomprehensible to the public, and the uncoordinated chaos of private examining bodies further reduced intelligibility and access within the system. Most notably, England delayed instituting a national curriculum years after other European countries with the consequence that, in the absence of those normative expectations which encourage achievement amongst all children, many were not reaching their potential.

There are clearly good reasons for avoiding some of the more monolithic aspects of central control in continental countries, such as the statutory prescription of textbooks. Thus far the liberal tradition has, as its many defenders claim, provided a useful safeguard against overweening central control. However, that same tradition has also been damaging in ways not fully recognized in our political culture. It has led to a fetishization of independence and flexibility at the expense of universalism and equality. It is the very lack of uniformity in our system which is one of the greatest barriers to educational equality. As French sociologist Raymond Boudon has cogently argued, in societies structured by class and other inequalities, the greater the variety of different routes through the education system, the more the 'branching-off' points, the greater the likelihood that differential class expectation, engendered from outside the education system, will structure student choices, even in a situation of ostensible equality of access, so that educational opportunities will be structured along class, race and gender lines.[2] It is not for the state to determine in minute detail what is taught and how in the classroom, but there is certainly a strong argument for intervention by the state, as has occurred in educationally progressive countries such as Sweden, to create more standardized educational structures which promote more uniform expectations amongst students and thus higher standards all round.

In the light of this argument it was promising that the government finally legislated for a national curriculum in 1988. Some form of legislation along these lines was certainly long overdue. However, the paradox was that this modernizing measure, which genuinely broke with past traditions, co-existed with other measures in the same legislation which were designed to give more financial and managerial autonomy to schools and to create a 'market' education system – that is, a system which returned to the *laissez-faire* traditions of the last century. Since then, all governments have sought to extend the quasi-market in education by increasing school choice and diversity and ratcheting up institutional competition through the use of school league tables and other measures. The recent promotion of 'free schools' and academies, institutions largely free from local education authority control, is but a further development of the agenda.

The results of all this over 25 years have been to markedly increase the divisions within the education system, so that England now has more unequal outcomes from schooling than most of the richer countries in the world. Social background has a large effect on how well children achieve, more than in all but 7 of the 34 OECD countries tested in the 2009 PISA survey.[3] Marketization in education has gone so far that many doubt whether a genuinely public system can be maintained at all. It would be a sad irony if the country which was last to create a national education system, and which never quite completed the job, should be the first to dismantle it. It remains to be seen whether, in the name of market liberalism, England again becomes the 'worst educated country in Europe'.

Postscript: Education and State Formation in East Asia

Part I: The State and Development in East Asia

The theory of education and state formation was developed to explain the uneven rise of national education systems in various countries in the West. It did not seek to generalize beyond its limited number of cases. The main countries considered were England, France, Prussia and the United States, with more or less passing consideration given to other German states, Denmark, Italy, the Netherlands and Sweden. The explanations provided were not put forward as a general theory of education and development which could be applied universally across contexts.

However, coterminous and subsequent research by myself[1] and others[2] does suggests that the theory has wider applicability – particularly in conjunction with cognate theories around 'late development,'[3] and 'developmental states'[4] – and is capable of contributing to the understanding of the role of education in economic development and state formation in a wider range of contexts than was originally conceived. This first became evident to me from reviewing the research on the role of education and skills formation in the rapid development of Japan in the decades of state-building following the Meiji Restoration in 1868 and in its post-war reconstruction and subsequent economic 'miracle' in the period after 1945.[5] The so-called East Asian 'tiger economies' or 'mini-dragons' – Hong Kong, South Korea, Singapore and Taiwan – provide further examples.[6] In each case, by general consent of historians and economists, education played a remarkable role in the accelerated process of state formation that preceded and accompanied rapid industrialization and general socio-economic development in the East Asian region, which is also arguably manifest more recently in the equally remarkable rise of China's economy.

In retrospect, then, one may say that the theory of education and state formation is a useful tool for analysing the role of education in state formation and development in new states per se. It works well with the East Asian states precisely because in the relevant period they were undergoing such rapid development. The theory has also been applied to Turkey under Atatürk and more recently,[7] and to the new post-colonial states in Africa where governments have also sought to harness the power of public education to the process of state-building. But in the latter case the efforts have usually been less successful and the linkages between education and state formation have generally been more opaque. If education as an instrument of state formation is essentially a phenomenon of new – or reconstructed – states, by the same token it should not be surprising that the theory has less to say about the developed states where state-building has ceased to be a primary concern. In these states, skills formation (for economic growth) now tends to take precedence over citizen formation in education and training policies and one cannot speak of this in the same way in the broader sense of state formation.[8]

This broader historical and spacial perspective on education and state formation necessarily brings the theory into contact with cognate or contiguous theories that were not very explicitly part of the original theoretical framework of *Education and State Formation*: most obviously, those of the 'late development' school, pioneered by the Russian-born economist Alexander Gerschenkron,[9] and of the various types of nationalism, and particularly those forms of 'reactive' or 'situational' nationalism which developmental state theorists, drawing on Gerschenkron, have used to explain rapid state-led development in East Asia.[10] Theoretically speaking this takes us onto new ground, although it is terrain which should have been explored more fully had it been possible to make the original work more comprehensive than it was.

That theories of nationalism were somewhat underplayed in the original account was attributable to some extent to the sheer complexity of scholarly work in this area, and to the fact that the historical focus of the work was on the period between 1780 and 1870 when forms of liberal and republican civic nationalism predominated in the West – that is, prior to the widespread dissemination of the imperialist and xenophobic types of nationalism which would become predominant thereafter.[11] For the purposes of the original work it was felt that the forces involved in liberal nationalism could be adequately conceptualized within the terms of state formation theory. However, when we come to the Age of Empire it becomes essential to consider the divergent doctrines of nationalism which were developing and shaped different modes of state formation.

It is the purpose of this postscript, therefore, to redress some of the theoretical lacunae in the original work and to explore further the applicability of the theory to new contexts with the benefit of cognate research that has been conducted on late development and developmental states.

State formation and 'late development' theory

State formation theory shares with 'late development' and 'developmental state' theory the basic premise that politics and economics are inseparable. Contrary to the abstract assumptions of neo-classical economics, markets cannot exist without states and history provides scant evidence of the unregulated market as a viable form of society.[12] Not surprisingly, these theories also tend to emphasize the key role of states in the development process.

Education and State Formation argued that one of the critical roles played by western states in development in the early nineteenth century lay in the formation of national education systems. These played a formative part not only in furnishing the skills necessary for economic growth but also more generally in shaping popular attitudes and beliefs in a way which was consistent with the new national identities which states sort to promote. 'Nation-building' was seen as a necessary condition of economic development and schooling had an important role to play in this.

The uneven development of national education systems could be seen to be related to the variable intensity of the state formation process in different countries. Where, as in Britain, state-building had occurred gradually over many centuries, and thus already by the late eighteenth century provided the institutional and ideological foundations for industrialization, less priority was then attached to state formation and the educational aspects of that process, and thus national education systems developed relatively slowly. However, some other countries, which lacked this long prior history of successful state-building, required a rapid and compacted process of state formation to create the conditions for economic development, and in these countries education was seen as peculiarly important to that process. Such countries tended in consequence to make deliberate and concerted efforts to create national education systems. Educational development was often closely associated with growing nationalist sentiments, and systems became fully fledged considerably earlier than in Britain, as I demonstrated earlier.

Three historical factors were particularly associated with this accelerated process of state formation in the West in the late eighteenth and early nineteenth centuries. One was the existence of external military threats, or territorial conflicts, which often propelled victim nations, such as Prussia after the Napoleonic invasion, into vehemently nationalistic responses and deliberate actions to strengthen their state machines.[13] Another was the occurrence of major internal transformations resulting from revolution, as in France, or from a successful struggle for national independence, as in North America. In each case the country concerned emerged from major conflagrations with an urgent task of national reconstruction, not only to repair the ruins of war but also to establish a new social order which would reflect the principles for which the struggle was originally undertaken. Lastly, there were situations where countries which were significantly underdeveloped in relation to leading countries in the region sought to 'catch up' economically through a process described by Barrington Moore as 'forced' industrialization.[14] In each type of case, development relied heavily on state action and schooling was one of the major spheres through which states sought to act.

The argument in *Education and State Formation* drew extensively on the theories of state formation and nationalism elaborated by writers in the Marxist tradition, such as Eric Hobsbawn, Perry Anderson and Tom Nairn, as well as on explanations of the peculiarities of British liberalism from within the social liberal and social democratic traditions, by, amongst others, David Marquand and Andrew Gamble. All of these accounts utilized versions of what may be called the 'logic of priority' thesis which asserts that Britain, as the first country to industrialize, was unique, and that 'successor' developing countries necessarily had to do things differently. Only passing reference was made to 'late development' theory and the works of Alexander Gerschenkron. However, the main tenets of the theory owed considerably, if inadvertently and indirectly, to the latter's original elaboration of arguments around the nature of 'late' development.

Writing in the post-Second World War period, and strongly influenced by his observations of development in Russia, Gerschenkron provided a highly influential account of the nature of economic development in what he called 'backward countries', which for him included virtually all countries industrializing after Britain. In his view, countries which were significantly underdeveloped economically with reference to the leading powers typically suffered from a number of crucial difficulties which they had to surmount in order to 'catch up'. A reliable, stable and disciplined industrial labour force tended to be in short supply and had to be developed in short order. There was a scarcity of entrepreneurial experience and skills which had to be rectified if new industries were to develop. And, most importantly, in the absence of the long-term capital accumulation such as had occurred through colonialism in countries such as Britain, there was a paucity of capital for industrial investment. The more underdeveloped a country was in these respects, according to Gerschenkron, the more concerted and dramatic had to be its mode of development if it were to catch up and compete with the advanced economies. As he wrote in *Economic Backwardness in Historical Perspective*, 'The more delayed the industrial development of a country, the more explosive was the great spurt of industrialisation, if and when it came.'[15]

Based on his observations of 'late' industrialization in France, Germany, Japan and Russia, Gerschenkron argued that reversing a history of 'economic underdevelopment' typically involved different means from those prevailing amongst early industrializers, such as Britain. Industrialization tended to be more rapid; it usually involved the creation of large-scale plants and firms, often organized through cartels; and it had to involve swift technology transfer which depended on the rapid generation of human capital. Typically, late industrializing countries could not rely on markets and individual entrepreneurs to achieve these conditions and needed greater support from institutions and from the state. The banks played a major role in providing institutional support in countries such as Germany. However, where, as in Japan, civil society was insufficiently developed to throw up 'organically' institutions, such as banks, which would play the key roles in directing investment capital to industry, the state had to play a more pronounced role. State-led development was a natural response, therefore, to underdevelopment, and the more backward a country was the more it would rely on the state. As Gerschenkron wrote,

> the more backward a country, the more likely its industrialisation was to proceed under some organised direction; depending on the degree of backwardness, the seat of such direction could be found in investment banks, in investment banking operating under the aegis of the state, or in bureaucratic controls. So viewed, the industrial history of Europe appears not as a series of repetitions of the 'first' industrialisation, but as an orderly system of graduated deviations from that industrialisation.[16]

Gerschenkron's account accurately identified the importance of the state and state-formed institutions in the development of countries such as Prussia, Japan and Russia. It was also correct in pointing out that 'later' developing countries have been able to industrialize much more rapidly than the first-comer industrializing nations. As Paul Morris has observed, from a later historical vantage point, it took Britain 58 years to double its real per capita income from 1780, at the start of the industrialization process.[17] The United States did it in 47 years from 1839; Japan in 34 years from 1900; and South Korea in 11 years from 1966. With the advance of information and communications technologies (ICT), this acceleration of the development process is even more evident now than when Gerschenkron first noted it. Whereas Meiji reformers in Japan had to send engineers to Britain, France and the United States to collect and bring home the secrets of western technology to kick start Japan's industrial revolution, knowledge codification though ICT now permits the virtual transfer of whole factory systems, albeit still requiring the skilled workers to operate efficiently.[18]

Gerschenkron was also right to emphasize how far the enhanced role of the state in late industrialization diverged from the paradigm case of British industrialization, or at least from the free-market, free-trade version of this which has become enshrined in neo-classical economics. The British liberal political economy of Adam Smith, Jeremy Bentham, John Stuart Mill, David Ricardo and the Manchester school, with its celebration of free markets, advocacy of free trade and opposition to extensive state intervention in the economy and society generally, had gained credence from Britain's global industrial dominance during the Victorian era and thus became a leading force both politically and later in the emerging discipline of liberal or neo-classical economics. The latter offered a paradigm of development based on the British case – or at least on its reading of the later phase of the British industrialization process – which emphasized the market role of private capital and entrepreneurialism in development and which downplayed the role of the state. Gerschenkron's thesis about the role of the state in later development thus pointed to discrepancies between 'classical' and 'late' development processes which he was obliged to explain by reference to the different conditions pertaining amongst these later developing states.

However, other accounts of the British development case cast doubt on how far the means for development adopted by later developing states did in fact diverge so much from the British case in the use of state power. Mid-Victorian Britain was indeed an exceptionally market-oriented and *laissez-faire* society; according to Eric Hobsbawn, the most *laissez-faire* society that had ever existed until that time.[19] It advocated the most limited role of the state in both society and economy and, since the 1850s at least, had indeed practised free trade, at least for a few decades until the turn of the century. This ideology was adopted because it well suited the interests of the dominant world power when it had already gone through its early phase of economic development. By this time, Britain could afford liberal economics which generally only benefits the powerful.[20] However, as Ha-Joon Chang has recently argued, it was only relatively late in its development that Britain espoused the classic free-market, free-trade policies which were later to become the liberal economic orthodoxy. Before Britain had secured its industrial dominance, it had for centuries been a mercantilist state which used the full armoury of state power to boost its fledgling manufacturing economy and to strengthen its position in world trade. It had pursued its mercantilist objectives by imposing tariffs to protect infant industries and to promote manufacturing exports, by exploiting its naval power to dominate trading routes, and by using diplomatic and military force to break open foreign markets to British trade, as it did most ruthlessly in India and China. The myths of liberal economics and development policy occlude this history but it is one well understood by contemporary developing states and also by those 'second wave' industrializing countries such as Germany and Japan, which, in practice, operated not according to the gospel of Adam Smith but according to the more practical and relevant prescriptions of the contemporary German theorist of the national economy, Friederich List.[21] The German historical school of economics, to which List belonged, was in many countries much better known than the classical school of political economy and much more influential.[22]

Friederich List and national economics

Friederich List was born in 1789, at the outset of the French Revolution, and grew up in Württemberg during the period of rising nationalism in the German states following the Napoleonic invasion of Prussia in 1806. He became an ardent liberal nationalist, arguing for a German national parliament, army and judiciary, and agitating against customs barriers between German states. By 1822, having served and then been forced to resign as a deputy to the Württemberg chamber, he had become known as a republican radical, and even, according to Greenfeld,[23] as a 'Jacobin republican revolutionary', and was subsequently imprisoned and then exiled to the United States (from 1825 to 1832). It was there that he became familiar with the works and policies of Alexander Hamilton, the country's first trade secretary, who was the first to lay out systematically the case for the protection of infant industries. This inspired List's interest in national economics. On his return to Leipzig in 1832, he became a vocal advocate of the state extension of the German railway system and of the Zollverein, the customs union which would help to unify German states into a common trading market. Not originally a trade protectionist, he became convinced, not least after Britain's adoption of free trade in 1846, that German manufactures could not develop under the free-trade system that advantaged British interests over those of the less developed continental nations. It was in this context that he wrote his famous work *National Systems of Political Economy* (1841),[24] which provided the first systematic account of the principles of the 'national economy', and which came to be recognized as the major alternative to the prevailing liberal theories of economics.

List was mainly motivated by practical concerns about ways of developing the economies of German states through building productive capacity in manufacturing and through the export of manufactured goods. These he rightly understood to be the key to economic strength in the world market. Unlike Adam Smith and his school, who relied mostly on deductive reasoning in the development of their economic theories, List developed his ideas through an historical inductive method, analysing the way in which states had developed their economies in the past and drawing general conclusions from this. Nevertheless, his analysis, based on the historical evidence, led to a systematic theory of national economics, laid out in the second book of his masterpiece, which diverged in important respects from the dominant ideas of Smith, which List criticized explicitly in his work.

For List, Adam Smith had concerned himself too exclusively with the motivation of individuals and the operations of firms, and had failed to understand the operation of the national economy as a whole, with its various different sectors, and the role of states as agents of national economic development. Smith, argued List, nullified 'nationality and state power [and exalted] individualism to the position of author of all effective power'. 'This', he claimed, was 'nothing more than...a mere shop-keepers'...theory – not a scientific doctrine showing how the productive powers of an entire nation can be called into existence, increased, maintained and preserved – for the special benefit of its civilization, welfare, might, continuance and independence.'[25]

Smith's theories, according to List, may have served Britain's interests as an already dominant economic power, but they had little to say about how nations actually began to develop their economies, including how Britain achieved its early manufacturing pre-eminence. For List, this could not be comprehended purely from an analysis of the market interaction of individuals, but only through an historical understanding of power and particularly of the uses of state power. As with the mercantilists before him, List recognized the indissoluble links between markets and the state, and economics and power. The source of economic development was the nurturing of productive capacity and this, as List explains, depends on power:

> Power is more important than wealth. And why? Simply because national power is a dynamic force by which new productive forces are opened out, and because the forces of production are the trees on which wealth grows, and because the tree which bears the fruit is of greater value than the fruit itself. Power is of more importance than wealth because a nation, by means of power, is enabled not only to open up new productive sources but to maintain itself in possession of former and recently acquired wealth, and because the reverse of power – namely feebleness – leads the relinquishment of all that we possess, not of acquired wealth alone. But of our power of production, of our civilization, of our freedom, nay of our national independence, into the hands of those who surpass us in might, as is abundantly attested by the history of the Italian Republics, of the Hanseatic League, of the Belgians, the Dutch, the Spaniards, and the Portuguese.[26]

List's was a realist's account of the ways and means of development in his period and those preceding. Adam Smith could largely take for granted the role of the state, institutions and international power in the achievement of British economic dominance, since such dominance had already been achieved, and since these processes of initial state formation belonged already to the past in his country. List could not afford to ignore such harsh realities since they still applied to his own native German lands for which they appeared as preconditions for development. For List, living in a German region still politically weak and fragmented into numerous small principalities, and lacking many of the institutions which only a long period of state formation could furnish, the political preconditions for development were necessarily very apparent. He understood the importance of state formation since he recognized that 'the unity of the nation forms the fundamental condition of lasting national prosperity'.[27] As he wrote at greater length, and clearly in contradiction of Smithian individualism,

> industry and thrift, innovation and enterprise, on the part of individuals, have not yet accomplished ought of importance where they are not sustained by municipal liberty, by suitable public institutions and laws, by state administration and foreign policy, but above all by the unity and power of the nation.[28]

List perhaps sometimes overplayed his differences with Smith (he did after all support free trade under certain circumstances), and he no doubt exaggerated the extent of Smithian individualism, since Smith, after all, did support state intervention for certain key public goods, such as education, just as List himself did. Indeed, as the economic historian Giovanni Arrighi[29] has recently reminded us, Smith also provided, if only in outline, an historical sociology of national economic development, and was certainly concerned with the role of the state in this. He believed that the state had important roles in underpinning the market, not least in relation to the maintenance of individual and national security, the administration of justice, the provision of physical infrastructures for trade and communications, the regulation of money and credit, and the provision of mass education. And despite his nineteenth-century reputation as a doctrinaire *laissez-faire*, free-trade liberal, he was not even invariably in favour of free trade, especially when its sudden adoption would jeopardize large sections of employment in any given economy.

However, there is no denying that List's was a fundamentally different approach to the question of national economic development from that of Smith, who, in his more prescriptive writings, often took for granted Britain's early development – including the long march of the institutions, the aggressive struggle for naval supremacy and the slow process of capital accumulation. Smith's doctrine of the minimal state and free trade, and his overriding belief in the beneficence of the 'hidden hand' of the market, may well have served Britain well at the time of its economic pre-eminence, but it was of little use to less developed countries. Whilst it is no wonder that powerful economies have given pride of place to Smith's liberal economics in the ensuing centuries, it is also not surprising that backward countries, struggling to get on the ladder of development, such as Germany and Japan in the nineteenth century, and the East Asian states in the twentieth, have often found List a more useful practical guide.[30] Like List before them, they have often tended to see the powerful states' prescriptions of free-trade and free-market economics for underdeveloped countries as so much hypocrisy, since countries such as Britain and the United States did not practise them themselves in their own periods of development.

List himself was quite savage in his denunciations of Victorian Britain's attempts to foist free trade on other countries when they were not ready for it, and when it could only harm their nascent manufacturing industries. Rich countries which preached it were simply trying to 'kick away the ladder... in order to deprive others of the means of climbing up after'.[31] He recognized this as a logical policy for strong states from a national point of view, but argued that weaker states could not accept it. 'Any nation', he wrote,

> which by means of protective duties and restrictions on navigation has raised up her manufacturing power and her navigation to such a degree of development that no other nation can sustain competition with her, can do nothing wiser than to throw away the ladders of her greatness, to preach to other nations the benefit of free trade, and to declare in penitent tones that she wandered into the paths of error, and has now for the first time succeeded in discovering the truth.[32]

What gives List's work its power and resonance in terms of development theory is its historical analysis of actual cases of development, including all of the major powers of the time. What he shows is that most of the great powers had used tariff protection to good effect at key moments in building up their manufacturing industries, and that those that had not, such as the Netherlands in its period of decline, had often paid a price. What is more, Britain and other strong powers had used the full might of their navies and militaries, as well as their powers of diplomacy, in gaining access to new markets and in ensuring their trading supremacy.

The 'source and origins of England's industry and commercial greatness', List argued, 'could be traced mainly to the breeding of sheep and to the woollen manufacture'.[33] The Tudor and Stuart monarchs had used protectionist measures to support both textile manufacture and shipbuilding, including, at various points, by imposing high tariffs or outright bans on imports of finished woollen goods, and by banning the export of unfinished cloth. Dutch wool manufacturers were driven to ruin by these measures,[34] but textile manufacturing industries grew so strongly in England that by James I's reign their products constituted nine-tenths of all exports. The woollen industry, which had given the English aristocracy an early interest in manufacturing, in turn stimulated the mining of coal, the export of which gave rise to coastal trade and fisheries, both of which constituted the basis of naval power and made possible the passing of the Navigation Acts, a measure which gave Britain a near monopoly of sea-borne transport of coal. These acts, argued List, secured the basis of Britain's maritime supremacy, which in turn led to the expansion of English trade with Northern Europe; an increase in contraband trade with Spain; an increase in herring and whale fisheries; and finally the conquest of the Caribbean Islands.

During the eighteenth century, Britain continued to use its political, naval and military power to advance its manufactures and trade in colonial and other markets. The 1703 Northern Treaty with Portugal excluded the Dutch and Germans from Iberian trade and made Portugal dependent on Britain, allowing Britain to build up its commercial wealth, which would allow the later development of the Asian Empire. At the same time, Britain continued to protect its own industries against foreign competition. The Wool Act of 1699 had prohibited the export of wool products from the colonies – a measure that had effectively killed off the Irish wool industry. Subsequently, Britain had tried to prevent the development of manufactures in the American colonies (with Adam Smith's approval), and did ban the import of cotton and silk goods from India, thus devastating the once-thriving calico industry in Bengal. List reports that in 1770, William Pitt the Elder, made uneasy by the first manufacturing attempts of the New Englanders, declared that 'the colonies should not be permitted to manufacture so much as a horseshoe nail'.[35]

List acknowledges that many factors contributed to Britain's early commercial and industrial success, including its insular geography, its early development of national institutions and the energy and 'love of liberty' of its people. However, the main point of his, inevitably selective, historical sketch of British development is to illustrate the great economic benefits it derived from the operation of state policy in support of the development of manufacturing. According to List, Britain became economically powerful by fostering 'productive power' (manufacturing capacity); using protective measures to nurture productive capacity, and particularly of infant manufacturing industries; importing only agricultural and raw materials and exporting nothing but manufactured goods; monopolizing exports to colonies and getting their imports on preferential terms; controlling navigation and trade; making wars only in the interest of trade; and granting freedom of trade only when in the interests of the national economy. These 'maxims of state policy,' which List derives from the English case, represented, for him, a kind of 'realpolitik' of the means for development. Furthermore, he claims that they are observable in most other cases of successful development, and that they are notably absent in cases where countries have declined.

List is primarily known for his critique of free trade and for his advocacy of protectionism to assist the development of infant manufacturing industries. However, his views on trade protection were, in fact, rather less ideological than is commonly thought, and were more guided by pragmatism than economic doctrine. He favoured whatever was good for the national economy at a given stage of development. Free trade, he argued, was beneficial for primitive economies wishing to export their primary goods. It was also clearly beneficial for those sectors in national economies which were sufficiently developed to compete successfully with foreign producers. Between countries at similar levels of development, free trade was the ideal. Furthermore, although he clearly resented the damage that British free trade did to his own region, List was clearly quite aware that it was a logical and beneficial policy for Victorian Britain. His emphasis on the virtues of protectionism derived from his own observations of what was needed by various continental economies, including his own, at their own stage of development.

However, he was far from advocating protectionism for all developing countries and in all their industries. Only manufacturing benefited from protection, he argued, and then only when it had developed to a point where it was possible, after a period of protection, to compete effectively with foreign producers. As he wrote, 'Protection is only beneficial to the prosperity of the nation so far as it corresponds with the degree of the nation's industrial development.'[36] In his view, so long as protective tariffs were applied moderately and in appropriate cases only, they could be beneficial and should be adopted in the long-term interests of national development. Contra Adam Smith, he did not believe that protectionism necessarily bred inefficiency, since competition amongst domestic firms could militate against this.

The myths of neo-liberal development theory

Friederich List's national economics has had powerful influences on countries developing after his time, as we shall see when we come to consider Japan and the East Asian tigers. It also influenced the leaders of the United States during the nineteenth century and arguably thereafter. However, in the post-Second World War era, and particularly since the 1980s, it has been Adam Smith and the tradition of liberal classical economics which has prevailed as the guiding economic ideology of the major powers. In the latter period, neo-classical economic theory has largely dominated amongst the international agencies which regulate the world economy, including the World Bank, the International Monetary Fund and the World Trade Organization.

These organizations, largely dominated by the interests of the United States and the major economic powers, have played a major part in setting the parameters for development, and they have done this almost entirely on the basis of the neo-liberal perspectives on free-trade and free-market economics. The economic policies which they favour, and which they have sought to impose on developing countries with increasing vigour, have been the policies of the so-called 'Washington Consensus'. These have generally prioritized low inflation and balanced budgets, the latter to be achieved if necessary through often draconian Structural Adjustment Policies which reduce state expenditure. They have also advocated free-trade policies, which involve the removal of import tariffs, export subsidies and restriction on capital movement, and opposed state interventionist economic policies, such as industrial policy. Wherever possible, they have sought to open up markets in developing countries to rich country exports and capital investment. In its recent rounds of negotiations, the World Trade Organization has sought to reinforce intellectual property rights and to encourage free trade in services (through the General Agreement in Trade of Services). The policies are clearly in the interests of the most developed countries. However, the claim that is made is that such policies are good for developing countries. List would clearly have scorned such claims, as do many of the currently developing countries.

Neo-liberal development policy is based on a number of abiding myths which world development agencies have come to believe, even if they were first proclaimed with outright cynicism, and which substantially obfuscate serious debate about what works in development policy. The myths are firstly that the rich countries followed such policies in their own paths to development, and secondly that they actually work for developing countries now.

The first myth, that today's rich countries developed through liberal economic policies, is easily dismantled. As Ha-Joon Chang has shown,[37] almost all countries which are now rich have at crucial points in their development adopted various forms of state intervention in their economies and in trade which go directly against the prescriptions of liberal development theory. These have often included substantial state intervention in industrial policy and forms of 'strategic trading' which include protectionist trade policies of various sorts, as well as measures to maintain currency competitiveness. From the longer historical vantage point, this is even more evident today than it was in the mid-nineteenth century when List first examined the issue. A focus on the history of tariffs makes the point fairly clearly.

The liberal myth claims that after Britain abandoned trade protection in 1846, the superiority of free-market and free-trade policies became apparent. Other countries then began to establish free trade after 1860, and by 1870 a liberal world order had been perfected based on *laissez-faire* industrial policies at home; low barriers to international flows of goods, capital and labour; and macro-economic stability, nationally and internationally guaranteed by the Gold Standard. Things started to go wrong with the onset of the First World War and the abandonment of free trade in the 1930s, led by the Smoot-Hawley tariff in 1930 in the United States. However, after the Second World War a liberal world economy was gradually re-established which, with the onset of a new wave of globalization in the late 1970s, brought increasing world prosperity.

As Chang shows, this picture is substantially distorted. Britain had kept high tariffs on most imported manufactures until the 1820s (averaging 45–55 per cent) but did later lead the way in liberalizing trade with the repeal of the Corn Laws in 1846. But it was not until the 1860s that a free-trade regime was fully in place (with only 48 dutiable items in 1869 compared with 1 146 in 1848, according to Chang).[38] In the following two decades, many leading economies did begin to reduce their tariffs, although in many cases these remained substantial. Average tariff rates on manufactured goods in 1875 were low in Switzerland (4–6 per cent), Sweden (3–5 per cent) and Germany (4–6 per cent), but still moderately high in Austria (15–20 per cent), Denmark (15–20 per cent), France (12–15 per cent) and Spain (15–20 per cent). This period of relatively free trade did not, in any case, last long. Tariff reform became a big issue in Britain again by the turn of the century, as in many other countries, and by 1913, 10 of the 14 leading economies again had tariffs averaging over 10 per cent, with only Britain and the Netherlands remaining strongly committed to free trade. Tariffs went higher still in the 1930s, and even by 1950 there remained 5 countries out of the 14 with tariffs averaging over 15 per cent (Austria, France, Germany, Italy and Britain). On Chang's account it would appear that the golden age of free trade was both rather short-lived and very partial.

However, it is the United States, which in the post-Second World War era has been the most vociferous advocate of free trade, that provides the most graphic rebuttal of the myth. Economic historian Paul Bairoch has called the United States 'the mother country and bastion of modern protectionism'[39] and it is easy to see why. The US economy grew up behind protectionist barriers and to this day has never fully, itself, embraced free trade. At the time of independence, southern agricultural interests opposed protection but northern manufacturing was in favour. The North won out. Alexander Hamilton, mentor of List, championed protection of infant industries in the 1790s, and the first federal tariff act in 1879 took tariffs to an average of 12.5 per cent, after which they rose even higher. By 1916 the average tariff on manufactured goods was already 35 per cent, so that the notorious Smoot-Hawley Tariff Act, which raised them to 40 per cent, was hardly a watershed.[40] The period 1846–61 had been one of modest protectionism but the victory of the North and the manufacturing interests in the Civil War ensured that the United States remained the most ardent practitioner of infant industry protectionism until well after the Second World War. Only during the period 1913–23 was there a regime of low protection, and this was reversed soon after. By 1950 the United States still had tariffs averaging 14 per cent.[41]

Contrary to the myth, the United States did not follow a liberal developmental path: it industrialized behind tariff walls. Protection was vital to the development of many of its key industries, including textiles, and iron and steel – indeed, subsidies still protect these industries. The United States only became converted to free trade, like Britain, when it had acquired global economic dominance after the Second World War, and even then it has maintained various forms of trade protection. These typically include voluntary export constraints, import quotas on textiles and clothes, subsidies for agriculture, including cotton, and unilateral trade sanctions (against so-called 'dumping').

From a vantage point 70 years after he was writing, it seems clear that List was substantially right in his main claims about the importance of state protection for the early development of manufacturing economies. Practically no states (perhaps excepting the Netherlands) have developed successfully without adopting such state-led protectionist policies at key points in their development. As Chang has argued,

> developed countries did not get where they are now through policies and institutions that they recommend to developing countries today. Most of them actively used 'bad' trade policies, such as infant industry protection and export subsidies – practises that these days are frowned up, if not actively banned, by the WTO.[42]

Given that rich countries did not develop successfully through liberal development policies, it should not be altogether surprising if the currently developing countries do not thrive through these policies. The second myth of the dominant world development agencies is that liberal market and free-trade policies are good for the development of poorer countries now. The evidence seems to contradict this myth. During the period from 1960 to 1980, when world trade regimes allowed protectionist policies and when many developing countries were still utilizing import substitution strategies, developing countries grew at an average rate of 3 per cent per annum. This was rather better, as Chang points out, than the average growth rate of 1–1.5 per cent for newly developing countries during the period 1820–1917. After the imposition of neo-liberal policies by the international bodies since the early 1980s, developing countries fared rather worse than in the earlier period. According to Chan, only in 13 of the 88 developing countries did average growth rates rise more than 0.1 per cent between the periods 1960–80 and 1980–2000.[43] The countries which have grown well during the later period have mostly been in Asia – and India aside – most of them East Asian. These, as we shall see in the next section, are precisely the countries which have, for the most part, ignored the prescriptions of liberal development policy.

State formation and development in East Asia

East Asia provides the outstanding example of a region which has achieved relatively successful economic and social development during the recent era of globalization. Not only have many of the East Asian states, and notably Japan and the four tiger economies of South Korea, Taiwan, Singapore and Hong Kong, achieved unprecedented levels of economic growth; they have also distributed the social benefits of growth quite widely. Income inequality was relatively low at the outset of industrialization and remained low, in most cases, relative to most developed countries until quite recently; poverty has declined substantially; and living standards and life quality have risen dramatically, with declining population growth and increased life expectancy. In 1960, South Korea's gross domestic product (GDP) per capita was similar to the Sudan's, and Taiwan's was similar to Zaire's.[44] Now these countries are amongst the most developed in the world. This regional phenomenon has not only encouraged countless studies of its particular developmental path(s) but has also promoted policy-makers in many other developing countries to examine the region for lessons that may be learnt and policies that may be transferred to their own countries.

Economic growth since 1960 in East Asia, and particularly in Japan and the tiger economies, has indeed been dramatic. During the 25 years from 1960, Japan and the tigers grew on average at over 8 per cent per annum.[45] Japan went into recession in the early 1990s but the tiger economies were still going strong between 1990 and 1995, with Korea registering an average annual growth of 7.2 per cent, Singapore of 8.7 per cent and Hong Kong of 5.6 per cent.[46] All East Asian economies were affected by the 1997 Asian financial crisis, although China, Singapore and Taiwan rather less than the others, but they generally subsequently returned to rapid growth, not quite at their formal levels in most cases, but at over 12 per cent in China. Before the rise of China, Japan and the tiger economies clearly had the most impressive records of sustained growth, in the Japanese case from the 1950s to 1990 and the tigers from 1960 to 1997. However, other East Asian economies have also performed well, including recently, of course, China. According to the World Bank's influential volume, *East Asian Economic Miracle*, eight High Performing Asian Economies (HPAEs), including Japan, the four tigers and the East Asian newly industrialized countries, Indonesia, Malaysia and Thailand, all grew exceptionally fast. Their average rate of growth between 1965 and 1990 was 5.3 per cent per annum, compared with 2.3 per cent in the rest of East Asia, 2.3 per cent in the OECD, 1.9 per cent in Latin America and 0.1 per cent in sub-Saharan Africa. The HPAEs grew at twice the rate of the rest of East Asia and at 25 times the rate of sub-Saharan Africa.[47]

Rapid economic growth in the HPAEs has generally been accompanied by rising real incomes, reduced poverty, declining inequality and improved quality of life. Real incomes per capita in Japan and the tigers increased fourfold between 1960 and 1998. The HPAEs were also the only countries during the period 1965–90 to have achieved both high growth and declining income inequality, with Japan and the four tigers recording the lowest levels (measured on the Gini coefficient) out of 14 countries in the region.[48] Income inequality, measured by the Gini coefficient, has fluctuated in some countries, increasing, for instance, in South Korea during the 1980s,[49] and it varies significantly between the different tiger economies, with Taiwan generally being the most equal[50] and Singapore the least, the latter with

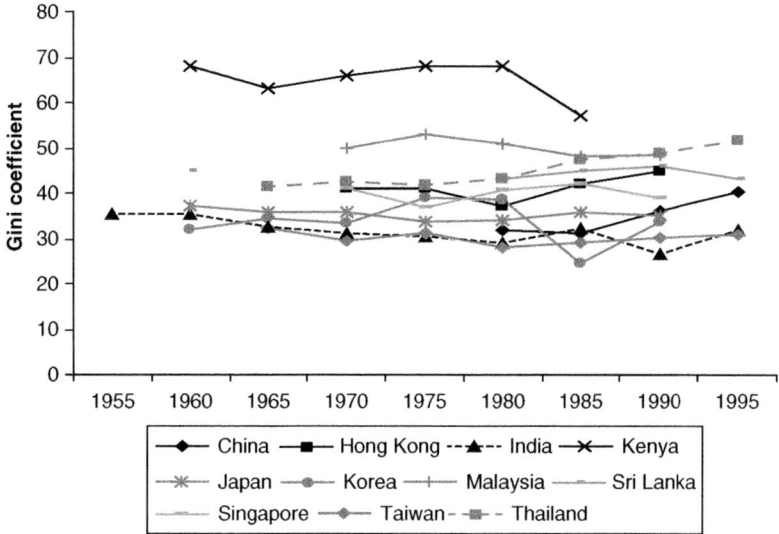

Figure P.1 Trends in income inequality in Asia

levels rather similar to the UK on some counts (see Figure P.1).[51] However, during the period 1960–90, Hong Kong, South Korea, Taiwan, Singapore and Malaysia all saw overall declines in their Gini coefficient.[52]

The relatively equitable distribution of the wealth from economic growth in many East Asian countries has been reflected in reduced levels of poverty. The tigers have generally reduced unemployment and poverty to quite low levels. The World Bank also cites the cases of Indonesia and Malaysia where the numbers of those living in absolute poverty declined, respectively, during the period from 1966 to 1990 from 58 per cent to 17 per cent and from 37 per cent to less than 5 per cent.[53] Growth with equity in the East Asian economies has also coincided with substantial declines in fertility rates, improved health and increased longevity. Life expectancy in the HPAEs rose from 56 years in 1960 to 71 years in 1990.[54] By 1995, life expectancy at birth was above 75 years in Japan, Hong Kong and Singapore, 71.7 years in South Korea and 69 years in China, against a world average of 63.6 years and an average for the developing world of 62 years.[55]

In terms of the more general indicators of well-being measured by the Human Development Index, Japan and the other HPAEs also appear to rate highly. Japan, Hong Kong, South Korea and Singapore were all in the top 20 per cent of the 174 countries for which the index was estimated by the United Nations Development Programme in 1998.[56]

Explanations of rapid growth with equity in East Asia.

Post-1960 rapid growth with equity is, to a large extent, a regional phenomenon. No region other than East Asia has been so successful during this period. Not surprisingly, therefore, much energy has been devoted by economists and sociologists to explaining the whys and wherefores of the East Asian 'economic miracle' as a regional phenomenon. The analyses offered do not necessarily assume that the countries involved adopted identical paths of development, and indeed it is quite clear that they differ in important ways. However, a regional phenomenon would seem to require an explanation that works at the regional level, so many explanations have focused on the commonalities of these countries. Overall we can say that these explanations focus predominantly on six areas: culture; colonial legacies; geography and geopolitics; historical timing; and policies, the latter covering both economic and social policies, including education. By far the most prominent amongst the types of explanation are those which focus on economic and human capital formation policies.

Cultural and institutional legacies

Cultural explanations of development in East Asia tend to focus on common aspects of Asian culture and values, and, most specifically, on the historical legacy of Confucianism. Various attempts have been made to associate these with identifiable and distinctive forms of what is sometimes called 'Asian' or 'Confucian' capitalism. Some scholars have argued that the stress on cooperation and group loyalty or harmony (*wa* in Japanese), said to be fundamental to Asian values, has been essential to the success of the large enterprises in Japan and elsewhere in Asia. In particular, group cooperation is said to be fundamental to the forms of 'just-in-time' manufacturing which were pioneered by Toyota in Japan after the 1960s and subsequently copied, more or less successfully, across the developed world.[57] To others, Asian values account more broadly for a whole form of capitalist organization. Sugihara argues that Japan developed and exported through East Asia a labour-intensive form of economic development, described as 'an industrious revolution', which contrasted with the capital intensive 'Industrial Revolution' of the West and which was more suited to the cultural traditions of the region.[58] The notion of a 'flying geese' pattern of 'late development', led by Japan and diffused throughout the region, has also been adopted widely in the literature.[59] Lucien Pye has pointed to the cultural roots of other key features of East Asian capitalism, including the reliance on market networks (*guanxi*), taking the long-run view, seeking market share rather than profits, and delaying profits and aggressively saving for the future.[60] Likewise, analyses of the role of the state and government have stressed the prevalence of the 'strong state' in East Asia[61] and of the importance placed on education.[62]

These accounts have undoubtedly been important in shaping analyses of East Asian economic and social development. However, the stress on cultural values as a primary determinant inevitably runs up against certain problems. Confucian values cannot provide a sufficient explanation of why successful development has occurred not only in predominantly Confucian societies but also in others (Malaysia, Indonesia, Thailand) where other religions predominate. An alternative recourse to 'Asian' values is often not very convincing since these are inevitably so diverse that they provide little explanatory purchase. Cultural values, Confucian or Asian, also say little about why rapid development in East Asia occurred when it did and not before. Older nineteenth-century traditions of sociological study of oriental societies tended to emphasize the centralized Confucian state as a barrier to development, as in Marx's notion of 'oriental despotism'. It is also not clear how far 'Asian values' can be seen as a determining factor and how far they have been used as post-hoc justification by certain Asian leaders, such as Singapore's Lee Kuan Yew, wishing to defend particular forms of state power.[63] Although it is often the case that cultural explanations stress the historically enduring and unchanging nature of cultures, cultures do, of course, change, and it is quite possible that the particular cultural forms evolving in modern Asia have been conducive to certain aspects of development, as Tu claims.[64] However, such anti-essentialist and contingent readings of culture inevitably face larger problems in explaining a contemporaneous regional phenomenon, such as rapid development in post-1960 East Asia.

Another explanation based on historical factors relates to colonial legacies, but this stresses the importance of institutions more than culture. In their writings on Japan and the East Asian region generally, Johnson and Cummings[65] have both consistently stressed the formative influence of Japan, both through the example set to later developing states in East Asia by the Meiji Restoration, Asia's first successful industrialization project, and through the effects of the subsequent history of Japanese colonialism in Korea and Taiwan. However, it is Atul Kohli who has propounded this argument most forcefully in relation to Korea.[66] His claim is that Japanese colonialism in Korea between 1905 and 1945 had a much more transformative effect than European colonialisms typically had. It not only developed the infrastructures of the modern state but also promoted the development of efficient agriculture and early industries. After independence, Kohli argues, Japan continued to be viewed as a developmental model by South Korean leaders and provided substantial advice, expertise and investment, which was decisive in the rapid re-industrialization after the devastation of the Korean Civil War.

The legacy of Japanese state-building during the colonial period was substantial. According to Kohli, 'the Korean state was transformed under Japanese influence from a relatively corrupt and ineffective agrarian bureaucracy into a highly authoritarian, penetrating organization, capable of controlling and penetrating Korean society.'[67] Before the Japanese colonial conquest, the old Yi dynasty of Chosun had been disintegrating – hobbled by the reactionary and entrenched Yangban landed aristocracy and with such weak state control that it had problems collecting taxes. After 1910 the Japanese colonial authorities broke the power of the Yangban elite and built a modern state bureaucracy which penetrated deep into Korean society and provided the organizational capacity for development. The architect of the reformed state was Ito Hirobumi, the former premier in Meiji Japan, who had set up the Prussian-style bureaucracy there and instigated Tokyo University as a school for bureaucrats. Ito, according to Kohli, performed the same feat in Korea. In short order he created a new, efficient and relatively uncorrupt state bureaucracy in Korea, with Japanese officials occupying top positions and Koreans occupying half of the official posts at the lower levels, and a new colonial police force. The latter, like the state bureaucracy, was controlled by the Japanese but with about half of the positions occupied by Koreans. It had extensive powers, including over tax collection and labour disputes. An elaborate spy system was also set up as an adjunct to the police, which gave the state extraordinary surveillance powers over Korean society down to the lowest levels. Kohli, whilst acknowledging the repressive nature of the regime, refers to this as the development of the 'cohesive state'.

The colonial Japanese state also contributed significantly to economic development in Korea. Unlike many colonizing states, such as Britain in India, which sought to restrict the growth of any competitor industries in their colonies, Japanese colonialism, argues Kohli, saw industrial development in neighbouring Korea as an extension of its own industrial strength and was therefore keen to support it. Initially, the colonial state concentrated on developing agriculture through land reform, legal reform of property rights, and improvements in irrigation, drainage and the use of fertilizers. Rice and other agricultural production grew substantially and agricultural productivity increased overall at an average of 2 per cent per annum during the colonial period. Koreans received little benefit from this since the additional produce was consumed by the Japanese or given to exports. But this left a technological legacy which could be built on later. Subsequently, the colonial state also developed the local infrastructure, with new roads and railways, and improved communications, and set up various industries in mineral extraction, tobacco, ginseng and power generation. Many of these industries were state owned or state controlled, often involving major Japanese companies, such as Mitsui, which got the ginseng franchise. But Korean entrepreneurs were also often involved. In fact, several of the modern Korean *chaebols* started life under Japanese tutelage. The Japanese colonial state also used many of the policy levers – such as import tariffs, export subsidies, licensing and the encouraging of mass savings through post-office accounts – which were to become the stock in trade for later developmental state leaders. Overall production grew at an impressive 10 per cent p.a. between 1910 and 1940. By the end of the colonial period there were 1.3 million industrial workers, representing 20 per cent of the population. Korea had already begun its industrialization process by the end of the colonial period. By the end of the Korean Civil War some two-thirds of the country's industry had been destroyed and South Korea had to start its industrialization anew. However, according to Kohli, it benefited substantially from the foundations laid during the colonial period, as well as from the close connection which leaders of independent South Korea maintained with the Japanese politicians and firms thereafter.

Kohli's account may well not be popular with Korean nationalists but it has considerable credibility, not least because the subsequent organization of the developmental state in South Korea followed the Japanese model so closely. Its main architect, a former communist party member and officer in the Japanese army, Park Chung-Hee, was an ardent and vociferous admirer of the Meiji model of development and collaborated closely with Japan during the 1960s and 1970s, despite the understandably strong anti-Japanese sentiments of most South Koreans at the time. Japanese contributions to Korean development, whether directly through its unusually developmentalist form of colonialism or simply through the example of its own development process, was clearly an important factor in South Korea's rapid industrialization after independence. The same argument can probably be made for Taiwan, where Japanese occupation (of what was then Formosa) lasted as long, and occurred on a similar model.

The Japanese influence on Singapore was less direct but nonetheless significant. The 1942–5 wartime occupation was short, brutal and destructive, and left lasting resentments against the Japanese, particularly amongst the Chinese population, and especially the communist sympathizers who were subject to draconian Japanese purges. The occupation left little in the way of institutional legacies, although the intense campaign of 'Nipponization' – spearheaded by the Japanese army in both Singapore and Malaya – may have left its mark, not least in terms of the Japanese values of loyalty to the state which were relentlessly promoted by the occupying forces. Most importantly, though, the Japanese occupation of Singapore – and its presence in South East Asia more generally under the pretext of creating an East Asian Co-Prosperity Zone – galvanized anti-colonial sentiments and nationalist ambitions, and, as Robin Ramcharan has argued,[68] acted as a long-term catalyst for independence, both in Singapore and elsewhere in the region. Chan Heng Chee, the former director of Singapore's Institute of South East Asian studies, has described the Japanese occupation as a watershed. According to his account, it

> changed the mind-set [and] facilitated a revolution in a generation of leaders and led to the creation of a modern and independent South East Asia . . . The Japanese occupation ushered in a great mental revolution, a

psychological revolution, in the people of the region. It created a desire among many members of the elite to run their own countries. Prior to that the superiority of the white man was uncontestible.[69]

Despite the lasting resentment of many Singaporeans towards the Japanese, diplomatic relations with Japan were quickly restored by the Singaporean leadership after independence in 1965. Both Lee Kuan Yew, the People's Action Party (PAP) leader and Prime Minister, and Goh Keng Swee, the architect of Singapore's economic development, were strong admirers of the Japanese model of nation-building and economic development. Japanese firms were enticed into Singapore, and investment and loans from Japan were strongly encouraged throughout the period of Singapore's economic development. By 1972, Japan had invested US$31.2 million in the country with loans amounting to US$11.8 million. By 1995 there were 1 500 Japanese companies in Singapore with a total of US$644 million of investments.[70] Japan's economic system, then in full flight and at the height of its international influence, was also used as a model for the Singaporean leadership in the early 1980s when it sought to drive its own economy up-market and away from the low-cost, low-skill model of competition which was under threat from lower-cost producers in the region. In an effort to promote high-productivity firms and industries, Singapore sought to import Japan's model of employment relations, at the same time as increasing its investment in skills. Workforce attitudes in Singapore were deemed to be too individualistic and job-hopping rates too high, so the 'Learn from Japan' campaign was instigated between 1977 and 1981 to introduce Japanese practices of team-work, quality-control circles, enterprise unionism and company welfarism. These pillars of Japanese employment relations did not really take root in Singapore, but the government was successful in driving up productivity through increasing wages and skills levels, as we shall see later. The Japanese exemplar of high value-added manufacturing remained the guiding model for Singapore's economic strategy for some time.

However, just as influential and not unconnected was the influence of the Japanese model of nation-building. Both Lee Kuan Yew and Goh Keng Swee were long-time admirers of Japan's cohesive social relations and saw national unity as the key to development. In a speech in Tokyo at the anniversary of the Meiji Restoration, Lee Kuan Yew reflected on the qualities he admired in Japan, including

the compactness and cohesiveness of society, the intense sense of national and community purpose, the keen group desire not to be left behind in the lower rungs of civilized societies, [and] the lack of natural resources which were compensated for by a keener human performance.[71]

The lessons for development were fundamental. In another speech extolling Japan, Lee argued that the country's 'remarkable record of high economic growth' was a 'tribute to her people's industrious nature, their sense of national unity and the quality of her leadership in government and enterprise'.[72]

The history of nation-building and development in Japan could also be used to justify Singapore's authoritarian state, as was made equally clear by Goh Keng Swee in a speech in 1966 when he reminded his audience that currently richer nations in the West, as well as Japan and the Soviet Union, had not had democracy when they first industrialized, and could not have done if they wanted rapid development. The political leadership in those cases, he argued, 'remained under tight control of the ruling elite. Hence it was possible to extract from the population sacrifices which no popularly elected government would dare even to contemplate.'[73]

Japan's model of nation-building was constantly invoked by the leadership in Singapore during this period, and indeed specific social policies that were introduced also owed much to the Japanese example. During the 1979–84 period, Singapore adopted Japan's *Koban* system of community policing, replete with neighbourhood police posts. After 1979 it also introduced moral education into the curriculum, influenced to some degree by Japan, and tried to promote Japanese-style social cohesion through re-emphasizing Confucian values. The campaign backfired but was followed by new measures to promote social cohesion through fostering 'Asian values'.

Korea, Taiwan and Singapore were all clearly strongly influenced by Japan, both during periods of colonization and occupation and afterwards. Another East Asian tiger, Hong Kong, was not, and one clearly cannot attribute the whole of the East Asian economic miracle to Japanese influence. Nevertheless, it was an important factor in the region, and not solely in terms of providing an economic model. More important, arguably, was the influence of the Japanese model of state formation, which was the crucial social underpinning of economic development.

Geopolitical factors

Geographical and geopolitical factors have undoubtedly also been important in East Asian development. Japan and the four tigers are all strategically located island or peninsular states with scarce natural resources. Their location on major trading routes has contributed historically to their development as centres of entrepôt trade and their long seaboards have encouraged the growth of coastal towns which became primary sites of commerce and later industrial development. The relative lack of natural resources obviated any development strategy based solely on agriculture and extraction industries, and made necessary the alternative path of development through manufacturing for export in the 1960s, which turned out to be the right way to go given the state of the global economy.[74] The lack of natural resources also, as Castells has argued, promoted the huge stress placed on skills and human capital which also coincided with the needs of the emerging knowledge economy.[75] Insular geography gave the East Asian states a measure of territorial security at certain historical periods, and has certainly contributed to the strong sense of national identity which these states share, and which has been an advantage for state-building, but their strategic location has also acted as a magnet for foreign incursions and, in the case of the tigers, for colonization, as we have seen, by either Japan or Britain or both.

Japan, virtually a United States satellite for much of the post-war period,[76] was the recipient of large-scale US aid during and after the American occupation, and this helped to restart its industrial economy. South Korea, Taiwan and Singapore also found themselves at the centre of Cold War tensions and consequently of large-scale aid from both the United States and Britain during the 1950s, 1960s and 1970s. Between 1953 and 1958, South Korea received an average of US$270 million a year in aid from the United States which amounted to nearly 15 per cent of gross national product (GNP).[77] The United States largely funded South Korea's defence costs and requisitioning for the Vietnam War later kick-started the *chaebols*, the future industrial giants.[78] Aid from the United States also helped Taiwan in the early stages of development, funding 49 per cent of public investment in infrastructure between 1953 and 1957.[79] Singapore also benefited economically from the presence of British military bases during the 1960s and from US requisitioning for the Vietnam War.[80]

Geography and geopolitics clearly provide only partial explanations for rapid East Asian development. Other Asian states caught up in Cold War tensions and benefiting from substantial US aid, such as the Philippines, have not prospered so well.[81] Nor economically, has another strategically placed island state, Sri Lanka, although it might be argued that this country suffered from the 'impediment' of having some rather abundant agricultural resources which deprived it of the incentive, acutely felt by the East Asian tigers, for a development policy based on export-led manufacturing.[82] Nevertheless, geography and geopolitics clearly did help Japan and the four tigers in the crucial periods of the economic development. Were it not for the geographical accident of their strategic locations and long coastlines, and for their economically fortuitous geopolitical positioning at the centre of Cold War tensions in the post-war era, it is unlikely that they would have developed when and in the way they did.

Lastly, amongst the historically contingent conditions of development, timing was clearly crucial for Japan and the East Asian tigers. Japan's second wave of industrialization in the 1950s and the first industrial take-off of the tiger economies in the 1960s coincided with a buoyant period in the world economy. Trade was increasing and liberalizing, but international agreements still allowed flexible trade regimes in different states.[83] As we shall see later, these countries made exemplary use of these favourable conditions, making the most for exports of the relatively open western markets and of the opportunities permissible for export subsidization, whilst at the same time shielding their economies from excessive capital penetration and imports through a variety of protective measures.[84]

Why these countries also managed to grow and maintain relatively low levels of income inequality can also to some extent be explained by the broader contexts which shaped the early stages of development. If we follow Kuznets' theories, increasing income inequality is likely to accompany industrialization because of growing sectoral imbalances between productivity in agriculture and manufacturing and between the rural and urban economies. This did not occur to the predicted degree in Japan and the tiger economies. Singapore and Hong Kong had little agriculture to speak of in any case, except for fisheries, so their entire economies quite rapidly became based on manufacturing, services and commerce. They are city states and therefore have no marked rural–urban divisions which elsewhere might have been the source of growing inequality. Japan, Taiwan and Korea all experienced substantial US-backed land reform in the 1950s, which decimated the old landed classes who might otherwise have provided blockages to reform, and created numerous smaller farmers. This reform arguably fostered social and political stability and enhanced the productivity of agriculture.[85] Taiwan, Korea and other states gave substantial support to the small farmers, particularly for irrigation, and taxed them lightly, and the development of a good infrastructure of roads, bridges, water and electricity supply also enhanced productivity.[86] According to the World Bank analysis the six HPAEs with substantial agriculture –Indonesia, Japan, Korea, Malaysia, Thailand and Taiwan – had considerably higher agricultural productivity than other regions in the 1960–80 period.[87] More broadly, the weakening of the old elites, including both the landowners and the industrial magnates of Japanese and Korean conglomerates, and the lack of well-established elites in Singapore, can be said to have advantaged the development of the meritocratic ideologies sponsored by post-war East Asian governments. This contributed to the social mobility and relatively 'classless' social relations which are reflected in the low levels of income inequality. Other factors have no doubt contributed to low income inequality, including the economic and social policies, encouraged by these meritocratic ideologies which will be discussed later, but land reform and the nature of the class structure which this promoted were certainly important contributors.

Economic policies

We have looked thus far at what one may call the more 'distal' causes of rapid growth in East Asia, focusing on the long-range cultural, geographical and geopolitical factors which may have been conducive to economic development. However, as the historian Eric Hobsbawm once observed in relation to the process of industrialization in nineteenth-century England, where economic outcomes are at issue it is generally better to find explanations in more directly economic causes where possible.[88] It is, of course, in the area of economic policy where there has been most debate about the so-called 'East Asian miracle', and it is on this that we now focus.

At one level the story of East Asian economic growth can be boiled down to a remarkable series of economic transitions made in similar sequence by all of the most successful East Asian states, albeit by Japan, in its second postwar phase of industrialization, 10 years or so ahead of the tiger economies. The larger countries each began their economic transformation in the 1950s, with reforms and productivity improvements in agriculture, and all of the countries went through an often brief phase of import substitution, in the case of the tiger economies in the late 1950s and early 1960s. However, all of these countries made a very rapid and determined transition to export-led manufacturing in the mid- to late 1960s or thereabouts. In most cases this involved the export of cheap, mass-produced manufactured goods, such as toys, shoes, fireworks and garments, in the markets for which these countries were highly competitive due to their low labour costs. Government support for exports helped to boost trade in many cases. This was the era of the Export Processing Zones, much criticized at the time for their exploitation of cheap young female labour under harsh factory regimes, and of the ubiquitous labels 'Made in Taiwan', and so forth, which produced almost the same mixture of awe and anxiety in the West as the tag 'Made in Germany' had made a century earlier. It was this transition to export-led manufacturing which kick-started the tiger economies as it had the Japanese one, and it was the critical moment for East Asian development.

Why this strategic shift was made here, and not in other regions which fatally stuck with the import substitution strategies for far longer, is somewhat obscure. It no doubt had something to do with the Japanese example as regional champion, and here the culturalist explanation of the 'flying geese' model may carry some weight. It also no doubt followed a certain logic of 'path dependency' since many of these countries had been long-standing trading nations. Equally, in some cases at least, it may have been the result of very pragmatic but nevertheless, as it turned out, strategic decision-making. Confirming Lew Kuan Yew's own autobiographical account,[89] Edgar Schein, in his fascinating chronicle of the shift in his book *Strategic Pragmatism*,[90] describes the time when the Prime Minister in Singapore realized that his – and Singapore's – post-independence political survival rested on reducing the massive unemployment then prevailing and his belief that he had no choice but to opt for export-led growth funded through foreign direct investment. Singapore had nothing else to run with. His subsequent employment of the Dutch economist Albert Wilsemmius to draw up a strategic plan, and the formation of the hugely instrumental Economic Development Board that issued from that process, set Singapore on a course of rapid growth which would transform it within a generation from what has been described as a poor swamp island with a trading post to one of the richest and most technologically sophisticated city states on earth.

The second transition, made by all of the countries, excepting perhaps Hong Kong, was the shift into heavy industrial production through oil refining, chemicals, steel production and, later, shipbuilding. This occurred in the late 1960s and early 1970s in Korea, Taiwan and Singapore, and signalled an important transition into higher value-added areas of export. In terms of natural comparative advantages there was often little to recommend this shift, and many countries were amazed to see South Korea investing in shipbuilding at a time when world markets for heavy vessels were saturated.[91] Nevertheless, the move worked in each case, not least due to the sustained competitiveness of East Asian labour costs, and helped to raise skills levels and incomes in each country. Exports in Korea had risen from less than 5 per cent of GDP in the 1950s to 35 per cent in the 1980s.[92] Wages increased in the 1970s by a multiple of 2.3.[93]

The third dramatic shift came in the late 1970s and early 1980s for the tigers when intensified competition amongst other East Asian economies in exporting low-cost manufactured goods threatened to erode their economic competitiveness. It was during this period that they all sought to move towards the more skills-intensive higher-end manufacture of electronic goods and components, including computer chips in Singapore and Korea, and PCs in Taiwan.[94] The move involved heavy investment in research and training, and it succeeded in raising productivity and incomes in the tiger economies at a rapid rate. Finally, as competitiveness in these areas was increasingly threatened by the rise of other East Asian electronic goods assemblers, not least China, in the 1990s, and particularly for higher-wage Singapore, a fourth economic transformation was engineered, this time into services and research-based areas of production, such as bio-technology. Singapore's strategic mission at this time came to be one of acting as the high-quality service hub for the region – providing a base for regional headquarters of transnational companies, complete with top-class IT and infrastructural services, and also a hub for regional medical and education provision. Singapore was to be the 'Boston of the East'.[95]

On this account what seems to mark out these economies is their sustained capacity to adapt to changing world circumstances both in terms of steering their economies away from declining or overcrowded markets and towards new areas of competitiveness, and in terms of upgrading their capacities to succeed in these new areas. The latter, of course, required massive investment in capital goods, infrastructure and human capital and, above all, the successful transfer of technologies. Joseph Stiglitz, writing about the lessons from East Asia, comments both on the extraordinary flexibility of these economies and on their capacity to invest. As he writes, 'East Asian success was based on a combination of factors, particularly the high savings rates interacting with high levels of capital accumulation, in a stable market-oriented environment – but with active government intervention – that was conducive to the transfer of technology.'[96] We will consider government intervention later, but for now it is important to note the key role of investment which was common to all of the East Asian success stories. On the World Bank estimate, two-thirds of all the growth in the HPAEs can be attributed to investment and human capital growth.[97] However, here we must also note that Japan and the tiger economies did not all take the same path. It is true that domestic savings rates were phenomenally high in all of these countries, and were often stimulated by similar government policies, as with the ubiquitous government-promoted post-office savings accounts. Savings rates amongst the four tigers generally averaged above 30 per cent of GDP between 1965 and 1990, varying from 17 to 37 per cent across the HPAEs more widely. This compared with 9–10 per cent in South Asia and 8–11 per cent in sub-Saharan Africa.[98]

However, the means of attracting foreign capital and, following that, the nature of company ownership varied substantially across Japan and the tiger economies. Singapore and Hong Kong relied substantially on foreign direct investment, and indeed probably had little choice but to do so since their home markets were small and indigenous capital was limited at the onset of industrialization. The economies of these states consequently became dominated by the foreign multinational corporations that provided most of the jobs and production for export. Japan and South Korea, on the other hand, took a different course. Until recently, foreign direct investment in these countries has been discouraged. Instead, Japan and South Korea built up their industries through domestic investment, largely from government-directed bank loans which channelled domestic savings to companies, and by ploughing back the profits from domestic sales (at often inflated prices) in their considerable home markets. Foreign capital was largely limited to loans and equity, with shares of the latter often restricted to ensure home control of companies.[99] Technology transfer came mostly not through multinational companies operating within their shores but through the buying of technology licences and the reverse-engineering of foreign goods.

These varied paths have led to quite different firm structures in the different countries. Japan and Korea developed their own large private enterprises, with considerable state support, including the huge vertically and horizontally integrated *keiretsu* and *chaebol* (conglomerates) which, respectively, dominate the Japanese and Korean economies (the top ten of which in Korea in 1984 accounted for 67 per cent of sales)[100] and spearhead their exports.[101] Singapore and Hong Kong, on the other hand, have been reliant on the large foreign-owned multinationals which account for much of their employment and export trade. Taiwan, again another case, took foreign direct investment and loans from abroad,[102] not only hosting foreign companies but also developing its own companies, both a multiplicity of small domestically-owned companies and in the form of the large, initially state-owned, conglomerates.[103] Both forms of capitalization seem to have worked, although South Korea, with its high levels of short-term loan debt, proved more vulnerable to the financial crisis of 1997 than either Taiwan or Singapore, which were less indebted to foreign banks and whose multinational companies were not as swift to remove their assets.[104]

That Japan and the tiger economies benefited from an export-led development strategy, underpinned by substantial investment from domestic savings and foreign capital, is not contested. In this sense these states were clearly adopting, by design or necessity, and ahead of their time, a strategy which was best-fit with the globalizing era which was soon to emerge in the 1970s. To this extent they were market-oriented regimes. However, a trade-based policy of development does not necessarily mean a liberal or free-market economic policy. It is here, around the specific nature of the economic policies adopted, that the debates about the East Asian developmental model have raged. Were the tiger economies paragons of free-trade, free-market liberal orthodoxy and was that the secret of their success? Or were they something rather different and strange to classical economic thinking: export-driven, capitalistic economies that nevertheless diverged from free-market orthodoxies in both their state-led industrial policies and their neo-mercantilist approach to trade? Were they successful because the state left major economic decisions to the market or because the state intervened in the markets in a *dirigiste* fashion which was anathema to orthodox economics?

The liberal orthodox economic view is that the tiger economies prospered by 'getting the basics right'.[105] They adopted an export-oriented growth policy that forced their nascent industries to be competitive; they invested heavily both in physical and human capital; and they adopted sound macroeconomic management policies. To Paul Krugman[106] there is no mystery at all about the growth of the tiger economies since almost all of the increases in outputs can be explained by rising inputs of labour and capital, without any increases in efficiency. In other words the success of the economies lay largely in mobilizing high levels of investment – although this begs the question of how the tigers attracted the investment in the first place. To other commentators adopting the neo-classical view, the ingredients of success also included reliable legal frameworks to promote competition, absence of price controls and a stable macro-economic environment. In particular, policies were adopted to keep inflation and fiscal deficits at reasonable levels, with inflation in the HPAEs averaging 9 per cent during the 1976–97 period compared with an average 18 per cent in other low- and middle-income countries.[107] The argument neglects the fact that during South Korea's most rapid phase of growth, inflation was running at in excess of 18 per cent.[108] Nevertheless, much of this account would remain unexceptional to economists of any persuasion. However, the problems arise when it comes to assessing other policies on trade and industrial policy. Martin Wolf's panegyric to globalization and free trade rightly centres his account of the East Asian development on the success of their trade-oriented policies which flourished in the liberalizing trade regime of the global era.[109] However, success in export does not necessarily equate with the adoption of free-trade policies. In fact, many would argue that Japan and the tigers had 'strategic trading' policies which were substantially at variance with free-trade principles. Likewise their industrial policies.[110]

Developmental states and state formation in East Asia

Critics of the neo-classical view have not found it hard to show where East Asian economic policies differed from free-market orthodoxy. Chalmers Johnson has described Japanese trade policy until the 1980s as anything but free trade; in fact, as a kind of neo-mercantilism whose main objective was capturing maximum shares of export markets, through whatever means, whilst at the same time limiting imports as far as it could manage. Certainly, on Perkin's comparative estimates, Japan's trading performance for many years was exceptional less for the size of its exports than for the modest extent of its imports.[111] Japan, and then Korea, Taiwan and Singapore, used all manner of policy levers and supports to promote exports, including export subsidies, preferential credit to exporters, preferential access to capital and foreign exchange, and the provision of market information.[112] Keeping their currencies competitive also greatly assisted their exports, even if it also caused international tensions – for instance, with the routine US and European denunciations of the undervaluing of the Japanese yen. At the same time, imports were regulated through quotas, taxes (particularly on luxury goods) and various complex regulations on standards, in the case of Japan, which served to keep foreign imports out of the retail outlets.[113] Protectionist policies were adopted in the early years, not only to protect infant industries but also to help the big corporations to recoup the losses that they made on subsidized sales on foreign markets, through high-priced sales of domestic goods[114] – in effect making the home consumers pay for the national export drive for market share.

Industrial policies were also adopted in Japan, Korea, Taiwan and Singapore which flouted neo-classical economic wisdom about letting markets determine investment decisions. Japan, through its celebrated Ministry for Trade and Industry (MITI), and Korea, Taiwan and Singapore, through similarly designed authorities, intervened substantially to promote particular industrial sectors and wind down others; to rationalize certain sectors by promoting company mergers; and to support the research and development which would strengthen chosen sectors. The so-called 'administrative guidance' offered by MITI in Japan did not usually involve 'picking winners and losers' in terms of particular firms, although MITI did famously try to dissuade Honda from entering what it considered to be the already over-crowded sector of auto production.[115] But in Korea and Taiwan the state did have a major hand in promoting certain companies and demoting others.[116] More usually, though, state intervention took the form of promoting par-ticular sectors and new areas for innovation through preferential credit and loans from state-controlled banks and through the award of technology and export licences.

If we share the view of Robert Wade,[117] in his detailed analysis of eco-nomic policy and development in Taiwan, that states were 'governing the market' in East Asia, then we are bound to ask where these states came from and what it was about them that enabled them to play this role so suc-cessfully. These are the questions that theorists of the 'developmental state' in East Asia have tried to answer. Their theories are generally anchored in the observations of Chalmers Johnson in his celebrated book *MITI and the Japanese Miracle*. For him the idea of the developmental state 'originated in the situational nationalism of the late industrialisers'.[118] As with Prussia in the early nineteenth century, which was arguably the first developmental state,[119] and Japan at the time of the Meiji Restoration, to which several recent East Asian leaders have looked for inspiration, developmental states have tended to emerge as a result of foreign invasion or threats of invasion, or, as with Japan after the Second World War, in the face of some major task of social and political reconstruction. They have also, as Johnson notes, gen-erally derived their goals from some other exemplary regional state. In the cases of South Korea, Taiwan and Singapore, they also arose as a project of state reconstruction at a time when the political viability of each of these states was in question: in South Korea because of hostility from its north-ern neighbour; in Taiwan because it was not recognized by mainland China; and in Singapore because it was a small and apparently unviable state sand-wiched between two states, China and Malaysia, with which its population had close ethnic ties, but with which it was on poor terms. In each case, state developmentalism was in the first place a political necessity rather than an economic priority. As Castells has written, for the developmental state, 'economic development was not a goal but a means ... the East Asian developmental state was born of a need for survival, and then it grew on the basis of a nationalist project of self-affirmation of cultural and political identity in the world system'.[120] What subsequently marked out these states was the sustained promotion of rapid economic development as a means of maintaining state legitimacy.

Developmental states have been characterized by their distinctive approach to what Kohli terms state-led economic development.[121] This has sometimes been attributed to the large and strategic vision of their lead-ers, some of which, such as Singapore's Lee Kuan Yew, certainly seemed to have possessed remarkable political will and strategic insight. However, what has been equally important about these states is their ability to exercise effective control. This has been put down to a number of causes. It is certainly the case, as Castells argues,[122] that the developmental states in Japan and the three independent tigers were able to conceive and implement strategic decisions partly because of their relative independence from narrow class interests. Each of these countries had comparatively weak or unorganized landed, and industrial capitalist classes and their labour movements were either weak or had been made weak by state action – including through outright repression in South Korea, and through a combination of repression and cooptation in Singapore. Governments, often formed from long-standing ruling parties, were relatively autonomous of sectional interests and so were better able to gain legitimacy by appealing to the national interest. At the same time, many of these states benefited from exceptionally competent bureaucracies which were largely free, at least in the cases of Japan, Taiwan and Singapore, from personal corruption.[123] Such was arguably one of the more positive legacies of the Japanese in Korea and Taiwan, and the British in Singapore. But it also owed much, at least in Singapore, to the tough laws on corruption, strictly meritocratic appointment procedures and rigorous systems of training for civil servants introduced since independence.[124] Without such levels of state autonomy and competence it is unlikely that these states would have been able to achieve so much.

However, effective state power also required legitimacy. This was certainly not guaranteed to the governments of these states, and for lengthy periods, especially in Taiwan and South Korea, there was considerable civil unrest and major challenges to state authority. However, developmental states typically rode many crises, not least because they could appeal to national sentiments by invoking the politics of national survival. The role of the state in fostering strong national identities and loyalties was crucial to ensuring support for the long and arduous process of economic development which they had undertaken. It is also important to remember this role since many of the initiatives in education have played as much to this imperative as to the need to develop skills for economic growth.

Developmental states, according to the leading accounts by Castells, Johnson, Amsden and Wade,[125] are states which, due to particular historical circumstances, and not least the contingencies of underdevelopment, adopt state-led strategies of capitalist development to catch up with more advanced economies and to secure their own political viability as states. They are capitalist in their fundamental economic relations and do not seek to avoid the fundamental logics of the market, but they use the state in specific ways to fashion market activities according to their long-term developmental priorities. As Johnson, Kohli and Castells argue, as political economies they are characterized by certain distinctive features: their states make an absolute priority of the long-term goals of national economic development on which the legitimacy of government depends; their political systems permit a leading economic role to their state bureaucracies, which are both competent and relatively autonomous, and which generally owe their position to strict meritocratic procedures; they allow and indeed encourage an exceptional degree of interpenetration and cooperation between the state bureaucracies and business; and they use multiple forms of intervention by the state not only in trade but also in shaping industrial policy.

Such states have arisen in specific circumstances where development is perceived to be possible only through such state-led strategies. In the case of Japan and the tiger economies of South Korea, Taiwan and Singapore, these circumstances, according to Johnson, included a lack of natural resources and raw material, a lack of capital accumulation, particularly in the absence of the build-up of colonial capital, an inexperienced merchant and entrepreneurial class, and considerable technological backwardness. These barriers to development gave rise to a number of what Johnson terms 'situational imperatives', including the need for the rapid development of manufacturing and trade in manufactured goods, and the need to achieve this through state-led policies. Although Johnson makes only passing reference to Gerschenkron and the German national school (Amsden does more), it is clear that the situational imperatives described are similar to those described by Gerschenkron and, before him, List. Notwithstanding the regional and temporal particularities which enabled these developmental states in East Asia to be so successful, it is clear that they represent in many ways the classic conditions of backwardness which List and Gerschenkron thought could be mitigated through policies which radically challenged the dominant nostrums of liberal economics. These policies were essentially neo-mercantilist policies, a modern version of the school of economic thinking in opposition to which liberal political economy developed in the first place. 'Mercantilism', according to Perry Anderson's account of late absolutist Europe, 'was precisely a theory of the coherent intervention of the political state into the working of the economy, in the joint interest of the prosperity of the one hand and the power of the other.'[126] The description could equally well be applied to the East Asian developmental states.

The reprise of mercantilism and the role of nationalism in state formation

Mercantilism, in its classic historical forms in sixteenth- to nineteenth-century Europe, placed equal emphasis on state power and economic prosperity: in fact, economic prosperity was seen as the means to state power, as well as state power being an essential means to achieve economic prosperity. Developmental state theorists have acknowledged the historical provenance of the policies which have guided developmental state leaders. They have also effectively identified the geopolitical conditions which have provoked the 'situational nationalism' which was the well-spring of modern developmental states. The situations which nurtured such nationalism included not only the international political and military threats that triggered the Meiji Restoration in Japan, and the Cold War setting in which the rise of the East Asian tigers occurred. Nationalism was also driven, more generally, by anti-imperialist forces. As Johnson's writings stress, communist nationalism in China arose as part of an anti-imperialist struggle against the Japanese. Despite being officially anti-communist ideologically, the nationalism of the East Asian tigers was also both a legacy of colonialism (British and Japanese) and, equally, anti-imperialist in character.

Developmental state theory thus provides hints of the historical contexts which have underpinned the rise of these extraordinary state forms. However, the analysis of state developmentalism has focused mainly on economic development, albeit that achieved through the state. Where the accounts are lacking is in a detailed analysis of the social and ideological dimensions of this process. In particular, the fundamental role of nationalism in the unfolding of the developmental projects is underplayed, albeit that situational nationalism is correctly identified as the source. For ultimately, as Castells recognizes,[127] the developmental states are nationalist political projects. In the broadest sense, they are examples of state formation in the most accelerated and concerted fashion imaginable.

The key political characteristic of developmental states, and specifically the developmental states in East Asia, then was nationalism. This was not the nationalism of the great power variety, such as in Britain in the days of Empire or of the United States during the post-war period of its global economic domination. Nor was it – except in Japan in the 1930s – an expansionist, or particularly aggressive, form of nationalism. It was a nationalism of smaller and underdeveloped states determined to assert their sovereign identities after years of colonialism and national humiliation at the hands of stronger powers, and to reverse their histories of economic backwardness. Theirs was, above all, a nationalism in the service of rapid economic development and accelerated state formation.

The role of nationalism in economic development has not always been appreciated. It has certainly been greatly underplayed in liberal theories of development, partly, perhaps, because it can lead to disastrous outcomes, as in Japan in its ultra-nationalist period, and partly no doubt because it does not obviously tally with the received understanding of the first and paradigm case of development, since nationalism was a fairly muted force in Britain during its industrial revolution. However, its importance was clearly understood by List and his followers. It has also been a subject of renewed scholarly interest in the past few decades, not least due to the work of the historical sociologist Liah Greenfeld.

In her major and controversial work *The Spirit of Capitalism: Nationalism and Economic Growth* (2001),[128] Greenfeld seeks to provide a new analysis of the motive forces behind the historical shift to capitalist ways of thinking and behaving. Accepting Max Weber's classic characterization of the spirit of capitalism as a mode of rational calculation allied to the pursuit of profit, she seeks to overturn Weber by arguing that it was not Protestantism that lay the foundation for this but rather the rise in national consciousness more generally. Nationalism was the primary factor in orienting societies towards economic growth, she argues, because nationalism, and the advocacy of national economic improvement, provided a higher purpose which could dignify and sanction the pursuit of individual profit, which in traditional societies had been scorned. In particular, she says, it was the liberal, civic form of nationalism, which she associates with England, and by extension the United States, which was most favourable to economic development because it celebrated individualism and individual improvement in a way that could be harnessed to entrepreneurialism. Thus it was Tudor England, she claims, which invented nationalism, and nationalist England which pioneered capitalist development. The German states, and Japan, by contrast, which did not discover nationalism until 1806 and 1868, respectively, were slower to adopt the spirit of capitalism and were more retarded in industrializing their economies.

Much of Greenfeld's account is anathema to mainstream historical scholarship and, particularly, to the historians of nationalism. As Krishan Kumar argues,[129] there is an embarrassing degree of anglophilia in her account, and much of her analysis of nationalism in Tudor England seems simply anachronistic. It is one thing to argue that the Tudors, and particularly Elizabeth I, aroused national consciousness in England, although it is highly debateable that it extended beyond the elites to the popular masses, as Greenfeld claims. However, to conflate national consciousness with nationalism as an ideology and political programme seems completely misguided. Others have associated the rise of Protestantism, and specifically Henry VIII's break with Rome, with new forms of national consciousness, which existed in the teeth of the undeniable internationalism of the Reformation as a movement, and one may even stretch this to identify forms of proto-nationalism in this period. But nationalism proper required a new equation of the nation with the people, where national sovereignty ultimately derived from the people, and this was not widely upheld before the eighteenth century and not systematically disseminated until the French Revolution. Greenfeld's identification of a nationalism rooted in individual rights and a new social egalitarianism in sixteenth-century England seems completely anachronistic. Furthermore, if early forms of national consciousness can be equated with nationalism in the way that Greenfeld wishes to do, and if nationalism is then seen as the incubator of the capitalist spirit, why then did not France, like England, make the early moves in this direction, since national consciousness can be discerned there as well in the seventeenth century?

As we can see, Greenfeld's comparative argument, as it relates to the chronology of the development of nationalism and the capitalist spirit in England and France, runs into considerable problems. However, her thesis works considerably better for Prussia and Japan, where the rise of nationalism proper and the transition to capitalist economic organization were indeed highly synchronized and closely connected. The Prussian educated middle class, the *bildungsburgertum*, were cosmopolitan internationalists during the Enlightenment. Germany was still a piecemeal scattering of small princedoms with little pretension to national status. It was only the Napoleonic victory in Jena in 1806, and the subsequent French occupation until 1812, which converted the German elites to nationalism, and this rapidly became a nationalism of a most rebarbative and xenophobic kind. The nationalism was, of course, to a large extent born of animosity to the French, but it was also allied to a powerful desire, most eloquently expressed by Fichte, to rebuild and modernize the Prussian state. This also meant developing the economy.

Like Prussia before 1806, Tokugawa Japan before the 1850s had no fully fledged popular nationalism, nor indeed any well-developed popular national consciousness. Before the mid-eighteenth century, indeed, ordinary people had little sense of Japanese identity (*nihonjin*) at all. As Morris-Suzuki points out, seventeenth-century world maps in Japan did not even represent all Japanese lands in the same colour and, up until the mid-eighteenth century at least, the modern word for 'country', *Kuni*, most often referred to the local region or domain.[130] It is true that since the early eighteenth century, Shinto scholars had sought to emphasize indigenous Japanese intellectual traditions and Japanese cultural uniqueness through reviling Confucian influences and promoting a cult of native learning, known as *Kokugaku*.[131] But this was a cultural movement confined largely to the elites. As Greenfeld writes

> Before the country was compelled to open up to the West, there was no national consciousness in Japan. Identity was defined, in the case of the Samurai, essentially by class – and to a lesser extent by feudal allegiances, however altered in significance during the Tokugawa period – and religion; in the case of the peasantry perhaps, essentially by religion.[132]

One may perhaps talk of proto-nationalism in this period but no more. It took the arrival of Commodore Perry's ships in 1853 to detonate the cultural explosion which was to see the rise of Japanese nationalism and one of the most remarkable surges in state formation that the world has seen.

As in Prussia half a century earlier, the impetus towards state formation in Japan was driven primarily by the fear of foreign domination. In this case, unlike in Prussia, the invasion was cultural and only putatively military, but it evoked no less a reaction for that, not least because it came after centuries of isolation such as no European state had experienced. The Meiji Restoration of 1868 was the result of a social movement triggered in part by the opening up of Japan to western influences during the 1840s and 1850s. It was the realization of the superiority and threat of western technology which prompted the formation of new social alliances dedicated to resisting foreign domination. This was to be achieved through the adoption of western technology and the reassertion of Japanese identity symbolized by the restoration of the Emperor.

Under the new Meiji regime it was the ex-Samurai reformers and the enlightened bureaucracy who spearheaded an intensive programme of modernization which drew on and adapted western principles to the Japanese context. With the abolition of the feudal class system in 1871, the adoption of a new constitution and the introduction of representative political institutions, a new order was established. Under the slogan of *shokusan kogyo* ('develop industry and private enterprise'), the reformers promoted a national banking system; built railways, harbours and telegraph networks; established and later sold off plants in the cement, silk, copper and glass industries; and provided start-up loans and subsidies to the private sector.[133] The explanation, says Greenfeld, for this remarkably speedy and successful modernization of Japan – that is, for the reconstruction of Japanese society, including the economy, along the lines of a novel, modern type of society – lies in the equally remarkable, speedy and successful articulation and spread of Japanese nationalism.[134]

Whatever the weaknesses of Greenfeld's chronology of nationalism in Western Europe, there can be no doubt that she is correct to identify nationalism as a major force behind the modernization drives in post-Napoleonic Prussia and Meiji Japan. It was nationalism which mobilized society for the extreme efforts required to propel a backward economy and society into modernity, both in Meiji Japan and later in the tiger economies. It provided the motive force behind the exertions of the masses, whose endless toil generated the profits and savings for investment in growth, and also for the political leaders whose unflinching will and determination shaped the development process. If we ask, as Kohli has done, from where the developmental states emerge, and what nurtured the extraordinary single-mindedness of many of their political leaders and senior bureaucrats, the answer has to be, in part at least, from nationalist (and anti-imperialist) convictions.

Nationalism as we know has taken many different forms, some of them very ugly. The nationalism of Meiji Japan was initially defensive rather than aggressive. It was born of a desire to build a secure modern state, not out of ambitions of conquest. However, the Meiji era coincided with the age of imperialism, in which major European powers vied for colonial expansion. Already by the latter half of the nineteenth century, nationalism had, in many regions, taken a decisive turn from the liberal and civic forms predominant in the first half of the century to more rebarbative ethno-cultural and racial forms. As Hobsbawm has argued,[135] this could be explained in part by the rise of pseudo race-science in the 1850s, and also by the intensification of class politics in the late nineteenth century in the context of the growth of mass democracy. Ruling elites increasingly sought to use the politics of race to trump the politics of class, which provided the greater danger to the state. Imperial rivalries between the great powers fanned the flames of ethno-nationalism further.

The fledgling modern state of Meiji Japan developed in this imperialist context, and it was not long before Japan developed its own imperial ambitions, driven, like Germany, by the belief that it should have its own share of the spoils of imperialism. At first this was often cloaked within a pan-Asian, anti-imperialist rhetoric. For a time, Tokyo became a Mecca for nationalists across Asia, and many Asian nationalists were thrilled at the assertion of Asian power with Japan's victory over Russia in 1905.[136] However, the notion of Japan leading Asia to liberation was not to last long. As a relatively closed and ethnically homogeneous nation, Japan had long-since cultivated a kind of popular cultural nationalism, based on notions of Japanese uniqueness (*nihonjinron*). Increasing rivalries with China over control of Korea, and the subsequent Sino-Japanese and Russo-Japanese wars of 1894 and 1905, saw Japan turn gradually into an overtly imperial power, with strong ambitions for domination in the region. A state-sanctioned and aggressive militaristic nationalism had developed whose final denouement was the ultra-nationalism of the pre-Second World War Showa period. The Japanese invasion of Manchuria in 1931 marked the beginning of what was only a prelude to a second Sino-Japanese war in 1937, which was to cost so many Chinese lives. It was only defeat in the Second World War which led to the resumption of the more pacific albeit still ethno-cultural, nationalism in Japan which then played its part in the reconstruction and subsequent rapid development of the post-war period.

The nationalisms of the independent tigers – South Korea, Taiwan and Singapore – had more of the defensive and non-expansionist character of the early Meiji era in Japan and, indeed, had learnt much from the achievements of that regime. They were certainly more benign than the nationalisms which prevailed in the pre-war period and no doubt played a positive role in mobilization for development, as argued above. In part they arose in popular forms as inevitable reactions to recent experiences of colonialism and underdevelopment. They were intensified by justified perceptions about the fragility of their new independent states, not least with the tensions remaining between South and North Korea and between Taiwan and mainland China. However, they were also assiduously cultivated by leaders. Both Lee Kuan Yew in Singapore and Park Chung-Hee in South Korea consistently played on national sentiments to mobilize support for their regimes and commitment to their national development projects. Most notably, in both cases, was the continual emphasis on threats to national survival and the need for extreme efforts needed to maintain it.[137] Nationalist aspirations were used to encourage hard work, personal savings and even consumption of national products, all key factors in the development of the economy. In the early years of development, personal rewards only gradually accrued to the workers in both countries. National aspiration as well as personal ambition were probably needed to motivate Korean workers for their gruelling 12-hour shifts, six days a week. When these were not sufficient, coercion was used, sanctified by appeals to national imperatives.

Nationalism, and specifically the kind of 'situational nationalism' described by Johnson, thus played a major part in economic development – and state formation more generally – in the tiger economies. However, it did not take identical forms for various obvious reasons. Hong Kong, still a British colony during its developmentalist stage, necessarily could not develop a fully fledged nationalism, although the colonial authorities did their best to inculcate a Hong Kong identity which they thought would help to safeguard its autonomy after the return of sovereignty to China without posing too many challengers to the delicate relationships which existed between Hong Kong, Britain and China at the time. An identity based around commerce and consumption seemed the safest bet. The case of Taiwan was equally complex given the divided loyalties (and politics) of the population, with some wishing to assert their independence vigorously and others wanting closer relationships with mainland China. The complex nature of identity politics in both cases prevent any cursory treatment here. However, South Korea and Singapore can be usefully contrasted.

Although divided from the North since the civil war, South Korea could claim a foundation of national unity on the basis of its long dynastic history, its relative ethnic homogeneity and its reasonably established institutional structures, albeit that these derived substantially from Japanese colonialism. A strong ethno-cultural identity could be promoted as a social cement so long as this was not too compromised by the leadership's continuing close relations with Japan, whose colonial role was still a source of popular resentment. The major divisions in South Korea were those of social class. Syngman Rhee had been toppled by a student uprising in 1960, paving the way for the military coup which brought General Park Chung-Hee to power in 1961.[138] Under Park there was long-lasting civil strife between workers, students and the government, at times overlaid with anti-Japanese sentiment amongst those who resented Japanese businessmen and officials still holding powerful positions. The strident assertion of Korean identity by the state, and the constant mobilization of national aspirations behind Korea's development goals, was the government's main response – alongside outright repression of dissent through the powerful secret service. Most notable was Park's instigation of the nationwide *Saemaul Undong* movement which, in Kohli's description, exhorted 'citizens in mass rallies and in the workplace to sacrifice and increase production for the sake of national security'.[139] This worked better with the peasants than the workers and students. Class conflict did not disappear, and in the longer term the former trade union leader and main political opponent of General Park, Kim Dae Jung, became the leader of the first democratic government. But nationalist mobilization no doubt did help to contain dissent and to maintain sufficient social order for economic development to proceed unhindered.

The Singaporean case was rather different. Firstly, at the time of independence in 1965, there was no history of the Singaporean national consciousness and, indeed, no prior history of Singapore as a sovereign state. Both national consciousness and national institutions had to be constructed *de novo*. Secondly, Singapore had an ethnically diverse population with multiple languages and several religions, and there had been a recent history of race riots. The PAP government thus had an urgent task in developing a new Singaporean national identity which would help to hold the fragile state together. Under the circumstances, only a state-centred identity, which was formally multicultural but which played down ethnic differences, could have any chance of working. Despite the historical prevalence of strong ethno-cultural identities in East Asia, not least in Japan, Korea and China, the government, through persistent efforts, did manage to cultivate an essentially civic state identity in Singapore,[140] albeit that this remained, to some extent at least, a somewhat artificial, top-down creation.

Education, as we shall see later, played a major part in this, but other social policies were also important. Most notable perhaps was the extraordinary feat of social engineering which produced Singapore's integrated public housing system. From very early on the government invested heavily in the construction of good-quality public housing estates. In time their apartments were made available for purchase at discounted rates to tenants, who later, with the substantial inflation in house prices, had good reason to be grateful to the government. In an ambitious – and largely successful – attempt to avoid residential ethnic ghettos, and to ensure maximum social integration, the government ensured that each estate consisted of homes of different sizes and prices, and imposed regulations on sales to ensure that the ethnic balance on each estate was kept approximately in line with the proportion of each ethnic group in the overall population. When the government later came to set up multiple member political constituencies, this dispersal of ethnic populations proved to be a boon to the PAP, since opposition parties were unlikely to be able to muster a majority based on ethnic minorities' votes in any area.

If the priorities of state formation in South Korea were overwhelmingly economic, albeit underpinned by the cultivation of nationalist ideology, in Singapore they were necessarily much more diverse since civic institutions had to be created from scratch and since broader efforts were needed to integrate the much more diverse population. Labour market institutions had to be developed, including employer associations and trade unions (the latter on the corporatist model); neighbourhood organizations had to be formed to share the burden of welfare services; and, gradually, elements of a welfare state had to be put in place. Perhaps most significantly, public education had to be created. Altogether, Singapore represented a more root-and-branch case of state formation.

However, in each case, in South Korea and Taiwan, as well as in Singapore, economic development was necessarily a process of intensive state formation, which required social as well as economic changes. Developmental states have been defined by their uniquely focused and sustained state-led projects for economic growth. But they cannot be reduced solely to this. Rapid economic growth depended on specific social and ideological conditions, not least on social order and constant political legitimization of the regimes. State direction of economic growth required state capacity. Both of these required an intensive process of state formation.

Part II: Education and state formation in East Asia

Education and economic development

All accounts of East Asian development have stressed the major role of education and skills. Indeed, for many analysts it was an educational miracle as much as an economic miracle in East Asia. Politicians in Japan, Singapore and elsewhere consistently stress the importance of skills, often pointing out that the East Asian states generally have few natural resources and therefore must rely on skills for their economic growth.[141]

The availability of a skilled workforce was a key condition for many of the economic factors that we have identified as critical for growth in the global economy. The early development of low-cost manufacturing industries required a well-socialized and highly disciplined labour force in all of our cases and this was also important in Singapore and Hong Kong for attracting foreign direct investment.[142] A rapidly expanding skills supply was also crucial to each phase of economic upgrading – for instance, in providing the skilled workers and managers for the development of heavy industry and electronic goods manufacture in the 1970s and 1980s, and for supplying the inputs of scientific and professional skills which were in increasing demand with the shift to higher value-added production and services in the 1980s and 1990s.[143] Greater skills, and the capacity for learning, were the essence of the ability to transfer knowledge and technology, which is ultimately what made integration into the global market work for these countries.[144] To maintain the dynamic of development, education and training had to be continuously upgraded. As Tilak argues, 'The East Asian miracle is attributed, amongst other things, to the region's sustained levels of investment in human capital over a long period.'[145]

Whether education was the primary cause of East Asian economic development – or a facilitating agent to other causal factors which were more unique to the region – is a hard to determine. Given the arguments above about the critical role of contextual determinants of East Asia's rapid regional growth pattern – that is to say, of the importance of geography, geopolitics, timing and the nature of the state and its economic policies – we may be more likely to say that education was a necessary but not sufficient cause of the unique developments in the region. Nevertheless, various accounts, not least those based on growth accounting, do place the role of education amongst the most important causes.

Using Denison's growth accounting methods, endogenous growth theorists Wang and Tallman estimate that education accounted for 45 per cent of growth in GDP in Taiwan during the 1965–89 period.[146] Tilak notes that data on both the wage returns to education and rates of return to investments in education for various East Asian countries is positive.[147] If we accept the human capital premise that earnings reflect employee productivity, then the evidence of substantial wage returns to qualifications suggests productivity enhancement from education. According to World Bank estimates, on average an additional year of schooling in South Korea increased earnings by 6 per cent.[148] Both private and social rates of return on investment in education were fairly high by comparison with other regions in the world, and, as is normally the case, were highest for the lower levels of education, as shown in Table P.1. Rates of return to women's education for various years in the 1960s and 1970s, according to Tilak, were higher than those for men in Japan, Korea and Taiwan, particularly in the case of higher education, although they were lower in Singapore.[149] Evidence also exists regarding the beneficial effects of education on agricultural productivity in East Asia. For instance, one year of additional education in South Korea is estimated to have increased productivity in agriculture by 2.2 per cent.[150]

Overall benefits of education to growth are estimated by the World Bank in *East Asian Economic Miracle*. Using growth accounting techniques it shows that 60 per cent of growth in HPAEs can be accounted for by accumulation of physical and human capital, initial income and population growth. The largest single contribution to HPAE growth came from primary education, with growth in primary school enrolments accounting for between 58 per cent (Japan) and 87 per cent (Thailand) of economic growth. 'Far and away the major difference in predicted growth rates,' according to the report, 'between HPAEs and Sub-Saharan Africa derives from variations in primary school enrolment rates.'[151]

Evidence on the effects of education on income distribution in the East Asian states is also generally positive, although the effects vary between

Table P.1   Rates of return to education in East Asia and elsewhere

Economy	Year	Social			Private		
		Primary	Secondary	Higher	Primary	Secondary	Higher
China	1993	14.4	12.9	11.3	18.0	13.4	15.1
Hong Kong	1976		15.0	12.4.		18.5	25.2
Japan	1976	9.6	8.6	6.9	13.4	10.4	8.8
Korea	1980	–	8.1	11.7	–	–	
Singapore	1970		26.5	15.0	–	17.6	18.4
Taiwan	1972	27.0	12.3	17.7	50.0	12.7	15.8
World		18.4	13.1	10.9	29.1	18.1	29.3
OECD		14.4	10.2	8.7	21.7	12.4	12.3
Asia*		19.9	13.3	11.7	39.0	18.9	19.9

* non-OECD Asia. Source: Tilak (2002) pp. 6–7

countries. Japan and the tigers all had near-universal enrolments in primary education in the early years of industrial take-off and rapidly expanded their enrolments in secondary education in the decade following take-off, at least in the case of the tiger economies. These rapid increases in access to education are likely, in principle, to have reduced any tendencies for income inequalities to rise in the early period of industrial development.[152] Tilak argues that inequality and poverty declined rapidly in South Korea during the early years of industrialization as a result of high spending on education and other social welfare areas. Other commentators have claimed similar effects in Japan (Passim),[153] Taiwan (Wade)[154] and East Asia generally (Weiss).[155] Several factors clearly affect income equality in addition to education, but research which decomposes the income distribution in terms of its different components – for example, in Taiwan – has found that education is either the most or the second most important determinant.[156]

The research suggests that the effects for different countries within Asia vary. Woo,[157] for instance, found that education had only a small equalizing potential in Singapore. However, this should be expected because it is not only average levels of education that may affect income equality but also how skills are distributed. Analyses of cross-sectional data on education and income for a range of countries, including those in East Asia, find strong correlations between educational distributions and income distributions.[158] Analysis of time series data on the same distributions also find that the effect holds over time. Thus differences between East Asian states in the effects of education on income distribution may well vary according to the degree to which educational outcomes have been equalized in those countries. As we shall see later, East Asian states vary considerably with regard to the degree of equality of outcomes achieved in their systems, with Singapore being one of the rather less education-equal states.

The comparative evidence on enrolments and spending on education suggests that East Asia had an advantage over other regions, which may have contributed to its superior growth rates. As Table P.2 shows, Japan and the Asian tigers all had universal, or near-universal, primary enrolment in 1960, at the point of economic take-off. As in many countries in Europe in the nineteenth century (see Chapter 2), educational expansion in these countries often preceded the economic need for it. By comparison, the average for primary enrolments for developing countries as a whole was far lower, at 73 per cent. Secondary enrolments in the tiger economies were still low by comparison with developed countries in 1960, at between 20 per cent (Hong Kong) and 33 per cent (Taiwan); but they were also considerably higher than the average for developing countries, at 15 per cent (and, incidentally, for European countries when they were at a similar stage of industrial take-off). By 1974–6, secondary enrolments had risen substantially in the tiger economies, to between 62 per cent (Singapore) and 96 per cent (South Korea), now far ahead of the average for developing countries (49 per cent). Thus, although the World Bank does not find that its sample of most globalizing countries (which were mostly East Asian) had higher levels of education at the outset of industrialization than its sample of less globalizing countries (mostly from other regions), it would seem clear that the tiger economies at least did have an advantage in levels of schooling compared with developing countries in general.[159] With a few exceptions, such as Sri Lanka, the Asian tigers were not only more educated than most developing countries when they started to industrialize but managed to increase their educational advantage as time went on. As Table P.3 shows, by 1990 the average years of schooling attained by the adult populations in the four tigers was relatively high. South Korea (at 9.94 years) and Hong Kong (at 9.15 years) already had average levels equal to those for the OECD countries (at 9.02 years). Taiwan (at 7.98 years) and, particularly, Singapore (at 5.89 years) still lagged behind the most developed nations somewhat, but even their populations had considerably more years of schooling than the average for countries in the Middle East and North Africa (at 4.47 years), and particularly those in sub-Saharan Africa (at 2.93 years). How far the latter was a result, rather than a cause, of growth is, of course, hard to determine.

Spending on education presents a more complex picture. As Tilak notes,[160] and as Table P.4 shows, public spending on education in East Asia, both as a proportion of GNP and as a proportion of total public expenditure, has risen substantially in the decades since 1960, and particularly in the last decade. But it has been only slightly higher than in other developing countries and is generally lower than in the most developed countries. However, other factors need to be taken into account. Firstly, private spending on education was high in many East Asian countries – including in all the tigers except for Singapore –[161] and considerably higher than in other developing regions

Table P.2 School enrolment ratios in East Asia and other regions

Economy	1960			1974–6		
	Primary	Secondary	Higher education	Primary	Secondary	Higher education
Hong Kong	87	20	4	91	71	22.7
Japan	103	74	10	100	99	40.3
Korea	94	27	5	100	96	52.0
Singapore	111	32	6	100	62	33.7
Taiwan	96	33	4	99	89	46.4
China	109	21	0.6*	99	69	5.7
Developing economies	73	15	2.0	99	49	8.9
Developed economies	102	62	13	103	99	51.0
World	62	38	8	100	58	16.2

Figures for Primary and Secondary are net enrolment rates, except for Secondary in the case of Singapore.
* 1975 Source Tilak, 2002, p. 57, Table A.2

Table P.3 Average years of schooling attained by population over 15, 1960 and 1990, regions and countries

Region/country	1960	1990
Latin America and Caribbean	3.26	5.24
Middle East/ North Africa	1.22	4.47
Sub-Saharan Africa	1.73	2.93
South Asia	1.51	3.85
OECD	7.05	9.02
HongKong	5.17	9.15
Singapore	4.33	5.89
South Korea	4.25	9.94
Taiwan	3.87	7.98

Source: Barro and Lee, 1996

and amongst the most developed countries. Secondly, GNP in the East Asian states rose far above that for other developing regions so per student expenditure rose also, even without taking into account private spending. Not only had more been invested in each student in education but, according to Tilak,[162] the money was spent more efficiently there than elsewhere. Investment in education was well balanced between the different sectors, with spending on secondary and then higher education following behind investment in primary education.

Table P.4 Public expenditure on education as a percentage
of GNP, 1960 and 1989, countries and region

Country/region	1960	1989
HongKong	–	2.8
South Korea	2.0	3.6
Singapore	2.8	3.4
Malaysia	2.9	5.6
Thailand	2.3	3.2
Indonesia	2.5	3.5
HPAE average	2.5	3.7
Brazil	1.9	3.7
Pakistan	1.1	2.63
Sub-Saharan Africa	2.4	4.1

Source: World Bank, East Asian Miracle, 1993

Competing explanations of educational contributions to development

Educational systems in East Asia are, of course, far from identical, and we shall be considering some of the significant differences later. However, there is a considerable literature on East Asian education and skill formation in general which seeks to analyse what common characteristics may account for the exceptional contributions these have made to economic and, to a lesser extent, social development. There are two main schools of thought which, although they share significant common ground, differ in important ways which are germane to policy. The first comes from the human capital school; the second from what is generally referred to as 'developmental skills formation' theory.

Accounts based on human capital theory and traditional neo-classical economics assume that education has been effective because it has supplied the skills demanded by the economy and done this efficiently. On this view, education and training, which we may refer to more generally in this context as skills formation, have been well attuned to the market, in terms of both the demands of consumers of skills (employers) and the consumers of education (parents and students). There has been efficient matching of supply and demand in both areas. Human capital accounts[163] argue that this has mainly been achieved through market mechanisms, with education and training systems being highly oriented to the market. In support of this they cite the high levels of private provision and the willingness of parents to invest heavily in education, a sign that the latter is being efficiently delivered and that its outcomes are valued in the labour market. The role of the state has been to ensure that these systems work efficiently and that they are

responsive to market demand. State intervention, over and above the organization of those parts of education which are seen as public goods – that is,
compulsory schooling – has not mainly gone beyond what has been necessary to rectify market failures, as when loans are provided to compensate for
the failures of markets to provide capital to fund student studies.

More specifically, human capital accounts note the success of East Asian
school systems in expanding at the right rate to meet the needs of the economy. The expansion of school systems in the tiger economies proceeded
sequentially, first with the universalization of primary schooling, then with
the rapid expansion of lower secondary education, and finally with the
growth of post-compulsory vocational education and training (VET) and
higher education. The initial priority given the state investment in primary
education was logical because this was where the social rates of return to
education were highest and this was what was most needed in the early
years of industrialization, when most of the growing demand was for semi-
skilled and disciplined manual labour. As the economies developed into
more highly skilled areas of manufacturing, there was increasing demand
for secondary education and VET graduates, and governments increasingly
invested in these areas. Further economic development created demand for
more post-secondary and higher-education graduates. The achievement of
near universal lower secondary schooling now created the basis for expansion of upper secondary and post-secondary provision. Since incomes had
risen, and with demand for post-secondary qualifications strong, parents
were willing and able to contribute to the cost of high school and university
education and did so substantially in Japan and all of the tiger economies,
barring Singapore, where education was largely free at all levels. This allowed
the very rapid expansion of higher education without excessive costs to
government. In this fashion, argue the human capital theorists, education
responded to changes in economic demands and continued to be provided
efficiently.

Developmental skills formation theorists[164] generally agree that skills
supply and demand were often well matched in the tiger economies and
that this was beneficial for growth. However, they tend to offer a different account from the human capital theorists as to how this was achieved.
In particular they argue that the state in these economies played a much
greater role than is acknowledged by human capital theory and that it went
well beyond the conventional notion of intervening in cases of market
failure. Ashton et al.[165] emphasize especially the major role that government manpower planning played in South Korea, Taiwan and Singapore,
and also the active role of government generally, not only in meeting skills
demands but in creating demand for greater skills through industrial and
other policies.

Manpower planning certainly played an important role in these countries
and was notably successful in some cases. Singapore was the outstanding

example. Here the high-level inter-ministerial government body, the Council for Professional and Technical Education, made detailed forecasts of future skills needs, based on market projections and on the expected outcomes of economic policy with regard to growth in different sectors, and developed policies for ensuring that the skills supply would meet these demands. These policies involved not only the development of new institutional capacity to meet demand – which was coordinated through the Ministry of Education, for schools and higher education, and the Ministry of Manpower and the Standards and Productivity Board, for workforce development. It also involved the setting of entry quotas for the different branches of vocational and higher education to ensure that the flows of skills from the system would meet future demand. Despite the scepticism towards manpower planning in most western countries, the process worked rather well in Singapore. Generally speaking, government skills targets were met and tended to be in line with the future needs of the economy. At each stage of its highly planned economic development, Singapore anticipated new skills demands and ensured that the skills supply adapted to these with remarkable accuracy.[166] Where miscalculations were made, targets and quotas were rapidly revised.

Manpower planning had not always been so successful in some of the other economies, however. South Korea used five-year plans in education throughout the 1960s and 1970s, like Singapore, trying to design policies to ensure that the future output of skills would be commensurate with the planned developments of the economy.[167] But it was not always able to achieve its goals. For example, it was notably unsuccessful in realizing its targets for graduates from vocational high schools, not least because with its proliferation of private high schools it was much less able than Singapore, or Taiwan, where schools were mostly state controlled, to regulate the intake. Additionally, in South Korea, deregulation of admissions to universities in the 1980s led to a substantial over-production of graduates and resulting graduate unemployment and declines in wage returns to a degree.[168] Highly regulated Singapore, by contrast, generally managed to avoid over-production of graduates and had stable returns to post-secondary qualifications. Manpower planning thus played a more significant role in Singapore, and possibly also in Taiwan, than in South Korea, where it was in any case abandoned in the late 1980s.

Perhaps more important for the developmental skills formation theory than manpower planning is the way in which governments in South Korea, Taiwan and Singapore acted to create demand for high skills through industrial and other policies. Singapore again provides some outstanding examples.

The Singaporean government was notoriously proactive in its dealings with multinational companies and its management of inward investment generally. One of its first acts after the first two crisis years of self-government, and once the decision had been made to seek export-led growth through foreign direct investment, was to set up the Economic Development Board in 1961. This body, whose work has been meticulously examined by Schein,[169] was charged with seeking out suitable foreign multinational companies and facilitating their location in Singapore. As a global organization with over 400 staff and offices in New York, London, Frankfurt and Milan (by the late 1980s), it used its international networks to obtain intelligence on companies, and to approach and negotiate with those selected on terms for locating in Singapore. It also acted as a 'one-stop-shop' in Singapore for organizing everything that relocation would demand, including providing turn-key factories, office space, preferential housing, deals on subsidies, and all of the infrastructure, including transport and IT, which the business would require. These arrangements also, crucially, involved forging agreements with regard to training (and skills transfer). The early multinational entrants into Singapore were encouraged to bring their own managers and technicians, who would train local staff on site or at the home country headquarters during secondments. Before long, however, the Singapore government was reaching agreements with the major multinationals for the joint development of training schools. In time, agreements were reached with the governments of the countries with the major investor firms to set up public training centres in Singapore which would supply the skills for the relevant sectors – hence the foundation of the German-Singapore Institute of Technology, the Japan-Singapore Institute of Software Technology and the French-Singapore Institute of Electro-Technology.[170]

Another example of state intervention in the demand for skills comes from Singapore during the so-called 'Second Industrial Revolution' in the early 1980s. In an attempt to drive up skills levels and encourage more productive use of labour, the PAP government deliberately forced up wages by instigating new wage minima and special taxes on low-wage companies. The revenues generated by the latter were ploughed into the Skills Development Fund, which was used to subsidize company training initiatives in targeted high-skills areas. This was part of a broader strategy to shift the Singaporean economy into higher value-added areas of manufacturing. Tax incentives and infrastructural improvements were also used by the Economic Development Board, which spearheaded the restructuring, to cajole foreign multinationals into upgrading their operations in Singapore.[171] At the same time, and in a coordinated process, large new investments were made in polytechnic education and training schemes to increase the supply of more skilled labour in anticipation of the upgrading. Major investments were also made in industrial parks and state-funded research and development (R&D) centres. In the end, the policy proved to be too successful since it drove up Singaporean wages to a point where they were no longer competitive, and it had to be abandoned. However, for a number of years it succeeded in pushing Singaporean industry up-market. Multinationals not wanting to upgrade their operations were encouraged to leave Singapore and did so. Others were willing to upgrade facilities from low-skilled assembly to higher-skilled manufacturing and did so. As Rodan shows,[172] productivity increased significantly as a result, if not to the levels hoped for by government.

Education and state formation

Theories of 'late development' and the 'developmental state' have brought us much closer to an adequate historical understanding of the remarkable rise of East Asian economies during the twentieth century than have the accounts of neo-liberal economics. Likewise, theories of developmental skills formation improve on traditional human capital theories by enhancing our understanding of the key role of the state in guiding educational development – including that of the private education markets – and in coordinating this with strategies for economic development. Without an understanding of this we cannot explain how Japan and the East Asian tiger economies have been so much more successful than other well-educated Asia states, such as Sri Lanka and the Philippines,[173] in placing skills formation at the service of economic development. Educational advance in Japan and the tigers was not only rapid, as in many other countries in Asia; it was also efficiently geared towards development, which was not always the case elsewhere.

However, developmental skills formation theories still fail to capture the full extent of the role played by education and training in the development of East Asian states. What was significant about East Asian education and training systems was not just how they managed to produce the right number of graduate engineers or mechatronic technicians at the right time and with the right technical skills. Also noteworthy are the kinds of values and attitudes that were developed through schooling and how these contributed to both economic and social development. In short, we need to understand more about the role of education and training in state formation in East Asia.

The process of state formation in Japan and the East Asian tigers involved both economic and social development, and these two aspects, as we have seen, were intimately related. Economic development in the early stages required a supply of disciplined workers with conforming social behaviours and the motivation to work hard in support of national economic improvement. It also required relative social and political stability – not least in order to attract foreign investors – and a competent bureaucracy led by highly motivated political leaders. Developmental states also required political legitimation to remain in power. This was achieved, by and large, through the mobilization of nationalist aspirations in support of their vision of rapid economic development; through gradual social reforms, which demonstrated that the benefits of growth would be shared; and through the cultivation of a meritocratic ethos, which promised individual rewards for those who worked hard. All of these necessary conditions for economic development thus rested on social foundations. Education not only provided the technical skills for economic development. It also nurtured the values and attitudes to underpin these social foundations.

Japan

Japan represents one of the classic historical cases of education in the service of a nationalist project of development. Indeed, the creation of a national education system soon after the 1868 Meiji Restoration was an integral part of the process of intensive state formation through which reformers sought to modernize Japan and save it from subjugation to the West. As Herbert Passim (1965) has written,

> educational reform ranks as one of the key measures in the transforma-
> tion of Japan from a feudal to a modern nation state.... Through the use
> of uniform teaching materials and the diffusion of a national language...,
> the schools helped promote a common sense of nationhood and the
> displacement of regional by national loyalties.[174]

During the pre-Meiji Tokugawa period, Japan had a thriving educational culture amongst the Samurai elite whose children were educated in the domain schools run by the feudal authorities, but less than 50 per cent of the population as a whole (by 1860) went to school and most of these in the privately run Terakoya basic schools.[175] Towards the end of the Shogunate, and after the arrival of Commodore Perry in 1853, Japanese culture began to be more open to western science, but the schools remained dominated by traditional Confucian values. It was the ex-Samurai reformers after the Meiji Restoration who sought to modernize Japan and saw education as a means of mobilizing the entire population in this process of rapid state formation.

Education was required to furnish the new bureaucratic elite so vital to the modernizing process; to inculcate new modernizing principles amongst the masses, whilst reinforcing traditional Japanese traditions and identity; and it was critical for the administrative and linguistic integration of a nation formerly divided into over 300 separate feudal units.[176] The Japanese author-ities proved themselves to be particularly adept at all of this, simultaneously emphasizing the importance of adapting western science and technology whilst stressing the uniqueness and historical continuity of Japanese cul-ture and traditions. As Burks has noted, 'In Japan, certainly, experience has demonstrated that an education system can be a powerful instrument in the forging of national unity.'[177]

With the establishment of a Ministry of Education in 1871, a new education system was developed which drew heavily on western influences, incorporating French principles of centralized administration and US mod-ern curricula. A later conservative backlash against westernization led to a return to traditional Japanese values in education, epitomized in the revised Education Ordinance of 1880 and later in the ultra-conservative Imperial Rescript, which stressed the role of education in promoting loyalty to the state and to the Emperor. After 1885, Japan's celebrated Education Minister, Mori Arinori, sought to reconcile modernity and tradition by promoting a westernized secondary education for the elite whilst preserving traditional values in popular education. Though later assassinated by nationalists, Arinori expressed his mission for education in classic nation-building terms, echoing the rhetoric of American republicans, such as Orville Taylor quoted in Chapter 5:

> In the administration of all schools...what is to be done is not for the sake of the pupils, but for the sake of the country...Our country must move from its third class position to second class, and from second class to first, and ultimately to the leading position amongst countries in the world.[178]

The nationalist objectives of Japanese education were increasingly emphasized during the pre-Second World War Showa period. Military training under the guidance of an officer was introduced in secondary schools. Textbooks in subjects such as history, Japanese and morals taught loyalty to the country and the Emperor, especially, as Peter Cave points out, after textbook production was made a monopoly of the Ministry of Education in 1903.[179] Before the 1930s, he writes, textbooks

> idealised soldiers as models for the entire population, presented the divine origins of the Emperor and of Japan as facts rather than myths, lauded self sacrifice while censuring self-interest, and represented Japan as a glamorous nation, undefeated in war, with special interest and responsibilities to the rest of East Asia.[180]

After defeat in the war and with the US occupation, nationalist elements were systematically purged from the curriculum. Moral education was banned and the teaching of history and geography was suspended until new, less nationalistic textbooks could be produced. Nevertheless, it did not take long after the US withdrawal before nationalist sentiments were reintroduced. The process of textbook certification was transferred back to the Ministry of Education in 1953, and in 1963 a law transferred textbook selection from schools to local boards. The nationalist elements in textbooks in Japan have remained to this day and are a matter of huge controversy.[181] Although a more objective view of Japan's wartime past began to creep in to history textbooks after the 1970s – with formerly forbidden subjects such as the Nanking Massacre and wartime sex slavery in China beginning to be mentioned – the curriculum has continued to be used to promote nationalist ends. As late as 1999 there was a new law which made flag-raising in schools compulsory. Japanese education was, and has remained, centrally about developing national consciousness.

Korea

The same was true of Korean education after independence. The national education system was created soon after the liberation from Japanese colonialism through a 1949 law which created a national, publically funded single-track school system, compulsory from the ages of 6–12. As Adams and Gottlieb note, the main purpose of the elementary schools was 'nation-building through education... to provide basic skills and general education in support of Korean culture and national integration'.[182] Nationalism was even more emphasized in the 1960s under the developmental state of General Park, which continually promoted the myth of the unitary nation in Korea with a 5 000-year history. As Yang Young-Kyan recalls,[183] every child in the 1970s was obliged to memorize the Charter of National Education, which began:

> We have been born into this land, charged with the historic mission of regenerating the nation. This is the time for us to establish a self-reliant posture within and contribute to the common prosperity of mankind without, by revitalising the illustrious spirit of our forefathers. We do hereby state the proper course to follow and set it up as the aim of our education.

In its 1985 publication on the vision for education for the year 2000, the Korean Education and Development Institute was still using the familiarly stentorian nationalistic tones: 'Korean education suffered setbacks in its development amid the political and social disturbances following territorial division. But the pounding of hammers steeled the will of the people to develop education as the driving force for national development.'[184] By 1988, the year after the transition to democratic rule, the Ministry of Education still listed amongst its objectives for high schools: 'To instil in students an awareness of the mission of the nation.'[185]

Singapore

Modern Singapore represents an equally clear case of education as an instrument of intensive state formation. Indeed, as a country with no prior history of nationhood or national identity, and one cast into independent statehood unexpectedly on its sudden exit from the Malaysian Federation in 1965, Singapore had an even more urgent need of nation-building than Japan and Korea, a task which the political leaders undertook in a characteristically dirigiste and comprehensive fashion. However, the model of statehood developed in Singapore was very different from that in Japan and Korea.

Japan and Korea could draw on their long histories as nations, stressing the relative ethnic homogeneity of their populations, and they developed essentially ethno-cultural understandings of nationhood. Singapore, by contrast, was characterized by considerable ethnic, religious and linguistic diversity, and the new state had to create a nation from scratch, from the top down. Since ethno-culturalism was unworkable amidst such cultural diversity, nationhood had to be constructed on a civic rather than an ethnic model. A statist, civic republican conception of citizenship, stressing political rather than cultural unity, and duties rather than individual rights, was more fitting than a liberal model for a paternalistic developmental state. Nevertheless, multiculturalism was at its heart from the beginning.

Singapore's leaders had always been multiculturalist cosmopolitans. The founding triumvirate of the People's Action Party (PAP), Lee Kuan Yew, Goh Keng Swee and Toh Chin Chye, were English-educated Chinese who had been active in anti-imperialist socialist politics in England in the late 1940s and early 1950s. As part of the Malayan Forum in 1949 they had campaigned against the British for an independent socialist Malaya, including Singapore.[186] Lee had allied with the unions and the Communist Party in Singapore in the mid-1950s, fighting Chinese chauvinism in a bid to promote the federation with Malaya and an end to British colonial rule. Following the PAP's resounding 1959 electoral victory in the newly self-governing Singapore, Lee, now as Prime Minister, adopted a pragmatic anti-communist line to dampen Cold War fears of a communist takeover in Singapore and to attract foreign investors. The left were forced out of the PAP, subsequently forming the opposition Barisan Socialis Party in 1961. But Lee maintained his commitment to a multi-racial Malaysian Federation, winning a referendum victory for Singapore's entry in 1963. Whilst inside the Federation, Lee campaigned against Malay-first exclusivism for a multicultural federation, but racial tensions did not abate and Singapore reluctantly exited the Federation for independent statehood in 1965. The Malaysian experiment had failed unhappily, but Lee's conviction of the necessity of a multicultural political solution was not diminished. In fact, after the experience of Singapore's Chinese-Malay race riots in 1964, it was only reinforced. At an emotional press conference after the secession, Lee declared resolutely: 'we are going to have a mutli-racial nation in Singapore ... we unite, regardless of language, religion and culture'.[187] A Constitutional Commission reporting in 1967 duly upheld multi-racialism as a founding principle in Singapore. According to the republican principle of *jus soli*, birthplace was the main criteria for citizenship.

If a harmonious multi-racialism was one of the founding myths of Singapore, and its creation a key task for education, 'survivalism' was its close ideological twin. The political theme was introduced by the political leadership immediately on independence and continued to be a constant *leitmotif* of political discourse thereafter. In his speech to parliament immediately after the declaration of independence, Lee warned that for Singapore 'survival has always been hazardous'. 'We tried to make it less so', he said 'by seeking a larger framework of Malaysia, but it was not to be. We are now on our own ... in the centre of an extremely tumultuous area of conflict.'[188] The Education Minister, Ong Pang Boon, echoed the refrain and drew lessons for education:

> Our young republic faces a number of problems, one of which is survival as an independent nation. To help solve this problem, our Republic needs people with the spirit of loyalty to the state, and a readiness to undergo training that will serve the country in good stead. Our ability to survive and prosper as individuals depends on our ability to survive as a nation and on our readiness to promote the collective interests of the people as a whole.[189]

In a later UNESCO speech in Paris in 1968, Ong linked the two key themes of multi-racialism and national survival and reasserted the importance of education:

> The other great task in Singapore is that of evolving a common multi-racial and multi-cultural society ... with Independence, came the task ... of forging a united nation out of many races and communities which had been brought together by colonial rule. Our objective in Singapore is the evolution of a multi-racial society out of our cosmopolitan population. In this evolution we have assigned education to a key role.

The fragility of national survival for a small country, surrounded by kindred – but often hostile – neighbours in China and Malaysia, has been repeatedly stressed by Singapore's leaders throughout the republic's history, and particularly at moments of perceived political instability. As Chua Beng-Huat has written, 'if Singapore were to survive, the population must be transformed into a tightly organized and highly disciplined citizenry all pulling together in the same direction with a sense of public spiritedness and self-sacrifice in the national interest'.[190] As he also notes, reminding the public of the ever-present dangers was also a way to bolster support for the ruling party and the state. Many social policies were adopted to promote the collective civic consciousness deemed necessary to maintain unity in a multi-racial society, not least in the measures on integrated social housing, corporatist trade unionism and group representation in extended multi-racial constituencies. But, arguably, the main burden of responsibility for promoting a united citizenship was placed on education.

Since self-government was introduced, the state in Singapore has been hyper-active in developing policies in education – language and civic education especially – which it believed would promote nation-building, and in so doing strengthen economic development. The reforms went through various 'twists and turns', reflecting, as Chia maintains, both the internal politics and the geopolitical climate of the time. We can broadly identify five phases: the period from self-government to independence (1959–65); the first phase of independence (1965–79); the period of Asian 're-culturation' (1979–89); the period of civic revival and 'shared values' (1989–97); and the era of national consolidation and 'national education' (1997–).

The period up to independence saw the laying of the foundations of an integrated education system. Schooling in Singapore had been mainly in the vernacular in the pre-war and early post-war period. English-medium education for the political elites, including the Straits Chinese, took place in Christian Mission schools; Tamil-medium education in estate-run schools; and Malay education in government-supported schools. There was also a plethora of Chinese-medium private schools. These had a history of support for the China mainland republicanism of Sun Yat-sen and during the 1950s had become increasingly nationalist, in some cases with student bodies also strongly influenced by the Communist Party of Malaya. As a means of defus-ing Chinese radical nationalism, and as a multi-racial solvent, the English colonial authorities had sought to promote English-medium education. Dur-ing the run-up to self-government, the All Party Committee on Education, comprising representatives from both the ruling Labour Party and the new PAP opposition, proposed a more integrated education system, with a com-mon nationally oriented curriculum and the teaching of civics, but with bi-lingual schools. In preparation for, and during, the Malaysian Federa-tion, the PAP had tactically supported Malay as the first language, including in schools. Moral education was also introduced in 1959 with a distinctly Malay nationalist orientation. The official aim of the syllabus was to fos-ter 'Malayan consciousness and common loyalty to the state in though and action'.[191] However, the main focus, at least for the younger students, was in promoting character-building and ethical behaviour, with primary topics including cleanliness, tidiness, politeness, obedience, honesty, courage and self-control.

The creation of a national education system per se occurred after indepen-dence, during the early years of consolidation of the new republic from 1965 to 1979. The PAP government sought to create a fully integrated education system, which would be bi-lingual, but where English-medium instruction would increasingly assume the dominant role. They wanted an English *lin-gua franca* in Singapore because, like the British, they thought it would promote racial harmony, and because they thought it would be beneficial for economic development. Parents mostly supported English as a medium for similar reasons and the integrated system which evolved increasingly adopted English as the medium for maths and the sciences, with the ver-nacular used for the 'softer' subjects, such as history and civics.[192] Creating an integrated system was a slow process, but it was largely complete by the end of this period. Tamil and Malay-medium streams gradually disappeared, and the Chinese-medium schools were gradually absorbed into the system. Before 1950, Chinese-medium students had outnumbered English-medium students by two to one. By 1978 there were nine English-medium students for every one Chinese-medium student.[193] Some 91 per cent of children were learning in English-medium schools.[194] The development of a Singaporean national identity also became a priority during this period. Flag-raising in school and the recitation of the loyalty pledge were introduced in 1966.[195] Following Prime Minister Lee's initiation of a Civic Training Subject Committee, civics was introduced into secondary schools in 1968. This was taught in Chinese and English, and it emphasized racial harmony, respect for law and order, and duties to the state. In 1974 the government also introduced a subject called 'Education for Living' into the curriculum. This combined civics with history and geography and was taught in the mother tongue to the different groups of students. Chia notes that it was seen as the epitome of the civics curriculum. As the Ministry of Education representative declared forthrightly in parliament, 'The aim of the subject is to inculcate social discipline and national identity and to imbue in pupils moral and civic values.'[196]

The cultural and political direction of educational reforms during the next phase seems, at first sight, somewhat contradictory. The politics of the 1980s were largely framed by debates about 'Asian values' and fears of 'deculturation', and various educational measures were taken to promote the first and counter the second. On the other hand, education in the period was also characterized by the increasing dominance of English.

The period can be said to begin with the Goh Report on education, which came out in 1979 and led to what became known as the New Education System. The report's main concern was the high rate of exam failure and dropout amongst lower-achieving students, with 60 per cent of children failing in both first and second languages in the primary school leaving exam (PSLE). This the report attributed to the fact that 85 per cent of children were taught in school in languages which they did not speak at home.[197] The recommendation, which formed the core of the New Education System reforms, was to introduce streaming in secondary schools and in primary schools from grade three (P3). Starting from P3, the lower-achieving students would receive only a monolingual education in English and would be given five years, rather than three, to complete their primary schooling. The measure was unpopular amongst many parents and the government was forced to make various amendments, but the principle of streaming remained largely intact. Pass rates in English at PSLE did subsequently improve and dropout from secondary schools declined.

Whilst English became more dominant as a medium in schools, Mandarin Chinese was promoted vigorously outside schools, and the values imparted by the curriculum became, in some measure, more asianized. The background to this was the growing angst amongst the political elites about the encroachment of unwanted western norms and behaviours, and of a gradual deculturation of Singaporean society. Since the late 1970s there had been increasing concern about rising crime, drug abuse and abortion, and more generally with what was perceived as a mounting individualism in society. The political leadership tried to stem the tide by promoting the merits of traditional Asian values. A 'Speak Mandarin' campaign was instigated at the end of the decade so that Singaporean Chinese, who spoke various Chinese dialects, could converse in a common language and also better maintain their heritage. At the same time there was a new drive to promote citizenship and Asian values in education.

The origins of this lay in Lee Kuan Yew's response to the Goh Report and can, in a sense, been seen as a rebalancing of the report's main thrust. In his letter, Lee stressed that exam results were not everything and that values too were important. The 'litmus test' of a good education, he wrote, were

> Whether it nurtures good citizens who can live, work, contend and cooperate in a civilized way. Is he loyal and Patriotic? Is he, when the need arises, a good soldier, ready defend his country, and so protect his wife and children and his fellow citizens? Is he filial, respectful to elders, law-abiding, human and responsible? ... Is he tolerant of Singapore's different races and religions?[198]

The final reference to tolerance underlines that multiculturalism was still the official rationale – and indeed future debates on values were invariably couched in terms of generic Asian values rather than Confucian values – and yet the values listed here had a distinctly Confucian ring to them. Nevertheless, the 'reculturation' of education promoted by the subsequent Ong Report on moral education remained scrupulously pan-Asian. The report led to a new moral education syllabus, taught to children up to 15. This was accompanied by a series of textbooks entitled *Good Citizens* that, in addition to moral themes, included topics on Singapore's pioneers, presidents past and present, the role of the military and police, the importance of national service and the multicultural nature of the country.[199]

Instead of moral education in secondary schools, a new subject, religious education, was introduced at the instigation of the Deputy Prime Minister, Goh Keng Swee. Students were offered the option of various topics, including bible knowledge, Bhuddist studies, Hindu studies, Islamic religious knowledge and Confucian ethics. This programme was not a success. Confucian ethics only attracted 18 per cent of students whereas Bhuddist studies attracted 44 per cent, thus hardly promoting the Confucian ideas which were seen to be at the heart of Singapore's Asian values. By the late 1980s there was growing government concern that religious education was causing ethnic divisions, fuelled by an Islamic Malay student protest about the visit of an Israeli president and by an alleged Catholic Marxist conspiracy supposedly uncovered by the security forces.[200] Claiming a rise in religious sectarianism, the government abruptly abandoned the programme. A new Religious Harmony Act came onto the statute books in 1990.

The next decade saw various attempts to revitalize civil society in Singapore, through the sanctioning and support of state-controlled community groups. This was partly the initiative of a new generation of political leaders who had taken note of the waning popularity of the PAP during the mid-1980s and sought to introduce a more participatory and consensual style of government to counter growing popular antagonism to the overweening and intrusive state which had grown up under the PAP.[201] At the same time, Japanese-style work practices were introduced into to the workplace to reinforce the collective spirit deemed to be lacking amongst employees, and new community policing tactics, again borrowed from Japan, were introduced onto the streets to further emphasize the need for collective discipline. In education there was a new drive to promote an indigenous sense of Singaporean citizenship, this time secularized to avoid escalating religious divisions. A Government Committee was set up to investigate Singapore's core values. The 'Shared Values' White Paper which issued from this in 1991 listed five shared values which neatly encapsulated many of the core beliefs of the political leadership:

Nation before Community and Society before Self;
Family as the Basic Unit of Society;
Regard and Community Support for Individuals;
Consensus instead of Contention [the latter later revised to Conflict];
Racial and Religious Harmony.

In a speech to the PAP youth wing in 1988, which is widely thought to have instigated this initiative, the forthcoming Prime Minister, Goh Chok Tong, had reviled the trend towards individualism in Singapore, calling instead for the 'formalisation' of Singaporean values (presumably those supported by the leadership) 'in a national ideology' which would then be taught in schools.[202] The new civic and moral education courses which were implanted in schools after the White Paper did just that.

The final phase of reforms in civic education, which occurred from 1997 onwards, can be seen as an intensification of the earlier measures for promoting the national ideology in schools. The reforms began at the time of another critical juncture, both in Singapore and in East Asia more generally. The Asian financial crisis had begun in 1997, raising serious doubts about the viability of the East Asian model of development. At the same time, Singaporean society was becoming increasingly internationalized – not least through policies of hiring foreign talents to make the economy more competitive – and political concerns were being raised about the emergence of a 'hotel society' in Singapore, where long-term loyalties to the state might be diminished. New measures were needed to remind Singaporeans of their history and of the ongoing need to strive to survive. The National Education programme was launched by the then Deputy Prime Minister, and future Prime Minister, Lee Hsien Loong, in 1997, with the aim 'to develop national cohesion, the instinct for survival and confidence in the future'.[203] Unlike previous civics education initiatives in schools which were implemented as discreet subjects, National Education was an ideological framework which was to be systematically 'infused' through the entire curriculum. Ironically, this new programme – probably the most overtly ideological of all the civic education programmes yet devised in Singapore – was launched at the same time as a programme entitled 'Thinking Schools', which aimed to promote more critical thinking and creativity amongst students. As ever, the Singaporean leadership was seeking to square the circle. A competitive economy was deemed to require more innovation and creative talent, at least amongst the professional elites. This suggested a need for a more open style of education, at least for some. At the same time, societal cohesion was seen as being under threat, and partly from the same globalizing trends which were encouraged in the economy. Globalization of the economy had to be balanced by intensified socialization of the citizen. National Education encouraged discussion of social and political issues, but only within strictly defined limits. The framework came replete with official markers for subjects which were 'out of bounds for discussion'.[204]

Commonalities of East Asian education and its social objectives

Promoting national identity and patriotism has been a major aim of education systems in Asia. Traditionally, moral education was at the centre of schooling in many Asian societies,[205] and the developmental states built on these foundations, adding to the curriculum various new subjects, such as civics, which dealt with more political themes, and national education, in Singapore, which was explicitly about political socialization and building loyalty to the Singaporean state. At the same time, practices were introduced which sought to enhance collective national consciousness amongst students. At a basic level these included practices designed to enhance cooperation between pupils, such as the undertaking of collective exercises, the singing of national anthems and the recital of loyalty pledges. In Japan, they included a practice whereby students took turns to prepare lunch for their classmates and to clean their own classrooms. Cooperation through group learning was also highly emphasized in both Japan and Korea where, typically, the faster students were encouraged to help the slower ones in class and performance was often measured on a group basis.[206] In Japan and South Korea, both relatively homogenous societies with fairly ethno-cultural notions of national identity, little concession was made to multicultural learning, and students were brought up with a largely mono-cultural version of their national identity. However, in Singapore, a multi-ethnic, multi-lingual and multi-faith state, more committed to a civic version of its national identity, the government sought to instil a more multicultural version of state identity.

Instilling a meritocratic culture was also important in all of these states. Although democracy was limited during the early years of the developmental states, governments had to gain legitimacy to govern effectively, and they did this not only by delivering improved living standards but also by ensuring that the fruits of development were reasonably fairly distributed. Cultivating a meritocratic ethos in education, where rewards and opportunities would come to those who worked hard, helped to encourage a belief that the system was equitable, as well as motivating students to achieve. Some of the East Asian states were more egalitarian than others in their education policies. But in all cases there was an emphasis on achievement through hard work, and rewards according to merit. Building on the traditional Confucian Mandarin system of meritocratic national examinations for the civil service entry, East Asian states developed national examination systems as the typical mode of selection for high school and higher education. The expanding opportunities available to those with qualifications during the boom years of economic expansion enhanced popular belief in education as the meritocratic route to individual advancement.

The way in which education and training have been organized in these countries has generally supported government social objectives, as well as the economic imperatives of development. East Asian education systems – during the years of developmental state formation and up, at least, until the end of the twentieth century – all had a number of structural features in common, as several commentators have observed.[207] These common features well served the state-forming functions of education.

School systems were generally highly centralized. Government ministries prescribed in some detail the curricula, standards and assessment tools for each stage and year of education. In most cases they also authorized textbooks, supplied teaching materials and provided detailed guidelines on teaching methods. Public schools generally had little managerial autonomy since government authorities generally appointed and allocated staff, determined the rules for student admissions and maintained tight control over spending. Strong central control, and the relatively uniform structures that went with it, allowed three important effects in the East Asian context.[208] Firstly, they allowed the government substantial control over the content of education; secondly, they facilitated the regulation of student flows through different tracks and subject areas, a process which in several countries is an integral part of manpower planning and control; and thirdly, they helped to promote the strong normative standards and expectations for all students[209] which were crucial to the high average levels of attainment observed in countries such as Japan, Singapore, Korea and Taiwan.[210]

A second common characteristic of East Asian education systems was the heavy emphasis placed on the core skills areas of literacy, maths and science. Primary school teaching concentrated heavily on literacy and numeracy;[211] maths and science generally occupied a large proportion of the secondary curriculum; and a large number of students took science and engineering subjects at university. This emphasis partly explains why students in countries such as Japan and Singapore invariably ranked so highly on the International Evaluation of Achievement (IEA) surveys of skills in maths and science, including in the Third International Maths and Science Study (TIMSS), and continue to rank so highly in the OECD Programme for International Student Assessment (PISA) surveys.[212] It also explains why so many young people in these countries went on to take and excel in maths, science and engineering subjects in high school and university. In Singapore during the 1990s over 20 per cent of the 18-year-old cohort regularly passed A-level in maths and over 10 per cent achieved a further maths A-level.[213] Of all the graduates from Singapore's polytechnics and universities in 1994, almost half (47 per cent) had studied engineering. Japan trained as many engineers in 1993 as the United States, with only half the population.[214] Lastly, all schools tended to place great stress on values and moral education, as the previous section demonstrates.

Central control, planning, and stress on values and core skills were all key features shared by the education systems of the East Asian states. Although policies in these areas began to change in the twenty-first century,[215] not least in response to the globalizing influences on education policy, they were highly important in the early years of industrialization. This form of mass, standardized education, with its strong socializing mission, served economies well during the first 30 years of growth, providing an expanding supply of labour market entrants with good work discipline, cooperative attitudes and sound basic skills.

Modalities of East Asian skills formation and the evolution of the developmental state

The account so far has concentrated on the common features of East Asian education and training systems, and how these supported the principal aims of the developmental states. However, there are also important differences between the systems in the different countries which it is important to understand. The remainder of this account therefore focuses on the different modalities of skills formation in East Asia and how these articulate in specific ways with the distinctive economic and social trajectories of their developmental states. The story ends with a consideration of the different challenges posed to the systems by the globalizing trends at the end of the twentieth century, by which time the developmental state itself was in transition, not least with the adoption of democratic political systems in Taiwan and South Korea.

The major differences in the skills formation systems in Japan and the tigers are along two axes. These relate, on the one hand, to the degree of social equality in the education systems and, on the other, to the forms of articulation between schooling, training and work. The first difference arises from the structure of school systems, with some having late selection and comprehensive schools, and others emphasizing early selection and differentiated schooling. The second difference arises out of the different industrial structures and forms of work organization which necessitate different types of linkage with education systems. Broadly speaking, countries which have large firms with strong internal labour markets rely heavily on enterprise-based occupational training and concentrate on general education in school. Countries with smaller firms or foreign firms, which do not have strong internal labour markets, are forced to provide more external occupational training, funded by the state, and will do more of this through the education system. Japan and Korea were at one extreme on both of these axes, having highly egalitarian compulsory school systems and extensive in-company training in large enterprises. Singapore occupies the opposite position, having rather selective schooling and a large provision of public vocational and occupational training to compensate for its relative lack of internal labour markets. Taiwan is in an intermediate position. Its educational structures are rather like those of Japan and Korea, unsurprisingly given the common Japanese and US influences. But it also has a predominance of small firms doing little training, which forces the public authorities to provide more vocational education.[216] In the following, I will contrast the model in Japan (and in passing Korea) with that in Singapore.

Japan

Japan has been the regional leader in East Asia since the pioneering modernization initiated by the Meiji reformers after 1868. It was the first country in Asia to adopt the developmentalist model of growth and skills formation and has remained the example to copy. As regional leader, and also former colonial power in Taiwan and Korea, it inevitably exercised enormous influence in the region, not least on its educational structures.[217] However, it is its close neighbour, South Korea, which most resembles it. There are good historical reasons for this in addition to the fact of colonization. Japan and Korea are both rather ethnically homogeneous societies and they both share certain historical characteristics which mark them out from Chinese societies in the region. Both Japan and Korea experienced a form of state-centred feudalism which had similarities with the absolutist states of the West and which left dense networks of hierarchical relations in civil society.[218] Family structures were also less inward-looking than in Chinese societies, allowing for the growth of professional organization beyond the bounds of kin. These shared characteristics arguably go some way towards accounting for the development in both cases of highly 'national' economies, dominated by large national firms, and characterized, particularly in Japan, by strong relations of trust.[219] In any event, both countries have developed educational systems which are remarkably similar and significantly different from others in the region.

The institutional structures of Japanese education are to a large extent, as we have seen, the product of the immediate post-Second World War period, when the traditional structures of education were initially reshaped, as part of the post-war settlement between the defeated Japanese and the victorious occupation authorities, and then subsequently 'renationalized' after the end of occupation. The American occupying powers (generally known as SCAP after General McArthur's title of Supreme Commander of the Allied Powers) proposed the democratization of Japanese schooling through the establishment of the characteristic US 6-3-3 system of public primary, secondary and high schools, and through the creation of decentralized local education authorities. To protect against any revival of the values associated with inter-war nationalism and militarism, moral education was removed from the curriculum. These measures were initially readily accepted by the Japanese authorities, and particularly by the teacher unions, which wanted to see a more liberal and egalitarian education system.[220] Not all of these measures survived, however, and the 1950s saw the reintroduction of moral education and the recentralization of education control in the central ministry, Monbusho. Even so, an egalitarian structure of neighbourhood public comprehensive primary and lower secondary schools did take root.

US influence through the 6-3-3 structure may be said to have been partly responsible for the relative equality of opportunity in the Japanese system. However, it took other more indigenous influences to achieve the high average levels of attainment and relative equality of outcomes for which Japanese education was particularly noted.[221] The Japanese authorities, strongly supported by Nikkyoso, the main teachers' union, introduced and maintained a tradition of unstreamed, mixed-ability classes and automatic grade promotion in line with their beliefs in the importance of all children learning together. Centralized control made possible the standardization of school resources (including of teachers and head teachers through the rotation system), and relative uniformity in curricula and teaching methods, all of which tended to minimize differences in student achievement. Last, but not least, the strong emphasis on whole-class teaching and cooperative learning encouraged the homogenization of student achievements. This, and the concentration on moral education and value formation, have been the most characteristic features of Japanese education.

These characteristics, however, were not only determined by school structures and processes. They also relied on certain underpinning social institutions and attitudes. The strong emphasis on cooperation in Japanese schooling was related to societal values generally. Both Confucian and Buddhist philosophies place great emphasis on the important of balance and harmony (*Wa*), notions which underpinned all Japanese social relations.[222] Furthermore, loyalty to the group was deeply embedded. The historical importance of household group *(ie)* in Japanese society was extended to a wide range of modern *iemoto* (family-like) groupings, the most significant of which was now the company (*Kaisha*).[223] Loyalty to the group, and subordination of individual interests to group interests, was axiomatic in social relations and extended to the behaviour of children in class.

Learning occurred through cooperation, with the faster students helping the slower ones, and with rewards often going to the group not the individual.[224] The elevation of group over self also had an important cultural corollary in notions of ability formation. Japanese teachers tended to pay little attention to notions of innate ability or IQ. Traditionally, almost all students were considered capable of achieving provided that they worked hard enough and provided that they got proper support. Susan Holloway's comparative study of ability formation in Japanese and American children bears this out.[225] Whereas American children tended to attribute success to individual talent, Japanese children tended to attribute it to working hard and having good support from family, friends and teachers. Learning and achievement in Japan were seen as collective and cooperative processes, unlike in more individualistic societies. Other aspects of collectivism and cohesiveness in Japanese society were possibly also important in supporting learning, not least during this period of exceptionally low rates of crime and divorce.[226]

The other essential social underpinning of education in Japan was meritocracy. Since the Second World War, Japan had tended to see itself as a relatively 'classless' society. This was true in the sense that despite the 'vertical' divisions between men and women and between those in different segments of the labour market (i.e. large and small firms), income distribution was more equal than in all other developed societies except for Taiwan.[227] In 1990, CEOs in Japan earned approximately 16 times the average workers' salary compared with 21 times in Germany and 150 times in the United States.[228] This relative equality of incomes, combined with the absence of old entrenched elites and the egalitarian structures of schooling, gave credence to the meritocratic notion that education could be the key to economic and social advancement. In Japan, since everyone was thought to have the potential to achieve, and since everyone was in the achievement game, competition for educational success was immense. Thus, notwithstanding the stress on cooperation in public schools, and particularly at the primary levels, there was a fierce competitiveness in Japanese education which forced up credential attainment. This also led to the proliferation of private crammer schools (*juku*) and serious problems of excessive competition, as we shall see later.[229]

High average standards and relative equality of outcomes in Japanese education clearly had a role in supporting the growth of the Japanese economy. Not least, they contributed to the availability of a growing pool of recruits to firms who had good basic skills. However, the nature of the articulation between education and the economy in Japan was more specific than this and requires an analysis of the connections between industrial structure, work organization, employment relations and the different forms of skills formation, including education and occupational training. To carry out this analysis we have to look first at singular structures of the Japanese economy.

Japan's economic development was driven by its large indigenous manufacturing companies. These occupied a central position in the economy and heavily determined the structure of the skills formation system. Three aspects of Japanese manufacturing were especially significant for skills formation since they provided the context for the high levels of investment in training and determined the kinds of skill that companies sought from the school system. These relate to company structure, industrial relations and work organization.

Large manufacturing companies were generally organized into conglomerates of firms (*keiretsu*) with high levels of cross-share ownership (in some cases restricting privately traded equity to as little as 20 per cent of the total). This protected the large companies from hostile takeovers and also shielded them from the demand of investors for short-term profits, thus allowing companies to take a long-term perspective and to invest heavily in R&D and training.[230] Industrial relations in the large companies involved a singular set of practices that many Japanese economists and executives believed were crucial to the high productivity of firms. These were the three so-called 'sacred pillars' of lifetime employment, seniority wages and company unionism. They were negotiated between employers and unions after the Second World War and are still at least partly in place, despite the pressures of economic recession and globalization. Lifetime employment, which in fact often applied only to core staff, was seen as important for high productivity because it encouraged employee commitment to the firm and willingness to adopt flexible working practices. Low labour turnover also meant that companies could invest heavily in worker training without fear of losing their investment.[231] The third factor was the specific forms of work organization in many large Japanese manufacturing firms which has been referred to as the Japanese Production System. This typically involved just-in-time systems for coordinating orders, production and deliveries; flexible team-working by multi-skilled employees; the use of quality circles for quality control; and worker improvement schemes which incentivized shop floor innovation.[232]

These systems required specific forms of human skill and placed enormous emphasis on collective organizational intelligence.[233]

The Japanese skills formation system was largely geared towards the large companies. Specific forms of articulation between schools and companies characterized this relationship. Large companies in Japan could afford to invest heavily in training because they were protected from the necessity to maximize short-term profits by the *keiretsu* system and because they had low labour turnover, which minimized the risk of losing the investment in training workers. Given that they provided very extensive occupational training in-house, they tended not to expect new recruits to have many occupationally specific skills. Instead they looked to the school systems to produce graduates who had good basic skills and were thus easily trainable, who had the right attitudes, including the ability to cooperate and work in teams, and who were prepared to be flexible. Companies were therefore content that the school system should concentrate on providing a broad general education with a strong emphasis on attitude formation. Companies recruited from schools and universities directly through their networks, paying particular attention to getting applicants who were deemed likely to fit in and who had the right attitude. Since the schools and universities did not grade their diplomas, companies tended to judge the academic abilities of recruits on the basis of the prestige of the university or school that they attended, which in turn was judged by the degree of selectivity of its intake,[234] hence the scramble in Japan for places in the most prestigious institutions.

The external skills formation system in Japan, however, could not concentrate exclusively on general education. Small companies could not afford to provide much of their own training and required recruits to have occupational skills on entry. Thus occupational training was also provided in the vocational high schools (although this was of a very general nature) and more extensively in government training centres and private vocational institutes (*senmon gakko*). Students in these institutions often took public tests which led to various vocational certificates which were based on national standards determined by the responsible ministries in conjunction with employers. These certificates acted as the portable passports for employment in the occupational labour markets of the small firms sector.

Korea

The Korean skills formation system during this period was remarkably similar to that in Japan. Large national conglomerates (*chaebol*) dominated the economy, with the major ten in 1984 accounting for 67 per cent of sales and the majority of employment.[235] Although not formally practising lifetime employment policies like Japan, they tended to retain their core staff and were therefore prepared to invest heavily in training. As in Japan, the schools concentrated on providing a broad general education, with relatively few students taking vocational courses in high school, where vocational high school programmes had, in any case, a high general education content. The institutional structures of schooling were also still highly egalitarian, with a 6-3-3 structure, including comprehensive, neighbourhood primary and lower secondary schools where places were largely allocated by lot. The Korean system had many of the same strengths of the Japanese system, including high average standards in basic skills and very high rates of staying-on. By the mid-1990s over 90 per cent of young people graduated from high school, and 60 per cent from higher education (39 per cent from four-year universities).[236] They also had many of the same problems, with overheated competition for credentials, a proliferating private tuition sector, and an emphasis on examination cramming which was thought by many to stunt student creativity and independent thinking.

Singapore

The skills formation system in Singapore had a number of features in common with those in Japan and Korea. Singapore had a highly centralized education system with no local education authorities and only a handful of private primary schools.[237] However, beyond this shared emphasis on central control, planning, and core skills and values there were significant differences which derived from the nature of economy and society.

Singapore is a small, highly internationalized, multi-ethnic state, with no strong history of national identity and with a majoritarian community of fairly recent Chinese immigrants with strongly familiaristic cultural traditions. As such it had not been able to build up the dense networks of civil association which, in Francis Fukuyama's terms, constitute the basis of 'high trust' societies.[238] Social cohesion in Singapore has been largely engineered, the product of government policy and continuing economic growth, rather than having been historically grounded in the traditions and institutions of civil society. In this sense it was highly contingent and fragile, and might easily erode with the increasing social differentiation and individualism which was likely to accompany further growth and continuing lifestyle change.[239]

Singapore's economy was also highly internationalized, compared with the 'walled' economies of Korea and Japan. As a small state with little domestic demand, it had initially little choice but to adopt an economic development strategy based on exports and large-scale foreign direct investment. Domestic capital was insufficient to stimulate growth, and the Chinese business community was unlikely to grow its own large corporations.[240] Systematic encouragement of foreign investment through government agencies, such as the Economic Development Board,[241] thus created an economy dominated by large foreign firms which employed over 50 per cent of the workforce. These were inevitably hybrid in their forms of work organization, industrial relations and human capital policies. Despite government efforts in the 1980s to reduce job-hopping and encourage Japanese-style practices of team-working, job mobility rates were at western levels and companies tended to lack the endogenous institutional bases for high levels of training investment, as found in Japan and Korea.[242] The structure of Singapore's economy was also distinctive, creating somewhat different demands for skills. Whilst manufacturing employed a comparable proportion of workers to Japan, there was practically no agricultural employment, and the economy consequently tended towards service sector employment.[243] The gradual 'hollowing' out of manufacturing, and the government's policy of developing Singapore as a business 'hub' in the region,[244] was reflected in the large proportion of the workforce employed in financial and business services.[245]

These economic and social peculiarities led to a number of distinguishing characteristics in the skills formation system. In the first place, the lack of strong internal labour markets, such as those in Japan and Korea, initially limited corporate motivation to invest in training. This situation meant that the government had to invest heavily in compensatory education for adult workers, public provision of occupational skills and various incentives to increase company training. Secondly, in terms of its social structures, Singapore did not have the basis for the type of egalitarian education system found in Japan and Korea. Income inequality was higher, values were somewhat more westernized[246] and there was a strong belief in policy-making circles in the importance of fostering elites through education. These factors led to significant differences in skills formation.

Japan and Korea placed great emphasis on promoting equality in education through mixed-ability teaching throughout the compulsory years of education. Singapore, on the other hand, developed a pragmatic 'meritocratic' ideology in education which involved early selection and differentiation amongst students. As we have seen, streaming was introduced following the recommendations of the Goh Report in 1979, which found an unacceptably high rate of dropout in secondary schools. The New Education System policy which was implemented after 1979 involved streaming pupils after their third year of primary school and throughout secondary school, so that only the highest streams (Special and Express streams in secondary schools) followed a full bi-lingual programme.[247] In addition to selection by streaming, there was considerable selection by schools, with a range of selective lower secondary schools, including Special Assistance Plan schools (mostly Chinese), and over 20 schools which had only Express streams (i.e. grammar-type schools). As a result of selection throughout the Singapore education system there was considerably more differentiation in qualification outcomes than in either Japan or Korea.

The elitist – or officially 'meritocratic' – system in Singapore was underpinned by a widely held view of 'natural' or genetic intelligence.[248] Whereas in Japan and, to a lesser extent, Korea it was generally believed that achievement is largely based on perseverance and hard work,[249] and that all therefore are capable of achieving, in Singapore educational policy-makers tended to believe that children are endowed with different natural abilities and must be educated accordingly. This geneticist view was equally apparent in population control policies which were applied to encourage higher fertility amongst middle class and educated Chinese women.[250] An elitist education policy was also rationalized on developmental grounds. Lee Kuan Yew repeatedly stressed the importance of cultivating the talents of the 5 per cent who will be the nation's future leaders:

> It is on this group that we must expand our limited and slender resources in order that they will provide that yeast, that ferment, that catalyst in our society which alone will ensure that Singapore shall maintain its pre-eminent place in the societies that exist in south East Asia – and the social organisation which enables us, with almost no 'natural resources', to provide the second highest standard of living in Asia.[251]

Singapore's selective educational policies, however, did not appear to create educational ghettoes or noticeably undermine the motivation of those placed in less favoured schools and streams. Considerable effort was expended in promoting quality and aspiration in every type of educational institution (and particularly the polytechnics, which were extremely well funded), and the system had been constructed so that it appeared that there were no 'dead-end' tracks which could not lead to further study. Every student had chances of progressing across streams (although this was rare) and to higher-level institutions (i.e. from Institute of Technical Education (ITE) courses to polytechnics, and from polytechnics to universities), and this system helped to maintain motivation. Education overseas also provided a safety valve for many. Also, in a dynamic economy there were well-paid jobs for graduates from all types of institution, and this kept up aspirations. Major problems would only appear when the economy slowed down, and if opportunities for social mobility then decreased.

Singapore's education system also differed substantially from that in Japan and Korea in the way in which it articulated with labour markets. There are several aspects to this. Singapore did not have a system of lifetime employment in the major companies like Japan and severance rates were at western levels. Large, well-established multinationals, and particularly those which were Japanese and Korean owned, were likely to try to follow their parent company's policies in providing high levels of training, despite the high levels of labour mobility. However, there were limits to how far this high training investment strategy could work in Singapore. In the first place, multinationals had to be enticed into Singapore which meant that they needed reassurance from the state that it would help to finance the level of training required to get production running. Secondly, a large proportion of workers in Singapore still had low levels of school education, which meant that there were exceptionally high costs to companies providing training in-house. Even by 1994, 34 per cent of the workforce had no more than primary education and the majority of workers over 50 had not even completed primary education,[252] compared with South Korea in 1997 where only 19 per cent had only primary education.[253] Thirdly, many companies did not have the same commitment to in-company training as the large Asian multinationals (particularly the small and medium-sized enterprises). For all of these – and some other – reasons, Singapore developed a different system of articulation between the education system and the labour market compared with Japan and Korea.

Unlike Japan and Korea, Singapore had most of its post-compulsory education system (the ITEs and polytechnics) devoted to developing entry-level occupational skills. Whilst government quotas limited the number of A-level students in Junior Colleges and Central Institutes to about 26 per cent of the cohort during the 1990s (1995 figures), a further 36 per cent of lower secondary school leavers entered polytechnic (about 30 per cent) and ITE courses (6 per cent).[254] Unlike Japan and Korea, again, Singapore had a well-developed system of portable national qualifications. Traditional O- and A-levels, degrees, polytechnic diplomas, and the broad range of craft and technician level certificates from the ITEs were all set to consistent national standards and thus provided passports for entry to, and movement between, jobs. Recruitment to firms was not based to the same extent as in Japan and Korea on networks and recommendations (although the status of schools attended was clearly significant). As in most western countries, qualifications played a major part in selection decisions. Lastly, the Singapore government intervened in adult workforce training far more than in Japan and Korea. Work-based training schemes in multinationals had been brokered by the government and were often partly funded by it (through the Skills Development Fund and other devices). The New Apprenticeship System operated through a collaboration between the state (ITEs) and enterprises. The government also funded and ran (through the ITEs) a whole host of off- and on-site adult re-education and retraining courses (with acronyms such as MOST, BEST and WISE).

Singapore is often credited with having had an exceptionally tight fit between its education and external training systems and the needs of the economy.[255] To the extent that it operated detailed manpower planning and quotas for courses, which few other countries did rigorously, this was probably true. Singapore also had a predominance of post-compulsory students in vocational courses (which is rare) and these, by and large, were learning skills that policy-makers, standard-setters and teachers deemed useful for the economy.

Challenges of globalization in the late 1990s

East Asian skills formation systems were now facing major challenges: what worked well in the past might not work so well in future, as global pressures made it more difficult for countries to maintain their distinctive national styles of economic and social management. Governments in each of the countries surveyed here were intensely aware of this and began to undertake major programmes of reform. The question was how far they could achieve change given the strength of indigenous traditions and given the collateral costs they might incur in dismantling institutional arrangements which had in the past provided part of their comparative advantage. Contradictions that had been suppressed during periods of rapid economic growth and nation-building might increasingly emerge.

The challenges facing these systems arose in part from social and economic changes that had been unfolding for some time in all advanced states, but these had been exacerbated in Asia by the effects of the financial crisis of 1997. Intensified global economic competition placed increased pressure on the advanced states to upgrade their economies through yet higher levels of skills and innovation. Asian economies which had 'caught up' with advanced western economies, through borrowing and incrementally improving foreign technology, products and processes, now had to be leading-edge innovators since imitation no longer sufficed when there was no one to catch up with or borrow from. The viability of national economies was increasingly threatened by the advance of global free markets. If weakened Asian economies bowed to western pressures for increased liberalization, many of the traditional forms of economic and social management exercised by the developmental state would become problematic.[256] Increasing penetration of foreign direct investment might be accompanied by diminished scope for national regulation, which would undermine the potential for developmental industrial policy and the concerted developmental skills formation strategies that had gone with it. At the same time, liberalization of equity markets and restrictions on cross-share-holding would be likely to increase shareholder power and demands for short-term profit, thus endangering the strategic approach which major companies in Japan and Korea had taken towards R&D and human capital development.[257] Other forms of liberalization would have the same effect. Labour market deregulation would increase labour mobility and undermine the institutional basis of large company training strategies further, putting greater pressure on the public sector to provide external training.

Social changes might also erode the foundations of East Asian skills formation systems. Rapid population ageing would deplete the stock of skills in companies at the same time as it increased, at least in Japan and Korea, the cost of the policies of long-term employment and seniority wage systems which had underpinned large company human resources strategies. Greying workforces could create promotion bottlenecks which would diminish the potential for social mobility and undercut the motivation of traditionally diploma-hungry youth and ambitious young employees. Economic slowdown and rising unemployment might further sap motivation in education systems whose dynamism has depended above all on the rising demand for skills. Growing demands for democratization, particularly amongst middle-class youth in Korea and Singapore, might make labour market control more difficult. Combined with the global pressures of economic liberalization, and the growing problems of economic forecasting in rapidly changing economies, they might make traditional forms of manpower planning and control increasingly difficult.

Some of these problems might not fully impact on some countries until the longer term and depended, in any case, on the outcome of the crisis in Asia. Demotivation of youth, for instance, was not yet very evident in Korea or Singapore, although it had been identified amongst lower achievers in Japan.[258] Whilst Japan and Korea had already abandoned detailed manpower planning and regulation of student flows, Singapore continued to believe that this was achievable with sufficient political will. However, the over-arching question of enhancing creativity and innovation was one that was being faced squarely in all of these states. Since the question went to the heart of the whole model of skills formation in Asian states, it was potentially quite revolutionary. It placed in question two of the three fundamentally distinguishing features of East Asian skills formation: the adherence to centralization and standardization, and the emphasis on social and moral education.

Japan had been debating the issue of creativity in education since 1984 when former premier, Nakasone, set up the Ad Hoc Council on Education (*Rinkyoshin*) to review the working of the whole education system. The Council came up with a programme of reforms which would enhance flexibility (*Junanka*) and extend diversity and choice in schools (*Jiyuka*).[259] These initiatives did not lead at the time to extensive reforms in the system, not least because of continuing support for the egalitarian principles of the 6-3-3 system both within the Ministry of Education and amongst the public at large. However, the debate continued and many now considered the time to be ripe for change. The Central Council on Education (CCE) was again playing a major role in rethinking the basic principles and objectives of the education system with its two major reports, both entitled *The Model for Japanese Education in the Perspective of the 21st Century.*[260] Korea was a relative latecomer to the debate, but it had now taken up the reforming mission with a vengeance, not least through the work of the influential Presidential Commission on Education.

Japan's Central Council on Education argued for radical reform of education for both social and economic reasons. Japanese children were thought to be suffering from over-heated examination competition which led to overwork, excessive use of private crammer schools (the *juku* and *yobiko*),and an overemphasis on rote-learning and memorization for examination subjects. The effects of this were seen to be a damaging syndrome where young people's personal development and 'zest for living' was marred by the lack of what the policy-makers called *yutori* (room for growth). This was thought to lie behind the rise in incidents of school bullying (*ijime*) and long-term school refusal (*futoko*). On the economic front, it was argued that long-term changes demanded new responses from education. The spread of IT created the need for new skills and allowed new possibilities for learning in flexible and diverse environments. Rapidly changing technology, new working methods and the waning of lifetime employment all put a greater premium upon flexibility and adaptability amongst adult employees. Above all, the intensification of economic competition in an increasingly global market placed greater pressure on the Japanese economy to increase its productive potential, and this made new demands on skills. According to the CCE, the Japanese economy had to move ever more rapidly towards the high-tech, high-value-added areas of production and services if it was to keep competitive, and this required greater skills and more innovation. As it put it,

> Japan has reached a stage where it will no longer be allowed to use the methods hitherto employed of skilfully making use of scientific and technological achievements of Western nations. Nowadays, it is being called upon to create its own scientific and technological achievements and to develop new frontiers for itself.[261]

In the view of the CCE, the education system failed to develop sufficient creativity and analytical thinking to meet the new economic challenges. It said:

> it is clear that to us that what children will need in the future... are the qualities and the ability to identify problem areas for themselves, to learn, think, make judgements and act independently and to be more adept at problem-solving.[262]

It also needed to develop a more international outlook so that Japan could work effectively in increasingly global environments.

The prescription for change advocated by the CCE involved a radical diversification and freeing-up of Japan's traditionally centralized and standardized education system. Government cautiously acted on these proposals through a gradual programme of reforms. The school week was shortened, the compulsory curriculum was slimmed down, and schools were being encouraged to diversify their curricula and teaching methods to pay more heed to the different abilities and aptitudes of individual children. Assessment methods were also gradually being diversified with high school and university entrance now depending somewhat less on test scores and more on school achievement records and performance at interviews. On 'school choice' the government was proceeding cautiously, but the direction was plain to see. Prefectures were being encouraged to set up new types of specialist and integrated high school (*sogo gakko*) where admissions systems were exempt from zone restrictions. New six-year all-through secondary schools were being developed, similarly exempt from neighbourhood recruitment policies, to allow more choice at the lower secondary level and – ostensibly at least – to reduce the pressures of high-school entry competition for 15-year olds, although this would probably only intensify competition at the end of primary school. Taken together, the measures, if widely implemented, would significantly extend school choice and diversity within and between schools.[263]

Korea was adopting similar measures. Lottery admission systems were being phased out in some areas and parents gradually being given more choice of schools. There was to be more diversity in curricula and methods of teaching, with setting introduced for some subjects in schools. New specialist vocational high schools were proliferating in order to encourage more diversity and to nurture particular talents, and universities were being given greater autonomy in curricula and admissions to encourage a move away from standardized and overly generalist, low-quality degree courses.

How far these reforms would go in either country remained to be seen. There were many obstacles to changing traditionally standardized systems. Teachers and parents tended to be conservative and were concerned that increasing school diversity and curriculum choice might disadvantage their children in the examination wars. Small classrooms and large class sizes made innovative forms of discovery learning and individualized teaching rather difficult and arguably impossible. Impetus for local level innovation was necessarily limited in centralized systems where schools had relatively little autonomy, and whilst policy-makers talked of decentralizing control, it was unlikely that systems so accustomed to using central powers to secure uniformity would easily tolerate much local management autonomy. Most critically, diversification threatened the relatively egalitarian nature of Japanese and Korean education systems and many were wary of this.[264] Japan's CCE explicitly recognized that this would be an effect, but argued that it is necessary:

Securing equality of opportunity in education is important in any age, and from now on as well, continuing efforts to this end are fundamental. However, until now in Japan, demands for formal equality have been *too strong* (my emphasis), and that an education which responds to individual abilities and aptitudes has not been given sufficient consideration must be rectified (sic). Up until now education was controlling and in all areas the idea was 'Everyone together and equal'; approaches must now be advanced to shift this idea to 'Contents, methods and approaches that respond to each person's individuality and abilities.'[265]

However, not everyone agreed that this is a price worth paying. Indeed, leading education researchers in Japan were soon to be arguing that educational inequality was already a problem in Japan and would become more so.[266]

The Singaporean education system was also going through a major overhaul. This, as ever, was being organized from the top and was designed to meet what were perceived to be major challenges in future social and economic development. There were three major areas. Firstly, there was the need to overcome skills shortages, particularly amongst technician and graduate-level engineers, and IT specialists. Secondly, there was a need to develop the new types of skill which would be demanded as the country's economy moved further into the higher value-added areas of production and services. These were chiefly thought to be flexibility, creative thinking, problem-solving, higher-level conceptual and analytical thinking, IT and research skills. Lastly, there was the need to promote national identity and loyalty, and social cohesion and discipline. Policy-makers believed that as Singapore became a more affluent and differentiated society, there was a danger of increasingly individualistic and 'selfish' attitudes taking hold. Additionally, policy-makers were concerned that as Singaporeans became more internationally mobile, there would be a danger that Singapore would become a kind of rootless 'hotel society'. Declining awareness of the nation's history amongst youth was thought to encourage complacency about the importance of collective effort and struggle.

Three interlinked programmes were devised at the national level to deal with these problems which were implemented through a rolling programme across the nation's schools.

The Thinking Programme (Thinking Schools – Learning Nation) was to be taught over a two-year period to lower secondary students and sought to develop what were taken to be the eight core thinking skills: analysing, organizing, remembering, information gathering, focusing, evaluating, generating and integrating. Two approaches were used. In the first, students were taught the thinking skills explicitly in non-curricula contexts for one period per week. According to the official government policy, students would 'learn the skills through teacher modelling, and then apply them in everyday situations and subject-related practice items'. They were required to keep 'thinking logs' to record their reflections on questions, which attempted 'to raise their metacognition and transfer'.[267] In the second approach the thinking skills were to be infused into the core subjects of English, science, maths, geography and history (about 30 per cent of the curriculum time). In preparation for this, teachers at participating schools were required to attend seven half-day training workshops to learn appropriate new teaching strategies. Other attempts to improve creativity in schools involved the encouragement of more project work and group work, allowing more options in the curriculum and encouraging more diversified forms of assessment. At the same time the government was concerned about maintaining the traditional function of schools in political socialization.

The National Education programme, as we have seen, was designed to raise awareness amongst students of the history and identity of their country. It was in addition to the civics element of the curriculum which was already well developed and was taught within civics lessons as well as being 'infused' elsewhere. The government supplied videos to schools about Singapore's history and development, as well as other learning materials. Schools organized special events, such as exhibitions, competitions and talks, as well as special days (e.g. 'Total Defence Day', 'Racial Harmony Day' and 'National Day'). Participating schools set up committees to promote National Education.

High priority was also given to be the IT Programme, which commanded a budget of S$2 billion. Most schools were already wired with local area network systems and had their own websites. Some elite schools (e.g. Raffles) had an e-mail address for each student. The target was now to have a computer for every two students in secondary schools by 2002 as well as a computer notebook for every two teachers. Schools involved in the pilots were encouraging teachers to put their learning materials on the website and to deliver 10–15 per cent of their teaching through IT.[268]

Lastly there was a major drive to reform school leadership through the School Leadership Programme. Singapore's Ministry of Education was looking to give more autonomy to schools to enhance school effectiveness and encourage more innovative practice. In preparation for this there was a large-scale school leadership training programme delivered by the National Institute of Education.

Singapore's schools have been very effective in promoting high general standards in basic skills areas and particularly in science and maths (they came top for 14-year olds in both maths and science scores in the IEA's TIMSS). However, in the view of many policy-makers in Singapore, they needed thoroughgoing reform. It was debateable, however, how far the new reforms would achieve the changes that were thought necessary. There were thought to be major impediments to change, including the traditional conservatism of teachers, especially with regard to teaching methods; the instrumental attitudes of students towards education which encouraged them to focus excessively on chasing diplomas; the low level of demand amongst students for taking up careers in research due to the greater rewards elsewhere; and the relative underdevelopment of humanities and creative arts areas of learning (by comparison with the very strong traditions of maths, science and engineering).

The Singaporean skills formation system was in some ways better placed to adapt to the demands of the future than those of Japan and Korea. Japan and Korea had highly generalist education systems which relied heavily on large companies for the delivery of occupational training. With increasing pressures on company profits and short-term performance, and with the increase in labour mobility between firms, there was a serious danger of the latter system unravelling and the public authorities not being able to fill the gap through provision of external public training. Singapore did not have this problem since the state has always had to play a major role in occupational skills training and since, unlike the other two countries, it had been able to contain the pressure towards academic drift that leads to graduate oversupply and shortages in other areas of skill. Singapore was probably also better placed to flex-up its system to develop more creative talents.

The school system was already quite diversified, and the routinization of tracking and selection, and the social legitimation of this, had allowed the system to avoid the development of the kind of monotonic or 'unidimensional' meritocracy which in Japan and Korea led to everyone chasing the same prizes with all of the excessive and mind-limiting examination preparation that this involves.[269] Changes were already in hand to give schools greater autonomy, by means of new clustering arrangements, and these facilitated innovations at the local level. On the other hand, the maintenance of strong central control in key areas, and the very proactive and systematic government approach to the retraining of teachers, might also lead to more rapid changes in teaching methods and goals than would be possible in Japan and Korea, with their deeply engrained pedagogic traditions and their more strongly organized interest groups in education. However, on the minus side, Singapore might develop a problem of motivation amongst lower-achieving pupils in this differentiated system, as economic down-turn reduced job entry and promotion prospects.

The major difficulty for all three countries was to maintain the traditional strengths of their systems at the same time as rectifying their faults. Policy-makers rarely admitted that there was a contradiction between developing more individual and creative talents and maintaining the emphasis on social cooperation and cohesion through education. It may be that the typical western polarization of these in terms of individualism and collectivism misreads the situation in these dynamic cultures. In Singapore, for instance, policy-makers talked of encouraging 'managed creativity' which, as the term implies, sought the economic benefits of flexible thinking without the social and political costs of creative individualism. However, it seemed unlikely that there would not be some tension between these policies.

Widespread adoption of school choice, and curriculum and pedagogic diversification policies in Japan and Korea would inevitably lead to greater differentiation between schools and within schools. This would not automatically lead to the weakening of traditional values of cooperation and social discipline in schools. This had not occurred in the selective system in Singapore, and Japan and Korea might well, in any case, seek to strengthen the moral and civic elements of their curricula to counteract this, just as Singapore had done with its National Education programme. However, school reform was not insulated from other social changes. Social divisions and inequalities were beginning to widen in all of these countries and would be reinforced by the economic recession. Where the social foundations of 'collective intelligence' and group cohesion begin to erode, education systems would find it harder to maintain their role in promoting these. If this was the case, and if East Asian societies were to become more individualistic and fragmented, then they might have gained in certain respects; but they might also lose some of the traditional strengths which had constituted a major part of their comparative economic advantage.

Coda

The fundamental lesson to be learnt from the rapid rise of the East Asian economies is about the importance of the state in development. Economic development, particularly in the early phases of industrialization, is always also a process of state formation. Rapid economic development, where the state has not already been largely established, is invariably accompanied by accelerated state formation. In fact, to put it more precisely, successful economic development rarely occurs without substantial prior state formation, and is only sustained through ongoing state-building activity. In one sense, this is to reiterate what Amartya Sen has most brilliantly argued – that successful development is always about both social and economic change. However, it also has another sense, since state formation refers not only to societal development in general but also, more specifically, to the shaping of the state apparatus itself.

National development, even in a globalized world, is still fundamentally about state power. Neo-liberal economics, the doctrine of the most powerful contemporary states, can afford to ignore the fact but, as the mercantilists and historical economists well understood, national economic strength does not occur from successful market competition alone. It is always also about relative geopolitical power and about the capacity and competence of states to support development and to engage with global markets on the most favourable terms.[270] As the East Asian development story illustrates, countries with 'strong' states have a substantial comparative advantage in the struggle for development. Behind the success of Japan and the independent tiger economies breathed 'the dragon of the developmental state'.[271]

The argument, of course, begs the question: what, exactly, is the 'strong' state which seems to favour rapid development? Comparative social science has for many years debated the relationship between political forms and economic development, with modernization theorists tending to assert the concurrence of capitalist development and democratic advance. But as the economic historians have shown – and particularly those from the national schools discussed earlier – democracy tends to follow industrial development rather than precede it. In the most statistically sophisticated analyses of the question to date, Przeworski et al. show that democracies are more likely to exist in richer countries, not because democracy caused development but because democracies are more likely to collapse in poorer countries.[272] At higher income levels, democracies tend to have higher rates of productivity than authoritarian states and incomes grow more quickly. But at lower income levels, growth has historically been similar in democracies and authoritarian states (for countries with per capita incomes of less than US$3000 p.a., according to Przeworski et al., at an average of 4.43 per cent in 'dictatorships' and 4.28 per cent in 'democracies').[273] But, as they also show, the fact is that most of the poorer states are not democracies and they do not industrialize as democracies. So the salient question is: what kind of pre-democratic state most favours social and economic development? Quantitative analysts cannot answer this question because data limitations force them to lump all non-democratic states together as 'dictatorships'.

For the modern period, theorists of the developmental state have been much better able to answer this question through detailed qualitative analysis of the process by which countries develop and the characteristics of the political states which have been most successful in engineering development. The 'strong' states which have been most successful have been states which have had the competence and political will to intervene extensively and effectively in economic development; which have made this their overwhelming priority; and which have managed to maintain their legitimacy through a relative absence of corruption and through their success in raising living standards and life quality. Invariably the process has been accompanied by intensive state formation in the broader sense, in terms of building the state apparatus and forging a national consciousness to mobilize popular support for the developmental goals.

Education has been at the heart of this process in all of the East Asian states considered here, just as it was in the nineteenth-century European states considered in the earlier chapters of this book. It has been key to the fostering of the national consciousness and relative cohesion favourable to development; to the development of 'modern' modes of thinking and behaving necessary for social advance, including population control; to the inculcation of the labour disciplines and values necessary in the early years of development; and, of course, to the formation of the specialist skills needed as the economies industrialized.

State-led development has been a common feature of successful, newly industrializing countries. But it tends not to survive – in a strong form at least – past the early stages of development. More democratic forms of state power tend, fortunately, to emerge over time. The developmental state, at least in the form we are familiar with, may have already past its zenith in East Asia, except in China and Singapore. It has been more or less abandoned in Japan, South Korea and Taiwan already, as global capital increasingly sidelines the formerly powerful financial bureaucracies which lack the flexibility to adjust in the modern information society. To Castells, these forces, and the rising tide of democracy in East Asia, make this state form increasingly redundant. 'The success of the developmental states in East Asia', he writes,

> ultimately led to the demise of their apparatuses and to the fading of their messianic dreams. The societies they helped to engender through sweat and tears are indeed industrialised, modern societies. But at the end of the millennium, their actual projects are being shaped by citizens, now in the open ground of history-making.[274]

However, for countries embarking on the early stages of industrialization, developmental states have proved highly effective. They have successfully promoted economic advance and the broader process of state formation, and made the most effective use of education in this process. Countries struggling to get on the developmental ladder can hardly afford to ignore the lesson that strong states tend to get there first.

Notes

Introduction

1. Chinese translation by Zhu Xudong, Education Science Publishing, Beijing, 2004; the Greek and Japanese translations forthcoming 2014.
2. See E. Hobsbawm, *Nations and Nationalism since 1780: Programme, Myth and Reality*, Cambridge University Press, 1990.
3. See A. Green, 'Education and State Formation Revisited', *Historical Studies in Education/Revue d'Histoire de l'Education*, Special Issue, 1994, pp. 1–19.
4. See I. Davey and P. Miller, 'Family Formation, Schooling and the Patriarchal State' in M. Theobald and D. Selleck (eds), *Family, School and State in Australian History*, Allen and Unwin; I. Davey and P. Miller, 'Patriarchal Transformations, Schooling and State Formation', 1991, Paper for Social Science History Association Conference, New Orleans.
5. E. Weber, *Peasants into Frenchmen: The Modernization of Rural France, 1870–1914*, Stanford University Press, 1976.
6. T.-H. Wong, *Hegemonies Compared: State Formation and Chinese School Politics in Postwar Singapore and Hong Kong*, Routledge, 2002.
7. Y. T. Chia, *The Loss of 'World Soul' in Education? Culture and the Making of the Singapore Developmental State, 1995–2004*, Palgrave, 2014.
8. See A. Green, A. Wolf and T. Leney, *Convergence and Divergence in European Education and Training Systems*, Institute of Education, 1999.
9. See A. Green, *Education, Globalization and the Nation-State*, Macmillan, 1997.
10. See C. Johnson, *MITI and the Japanese Miracle: The Growth of Industrial Policy 1925–1975*, Stanford University Press, 1982.
11. See P. Brown, A. Green and H. Lauder, *High Skills: Globalisation, Competitiveness and Skill Formation*, Oxford University Press, 2001.
    A. Green, A., Little, S., Kamat, M., Oketch and E. Vickers, *Education and Development in a Global Era: Strategies for Successful Globalisation*, Department for International Development, London, 2007.
12. A. K. Sen, *Development as Freedom*, Oxford University Press, 1999.
13. T. Skocpol and M. Somers, 'The Uses of Comparative History in Macrosocial Inquiry', *Comparative Studies in the Society and History*, 22, 2, pp. 174–197, 1980.
14. T. Landman, *Issues and Methods in Comparative Politics*, Routledge, 2008.
15. C. Ragin, *The Comparative Method: Moving Beyond Qualitative and Quantitative Strategies*, University of California Press, 1987.
16. See J. S. Mill, *A System of Logic*, University Press of the Pacific, 2002.
17. See Ragin, op. cit.
18. See Landman, op. cit. on the latter point.

1 The Uneven Development of National Education Systems

1. M. Katz, 'The Origins of Public Education: A Reassessment', *History of Education Quarterly*, 16, 4, 1976, p. 383–407.
2. E. Levasseur, *L'Enseignement Primaire dans les Pays Civilisés*, 1896, pp. 98–100.

3. See P. Sawin, *Nationalism and the Control of Education in Prussia, 1800–1871*, unpublished PhD thesis, University of Wisconsin, 1954.
4. J. Bowen, *A History of Western Education*, vol. 3, 1981, p. 322.
5. R. Samuel and R. Thomas, *Education and Society in Modern Germany*, 1949, p. 41.
6. Ibid., p. 36.
7. E. Levasseur, *L'Enseignenment Primaire*, pp. 98–100.
8. J. Moody, *French Education since Napoleon*, 1978, p. 43.
9. E. Levasseur, *L'Enseignement Primaire*, p. 91.
10. P. Harrigan, *Mobility, Elites and Education in French Society of the Second Empire*, 1980, p. 13, fn. 3.
11. There were, in addition, 278 Catholic secondary schools, 137 *petit-seminaires* and 657 lay private schools in 1865. See R. D. Anderson, 'Secondary Education in Mid-Nineteenth Century France: Some Social Aspects', *Past and Present*, no. 53, November, 1971 and A. Prost, *L'Enseignement en France*, Paris, 1968, p. 33.
12. L. Cremin, *American Education: The National Experience, 1783–1876*, 1982, p. 179.
13. C. F. Kaestle, *Pillars of the Republic: Common Schools and American Society, 1780–1860*, 1983, pp. 111, 68.
14. E. P. Cubberley, *Public Education in the United States*, 1934, p. 205.
15. A. Fishlow, 'Levels of 19th Century Investment in Education', *The Journal of Economic History*, vol. xxvi, no. 4, 1966, p. 420.
16. B. Simon, *Education and the Labour Movement, 1870–1920*, 1965, p. 112.
17. E. G. West, *Education and the Industrial Revolution*, 1975, p. 41; A. S. Bishop, *The Rise of a Central Authority in English Education*, 1971, p. 11.
18. The voluntary schools had 2 008 000 students and the board schools 856 000 students. See M. Mulhall, *Dictionary of Statistics*, 1884, p. 111.
19. Quoted in J. Murphy, *The Education Act of 1870*, Text and Commentary, 1972, p. 9.
20. J. Hurt, *Education in Evolution: Church, Society, State and Popular Education, 1800–1870*, 1971, p. 17.
21. See E. Baines, jnr., Letters to the Right Honorable John Russell *On State Education*, 1846; J. A. Roebuck, *Speech on Education Bill* in House of Commons, Hansard, 30 July 1833, c.148.
22. J. Orville Taylor, *The District School*, 1835, p. iv.
23. A. Potter and G. Emerson, *The School and the School Master*, 1846, pp. 241–2.
24. Ibid., p. 10.
25. M. Arnold, *The Popular Education of France*, 1861; T. Huxley, Address on Behalf of the National Association for the Promotion of Technical Education, 1887, in C. Bibby (ed.), *T. H. Huxley on Education*: A Selection of his Writings, 1971; L. Playfair, *Industrial Education on the Continent*, lecture at the Government School of Mines, Science and Applied Arts, 1852.
26. H. Brougham, Speech on Education Bill, House of Commons, June 28th 1820, *Hansard*, c.49; A. J. Balfour, Speech on 1902 Education Bill in House of Commons, quoted in J. Stuart Maclure, *Educational Documents, England and Wales, 1816 to the Present Day*, 1986, p. 152.
27. Quoted in L. Stone, 'Literacy and Education in England, 1600–1900', *Past and Present*, no. 42, 1969, p. 129.
28. Quoted in V. Cousin, *Education in Holland as Regards Schools for the Working Classes and for the Poor*, trans. L. Horner, 1838, p. xix.
29. Quoted in C. Kaestle, *Pillars of the Republic*, p. 34.
30. A. Potter and G. Emerson, *The School and the School Master*, p. 116.
31. E. G. West, *Education and Industrial Revolution*.

32. W. Brewer, *Victor Cousin as a Comparative Educator*, 1971; E. Levasseur, *L'Enseignement Primaire*, pp. 102–3.
33. A. Fishlow, 'The American School Revival, Fact or Fancy ?' in H. Rosdovsky (ed.), *Industrialization in Two Systems*, 1966, pp. 51, 43.
34. C. Kaestle, *Pillars of the Republic*, pp. 60, 107.
35. Attendance given as 4283 out of 5432. See L. Cremin, *American Education*, p. 417.
36. Ibid., pp. 15, 179.
37. E. Levasseur, *L'Enseignenment Primaire*, pp. 102, 91. The population of France was 34.1 million in 1850 whilst the population of Prussia was only 11.7 million. See E. J. Hobsbawm, *Age of Capital*, 1977, p. 360.
38. Jules Ferry's 1882 law introduced compulsory attendance.
39. E. G. West, *Education and the Industrial Revolution*, p. 27, n. 4.
40. Ibid., p. 96.
41. E. Levasseur, *L'Enseignement Primaire*, p. 6.
42. M. Mulhall, *Dictionary of Statistics*, p. 158.
43. E. G. West, *Education and the Industrial Revolution*, p. 29. Richard Johnson argues that Kerry underestimated attendance figures. See R. Johnson, *The Education Movement*, unpublished paper, Birmingham University, Department of Cultural Studies, p. 12.
44. According to Victor Cousin, Dutch elementary schools had 32 per cent of all children in school where 42 per cent were of school age – that is, 76 per cent enrolment. In 1848 the ratio of children enrolled in school to total population was 1 to 7.78. See Matthew Arnold's summary of the report by Cousin and Cuvier on Dutch education in M. Arnold, *The Popular Education of France*, 1861, p. 209.
45. See doctoral research by Ann Doyle, Institute of Education, London.
46. L. Cremin, *American Education*, p. 488.
47. Ibid., p. 488. The Newcastle Commission Report of 1861, based on returns from church schools in sample areas covering one-eighth of the total population, estimated that 13 per cent of the population were at school. Horace Mann appears to have accepted this figure but Matthew Arnold, later inspector of schools, considered it over-optimistic. See E. G. West, *Education and Industrial Revolution*, p. 108. See also Levasseur's figures for 1873: Saxony (17.5 per cent); United States (17 per cent); Prussia (15 per cent); Denmark (15 per cent); Sweden (13.75 per cent); France (13 per cent); England (12 per cent), in *L'Enseignement Primaire*, p. 565.
48. Some 90 per cent of males had eight years of schooling in Prussia in 1864, according to P. Lungreen, 'Industrialization and the Formation of Manpower in Germany', *Journal of Economic History*, vol. 9, no. 1, 1975. Horace Mann believed that four years of education in England was typical, whereas the Newcastle Commission gave 5.7 years as the average. See E. G. West, *Education and the Industrial Revolution*, p. 83.
49. R. D. Anderson, *Education in France, 1848–1870*, 1975, p. 35.
50. R. Samuel and R. Thomas, *Education and Society*, pp. 41, 44.
51. E. P. Cubberley, *Public Education*, pp. 268, 247; L. Cremin, *Traditions in American Education*, 1977, p. 8; M. Mulhall, *Dictionary of Statistics*, p. 161.
52. M. Katz, *The Irony of Early School Reform*, 1968, p. 244, Table A.7.
53. B. Simon, *The Two Nations*, p. 320; T. W. Bamford, *The Rise of the Public Schools*, 1967, p. 175.
54. Chapter 6 will consider this in greater detail.

55. This assumes Mulhall's figure for total population of 37 290 000 in 1884, *Dictionary of Statistics*, p. 356; see also R. D. Anderson, 'Secondary Education in Mid-Nineteenth Century France: Some Social Aspects', *Past and Present*, no. 53, November 1971; P. Harrigan, *Mobility, Elites and Education*, p. 148, note 10.
56. R. D. Anderson, *Education in France*, p. 20.
57. F. K. Ringer, *Education and Society in Modern Europe*, 1979, p. 46.
58. Ibid., pp. 57, 140.
59. These figures assume Mulhall's figure of 51 410 000 for US population in M. Mulhall, *Dictionary of Statistics*, p. 357; B. Tyack, *The One Best System*, 1974, p. 57.
60. M. Katz, *The Irony*, p. 39.
61. D. Tyack, *One Best System*, p. 57.
62. F. K. Ringer, *Education and Society*, p. 221.
63. T. W. Bamford, *The Rise of the Public Schools*, p. 36.
64. This assumes a figure of 25 million for the population of England and Wales.
65. L. Stone, 'Literacy and Education', pp. 134–5.
66. F. K. Ringer, *Education and Society*, p. 220.
67. M. Arnold, Popular Education in France in *Selected Prose*, 1970, p. 118.
68. T. W. Bamford, *The Rise of the Public Schools*, p. 6.
69. P. Harrigan, *Mobility, Elites and Education*, p. 14.
70. F. K. Ringer, *Education and Society*, p. 71.
71. M. Katz, *The Irony*, p. 271.
72. F. K. Ringer, *Education and Society*, pp. 34, 60.
73. J. Moody, *French Education since Napoleon*, p. 56.
74. T. Zeldin, *France, 1848–1945, Intellect and Pride*, 1980, p. 159.
75. E. Levasseur, *L'Enseignement Primaire*, pp. 88, 98.
76. T. Zeldin, *Intellect and Pride*, p. 161.
77. C. F. Kaestle, *Pillars of the Republic*, pp. 20, 130.
78. B. Tyack, *The One Best System*, p. 59.
79. C. F. Kaestle, *Pillars of the Republic*, p. 131.
80. A. Potter and G. Emerson, *The School and the School Master*, p. 236.
81. C. F. Kaestle, *Pillars of the Republic*, p. 21.
82. J. Hurt, *Education in Evolution*, pp. 122, 142.
83. In 1875 there were 20 940 certificated teachers and 29 667 pupil-teachers. See E. Levasseur, *L'Enseignement Primaire*, p. 12.
84. M. Mulhall, *Dictionary of Statistics*, p. 159.
85. L. Stone, 'Literacy and Education', p. 119.
86. L. Cremin, *American Education*, p. 491.
87. C. Cipolla, *Literacy and Development in the West*, 1969, p. 115.
88. Quoted in L. Cremin, *American Education*, p. 491.
89. L. Stone, 'Literacy and Education', p. 128.
90. C. Cipolla, *Literacy and Development*, pp. 106, 110.

2 The Social Origins of National Education Systems

1. M. Archer and M. Vaughan, *Social Conflict and Educational Change in England and France, 1789–1848*, 1971; M. Archer, *The Social Origins of Educational Systems*, 1979.
2. M. Katz, 'The Origins of Popular Education: A Reassessment', *History of Education Quarterly*, Winter, 1976, p. 384.

3. L. Stone, 'Literacy and Education', p. 70.
4. See H. Butterfield, *The Whig Interpretation of History*, 1931.
5. L. Stone, 'Literacy and Education', p. 78.
6. C. M. Cipolla, *Literacy and Development in the West*, 1969, p. 61.
7. Quoted in J. Cavenagh (ed.), *John Stuart and James Mill on Education*, 1931, p. 12.
8. B. Simon, *The Two Nations*, p. 45.
9. A. J. P. Taylor, *The Course of German History*, 1982, p. 37.
10. See ibid., Chapter 4.
11. Quoted in L. Stone, 'Literacy and Education', p. 87.
12. See H. Perkins, *The Origins of Modern English Society*.
13. This argument will be developed in Chapter 6.
14. E. P. Cubberley, *Public Education in The United States*, 1934.
15. M. Katz, *The Irony*, pp. 1–2.
16. See E. Durkheim, *The Division of Labour in Society*, trans. G. Simpson, 1933.
17. E. Durkheim, *Education and Sociology*, trans. S. D. Fox, 1956, p. 81.
18. Ibid., p. 70.
19. E. Durkheim, *Professional Ethics and Civic Morals*, 1957, pp. 49–50.
20. E. Durkheim, *Education and Sociology*, p. 80.
21. Quoted in H. Haralambos, *Sociology: Themes and Perspectives*, 1980, p. 176.
22. A. H. Halsey et al., *Education, Economy and Society*, 1961, p. 1.
23. R. Collins, 'Some Comparative Principles of Educational Stratification' in R. Dale et al., *Schooling and the National Interest*, 1981, p. 278.
24. See, for instance, S. Bowles and H. Gintis, *Schooling in Capitalist America*, 1976.
25. Quoted in M. Archer and M. Vaughan, *Social Conflict and Educational Change*, p. 206.
26. E. G. West, *Education and the Industrial Revolution*, p. 256.
27. M. Sanderson, *Education, Economic Change and Society in England, 1700–1870*, 1983.
28. E. J. Hobsbawm, *Industry and Empire*, 1969, p. 173; D. Landes, *The Unbound Prometheus. Technological Change and Industrial Development In Western Europe From 1750 to the Present*, 1969, pp. 339–48.
29. C. M. Cipolla, *Literacy and Development*, p. 102.
30. E. J. Hobsbawm, *Industry and Empire*, p. 174.
31. D. Landes, *The Unbound Prometheus*, pp. 339–48.
32. S. Cotgrove, *Technical Education and Social Change*, 1958, p. 58.
33. E. Ashby, 'Technology and the Academies. An Essay on Universities and the Scientific Revolution', in A. H. Halsey et al., *Education, Economy and Society*, pp. 446–75; M. J. Wiener, *English Culture and the Decline of the Industrial Spirit, 1850–1980*, 1984; G. Allen, *The British Disease*, 1967; A. Gamble, *Britain in Decline*, 1981.
34. W. W. Rostow, *Stages of Economic Growth*, 1960, p. 38.
35. M. Mulhall, *Dictionary of Statistics*, p. 331.
36. Quoted in R. Aminzade, 'Reinterpreting Capitalist Industrialization: A Study of 19th century France', *Social History*, vol. 9, no. 4, 1984.
37. F. K. Ringer, *Education and Society in Modern Europe*, 1979, pp. 45–52.
38. Ibid.
39. For an analysis of the advances of French technical education, see F. B. Artz, *The Development of Technical Education in France, 1500–1850*, 1966.
40. E. J. Hobsbawm, *The Age of Capital*, 1977, p. 212.
41. W. W. Rostow, *Stages of Economic Growth*, p. 48.

42. A. Potter and G. Emerson, *The School and the School Master*, pp. 118–22.
43. S. Bowles and H. Gintis, *Schooling in Capitalist America*, p. 169.
44. C. F. Kaestle, *Pillars of the Republic*, p. 26.
45. L. Stone, 'Literacy and Education', p. 95; R. Johnson, 'Notes on the Schooling of the English Working Class. 1780–1850', in R. Dale and G. Esland (eds), *Schooling and Capitalism*, p. 47.
46. S. Bowles and H. Gintis, *Schooling in Capitalist America*; M. Katz, *The Irony*; R. Johnson, 'Educating the Educators: Experts and the State', in A. P. Donagrodsky (ed.), *Social Control in Nineteenth Century England*, 1977.
47. H. Perkin, *The Origins of Modern English Society*, 1985, p. 117.
48. Quoted in K. Kumar, *Prophecy and Progress*, 1983, p. 64.
49. Quoted in B. Simon, *The Two Nations*, p. 116.
50. Quoted in K. Kumar, *Prophecy and Progress*, p. 44.
51. Quoted in D. Levine, 'Industrialization and the Proletarian Family in England', *Past and Present*, no. 107, May 1985, p. 178. See also E. Zaretsky, *Capitalism, the Family and Personal Life*, 1976; L. Davidoff and C. Hall, *Family Fortunes. Men and Women of the English Middle Class, 1780–1850*, 1987.
52. F. Engels, *The Condition of the Working Class in England*, 1969, pp. 172–3.
53. R. Johnson, 'The State and the Politics of Education', p. 30.
54. D. Levine, 'Industrialization and the Proletarian Family', p. 195.
55. Quoted in ibid., p. 195.
56. D. Wardle, *English Popular Education, 1780–1975*, 1976, p. 87.
57. R. Johnson, 'Education and Popular Politics', Unit one in H. Cathcart et al., *The State and the Politics of Education*, Open University reader for E353, Milton Keynes, 1981, p. 30.
58. R. Johnson, *The Education Movement, 1780–1840*, unpublished paper, Centre for Contemporary Cultural Studies, University of Birmingham, pp. 15–23.
59. L. Stone, 'Literacy and Education', p. 125.
60. M. Sanderson, 'Literacy and Social Mobility in the Industrial Revolution in England', *Past and Present*, no. 56, August 1972, p. 79.
61. C. M. Cipolla, *Literacy and Development*, p. 74.
62. M. Mulhall, *Dictionary of Statistics*, p. 356.
63. H. Medick, 'The Proto-Industrial Family Economy: The Structures of Household and Family during the Transition to Industrial Capitalism', *Social History*, 1976, no. 3, p. 296.
64. Ibid., p. 297.
65. Ibid., p. 303.
66. J. Melton, *Absolutism and the Eighteenth-Century Origins of Compulsory Schooling*, 1988.
67. Ibid., pp. 120–3.
68. Ibid., p. 154.
69. Ibid., pp. 142–3.
70. Ibid., pp. 149–50, 159–60.
71. Ibid., p. 158.
72. Ibid., p. 165.
73. M. Katz, *The Irony*, p. 11.
74. Ibid., p. 112.
75. S. Bowles and H. Gintis, *Schooling in Capitalist America*, pp. 178–9.
76. D. Tyack, *The One Best System*, p. 30.
77. M. Katz, *The Irony*, p. 221.

78. F. Carlton, *Economic Influences upon Educational Progress in the United States, 1820–1850*, 1965, p. 34.
79. C. F. Kaestle, *Pillars of the Republic*, p. 63.
80. M. Katz, *The Irony*, pp. 121, 222.
81. S. Bowles and H. Gintis, *Schooling in Capitalist America*, p. 157.
82. C. F. Kaestle, *Pillars of the Republic*, p. 103.
83. S. Hirsch, *The Roots of the American Working Class, 1800–1860*, 1978, p. 78.
84. C. F. Kaestle, *Pillars of the Republic*, p. 64.
85. E. P. Cubberley, *Public Education in the United States*, p. 149.
86. M. Katz, 'The Origins of Public Education: A Reassessment', p. 398.
87. Quoted in M. Katz, *Class, Bureaucracy and Schools*, 1971, p. 31.
88. Ibid., p. 31.
89. Quoted in M. Katz, *The Irony*, p. 42.
90. Quoted in ibid., p. 120.
91. According to Dawley there were two slaves, two servants or tenant farmers and one industrial worker for every five freeholders at the mid-century. See A. Dawley, *Class and Community: The Industrial Revolution in Lynn*, 1976, p. 11.
92. A. Fishlow, 'The American School Revival, Fact or Fancy?' in H. Rosovsky (ed.), *Industrialization in Two Systems*, 1966, pp. 49–51.
93. Ibid.
94. S. Hirsch, *Roots of the American Working Class*, p. 54.
95. Ibid., pp. 40, 65.
96. A. Fishlow, 'Levels of 19th Century Investment', p. 65.
97. M. Archer and M. Vaughan, *Social Conflict and Educational Change*; M. Archer, *The Social Origins of Educational Systems*.
98. M. Archer and M. Vaughan, *Social Conflict and Educational Change*, p. 14.
99. M. Archer (ed.), *The Sociology of Educational Expansion*, 1982, pp. 3–4.
100. M. Archer, *Social Origins*, p. 2.
101. Ibid., p. 68.
102. Ibid., p. 121.
103. Ibid., p. 157.
104. Ibid., p. 160.
105. Ibid., p. 174.
106. Ibid., p. 176.
107. Ibid., p. 179.
108. Ibid., p. 187.
109. Ibid., p. 175.
110. Ibid., p. 200.
111. Ibid., p. 195.
112. Ibid., p. 1.
113. Ibid., p. 4.

3 Education and State Formation

1. B. Bailyn, *Education in the Forming of American Society*, p. 10.
2. Ibid., p. 14.
3. P. Corrigan and D. Sayer, *The Great Arch: English State Formation as Cultural Revolution*, 1985, p. 3.
4. K. Marx, 'Contribution to the Critique of Hegel's Philosophy of Law', *Collected Works*, vol. 3, 1975, p. 32.

5. K. Marx and F. Engels, *The German Ideology*, E. J. Arthur (ed.), 1970, p. 53.
6. Ibid., p. 80.
7. K. Marx, Preface to *A Contribution to the Critique of Political Economy* (1859), *Marx and Engels Selected Works* (hereafter, Selected Works), 1973, p. 181.
8. K. Marx, *Capital*, vol. 3, 1972, p. 791.
9. B. Jessop, *The Capitalist State*, 1982.
10. K. Marx and F. Engels, *The Communist Manifesto, Selected Works*, p. 37.
11. F. Engels, *Socialism: Utopian and Scientific, Selected Works*, p. 422.
12. S. Hall, 'Re-thinking the Base-superstructure Metaphor', in J. Bloomfield (ed.), *Class, Hegemony and Party*, 1977.
13. K. Marx, 'The British Constitution', in D. Fernbach (ed.), *Surveys from Exile*, 1973, pp. 281–2.
14. Quoted in T. Bottomore and M. Rubel (eds), *Karl Marx on Sociology and Social Philosophy*, 1963, p. 233.
15. F. Engels, letter to J. Block, September 1890, *Selected Works*, p. 682.
16. Ibid., p. 683.
17. F. Engels, *The Origins of the Family, Private Property and the State*, 1972, p. 231.
18. K. Marx, *The Eighteenth Brumaire of Louis Napoleon*, in *Selected Works*, p. 168.
19. K. Marx and F. Engels, *The German Ideology*, pp. 65–6.
20. K. Marx, *The Critique of the Gotha Programme*, in *Selected Works*, p. 329.
21. K. Marx and F. Engels, *The Communist Manifesto*, in *Selected Works*, p. 53.
22. K. Marx, *Capital*, vol. 1, 1976, p. 613.
23. To French Marxist Louis Althusser, Gramsci's theoretical writings remain in a 'practical state'. See his *For Marx*, 1969.
24. A. Gramsci, *Selections from the Prison Notebooks*, Q. Hoare and G. Nowell Smith (eds), 1971, p. 408.
25. The so-called Third Period of the Comintern – or Communist International – was inaugurated in 1928 and lasted until 1935. The Comintern proclaimed that the capitalist system was entering the period of final collapse, and that as such, the correct stance for all Communist parties was that of a highly aggressive, militant, ultra-left line. Communists were urged to oppose all moderate parties of the Left which were described as 'Social Fascist'. With the rise of the Nazi movement in Germany after 1930, this stance became highly controversial because it appeared to mistake the real enemy, and popular front movements became more common on the left in the middle of the decade.
26. Ibid., p. 407.
27. Ibid., p. 244.
28. See P. Anderson, 'The Antinomies of Antonio Gramsci', *New Left Review*, no. 100, 1976, pp. 12–13.
29. A. Gramsci, *Prison Notebooks*, pp. 235–8.
30. Ibid., p. 57.
31. Gramcsi uses the term 'Modern Prince' – derived from book of that name by the Italian political philosopher Niccolò Machiavelli – as a synonym for the revolutionary party. The usage signals his philosophical debt to Machiavelli but also, possibly, his desire to evade his prison censors.
32. Quoted in P. Anderson, 'Antinomies', p. 22.
33. A. Gramsci, *Prison Notebooks*, p. 161.
34. Ibid., p. 182.
35. Ibid., p. 247.

36. Ibid., p. 258.
37. Quoted in P. Anderson, 'The Antinomies', p. 22.
38. Ibid., pp. 33–4.
39. Ibid., p. 43.
40. Ibid., p. 328.
41. Ibid., p. 42.
42. A. Gramsci, *Political Writings*, Q. Hoare (ed.), 1977, p. 27.
43. A. Gramsci, *Prison Notebooks*, p. 377.
44. See the discussion around this question in B. Jessop, *The Capitalist State*, pp. 28–30.
45. See Engels' footnote to the 1888 English edition of the Communist Manifesto: 'Generally speaking, for economic development of the bourgeois, England is taken to be the typical country; for its political development, France.' Quoted in K. Kumar, *Prophecy and Progress*, 1978, p. 142.
46. F. Engels, 'On Certain Peculiarities of the Economic and Political Development of England' in *Marx and Engels on Britain*, Moscow, 1962, p. 529.
47. Quoted in K. Kumar, *Prophesy and Progress*, p. 142.
48. K. Marx, *The Eighteenth Brumaire of Louis Napoleon*, in *Selected Works*, p. 186.
49. Ibid., pp. 167–70.
50. K. Marx, Review of Guizot's book on the English Revolution, in J. Fernbach (ed.), *Surveys from Exile*, p. 254.
51. Ibid., p. 255.
52. Ibid., p. 282.
53. Ibid., p. 263.
54. Quoted in K. Kumar, *Prophesy and Progress*, p. 142.
55. A. Gramsci, *Prison Notebooks*, p. 79.
56. Ibid., p. 78.
57. Ibid., p. 57.
58. Ibid., p. 131. See also D. Forgacs, 'National Popular: Genealogy of a Concept', in D. Forgacs (ed.), *Formations of Nations and People*.
59. 'Thermidor' refers to the overthrow of the Committee of Public Safety led by Maximilien Robespierre and the end of the so-called Reign of Terror.
60. Quoted in A. Gramsci, *Prison Notebooks*, p. 216, footnote.
61. Ibid., pp. 159–60.
62. Quoted in ibid., p. 186, footnote.
63. Ibid., p. 160.
64. E. J. Hobsbawm, *The Age of Capital*, 1977, p. 120.

4   Education and Statism in Continental Europe

1. J. Simon, *Education and Society in Tudor England*, p. 133.
2. J. Melton, *Absolutism*, p. 4.
3. J. Bowen, *A History of Western Education*, vol. 3, p. 24.
4. Ibid., p. 126.
5. P. Anderson, *Lineages of the Absolutist State*, p. 18.
6. Ibid., p. 15.
7. Ibid., p. 19.
8. Ibid., p. 31.
9. Ibid., p. 33.
10. J. Melton, *Absolutism*.

11. For technical education in France, see F. Artz, *The Development of Technical Education.*
12. See J. Melton, *Absolutism.*
13. P. Anderson, *Lineages of the Absolutist State*, p. 195.
14. Ibid., p. 223.
15. Ibid., pp. 236–78.
16. J. Melton, *Absolutism*, p. 59.
17. Ibid., pp. 30–4.
18. R. H. Samuel and R. H. Thomas, *Education and Society in Modern Germany*, p. 99.
19. A. J. P. Taylor, *The Course of German History*, p. 37.
20. Ibid., p. 33.
21. P. Anderson, *Lineages*, p. 271.
22. Ibid., p. 271.
23. Quoted in J. Bowen, *A History of Western Education*, vol. 111, pp. 258–9.
24. Quoted in H. Pollard, *Pioneers of Popular Education*, 1956, p. 88.
25. Quoted in ibid., p. 88.
26. J. Gillis, 'Aristocracy and Bureaucracy in Nineteenth-Century Prussia', *Past and Present*, no. 41, 1968, pp. 105–29.
27. P. Anderson, *Lineages*, pp. 273–4.
28. Barrington Moore Jr, *Social Origins of Dictatorship and Democracy*, p. 433.
29. Quoted in R. Samuel and R. Thomas, *Education and Society in Modern Germany*, p. 4.
30. F. K. Ringer, *Education and Society in Modern Europe*, p. 34.
31. Ibid., pp. 37–8.
32. Ibid., p. 221.
33. Ibid., pp. 77–8.
34. Ibid., p. 74.
35. Ibid., p. 71. See also P. Harrigan, *Mobility, Elites and Education*, p. 14.
36. F. Ringer, *Education and Society in Modern Europe*, p. 74.
37. D. Landes, *The Unbound Prometheus*, p. 348.
38. A. Gramsci, *Prison Notebooks*, p. 19. Gramsci's reference to the more productive nature of Junker agriculture presumably refers to the close involvement of the Junkers in agricultural production and not to any greater efficiency in the process itself.
39. P. Anderson, *Lineages*, pp. 100–2.
40. A. de Tocqueville, *The Old Regime and the French Revolution*, trans. Stuart Gilbert, 1955, p. 57.
41. F. B. Artz, *The Development of Technical Education in France, 1500–1850*, 1966, p. 25.
42. H. Seton-Watson, *Nations and States. An Enquiry into the Origins of Nations and the Politics of Nationalism*, 1977, pp. 42–6.
43. Barrington Moore Jr, *Social Origins of Dictatorship and Democracy*, pp. 70–3.
44. A. Prost, *Histoire de L'Enseignement en France, 1800–1967*, p. 99.
45. F. B. Artz, *The Development of Technical Education*, for the early development of technical education in France.
46. Barrington Moore Jr, *Social Origins of Dictatorship and Democracy*, p. 59.
47. A. de Tocqueville, *The Old Regime and the French Revolution*, p. 105.
48. F. B. Artz, *The Development of Technical Education*, p. 28.
49. Ibid., pp. 26–30.

50. Quoted in ibid., p. 43.
51. Ibid., p. 56.
52. P. Anderson, *Lineages*, p. 110.
53. F. B. Artz, *The Development of Technical Education*, pp. 82–3.
54. Ibid., p. 88.
55. Ibid., p. 86.
56. Ibid., p. 76.
57. Ibid., p. 80.
58. Ibid., p. 97.
59. Ibid., pp. 104–5.
60. Ibid., p. 111.
61. Quoted in R. Bendix, *Nation-Building and Citizenship*, 1964, p. 110.
62. Quoted in M. Archer and M. Vaughan, *Social Conflict and Educational Change*, P. 154.
63. Quoted in ibid., p. 150.
64. Quoted in ibid., p. 150.
65. Quoted in ibid., p. 158.
66. Quoted in ibid., p. 158.
67. See discussion of this point in R. D. Anderson, *Education in France*, p. 25.
68. A. de Tocqueville, *The Old Regime and the French Revolution*, p. 209.
69. A. Soboul, *The French Revolution, 1787–1799*, 1974, p. 554.
70. Ibid., p. 601.
71. Quoted in H. C. Barnard, *Education and the French Revolution*, 1969, p. 82.
72. Quoted in M. Archer and M. Vaughan, *Social Conflict and Educational Change*, p. 164.
73. Quoted in A. Soboul, *The French Revolution*, p. 602.
74. M. Archer and M. Vaughan, *Social Conflict and Educational Change*, p. 172.
75. Ibid., p. 122.
76. A. Soboul, *The French Revolution*, p. 602.
77. F. B. Artz, *The Development of Technical Education*, p. 129.
78. Ibid., p. 129.
79. A. Soboul, *The French Revolution*, p. 604.
80. F. B. Artz, *The Development of Technical Education*, p. 159.
81. Ibid., p. 181.
82. A. Soboul, *The French Revolution*, pp. 553–63.
83. A. Cobban, *A History of Modern France*, 1984. p. 27.
84. Ibid., p. 31.
85. A. Gramsci, *Prison Notebooks*, p. 219.
86. Ibid., p. 211.
87. K. Marx, *The 18th Brumaire of Louis Bonaparte*, in F. Fernbach (ed.), *Surveys from Exile*, p. 147.
88. Quoted in M. Archer, *Social Origins*, p. 152.
89. M. Archer and M. Vaughan, *Social Conflict and Educational Change*, pp. 142–5.
90. R. D. Anderson, *Education in France*, p. 8.
91. T. Zeldin, *France, 1848–1945. Politics and Anger*, pp. 157–9.
92. Cited in F. B. Artz, *The Development of Technical Education*, p. 132.
93. M. Archer, *Social Origins*, pp. 202–04.
94. Numerous other écoles des arts et métiers were set up along the lines of this original version. See F. B. Artz, *The Development of Technical Education*, p. 131.

95. Villemain's retrospective figures cited in F. K. Ringer, *Education and Society in Modern Europe*, p. 132.
96. A. Cobban, *A History of Modern France*, p. 34.
97. F. B. Artz, *The Development of Technical Education*, p. 136.
98. A. Cobban, *A History of Modern France*, p. 136.
99. Quoted in M. Archer and M. Vaughan, *Social Conflict and Educational Change*, p. 184.
100. T. Zeldin, *France, Politics and Anger*, p. 172.
101. K. Marx, *The 18th Brumaire of Louis Napoleon*, in *Selected Works*, pp. 160–70. See also K. Marx, *The Civil War in France* in ibid.
102. J. Moody, *French Education since Napoleon*, pp. 23–4.
103. R. D. Anderson, *Education in France*, pp. 17–19.
104. F. B. Artz, *The Development of Technical Education*, p. 188.
105. In 1847 there were 3 213 communes without schools. See A. Prost, *Histoire de L'Enseignement*, p. 97.
106. F. B. Artz, *The Development of Technical Education*, pp. 188, 190.
107. Quoted in J. Moody, *French Education since Napoleon*, pp. 33–4.
108. F. B. Artz, *The Development of Technical Education*, p. 191.
109. R. D. Anderson, 'Secondary Education in Nineteenth Century France', p. 121.
110. T. Zeldin, *France, Intellect and Price*, pp. 250–1.
111. Ibid., p. 207.
112. F. K. Ringer, *Education and Society in Modern Europe*, p. 134.
113. T. Zeldin, *France. Intellect and Pride*, p. 141.
114. Quoted in A. Soboul, *The French Revolution*, vol. 2, p. 593.
115. T. Zeldin, *France. Intellect and Pride*, p. 19.
116. Quoted in J. Moody, *French Education since Napoleon*, p. 34.
117. T. Zeldin, *France. Intellect and Pride*, p. 148.
118. Quoted in ibid., p. 150.
119. Quoted in J. Moody, *French Education since Napoleon*, p. 43.
120. Quoted in R. D. Anderson, *Education in France*, p. 40.
121. Quoted in R. D. Anderson, 'Secondary Education in Mid-Nineteenth Century France', p. 124.
122. Quoted in R. D. Anderson, *Education in France*, p. 124.
123. P. Harrigan, *Mobility, Elites and Education*, p. 14.
124. Ibid., p. 79.
125. Ibid., p. 31.
126. Quoted in T. Zeldin, *France. Politics and Anger*, p. 117.
127. Quoted in R. D. Anderson, 'Secondary Education in Mid-Nineteenth Century France', p. 145.
128. Ibid., p. 145.
129. D. Marquand, *The Unprincipled Society*, 1988, p. 13.

5 The US Experience: Education, Nationhood and the Decentralized State

1. L. Cremin, *American Education*, p. 11.
2. E. J. Hobsbawm, *The Age of Capital*, p. 120.
3. S. Showronek, *Building a New American Nation: The Expansion of National Administrative Capacities, 1877–1920*, 1982.
4. De Tocqueville, *Democracy in America*, p. 62.

5. See also, G. Myrdal, *An American Dilemma*, 1944.
6. Quoted in D. Tyack and T. James, 'The Law and the Shaping of Public Education. Explorations in Political History', unpublished monograph, 1986.
7. De Tocqueville, *Democracy in America*, p. 70.
8. Ibid., p. 117.
9. F. Engels, 'Origins of the Family', quoted in B. Held (ed.), *States and Societies*, 1985, pp. 103–4.
10. K. Marx and F. Engels, *The German Ideology*, p. 80.
11. S. Showronek, *Building a New American Nation*.
12. Ibid.
13. E. P. Cubberley, *Public Education*, p. 212.
14. See D. Tyack and T. James, 'The Law and the Shaping'.
15. B. Bailyn, *Education in the Forming of American Society*, pp. 15–18.
16. Ibid., pp. 21–36.
17. C. F. Kaestle, *Pillars of the Republic*, pp. 4, 31.
18. E. P. Cubberley, *Public Education*, p. 59.
19. Ibid., p. 19.
20. Quoted in B. Bailyn, *Education in the Forming of American Society*, p. 26.
21. Ibid., p. 27.
22. L. Cremin, *Tradition in American Education*, p. 35.
23. Quoted in C. F. Kaestle, *Pillars of the Republic*, title page.
24. D. Tyack, 'Forming the National Character', p. 30.
25. Quoted in ibid., p. 30.
26. Quoted in ibid., p. 30.
27. Quoted in ibid., p. 29.
28. Quoted in ibid., p. 31.
29. Quoted in ibid., p. 35.
30. Quoted in ibid., p. 35.
31. B. Rush, *Thoughts upon Female Education* in F. Rudolph (ed.), *Essays on Education in the Early Republic*, 1965, p. 28.
32. Ibid., p. 28.
33. N. Webster, *On the Education of Youth in America* in F. Rudolph (ed.), *Essays on Education in the Early Republic*, p. 68.
34. Quoted in L. Cremin, *American Education*, p. 3.
35. D. Tyack, 'Forming the National Character', p. 40.
36. C. F. Kaestle, *Pillars of the Republic*, p. 13.
37. E. P. Cubberley, *Public Education*, p. 219.
38. C. F. Kaestle, *Pillars of the Republic*, p. 22.
39. Ibid., p. 56.
40. Ibid., p. 30.
41. Ibid., p. 5.
42. Ibid., p. 30.
43. Ibid., p. 37.
44. Ibid., pp. 57–8.
45. Ibid., p. 58.
46. E. P. Cubberley, *Public Education*, pp. 22–5.
47. C. F. Kaestle, *Pillars of the Republic*, p. 24.
48. A. Fishlow, 'The American School Revival. Fact or Fancy', p. 45.
49. D. Tyack and T. James, 'State Government and American Public Education: Exploring the "Primeval Forest" ', *History of Education Quarterly*, vol. 26, no. 1, Spring 1986, p. 64.

50. Ibid., p. 64.
51. Ibid., pp. 56–61.
52. E. P. Cubberley, *Public Education*, pp. 163–6.
53. C. F. Kaestle, *Pillars of the Republic*, p. 152.
54. Ibid., p. 149.
55. L. Cremin, *American Education*, p. 173.
56. Cubberley first asserted this point and it has recently been generally endorsed by educational historians as diverse as Cremin, Tyack and Kaestle. See in particular Tyack's remarks on this subject in a review of Kaestle's recent book, 'The Common school and American Society: A Reappraisal', in *History of Education Quarterly*, vol. 26, no. 2, Summer 1986. Michael Katz has been the main dissenting voice and even he has recently reviewed his position to account for the 'hegemony' of the ideology of public schooling. See his 'The Origins of Public Education: A Reassessment'.
57. C. F. Kaestle, *Pillars of the Republic*, p. 140.
58. E. P. Cubberley, *Public Education*, p. 174.
59. Ibid., p. 174.
60. E. Foner, *Free Soil, Free Labour, Free Men*, Oxford University Press, 1982, p. 15.
61. C. F. Kaestle, *The Pillars of the Republic*, p. 146.
62. Ibid., p. 181.
63. Ibid., p. 116.
64. Quoted in ibid., p. 91.
65. A. Potter and G. Emerson, *The School and the School Master*, pp. 1–2.
66. E. Pesan, 'The Egalitarian Myth and the American Social Reality. Wealth, Mobility, and Equality in the "Era of the Common Man" ', *American Historical Review*, October 1971.
67. Ibid.
68. For a full discussion of this see S. Thernstrom, *The Other Bostonians: Poverty and Progress in the American Metropolis, 1880–1970*, pp. 76–96.
69. According to Dawley, 10 per cent of shoemakers moved into other jobs. See A. Dawley, *Class and Community*, p. 163. See also S. Hirsch, *Roots of the American Working Class*, p. 81.
70. W. Sombart, *Why Is There No Socialism in the United States*, p. 118.
71. E. Foner, *Free Soil, Free Labour, Free Men*, pp. 27–30.
72. M. Davis, 'Labour in American Politics', *New Left Review*, no. 123, September/October 1980, pp. 18–19.
73. Ibid., p. 20.
74. Ibid., p. 10.
75. S. Thernstrom, *The Other Bostonians*.
76. H. Brogan, *The Pelican History of the United States of America*, p. 295.
77. C. F. Kaestle, *Pillars of the Republic*, p. 197.
78. S. M. Elkins, *Slavery*, 1976, p. 60.
79. C. F. Kaestle, *Pillars of the Republic*, p. 195. Advertisements for runaway slaves are discussed in E. Genovese, *Roll Jordan Roll. The World the Slaves Made*, 1976.
80. L. Cremin, *American Education*, p. 229.
81. H. Brogan, *History of the United States*, p. 89.
82. C. F. Kaestle, *Pillars of the Republic*, p. 179.
83. Ibid., p. 177.
84. M. Katz, *The Irony*, p. 112. See also the discussion in Chapter 2.
85. M. Katz, 'The Origins of Public Education', p. 394.
86. C. F. Kaestle, *Pillars of the Republic*, p. 163.

87. J. Orville Taylor, *The District School*, p. 82.
88. C. F. Kaestle, *Pillars of the Republic*, p. 82.
89. Quoted in ibid., p. 82.
90. Quoted in ibid., p. 99.
91. J. Orville Taylor, *The District School*, p. 24.
92. Ibid., p. 293.
93. Ibid., p. 293.
94. B. Rush in F. Rudolph, *Essays on Education*, p. 28.
95. Quoted in C. F. Kaestle, *Pillars of the Republic*, p. 87.
96. Quoted in ibid., pp. 86–7.
97. C. F. Kaestle, *Pillars of the Republic*, p. 85.
98. A. Potter and G. Emerson, *The School and the School Master*, pp. 51–4.
99. Ibid.
100. Quoted in D. Tyack, 'Forming the National Character'.
101. Quoted in C. F. Kaestle, *Pillars of the Republic*, p. 94.
102. J. Orville Taylor, *The District School*, p. 333.

6   English Education and the Liberal State

1.   D. Landes, *The Unbound Prometheus*, p. 348.
2.   Quoted in A. S. Bishop, *The Rise of a Central Authority*, p. 270.
3.   H. Perkin, *Origins of Modern English Society*, p. 352.
4.   D. Fraser, *The Evolution of the British Welfare State*, 1985, pp. 78–89.
5.   P. Anderson: 'The Origins of the Present Crisis', *New Left Review*, no. 23, January/Feburary 1964; 'Socialism and Pseudo-Empiricism', *New Left Review*, no. 35, January/February 1966; 'The Figures of Descent', *New Left Review*, no. 161, January/February 1987; E. P. Thompson, 'The Peculiarities of the English', *The Socialist Register*, 1965. (An extended version of this in his *The Poverty of Theory*, 1978); T. Nairn, *The Break-Up of Britain*, 1981; E. J. Hobsbawm, *Industry and Empire*, 1969; D. Marquand, *The Unprincipled Society*, 1988; M. Weiner, *English Culture and the Decline of the Industrial Spirit*.
6.   P. Anderson, 'The Origins of the Present Crisis', p. 28.
7.   Ibid., p. 30.
8.   Ibid., p. 33.
9.   T. Nairn, *The Break-Up of Britain*.
10. Ibid., p. 15.
11. Ibid., p. 22.
12. E. P. Thompson, 'The Peculiarities of the English', in *The Poverty of Theory*, p. 62.
13. R. Johnson, 'Barrington Moore, Perry Anderson and English Social Development' in C.C.C.S. *Culture and Domination*, WPCS 9, Spring 1976, p. 21.
14. Ibid., p. 26.
15. P. Anderson, 'The Figures of Descent', p. 40.
16. Ibid., pp. 28–32.
17. Ibid., pp. 34–5.
18. Ibid., pp. 39–40.
19. Ibid., p. 41.
20. Ibid., p. 37.
21. E. J. Hobsbawm, article in *Marxism Today*, April 1988.
22. N. Poulantzas, 'Marxist Political Theory in Great Britain', *New Left Review*, no.43, May/June 1967, p. 67.

23. P. Anderson, 'Figures of Descent', p. 36.
24. Quoted in ibid., p. 24.
25. Ibid., p. 35.
26. R. Gray, 'Bourgeois Hegemony in Victorian Britain', in J. Bloomfield (ed.), *Class, Hegemony and Party*, 1976, p. 80.
27. E. J. Hobsbawm, *Industry and Empire*, p. 81.
28. Ibid., pp. 81–3.
29. Ibid., p. 185.
30. Ibid., p. 187.
31. Ibid., p. 40.
32. Ibid., p. 233.
33. Ibid., p. 233.
34. Ibid., p. 231.
35. D. Marquand, *The Unprincipled Society*, p. 7.
36. A. Gamble, *Britain in Decline*, p. 84.
37. Ibid., pp. 74–5.
38. D. Marquand, *The Unprincipled Society*, p. 154.
39. Ibid., pp. 7, 211.
40. J. Simon, *Education and Society in Tudor England*, 1966.
41. Ibid., p. 196.
42. R. O'Day, *Education and Society, 1500–1800*, 1982; B. Simon, *The Two Nations and the Educational Structure*, p. 27.
43. See L. Stone, 'The Educational Revolution in England, 1560–1640', *Past and Present*, no. 28, July 1964.
44. Quoted in J. Bowen, *A History of Western Education*, vol. 3, p. 143.
45. H. Seton-Watson, *Nations and States*, p. 33.
46. E. Reisner, *Nationalism and Education since 1789. A Social and Political History of Modern Education*, 1925.
47. A. Gamble, *Britain in Decline*, p. 71.
48. Quoted in B. Simon, *The Two Nations*, p. 49.
49. M. Archer and M. Vaughan, *Social Conflict and Educational Change*, pp. 81–4.
50. B. Simon, *The Two Nations*, p. 70.
51. *Westminster Review*, vol. 649, no. 12, October 1826, p. 269.
52. Quoted in B. Simon, *The Two Nations*, p. 90.
53. Ibid.
54. T. Wyse, *Education in the United Kingdom*, Central Society of Education, 1837, pp. 59–60.
55. B. Simon, *The Two Nations*, pp. 79–4.
56. Ibid., pp. 62–4.
57. Smith, *An Inquiry into the Nature and Causes of the Wealth of Nations*, 1785, Book v, Chapter 1, pp. 276–305.
58. Ibid., p. 305.
59. T. Malthus, *An Essay on the Principles of Population As It Effects the Future Improvement of Society*, quoted in B. Simon, *The Two Nations*, p. 142.
60. Quoted in F. Cavenagh (ed.), *James and John Stuart Mill on Education*, 1931, pp. 1, 29, 12.
61. Ibid., pp. 61–2.
62. L. Horner, Letter to N. Senior (1837), quoted in D. Fraser, *The Evolution of the British Welfare State*, p. 80.
63. A. Roebuck, Speech in the House of Commons in defense of his Bill for National Education, *Hansard*, 30 July 1833, col. 159.

64. Quoted in A. J. Taylor, *Laissez-Faire and State Intervention in Nineteenth Century Britain*, 1972, p. 23.
65. Quoted in ibid., p. 34.
66. Quoted in H. Perkin, *The Origins of Modern English Society*, p. 322.
67. K. Polanyi, *The Great Transformation*, 1957, p. 140.
68. Quoted in D. Fraser, *The Evolution of the British Welfare State*, p. 101.
69. Quoted in ibid., p. 47.
70. A. Smith, *The Wealth of Nations*, Book v, pp. 276–305.
71. Quoted in A. J. Taylor, *Laissez-Faire*, p. 47.
72. Quoted in F. Cavenagh (ed.), *James and John Stuart Mill on Education*, p. 67.
73. Quoted in A. J. Taylor, *Laissez-Faire*, pp. 46–7.
74. J. S. Mill, *On Liberty*, in *Utilitarianism*, M. Warnock (ed.), 1986, pp. 239–40.
75. This is the main theme of E. Halévy, *The Growth of Philosophical Radicalism*, 1928.
76. A. J. Taylor, *Laissez-Faire*, p. 56.
77. Quoted in R. Johnson, ' "Really Useful Knowledge": Radical Education and Working-Class Culture' in J. Clarke, C. Critcher and R. Johnson (eds), *Working Class Culture. Studies in History and Theory*, 1979, p. 89.
78. Quoted in P. Anderson, 'Figures of Descent', p. 50.
79. Quoted in B. Simon, *The Two Nations*, p. 250.
80. Ibid., p. 270.
81. Quoted in D. Vincent, *Bread, Knowledge and Freedom: A Study of 19th Century Working Class Autobiography*, 1981, p. 135.
82. Quoted in B. Simon, *The Two Nations*, p. 258.
83. Quoted in ibid., p. 259.
84. Quoted in ibid., p. 262.
85. E. P. Thompson, *The Making of the English Working Class*, 1968, p. 824.
86. Quoted in B. Simon, *The Two Nations*, p. 207.
87. W. Lovett, Chartism: A New Organization of the People (1840), in B. Simon (ed.), *The Radical Tradition of Education*, pp. 247–8.
88. Quoted in B. Simon, *The Two Nations*, p. 268.
89. Ibid., p. 341.
90. D. Giddy, Speech in Parliament, in *Cobbet's Parliamentary Papers*, 13 July 1807, p. 798.
91. B. Simon, *The Two Nations*, pp. 149–50.
92. Quoted in *Hansard*, July 30th 1833, col. 169.
93. R. Johnson, 'Notes on Schooling', p. 45.
94. P. McCann, 'Popular Education, Socialization and Social Control: Spitalfields 1812–1824', in P. McCann (ed.), *Popular Education and Socialization in the 19th Century*, pp. 12–13.
95. J. M. Goldstrom, 'The Content of Education and the Socialization of the Working Class Child', in P. McCann (ed.), *Popular Education*, p. 101.
96. B. Simon, *The Two Nations*, p. 105.
97. See Chapter 3.
98. A. Roebuck, Speech in House of Commons, *Hansard*, 30 July 1833, col. 140; J. Hume, Speech in House of Commons, *Hansard*, 25 July 1843, col. 1345.
99. Quoted in A. S. Bishop, *The Rise of a Central Authority*, p. 17.
100. H. Perkins, *The Origins of Modern English Society*, p. 27.
101. A. J. Taylor, *Laissez-Faire*, p. 64.
102. E. J. Hobsbawm, *Industry and Empire*, p. 186.

103. S. Smiles, *Self-Help*, 1969, p. 35.
104. Ibid., p. 284.
105. J. S. Mill, *On Liberty* in M. Warnock (ed.), *Utilitarianism*, p. 249.
106. Quoted in J. Roach, *Public Examinations in England. 1850–1900*, 1971, p. 41.
107. Ibid., p. 49.
108. Quoted in B. Simon, *The Two Nations*, p. 170.
109. J.S. Mill, *Autobiography*, J. Stillinger (ed.), 1971, p. 37.
110. This constant theme of M. Arnold, *Culture and Anarchy*, J. Dover Wilson (ed.), 1981.
111. Quoted in B. Simon, *The Two Nations*, p. 166.
112. Quoted in H. Perkins, *The Origins of Modern English Society*, p. 293. For the rich culture of middle-class philanthropy, see also L. Davidoff and C. Hall, *Family Fortunes*, 1987.
113. J. S. Mill, *Autobiography*, p. 116.
114. M. Arnold, *Culture and Anarchy*, p. 75.
115. E. Baines Jr, Letters to Lord John Russell *On State Education*, Letter (i), August 1st, 1846.
116. Ibid., Letter (ii).
117. Ibid., Letter (i).
118. Ibid., Letter (viii).
119. Ibid., Letter (x).
120. Ibid., Letter (x).
121. H. Perkin, *The Origins of Modern English Society*, p. 269.
122. Quoted in D. Fraser, *The Evolution of the British Welfare State*, p. 151.
123. Quoted in H. Perkin, *The Origins of Modern English Society*, p. 324.
124. K. Polanyi, *The Great Transformation*, p. 141.
125. These retrospective figures from Horace Mann's supplement to the 1851 census refer to the founding dates of then existing schools by the decade. The figures cannot give an accurate picture of the number of public day schools in existence since they ignore the number of schools that had started up and become defunct before the date of the census. See R. Johnson, 'The Education Movement', p. 20, table Table 4 and comments on p. 119.
126. E. G. West, *Education and the Industrial Revolution*, p. 41.
127. A. S. Bishop, *The Rise of A Central Authority*, p. 18.
128. Quoted in ibid., p. 34.
129. Ibid., p. 24.
130. Ibid., p. 78.
131. J. Hurt, *Education in Evolution*, pp. 59, 67.
132. Ibid., p. 122.
133. Principal of St Marks College, Chelsea to HMI Allen, quoted in ibid., p. 119.
134. Ibid., p. 144.
135. Quoted in J. Stuart Maclure, *Educational Documents, 1816–1963*, p. 81.
136. F. K. Ringer, *Education and Society in Modern Europe*, p. 231.
137. Quoted in R. Warner, *English Public Schools*, 1945, p. 25.
138. Quoted in B. Simon, *The Two Nations*, p. 312.
139. Quoted in M. Wiener, *English Culture and the Decline of the Industrial Spirit*, p. 19.
140. Quoted in ibid., p. 19.
141. T. W. Bamford, *The Rise of the Public Schools*, pp. 209–47.
142. Quoted in ibid., p. 92.

143. Quoted in M. Wiener, *English Culture and the Decline of the Industrial Spirit*, p. 18.
144. H. Perkin, *The Origins of Modern English Society*, pp. 154 and 430.
145. W. Gladstone letter to Russell, quoted in J. Roach, *Public Examinations*, p. 193.
146. B. Simon, *The Two Nations*, p. 318.
147. See ibid., p. 333. and S. Maclure, *Educational Documents*, pp. 92–5.
148. L. Davidoff and C. Hall, *Family Fortunes*, p. 290.
149. C. Dyhouse, *Girls Growing up in Late Victorian and Edwardian England*, 1981, p. 68.
150. Quoted in ibid., p. 51.
151. Report of the Council of Civil Engineers (1868), quoted in G. Roderick and M. Stephens 'The Higher Education of Engineers in England in the Nineteenth Century, With Observations on Engineering Training on the Continent and in America', in *Paedagogia Historica* xvi/2, 1976.
152. A. S. Bishop, *The Rise of a Central Authority*, p. 153.
153. Quoted in E. Ashby, *Technology and the Academics*, 1958, p. 37.
154. E. J. Hobsbawm, *Industry and Empire*, p. 173.
155. Select Committee on the Provision for Giving Instruction in Theoretical and Applied Science to the Industrial Class, *Report*, 1867–1868, Evidence from D. Kitson, p. 248.
156. L. Playfair, *Industrial Instruction on the Continent*, 1952, p. 6.
157. Board of Trade letter to the Treasury, quoted in A. S. Bishop, *The Rise of a Central Authority*, p. 161.
158. Ibid., p. 159.
159. Ibid., p. 167.
160. Ibid., p. 174.
161. L. Playfair, Open Letter to Lord Taunton, quoted in A. S. Bishop, *The Rise of a Central Authority*, p. 174.
162. L. Playfair, Two Lectures Delivered to the Philosophical Institution of Edinburgh *On Primary and Technical Education*, 1870, p. 51.
163. F. Engels, *Socialism, Utopian and Scientific* in *Selected Works*, pp. 102–3.
164. T. Huxley, Address on Behalf of National Association For the Promotion of Technical Education, 1887.
165. Royal Commission on Technical Instruction, *Second Report*, 1884, vol. 1, pt. iv, p. 508.
166. Select Committee, 1867–1868, *Report*, p. vii.
167. Royal Commission on Technical Instruction and the Advancement of Science, *Sixth Report*, Preliminary Remarks, p. 1.
168. Quoted in A. S. Bishop. *The Rise of a Central Authority*, p. 179.
169. Royal Commission on Technical Instruction, *Second Report*, 1875, vol. 1, pt. 1., p. 23.
170. Select Committee, 1867–1868, *Report*, minutes of evidence, p. 130.
171. Quoted in E. G. West, *Education and the Industrial Revolution*. pp. 169–70.
172. Quoted in B. Simon, *The Two Nations*, p. 355.
173. Quoted in A. S. Bishop, *The Rise of a Central Authority*, p. 1.
174. B. Simon, *The Two Nations*, pp. 363–4.
175. W. E. Foster, Speech in House of Commons on 1870 Education Bill, quoted in J. Murphy, *The Education Act, 1870, Text and Commentary*, 1972, p. 39.
176. Quoted in E. G. West, *Education and the Industrial Revolution*, p. 165.
177. Quoted in ibid., pp. 173–4.
178. Quoted in ibid., p. 184.

179. In 1881 the average attendance in voluntary schools was 2 008 000 as against 856 000 in board schools. See M. Mulhall, *Dictionary of Statistics*, p. 161. In 1902 there were 1 400 voluntary schools to 6 000 board schools. See M. Archer, *The Sociology of Educational Expansion*, p. 14.
180. Quoted M. Archer, *Social Origins*, p. 211, fn. 43.
181. Quoted in ibid., p. 187.
182. Ibid., p. 188.
183. S. Maclure, *Educational Documents*, p. 142.
184. M. Archer, *Social Origins*, pp. 193–4.
185. Quoted in S. Maclure, *Educational Documents*, p. 147.
186. R. H. Tawney, *Equality*, 1931, p. 142.

Conclusion: Education and State Formation in the West

1. Quoted in C. Chitty, *Redefining the Comprehensive Experience*, 1987, p. 7.
2. R. Boudon, *Education, Opportunity and Social Inequality*, 1984.
3. See A. Green, 'Lifelong Learning, Equality and Social Cohesion', *European Journal of Education*, vol. 46, no. 2, 2011, pp. 228–248.

Postscript: Education and State Formation in East Asia

1. A. Green, 'Education and State Formation Revisited', *Historical Studies in Education/Revue D'Histoire De L'Education*, Special Issue, 1994, pp. 1–19; A. Green, 'East Asian Skills Formation Systems and the Challenge of Globalization', *Journal of Education and Work*, 21 (3), pp. 253–79; A. Green, 'Education and Globalization in Europe and Asia: Convergent and Divergent Trends', *Journal of Education Policy*, 14 (1), 1999, pp. 55–71; A. Green, *Education, Globalization and the Nation State*, Macmillan, 1997; A. Green and J. Janmaat, *Regimes of Social Cohesion: Societies and The Crisis of Globalisation*, Palgrave, 2011; P. Brown, A. Green and H. Lauder, *High Skills: Globalization, Competitiveness and Skills Formation*, Oxford University Press, 1999.
2. D. Ashton and J. Sung, *The State, Economic Development and Skill Formation: A New East Asian Model?*, Centre for Labour Market Studies: University of Leicester, 1994; D. Ashton, F. Green, D. James and J. Sung, *Education and Training for Development: The Political Economy of Skills Formation in East Asian Newly Industrialized Economies*, Routledge, 1999; N. Hovsepian, *Palestinian State Formation: Education and the Construction of National Identity*, Cambridge Scholars Publishing, 2008; Y. T. Chia, *The Loss of 'World Soul' in Education? Culture and the Making of the Singapore Developmental State, 1995–2004*, Doctoral Dissertation, 2010, University of Toronto; B. Curtis, *Building the Educational State: Canada West, 1836–1871*, Falmer Press, 1988; B. Curtis, *The Politics of Population: State Formation, Statistics and the Census of Canada, 1840–1875*, University of Toronto Press, 2001; I. Davey and P. Miller, 'Family Formation, Schooling and the Patriarchal State' in M. Theobald and D. Selleck (eds) *Family, School and the State in Australian History*, Allen and Unwin, 1991; I. Davey and P. Miller, Patriarchal Transformation, Schooling and State Formation, Paper for Social Science History Association Conference, New Orleans, 1991; S. Gopinathan, *Educational Development in a Strong-Developmentalist State: The Singapore Experience*, Paper presented at the Australian Association for Research in Education Annual Conference, 1994.

A. Hunt and C. Tokluoglu, 'State Formation from Below: The Turkish Case', *The Social Science Journals*, 39, 4, 2002, pp. 617–24; D. Polomba, 'Education and State Formation in Italy', *International Handbook of Comparative Education, Springer International Handbooks of Education*, Volume 22, 2009, pp. 195–216; S. Wiborg, *Education and Social Integration. Comprehensive Schooling in Europe*, Palgrave Macmillan, 2009; T.-H. Wong, *Hegemonies Compared: State Formation and Chinese School Politics in Post-War Singapore and Hong Kong*, Routledge, 2002.

3. See particularly A. Amsden, *Asia's Next Giant: South Korea and Late Industrialisation*, Oxford University Press, 1992; A. Gerschenkron, *Economic Backwardness in Historical Perspective: A Book of Essays*, Belknap Press, 1966.

4. See particularly M. Castells, 'Four Asian Tigers with a Dragons' Head: A Comparative Analysis of the State, Economy and Society in the Asian Pacific Rim' in R. Appelbaum and J. Henderson (eds), *States and Development in the Asia Pacific Rim*, Sage, 1992; C. Johnson, *MITI and the Japanese Miracle: The Growth of Industrial Policy 1925–1975*, Stanford University Press, 1982; A. Kohli, *State Directed Development: Political Power and Industrialisation in the Global Periphery*, Cambridge University Press, 2004; M. Woo-Cumings (ed.), *The Developmental State*, Cornell University Press, 1999.

5. See particularly H. Passim, *Society and Education in Japan*, Teachers College Press, 1965.

6. See particularly Y. T. Chia, *The Loss of 'World Soul' in Education? Culture and the Making of the Singapore Developmental State, 1995–2004*, Doctoral Dissertation, University of Toronto, 2010; S. Gopinathan, '*Educational Development in a Strong-Developmentalist State: The Singapore Experience*', Paper presented at the Australian Association for Research in Education Annual Conference, 1994; T. H. Wong, *Hegemonies Compared: State Formation and Chinese School Politics in Post-War Singapore and Hong Kong*, Routledge, 2002.

7. See Hunt and Tokluoglu, 'State Formation from Below: The Turkish Case', op. cit.; A. Kazamias, *Education and the Quest for Modernity in Turkey*, Allen and Unwin, 1966.

8. See A. Green, *Education, Globalisation and the Nation State*, Macmillan, 1997.

9. A. Gerschenkron, *Economic Backwardness in Historical Perspective*: op. cit., 1996.

10. See endnote 4.

11. See E. Hobsbawm, *Nations and Nationalism since 1780: Programme, Myth and Reality*, Cambridge University Press, 1990.

12. See E. Hobsbawm, *Industry and Empire*, Penguin, 1969.

13. See L. Greenfeld: *Nationalism: Five Roads to Modernity*, Harvard University Press, 1992; *The Spirit of Capitalism: Nationalism and Economic Growth*, Harvard University Press, 2001.

14. See B. Moore, Jr, *Social Origins of Dictatorship and Democracy*, Beacon Press, 1966.

15. A. Gerschenkron, *Economic Backwardness in Historical Perspective: A Book of Essays*, Belknap Press, 1966, p. 44.

16. Ibid. p.44.

17. P. Morris, Introduction to P. Morris and A. Sweeting (eds) *Education and Development in East Asia*, Garland Press, 1995, p. 38.

18. See Amsden, 1988, op. cit.

19. See Hobsbawm, 1969, op. cit.

20. Ibid.

21. M. Woo-Cumings (ed.), *The Developmental State*, Cornell University Press, 1999.

22. See L. Greenfeld, *The Spirit of Capitalism: Nationalism and Economic Growth*, Harvard University Press, 2001.

23. Ibid.
24. F. List, *National Systems of Political Economy*, Cosmo Classic, 2005.
25. Quoted in Greenfeld, 2001, op. cit., p. 205.
26. F. List, 2005, op. cit., p. 59.
27. Ibid., p.57.
28. Ibid., p. 132.
29. G. Arrighi, *Adam Smith in Beijing*, Verso, 2007.
30. M. Woo-Cumings, 1999, op. cit.
31. F. List, 2005 op. cit., p. 47.
32. Ibid.
33. Ibid., p. 51.
34. See also H.-J. Chang, 2003, op.cit.
35. Quoted in ibid., p. 51.
36. F. List, 2005, op. cit., p. 244.
37. H.-J. Chang, 2003, op.cit.
38. Ibid., p.23
39. Quoted in H.-J. Chang, op. cit., p. 24.
40. Ibid., p. 26.
41. Ibid., p. 17, Table 2.1.
42. Ibid., p. 2.
43. Ibid., p.128.
44. See P. Morris, 1995, op. cit.
45. See R. Wade, *Governing the Market, Economic Theory and the Role of Government in East Asian Industrialisation*, Princeton University Press, 1990.
46. See J. Tilak, *Building Human Capital in East Asia: What Others Can Learn*, National Institute of Educational Planning and Administration, New Delhi, 2002.
47. World Bank, *East Asian Economic Miracle*, Geneva, World Bank, 1993.
48. Ibid.
49. See M. Castells, *The Power of Identity: The Information Age: Economy, Society and Culture*, Volume 11, Blackwell, 1997.
50. See R. Wade, *Governing the Market, Economic Theory and the Role of Government in East Asian Industrialisation*, Princeton University Press, 1990.
51. See P. Brown, A. Green and H. Lauder, *High Skills: Globalisation, Competitiveness and Skill Formation*, Oxford University Press, 2001.
52. See M. Castells, 1997, op. cit., p. 80.
53. World Bank, 1993, op. cit., p. 5.
54. Ibid., p.4.
55. J. Tilak, 2002, op. cit., p.2.
56. Ibid.
57. See T. Elger and C. Smith, C., *Global Japanisation*, Routledge, 1994; C. Hampden-Turner and F. Trompenaars, *The Seven Cultures of Capitalism: Value Systems for Creating Wealth in Britain, the United States, Germany, France, Japan, Sweden and the Netherlands*, Piaticus Books, 1995; H. Perkin, *The Third Revolution: Professional Ethics in the Modern World*, Routledge, 1996.
58. K. Sugihara, 'The East Asian Path of Economic Development' in A. Arrighi, H. Takeshi and M. Seldon, *The Resurgence of East Asia*, Routledge, 2003, pp. 78–123.
59. See F. Furoka, 'Japan and the "Flying Geese" Pattern of East Asian Integration', *eastasia.at*, 4(1), 2005; C. H. Kwan, *The Rise of China and Asia's Flying-Geese*

Pattern of Economic Development: An Empirical Analysis Based on US Import Statistics, RIETI Discussion Paper Series, 02-E-009, July 2002.

60. L. Pye, '"Asian Values": From Dynamos to Dominoes' in L. Harrison and S. Huntington (eds), *Culture Matters: How Values Shape Human Progress*, Basic Books, 2000, pp. 244–55.

61. See B.-H. Chua, *Communitarian Ideology and Democracy in Singapore*, Routledge, 1995; Tu, Wei-Ming, 'Multiple Modernities: A Preliminary Inquiry into the Implication of East Asian Modernity' in L. Harrison and S. Huntington (eds) *Culture Matters: How Values Shape Human Progress*, Basic Books, 2000, pp. 256–67.

62. W. Tu, 2000, op. cit.

63. See B.-H. Chua, 1995, op. cit.

64. W. Tu, 2000, op. cit.

65. See W. K. Cummings, 'The Asian Human Resource Approach in Global Perspective,' *Oxford Review of Education*, 21, 1995; C. Johnson, *MITI and the Japanese Miracle: The Growth of Industrial Policy 1925–1975*, Stanford University Press, 1982; and C. Johnson, *Japan Who Governs? The Rise of the Developmental State*, W. W. Norton, 1995.

66. A. Kohli, *State-Directed Development: Political Power and Industrialisation in the Global Periphery*, Cambridge University Press, 2004.

67. Ibid., p. 27.

68. R. Ramcharan, *Forging a Singaporean Statehood, 1965–1995: The Contribution of Japan*, Kluwer Law International, 2002.

69. Chan Heng Lee quoted in ibid., p. 94.

70. R. Ramcharan, 2002, op. cit., p. 297.

71. Lee Kuan Yew quoted in R. Ramcharan, 2002, op. cit., p.130.

72. Lee Kuan Yew quoted in ibid., p. 131.

73. Goh Keng Swee quoted in ibid., p. 131.

74. See E. Schein, *Strategic Pragmatism: The Culture of Singapore's Economic Development Board*, MIT Press, 1996.

75. M. Castells, *The Power of Identity: The Information Age: Economy, Society and Culture*, Volume 11, Blackwell, 1997.

76. C. Johnson, *Blowback: The Costs and Consequences of American Empire*, Time Warner Paperbacks, 2000.

77. A. Amsden, *Asia's Next Giant: South Korea and Late Industrialisation*, Oxford University Press, 1992, p. 39.

78. M. Castells, 1997, op. cit.

79. World Bank, 1993, op. cit.

80. See G. Rodan, *The Political Economy of Singapore's Industrialisation*, Macmillan, 1989.

81. M. Maca, *Education and the Failure of the Philippines to Achieve its Developmental Potential: A Comparison with the East Asian Tigers*, MA thesis, Institute of Education, London, September 2009.

82. A. Green, A. Little, G. Kamat, M. Oketch, and E. Vickers, *Education and Development in a Global Era: Strategies for 'Successful Globalisation*, Department for International Development, London, 2007.

83. See A. Amsden, *Escape from Empire*, MIT Press, 2007.

84. See C. Johnson, *Blowback: The Costs and Consequences of American Empire*, Time Warner Paperbacks, 2000.

85. See J. Stiglitz, 'Some Lessons from the East Asian Miracle', *The World Bank Research Observer*, 11 (2), 1996, pp.151–77; World Bank, 1993, op. cit.

86. World Bank, 1993, op. cit.
87. Ibid.
88. Hobsbawm, 1969, op. cit.
89. K. Y. Lee, *From Third World to First: The Singapore Story: 1965–2000*, Harper Collins, 2000.
90. E. Schein, 1996, op. cit.
91. See A. Amsden, 1992, op. cit. and A. Kohli, 2002. op. cit.
92. A. Amsden, 1992, op cit., p. 72.
93. Ibid., p.204.
94. G. Rodan, 1989, op. cit.
95. Government of Singapore, *Singapore: The Next Lap*, Times Editions, Singapore, 1991.
96. J. Stiglitz, 'Some Lessons from the East Asian Miracle', *The World Bank Research Observer*, 11 (2), 1996, pp.151–77.
97. World Bank, 1993, op. cit.
98. Ibid., p. 38.
99. C. Johnson, 1982, op. cit.; H. Perkin, 1996, op. cit.
100. A. Amsden, 1992, op. cit., p.108.
101. H. Perkin, 1996, op. cit.; Dore, 2000, op. cit.
102. R. Wade, 1990, op. cit.
103. See F. Fukuyama,1996, op. cit.
104. See R. Wade, and F. Veneros, 'The Asian Crisis: The High Debt Model versus the Wall Street-Treasury-IMF Complex', *New Left Review*, 228, 1998, pp. 3–23.
105. World Bank, 1993, op. cit.
106. P. Krugman, 'Competitiveness: A Dangerous Obsession', *Foreign Affairs*, March/April, 1994.
107. World Bank, 1993, op. cit., p. 12.
108. A. Amsden, 1992, op. cit.
109. M. Wolf, *Why Globalisation Works*, Yale University Press, 2004.
110. J. Stiglitz, *Globalisation and its Discontents*, Allen Lane, 2002.
111. H. Perkin, 1996, op. cit.
112. J. Stiglitz, 1996, op. cit.
113. C. Johnson, 1982, op. cit.; C. Johnson, 1995, op. cit.
114. C. Johnson, 1982, op. cit.
115. Ibid.
116. A. Amsden, 1992, op. cit.; Wade, 1990, op. cit.
117. R. Wade, 1990, op. cit.
118. C. Johnson, 2002, op. cit., p. 24.
119. See D. Marquand, 1988, op. cit.
120. M. Castells, 1992, op. cit., 1992, pp.57–8.
121. A. Kohli, 2004, op. cit.
122. C. Castells, 1992, op. cit.
123. See A. Kohli, 2004, op. cit.; C. Johnson, 1982, 1995, op. cit. Also, for Singapore, J. S. T. Quah, 'The Public Policy-Making Process in Singapore', *Asian Journal of Public Administration*, 6 (2), 1984, pp. 108–26.
124. See B. S. Neo and G. Chen, *Dynamic Governance: Embedding Culture, Capabilities and Change in Singapore*, World Scientific Publishing, 2007.
125. A. Amsden, 1992, op. cit.; M. Castells, 1992, op. cit.; A. Kohli, 2004, op, cit.; R. Wade, 1990, op. cit.
126. Quoted in M. Woo-Cumings, 1999, op. cit., p. 5.

127. M. Castells, 1992, op. cit.
128. L. Greenfeld, *The Spirit of Capitalism: Nationalism and Economic Growth*, Harvard University Press, 2001.
129. K. Kumar, *The Making of English National Identity*, Cambridge University Press, 2006.
130. T. Morris-Suzuki, *Re-inventing Japan: Time Space and Nation*, M. E. Sharp, East Gate Books, 1998.
131. L. Greenfeld, 2001, op. cit. p. 251.
132. Ibid, p.268.
133. D. Marquand, 1988, op. cit. p. 102–3.
134. L. Greenfeld, 2001, op. cit. p. 228.
135. E. Hobsbawm, 1990, op. cit.
136. P. Mishra, *From the Ruins of Empire: The Revolt against the West and the Remaking of Asia*, Allen Lane, 2012.
137. For Singapore see B.-H. Chua, *Communitarian Ideology and Democracy in Singapore*, Routledge, 1995.
138. See M., Castells, *End of the Millennium: The Information Age*, Vol. 111, John Wiley and Sons, 2000.
139. A. Kohli, 2004, op. cit. p. 93.
140. See M. Hill and L. K. Fee, *The Politics of Nation-Building and Citizenship in Singapore*, Routledge, 1995.
141. K. Y. Lee, 2000, op. cit.
142. A. Green, 'Education and Globalisation in Europe and East Asia: Convergent and Divergent Trends', *Journal of Education Policy, 1999*; D. Ashton et al., 1999, op. cit.
143. G. Rodan, 1989, op. cit.
144. P. Brown, A. Green and H. Lauder, *High Skills: Globalization, Competitiveness and Skills Formation*, Oxford University Press, 2001.
145. J. Tilak, 2002, op. cit. p. 3.
146. P. Wang, and E. W. Tallman, 'Human Capital and Endogenous Growth: Evidence from Taiwan', *Journal of Monetary Economics*, 34, 1994, pp. 101–24.
147. J. Tilak, 2002, op. cit.
148. World Bank, 1993, op. cit., p.57.
149. J. Tilak, 2002, op. cit.
150. D. Jamieson and L. Lau, 1982, cited in J. Tilak, 2002, op. cit.
151. World Bank, 1993, op. cit., p. 54.
152. See D. Checchi, *Education, Inequality and Income Inequality*, Discussion Paper 52, London: DARP, London School of Economics; W. McMahon, *Education and Development*, Oxford University Press, 1999.
153. H. Passim, *Society and Education in Japan*, Teachers College Press, 1965.
154. R. Wade, 1990, op. cit.
155. A. Weiss, 1996, cited in J. Tilak, 2002, op. cit.
156. G. Fields, 1980, cited in J. Tilak, 2002, op. cit.
157. L. K. Woo, 'Equalising Education and Earnings amongst Ethnic and Socioeconomic Groups in Singapore', PhD thesis, Stanford University.
158. A. Green, J. Preston, J. G. Janmaat, *Education, Inequality and Social Cohesion*, Palgrave, 2007; S. Nickel and R. Layard, *Institutions and Economic Performance*, LSE Discussion Paper, London School of Economics, 1998.
159. World Bank, *Globalisation, Growth and Poverty: Building an Inclusive World Economy*, World Bank, 2002.
160. J. Tilak, 2002, op. cit.

161. M. Bray, 'Private Tutoring: Supplementary Function or Conflicting Alternatives', in *Sixty Years of Korean Education: Achievements and Challenges*, Korean Educational Development Institute, 2005, pp.155–68.
162. J. Tilak, 2002, op. cit.
163. J. Tilak, 2002, op. cit; World Bank, 1993, op. cit.
164. D. Ashton et al., 1999, op. cit.; P. Brown et al., 2001, op. cit,
165. D. Ashton et al., 1999, op. cit.
166. Ibid; G. Rodan, 1989, op. cit.
167. D. Adams and E. Gottlieb, *Education and Change in Korea*, Garland Press, 1993.
168. P. Brown et al., 2001, op. cit.
169. E. Schein, 1989, op. cit.
170. P. Brown et al., 2001, op. cit.
171. G. Rodan, 1989, op. cit.; E. Schein, 1996, op. cit.
172. G. Rodan, 1989, op. cit
173. For Sri Lanka see A. Little in 'Paradoxes of Economic and Social Development in Sri Lanka: The Wages of Civil War' in A. Green et al., *Education and Development in a Global Era: Strategies for 'Successful Globalisation*, Department for International Development, London, 2007, pp. 163–209. For the Philippines see M. Maca, *Education and the Failure of the Philippines to Achieve its Developmental Potential: A Comparison with the East Asian Tigers*, MA thesis, Institute of Education, London, September 2009.
174. H. Passim, *Education and Society in Japan*, Teachers College Press, 1965.
175. R. Dore, *Education in Tokugawa Japan*, Routledge and Kegan Paul, 1965.
176. W. K. Cummings, *Education and Equality in Japan*, Princeton University Press, 1980.
177. A. Burks, *The Modernizers: Overseas Students, Foreign Employees, and Meiji Japan*. Westview Press, p. 257.
178. Quoted in H. Passim, op. cit., pp. 88 and 68.
179. P. Cave 'The Inescapability of Politics: Nationalism, Democratisation and Social Order in Japanese Education', in M. Lall and E. Vickers (eds), *Education as a Political Tool in Asia*, Routledge, 2009.
180. P. Cave, ibid., p. 35.
181. See T. Horio, *Educational Thought and Ideology in Modern Japan*, edited and translated by S. Platzer, University of Tokyo Press, 1988.
182. D. Adams and E. Gottlieb, *Education and Social Change in Korea*, Garland Press, 1993, p. 26.
183. Yang Young-Kym, 'Nationalism, Transnationalism and Globalisation in Korean Society', *The Review of Korean Studies*, 7, 2, pp. 3–10.
184. Korean Education and Development Unit, *Education 2000*, 1985, p. 33.
185. Quoted in D. Adams and E. Gottlieg, op. cit., p. 50.
186. See M. Hill and Lian Kwen Fee, *The Politics of Nation-Building and Citizenship in Singapore*, Routledge, 1995.
187. Quoted in Y.-T. Chia, *The Loss of 'World Soul' in Education? Culture and the Making of the Singapore Developmental State, 1995–2004*, Doctoral Dissertation, University of Toronto, 2010, p. 63.
188. Quoted in ibid., p. 67.
189. Quoted in ibid., p. 67.
190. B.-H. Chua, *Communitarian Ideology and Democracy in Singapore*, Routledge, 1995, p. 18.
191. See B.-H. Chia, op. cit., p. 50.
192. See M. Hill and L. K. Fee, 1995, op. cit. and S. Gopinathan, 1994, op. cit.

193. See M. Hill and L. K. Fee, op. cit., p. 81.
194. See S. T. Wong, *Singapore's New Education System: Education Reform for Economic Development*. Institute of South East Asian Studies, 1988.
195. See Y.-T. Chia, op. cit., p.72.
196. See Y.-T. Chia, op. cit., p. 71.
197. See S.-T. Wong, op. cit., p.6.
198. Quoted in M. Hill and L. K. Fee, op. cit., p. 89–90.
199. See Y.-T. Chia, op. cit., p. 139.
200. See M. Hill and L. K. Fee, op. cit.
201. See Chua, op. cit.
202. S.-T. Chia, op.cit., p. 167.
203. Lee Hsien Loong quoted in Chia, op. cit., p. 199.
204. See C. Han, 'National Education and "Active Citizenship" ': The Implications for Citizenship and Citizenship Education in Singapore', *Asia Pacific Journal of Education*, 20 (1), 2000, pp. 63–73.
205. See W. O. Lee, *Social Change and Educational Problems in Japan, Singapore and Hong Kong*, Macmillan, 1991.
206. M. White, *The Japanese Educational Challenge*, Macmillan, 1987.
207. W. K. Cummings, 'The Asian Human Resource Approach in Global Perspective', *Oxford Review of Education*, 21, 1995.
208. A. Green, A. Little, G. Kamat, M. Oketch and E. Vickers, *Education and Development in a Global Era: Strategies for 'Successful Globalisation*, Department for International Development, London, 2007.
209. A. Green and H. Steedman, *Educational Provision, Educational Attainment and the Needs of Industry: A Review of the Research for Germany, France, Japan, the USA and Britain* Report Series 5, National Institute of Economic and Social Research, 1993.
210. A. Green and H. Steedman, 1993, op. cit; D. Reynolds and S. Farrell, *Worlds Apart? A Review of International Surveys of Educational Achievement Involving England*, OFSTED, London, 1996.
211. D. Reynolds and S. Farrell, 1996, op. cit.
212. OECD, *PISA 2009 Results: Overcoming Social Background: Equity in Learning Opportunities and Outcomes* (Volume II), OECD, 2010.
213. A. Green, 1997, op. cit.
214. W. Cummings, 1995, op. cit., p.74.
215. K-H. Mok, 'Similar Trends: Diverse Agendas: HE Reforms in East Asia', *Globalisation, Societies and Education*, 1 (2), 2003; K.-H. Mok and M. Lee 'Globalisation or Glocalisation? High Education Reforms in Singapore', *Asia Pacific Journal of Education*, 23 (1), 2003, pp. 15–42.
216. F. Fukuyama, 1996, op. cit.
217. W. Cummings, 1995, op. cit.
218. B. Moore, 1967, op. cit.
219. F. Fukuyama, 1996, op. cit.
220. J. Schoppa, 1991, op. cit.
221. See W. Cummings, 1995, op. cit.; M. White, 1987, op. cit.; W. K. Cummings, *Education and Equality in Japan*, Princeton University Press, 1980.
222. H. Perkin, 1996, op. cit.
223. F. Fukuyama, 1996, op. cit.
224. See P. Brown *et al.*, 2001; M. White, 1987, op. cit.
225. S. Holloway, 'Concepts and Effort in Japan and the United States', *Review of Educational Research*, 58 (3), 1988, pp. 327–45.

226. The male homicide rate in Japan in 1993 was 0.9 per 100 000 compared with 12.4 per 100 000 in the United States. Rape and robbery convictions were equally low by US standards with 1.5 rape convictions per 100 000 in Japan compared with 42.8 in the United States, and 1.75 robbery convictions per 100 000 compared with 255.8. See J. Gray, 1998, p. 118.

227. N. Birdsall, D. Ross, and R. Sabot, 'Inequality and Growth Reconsidered: Lessons from East Asia', *The World Bank Economic Review*, 9 (3), 1995, pp. 477–508.

228. The ratio between the top and bottom quintiles of household income in Japan in 1980 was ×4 compared with West Germany (×5); Britain (×8); France (×9) and the United States (×12). See H. Perkin, 1996, op. cit.

229. See Y. Kudomi, 'The Competitive Education in Japan', *Hitotsubashi Journal of Social Studies*, 26, 1 and 2, 1994.

230. W. Hutton, 1995, op. cit.

231. According to Martin Wolf's data, 43 per cent of employees in Japan had worked for the same employer for more than a decade in 1991 compared with 33.5 per cent in a range of OECD countries ('Too Great a Sacrifice', FT, 14 January 1997). This will understate the relative longevity of employment in large Japanese firms which will be a long way from the average for Japan as a whole.

232. H. Elger and T. Smith, 1994, op. cit.

233. C. Hampden-Turner and F. Trompenaars, *The Seven Cultures of Capitalism*, Piatkus, 1995.

234. I. Amano, 'Education in More Affluent Japan', *Assessment in Education: Principles, Policy and Practice*, 4, 1, 1997.

235. A. Amsden, 1992, op. cit.

236. P. Brown et al., 2001, op. cit.

237. W. O. Lee, *Social Change and Educational Problems in Japan, Singapore and Hong Kong*, Macmillan, 1991.

238. F. Fukuyama, 1995, op. cit.

239. B.-H. Chua, 1995, op. cit.

240. G. Rodan, 1989, op. cit.

241. E. Schein, 1996, op. cit.

242. G. Rodan, 1989, op. cit.

243. A. Sakamoto and A. Green (1998) *Japan's Human Resources Response to the Challenge of the 1990s*, Working Paper 1, IOE/University of Bath/University of Cardiff, pp. 1–40.

244. Singapore Government, *The Next Lap*, Times Editions Pte Ltd, 1991.

245. 14.98 per cent in 1997 according to Ministry of Labour figures. See Ministry of Labour (1998) Labour News: Key Findings from the Labour force Survey of Singapore 1997, January 1998, at website: http://www.gov.sg/mom/gen/Ibn0198/survey.html.

246. B.-H. Chua, 1995, op. cit.

247. S. T. Wong, *Education Reform for Economic Development*, Institute of East Asian Studies, 1988.

248. Interview with Soon Teck Wong.

249. S. Holloway, 1988, op. cit; M. White, 1987, op. cit.

250. B.-H. Chua, 1995, op. cit.

251. Lee Kuan Yew quoted in B.-H. Chua, 1995, op. cit., p. 64.

252. A. Green and H. Steedman, 1997, op. cit.

253. National Statistical Office, *Annual Report on the Economically Active Population Survey*, Republic of Korea Government, Seoul, 1998.
254. These figures are estimates made by Green and Steedman for the DTI's Skills Audit (H. Steedman and A. Green, 1995).
255. D. Ashton and J. Sung, *The State, Economic Development and Skill Formation: A New East Asian Model?* Centre for Labour Market Studies, University of Leicester, 1994.
256. R. Wade and F. Veneros, 1998, p. cit.
257. Recent legislation in Japan has increased the rights of private shareholders in companies in Japan in an attempt to increase the ratio of private equity to cross shareholdings in companies. Lecture by Ronald Dore at the School of African and Oriental Studies, 13 October 1998.
258. I. Amano, 1997, op. cit.
259. J. Schoppa, 1991, op. cit.
260. Central Council on Education, *The Model for Japanese Education in the Perspective of the 21st Century*, First Report, Monbusho, Tokyo, 1996; Central Council on Education, *The Model for Japanese Education in the Perspective of the 21st Century*, Second Report, Monbusho, Tokyo, 1997.
261. Central Council on Education, 1996, op. cit., p.13.
262. Ibid., p.18.
263. A. Green, J. Ouston and A. Sakamoto, *Comparisons of English and Japanese Schooling*, Report for Embassy of Japan London, London University Institute of Education, 1998.
264. See discussion of CEE proposals and their impacts on equality of opportunity in A. Okada, 'Secondary Education Reform and the Concept of Equality of Opportunity in Japan.' *Compare*, 29, 2, 1999, pp. 171–89.
265. Central Council on Education, 1997, p.7.
266. For instance, Takehiko Kariya. See account in T. Kariya, 'The End of Egalitarian Education in Japan? The Effect of Policy Changes in Resource Distribution on Compulsory Education', in J. A. Gordon, H. Fujita, T. Kariya, and G. LeTendre, *Challenges to Japanese Education: Economics, Reform, and Human Rights*, Teachers College Press, 2010.
267. Singapore Government Ministry of Education (MOE), *The Thinking Programme – An Overview*, MOE, Singapore, 1998.
268. Information from interview at Temasek Junior College.
269. T. Horio, 'Problems of Unidimensional Meritocracy and Conformism in Society and Education', *Harmonie und Konformidät Herg. Agi Schründerlenzen Indicum*, 1996.
270. See A. Green, A. Little, G. Kamat, M. Oketch, and E. Vickers, *Education and Development in a Global Era: Strategies for 'Successful' Globalisation*, Department for International Development, London, 2007.
271. M. Castells, 1992, op. cit.
272. A. Przeworski, M. Alvarez, J. Cheibub and F. Limongi, *Democracy and Development: Political Institutions and Well-Being in the World, 1950–1990*, Cambridge University Press, 2000.
273. Ibid., p. 158.
274. M. Castells, 1997, op. cit., p.286.

Bibliography

General Theoretical and Comparative Works

Abrams, P., *Historical Sociology*, Open Books Publishing, 1982.

Althusser, L., *For Marx*, Penguin Press, 1969.

Althusser, L. and Balibar, E., *Reading Capital*, New Left Books, 1970.

Althusser, L., *Essays in Self-Criticism*, New Left Books, 1976.

Anderson, B., *Imagined Communities*, Verso, 1985.

Anderson, M., *Approaches to the History of the Western Family, 1500–1914*, Cambridge University Press, 1986.

Anderson, P., 'The Origins of the Present Crisis', *New Left Review*, no. 23, January/February 1964.

Anderson, P., 'Socialism and Pseudo-Empiricism', *New Left Review*, no. 35, January/February 1966.

Anderson, P., 'Components of an English National Culture', in A. Cockburn and R. Blackburn (eds), *Student Power*, Penguin, 1969, pp. 214–287.

Anderson, P., 'The Antinomies of Antonio Gramsci', *New Left Review*, no. 100, November 1976.

Anderson, P., *Considerations on Western Marxism*, New Left Books, 1976.

Anderson, P., *Arguments within Marxism*, Verso, 1980.

Anderson, P., *In the Tracks of Historical Materialism*, Verso, 1983.

Anderson, P., 'Figures of Descent', *New Left Review*, no. 161, January/February 1987.

Barrett, M., *Women's Oppression Today*, Verso, 1980.

Bendix, R., *Nation-Building and Citizenship*, University of California Press, 1964.

Boggs, C., *Gramsci's Marxism*, Pluto Press, 1976.

Bottomore, T. and Rubel, M. (eds), *Karl Marx on Sociology and Social Philosophy*, McGraw Hill, 1963.

Braverman, H., *Labour and Monopoly Capital*, Monthly Review Press, 1974.

Butterfield, H., *The Whig Interpretation of History*, G. Bell and Sons, 1931.

Dobb, M., *Studies in the Development of Capitalism*, Routledge and Kegan Paul, 1975.

Durkheim, E., *Professional Ethics and Civic Morals*, Routledge, 1957.

Durkheim, E., *The Division of Labour in Society*, trans. G. Simpson, Free Press, 1964.

Engels, F., *The Condition of the Working Class in England*, Panther Books, 1969.

Engels, F., *The Origins of the Family, Private Property and the State*, Pathfinder Press, 1972.

Engels, F., letter to J. Block, September 1890, *Marx and Engels Selected Works in One Volume* (hereafter, Selected Works), Progress Publishers, 1973.

Engels, F., *Socialism, Utopian and Scientific* in *Selected Works*, Progress Publishers, 1973.

Gramsci, A., *Selections from the Prison Notebooks*, edited and translated by Q. Hoare and G. Nowell Smith, International Publishers, 1971.

Gramsci, A., *Political Writings*, edited and translated by Q. Hoare, 1977.

Hall, S., 'Re-thinking the "Base-Superstructure Metaphor"', in J. Bloomfield (ed.), *Class, Hegemony and Party*, Lawrence and Wishart, 1977, pp. 43–73.

Hall, S. and Jacques, M. (eds), *The Politics of Thatcherism*, Lawrence and Wishart, 1983.

Haralambos, H., *Sociology: Themes and Perspectives*, University Tutorial Press, 1980.

Held, D. (ed.), *States and Societies*, Open University Press, 1983.

Hobsbawm, E. J., *Revolutionaries*, Pantheon Books, 1973.

Hobsbawm, E. J., *The Age of Revolution*, Abacus, 1977.

Hobsbawm, E. J., *The Age of Capital, 1845–1875*, Abacus, 1977.

Hobsbawm, E. J., *Age of Empire, 1875–1914*, Weidenfeld and Nicholson, 1987.

Hobsbawm, E., *Nations and Nationalism since 1780: Programme, Myth and Reality*, Cambridge University Press, 1990.

Hunt, A. (ed.), *Class and Class Structure*, Lawrence and Wishart, 1977.

Jessop, B., *The Capitalist State*, Martin Robertson and co., 1982.

Johnson, R., 'Barrington Moore, Perry Anderson and English Social Development', in C.C.C.S. *Culture and Domination*, WPCS 9, Birmingham, Spring 1976.

Koestler, A., *The Sleepwalkers, A History of Man's Changing Vision of the Universe*, Penguin, 1968.

Kumar, K., *Prophecy and Progress*, Penguin, 1983.

Kumar, K., *The Making of English National Identity*, Cambridge University Press, 2006.

Landes, D., *The Unbound Prometheus. Technological Change and Industrial Development in Western Europe from 1750 to the Present*, Cambridge University Press, 1969.

Landman, T., *Issues and Methods in Comparative Politics*, Routledge, 2008.

Lipset, S. M. and Bendix, R., *Social Mobility in Industrial Society*, University of California Press, 1967.

Marx, K. and Engels, F., *The German Ideology*, C. J. Arthur (ed.), Lawrence and Wishart, 1974.

Marx, K., *Capital*, Volume One, Penguin/New Left Review, 1972.

Marx, K. and Engels, F., *The Communist Manifesto*, in *Selected Works*, Progress Publishers, 1973.

Marx, K., Preface to *A Contribution to the Critique of Political Economy* (1859), *Selected Works*, Progress Publishers, 1973.

Marx, K., *Surveys from Exile*, J. Fernbach (ed.), Penguin/New Left Review, 1973.

Marx, K., *The Critique of the Gotha Programme*, in *Selected Works*, Progress Publishers, 1973.

Marx, K., *The Eighteenth Brumaire of Louis Napoleon*, in *Selected Works*, Progress Publishers, 1973.

Marx, K., 'The British Constitution', in D. Fernbach (ed.), *Surveys from Exile*, Penguin/New Left Review, 1973.

McLennan, G., Held, D. and Hall, S., *State and Society in Contemporary Britain*, Polity Press, 1984.

Medick, H., 'The Proto-Industrial Family Economy: The Structures of Household and Family during the Transition to Industrial Capitalism', *Social History*, no. 3, 1976.

Miliband, R., *The State in Capitalist Society*, Basic Books, 1969.

Miliband, R., *Marxism and Politics*, Oxford Paperbacks,1977.

Mill, J. S., *A System of Logic*, University Press of the Pacific, 2002.

Mitchell, J. and Oakley, A., *The Rights and Wrongs of Women*, Penguin, 1976.

Moore, B. Jr, *Social Origins of Dictatorship and Democracy*, Beacon Press, 1966.

Nairn, T., *The Break-up of Britain*, Verso, 1981.

Poulantzas, N., 'Marxist Political Theory in Great Britain', *New Left Review*, no. 43, May/June 1967.

Poulantzas, N., *Political Power and Social Classes*, New Left Books, 1973.

Poulantzas, N., *Classes in Contemporary Capitalism*, Verso, 1975.

Poulantzas, N., *State, Power, Socialism*, Verso, 1978.

Ragin, C., *The Comparative Method: Moving Beyond Qualitative and Quantitative Strategies*, University of California Press, 1987.

Rostow, W. W., *Stages of Economic Growth*, Cambridge University Press, 1960.

Rowbotham, S., *Hidden from History*, Pluto Press, 1974.

Rowbotham, S., Segal, L. and Wainwright, H., *Beyond the Fragments*, Merlin Press, 1979.

Sayer, D., *Marx's Method: Ideology, Science and Critique in Capital*, Harvester Press, 1979.

Seton-Watson, H., *Nations and States. An Enquiry into the Origins of Nations and the Politics of Nationalism*, Westview Press, 1977.

Sen, A. K., *Development as Freedom*, Oxford University Press, 1999.

Skocpol, T. (ed.), *Vision and Method in Historical Sociology*, Cambridge University Press, 1984.

Thompson, E. P. 'The Peculiarities of the English', *The Socialist Register*, 1965.

Thompson, E. P., *Poverty of Theory and Other Essays*, Merlin Press, 1978.

Weber, M., *The Protestant Ethic and the Spirit of Capitalism*, Charles Scribners and sons, 1958.

Weber, M., *From Max Weber: Essays in Sociology*, translated by H. H. Gerth and C. Wright Mills, Oxford University Press, 1946.

Williams, G., *Proletarian Order*, Pluto Press, 1975.

Williams, R., *Culture and Society, 1780–1950*, Penguin, 1984.

Women's Studies Group, *Women Take Issue. Aspects of Women's Subordination*, Centre for Contemporary Cultural Studies, 1978.

Working Papers in Cultural Studies, *On Ideology*, Working Papers in Cultural Studies no. 10, Birmingham, 1977.

Zaretsky, E., *Capitalism, the Family and Personal Life*, Harper and Row, 1976.

General and Comparative Works on Education

Apple, M. (ed.), *Cultural and Economic Reproduction in Education*, Routledge and Kegan Paul, 1982.

Apple, M., *Education and Power*, Routledge and Kegan Paul, 1982.

Archer M. and Vaughan, M., *Social Conflict and Educational Change in England and France, 1789–1848*, Cambridge University Press, 1971.

Archer, M., *The Social Origins of Educational Systems*, Sage, 1979.

Archer, M. (ed.), *The Sociology of Educational Expansion*, Sage, 1982.

Berg, I., *Education and Jobs: The Great Training Robbery*, Praeger, 1970.

Boudon, R., *Education, Opportunity and Social Inequality*, John Wiley and Sons, 1974.

Bourdieu, P., 'The School as a Conservative Force', in R. Dale et al. (eds), *Schooling and Capitalism*, Routledge and Kegan Paul, 1976.

Bourdieu, P. and Passeron, J.-C., *Reproduction in Education, Society and Culture*, trans. R. Nice, Sage, 1977.

Bowles S. and Gintis, H., *Schooling in Capitalist America*, Routledge and Kegan Paul, 1976.

Bowles, S., 'Unequal Education and the Reproduction of the Social Division of Labour', in R. Dale et al. (eds), *Schooling and Capitalism*, Routledge and Kegan Paul, 1976.

Brewer, W., *Victor Cousin as a Comparative Educator*, Teachers College Press, 1971.

Broadfoot, P. (ed.), *Selection, Certification and Control*, Falmer Press, 1984.

Castles, S. and Wustenberg, W., *The Education of the Future*, Pluto Press,1979.

Chitty, C. (ed.), *Redefining the Comprehensive Experience*, Bedford Way Papers 32, Institute of Education, London.

Collins, R., 'Some Comparative Principles of Educational Stratification', in R. Dale et al., *Schooling and the National Interest*, Falmer Press, 1981.

Curtis, B., *Building the Educational State: Canada West, 1836–1871*, Falmer Press, 1988.

Curtis, B., *The Politics of Population: State Formation, Statistics and the Census of Canada, 1840–1875*, University of Toronto Press, 2001.

Dale R., Esland, G. and Macdonald, M. (eds), *Schooling and Capitalism*, Routledge and Kegan Paul, 1976.

Dale, R. et al. (eds), *Education and the State: Schooling and the National Interest*, Falmer Press, 1981.

Davey and Miller, P., 'Family Formation, Schooling and the Patriarchal State', in M. Theobald and D. Selleck (eds), *Family, School and the State in Australian History*, Allen and Unwin, 1991.

Davey, I. and Miller, P., 'Patriarchal Transformation, Schooling and State Formation', *Paper for Social Science History Association Conference*, New Orleans, 1991.

Durkheim, E., *Education and Sociology*, trans. S. D. Fox, Free Press, 1956.

Education Group, *Unpopular Education*, Centre for Contemporary Cultural Studies, Birmingham University, 1981.

Entwistle, H. (ed.), *Antonio Gramsci, Conservative Schooling for Radical Politics*, Routledge and Kegan Paul, 1979.

Gintis, H. and Bowles, S., 'Contradiction and Reproduction in Educational Theory', R. Dale et al. (eds), *Education and the State*, vol. 1, Falmer Press, 1981.

Green, A., 'In Defence of Anti-Racist Teaching: A Reply to Recent Critiques of Multicultural Education', *Multiracial Education*, Spring 1982.

Green, A., 'Education and Training: Under New Masters', in A. M. Wolpe and J. Donald (eds), *Is There Anyone Here from Education*, Pluto Press, 1983.

Green, A., 'The MSC and the Three-tiered Structure of Further Education', in C. Benn and J. Fairley (eds), *Challenging the MSC*, Pluto Press, 1986.

Green, A., 'Lessons in Standards', *Marxism Today*, January 1988.

Green, A., 'The Price of Educational Fragmentation', *Comprehensive Education*, no. 51, 1989.

Green, A., 'The Peculiarities of English Education', in Education Group II, *Education Limited, Schooling and Training since 1979*, Unwin Hyman, 1990.

Green, A., 'Comprehensive Post-Compulsory Education and Training: Policies and Prospects', in C. Chitty (ed.), *Post-Sixteen Education: Studies in Access and Achievement*, Kogan Page, 1991.

Green, A., 'Education and State Formation Revisited', *Historical Studies in Education/Revue D'Histoire De L'Education*, Special Issue, 1994, pp. 1–19.

Green, A., Preston, J. and Janmaat, J. G., *Education, Inequality and Social Cohesion*, Palgrave, 2007.

Green, A., 'Lifelong Learning, Equality and Social Cohesion', *European Journal of Education*, vol. 46, no. 2, 2011, pp. 228–248.

Halsey, A. et al., *Education, Economy and Society*, Free Press, 1961.

Halsey, A., Heath, A. and Ridge, J. M., *Origins and Destinations*, Clarendon Press, 1980.

Hans, N., *Comparative Education. A Study of Educational Factors and Traditions*, Routledge, 1958.

Hardy, C., *The Making of Managers: A Report on Management Education, Training and Development in the United States, West Germany, France, Japan and the UK*, NEDO, 1988.

Holmes, B., *Comparative Education. Some Considerations on Method*, Allen and Unwin, 1981.

Institute for Manpower Studies, *Competence and Competition*, MSC/NEDC, 1984.

Lauglo, J. and McLean, M. (eds), *The Control of Education*, Heinemann, 1985.

Mallinson, V., *An Introduction to the Study of Comparative Education*, Heinemann, 1975.

Mallinson, V., *The Western European Idea in Education*, Pergamon Press, 1980.
Prais, S. J., 'Vocational Qualifications of the Labour Force in Britain and Germany', *National Institute Economic Review*, November 1981.
Prais, S. J. and Wagner, K., *Schooling Standards in Britain and Germany: Some Summary Comparisons Bearing on Economic Efficiency*, Discussion Paper No. 60, National Institute for Economic and Social Research, June 1983.
Ringer, F. K., *Education and Society in Modern Europe*, Indiana University Press, 1979.
Sarup, M., *Marxism and Education*, Routledge and Kegan Paul, 1978.
Sexton, S., *Our Schools; A Radical Policy*, Institute of Economic Affairs, 1986.
Simon, B., *Does Education Matter?*, Lawrence and Wishart, 1985.
Simon, B., *Bending the Rules*, Lawrence and Wishart, 1988.
Skocpol, T. and Somers, M., 'The Uses of Comparative History in Macrosocial Inquiry', *Comparative Studies in the Society and History*, vol. 22, no. 2, 1980, pp. 174–97.
Steedman, H., 'Vocational Training in France and Britain: Mechanical and Electrical Craftsmen', *National Institute Economic Review*, November 1988.
Whitty, G., *Sociology and School Knowledge. Curriculum Theory, Research and Politics*, Methuen, 1985.
Williamson, B., *Education, Social Structure and Development*, Holmes & Meier Publishers, 1979.
Willis, P., *Learning to Labour*, Routledge and Kegan Paul,1978.

Historical Works on European Education and Society

Aminzade, R., 'Reinterpreting Capitalist Industrialization: A Study of 19th Century France', *Social History*, vol. 9, October 1984.
Anderson, R. D., 'Secondary Education in Mid-Nineteenth Century France: Some Social Aspects', *Past and Present*, no. 53, November 1971.
Anderson, P., *Lineages of the Absolutist State*, Verso, 1974.
Anderson, R. D., *Education in France, 1848–1870*, Clarendon Press, 1975.
Aries, P., *Centuries of Childhood*, Penguin, 1979.
Artz, F. D., *The Development of Technical Education in France, 1500–1850*, The MIT Press, 1966.
Barnard, H. C., *Education and the French Revolution*, Cambridge University Press, 1969.
Boucher, L., *Tradition and Change in Swedish Education*, Pergamon Press, 1982.
Bourdieu P. and Passeron, J-C., *Les Héritiers*, Les Éditions de Minuit, 1964.
Bowen, J., *A History of Western Education*, vol. 3, Methuen, 1981.
Caute, D., *The Left in Europe since 1789*, Weidenfeld and Nicolson, 1966.
Cipolla, C. M., *Literacy and Development in the West*, Penguin Books, 1969.
Cobban, A., *A History of Modern France*, 2 vols, 1984.
Cousin, V., *Education in Holland as Regards Schools for the Working Classes and for the Poor*, Trans. L. Horner, John Murray, 1838.
Crew, D., 'Definitions of Modernity: Social, Mobility in a German Town, 1880–1901', *Journal of Social History*, no. 7, Autumn 1973.
Gillis, J., 'Aristocracy and Bureaucracy in Nineteenth-Century Prussia', *Past and Present*, no. 41, December 1968.
Harrigan, P., *Mobility, Elites and Education in French Society of the Second Empire*, Wilfrid Laurier University Press,1980.
Hazard, P., *The European Mind, 1680–1715*, trans. J. Lewis May, Penguin, 1964.
Hazlett, J. S., 'A French Conception of Republican Education: The Carnot Ministry, 1848', *Paedagogia Historica*, vol. 10, no. 2, 1973.

Kazamias, A., *Education and the Quest for Modernity in Turkey*, Allen and Unwin, 1966.
Levasseur, E., *L'Enseignement Primaire dans les Pays Civilisés*, Berger-Levrault and Cie,1896.
Lüdtke, A., 'The Role of State Violence in the Transition to Industrial Capitalism: The Example of Prussia from 1815–1848', *Social History*, vol. 4, no. 2, May 1979.
Lundgreen, P., 'Industrialization and the Educational Formation of Manpower in Germany', *Journal of Social History*, vol. 9, no. 1, Autumn 1975.
Melton, J. Van Horn, *Absolutism and the Eighteenth-Century Origins of Compulsory Schooling in Prussia and Austria*, Cambridge University Press, 1988.
Moody, J. N., *French Education since Napoleon*, Syracuse University Press, 1978.
Mulhall, M., *Dictionary of Statistics*, Routledge and sons, 1884.
O'Boyle, L., 'The Problem of Excess of Educated Men in Western Europe, 1800–1850', *Journal of Modern History*, vol. 42, no. 4, December 1970.
O'Brien, G., 'Maria Theresa's Attempt to Educate an Empire', *Paedagogia Historica*, no. 3, 1970.
Paulston, R. G., *Educational Change in Sweden*, Teachers College Press, 1968.
Pollard, H., *Pioneers of Popular Education*, John Murray, 1956.
Polomba, D., 'Education and State Formation in Italy, International Handbook of Comparative Education', *Springer International Handbooks of Education*, vol. 22, 2009, Springer, pp. 195–216.
Prost, A., *Histoire de l'Enseignement en France, 1800–1967*, Armand Colin, 1968.
Rath, R., 'Training for Citizenship in Austrian Elementary Schools during the Reign of Francis 1st', *Journal of Central European Affairs*, vol. iv, July 1944.
Reisner, E., *Nationalism and Education Since 1789. A Social and Political History of Modern Education*, The Macmillan Company, 1922.
Rousseau, J-J., *Emile*, trans. B. Foxley, Dent, 1982.
Samuel, R. H. and Thomas, R., *Education and Society in Modern Germany*, Routledge and Kegan Paul,1949.
Sawin, P. Q., *Nationalism and the Control of Education in Prussia, 1800–1871*, unpublished PhD, University of Wisconsin, 1954.
Soboul, A., *The French Revolution*, two volumes, New Left Books, 1974.
Taylor, A. J. P., *The Course of German History*, Routledge, 1982.
Tocqueville, A. de, *The Old Regime and the French Revolution*, trans., Stuart Gilbert, Doubleday, 1955.
Zeldin, T., *France, 1848–1945, Intellect and Pride*, Oxford University Press, 1980.
Zeldin, T., *France, 1848–1945, Politics and Anger*, Oxford University Press, 1984.
Weber, E., *Peasants into Frenchmen: The Modernization of Rural France, 1870–1914*, Stanford University Press, 1976.
Wiborg, S., *Education and Social Integration. Comprehensive Schooling in Europe*, Palgrave MacMillan, 2009.

Historical Works on North American Education and Society

Adams, H., *The Education of Henry Adams*, Random House Modern Library, 1946.
Alger, H., *Ragged Dick and Mark, the Match Boy*, Collier Books, 1962.
Bailyn, B., *Education in the Forming of American Society*, Vintage Books, 1960.
Bailyn, B., *The Ideological Origins of the American Revolution*, Harvard University Press, 1977.
Bowles S. and Gintis, H., *Schooling in Capitalist America*, Routledge and Kegan Paul, 1976.

Bibliography   421

Brogan, H., *The Pelican History of the United States of America*, Penguin Books, 1986.

Carlton, F. T., *Economic Influences upon Educational Progress in the United States, 1820–1850*, Teachers College Press, 1965.

Cremin, L., *Traditions in American Education*, Basic Books, 1977.

Cremin, L., *American Education: The National Experience, 1783–1876*, Harper and Row, 1982.

Cubberley, E. P., *Public Education in the United States*, Houghton Mifflin, 1934.

Dangerfield, G., *The Awakening of American Nationalism, 1815–1828*, Harper-Collins, 1965.

Davis, M., 'Labour in American Politics', *New Left Review*, no. 123, September/October 1980.

Dawley, A., *Class and Community: The Industrial Revolution in Lynn*, Harvard, 1976.

Elkins, S. M., *Slavery*, University of Chicago Press, 1976.

Fishlow, A., 'Levels of 19th Century Investment in Education', *The Journal of Economic History*, vol. xxvi, no. 4, December 1966.

Fishlow, A., 'The American School Revival, Fact or Fancy?', in H. Rosdovsky (ed.) *Industrialization in Two Systems*, John Wiley and Sons, 1966.

Foner, E., *Free Soil, Free Labour, Free Men*, Oxford University Press, 1982.

Franklin, B., *The Autobiography and Other Writings*, Penguin, 1986.

Genovese, E., *Roll Jordan Roll. The World the Slaves Made*, Vintage, 1976.

Hirsch, S., *The Roots of the American Working Class, 1800–1860*, University of Pennsylvania Press,1978.

Kaestle, C. F., *Pillars of the Republic: Common Schools and American Society, 1780–1860*, Hill and Wang, 1983.

Katz, M., *The Irony of Early School Reform*, Harvard University Press, 1968.

Katz, M., *Class, Bureaucracy and Schools*, Praeger, 1971.

Katz, M., 'The Origins of Public Education: A Reassessment', *History of Education Quarterly*, Winter 1976.

Katz, M., 'The Origins of Popular Education: A Reassessment', *History of Education Quarterly*, Winter 1976.

Messerli, J., 'Localism and State Control in Horace Mann's Reform of the Common Schools', *American Quarterly*, vol. 17, no. 1, Spring 1965.

Myrdal, G., *An American Dilemma*, Harper, 1944.

Pesan, E., 'The Egalitarian Myth and the American Social Reality. Wealth, Mobility, and Equality in the "Era of the Common man"', *American Historical Review*, October 1971.

Potter, A. and Emerson, G., *The School and the School Master*, W. B. Fowle and N. Capen, 1846.

Showronek, S., *Building a New American Nation: The Expansion of National Administrative Capacities, 1877–1920*, 1982.

Sombart, W., *Why Is There No Socialism in the United States*, Macmillan, 1976.

Stamp, K.(ed.), *The Causes of the Civil War*, Prentice Hall, 1965.

Taylor, J. Orville, *The District School*, Carey, Lea & Blanchard, 1835.

Thernstrom, S., *The Other Bostonians: Poverty and progress in the American Metropolis, 1880–1970*, Harvard University Press, 1964.

Tocqueville, A. de, *Democracy in America*, trans. R. Heffner, Mentor Books, 1956.

Tyack, D., 'Forming the National Character: Paradox in the Thought of the Revolutionary Generation', *Harvard Educational Review*, vol. 36, no. 1, 1966.

Tyack, D., *The One Best System*, Harvard University Press, 1974.

Tyack, D., 'The Common school and American Society: A Reappraisal', *History of Education Quarterly*, vol. 26, no. 2, Summer 1986.
Tyack, D. and James, T., 'State Government and American Public Education: Exploring the "Primeval Forest" ', *History of Education Quarterly*, vol. 26, no. 1, Spring 1986.
Tyack, D. and James, T., 'The Law and the Shaping of Public Education. Explorations in Political History'. Unpublished monograph, 1986.

Historical Works on English Education and Society

Allen, G., *The British Disease*, Institute of Economic Affairs,1976.
Annan, N., *Leslie Stephen. His Thought and Character in Relation to His Time*, MacGibbon & Kee, 1951.
Arnold, M., *Culture and Anarchy*, J. Dover Wilson (ed.), Cambridge University Press, 1981.
Ashby, E., 'Technology and the Academies. An Essay on Universities and the Scientific Revolution', in A. H. Halsey et al., *Education, Economy and Society*, Free Press, 1961.
Ashley, W., *Commercial Education*, Williams and Norgate, 1926.
Ashton, T. S., *The Industrial Revolution*, Oxford University Press, 1968.
Babbage, C., *Reflections on the Decline of Science*, B. Fellows and J. Booth, 1830.
Bailey, B., 'The Technical Education Movement: A Late Nineteenth Century Lobby', *Journal of Further and Higher Education*, no. 3, Autumn, 1983.
Bailey, B., 'The Development of Technical Education, 1934–1939', *History of Education*, vol. 16, no. 1, 1987.
Baines Jr, E., *Letters to the Right Honorable John Russell On State Education*, Simpkin, Marshall, 1846.
Bamford, T. W., *The Rise of the Public Schools, 1837 to the Present Day*, Nelson, 1967.
Bantock, G., *Education in an Industrial Society*, Faber and Faber, 1963.
Bibby, C. (ed.), *T. H. Huxley: A Selection of His Writings*, Cambridge University Press, 1971.
Bishop, A. S., *The Rise of a Central Authority in English Education*, Cambridge University Press, 1971.
Brougham, H., *Speech on Education Bill, House of Commons*, Hansard, June 28.
Carlyle, T., *Selected Writings*, ed. A. Shelston, Penguin, 1971.
Cavenagh, J., (ed.), *John Stuart and James Mill on Education*, Cambridge University Press, 1931.
Clarke, F., *Education and Social Change. An English Interpretation*, Sheldon Press, 1940.
Clarke, J., Critcher, C. and Johnson, R. (eds) (1979) *Working-Class Culture*, Hutchinson, 1979.
Corrigan, P. and Sayer, D., *The Great Arch: English State Formation as Cultural Revolution*, Basil Blackwell, 1985.
Cotgrove, S., *Technical Education and Social Change*, Allen and Unwin, 1958.
Davidoff, L. and Hall, C., *Family Fortunes. Men and Women of the English Middle Class, 1780–1850*, Hutchinson, 1987.
Dickens, A. G., *The English Reformation*, Schocken Books, 1964.
Donagrodski, A. P., *Social Control in Nineteenth Century England*, Croom Helm, 1977.
Dyhouse, C., *Girls Growing up in Late Victorian and Edwardian England*, Routledge and Kegan Paul, 1981.
Elton, G. R., *Reformation Europe, 1517–1559*, Collins, 1970.
Foster, J., *Class Struggle and the Industrial Revolution*, Weidenfeld and Nicholson, 1974.
Fraser, D., *The Evolution of the British Welfare State*, Macmillan, 1985.

Gamble, A., *Britain in Decline*, Macmillan, 1981.

Giddy, D., *Speech in Parliament, in Cobbet's Parliamentary Papers*, 13 July 1807.

Goldstrom, J. M., 'The Content of Education and the Socialization of the Working Class Child', in P. McCann (ed.), *Popular Education and Socialization in the Nineteenth Century*, Methuen, 1977.

Grace, G., *Teachers, Ideology and Control*, Routledge and Keegan Paul, 1978.

Gray, R., 'Bourgeois Hegemony in Victorian Britain', in J. Bloomfield (ed.), *Class, Hegemony and Party*, 1976.

Halévy, E., *The Growth of Philosophical Radicalism*, Faber, 1928.

Halévy, E., *A History of the English Speaking People in the Nineteenth Century, The Triumph of Reform, 1831–1841*, Barnes and Noble Inc., 1961.

Halévy, E., *The Liberal Awakening, 1815–1830*, Ark, 1987.

Hill, C., *The English Revolution*, Penguin, 1968.

Hill, C., *Reformation to Industrial Revolution*, Penguin, 1969.

Hill, C., *Puritanism and Revolution*, Viking, 1986.

Hobsbawm, E. J., *Industry and Empire*, Penguin, 1969.

Hobsbawm, E. J. and Rude, G., *Captain Swing*, Penguin, 1985.

Hume, J., *Speech in House of Commons*, Hansard, 25 July 1843, col. 1345.

Hurt, J., *Education in Evolution: Church, Society, State and Popular Education, 1800–1870*, Rupert Hart-Davis, 1971.

Huxley, T., Address on Behalf of the National Association for the promotion of Technical education, 1887, in C. Bibby (ed.), *T. H. Huxley on Education*, Cambridge University Press, 1971.

Johnson, R., The Education Department, 1839–1864, unpublished PhD, Cambridge, 1968.

Johnson, R., 'The Education Movement, 1780–1840,' unpublished paper, Centre for Contemporary Cultural Studies, University of Birmingham.

Johnson, R., 'Notes on the Schooling of the English Working Class. 1780–1850', in R. Dale and G. Esland (eds), *Schooling and Capitalism*, Open University Press, 1976.

Johnson, R., 'Educating the Educators: Experts and the State', in A. P. Donagrodsky (ed.), *Social Control in Nineteenth Century England*, Croom Helm, 1977.

Johnson, R., ' "Really Useful Knowledge": Radical Education and Working-Class Culture', in J. Clarke, C. Critcher and R. Johnson (eds), *Working Class Culture. Studies in History and Theory*, Hutchinson, 1979.

Johnson, R., 'Education and Popular Politics', Unit One in H. Cathcart et al. *The State and the Politics of Education, Open University Rreader for E353*, Milton Keynes, 1981.

Langan, M. and Schwartz, B. (eds), *Crisis in the British State, 1880–1930*, Hutchinson, 1985.

Lawson, J. and Silver, H., *A Social History of Education in England*, Methuen, 1973.

Levine, D., 'Industrialization and the Proletarian Family in England', *Past and Present*, no. 107, May 1985.

Locke, J., *Two Treatises on Civil Government*, J. M. Dent and sons, 1955.

Locke, J., *An Essay Concerning Human Understanding*, Clarendon Press, 1968.

Lovett, W., 'Chartism: A New Organization of the People', (1840), in B. Simon (ed.), *The Radical Tradition of Education*, Lawrence and Wishart, 1972.

Maclure, J. S., *Educational Documents, England and Wales, 1816 to the Present Day*, Methuen, 1986.

Marquand, D., *The Unprincipled Society*, Jonathan Cape, 1988.

McCann, P. (ed.), *Popular Education and Socialization in the 19th Century*, Methuen, 1977.

Mill, J., *Autobiography*, J. Stillinger (ed.), Clarendon Press, 1971.

Mill, J., *Utilitarianism*, M. Warnock (ed.), Fontana, 1986.

Murphy, J., *The Education Act, 1870*, Text and Commentary, David and Charles, 1972.

Musgrave, P., *Society and Education in England Since 1800*, Chapman and Hall, 1968.

O'Day, R., *Education and Society, 1500–1800*, Longman, 1982.

Paine, T., *Rights of Man*, Penguin, 1983.

Perkin, H., *The Origins of Modern English Society*, Ark, 1985.

Playfair, L., *Industrial Education on the Continent, Lecture at the Government School of Mines, Science and Applied Arts*, 1852.

Playfair, L., *Two Lectures Delivered to the Philosophical Institution of Edinburgh On Primary and Technical Education*, 1870.

Polanyi, K., *The Great Transformation*, Beacon Press, 1957.

Reeder, D., 'A Recurring Debate: Education and Industry', in R. Dale et al. (eds), *Schooling and the National Interest*, 1981.

Report from the Select Committee On the Provision for Giving Instruction in Theoretical and Applied Science to the Industrial Class, 1867–1868.

Reports of the Royal Commission On Scientific Instruction and the Advancement of Science (The Devonshire Report), 1872–1875.

Reports of the Royal Commission On Technical Instruction (The Samuelson Report), 1881–1884.

Roach, J., *Public Examinations in England*, 1850–1900, Cambridge University Press, 1971.

Roderick, G. and Stephens, M., 'The Higher Education of Engineers in England in the Nineteenth Century, With Observations on Engineering Training on the Continent and in America', *Paedagogia Historia*, xv 1/2, 1976.

Roderick, G. and Stephens, M. (eds), *Where Did We Go Wrong?*, Falmer Press, 1981.

Roebuck, A., Speech in the House of Commons in defense of his Bill for National Education, Hansard, 30 July 1833, col. 159.

Sanderson, M., 'Literacy and Social Mobility in the Industrial Revolution in England', *Past and Present*, no. 56, August 1972.

Sanderson, M., *Education, Economic Change and Society in England, 1700–1870*, Macmillan, 1983.

Silver, H., *The Concept of Popular Education*, Macgibbon and Kee, 1965.

Silver, H., *Education as History*, Methuen, 1983.

Simon, B., *The Two Nations and the Educational Structure, 1780–1870*, Lawrence and Wishart, 1960.

Simon, B., *Education and the Labour Movement, 1870–1920*, Lawrence and Wishart, 1965.

Simon, J., *Education and Society in Tudor England*, Cambridge University Press, 1966.

Simon, B., *The Radical Tradition of Education in Britain*, Lawrence and Wishart, 1972.

Simon, B., *The Politics of Educational Reform, 1920–1940*, Lawrence and Wishart, 1974.

Smiles, S., *Self-Help*, John Murray, 1859.

Smith, A., *An Inquiry into the Nature and Causes of the Wealth of Nations*, W. Strahan and T. Cadell, 1776.

Spencer, H., *State Education Self Defeating. A Chapter from Social Statistics; or, The Conditions Essential to Human Happiness Specified, and the First of them Developed*, John Chapman, 1851.

Stone, L., 'The Educational Revolution in England, 1560–1640', *Past and Present*, no. 28, July 1964.

Stone, L., 'Literacy and Education in England, 1600–1900', *Past and Present*, no. 42, February 1969.

Strachey, L., *Eminent Victorians*, Chatto and Windus, 1981.

Tawney, R. H., *The School-Leaving Age and Juvenile Unemployment*, Workers Education Authority, 1933.

Taylor, A. J., *Laissez-Faire and State Intervention in Nineteenth Century Britain*, Macmillan, 1972.

Tholfsen, T., *Working Class Radicalism in Mid-Victorian England*, Croom Helm, 1976.

Thompson, E. P., *The Making of the English Working Class*, Penguin, 1968.

Thompson, E. P., 'Patrician Society, Plebian Culture', *Journal of Social History*, 1974.

Trevelyan, G. M., *English Social History*, Penguin, 1944.

Vincent, D., *Bread, Knowledge and Freedom: A Study of 19th Century Working-Class Autobiography*, Europa, 1981.

Wardle, R. D., *English Popular Education, 1780–1975*, Cambridge University Press, 1976.

Warner, R., *English Public Schools*, Collins, 1945.

West, E. G., *Education and the Industrial Revolution*, Batsford, 1975.

Wiener, M. J., *English Culture and the Decline of the Industrial Spirit, 1850–1980*, Pantheon Books, 1984.

Wyse, T., *Educational Reform; On the Necessity of a National System of Education*, 1836.

Wyse, T., *Education in the United Kingdom*, Central Society of Education, 1837.

Young, G. M., *Victorian England. A Portrait of an Age*, Oxford University Press, 1960.

Works on Development and State Formation in East Asia

Amsden, A., *Asia's Next Giant: South Korea and Late Industrialisation*, Oxford University Press, 1992.

Amsden, A., *Escape from Empire: The Developing World's Journey through Heavan and Hell*, MIT Press, 2007.

Arrighi, G., *Adam Smith in Beijing*, Verso, 2007.

Birdsall, N., Ross, D. and Sabot, R., 'Inequality and Growth Reconsidered: Lessons from East Asia', *The World Bank Economic Review*, vol. 9, no. 3, 1995, pp. 477–508.

Burks, A., *The Modernizers: Overseas students, Foreign Employees, and Meiji Japan*. Westview Press, 1985.

Castells, M., 'Four Asian Tigers with a Dragons' Head: A Comparative Analysis of the State, Economy and Society in the Asian Pacific Rim', in R. Appelbaum and J. Henderson (eds), *States and Development in the Asia Pacific Rim*, Sage, 1992.

Castells, M., *The Power of Identity: The Information Age: Economy, Society and Culture*, vol. 11, Blackwell, 1997.

Castells, M., *End of the Millennium: The Information Age*, vol. 111, John Wiley and Sons, 2000.

Chang, H.-J., *Kicking away the Ladder: Development Strategy in Historical Perspective*, Athlone Press, 2003.

Checchi, D., *Education, Inequality and Income Inequality*, Discussion Paper No. DARP 52, London School of Economics, London, 2001.

Chua, B.-H., *Communitarian Ideology and Democracy in Singapore*, Routledge, 1995.

Denison, E. F., *Why Growth Rates Differ: Post War Experience in Nine Western Countries*, Brookings Institution, 1967.

Denison, E. F., *Accounting for Slower Economic Growth: The United States in the 1970s*, Brookings Institution, 1979.

Dore, R., *Stock Market Capitalism: Welfare Capitalism: Japan and Germany versus the Anglo-Saxons*, Oxford University Press, 2000.

Elger, T. and Smith, C., *Global Japanisation*, Routledge, 1994.

Fei, J., Ranis, G and Kuo, S., *Growth with Equity: The Taiwan Case*, Oxford University Press, 1979.

Fukuyama, F., *Trust: The Social Virtues and the Creation of Prosperity*, Hamish Hamilton, 1996.

Furoka, F., 'Japan and the "Flying Geese" Pattern of East Asian Integration', *eastasia.at*, vol. 4, no. 1, 2005.

Gerschenkron, A., *Economic Backwardness in Historical Perspective: A Book of Essays*, Belknap Press, 1966.

Government of Singapore, *Singapore: The Next Lap*, Times Editions, 1991.

Gray, J., *False Dawn: The Delusions of Global Capitalism*, Granta, 1998.

Green, A. and Janmaat, J.-G., *Regimes of Social Cohesion: Societies and The Crisis of Globalisation*, Palgrave, 2011.

Greenfeld, L., *Nationalism: Five Roads to Modernity*, Harvard University Press, 1992.

Greenfeld, L., *The Spirit of Capitalism: Nationalism and Economic Growth*, Harvard University Press, 2001.

Hampden-Turner, C. and Trompenaars, F., *The Seven Cultures of Capitalism*, Piatkus, 1995.

Hill, M. and Lian Kwen Fee, *The Politics of Nation-Building and Citizenship in Singapore*, Routledge, 1995.

Hovsepian, N., *Palestinian State Formation: Education and the Construction of National Identity*, Cambridge Scholars Publishing, 2008.

Hutton, W., *The State We're In*, Jonathan Cape, 1995.

Jameson, S., 'Japan: Confronting an Uncertain Future', *Asian Perspective*, vol. 21, no. 1, Spring-Summer 1997, pp. 103–124.

Johnson, C., *MITI and the Japanese Miracle: The Growth of Industrial Policy 1925–1975*, Stanford University Press, 1982.

Johnson, C., *Japan Who Governs? The Rise of the Developmental State*, W. W. Norton, 1995.

Johnson, C., *Blowback: The Costs and Consequences of American Empire*, Time Warner Paperbacks, 2000.

Kohli, A., *State-Directed Development: Political Power and Industrialisation in the Global Periphery*, Cambridge University Press, 2004.

Krugman, P. 'Competitiveness: a Dangerous Obsession', *Foreign Affairs*, March/April 1994.

Kwan, C. H., 'The Rise of China and Asia's Flying-Geese Pattern of Economic Development: An Empirical Analysis Based on US Import Statistics', *RIETI Discussion Paper Series*, 02-E-009, July 2002.

Kuznets, S., 'Economic Growth and Income Inequality', *American Economic Review*, 45, 1995, pp. 1–28.

Lee, K. Y., *From Third World to First: The Singapore Story: 1965–2000*, Harper Collins, 2000.

List, F., *National Systems of Political Economy*, Cosmo Classic, 2005.

Mishra, P., *From the Ruins of Empire: The Revolt against the West and the Remaking of Asia*, Allen Lane, 2012.

Morris-Suzuki, T., *Re-Inventing Japan: Time Space and Nation*, M. E. Sharp, East Gate Books, 1998.

Neo, B. S. and Chen, G., *Dynamic Governance: Embedding Culture, Capabilities and Change in Singapore*, World Scientific Publishing, 2007.

Nickel, S. and Layard, R., *Institutions and Economic Performance*, LSE Discussion Paper, London School of Economics, London, 1998.

Perkin, H., *The Third Revolution: Professional Ethics in the Modern World*, Routledge, 1996.

Przeworski, A., Alvarez, M., Cheibub, J. and Limongi, F., *Democracy and Development: Political Institutions and Well-Being in the World, 1950 –1990*, Cambridge University Press, 2000.

Pye, L., 'Asian Values': From Dynamos to Dominoes', in L. Harrison and S. Huntington (eds), *Culture Matters: How Values Shape Human Progress*, Basic Books, 2000, pp. 244–55.

Quah, J.S.T., 'The Public Policy-Making Process in Singapore', *Asian Journal of Public Administration*, vol. 6, no. 2, 1984, pp.108–26.

Rodan, G., *The Political Economy of Singapore's Industrialisation*, Macmillan, 1989.

Schein, E., *Strategic Pragmatism: The Culture of Singapore's Economic Development Board*, MIT Press, 1996.

Singapore Government, *The Next Lap*, Times Editions Pte Ltd, 1991.

Stiglitz, J., 'Some Lessons from the East Asian Miracle', *The World Bank Research Observer*, vol. 11, no. 2, 1996, pp.151–77.

Stiglitz, J., *Sound Finance and Sustainable Development in Asia: Address to Asian Development Forum*, Manila, 1998.

Stiglitz, J., *Globalisation and its Discontents*, Allen Lane, 2002.

Streek, W., 'Skills and the Limits of Neo-Liberalism: The Enterprise of the Future as a Place of Learning', *Work, Employment and Society*, vol. 3, no. 1, 1987, pp. 89–104.

Sugihara, K., 'The East Asian Path of Economic Development', in A. Arrighi, H. Takeshi and M. Seldon (eds), *The Resurgence of East Asia*, Routledge, 2003, pp. 78–123.

Tu, Wei-Ming, 'Multiple Modernities: A Preliminary Inquiry into the Implication of East Asian Modernity', in L. Harrison and S. Huntington (eds), *Culture Matters: How Values Shape Human Progress*, Basic Books, 2000, pp. 256–67.

Wade, R., *Governing the Market, Economic Theory and the Role of Government in East Asian Industrialisation*, Princeton University Press, 1990.

Wade, R. and Veneros, F. 'The Asian Crisis: The High Debt Model versus the Wall Street-Treasury-IMF Complex', *New Left Review*, 228, 1998, pp. 3–23.

Wang, P. and Tallman, E. W., 'Human Capital and Endogenous Growth: Evidence from Taiwan', *Journal of Monetary Economics*, 34, 1994, pp. 101–24.

Wolf, M., *Why Globalisation Works*, Yale University Press, 2004.

Woo, L. K., 'Equalising Education and Earnings amongst Ethnic and Socioeconomic Groups in Singapore', PhD thesis, Stanford University.

Woo-Cumings, M. (ed.), *The Developmental State*, Cornell University Press, 1999.

World Bank, *East Asian Economic Miracle*, World Bank, 1993.

World Bank, *Globalisation, Growth and Poverty: Building an Inclusive World Economy*, World Bank, 2002.

Works on Education, Training and Skills in East Asia

Adams, D. and Gottlieb, E., *Education and Change in Korea*, Garland Publishing, 1993.

Amano, I., 'Education in More Affluent Japan', *Assessment in Education: Principles, Policy and Practice*, vol. 4, no. 1, 1997.

Ashton, D. and Green, F., *Education, Training and the Global Economy*, Edward Elgar, 1996.

Ashton, D., Green, F., James D. and Sung, J., *Education and Training for Development: The Political Economy of Skills Formation in East Asian Newly Industrialized Economies*, Routledge, 1999.

Ashton, D. and Sung, J., *The State, Economic Development and Skill Formation: A New East Asian Model? Centre for Labour Market Studies*, University of Leicester, 1994.

Bray, M., 'Private Tutoring: Supplementary Function or Conflicting Alternatives', in *Sixty Years of Korean Education: Achievements and Challenges*, Korean Educational Development Institute, 2005, pp. 155–68.

Brown, P., Green, A. and Lauder, H., *High Skills: Globalisation, Competitiveness and Skill Formation*, Oxford University Press, 2001.

Cave, P., 'The Inescapability of Politics: Nationalism, Democratisation and Social Order in Japanese Education', in M. Lall and E. Vickers (eds), *Education as a Political Tool in Asia*, Routledge, 2009.

Central Council on Education, *The Model for Japanese Education in the Perspective of the 21st Century*, First Report, Monbusho, 1996.

Central Council on Education, *The Model for Japanese Education in the Perspective of the 21st Century*, Second Report, Monbusho, 1997.

Chia, Y. T., *The Loss of 'World Soul' in Education? Culture and the Making of the Singapore Developmental State, 1995–2004*, Palgrave, 2014.

Cummings, W. K., *Education and Equality in Japan*, Princeton University Press, 1980.

Cummings, W. K., 'The Asian Human Resource Approach in Global Perspective', *Oxford Review of Education*, 21, 1995.

Dore, R., *Education in Tokugawa Japan*, Routledge and Kegan Paul, 1965.

Dore, R. and Sako, M., *How the Japanese Learn to Work*, Routledge, 1989.

Gopinathan, S., 'Educational Development in a Strong-Developmentalist State: The Singapore Experience', Paper Presented at the Australian Association for Research in Education Annual Conference, 1994.

Green, A., 'Education and State Formation Revisited', *Historical Studies in Education/Revue D'Histoire De L'Education*, Special Issue, 1994, pp. 1–19.

Green, A., *Education, Globalisation and the Nation State*, Macmillan, 1997.

Green, A., 'Education and Globalisation in Europe and East Asia: Convergent and Divergent Trends', *Journal of Education Policy*, 1999.

Green, A., 'East Asian Skills Formation Systems and the Challenge of Globalization', *Journal of Education and Work*, vol. 21, no. 3, 1999, pp. 253–79.

Green, A., Little, A., Kamat, G., Oketch, M. and Vickers, E., *Education and Development in a Global Era: Strategies for 'Successful Globalisation'*, Department for International Development, London, 2007.

Green, A., Ouston, J., and Sakamoto, A., *Comparisons of English and Japanese Schooling*, Report for Embassy of Japan London, London University Institute of Education, 1998.

Green, A. and Steedman, H., 'Educational Provision, Educational Attainment and the Needs of Industry: A Review of the Research for Germany, France, Japan, the USA and Britain' Report Series 5, National Institute of Economic and Social Research, 1993.

Han, C., 'National Education and "Active Citizenship": The Implications for Citizenship and Citizenship Education in Singapore', *Asia Pacific Journal of Education*, vol. 20, no. 1, 2000, p. 63–73.

Han, C., 'History Education and "Asian" Values for an "Asian" Democracy: The Case of Singapore', *Compare*, vol. 37, no. 3, 2007, pp. 383–98.

Holloway, S. D., 'Concepts of ability and Effort in Japan and the United States', *Review of Educational Research*, vol. 58, no. 3, 1988, pp. 327–45.

Horio, T., *Educational Thought and Ideology in Modern Japan*, edited and translated by S. Platzer, University of Tokyo Press, 1988.

Horio, T., 'Problems of Unidimensional Meritocracy and Conformism in Society and Education', *Harmonie und Konformidät Herg. Agi Schründerlenzen Indicum*, 1996.

Hunt, A. and Tokluoglu, C., 'State Formation from Below: The Turkish Case', *The Social Science Journals*, vol. 39, no. 4, 2002, pp. 617–24.

Kariya, T., 'The End of Egalitarian Education in Japan? The Effect of Policy Changes in Resource Distribution on Compulsory Education', in Gordon, J. A., Fujita, H., Kariya, T. and LeTendre, G., *Challenges to Japanese Education: Economics, Reform, and Human Rights*, Teachers College Press, 2010.

Koike, K. and Inoki, T. (eds), *Skill Formation in Japan and South East Asia*, University of Tokyo Press, 1990.

Korean Education and Development Unit, *Education 2000*, 1985.

Korean Education Development Institute, The Korean Education System, Ministry of Education, 1996.

Kudomi, Y., 'The Competitive Education in Japan', *Hitotsubashi Journal of Social Studies*, vol. 26, nos. 1 and 2, 1994.

Lee, W. O., *Social Change and Educational Problems in Japan, Singapore and Hong Kong*, Macmillan, 1991.

Lewin, K., Education in Emerging Asia: Patterns, policies and Futures into the 21st Century, Paper to Comparative Education Conference at New College Oxford, September, 1997.

Maca, M., *Education and the Failure of the Philippines to Achieve its Developmental Potential: A Comparison with the East Asian Tigers*, MA Thesis, Institute of Education, London, September 2009.

McMahon, W., *Education and Development*, Oxford University Press, 1999.

Ministry of Labour, 'Labour News: Key Findings from the Labour Force Survey of Singapore 1997', January 1998, at website: http://www.gov.sg/mom/gen/ Ibn0198/ survey.html.

Mok, K.-H., 'Similar Trends: Diverse Agendas: HE Reforms in East Asia', *Globalisation, Societies and Education*, vol. 1, no. 2, 2003.

Mok, K.-H. and Lee, M. 'Globalisation or Glocalisation? High Education Reforms in Singapore', *Asia Pacific Journal of Education*, vol. 23 no. 1, 2003, pp. 15–42.

Morishima, M., 'Work Organisation and Training systems for Technical Employees: A Comparison of Japan, the UK and Germany', *Keio Business Review*, 33, 1997.

Morris and Sweeting, A. (eds), *Education and Development in East Asia*, Garland Press, 1995.

National Statistical Office, *Annual Report on the Economically Active Population Survey*, Republic of Korea Government, Seoul, 1998.

OECD, *PISA 2009 Results: Overcoming Social Background: Equity in Learning Opportunities and Outcomes (Volume II)*, OECD, 2010.

Okada, A., 'Secondary Education Reform and the Concept of Equality of Opportunity in Japan', *Compare*, vol. 29, no. 2, 1999, pp.171–189.

Passim, H., *Society and Education in Japan*, Teachers College Press, 1965.

Presidential Commission on Education Reform (PCER), *Education Reform for a New Education System*, Republic of Korea Government, Seoul, 1996.

Reynolds, D. and Farrell, S., *Worlds Apart? A Review of International Surveys of Educational Achievement Involving England*, OFSTED, 1996.

Sakamoto, A., Green, A., Brown, P. and Lauder, H., 'Japan's Human Resource Response to the Challenges of the 1990s,' High Skills Working Paper No. 1, London University Institute of Education, 1998.

Schoppa, J., *Education Reform in Japan: A Case of Immobilist Politics*, Routledge, 1991.

Singapore Government Ministry of Education (MOE), *The Thinking Programme – An Overview*, MOE, 1998.

Singapore Government Ministry of Labour, *Labour News: Key Findings from the Labour Force Survey of Singapore 1997*, January 1998, at website: http://www.gov.sg/mom/gen/lbn0198/survey.html.

Tilak, J., *Building Human Capital in East Asia: What Others Can Learn*, National Institute of Educational Planning and Administration, 2002.

White, M., *The Japanese Educational Challenge*, Macmillan, 1987.

Wielemans, W. and Choi-Ping Chan, P. (eds), *Education and Culture in Industrialising Asia. The Interaction between Industrialisation, Cultural Identity and Education*, Leuven University Press, 1994.

Wong, S. T., *Singapore's New Education System: Education Reform for Economic Development*, Institute of South East Asian Studies, 1988.

Wong, S. T., *Education Reform for Economic Development*, Institute of East Asian Studies, 1988.

Wong, T. H., *Hegemonies Compared: State Formation and Chinese School Politics in Postwar Singapore and Hong Kong*, Routledge, 2002.

Woo, L. K., Equalising Education and Earnings amongst Ethnic and Socioeconomic Groups in Singapore, PHD thesis, Stanford University, 1982.

Yang Young-Kym, 'Nationalism, Transnationalism and Globalisation in Korean Society', *The Review of Korean Studies*, vol. 7, no. 2, pp. 3–11.

Index

432 *Index*

Printed by Printforce, the Netherlands